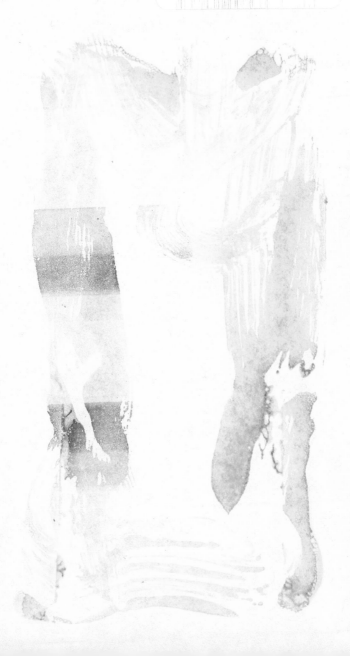

THE EVOLUTION OF UN PEACEKEEPING

*Also published by St. Martin's Press
in association with the Henry L. Stimson Center*

NAVAL ARMS CONTROL: A Strategic Assessment
Barry M. Blechman, William J. Durch, W. Phillip Ellis,
and Cathleen S. Fisher

THE POLITICS OF ARMS CONTROL TREATY RATIFICATION
Edited by Michael Krepon and Dan Caldwell

OPEN SKIES, ARMS CONTROL, AND COOPERATIVE
SECURITY
Edited by Michael Krepon and Amy E. Smithson

TECHNOLOGY POLICY AND AMERICA'S FUTURE
Steven M. Irwin

THE AMERICAN MILITARY IN THE TWENTY-FIRST
CENTURY
Barry M. Blechman, William J. Durch, David R. Graham, John H.
Henshaw, Pamela L. Reed, Victor A. Utgoff, and Steven A. Wolfe

THE EVOLUTION OF UN PEACEKEEPING

Case Studies and Comparative Analysis

Edited by William J. Durch

St. Martin's Press

© Henry L. Stimson Center 1993

All rights reserved. For information, write:
Scholarly & Reference Division,
St. Martin's Press, Inc., 175 Fifth Avenue,
New York, NY 10010

First published in the United States of America 1993
Paperback edition 1993

Printed in the United States of America

The editor and publishers thank the United Nations for
permission to reproduce UN maps in this book.

ISBN 0-312-06600-7 (cloth)
ISBN 0-312-10401-4 (paperback)

Library of Congress Cataloging-in-Publication Data

The Evolution of UN peacekeeping: case studies and
  comparative analysis / edited by William Durch.
    p. cm.
  "A Henry L. Stimson Center book."
  Includes bibliographical references and index.
  ISBN 0-312-06600-7
  1. United Nations—Armed Forces. I. Durch, William J.
JX1981.P7E92   1992
341.5' 8—dc20   92-36820
                               CIP

Contents

List of Figures

List of Tables

Preface and Acknowledgments

In the spring of 1990, the Henry L. Stimson Center received a grant from the Ford Foundation to study UN peacekeeping to see how it might be improved. For many years, peacekeeping was a slow-to-change endeavor that involved a handful of missions seemingly fixed in time and space, locked between Israel and its neighbors, between Greeks and Turks on Cyprus, and between Hindus and Muslims in Kashmir. But as the Cold War wound down in the late 1980s and regional conflicts sustained by the Cold War came to an end, the demand for UN peacekeepers began to increase geometrically. Shortcomings in planning, training, technology, and finance, which could be worked around when there were just a few missions, suddenly needed to be addressed. Indeed, the pace of change demanded a serious look at the whole enterprise of peacekeeping.

The Stimson Center is a nonprofit research and educational institution that strives to promote better understanding of complex public policy problems and to make recommendations that address those problems directly and pragmatically. To do this for peacekeeping, we established a research design that combined a search for the lessons of the past with an effort to tap the contemporary experience of UN and government officials familiar with peacekeeping and its politics. Since most of these individuals remain active in UN or government service, we agreed to conduct our interviews on background: hence, interviews are identified in the notes only by number and date, although a complete list of those interviewed is included at the back of the book. The bibliography also contains a complete list of UN documents that are cited in short form in the notes.

The results of twenty structured case studies of UN operations from 1947 to 1991 were combined with the results of roughly one hundred interviews conducted in 1990 and 1991 to produce a policy report released in March 1992. A condensed version of the analysis in that report (*Keeping the Peace: The United Nations in the Emerging World Order*, by William J. Durch and Barry M. Blechman) appears as Part One of this book. The case studies constitute Parts Two through Five. The epilogue briefly examines four new missions responsible for the explosion in the size and cost of UN peacekeeping in 1992, and what they bode for the future of the enterprise.

This study is closely focused on peacekeeping and does not address peace enforcement, the UN's term for the coercive use of force, although it is increasingly fashionable to do so. In our view, the UN needs to walk before it can run. Peacekeeping is primarily a political task that uses military symbols and some military tools, including force in certain circumstances (self-defense, for example). Its material requirements, while substantially less than the requirements of war, still tax the Organization to the utmost; the costs and risks of enforcement operations would be greater by orders of magnitude.

The range of situations in which peacekeepers have worked leads some to label each operation "unique" and thus immune to probing for useful generalizations. But if each new operation has had unique elements, each also has shared many elements with missions that have gone before it, namely, political and military origins, a geopolitical context, and a set of tasks to perform that are drawn from a basic repertoire of observation, mediation, and conflict management. These common elements can be compared analytically across missions to glean lessons from history, and the results can be used, as they are here, to answer some basic questions about what makes peacekeeping work.

This book is intended to fill a gap in the peacekeeping literature, which tends either toward single case studies or toward collections of essays that are but loosely tied together. It avoids both shortcomings by offering both comparative analysis and a comprehensive set of cases. It is designed for an advanced undergraduate or graduate course in conflict management, conflict resolution, international organization, or, of course, peacekeeping. It assumes basic familiarity with international relations, the history of the Cold War, and the basic structure and purposes of the United Nations. It assumes that readers know the basic makeup and functions of the General Assembly, Security Council, and Secretariat. The cases, in particular, take such knowledge for granted.

The case studies are organized by region and listed chronologically within region. They can be taught geographically, historically, or developmentally, comparing regions, periods, or mandates (tracing the evolution of peacekeeping from basic border monitoring tasks to complex nation- or peace-building).

Peacekeeping is a work in progress. Of the twenty cases detailed in the book, nine are of necessity unfinished because they deal with continuing operations. As this printing of the book went to press, the list of operations continued to expand. The largest and most consequential are treated briefly in the epilogue. They demonstrate that the end of the Cold War has not produced Utopia. However, as we cast about for models to use in coping with the conflict we see all around us, we can do worse than draw upon four decades of UN experience. This volume offers a composite of that experience.

The Stimson Center was fortunate, in the course of its study of peacekeeping, to have had the advice of a group of experienced individuals who served as an advisory committee. They included General George L. Butler, currently commander of the US Strategic Command; Dr. David Cox, director of a study of UN peacekeeping at the Canadian Centre for Arms Control and Disarmament in Ottawa; the Hon. Jan Eliasson, now UN Under-Secretary General for Humanitarian Affairs; Representative Lee Hamilton, Chair of the Subcommittee on Europe and the Middle East of the House Foreign Affairs Committee, United States Congress; Dr. Marianne Heiberg, director of a study of UN peacekeeping at the Norwegian Institute of International Affairs in Oslo; Dr. Patricia Lewis, director of the Verification Technology Information Centre in London; Ambassador Olara Otunnu, President of the International Peace Academy in New York; the Hon. Thomas Pickering, former US Ambassador to the United Nations, now Ambassador to Russia; Dr. Enid Schoettle, director of a program on international organizations at the Council on Foreign Relations; Sir Brian Urquhart, former UN Under-Secretary General for Special Political Affairs; and the Hon. Cyrus Vance, former US Secretary of State and, for nearly two years, UN Special Representative on the crisis in the Balkans. I would like to extend additional thanks to John Mackinlay and James Schear for their comments on early drafts of the policy report; to Jack Child, Richard Nelson, Jane Stromseth, and Abiodun Williams for their critical comments on the case studies; to Page Fortna and Pamela Reed for their invaluable research assistance; to Scott Hamilton for his indefatigable editing of a difficult manuscript; and to Robert McKay for his invaluable assistance with the maps.

Needless to say, responsibility for the content of this study, and for any errors or omissions, rests solely with the authors. In particular, its recommendations should not be attributed to any of the individuals mentioned above, who may or may not agree with them.

The Stimson Center would like to extend special thanks to the Ford Foundation, Enid Schoettle, its director of international programs at the time this study was initiated, and Shepard Forman, the current director. Without Ford's generous support, this study would not have been possible. I, in turn, would like to express my appreciation to the Stimson Center, its Chairman, Barry Blechman, and its President, Michael Krepon, for their unstinting support and encouragement of this project.

Finally, on a personal note, I would like to thank Jane Stevenson Durch, my best friend and spouse of twenty years, for her patience and support over the course of this project, and I would like to dedicate this book to her. We have learned, bit by bit, a good deal about what it takes to keep the peace and make it grow.

W.J.D.
Arlington, Virginia
August 1993

1 Introduction

by William J. Durch

During the Cold War, the United Nations could not do the job for which it was created. Global collective security, the organizing precept of its Charter, was impossible in a world divided into hostile blocs. But the UN did manage to carve out a more narrow security role. As a "neutral" organization, it could sometimes help to bring smaller conflicts to an end, keep them from flaring anew, and keep them from leading to a direct and potentially catastrophic clash of US and Soviet arms. Thus, the UN came to be associated over the years with more modest but, under the circumstances, more realistic objectives: the mediation of isolated and idiosyncratic conflicts, the monitoring of cease-fire arrangements, and the separation of hostile armed forces. Novel kinds of field operations were developed to support this work, which can be grouped into two categories: unarmed military observer missions (first utilized in the Balkans in 1947) and armed peacekeeping missions (first utilized in the Sinai in 1956). In this study, the term "peacekeeping" is used as a shorthand reference to both.

Over the years, the United Nations has undertaken nearly two dozen such missions of varying scope, duration, and degree of success, most of them involving conflicts whose origins can be traced to the end of colonial empires. In Africa, the Middle East, and South and East Asia through the 1970s, and currently in southern Europe and Central Asia, decolonization has often unleashed ethnic and nationalist forces that challenge state authority and old imperial boundaries. Many new states must struggle to balance the interests and demands of multi-ethnic populations. Indeed, subnational groups' demands for empowerment, autonomy, and even independence represent a new stage in the struggle for self-determination that, like the first, has often turned violent and may yet fragment the globe into ever smaller, and ultimately vulnerable, polities. The UN has contributed frequently to the containment or resolution of first-stage conflicts and wars between states, but it now faces permanent entanglement in second-stage conflicts over territory, resources, and political control where emotions run high and there are no rules. Two searing examples of such conflict are Somalia, where government has virtually disappeared and armed gangs roam at will, and the killing field that once was Yugoslavia, where civilians are the targets of "ethnic cleansing."

The end of the Cold War and the rise of ethnic conflict has led some to suggest that the time is ripe for the UN to move beyond peacekeeping and into peace enforcement.[1] But the financial, organizational, and operational requirements of peace enforcement would be orders of magnitude greater than what today's peacekeeping currently needs, which is a great deal. Moreover, if and when the UN does decide to intervene more actively in conflicts around the world, the need to sustain postwar cease-fires and to implement settlement agreements will be, if anything, even greater than at present, and well-trained, well-funded, and well-equipped peacekeepers will be in even greater demand. Indeed, the UN offices responsible for designing and supporting these missions already feel besieged.

Many of peacekeeping's problems are caused by its growing popularity as the international community's tool of choice for conflict containment in an age of growing violence. Every new or newly rediscovered tool is subject to the "law of the instrument": people and states want to use it on everything. But peacekeepers cannot do everything; they serve a niche market: states and groups who are sick of conflict and want to get on with their lives, but who don't trust erstwhile enemies to live up to a settlement or a cease-fire without supervision.

It is, unfortunately, a very big niche. Demand for UN peacekeeping since early 1992 has begun to outstrip the supply, whether that supply is measured in money or in national political will. By mid-1992, the UN Security Council and the UN's Secretary General, its chief executive officer, were arguing in public about how best to implement triage: where to intervene, where to stay away, and where to administer palliatives.

Such choices will be with us always, and the 178 states (at last count) that make up the UN must face up to them. Their past choices are the focus of chapter two, which examines the political and military context of peacekeeping operations. Yet the Organization can only be asked to do as much or as little as its members are willing to agree on and pay for. The difficulty of late is that they have been agreeing much more readily than they have been paying. Peacekeeping is much cheaper than warfare, but it isn't free. Chapter three looks at the UN's money problems and the difficulty of convincing governments that somebody else can't pay for everything.

Part of the UN's problem is its basic lack of autonomy and its habituation to rhetoric, a learned response from its first forty years of political stalemate (first East-West, and then North-South). The Organization has rarely seemed more than the sum of its arguing parts. Its "executive" branch really *is* a secretariat, used for the most part to set up conferences, publish transcripts of meetings, and track, rather than carry out, activities related to economic and social development; quasi-independent operating agencies like UNICEF do the actual field work. Out of a headquarters bureaucracy of several thousand people, fewer than 150 plan, recruit, and manage peacekeeping operations that, as of 1992, have more than 40,000 people in the field under frequently dangerous conditions, and that cost more than the rest of the regular UN budget combined. Chapter four examines the problem of planning and implementing a peacekeeping operation.

But before proceeding to a chronological overview of peacekeeping during and after the Cold War (which, we hope, will provide a stable reference point from which to venture into the comparative analysis of Part One), we need to better define what peacekeeping is, what it does, and where it fits into the larger array of tools for conflict management (and conflict suppression) that are built into the UN Charter.

DEFINING TERMS

In the idiom of international relations theory, peacekeeping supplements the self-help system of international politics with an element of disinterested outside assistance that can help the parties to a conflict disengage themselves from it. Peacekeeping missions may involve, in ascending order of complexity and intrusiveness: uncovering the facts of a conflict; monitoring of border or buffer zones after armistice agreements have been signed; verification of agreed-upon force disengagements or withdrawals; supervision of the disarming and demobilization of local forces; maintenance of security conditions essential to the conduct of elections; and even the temporary, transitional administration of countries.[2] Peacekeepers may be armed, but only for self-defense; what constitutes appropriate self-defense will vary by mission, but because they are almost by definition outgunned by the disputants they are sent out to monitor, any recourse to force must be calibrated to localize and defuse, rather than escalate, violence.

By observing both sides' behavior, by reporting on what they see, and by resolving violations before they generate local military reactions, peacekeeping forces can assure conflicting parties, for example, that a cease-fire will remain a cease-fire. Their presence provides a mechanism for limiting the consequences of disputes that will inevitably arise when implementing a cease-fire or political settlement between groups who remain basically hostile to, or mistrustful of, one another. International peacekeepers can verify, for example, that one side's willingness to lay down its arms is reciprocated by the other. They can monitor the repatriation of dispossessed populations and property, and provide the public security and administrative coherence necessary to restore the basic amenities of life. They can verify that election processes are free from bias and voter intimidation, and that election outcomes are valid reflections of the votes cast.

In short, while peacekeepers cannot do all things, they can do some very valuable things that local parties cannot do for themselves under the prevailing circumstances (which, in the places that peacekeepers frequent, means very recent warfare, accompanied more and more by substantial displacement or deaths of civilians). Peacekeeping is a confidence-building measure, providing a means for nations or factions who are tired of war, but wary of one another, to live in relative peace and eventual comity.

PEACEKEEPING AND THE SPECTRUM OF CONFLICT

Peacekeeping is a subset of a much larger spectrum of operations that the UN might undertake to sustain or restore peace and security under the terms of its Charter. Figure 1.1 shows how peacekeeping and related operations fit into this larger universe. The level of military force involved in a UN operation can range from zero (as in mediation or preventive diplomacy) to quite considerable (for a peace enforcement action like the 1991 Gulf War). The level of local consent to a UN operation can vary as well.

Most UN operations are undertaken with full local consent. In a multiparty conflict, however, some parties' consent can be hard to maintain, so we depict it in Figure 1.1 as a continuum.

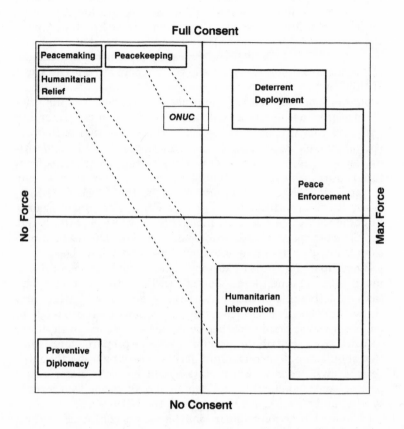

**Figure 1.1. Level of Consent and Use of Force
in UN Field Operations**

As a working definition, we take "consent" to mean the agreement of a host government to a UN mission's presence. Some factions within the host country, including armed elements, may object to that presence, and on occasion peacekeepers may need to use force as a last resort to defend themselves or restore order to a deteriorating field situation. We illustrate this possibility using the UN's 1960–64 operation in the Congo (ONUC) as an example.

"Deterrent deployments" include actions that are sometimes dubbed "preventive peacekeeping," which is a misnomer. Such deployments would be intended to deter aggression by signaling the international community's willingness to counter it militarily. The UN would deploy with the consent of the threatened party but with capabilities (and orders) to engage in combat as may be necessary. This task distinguishes such preventive combat deployments from peacekeeping and places them outside the scope of this study.

Similarly outside the scope of peacekeeping, but meriting brief discussion nonetheless, are still more coercive means of enforcing collective security, such as the 1990–91 intervention to liberate Kuwait, which employed economic sanctions, blockade, and ultimately air, ground, and naval warfare to oust Iraqi forces from that country. The fact that there have been very few such actions to date—the 1950 Korean intervention, the 1965 blockade of Rhodesia, Kuwait, and the 1992 Security Council sanctions against Yugoslavia (Serbia)—does not make them any less important. But the Charter specifies that enforcement actions should be measures of last resort, and to date that is what they have been.

By comparison to peacekeeping, enforcement actions impose much higher human and monetary costs on the countries who take an active role in the operation. The hotter the conflict and the sooner the UN intervenes, the higher those costs are likely to be. Even where action is taken to deter rather than to suppress conflict, troop contributors would have to be prepared for casualties should the deterrent effort fail. Operations undertaken to restore civil order within a state would be particularly risky, prone to entanglement in local factional politics and to terrorist-type assault by factions unhappy with the UN presence.

Delaying UN action reapportions the costs of conflict. Early and active intervention imposes increased costs on the international community but reduces the burdens of conflict on noncombatant local populations (assuming that international intervention does indeed suppress the fighting). Late intercession—helping to mediate a conflict, to maintain a cease-fire, or to pick up the pieces after conflict has burned itself out—implies fewer risks for the outsiders but greater suffering by noncombatants. But unless the international community (including the major powers, and specifically the United States) is willing to jump into potentially long-running conflicts in many places at once, it may have little choice but to avoid direct military involvement, waiting instead until one side wins or until all sides' will to fight is exhausted; in this scenario, it would limit itself to supporting persons displaced or made refugees by the fighting and, perhaps, protecting humanitarian assistance to civilians caught in the cross-fire. We have drawn a line in Figure 1.1, a "slippery slope," if you will, from humanitarian assistance to humanitarian intervention (forceful measures taken, for example, to protect a local populace from a genocidal regime). This will be, we suggest, the way in which the UN will most likely be drawn into regional conflicts in the future, not thundering over the beach, but slipping in through a side door.[3]

To date, however, with the exception of the Korean War, which was under de facto American control, UN operations have all been intercessions after the fact.[4] During the Cold War, UN efforts to terminate conflicts at an early stage were confined to diplomatic initiatives and occasional economic sanctions. On relatively rare occasions, cease-fires imposed by threats of Great Power military intervention were later overseen by UN peacekeepers.[5]

PEACEKEEPING DURING THE COLD WAR

From 1947 to 1985, the United Nations undertook thirteen peacekeeping operations of varying scope, duration, and degree of success. They are listed in Table 1.1. Many of these Cold War operations were politically possible because they helped to avoid direct clashes of US and Soviet arms. As was frequently the case then, both countries' principal interest in most Third World states was to keep the other power's influence to a minimum. The UN offered a nominally impartial alternative that could meet this objective—an important one, especially from the West's perspective. Peacekeeping missions more often served the West's interests in regional stability. Since Moscow's interest at that time was to foster regional instability, which would, in turn, lead to radical political change and greater Soviet regional influence, Soviet support for UN peacekeeping was intermittent at best throughout this period.

The first mission explicitly labelled "peacekeeping" was the UN Emergency Force (UNEF) dispatched to the Sinai peninsula following the Suez Crisis of 1956. UNEF oversaw the withdrawal of British, French, and Israeli forces from the Sinai, and it monitored a buffer zone between Egypt and Israel. UNEF remained in place for eleven years until it was asked by Egypt to withdraw on what turned out to be the eve of the Six Day War. Peacekeepers returned to the Sinai six years later, after the October 1973 War, and remained in place as UNEF II until Egypt and Israel signed

their historic peace treaty in 1979. These two operations are what
most refer to when they talk about "classical" peacekeeping.

Table 1.1. UN Peacekeeping Operations
During the Cold War, 1945–1985

Missions	Description
UN Special Committee on the Balkans (UNSCOB) 1947–51	Investigate outside support for guerrillas in Greece
UN Truce Supervision Organization (UNTSO) 1948–	Monitor cease-fires along Israeli borders
UN Military Observer Group in India and Pakistan (UNMOGIP) 1949–	Monitor cease-fire in Jammu and Kashmir
UN Emergency Force (UNEF I) 1956–67	Separate Egyptian & Israeli forces in Sinai
UN Observation Group in Lebanon (UNOGIL) 1958	Monitor infiltration of arms & troops into Lebanon from Syria
UN Operation in the Congo (ONUC) 1960–64	Render military assistance, restore civil order
UN Temporary Executive Authority (UNTEA) 1962–63	Keep order and administer W. New Guinea pending transfer to Indonesia
UN Yemen Observation Mission (UNYOM) 1963–64	Monitor infiltration into Yemen via Saudi border
UN Force in Cyprus (UNFICYP) 1964–	Maintain order; from 1974 monitor buffer zone
UN India Pakistan Observer Mission (UNIPOM) 1965–66	Monitor cease-fire in 1965 India-Pakistan War
UN Emergency Force II (UNEF II) 1974–79	Separate Egyptian & Israeli forces in Sinai
UN Disengagement Observer Force (UNDOF) 1974–	Monitor separation of Syrian & Israeli forces on Golan Heights
UN Interim Force in Lebanon (UNIFIL) 1978–	Establish buffer zone between Israel & Lebanon

The UN's second armed peacekeeping force was sent to the
Congo in 1960 to help preserve order and avoid a direct US-Soviet
confrontation. The Congo force, known by its French initials
(ONUC), later worked to control a major secessionist movement
and thus to end an emerging civil war. It set a potential precedent
for coercive UN operations elsewhere, but the political trauma
that it caused led many in the UN to view it as "the UN's
Vietnam," as an experience never to be repeated. In mid-1992,
when UN officials looked at Bosnia-Herzegovina, they saw the
Congo.

A third large UN force was placed on Cyprus in 1964. It was
still there in 1992, separating Greek and Turkish factions along

the so-called Green Line. UNFICYP is an example to many impatient troop-contributing nations of how peacekeeping operations can sometimes have unintended adverse effects, suppressing open conflict without resolving its underlying causes.

The last major UN mission launched during the Cold War was the UN Interim Force in Lebanon (UNIFIL). Deployed after the Israeli invasion of Lebanon in early 1978, UNIFIL was given a mandate that it could not fulfill: to escort the powerful Israelis out and to restore the authority of the disintegrating Lebanese government. Once ensconced, however, the UN was unable to free itself, worried that precipitate withdrawal would cause substantial loss of civilian life.

PEACEKEEPING IN THE NEW ERA

In the second half of the 1980s, the United Nations was inundated by requests for new peacekeeping missions in the Persian Gulf, Southern Africa, South Asia, and Central America. Several of these new operations were precedent shattering. In Namibia in 1989, the UN undertook its first peace-building operation, both overseeing the withdrawal of hostile armed forces and monitoring that nation's first free election. Shortly thereafter, the UN began its first mission in the Western Hemisphere, helping to disarm the Nicaraguan Contras after Nicaraguans voted the Sandinista movement out of office in February 1990.

A second and even larger surge of demand for UN peacekeeping operations began in mid-1991. Added to long-anticipated new missions in the Western Sahara, El Salvador, and Angola were a monitoring operation on the Iraq-Kuwait border after the second Gulf War; the Special Commission implementing the disarmament provisions of the cease-fire with Iraq; and the policing and relief operation for the Kurdish populations in northern Iraq.[6] In early 1992, the two largest missions in three decades began simultaneously, one to oversee the rebuilding of war-torn Cambodia and the other to monitor the cease-fire in Croatia (an independent former province of Yugoslavia).

All told, thirteen missions were begun between 1988 and 1992 (Table 1.2), equal to the number undertaken in the previous forty years of the UN's existence. Considering the typically more ambitious mandates of the new missions, it is clear that UN-peacekeeping requirements have increased by orders of magnitude since 1985. More missions are sure to follow as the Security Council acts to quell cross-border and other conflicts and as the

Introduction

Secretary General's teams of mediators produce more settlement agreements.

Table 1.2. UN Peacekeeping Operations in the New Era, 1985–1992

Missions	Description
UN Good Offices Mission in Afghanistan and Pakistan (UNGOMAP) 1988–89	Monitor Soviet pullout from Afghanistan.
UN Iran-Iraq Military Observer Group (UNIIMOG) 1988–91	Monitor cease-fire in Iran-Iraq War.
UN Angola Verification Mission I (UNAVEM I) 1988–91	Monitor Cuban pullout from Angola.
UN Transition Assistance Group (UNTAG) 1989–90	Supervise transition of Namibia from South African rule to independence.
UN Observer Group in Central America (ONUCA)1989–91	Monitor compliance with Esquipulas II agreement; demobilize Nicaraguan contras.
UN Angola Verification Mission II (UNAVEM II) 1991–	Monitor general cease-fire and creation of new joint army.
UN Iraq-Kuwait Observation Mission (UNIKOM) 1991–	Monitor buffer zone after Gulf War. Temporary armed component.
UN Mission for the Referendum in Western Sahara (MINURSO) 1991–	Conduct referendum on independence from Morocco.
UN Observer Mission in El Salvador (ONUSAL) 1991–	Monitor human rights, elections, government restructuring.
UN Advance Mission in Cambodia (UNAMIC) 1991–March 92 UN Transitional Authority in Cambodia (UNTAC) 1992–	Supervise government functions and eventual elections while rebuilding the country and disarming the factions.
UN Protection Force in Yugoslavia (UNPROFOR) 1992–	Replace Yugoslav forces in Serbian-controlled areas of Croatia.
UN Operation in Somalia (UNOSOM) 1992–	Security for humanitarian shipments to victims of civil war.

It is also likely that the UN will function increasingly as the midwife of political transitions. Nine of the missions undertaken since 1988 have facilitated resolution of "domestic" conflicts and the establishment of democratic regimes. As an organization that represents the entire international community, and as an entity with no armies of its own and no vested interest other than the success of the peace process, the UN may be ideally suited for this role. It is guaranteed to leave when its work is finished, but its presence can deter and, if necessary, expose unfair election practices, thus ensuring the credibility of, and conferring automatic legitimacy upon, the new political processes and regimes it creates.

However, UN involvement in national affairs is a potential political minefield for the Organization. Whatever the constellation of forces that permits a UN peacekeeping operation to be mounted, the resolution of internal conflicts involves the apportionment of power among recently hostile parties with sometimes long histories of bloodshed and violence. Referenda have losers as well as winners, and regardless of the "fairness" of an election, to the degree that the UN is involved it runs the risk of being seen as a hostile force by the losing side. Once a perception of bias is established, the UN's effectiveness is greatly hampered.

Deteriorating field situations may force the UN to choose between ignominious withdrawal and onerous persistence in a mission, the latter course perhaps requiring coercive enforcement of a settlement. Such a step, as noted earlier, would transform peacekeeping into peace enforcement, an operation with completely different political, financial, and operational requirements which the UN is not yet prepared to meet. Although it has become involved in several risky "domestic" operations, including those in Cambodia and the former Yugoslavia, the UN has no plans as yet for effecting such a transformation, or for safely extracting a peacekeeping mission under fire. As a result, the Organization risks disaster in one or more missions, which could cast doubts on its credibility with troop contributors, and thus cast a shadow on the future of peacekeeping. Without continued caution and substantially better capabilities to plan ahead, gather funds, and support its field operations, the UN could be headed for an unpleasant fall, and its "renaissance" could be short lived.

This need not be so. Although the UN is grappling with a growing list of responsibilities and is hard-pressed to keep up, the efforts begun in the spring of 1992 to reform the Organization may indeed result in the enhanced "capacity...for preventive diplomacy, for peacemaking, and for peacekeeping," sought by the January 1992 Security Council "summit."[7] To improve substantially the UN's capacity in the realm of peace and security, member states will need to change the way they view the Organization, to give it greater resources, and to attend to the lessons of history.[8]

EVALUATING UN OPERATIONS

Part one of this book seeks to answer the question, "When should peacekeeping be used as an instrument of conflict containment or resolution, and when should it be avoided?" A related question, of course, is "When does it work and when does it fail?" As readers will discover as they look at the cases, success and failure in peacekeeping are not readily definable in black and white terms. Is a mission that keeps foes apart for ten years, but whose involuntary departure is followed by war, a success for what it sustained for a decade or a failure for what happened afterward? Is a mission that keeps foes apart indefinitely a success for having spared them new bloodshed, or a failure for having made them dependent on its presence, for having removed the need to settle old grievances?

Over the years, peacekeeping practitioners have evolved certain rules of thumb to help answer basic questions about when peacekeeping should be attempted and what makes it work. They can be considered the basic hypotheses of peacekeeping:[9]

- First hypothesis: Peacekeeping requires local consent, and consent derives from local perceptions of the impartiality and moral authority of the peacekeepers' sponsoring organization.

- Second hypothesis: Peacekeeping requires the support of the Great Powers and the United States in particular.

- Third hypothesis: Peacekeeping requires a prior alteration of the local parties' basic objectives, from winning everything to salvaging something; a frequent corollary of attitude change is combat exhaustion or battlefield stalemate.

We investigated these hypotheses through structured and focused comparisons of all cases of UN peacekeeping since World War II.[10] Thus the cases follow a common format. Each outlines the political, military, and geographic setting for the operation, examines the sources of UN involvement in the conflict, the scope of political support for that involvement, the operation's mandate (or marching orders), its source(s) of funding, how it was set up, and the operational problems it faced. Each case includes an assessment of how well the UN force fulfilled the mandate it was given, and a concluding section places the operation in a larger political context. The cases are grouped by region, and cover 1947–1991.[11]

Notes

1. See, for example, John M. Lee, Robert von Pagenhardt, and Timothy W. Stanley, *Strengthening United Nations Peacekeeping and Peacemaking: A Summary* (Washington, D.C.: International Economic Studies Institute, April 1992); and United Nations Association-National Capital Area, *The Common Defense: Peace and Security in a Changing World* (Washington, D.C.: UNA-USA, June 1992).

2. Holst's typology of missions is somewhat similar: observation, reporting, prevention of incursions, supervision of implementation of agreements, disarmament of contestants, and decompression of tensions (Johan Jørgen Holst, "Enhancing Peacekeeping Operations," *Survival* [May–June 1990]: 265-266).

3. For a discussion of international military intervention to protect civilian populations or to safeguard human rights, and for recommendations on reforming UN organizational structure, funding, and training for peacekeeping, see William J. Durch and Barry M. Blechman, *Keeping the Peace: The United Nations in the Emerging World Order* (Washington, D.C.: The Henry L. Stimson Center, March 1992), especially chapter three. For a wide-ranging discussion of human rights and international responsibilities, see Lori Fisler Damrosch and David J. Scheffer, eds., *Law and Force in the New International Order* (Boulder, Co.: Westview Press, 1991); and David P. Forsythe, *The Internationalization of Human Rights* (Lexington, Mass.: Lexington Books, 1991).

4. Operation Desert Storm was not under UN command, either technically or legally.

5. These were most effective where the United States and the Soviet Union wielded great influence with the opposing sides, and both worked to smother the fighting. The best example is the 1973 Middle East War. See the discussion, below, in the case on the Second UN Emergency Force (UNEF II).

6. For a summary of activities, see Johan Molander, "The Lessons of Iraq: Unconventional Weapons, Inspection and Verification, and the United Nations and Disarmament," transcript of a briefing at The Committee on National Security, Washington, D.C., November 13, 1991. Mr. Molander served as special adviser to the Chairman of the Special Commission.

7. "Security Council Summit Declaration," *New York Times*, February 1, 1992, 4.

8. In June 1992, the Secretary General published the report sought by the Security Council, entitled *An Agenda for Peace*. In it, and in subsequent speeches and writing about peacekeeping, the Secretary General urged regional organizations to play a greater role. The activities of regional organizations are beyond the scope of this volume, but a summary

study of regional peacekeeping efforts is available. See, Virginia Page Fortna, *Regional Organizations and Peacekeeping*, Occasional Paper No. 11 (Washington, D.C.: The Henry L. Stimson Center, October 1992).

9. Reflecting its pragmatic evolution, peacekeeping is rarely cast by practitioners in explicitly theoretical terms. Thus Marrack Goulding, UN Under-Secretary General for Peacekeeping Operations, defines peacekeeping in terms of what has worked historically, and what distinguishes it from other activities using military personnel. Peacekeeping is an operation that "requires the consent of the parties," does "not involve military enforcement measures," but does "involve the deployment in the field of UN personnel...to help control and resolve actual or potential international conflicts or...internal conflicts which have a clear international dimension" ("The Evolving Role of United Nations Peacekeeping Operations," in the *The Singapore Symposium, The Changing Role of the United Nations in Conflict Resolution and Peacekeeping*, United Nations Document DPI/1141 [New York: United Nations Department of Public Information, September 1991], 25).

10. See Alexander L. George, "Case Studies and Theory Development: The Method of Structured, Focused Comparison," in Paul Gordon Lauren, ed., *Diplomacy: New Approaches in History, Theory, and Policy* (New York: The Free Press, 1979), 43-68.

11. Case studies of UN peacekeeping operations begun since mid-1991 will be available directly from The Henry L. Stimson Center in late 1993.

Part One:

Lessons Learned

2 Getting Involved: The Political-Military Context

by William J. Durch

This chapter looks at how and why the UN becomes involved in peacekeeping and at how variations in local and international political support, the nature of the conflict, and the character of the marching orders given to the force (its "mandate") affect the feasibility and effectiveness of operations. Chapters three and four examine questions of funding and issues of planning, command and control, training, and equipment, and how they affect the ability of UN peacekeepers to do their jobs. The analysis draws on the case studies unless otherwise noted.

SOURCES OF INVOLVEMENT

How the UN becomes involved in a mission affects the operation's structure, objectives, and likelihood of success. Of the nearly two dozen UN operations studied here, about one-fourth resulted from Security Council initiatives to quell a conventional conflict. Another one-fourth originated with an independent request for UN assistance by the local parties to a conflict; all of these were made in the first half of the Cold War and involved situations best characterized as disputes over local political control. Fully one-half of all UN peacekeeping operations, some old, but most of them new, grew out of agreements brokered by third parties that sought UN assistance for implementation. The United States participated in brokering seven of these eleven cases. (See Table 2.1 for missions categorized by source of UN involvement.)

Table 2.1. Sources of UN Peacekeeping Operations

Security Council Initiatives

1. War for Palestine, 1948 *UN Truce Supervision Organization*
2. Suez Crisis, 1956 *UN Emergency Force I*
3. October War, 1973 *UN Emergency Force II*
4. Operation Litani, 1978 *UN Interim Force in Lebanon*
5. Iran-Iraq War, 1980–88 *UN Iran-Iraq Military Observer Group*
6. Gulf War, 1990–91 *UN Iraq-Kuwait Observation Mission*

Local Initiatives (source of initiative)

1. Greek Civil War, 1947 *UN Special Committee on the Balkans* (Greece)
2. Kashmir Dispute, 1948 *UN Military Observer Group in India and Pakistan* (India)
3. Lebanon Crisis, 1958 *UN Observation Group in Lebanon* (Lebanon)
4. Congo Crisis, 1960 *UN Operation in the Congo* (Congo)
5. Cyprus Dispute, 1964 *UN Force in Cyprus* (Cyprus and UK)

Brokered Requests for UN Assistance

1. West New Guinea, 1962–63 *UN Temporary Executive Authority* (US mediated)
2. Yemen Civil War, 1963–67 *UN Yemen Observation Mission* (US, UN mediated)
3. October War, 1973 *UN Disengagement Observer Force* (US mediated)
4. Afghan Civil War, 1988 *UN Good Offices Mission in Afghanistan and Pakistan* (UN mediated)
5. Cuban troops in Angola, 1975–91 *UN Angola Verification Mission I* (US mediated)
6. Namibian Independence, 1978–90 *UN Transition Assistance Group* (Western Contact Group Initiative, US mediated)
7. Conflict in Central America, 1980–90 *UN Observer Group in Central America* (UN mediated)
8. El Salvador Civil War, 1979–91 *UN Observer Mission in El Salvador* (UN mediated)
9. Angola Civil War, 1974–91 *UN Angola Verification Mission II* (Portugal/US/Soviet mediated)
10. W. Sahara Conflict, 1975–91 *UN Mission for the Referendum in W. Sahara* (UN Mediated)
11. Cambodia Civil War, 1969–91 *UN Advance Mission in Cambodia, UN Transitional Authority in Cambodia* (Perm Five initiative)
12. Yugoslav Conflict, 1991– *UN Protection Force* (UN mediated)
13. Somali Civil War, 1991– *UN Operation in Somalia* (UN mediated)

Security Council Initiatives

In six cases, the Council has taken the initiative to demand the conclusion of cease-fires in major regional conflicts and has followed up by dispatching UN peacekeeping operations. Those initiatives have all come in response to wars in the Middle East, including three of the four Arab-Israeli wars, the 1978 Israeli invasion of Lebanon, and the two recent Persian Gulf wars. The first Arab-Israeli conflict in 1948 led to the establishment of the UN Truce Supervision Organization (UNTSO); the second, in 1956, led to the UN Emergency Force (UNEF), the first armed peacekeeping mission, deployed in the Sinai following the Suez Crisis. The Israeli Defense Force drove through the remnants of UNEF in June 1967 at the start of the third Arab-Israeli war, and from 1967 to 1973 the UN presence in the Middle East was limited to the still-deployed, unarmed UNTSO observers. The fourth Arab-Israeli war, in October 1973, led to deployment of UNEF II, which helped implement a Security Council cease-fire devised by the US and USSR, and later supervised a US-brokered separation of Egyptian and Israeli forces. Similar mediation by the United States led to a 1974 agreement to separate Syrian and Israeli forces and to a spin-off operation, the UN Disengagement Observer Force (UNDOF) on the Golan Heights.[1]

In March 1978, the Israeli invasion of southern Lebanon sparked a US-sponsored Security Council resolution that called for a cease-fire, Israeli withdrawal, and a peacekeeping operation called the UN Interim Force in Lebanon (UNIFIL) to supervise both. Ten years later, a Council-mandated cease-fire created the Iran-Iraq Military Observer Group (UNIIMOG), which supervised the separation of Iraqi and Iranian forces along their 1,400-kilometer frontier. UNIIMOG's work wound down after Iraq's August 1990 invasion of Kuwait and formally ended as UN-sanctioned military operations to reverse that invasion began. Many of UNIIMOG's assets were redeployed a few months later to the UN Iraq-Kuwait Observer Mission (UNIKOM), whose task was to monitor the buffer zone established between Kuwait and Iraq by Security Council Resolution 687.

All of the operations initiated by the Security Council have involved "traditional" peacekeeping. Military units were sent to separate forces, monitor borders, and to investigate, mediate, and report on cease-fire violations. Usually dispatched in the immediate aftermath of major wars, they have rarely had the benefit of either long-range planning or a peace settlement, and have been primarily holding actions intended to prevent renewed outbreaks of fighting. The effectiveness of four of the six operations was ended by new conflicts. Only one of the operations (UNEF II) ended with a peace accord, the 1979 peace treaty between Egypt and Israel. A second (UNIKOM) is still operational at this writing and, as an outgrowth of a UN collective security enforcement action, has unique parentage and unique military support by the Great Powers. It is thus likely to fulfill its limited border-monitoring mandate successfully.

Unbrokered Local Requests

Independent requests for UN peacekeepers from local parties were more prominent in earlier decades than they are today. In 1947, Greece asked for UN observers to investigate outside arms shipments to Greek Communist guerrilla forces. In 1948, India sought UN condemnation of Pakistani aggression in Kashmir. A small force, the UN Military Observer Group in India and Pakistan

(UNMOGIP) was dispatched and remains there today after more than 40 years. In 1958, Lebanon asked the UN to document infiltration of arms and insurgents from Syria. The UN Observer Group in Lebanon (UNOGIL) withdrew within six months when the immediate crisis passed. In July 1960, leaders of the newly independent Congo issued several calls for UN assistance to repel "external aggression" when army mutinies threatened internal order and triggered Belgian military moves to safeguard European lives and property in the former Belgian colony. That operation lasted four years. Finally, communal strife in Cyprus in early 1964, and the country's refusal to accept a NATO peacekeeping force, led its Greek Cypriot-dominated government, along with Cyprus' guarantor power and former colonial master Great Britain, to request establishment of the UN Force in Cyprus (UNFICYP), which remained in place through 1992.

Two of these cases (Greece and the Congo) involved civil conflicts that were seen to have major Cold War implications. Aid to Greek insurgent forces was believed to be coming from Greece's Communist northern neighbors, and the strife-torn Congo was considered at the time to be a looming battleground between East and West in their contest for influence among the emerging new states of Sub-Saharan Africa. Two other cases, Lebanon and Cyprus, involved civil conflicts with religious roots far deeper than the Cold War, but the US and its allies supported the dispatch of peacekeeping missions to maintain political stability and thus minimize Soviet influence. Troubles in Jammu and Kashmir also had religious as well as political origins in the struggles between Hindus and Muslims to sort out the boundaries of their respective states in a region that, from the late 18th century until 1947, had been British-ruled India.

With the exception of Kashmir, therefore, UN responses to independent requests for peacekeeping forces served primarily the West's interests in regional stability. This perceived bias was one reason for Soviet hostility to peacekeeping prior to 1986 and was an important constraint on the potential of the UN system to contribute to world peace.

The policies of the USSR in the late 1980s made these issues moot, making possible a far greater role for UN peacekeeping. On the other hand, with the anti-Soviet, anti-Communist motivation removed, Western willingness to become involved in such situations is much reduced. The US showed great initial reluctance to support UN involvement in Croatia, for example. The UN itself did not move to end fratricidal violence in Somalia until the carnage reached epic proportions. Perhaps most telling of all, the political and economic situation in Zaire at the end of 1991 was roughly as chaotic as in mid-1960, and in many ways eerily parallel (mutinous soldiers, threats to foreigners, collapsing infrastructure, paralyzed government), but the upheavals have not yet produced "ONUC II."

Brokered Requests

This category includes roughly half of all the peacekeeping operations undertaken by the United Nations. The first one, the UN Transitional Executive Authority (UNTEA), stepped between the Netherlands and Indonesia to assist the transfer of West New Guinea from Dutch to Indonesian control over a seven-month period in 1962–1963. The bilateral agreement authorizing UNTEA was a product of talks brokered by then-retired US Ambassador Ellsworth Bunker, serving officially as the Special Representative of the Secretary General. Bunker was subsequently involved, along with UN Under-Secretary General Ralph Bunche, in mediating a Saudi-Egyptian dispute involving the two countries' material support for opposite sides in a civil war in North Yemen. An agreement to cease that assistance called for the UN Yemen Observer Force (UNYOM), which was duly dispatched in July 1963.

The US role in separating forces after the October 1973 Middle East War has already been noted. After that came a 14-year gap in brokered requests for UN peacekeeping operations. This gap resulted in large part from the continuing decay in US-Soviet relations that saw increased Soviet activism in regional conflicts and increasingly assertive US responses. During this period, the United States tried peacekeeping missions outside UN channels, sometimes with success but other times straying into miscalculated efforts to enforce preferred solutions to local conflicts. The Multinational Force and Observers, for example, is a US-led organization jointly supported by US, Egyptian, and Israeli funds that successfully deployed in January 1982 to monitor the Sinai under a protocol to the Egypt-Israel Peace Treaty. It remains a quiet success. Similarly, the first Multinational Force (MNF) for Lebanon, composed of US, French, and Italian troops, grew out of talks mediated by US presidential representative Philip Habib. MNF successfully monitored the withdrawal from Lebanon of Palestinian (and some Syrian) fighters pinned in Beirut by the rapid advance of Israeli forces in the summer of 1982. It then quickly departed, only to return just as quickly in the wake of massacres of Palestinian civilians by Christian Phalangist militiamen. French and American units of "MNF II" soon became too closely identified with Lebanon's Christian government, however, and in October 1983, both French and US contingents became targets of suicide bombers, with heavy loss of lives. Several months later both withdrew their forces from the country.[2]

By 1988, the waning Cold War facilitated a series of agreements, some settling longstanding disputes, others permitting the graceful—and verified—withdrawal of foreign forces from regional conflicts. UN peacekeeping operations to observe such withdrawals included the UN Good Offices Mission in Afghanistan and Pakistan (UNGOMAP), which monitored Soviet withdrawals from Afghanistan in 1988–1989, and the UN Angola Verification Mission (UNAVEM), which did the same for Cuba's withdrawal from Angola. The Soviet pull-out was based on regional multilateral agreements mediated by the UN in Geneva. The Cuban pull-out was based formally on a bilateral agreement between Cuba and Angola signed in late 1988, one result of a long US mediation effort that included Angola, Cuba, and South Africa (whose forces withdrew from Angola the previous year).

Other recent agreements calling for UN assistance include Esquipulas II, the Central American presidents' vehicle for conflict resolution in that region. The UN's first operation in Central America (ONUCA) was deployed in late 1989 in the five countries of that region to support Esquipulas' ban on harboring or supplying "extra legal" military forces. UN mediation also produced the UN Operation in El Salvador (ONUSAL) in July 1991, which was a multipartite mission to monitor and investigate human rights issues. Starting in January 1992, ONUSAL's mandate was enlarged to monitor a cease-fire in that country's twelve-year civil war, leading toward implementation of an accord that will demobilize guerrilla forces and reintegrate them into national life. Finally, a 1989 initiative by the five permanent members of the Security Council, brokered through the Paris Conference on Cambodia, led to authorization of a UN Transitional Authority in Cambodia (UNTAC), designed to rebuild the country and oversee its transition to democratic rule. Such settlements allow peacekeeping operations to be more than temporary palliatives.[3]

In every instance in which there has been a political settlement, the conflicting parties' objectives have changed from winning *everything* to a more modest objective, winning *something*. Openness to settlement may stem from stalemate on the battlefield or from the mutual exhaustion of the local parties, which leads them to look more favorably at alternatives to fighting. Movement toward a deal may also be a function of pressures exerted by outside powers who see their own interests placed at risk by continued conflict. Whatever the source of the shift, the parties reach the conclusion that pure victory is unattainable and, equally important, that settling for less than total victory does not mean risking total defeat.[4]

Noncoercive, third party peace*making*, or mediation, can play a crucial role in this process. Intermediaries can bring in new ideas and facilitate communications between the parties without requiring politically difficult face-to-face talks. Of course, where one party does not recognize the legal existence of the other, any progress made in indirect talks may be illusory. The case of Western Sahara is illustrative. Through six years of UN mediation, and right through the initial deployments of the UN's referendum-conducting team in 1991, Morocco refused to recognize the POLISARIO independence movement as anything more than an internal phenomenon, even though POLISARIO's state-in-exile had been accorded diplomatic recognition by many African countries. Morocco's calculus of victory clearly had not yet been altered.

Mediation cannot produce peace overnight, particularly where the perceptions of the local parties are conditioned by years, and occasionally centuries of ethnic, religious, or national grievances, as in the Middle East. Yet mediation has produced peace over time, especially when shifts in external support have paralleled battlefield exhaustion. The Namibia mediation effort, for example, was begun by the so-called Western Contact Group (Canada, France, then-West Germany, the United Kingdom, and the United States) in the 1970s. Talks stalled in the early 1980s, but finally bore fruit late in the decade, when a combination of rising costs (on South Africa's part), dwindling outside support (on Angola's part), and the opportunity to achieve through diplomacy what combat could not, led Angola, South Africa, and Cuba to agree to Cuban and South African withdrawals from Angola, South African withdrawal from Namibia, and a UN-supervised transition to Namibian independence.[5]

POLITICAL SUPPORT

Peacekeeping operations require complementary political support from the Great Powers and the local parties. If either is missing or deficient, an operation may never get underway or may fail to achieve its potential once deployed.

Great Power Support

The changing face of UN peacekeeping is a function of the changing nature of international relations at the Great Power level. A few past peacekeeping operations benefitted from the tactical confluence of US and Soviet regional interests during the Cold War, as in the case of UNTEA, where both sides backed Indonesian claims to West New Guinea, although for different reasons. It was also the case for UNEF II. Both sides wanted to end the fighting in the October 1973 War. In the last few years, however, Moscow and Washington have consistently followed complementary foreign policies, and the positive results have been apparent in southern Africa, Central America, Southeast Asia, and most visibly, in the Persian Gulf.

US support has been particularly crucial for peacekeeping in the past. In 45 years of UN peacekeeping operations, all that have gone forward have had US support, while others that were still-born suffered a lack of such support. Nicaraguan requests for observers to monitor the activities of Contra guerrillas, for example, or France's proposal to have UN troops secure the PLO's withdrawal from Beirut in 1982, were both blocked by the United States. As it demonstrated in the prologue to the Gulf War, Washington can marshall an awesome array of political, military, and financial resources when its governmental machinery is bent to the task.

In the new era, US leadership may sometimes be most effective when exercised quietly, behind the scenes, in concert with other powers. Such efforts can and have spelled the difference between success or failure of peacekeeping missions at critical junctures. For example, when deployment of the military component of UNTAG was delayed in late March 1989, fighters of the Southwest African People's Organization (SWAPO) poured into Namibia from their bases in Angola, threatening the settlement agreement. UNTAG's leaders felt compelled to let South African military forces leave their Namibian bases to contain the incursion, which resulted in several hundred casualties. Intercession by the Joint Commission of Angolan, Cuban, and South African officials established by their tripartite agreement of December 1988, on which US and Soviet officials sat as interested observers, helped to bring the fighting to a halt, induced SWAPO to withdraw with promises of safe passage back into Angola, and allowed the peacekeeping mission to proceed. Quiet US leadership was exerted in this action. Even if UN forces had been fully deployed in Namibia at the time, it is not clear that they would have been willing or able to accost SWAPO, let alone throw themselves between SWAPO's fighters and South African guns.

Local Support

Although support by the Great Powers, and especially the Security Council's five permanent members, is necessary for successful peacekeeping, it is far from sufficient. The need for "consent of the local parties," although recited often enough to appear a cliché, is also crucial if an operation is to be both politically effective and financially supportable. Peacekeeping is cheap compared to war because it does not require such expensive military accoutrements as armored brigades, advanced air forces, or 30-day supplies of smart munitions. Peacekeepers don't require such things because they don't have to force their way into disputed territory; they are invited to deploy there with the consent of the local parties. Consent also makes peacekeeping operations more effective politically, because they can build trust faster with parties who want them than with parties who don't, or parties who are ambivalent.

Impartiality is important to maintain local consent. When it falters, the consequences can be fatal, as happened to MNF II in Beirut. But impartiality itself, in the views of some partisan observers, may be evidence of bias (as in, "he who is not with me, is against me").

Iran, for example, treated UNIIMOG with marked suspicion. Part of UNIIMOG's difficulties could be attributed to Tehran's initial lack of familiarity with UN peacekeeping, and to a general wariness of foreigners "spying" near its most sensitive military dispositions. Iraq had the benefit of Egyptian briefings about what to expect before UN personnel arrived, and Iran had no such coaching. Continuing Iranian suspiciousness, however, suggests a more fundamental problem than unclear initial expectations.

Iran was suspicious of all outside UN communications, and especially suspicious of communication links between UNIIMOG elements in Iran and those in Iraq, concerned perhaps that military secrets derived from UN inspections were being funnelled to Iraqi authorities. As a result, Iranian officials impounded the operation's main INTELSAT transmission dish, used to talk to New York, and shut down the smaller INMARSAT terminal used to communicate with UNIIMOG-Baghdad. Ground observers assigned to the Iranian side of the international border were not permitted to cross into Iraq, nor observers on the far side to cross into Iran. Indeed, ground observers were restricted to a very narrow strip of border zone and generally were not allowed to venture inland. Even when permission came down from Tehran to allow such visits, local commanders often failed to act on it. And observers were usually accompanied by members of a specially raised, politically correct group of escort-interpreters. Restrictions applied to air patrols as well. The UN was forbidden to bring any of its own observation helicopters into Iran, and suitable Iranian helicopters were not always available when needed. Having had only their removable doors painted "UN white," they could be reassigned to military tasks on short notice.

Unhappiness with peacekeeping operations may be even more pronounced when a local party feels that its arm was twisted to accept the operation. When that party is particularly well armed, the peacekeepers' mission can become impossible, as happened to UNIFIL. Never fully accepted by Israel, UNIFIL was not able to extend its area of operations to the Lebanese-Israeli border (nor, to be strictly fair, into Palestinian strongholds around Tyre). In 1982, UNIFIL was brushed aside by Israel's reinvasion of Lebanon, and today has a limited role and limited freedom of movement, even within its nominal area of operations. Israel might have supported the operation had UNIFIL been willing and able to seal its area to all "armed elements" hostile to Israel, meaning Palestinians and extremist Lebanese factions, at the risk of firefights and continuing casualties. Dissatisfied with UNIFIL, Israel retained the Lebanese proxy force it had created to enforce "security," as it saw it, in southern Lebanon. After its troops withdrew from Lebanon, they left behind a "security zone" patrolled by their proxies that overlapped UNIFIL's area to a significant degree, especially near the Syrian border. Both developments have made life difficult for the UN peacekeepers.[6]

In some cases, certain armed groups may be less than happy to see peacekeepers appear. Like El Salvador's *Farabundo Marti National Liberation Front* (FMLN), they may perceive the UN force to be deployed against their interests. The five Central American presidents' Esquipulas II accord called for an end to cross-border arms aid to insurgent movements in the region, and a UN force deployed there (ONUCA) had the job of monitoring regional compliance. Particularly after the Nicaraguan Contras demobilized, the FMLN felt (rightly, in fact) that ONUCA's principal remaining mission was to abet the shutdown of FMLN arms supplies. ONUCA's leadership was told that the FMLN did not want to see any of ONUCA's white Toyotas or UN helicopters on or over its areas of influence—and they didn't. When the Salvadoran conflict reached the stage, in the summer of 1991, where a settlement seemed possible, an entirely separate UN operation was established to help implement it. And when eleventh-hour negotiations in New York at the end of 1991 produced a peace accord, ONUCA was immediately terminated, and most of its personnel and equipment were transferred to the new operation, ONUSAL.

In Afghanistan, government forces and the *mujahedeen* fought on while the UN monitored the withdrawal of Soviet combat forces. As the guerrillas were neither party to the withdrawal agreement nor much interested in making UNGOMAP's job easy, the UN's observers did not venture much into the field. In Angola, a similar withdrawal agreement covering Cuban forces was somewhat easier to verify because guerrilla forces there recognized that interfering with UN personnel would not benefit their cause.

GROUND TRUTH, MANDATE, AND FEASIBILITY

The characteristics of the field situation, what peacekeepers call the "ground truth," carry their own implications for the success or failure of a mission. A border war presents UN forces with one set of circumstances, an internal struggle a different one. In this section, we look at the impact of ground truth, at how an operation is instructed to deal with it (i.e., its "mandate"), and at how the UN copes with operations that run off the rails.

Clarity of the Mandate

Although studies of peacekeeping often note the importance of a clear mandate to a successful peacekeeping operation, the attitudes of the local parties and the support of the Great Powers, as suggested above, seem to be more important determinants of a mission's likely success. An ambiguous or incomplete mandate can indeed make a straightforward mission difficult, or a difficult mission impossible, but the clearest mandate in the world cannot make an impossible mission more feasible. It merely paints the impossible task in high-contrast colors.

Mandates tend to reflect the political play in the Security Council. Ambiguous mandates are often a sign that the Great Powers' perceived interests in the situation diverge, but that each of the potential veto-wielders is willing to go along with the operation for the time being, so long as its duties are fudged.[7] It is this fragile political consensus behind the operation, and not the ambiguity of its instructions per se, that may endanger a field force should its operational circumstances deteriorate. In such cases, the energetic interpretation and implementation of a mandate by field personnel can create even more turmoil in New York and a backlash in the field, as happened to UN officials in the Congo whenever they took forceful actions.

With a peak strength of 20,000 troops, ONUC was the largest peacekeeping force so far deployed by the United Nations. Its initial mandate of July 1960 authorized Secretary General Hammarskjöld to "provide the Government [of the Congo] with such military assistance as may be necessary until...the national security forces may be able, in the opinion of the Government, to fully meet their tasks."[8]

ONUC had the strong support of the United States and, initially, the support of the USSR as well, until it became clear that UN troops were not going to suppress the foreign-supported secession of the country's richest province, Katanga, as Prime Minister Patrice Lumumba wished. (In Hammarskjöld's view, ONUC did not then have the authority to use force.) Lumumba then sent his own troops toward Katanga in Soviet-provided transport aircraft. When they killed large numbers of civilians en route, Lumumba was sacked by the Congo's pro-Western president. When he attempted to fly his troops back to the capital to seize control, UN officials closed the capital's airport and seized its radio station. In the ensuing political turmoil, the government dissolved, Soviet General Secretary Nikita Khrushchev demanded Hammarskjöld's resignation, and ONUC occupied itself trying to minimize death and destruction in the country while gingerly gluing its fragments back together. When ONUC failed to prevent Lumumba's assassination in early 1961, one-third of its troop contingents were pulled out by their governments, but within a month its mandate was expanded to include the deportation of foreign mercenaries and the use of force to prevent civil war.

This ambitious order was not exercised for six months while a new central government was built under UN protection. When ONUC officials in Katanga did act to seize and deport European mercenaries, they did so haltingly, since whatever they did displeased some UN member governments. Partly as a result, three separate skirmishes over a period of sixteen months, and a further mandate amendment in November 1961 that explicitly ordered an end to Katanga's revolt, were needed before ONUC could complete its task.

The Security Council is unlikely ever again to dispatch such a sizable force under UN command with such a similarly undefined initial mandate. ONUC did permit the expeditious withdrawal of Belgian troops from most of the country, thus removing one source of tension, and did prevent the country from deteriorating into wholesale civil war and political breakup.[9] But at one time or another in its first nine months of operation, ONUC was the focus of harsh words and physical violence from every faction in the country. The experience was traumatic for the UN, and it cost Secretary General Hammarskjöld his life in a plane crash en route to Katanga. Thirty years would elapse before the Organization would undertake a peacekeeping operation remotely as large or as broad in scope.

Yet an ambiguous mandate is not without advantages and can serve as a vehicle for broadening political support for a controversial operation. Under such circumstances, vagueness may allow states to lend their support without appearing to endorse (indeed, leaving them free to denounce) specific actions taken under color of the mandate. Members used such freedom in the case of ONUC.

A second way to gain such sometimes necessary political cover is to have a major nation run an operation with UN blessing, much as Operations Desert Shield and Desert Storm were run in 1990–91. But future delegated mandates should probably be a good deal more specific than Resolution 678, which authorized the use of "all necessary means" to reverse Iraq's invasion of Kuwait. The United States chose to stop the war once that objective had been achieved, but a different political calculus on the part of a coalition leader could have sent its forces on to Baghdad. If that leader (or an ally) wielded a veto in the Security Council, then the Organization would find itself in the uncomfortable position of sponsoring an operation that it could neither control effectively nor terminate. Delegated mandates should therefore be used with extreme caution.

Scope of the Mandate

What an operation is asked to do can have as much to do with its success or failure as how clearly it is asked to do it. Over time, the UN has demonstrated that it is good at fulfilling certain mandates, among them monitoring national borders for large-scale troop movements, verifying cease-fires between conventional armed forces, overseeing the subsequent separation of such forces, monitoring or supervising elections, and mediating political transitions where all sides are happy enough to have the transition take place.

Mandates for which the historical record is less consistently successful include attempts to restore governmental authority that has been seriously eroded by civil unrest. Lebanon is the clearest historical example.

Mandates for which the record is decidedly negative involve border monitoring to detect illicit infiltration of people or weaponry. Not since the UN Special Commission on the Balkans helped to verify outside support for Greek Communist guerrillas in 1947 has the UN managed to deploy a force that has been effective in monitoring arms trafficking. The observers dispatched to Lebanon in 1958, to Yemen in 1963, and to Central America in 1989 generated little or no evidence of contraband. All of these missions experienced problems of access, and none was either equipped or particularly willing to watch for illicit activity after dark. Indeed, the very premise of such missions violates the requirement for impartiality, which is one of the basic principles of successful peacekeeping (unless, of course, the gun-runners in question are merely smugglers whose activities are devoid of political content, in which case their activities are the proper purview of national police authorities, not the UN).

The UN's first peacekeeping mission in Central America, ONUCA, was supposed to monitor border regions to verify states' compliance with obligations to cease all assistance to regional insurgent forces. Once ONUCA had been deployed for a few months, however, the UN realized that neither arms traffickers nor the local populace who might see their comings and goings were about to impart potentially life-threatening information to UN officers, who could neither stop infiltrators nor protect informers. Thus, in late 1990, the operation was reduced in size and its mandate was reinterpreted to focus on local authorities' own implementation of Esquipulas II. The new mandate was a change for the better, as the increased scrutiny prompted those governments to improve their own border monitoring.

Options for Problematic Missions

Mandate revision is one of the UN's three principal options when a force is not contributing to the solution of a conflict or cannot otherwise fulfill its original tasking. The other options include soldiering on with an unrevised and unsuccessful mandate (as on Cyprus) and withdrawal (as did the first Sinai force).

A revised mandate might ask less of a force or, under appropriate conditions, might ask more.

Soldiering On. Soldiering on is the path of least resistance and regret (except on the part of the middle powers who contribute most of the troops and pay most of the bills). The UN does not want to appear to be declaring a dispute insoluble by withdrawing its force, nor does it want to risk blame for outbreaks of violence that might follow such withdrawal. Such charges of dereliction were levelled at the Organization by critics of UNEF's pull-out from the Sinai in 1967 just before the outbreak of the June War, even though the UN had no legal recourse but to leave Egyptian territory when Cairo requested it. Since Israel refused to accommodate a UN presence on its soil, UNEF had nowhere to go but home.

Another operation, UNFICYP, intended as a temporary palliative, became a political fixture. Inserted to separate conflicting parties, the Cyprus force treated the symptoms of Greek-Turkish strife so well that the local parties lost incentive to treat the causes. The human cost of this political recalcitrance has been reduced without creating or requiring any changes in basic local attitudes. UNFICYP's presence removes the need for compromise. Not happy with this situation, the UN nonetheless chose to stay in Cyprus for nearly three decades, rather than to leave and force the local parties either to resolve their dispute or to face further bloodshed.

The UN would also prefer not to face a "snap back" operation, in which peacekeeping forces are rapidly returned to a situation worse than the one they left, as were the contingents of MNF II. Perhaps overly sensitive to what they perceive as the Organization's limited reserves of credibility in international affairs, UN officials prefer to hang tight, even when staying may be damaging to the image of peacekeeping, as well as to real resolution of an underlying conflict.

Lowering Expectations. In 1978, UNIFIL deployed into a situation as unsettled as the Congo or Cyprus, and one that met none of the conditions for mandate strengthening. UNIFIL's operating area was limited (and Israel opposed extending it to Beirut). Israel and Syria were far stronger than UNIFIL militarily, and Great Power support did not extend to military intervention on the UN's behalf.[10] However, UNIFIL illustrates the other alternative for mandate revision, namely, reduction in scope.

Prevented from carrying out its original, arguably impossible, instructions to restore the authority of a then-crumbling government in the southern part of the country, UNIFIL became an essential provider of basic services and political protection to the populace within its area of operations. When UNIFIL first deployed in 1978, the population in its area of operations was about 50,000. As fighting in and around Beirut escalated during the 1980s, the UN area's population peaked at 300,000, serving as a sanctuary from Beirut's violence. This is a population that the UN is loathe to abandon. Since the Lebanese government, gradually rebuilding its power since the Saudi-brokered Ta'if accords of 1989, also prefers a weak buffer force in the south to none at all, UNIFIL is likely to remain in place with a narrow, largely humanitarian, agenda.

Strengthening the Mandate. In principle, the Secretary General can approach the Security Council to seek a stronger mandate, but for the UN forces to make effective use of a new mandate with, say, quasi-enforcement powers, several political-military conditions should be met first. The UN force must operate throughout a country's territory and not just in a border region, and it must have substantial military power relative to local combatants, or be able to invoke such power reliably. Thus, it must have the active cooperation of the relevant Great Powers and not just their acquiescence. Finally, it must have the cooperation of regional powers to deny an uncooperative party sanctuary and support. These conditions are difficult to meet.

ONUC was the first, and so far the only, peacekeeping operation to have had its mandate successively strengthened to cope with deteriorating field conditions.[11] However, the military balance in the Congo was no more than merely adequate from ONUC's perspective, and in 1960–62 the country was nearly surrounded by European colonies, including Portuguese Angola and British Northern Rhodesia (now Zambia), through which Katanga's rebels could be supplied with arms. France and the Soviet Union were largely hostile to the operation and refused to support it financially, and British official opinion was divided, as was Belgian. US support was consistent, but its attention was not, as it weathered both the Berlin Wall Crisis and the Cuban Missile Crisis while ONUC wrestled with Katanga. All of these factors contributed to the uneven and hesitant manner in which ONUC went about its tasks, and made the Congo experience nearly as searing for the UN as Vietnam was for the United States.

Member states' objections to entanglement in comparable situations of civil unrest helped prevent the operation in Cyprus (begun three months before ONUC ended) from being funded as an obligatory "expense of the Organization." Moreover, conditions surrounding UNFICYP were not conducive to strengthening its mandate when local conditions deteriorated. Regional powers Greece and Turkey, two of three guarantors of Cypriot independence, not only failed to inhibit, but even encouraged, armed elements within their respective Cypriot communities. (The third guarantor was Great Britain.) Prospects for Soviet support of a stronger mandate for UNFICYP when unrest increased in the late 1960s and early 1970s were thus nil, and Cyprus' stipulation that no people "of color" serve in the UN peacekeeping force doubtless left much of the nonaligned world indifferent to its troubles.

Of the newer UN operations, those in Iraq (taking together the relief operations, the weapons-hunting of the Special Commission, and UNIKOM) meet most of the conditions for mandate expansion. The operation in Cambodia (UNTAC), where Khmer Rouge resistance to UN plans was an early source of concern, may meet some of the conditions. UNTAC's ability to adapt to problems will depend on whether its modest military capability can be reinforced; on the willingness and ability of Thailand, Laos, and Vietnam to seal their borders to weapon infiltration; and on the continued support of the permanent members of the Security Council, and of China, in particular, as chief external patron of the Khmer Rouge.

Risks in Settlement

The UN has undertaken several operations since 1989 in support of national political settlements. But implementation of a settlement plan is not risk free. Some local factions may remain disgruntled or may hope to use the settlement for their own ends. In Namibia, for example, considered the UN's greatest implementation success to date, the incursion by SWAPO, which wasn't party to the settlement, nearly wrecked it at the outset, and right-wing elements of the old Southwest Africa security police harassed potential black voters well after UNTAG deployed. South African security forces worked covertly to manipulate the election, and busloads of new-found "Namibians" were trucked across the border from South Africa to help dilute SWAPO's expected electoral majorities.

The implementation of a settlement plan contains three particular risks: some agreements only appear to embody a political settlement; the UN cannot guarantee that it has fully disarmed fighting forces that are demobilized as part of a settlement; and a settlement can begin to come apart after UN forces depart.

Expedient Agreements. Many peacekeeping forces, even some growing out of brokered requests for UN help (Table 2.1, above), deploy as expedients and are neither billed nor perceived as permanent solutions to conflict. However, some negotiated agreements masquerade as settlement plans, providing the appearance of settlement without its substance.

One example of an expedient agreement would be the Dutch-Indonesian accord that effectuated transfer of West New Guinea from Dutch to Indonesian control in 1962–63. The agreement, and the UN operation that managed the transition, UNTEA, kept the two powers from outright warfare over this territory and in those terms was quite successful. But the agreement settled little from the perspective of the local Papuan population. Having ousted the Dutch, Indonesia remained determined to control the territory, and six years after the UN force withdrew, a series of local conclaves, tightly controlled by Indonesian authorities, endorsed union with Indonesia.[12]

A second example would be Western Sahara, where de facto political control passed from a European colonial power (Spain) to Morocco in the mid-1970s. Armed resistance to the new regime was far better organized than in West New Guinea, but stalemate ensued by the mid-1980s, opening a window for UN mediation. After six years of UN mediation, Morocco and Polisario agreed to have the UN conduct a referendum on the political fate of the territory. It is difficult to craft a settlement when both sides want all of the land. UN mediators drafted an agreement that would give all of it to one party or the other. If a majority of voters cast their lot with Morocco, the well-organized POLISARIO movement was to bow out gracefully after nineteen years, with the UN supervising its disarmament. If a majority voted for POLISARIO, on the other hand, Morocco was to withdraw its forces, relinquish territorial claims that were overwhelmingly popular with Moroccan politicians and public alike, and leave behind several hundred thousand recent Moroccan settlers to a political future about which the agreement said nothing. It said only that Morocco would leave, followed by the UN, at which point the strongest armed factions in the territory would be free to do as they liked. The basic terms of the accord were thus a recipe for continuing turbulence, whatever the outcome of the referendum. As of this writing, the referendum plan is in abeyance while the parties wrangle over the question of who is eligible to vote (the answer to which would determine the outcome of the election). The peoples of West New Guinea and Western Sahara had the misfortune to live in places coveted first by colonial powers and then by imperious neighbors. In both cases, political agreements appeared to offer a choice to the local peoples, but the realities of regional power made that choice more apparent than real. If the UN wishes to continue or expand its role in fostering democratic transitions, it must come equipped to assure a level political playing field and to truly guarantee the outcome of free and fair votes, lest its role in such transitions appear merely cosmetic.

Demobilizing Armed Elements. Where a settlement calls for the UN to disarm and demobilize "armed elements," like the Contras (or the Khmer Rouge, or the POLISARIO), it is difficult to verify that this actually happens. In Nicaragua, the UN understood that significant quantities of arms would remain in the bush and that it had neither the authority nor the manpower to search for or seize those arms. In Cambodia, it was given the authority to conduct such searches, but not the manpower (or the firepower). In Croatia, the UN was to rely on the Serbian-dominated Yugoslav federal army to disarm Serbian militias in the areas of the country to be monitored by UN forces. In such cases, the Organization can only hope that the hedging party finds the new political situation sufficiently congenial that it does not create secret arms caches or, more realistically, feels no need to use them.

Even if all local parties formally support an accord, there may be splinter groups who do not, or remnants of armed elements who have turned to banditry in the countryside. Countries on the rebound from lengthy civil wars may also have largely demolished or deteriorated physical infrastructures that make the reestablishment of civil order all the more difficult. UN peacekeepers sent into such circumstances must be prepared, therefore, to face hostilities that neither emanate from nor are amenable to political solution. Activities such as mine clearing may require active protection, as may the local populace.

In short, despite every effort politically to avoid placing its forces in harm's way, a UN force deployed into a situation of recent civil war may find it necessary to undertake, at least locally and on a small scale, operations not unlike those required in counterinsurgency. The alternative may be to suffer continuing casualties, among populace and peacekeepers alike, that threaten the success of the mission. As Mackinlay observes, for such operations to succeed, the peacekeepers must be seen to be acting with the support of the people, and any use of force must be "precise" in its effects. But such responses will be viable only against splinter groups and outlaws. Should a major local party renege on the settlement agreement, the force may have little choice but to withdraw.[13]

Dealing with Backsliding. Political settlements can begin to come unstuck after the UN departs the scene. Two examples illustrate the problem.

In Nicaragua, the Sandinista Front was unexpectedly voted out of office in February 1990 national elections closely monitored by the Organization of American States and the UN's own Mission to Verify the Election in Nicaragua (ONUVEN). ONUCA helped demobilize the Nicaraguan Resistance thereafter. But tensions remained between the new government and the Sandinistas, who were still a powerful political force with effective control of the army. Former members of the Resistance clearly retained access to armaments, and the most active cells of "recontras" did not lay down their arms until early 1992.

In December 1990, the United Nations Mission to Verify the Election in Haiti (ONUVEH) helped to monitor that country's first free and fair presidential election. Although not designated a peacekeeping mission (at the Haitian government's request), ONUVEH did have a small component of military officers who advised the Haitian military on conduct during the election, which unleashed an unexpected flood of support for social activist Bertrand Aristide. An early coup attempt against the new government was turned aside, but nine months after the vote, and long after UN and other election monitors had gone home, a more powerful coup ousted President Aristide. The Organization of American States voted economic sanctions and, after long negotiations to return Aristide to power, devised a plan to oversee implementation of the new political settlement. But as of mid-1992, Haiti continued to languish under military rule, and thousands of Haitians had fled the island by any means available.

Similar problems may occur on a much larger scale in other places in the future, and the UN needs to devote more thought to following up its peace-building operations with efforts to shore up the new polities that they create and leave behind. The shoring-up process might involve continued monitoring by a small, free-roving observer group. Or it might involve technical advice, integrated development assistance, or some combination of all three. Having intervened once to halt conflict or to help a people establish democracy, the international community has an interest in preserving what it has wrought, if not an obligation.

SUMMARY

Peacekeeping missions do not get off the ground without Great Power support, and they do not fare well *on* the ground without local consent. The more complex the local situation, the more opportunities to lose the consent or the trust of one or more parties. When that happens, an operation is in jeopardy. A peacekeeping mission that loses a substantial element of local support can no longer do its original job.

Ambiguous mandates can make a difficult mission harder, but the clearest of orders cannot make an impossible mission feasible. Rapid UN deployments to contain conflicts or reinforce ceasefires do immediate good, but they may leave the UN bogged down indefinitely in costly operations. Mediation offers the UN a chance to resolve, rather than simply contain, local conflicts, but containment may be all that is feasible in many situations.

For the future, the Organization needs to decide where to put most of its peacekeeping money and how many new, long-term commitments it can realistically afford. In addition, the UN needs to think harder about the implications of its growing involvement in implementing political settlements and rebuilding countries, the ways in which such operations can go wrong, its options if they do, and the sorts of reserve capabilities that it will need in such cases. The most difficult reserve capacity of all to maintain, however, is likely to be financial.

Notes

1. UNDOF remains in place. UNEF II would still be in the Sinai, helping to implement the 1979 Egypt-Israel Peace Treaty, but for Soviet objections at the time. When its mandate expired in 1979, UNEF II's role was filled, ad interim, by the U.S. Sinai Support Mission, a group of civilian observers and technicians originally tasked to monitor the Midi and Gitla passes. In early 1982, the Sinai monitoring role passed to the Multinational Force and Observers (MFO).

2. For details on these non-UN cases, see Mona M. Ghali, *The Multinational Forces: Non-UN Peacekeeping in the Middle East*, Occasional

Paper No. 12 (Washington, D.C.: The Henry L. Stimson Center, October 1992).

3. Stimson Center Occasional Papers on ONUSAL and UNTAC are forthcoming in 1993.

4. Brian Urquhart, "International Peace and Security: Thoughts on the Twentienth Anniversary of Dag Hammarskjold's Death," *Foreign Affairs* (Fall 1981): 11. Arrangements motivated solely by outside pressure, however, are unlikely to produce durable settlements, as the shifts in the local political calculus that they induce are likely to be expedient and temporary, rather than fundamental.

On the general topic of negotiations and conflict resolution, there is a large literature. Relevant works with a practical bent include Raymond Cohen, *Negotiating Across Cultures: Common Obstacles in International Diplomacy* (Washington, D.C.: US Institute of Peace, 1991); Francis M. Deng and I. William Zartman, eds., *Conflict Resolution in Africa* (Washington, D.C.: The Brookings Institution, 1991); Roger Fisher and William Ury, *Getting to Yes: Negotiating Agreement Without Giving In* (Boston: Houghton Mifflin Co., 1981); and I. William Zartman and Maureen R. Berman, *The Practical Negotiator* (New Haven and London: Yale University Press, 1982).

5. South Africa's original stake in Namibia changed as its apartheid policies relaxed under domestic and international pressure, and as the financial and human costs of maintaining forces in Angola increased. The decline of Soviet activism and influence in the Third World also reduced South Africa's perceived need to buffer itself against encroaching Communist influence. Cuba agreed to leave Angola after South Africa pulled back and promised to leave Namibia as well. In a real sense, the settlement allowed all sides to declare victory and go home, except for SWAPO, which went home and then declared victory, although its percentage in the constitutional elections monitored by the UN fell short of a controlling two-thirds.

6. Most recently, exchanges of fire between Iranian-supported Hezballah fighters and the Israeli Defense Force escalated into a 24-hour Israeli ground incursion that pushed through UNIFIL checkpoints to engage Hezballah within the UN's area of operations. Several peacekeepers were wounded (*New York Times*, February 16, 1992, 3; February 17, 1992, A1; February 18, 1992, A8; February 22, 1992, A1; and the *Washington Post*, February 21, 1992, A1).

7. Paul F. Diehl, "Peacekeeping Operations and the Quest for Peace," *Political Science Quarterly* 103, no. 3 (1988): 497.

8. Security Council Resolution S/4387, July 14, 1960. China (Taiwan), France, and the UK abstained. Quoted in Rosalyn Higgins, *United Nations Peacekeeping, Vol. III: Africa* (Oxford: Oxford University Press, 1980), 15.

9. The US also wished to prevent a direct US-Soviet military clash in the Congo, although this objective was never a formal part of ONUC's mandate.

10. The US was busy brokering the Israeli-Egyptian peace accord and, in any case, was still flush with Vietnam Syndrome, prompting reluctance about ground involvement in Lebanon that seemed quite appropriate when viewed from the perspective of the MNF II disaster five years later.

11. ONUCA's mandate was also expanded temporarily, but to adapt to new opportunities, such as disarming the Nicaraguan Contras, and not to salvage the mission.

12. Arend Lijphart, *The Trauma of Decolonization: The Dutch and West New Guinea* (New Haven: Yale University Press, 1966), especially 285-291; Brian May, *The Indonesian Tragedy* (London and Boston: Routledge & Kegan Paul, 1978), chapter five; and Christopher J. McMullen, *Mediation of the West New Guinea Dispute, 1962, A Case Study* (Washington, D.C.: Institute for the Study of Diplomacy, Georgetown University, 1981), 71.

13. John Mackinlay, "Powerful Peacekeepers," *Survival* (May–June 1990): 246-248.

3 Paying the Tab: Financial Crises

by William J. Durch

It takes money to keep the peace, and money for peacekeeping is in chronically short supply. This chapter looks at past and present UN funding crises, the present and likely future cost of peacekeeping, the UN system for covering these costs, and how the Organization repays the countries who send troops to UN operations.

To fund its operations, the United Nations collects dues (or "assessments") from each of its member states. Although UN assessments are treaty obligations that members are bound to pay under international law, the Organization has little leverage in this critical area. The only sanction in the UN Charter against nonpayment of dues (Article 19) is loss of one's vote in the General Assembly after accumulating the equivalent of two years' arrearages, but even that sanction is not automatic. Moreover, the bigger the country, the harder to implement sanctions. In 1961, France and the USSR refused to pay their shares of peacekeeping costs, which had escalated sharply for operations in the Sinai and the Congo. Although the UN sought and won an advisory opinion from the International Court of Justice that peacekeeping costs were legitimate "expenses of the Organization," neither country paid up. But neither lost its vote. Instead, the Assembly agreed to proceed for two sessions without taking any votes.[1]

Today, because the Assembly passes its budgets by consensus (at US insistence), Article 19 sanctions might actually mean something if applied, since they would rob a state of its "veto" on spending issues. In reality, however, Article 19 is unlikely to be revived.

There is no typical peacekeeping operation, financially speaking. The cost of a mission varies with the number of people involved, the mix of military to civilians, and the type of equipment required. Member nations contributing units for peacekeeping missions are compensated at the flat rate of $30-$40 per day per soldier regardless of rank (the higher rate is for technical specialists), while civilian specialists and military observers (usually officers) serving individually in missions receive a per diem ("mission subsistence allowance") that may exceed $100 per day. Thus, the missions in Lebanon (UNIFIL) and on the Golan Heights (UNDOF), each consisting almost exclusively of troops in units, cost between $20,000 and $30,000 per person on the ground per year. Missions featuring individual observers, like UNIIMOG (Iran-Iraq) and ONUCA (Central America), cost around $90,000 per person on the ground per year.

These financial estimates, moreover, greatly understate the true cost of peacekeeping, as they neglect the contributions in kind often made to peacekeeping missions, including some air and sea lift, intelligence, planning, and logistical support. Most importantly, some of the countries contributing troops to peacekeeping missions provide an implicit subsidy to the UN, both by bearing the expense of the specialized training necessary to prepare their forces for UN work and because the rates at which they pay their soldiers exceed the troop reimbursement rates used by the United Nations. In an extreme case, the bulk of actual operating costs on Cyprus are borne by the troop contributors themselves.[2]

Because each peacekeeping operation is now separately funded, with its own Special Account, member states receive separate assessment letters for each mission; since ongoing missions are frequently mandated for six-month periods, states receive two letters per mission per year. Because operations' "fiscal years" follow their mandate periods, which started on the date they were authorized by the Security Council, letters arrive at member states' treasuries year-round. It is sheer luck if they coincide with states' budget cycles. Unless there is a national fund set aside for anticipated UN requests for money, states either must work these requests into their budgets as best they can or must seek special appropriations.[3]

THE FUNDING CRISIS

Since 1985, the UN has been coping with a funding crisis precipitated in part by the United States Congress, in the form of the Kassebaum-Solomon amendment, which threatened to choke off successively larger fractions of US contributions to international organizations unless they undertook significant administrative reforms.[4] As a result, the United States accumulated several hundred million dollars in arrearages, which the Congress agreed to repay over five years, starting with fiscal year 1991. Since 1981, moreover, the United States has budgeted its regular UN dues a year later than when they are due. Thus, the fiscal 1992 US budget, passed in October 1991, contained money for the United States' calendar year 1991 UN obligations, assessed the previous January. Under this system, one quarter of the UN's regular budget (the US share) is never available until the last quarter of the UN's fiscal year, so every fall, the Organization begins to run critically short of cash.[5]

If all other UN member states paid their dues in a timely fashion, Washington's tardiness would not matter quite so much, but the United States has company. As of December 31, 1991, nearly 40 percent of the assessments for the regular 1991 UN budget had yet to be paid; by the following June, over 35 percent of 1991 assessments remained outstanding *along with* 65 percent of 1992 dues, meaning that the UN was short a full year of funding. Unlike the US government, the UN has no borrowing authority; when assessments are not paid, neither are salaries and creditors.[6]

There has been a similar crisis with peacekeeping, where it has proven far easier to excite the Security Council into supporting new missions than to get member states to pay their share of the cost on time (or at all). For example, only twenty-five percent of 1992's heavy peacekeeping assessments had been paid by June, most likely because members' budgets hadn't made allowance for the new year's sharp increase in spending. The United States, however, was for once ahead of the pack, paying nearly 85 percent of its 1992 peacekeeping dues by June.[7] Russia, on the other hand, which inherited the debts of the USSR and is hard-pressed for hard currency, owed $110 million in peacekeeping back dues and $97 million in current assessments, toward which it had paid nothing. The number two financial contributor to peacekeeping, Japan, withheld 85 percent of its peacekeeping payment until the last minute in 1991, but began paying promptly after assuming a two-year seat on the Security Council in January 1992. Tokyo's payments had a regional twist, however; contributions for Cambodian operations were made in full by June, while just one-third of its assessments for Lebanon and Angola had been paid, and nothing had been sent to the UN for the force in Croatia.[8]

The UN weathered its 1961 crisis partly by issuing $200 million in 25-year bonds, of which $169 million were actually purchased, 45 percent by the United States (in accordance with limits imposed by the Congress). The bond issue kept the Organization and its two major peacekeeping missions going for a year. Although the Secretary General has periodically sought borrowing authority in recent years, as well as the authority to charge interest on overdue assessments, his requests have been denied by the General Assembly, even though penalties for late payment are so common in business and government alike as to be unremarkable, and are used by other agencies in the UN system.[9]

Over the years, various voluntary funds have also been proposed or established to ease the Organization's financial problems. For example, the UN has always maintained a Working Capital Fund as its basic cash reserve. Last increased to $100 million in 1982, the Fund has been regularly depleted of late to cover arrearages.

In 1965 and again in 1972, the General Assembly established a Special Account intended to allow states that had withheld their assessed contributions to peacekeeping operations to make voluntary contributions to those operations. Although nominally worth well over $100 million by 1989, counting contributions and accumulated interest, the Special Account has been drained along with the Working Capital Fund to pay the daily expenses of the Organization.[10]

More recently, a Trust Fund in Support of United Nations Peacemaking and Peacekeeping Activities was established with initial financial support from Japan, Australia, Sweden, and others. As of the end of 1991, it contained six million dollars.[11] A separate trust fund was created for advance voluntary contributions to peacemaking and peacekeeping in Cambodia. Finally, in late 1991, the Secretary General urged the establishment of a one billion dollar Peace Endowment Fund, with roughly one-third of the money to be provided by governments, and the remainder to be raised from the private sector.[12]

It is not clear, however, that states will contribute voluntarily what they fail to contribute under legal obligation. Unless the UN becomes more widely viewed as a source of indispensable services, like the International Monetary Fund, late-paying member states will continue to pay late and also refuse to give the Organization a bigger stick to use against those in arrears. Peacekeeping can and should be viewed as such an indispensable service, not the only one that the UN provides, but an important one that serves member states' national interests in a stable and peaceful international political environment.

In the wake of the 1960s financial crisis, the only new peacekeeping missions undertaken for ten years were those paid for by the disputants themselves, or those supported by voluntary contributions. In the current crisis, the Organization may not be loathe to initiate new missions, but those missions may be cut back in size and face delays because they lack start-up funding. Moreover, the UN will have to rely upon the continuing good will and patience of troop contributing governments, whose costs may not be reimbursed for years. Because of the way the UN structures its missions and pays its forces (discussed shortly), operations organized around military units may be the only readily affordable ones in the near future.

Table 3.1 Cost of UN Peacekeeping, 1989–1991, and Payments Outstanding at the End of 1991

Mission and Starting Date	Cost ($US mil)			Outstanding ($US mil)	
	1989	1990	1991	To 1990	1991
UNTSO (1948, Israeli borders)	21	22	24(a)	—	
UNMOGIP (1949, Kashmir)	4	4	5	(a)	—
UNFICYP (1964, Cyprus)	26	28	29	(b)	(b)
UNDOF (1974, Golan Heights)	36	37	38	6	10
UNIFIL (1978, Lebanon)	141	142	152	167	98
UNGOMAP (1988, Afghanistan)	7	7	—	(a)	—
UNIIMOG (1988, Iran-Iraq)	95	44	8	1	—
UNAVEM I/II (1988, Angola)	9	5	52	1	14
UNTAG (1989, Namibia)	294	71	—	(c)	—
ONUCA (1989, Cent. America)	—	49	23	3	4
ONUVEN (1990, Nicaragua)	2	—	—	(a)	—
ONUVEH (1990, Haiti)	—	5	—	(a)	—
UNIKOM (1991, Iraq-Kuwait)	—	—	60	—	9
ONUSAL (1991, El Salvador)	—	—	13	—	6
MINURSO (1991, W. Sahara)	—	—	141	—	55
UNAMIC (1991 Cambodia advance mission)	—	—	10	—	—
Secretariat Support Costs	3	3	4	(a)	—
Totals:	638	417	559	178	196

Note: Table includes payments outstanding as of 12/31/91. Table notes: (a) Regular budget; (b) Voluntary contributions (as of May 31, 1991, UNFICYP had a $188 million deficit); (c) Surplus, being distributed to other accounts as the creditor states direct.

Source: Authors' estimates based on information from Fred Schottler, DPI/CPMD/PSPS (Fax, October 4 & 14, 1991), *Proposed Programme Budget for the Biennium 1992-93*, Vol. 1 (A/46/16/Rev.1), part II, *Report of the Secretary General on Cambodia* (S/23097/Add.1, September 30, 1991), and *Status of Contributions as at December 31, 1991* (Document ST/ADM/SER.B/364, January 8, 1992).

CURRENT COSTS

Through 1988, the United Nations typically spent less than
$300 million annually for peacekeeping. In more recent years, as
the demand for peacekeeping missions has increased, total annual
peacekeeping costs have risen sharply, although they still remain
small by the standards of contemporary military operations. All
told, the UN probably spent close to $640 million on peacekeeping
in 1989, the first year of really big demands since the early 1960s.
Costs declined in 1990, but rose again in 1991, exceeding $550
million (see Table 3.1), and truly zoomed in 1992, as the most
expensive ongoing missions in Lebanon, Western Sahara, and
Kuwait were joined by the missions in El Salvador, Croatia, and
Cambodia. Annualized costs had reached nearly $2 billion.[13]

Nonetheless, peacekeeping remains cheap when compared to
the cost of modern militaries. The $638 million spent by the UN
for peacekeeping in 1989, for example, was less than the annual
operating cost of a single US Army division that is *not* engaged in
battle. Even 1992's much larger budget only equalled the cost of
one nuclear-powered attack submarine. The United States pays
the largest share of UN peacekeeping costs (just over 30 percent),
but it would have to save its 1992 share for eight years to have
enough money to pay for a single aircraft carrier, and then it
would have to wait another three years to buy the air wing to
operate from that carrier.

The cost of peacekeeping should also be compared to the costs
of war itself. The United States' expenditures in the 1991 war
against Iraq, for example, totalled approximately $63 billion—
more than 100 times the amount spent for UN peacekeeping
worldwide in that same year. If the opportunity had presented
itself prior to the Iraqi invasion, the $100 million that it might
have cost to place a large UN monitoring force on the Iraq-Kuwait
border, in conjunction with intense preventive diplomacy, would
have been a bargain for this country and the financial backers of
Operation Desert Storm, and an even sounder investment for
both Iraq and Kuwait, if it served to prevent a war.[14]

Evaluated in such a context, annual peacekeeping budgets of
$2 to $3 billion remain a bargain for the world. A budget of this
size would permit the UN, each year, to conduct one large
operation with high administrative content, like the one planned
for Cambodia, two good-sized operations consisting primarily of
troops in units, like the one in Lebanon, and dozen or so smaller
missions, like those in Central America, which seem likely to be

on the UN's agenda in the years ahead. If the budget were raised to $3 billion, the United Nations could reimburse countries for more of the in-kind services they contribute to peacekeeping, an innovation that would make calculations of assessments more fair to major national contributors of military units and support services.

Nonetheless, the cost of UN peacekeeping and related activities has grown so fast in the last two years that the system that finances them is experiencing extreme stress.

PAYING THE TAB

Article 17 of the Charter empowers the General Assembly to approve the budget of the Organization and states that "expenses of the Organization shall be borne by the Members as apportioned by the General Assembly." The apportionment is called the "scale of assessment." The regular budget scale is steeply progressive, based on ability to pay. Assessments for the richer half of UN members are proportional to their Gross National Product (GNP), while assessments for the poorer half are adjusted for low per capita GNP and for external debt. There is a maximum regular assessment (25 percent, paid by the US) and a minimum (0.01 percent, paid by the 78 poorest states).

Over the years, a few small observer missions like UNTSO (with about 260 military observers in the Middle East) have been paid for out of the regular UN budget. "Good offices" and technical survey missions, as well as peacemaking and the office staffs who support the activities of Special Representatives of the Secretary General (his impromptu alter egos for conflict mediation and other important missions), are also funded from the regular budget, for about $2 million annually, as is the small staff in the Office of Peacekeeping Operations ($4 million).

All other UN peacekeeping missions are financed through special arrangements. The mission on Cyprus, UNFICYP, which cost about $29 million in 1991, is paid for by strictly voluntary contributions from a relative handful of states. The others are budgeted and paid for out of special accounts and financed according to special assessments on all member states. This has been the custom since the Second UN Emergency Force was sent to the Sinai in the wake of the October 1973 Middle East War.[15]

Special assessments for peacekeeping charge the five permanent members of the Security Council (known for this purpose as "Group A") about 22 percent more than the regular scale.[16]

Other developed industrial states (Group B) pay the same share for peacekeeping as for the regular budget. Wealthier developing countries (Group C) pay just one-fifth of their regular budget share for peacekeeping, while the poorest countries (Group D) pay just one-tenth of their regular share (or 0.001 percent). For 1991, the 78 countries in Group D were assessed about $5,000 apiece for peacekeeping (see the Appendix to this chapter for a complete listing).

There are some curious anomalies in the assignment of states to Group C, particularly the fifteen states with per capita GNPs of $5,000 or more (see Table 3.2). These states, it would seem, could readily afford to make a full contribution to the UN's peacekeeping accounts. This would be desirable, as a matter of equity. Were they to move to Group B, its share of peacekeeping costs would rise two percent, to roughly 43 percent; the Perm Five's share would drop two percent, to about 55 percent; and Group C's share would drop one-half percent, to less than two percent. To its credit, one country (Spain) voluntarily made the switch from Group C to B when one of its countrymen took command of ONUCA in 1989; it will pay a full regular share of peacekeeping expenses starting in 1992.

Table 3.2 Fifteen Wealthiest States Paying Reduced Assessment for Peacekeeping

Country	Per Capita GNP ($US)	Est'd Pct World GNP	Pct Regular Assessment	Peacekeeping Assessment
UAE	19860	.15	.19	.038
Kuwait	16160	.16	.29	.058
Qatar	15860	.03	.05	.010
Brunei	14100	.02	.04	.008
Singapore	12310	.16	.11	.022
Bahamas	11510	.01	.02	.004
Israel	10970	.24	.21	.042
Cyprus	8040	.03	.02	.004
Barbados	6540	.01	.01	.002
Bahrain	6380	.02	.02	.004
Saudi Arabia	6200	.42	1.02	.204
Malta	6020	.01	.01	.002
Greece	6000	.29	.40	.080
Libya	5310	.11	.28	.056
Oman	5220	.04	.02	.004

Note: Gross National Product per capita from latest available year. **Sources**: *World Bank Atlas*, 1989 and 1991 eds. (Washington, D.C.: International Bank for Reconstruction and Development, 1990, 1991). United Nations, *Status of Contributions as at 31 December 1991*, ST/ADM/SER.B/364, January 8, 1992.

The rationale for the special scale rests on the argument that the Permanent Five, with privileged positions as veto-wielders on the Security Council, have greater than average influence over Council decisions, and greater than average responsibility for international peace and security. With greater influence and voting privileges, it is argued, comes heavier than usual political and financial responsibility for Council actions.

However, in the regular scale of assessments the majority of the General Assembly already have a steeply progressive system of dues, although for some of the poorest and smallest even 0.01 percent may be a burdensome assessment. If so, the desirability of a minimum contribution needs to be revisited, and their burden reduced. Still, at present, 125 UN member states together provide just six percent of the UN's regular budget, and just two percent of the contributions to peacekeeping accounts. Ninety-eight percent is financed by the Permanent Five and the developed states.

Moreover, while officials of developing countries argue that their governments are too strapped for cash to be dunned for any larger share of global peacekeeping costs, the same countries spend, on average, several thousand times more per year on domestic military expenditures than they do on peacekeeping. A fractional reduction in these countries' military spending would fully fund a greater commitment to peacekeeping, even if annual costs reach the $3 billion projected above *and* the regular scale were to become the basis of assessment.[17]

MISSION START-UP

A peacekeeping mission is created in a series of steps whose sequence depends in part on the source of request for the mission. Security Council initiatives tend to be a direct response to a crisis, so the processes of mission structuring, contributor recruitment, and mission budgeting occur more or less simultaneously. With more time, the sequence is usually the following:

- Mediation, with one or more field survey missions conducted as political settlement nears, or soon after it is reached.

- Presentation of the mission concept to the Security Council for its preliminary approval.

- A directive from the Council to the Secretary General to report back with a plan for the peacekeeping mission that indicates its overall size, structure, duties, and timing.

- Creation of that plan by the Office of Special Political Affairs (SPA) with assistance from the Field Operations Division (FOD) in the Office of General Services.

- Council approval of the plan.

- Creation of the mission budget by FOD.

- Review of cost justifications by the Special Peacekeeping Unit in the Office of Planning, Programming, Budgeting, and Finance (PPBF).

- Submission of the mission budget by PPBF to the Advisory Committee on Administrative and Budgetary Questions (or ACABQ, the standing budget review unit of the General Assembly's Fifth, or Financial, Committee).

- ACABQ recommendations to the Fifth Committee (which includes all member states).

- Fifth Committee consensus and referral to the General Assembly for final, consensus approval.

Once the budget has been approved by the GA, the UN sends out assessment letters to member states. Until then, the Secretariat can make no contracts for equipment, transport services, or the like, that exceed the current $10 million cumulative annual limit on the Secretary General's independent spending authority for "unforeseen and extraordinary circumstances."[18]

This constraint can prove dangerous. In the case of UNTAG, a lag of six weeks between authorization and budget approval—caused by haggling over the size, structure, and cost of the operation—left the UN with just four weeks to order all of the materials, the new field equipment, and the transport needed to meet a mission start-up date that had been fixed by agreement among Angola, Cuba, and South Africa. Troop contributor Finland was prepared to send its battalion to Namibia some three weeks before it was eventually dispatched in an emergency US airlift, the source of urgency being the sudden incursion of SWAPO forces into Namibia discussed in an earlier section.

In the case of Cambodia, the relatively long delay between signature of the Paris Agreement in late October 1991 and the deployment of the main body of UNTAC left the country in unstable political equilibrium, its civil order and infrastructure continuing to deteriorate, and a spring monsoon season approaching that promised to make most rural areas inaccessible by road for many months.[19]

As one way to cope with the problem of start-up squeeze, the Secretariat has developed the flexible mission timeline, which does not start to run until the budget is approved. This approach was used for ONUCA and MINURSO, the mission to Western Sahara, and shows promise for future operations where time is not at a premium.[20] Where time *is* at a premium, however, particularly for large missions whose start-up costs exceed the SG's current autonomous spending authority, a mechanism needs to be developed whereby the Secretariat can enter into contractual commitments after a mission is authorized but before its budget is approved. This may entail larger discretionary spending authority for the SG, and/or submission of preliminary budget estimates to the Security Council along with the mission plan. The latter approach tends to raise hackles in the legislative bodies if it appears to usurp their prerogatives in financial matters.

A second time-lag affects the UN's ability to field and sustain a full-size operation quickly. It is not coincidental that the UN operations in Cambodia got underway in piecemeal fashion, first with a 260-person advance mission, then with 1,000 additional mine-clearing personnel. In late 1991, the Secretary General appealed to member states to advance up to $200 million to fund the start-up of UNTAC, saying that the Organization needed assurance of such funding before it made the great leap to a full-fledged effort to rebuild the country. The scope and sensitivity of the operation were such that the UN could not afford to have its activities grind to a halt in three months' time because it had run short of funds. The General Assembly, in mid-February 1992, finally authorized the Secretary General to enter into contractual obligations for UNTAC worth up to $200 million. At that point, the recruitment of the operation's large civilian components got underway in earnest.

UNTAC's situation was the most acute because the operation was so ambitious, but it is not unique, and the problem cannot be laid entirely at the doorsteps of member states. Delays stem in part from the way the UN assesses and accounts for its peacekeeping funds.

REIMBURSING TROOP CONTRIBUTORS

As noted earlier, governments are reimbursed directly at a flat per-person rate for the troop units (such as infantry or logistics battalions) contributed to UN peacekeeping operations. The middle industrial powers, who are the most frequent contributors to UN peacekeeping and whose troops are the most expensive to support, never fully recoup the costs of their participation in UN operations. Poorer troop contributing countries, who send the lowest-paid forces with the least technical skills, are reimbursed much more than their actual costs. A 1990 survey of troop contributors revealed that their monthly per-person cost averaged $2,300, so the average contributor absorbed about 59 percent of the actual costs of keeping its troops in the field. But actual costs varied by $2,000 in either direction, from as little as $280 per month to as much as $4,400. The lowest-cost contributor is thus "reimbursed" roughly 3.5 times as much as it spends, and the highest-cost contributor a bit less than one-fourth of its costs. The fixed reimbursement system functions, in effect, to redistribute resources to developing countries' militaries, but without requiring that surpluses be invested in equipment or training that could be useful to the UN at a future date.[21]

Individuals who participate in peacekeeping missions outside of formed military units are paid salary and per diem if they are full-time UN employees, or just per diem if they have been seconded by governments as election observers, police, or military observers. Paying them requires the continuous and timely distribution of cash. Commercial vendors must also be paid in good time, lest they refuse in the future to sell items or lease services to the UN. Governments tend to have more patience than the market, so governments that contribute troop units, and especially governments of wealthier countries, tend to be the last to receive reimbursement from the UN.

Despite their commitment to the concept of peacekeeping, some middle powers have been growing disenchanted with the idea of doing it essentially for free. Most of that disenchantment appears to be directed not at countries that profit financially from peacekeeping, but at the wealthiest countries that withhold or otherwise delay their payments to the UN. US repayment of its old debts in particular will do much to reduce the middle powers' sense of having been exploited (particularly in Lebanon and Cyprus) because of their commitment to peacekeeping.

SUMMARY AND CONCLUSIONS

The financial situation in peacekeeping currently depends crucially on the timely and regular contributions of a relatively small handful of countries—the Permanent Five—and on the contributions in cash and in kind of roughly twenty other developed states. The special scale of assessments for peacekeeping reflects General Assembly decisions made in 1973 to relieve developing states of most of their obligations to support these UN operations. However, ratios of military spending to spending on peacekeeping in many developing countries are much higher than in developed states, suggesting that a reexamination of national spending priorities in the Third World is in order. Such an examination might suggest that there would be a net benefit in trading some military spending (far less than one percent) for higher contributions to UN peacekeeping, that is, for making the rate of contributions, over time, the same as that found in the regular UN scale of assessments. Countries making the change should be accorded greater opportunities for equipment, training, and participation in UN operations, which would return more to national coffers than higher monetary contributions to peacekeeping would take away.

Finally, the UN's ability to dispatch peacekeepers promptly is hampered by internal financial constraints, and by its year-round billings to member states. Both need to be redressed if peacekeeping is to evolve from its old status of emergency activity to one that is fully integrated into the functions of the United Nations.

Notes

1. Rosalyn Higgins, *United Nations Peacekeeping, 1946–1967, Documents and Commentary, Vol. III: Africa* (Oxford: Oxford University Press, 1980), 282-85, 294-300.

2. For costs and reimbursements for UNFICYP, see UN Security Council Documents S/18431, November 1986, and S/22665, June 1991.

3. For example, the United States budgeted $90.6 million for peacekeeping for its fiscal year 1991, which ran from October 1990 through September 30, 1991. Although the money for the United States' regular UN payment is budgeted a year behind UN assessments, an effort is made in the State Department to budget ahead for peacekeeping. But the 1991 budget, submitted to the Congress in February 1990, was based on planning begun in the spring of 1989. The US initially owed $92.3 million for calendar year 1991, very close to the amount requested from Congress, but new missions begun in mid-year added $67 million to the tab. Of that added amount, the United States' $19 million share of costs for

UNIKOM, the operation on the Iraq-Kuwait border that began in late April, was appended to an emergency appropriation for war refugees, sailed through the Congress, and was sent to the UN by July. But there is very little money available for the other new missions. State had budgeted just $69 million for peacekeeping in fiscal year 1992, evidently not foreseeing diplomatic breakthroughs in Angola or El Salvador, and discounting prospects for operations in Western Sahara, Cambodia, and the Gulf. Although the full $69 million fiscal 1992 request was approved by the Congress, after State finished paying 1991 assessments it had just $20 million in hand for peacekeeping payments in 1992, a year that pushed the US share for peacekeeping past $500 million. State went back to the Congress with a supplemental request for another $350 million for 1992, received $270 million, and budgeted another $350 million for fiscal 1993 (US Department of State, *The Budget in Brief, Fiscal Year 1993*, February 1992, 63).

4. For text of the Kassebaum Amendment, see US House of Representatives, Committee on Foreign Affairs, *The US Role in the United Nations, Hearings before the Subcommittee on Human Rights and International Organizations*, 98th Cong., 1st sess., October 3, 1983, 85. As modified in 1988, the amendment stipulates withholding 20 percent of US contributions to organizations that do not create their budgets by consensus. Also, by Administration policy, the US seeks to avoid real (inflation- and exchange rate-adjusted) growth in international organizations' budgets; the US will withdraw from consensus on budgets that exhibit such growth, which would trigger the Kassebaum withholding mechanism.

5. The US paid its regular 1991 assessment in two parts, $223 million in October and $79 million on December 31st, retaining enough to cover the requirements of the Kassebaum Amendment until assured that the General Assembly would pass the 1992 UN budget by consensus. Because the UN credits payments first against arrearages (overdue payments) and then against current assessments, how the UN and how a member state views its debits may be rather different. Thus, at year's end, the UN showed the United States without arrearages on the regular budget, but still owing $266 million for 1991 (71 percent of the total owed by all member states). The United States considers its 1991 assessment fully paid, while its back dues continue to be paid off in stages (United Nations Document ST/ADM/SER.B/364, January 8, 1992, 7).

6. United Nations Documents ST/ADM/SER.B/364, January 8, 1992, 7; and ST/ADM/SER.B/380, June 4, 1992, 6.

7. The US still owed more than $100 million for UNIFIL, however, of which $80 million was for back dues being remitted over a five year period.

8. ST/ADM/SER.B/380, 6.

9. To encourage prompt payment by their member states, the International Telecommunications Union and the Universal Postal Union— both UN specialized agencies—charge interest on "contributions not received by 1 January" of the year after assessments are made. The

International Civil Aviation Organization uses an incentive approach whereby the organization's interest income is "distributed to member states on a weighted scale which takes into account the dates of payment and amounts of current year contributions actually made." The incentive payment is proportionately greater for states paying in the first half of the year.

The 36th and 40th UN General Assemblies rejected Secretariat proposals for comparable incentive or penalty plans (*Financial Emergency of the United Nations, Report of the Secretary General*, United Nations Document A/C.5/42/31, November 5, 1987, especially 7-9).

10. Susan R. Mills, *The Financing of United Nations Peacekeeping Operations*, Occasional Paper No. 3 (New York: International Peace Academy, 1989), 13-14.

11. Unit for Peacekeeping Matters, Office of Program Planning, Budget and Finance, United Nations, telephone interview, January 22, 1992.

12. Paul Lewis, "UN Asks Billion for Peacekeeper Fund," *New York Times*, November 25, 1991, A3. Several of these ideas were also contained in the Secretary General's report, *An Agenda for Peace*, United Nations Document A/47/277, June 17, 1992.

13. By mid-year, moreover, the UN was conducting a humanitarian airlift into Sarajevo, Bosnia, and inching closer to armed humanitarian intervention in Somalia. Costs for 1992 were extrapolated from part-year assessments for ongoing missions listed in ST/ADM/SER.B/380, June 4, 1992.

14. The force described above is not conceived of as a deterrent force or a tripwire, but as expert eyes and ears for the Secretary General, and as a symbol of focused global attention on the budding crisis. Should diplomacy manage to defuse the immediate crisis, the force could either be withdrawn, or reconfigured as needed into a more permanent border monitoring operation.

Such a force would need substantial reconnaissance capability; in such a potentially dangerous situation, that capability might best be provided by drone aircraft, discussed below.

15. David W. Wainhouse, *International Peacekeeping at the Crossroads* (Baltimore: The Johns Hopkins University Press, 1973), 575.

16. The five states pay the following shares of the regular and peacekeeping budgets, respectively, for 1992: China, 0.77 and 0.94 percent; France, 6.0 and 7.29 percent; the former USSR, 9.41 and 11.44 percent; the UK, 5.02 and 6.10 percent; and the US, 25 and 30.39 percent.

17. Again, it is important to place the numbers in proper context. Toward a budget of $3 billion, a country in Group D would pay $30,000 under the current special peacekeeping scale, and $300,000 under the regular scale of assessments, if the floor on contributions in the regular scale remains at 0.01 percent. For a state like Tanzania, with per capita military spending of just $7 annually, the larger amount represents about two-tenths percent of its military budget. For a country in Group C with higher per capita military spending, like Syria ($242/year), whose

regular assessment is 0.04 percent, the full contribution would be $1.2 million, equal to about 0.04 percent of its military budget.

On average, in the late 1980s the Perm Five spent about $2,400 on armaments for every dollar they spent on peacekeeping. Countries in Group B averaged $750 in arms for each dollar devoted to peacekeeping. But countries in Group C averaged $20,000, and countries in Group D averaged $40,000 in military spending for every dollar spent on peacekeeping. Were they to contribute to peacekeeping on the basis of the regular scale of assessments, the ratios of military to peacekeeping expenditures in the latter two groups of countries would drop to 4,000:1, still well above the average of the developed industrial states.

Data on military spending was drawn from Ruth Leger Sivard, *World Military & Social Expenditures*, 14th ed. (Washington, D.C.: World Priorities, 1991), 54-59; data on the 1991 scales of assessment for the regular UN budget and peacekeeping were drawn from United Nations Secretariat Document ST/ADM/Ser.B/364, January 8, 1992.

18. Any expenditures exceeding $3 million in one year must be approved by the ACABQ under current General Assembly rules set at the start of each biennium. See United Nations Document A/RES/44/203, December 21, 1989.

19. *Far Eastern Economic Review*, February 27, 1992, 22-28.

20. See United Nations Documents S/22464, April 19, 1991, and A/45/241/Add.1, May 8, 1991.

21. For the history of troop reimbursement levels and policy, see United Nations Documents A/44/605/Add.1, October 12, 1989, and A/45/582, October 10, 1990, 5.

Appendix A. United Nations Member States and Assessments, 1991

	Regular Assessment (%)	Peacekeeping Category	Peacekeeping Assessment (%)
Afghanistan	0.01	D	0.001
Albania	0.01	C	0.002
Algeria	0.15	C	0.030
Angola	0.01	D	0.001
Antigua	0.01	D	0.001
Argentina	0.66	C	0.132
Australia	1.57	B	1.570
Austria	0.74	B	0.740
Bahamas	0.02	C	0.004
Bahrain	0.02	C	0.004
Bangladesh	0.01	D	0.001
Barbados	0.01	C	0.002
Belgium	1.17	B	1.170
Belize	0.01	D	0.001
Benin	0.01	D	0.001
Bhutan	0.01	D	0.001
Bolivia	0.01	C	0.002
Botswana	0.01	D	0.001
Brazil	1.45	C	0.290
Brunei	0.04	C	0.008
Bulgaria	0.15	C	0.030
Burkina Faso	0.01	D	0.001
Burundi	0.01	D	0.001
Belarus	0.33	B	0.330
Cambodia	0.01	C	0.002
Cameroon	0.01	C	0.002
Canada	3.09	B	3.090
Cape Verde	0.01	D	0.001
Cent.Afr.Rep	0.01	D	0.001
Chad	0.01	D	0.001
Chile	0.08	C	0.016
China	0.79	A	0.970
Colombia	0.14	C	0.028
Comoros Is	0.01	D	0.001
Congo	0.01	C	0.002
Costa Rica	0.02	C	0.004
Cote d'Ivoire	0.02	C	0.004
Cuba	0.09	C	0.018

	Regular Assessment (%)	Peacekeeping Category	Peacekeeping Assessment (%)
Cyprus	0.02	C	0.004
Czech & Slovak	0.66	B	0.660
Denmark	0.69	B	0.690
Djibouti	0.01	D	0.001
Dominica	0.01	D	0.001
Dominican Rep	0.03	C	0.006
Ecuador	0.03	C	0.006
Egypt	0.07	C	0.014
El Salvador	0.01	C	0.002
Equ. Guinea	0.01	D	0.001
Ethiopia	0.01	D	0.001
Fiji	0.01	C	0.002
Finland	0.51	B	0.510
France	6.25	A	7.680
Gabon	0.03	C	0.006
Gambia	0.01	D	0.001
Germany	9.36	B	9.360
Ghana	0.01	C	0.002
Greece	0.40	C	0.080
Grenada	0.01	D	0.001
Guatemala	0.02	C	0.004
Guinea	0.01	D	0.001
Guinea Bissau	0.01	D	0.001
Guyana	0.01	C	0.002
Haiti	0.01	D	0.001
Honduras	0.01	C	0.002
Hungary	0.21	C	0.042
Iceland	0.03	B	0.030
India	0.37	C	0.074
Indonesia	0.15	C	0.030
Iran	0.69	C	0.138
Iraq	0.12	C	0.024
Ireland	0.18	B	0.180
Israel	0.21	C	0.042
Italy	3.99	B	3.990
Jamaica	0.01	C	0.002
Japan	11.38	B	11.380
Jordan	0.01	C	0.002
Kenya	0.01	C	0.002
Kuwait	0.29	C	0.058
Laos	0.01	D	0.001
Lebanon	0.01	D	0.001

	Regular Assessment (%)	Peacekeeping Category	Peacekeeping Assessment (%)
Lesotho	0.01	D	0.001
Liberia	0.01	C	0.002
Libya	0.28	C	0.056
Liechtenstein	0.01	D	0.001
Luxembourg	0.06	B	0.060
Madagascar	0.01	C	0.002
Malawi	0.01	D	0.001
Malaysia	0.11	C	0.022
Maldive Is.	0.01	D	0.001
Mali	0.01	D	0.001
Malta	0.01	C	0.002
Mauritania	0.01	D	0.001
Mauritius	0.01	C	0.002
Mexico	0.94	C	0.188
Mongolia	0.01	C	0.002
Morocco	0.04	C	0.008
Mozambique	0.01	D	0.001
Myanmar	0.01	D	0.001
Namibia	0.01	D	0.001
Nepal	0.01	D	0.001
Netherlands	1.65	B	1.650
New Zealand	0.24	B	0.240
Nicaragua	0.01	C	0.002
Niger	0.01	D	0.001
Nigeria	0.20	C	0.040
Norway	0.55	B	0.550
Oman	0.02	C	0.004
Pakistan	0.06	C	0.012
Panama	0.02	C	0.004
Pap. New Guinea	0.01	D	0.001
Paraguay	0.03	C	0.006
Peru	0.06	C	0.012
Philippines	0.09	C	0.018
Poland	0.56	C	0.112
Portugal	0.18	C	0.036
Qatar	0.05	C	0.010
Romania	0.19	C	0.038
Rwanda	0.01	D	0.001
Samoa	0.01	D	0.001
SaoTomé/Princ	0.01	D	0.001
Saudia Arabia	1.02	C	0.204
Senegal	0.01	D	0.001

	Regular Assessment (%)	Peacekeeping Category	Peacekeeping Assessment (%)
Seychelle Is	0.01	D	0.001
Siera Leone	0.01	D	0.001
Singapore	0.11	C	0.022
Solomon Is	0.01	D	0.001
Somalia	0.01	D	0.001
South Africa	0.45	B	0.450
Spain	1.95	B	1.560
Sri Lanka	0.01	C	0.002
St. Kitts & Nevis	0.01	D	0.001
St. Lucia	0.01	D	0.001
St. Vincent	0.01	D	0.001
Sudan	0.01	D	0.001
Surinam	0.01	D	0.001
Swaziland	0.01	C	0.002
Sweden	1.21	B	1.210
Syria	0.04	C	0.008
Tanzania	0.01	D	0.001
Thailand	0.10	C	0.020
Togo	0.01	D	0.001
Trinidad	0.05	C	0.010
Tunisia	0.03	C	0.006
Turkey	0.32	C	0.064
Uganda	0.01	D	0.001
Ukraine	1.25	B	1.250
USSR (Russia)	9.99	A	12.290
Uruguay	0.04	C	0.008
UAE	0.19	C	0.038
United Kingdom	4.86	A	5.970
United States	25.00	A	30.400
Vanuatu	0.01	D	0.001
Venezuela	0.57	C	0.114
Vietnam	0.01	C	0.002
Yemen	0.01	D	0.001
Yugoslavia	0.46	C	0.092
Zaire	0.01	C	0.002
Zambia	0.01	C	0.002
Zimbabwe	0.02	C	0.004

Sources: Derived from United Nations, *Status of Contributions as at 30 November 1991*, ST/ADM/SER.B/362, December 4, 1991, Annex II.

4 Running the Show: Planning and Implementation

by William J. Durch

The UN's structure for undertaking peacekeeping operations evolved slowly over three decades. Until 1992, Peacekeeping Operations (PKO) was known as the Office of Special Political Affairs. Originally, Secretary General Dag Hammarskjöld (1953–1961) established two "Under-Secretaries Without Portfolio," who were retitled Under-Secretaries General (USG) for Special Political Affairs in 1961. One post was held by Ralph Bunche until his death in 1971, the other by José Rolz-Bennet until his death the same year.

Bunche was replaced by his long-time aide Brian Urquhart. For many years, Urquhart's side of Special Political Affairs oversaw the UN's operations in the Middle East, which then included virtually all of the ongoing peacekeeping missions. He oversaw both field operations and mediation efforts within his sphere of interest. In UN parlance, he had an "empire." When he retired at the end of 1985, Urquhart was succeeded by fellow Briton Marrack Goulding, making the position, by the UN tradition of successive appointments, a "British slot." But the office soon began to lose (or to relinquish) control over disparate bits of the peacekeeping business.

The other USG position in the office had become a Latin American slot by a parallel process of successive appointment. The officeholder served as a mediator and troubleshooter for the Secretary General (SG). Javier Pérez de Cuéllar held this post when selected to be SG in late 1981. His work as UN mediator for the crisis in Afghanistan passed to his successor, Diego Cordovez of Ecuador. After the agreements on Afghanistan were signed in 1988, friction over Cordovez's independent management style evidently led to his departure from UN service.

Soon after, Cordovez's post was abolished, and all peacemaking (that is, conflict mediation and political negotiation) functions were drawn into the SG's Executive Office and strictly separated from the operational side of peacekeeping—a separation that many viewed as unfortunate. As various peacemaking efforts bore fruit between 1988 and 1991, the offices charged with planning and implementing field operations frequently had no role in the crucial political prologue to deployment, nor did the Special Representatives of the Secretary General (SRSGs) tapped to head the operations. There was no requirement that peacemakers check with the operational offices before making or accepting proposals in their negotiations.[1]

Although peacekeeping is a quasi-military function, the UN has never possessed much of a military staff. Indeed, from the days of Hammarskjöld, who was dedicated to non-violent conflict resolution, the UN Secretariat evolved a culture that has tended to separate the concepts "peace" and "military."[2] Although the Military Advisor nominally has remained the Secretary General's principal source of military advice, he and his small staff of four or five officers function, for all practical purposes, as the military operations staff of PKO.

In the latter 1980s, with peacemaking done elsewhere and just a handful of long-term missions to run, the small staff of then-Special Political Affairs managed quite well for awhile, especially since day-to-day mission support was the job of another part of the bureaucracy entirely: the Field Operations Division (FOD) in the Department of Administration and Management, which generates requirements for transport, logistical support, and communications, draws up mission budgets, and tends to these aspects of each operation once it deploys.[3]

This structure was jostled by the upsurge of missions in 1988–89 and showed increasingly serious signs of strain by mid-1991. The peacekeeping staff, still fewer than two dozen in number, was attempting to cope with all political and military planning, military recruiting, and political backstopping for more than twice as many operations as in 1985, most of which were more complex than traditional border monitoring. Planning for some missions was interrupted by competing demands from others and, once launched, some important missions found themselves operating virtually without backstopping in New York.[4] Whatever margin the planning and implementation system may once have had was eaten up by the continuing crush of new missions.

Although the UN took a first step toward much-needed revamping of its basic administrative structure in early 1992, the impact on peacekeeping was not immediate. The new organization

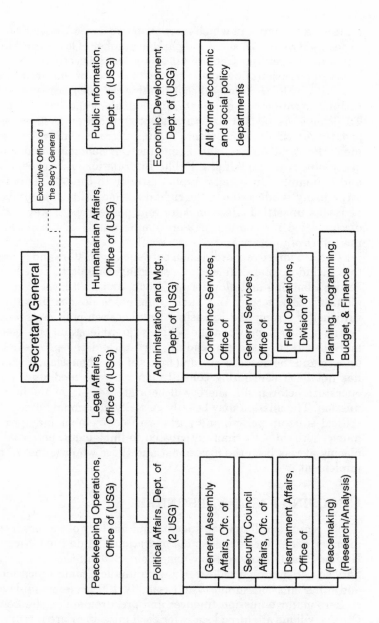

Figure 4.1. Organization Chart of the United Nations Secretariat, as of February 1992

replaced a structure in which more than two dozen Under-Secretaries General (USGs) and a comparable number of lower-ranking Assistant-Secretaries General (ASGs) reported directly to the SG. Ideas and decisions flowed all the way to the top of the Organization with little or no lateral coordination between bureaus, and little or no winnowing of wheat from chaff along the way.[5] Figure 4.1 depicts the revised structure adopted in March 1992, where just three "super departments" (Administration and Management, Political Affairs, and Economic Development) and four other offices (Legal Affairs, Public Information, Peacekeeping, and Humanitarian Affairs) report directly to the SG.[6] This restructuring, while a step in the right direction, still left a number of issues unsettled. Peacemakers and peacekeepers were still disconnected, for example, as were planners and logisticians, and recruiters of military and civilian staff.

Efforts to improve coordination between negotiators and operators included establishment of a standing committee called the Senior Planning and Monitoring Group, and high level mission planning task forces. But such committees do not provide a sufficiently strong and consistent link between politics and operations, that is, between the people who understand the needs and priorities of the contending parties, and the people who understand the needs, costs, and limits of a field mission. If there has not been continuing consultation between mediators and operators beforehand, there will be a greater lag in fielding a mission. The mission may be only partially functional during its critical start-up period, and parts of the agreement may prove much more difficult than anticipated to implement, potentially placing at risk both the agreement and those who are tasked to implement it.

CHOOSING FIELD PERSONNEL

PKO recruits military contingents and military observers from member states for peacekeeping operations, while the Office of Human Resources recruits civilians. Some 840 full-time FOD Field Service personnel provide world-wide mission communications and other mission support, and roughly 160 professional-level staffers manage mission finances and procurement in the field. Other civilians are hired locally for each mission or are recruited from member state governments.

In staffing a peacekeeping operation, all offices pay attention to "geographic distribution" to ensure recruitment opportunities for each of the UN's regional caucuses, even though there is no master list of countries, contingents, or expertise. Indeed, a questionnaire distributed to member states in 1990 asking what military capabilities, equipment, and forces they might make available to the UN, if requested, produced a rather disappointing return, and there has been no similar questionnaire for civilians. Still, more than 80 countries have at one time or another contributed at least individual observers, support personnel, or equipment to UN peacekeeping missions. Fewer countries have contributed military units (support units, infantry battalions or, on occasion, entire brigades). Support units have included air and ground transport, logistics, communications, engineering, and medical. As few developing states can provide more than basic infantry contingents, specialized units tend to be drawn from the middle industrial powers. Until recently, the Security Council's five permanent members have contributed primarily financial and logistical support to peacekeeping. However, several new operations, including MINURSO, UNIKOM, and UNTAC, have included military observers from all five.

Generally, when the need arises for contributors to a new operation, the Secretariat informally approaches diplomatic missions to the UN, outlining the capabilities that it needs and sounding out countries' willingness to provide them. The missions in turn ask their capitals, pass on replies to the Secretariat and note, when the reply is favorable, any national conditions on the size or type of unit, duration of deployment, and so on. If the conditions fit the UN's plans (or the plans can be adapted to the conditions), the Secretariat then makes a written request for the unit in the stated terms. This procedure allows both sides of the transaction to avoid saying "no," and mirrors decision-making elsewhere in an organization that routinely goes to great lengths to avoid loss of face for itself or its members.

When the Force Commander and the troop contributors for a traditional (all-military) operation have been selected, the highest echelons of the operation may be brought to New York for a week-long familiarization meeting. In most cases the Force Commander, who has had nothing to do with the planning of the operation he is to head or the choice of troop contributors, meets his second-level officers here for the first time. They may or may not meet, in turn, the personnel from FOD who will support the mission, or the UN civilians who will control all the funds and administer the operation in the field on behalf of FOD. Nor is there formal training for the military officers who will serve on the operation's headquarters staff to familiarize them with the FOD's voluminous field manual.

For multicomponent missions, which include civilian components as well as military units, predeployment coordination and familiarization is even murkier. All professional personnel, civilian and military, other than those deploying in self-contained military units, are recruited and supported by the UN as individuals (although governments may nominate their nationals in groups). Only the heads of the police or electoral components of such missions are likely to be briefed in New York about the mission. They, like the military, receive a mission plan drafted by someone whom they do not know, and they will not meet the people whom they are to lead until they reach the mission area. The latter individuals may or may not have prior experience working with a UN field mission, and are unlikely to be briefed on their duties before they reach the mission area. This can contribute to mission delay and reduce local confidence in the UN's ability to do its job, yet credibility with the local parties is established, or lost, according to experienced hands, in the first six weeks of a new operation. The tenser the local situation, the more likely it is that peacekeepers will be deployed in some haste, and the more critical it is that they be seen as competent and effective from the outset. This is particularly true for all-military missions that may be sent to exploit and expand temporary lulls in fighting. Multicomponent operations are likely to have been planned further in advance.

The UN's recruitment of countries and people for peacekeeping operations may always have an ad hoc air to it, as an unavoidable consequence of dealing with sovereign states and their prerogatives. But the impact of such recruitment on the start of new missions could be reduced by a training program that familiarizes military and civilian leadership cadres with UN mission goals and procedures before they participate in UN field operations. Eventually, such training should be required of most mission participants.

COMMAND AND CONTROL IN THE FIELD

Although peacekeeping operations are under UN command, officials in New York are well aware of the basically tenuous nature of their control over military contingents in the field. Most national contingents maintain radio contact with their home governments. Particularly in situations that may pose increased danger to their troops, governments are not averse to second-guessing UN field commanders if contingents "phone home" to clear orders, a process that can complicate operations and even increase the level of danger posed to troops in the field.

The UN, historically, has striven to reinforce its control over field missions by giving every mission a career UN Chief Administrative Officer to mind the money and dispense supplies, as well as FOD civilians to manage communications with New York. The Chief Administrative Officer reports back to FOD, whereas the Force Commander or Chief Military Observer reports to Peacekeeping Operations. The argument for this dual chain of command, the so-called "Middle East Model," rests in part on the need to have people in the mission who understand UN procurement and financial regulations, but also reflects the Organization's perceived need to maintain control and continuity in operations staffed in their view largely by "temps," that is, non-UN personnel who are typically on the scene for six months to a year, but no more than that.

Astute Force Commanders recognize the stability and expertise that the UN civilian presence imparts to longer-term peacekeeping operations. But their lack of control over spending can place an administrative straitjacket on operations that face a difficult or changing field situation. Logistics and finance are critical functions—an operation can fail for lack of food, water, transport, or spare parts—but they remain support functions tangential to the main mission, which is to contain conflict. Moreover, they are functions that modern military staff officers are fully capable of performing, given the time and advance opportunity to learn the basics of the UN procurement system.

With respect to relatively short-duration, multicomponent missions, like the one in Namibia, where a good fraction of the military, police, and other personnel are new to UN work and the SG's Special Representative is civilian, the Secretariat's argument for close UN staff control is on firmer ground. But as more of those missions are undertaken, the cadre of national personnel, both civilian and military, who are familiar with the UN *modus operandi* will broaden and deepen, allowing UN staff to be supplemented regularly by persons seconded from governments.

Civilian control of multicomponent missions represents not so much continuing "military allergy" on the part of the Secretariat as a judgment that, where UN operations facilitate political transitions, such operations must consistently demonstrate military subordination to civilian control. Given the prevalence of military regimes and the continuing fragility of democratic civilian control in many countries, this concern is legitimate and important for both operational and symbolic reasons. The UN correctly views such operations as primarily political. Politics is about power, and settlement agreements reallocate power or provide methods (usually elections) to bring about its reallocation. Nonetheless, military commanders (and troop contributing governments, who are often consulted by their contingents and may influence them directly) need to have sufficient confidence in UN leadership that they are willing to follow UN orders in instances where a local group may choose to dissent forcefully from a settlement accord.[7] To generate and maintain such confidence, the UN should appoint a general officer with UN field experience to work within an enlarged Department of Peacekeeping and International Security. For unless UN civilian-military relations are sorted out, there remains the potential for friction, even tragedy, as the UN embarks upon missions where civil conflict may not be fully extinguished or civil order has yet to be restored.[8]

EQUIPMENT AND TRAINING

Obtaining equipment for a new peacekeeping operation is a costly endeavor that may also delay the start of time-critical missions. Deployment of government-provided personnel without experience in peacekeeping can further delay the effective start of operations as these individuals are familiarized with the field situation and learn what is expected of them as members of a UN team. This combination of equipment delays and unacquainted, inexperienced personnel can create start-up problems that reduce the confidence of local parties in the UN's ability to sustain a peace or rebuild a society.

Equipping the Force

When the United Nations recruits a military unit for peacekeeping, it requests that the unit bring needed equipment with it (such as trucks, armored personnel carriers, communications gear).[9] Units from wealthier countries generally arrive well equipped, whereas units from poorer countries may arrive with rifles in hand and not much more. Transport and other support for them is provided either through donations from wealthier countries or through the UN procurement system. Equipment also must be purchased for new observer missions, which do not involve formed military units. There may be delays of weeks to months while the equipment is acquired and delivered.

With the rush of new missions since 1988, the Secretariat has therefore been interested in enlarging the role of the UN's storage depot at Pisa, Italy. Established in the 1950s as a way station for equipment bound for active missions, it remains essentially that. Nonperishable items such as uniforms and other personal accoutrements are stored there, along with items used by the UN's Disaster Relief Office (tents, blankets, plastic sheeting, buckets, and the like). A 1990 request that $15 million be authorized to create a revolving stock of vehicles, maintenance equipment, communications equipment, prefabricated housing, and the like, was denied by the Assembly's funding watchdog committee, which recommended that equipment be recycled from ongoing missions.[10]

Only with the advent of short-term missions like UNTAG, UNII-MOG, or UNAVEM I has this alternative emerged, as long-term missions will inevitably tend to wear out equipment. The mandates of UNIIMOG and UNAVEM I specified that surplus equipment be sent to Pisa upon completion of the mission. However, these operations were followed immediately by new ones (UNIKOM and UNAVEM II) that deployed nearby and absorbed their surplus. The same was true for ONUCA, whose personnel and equipment were shifted immediately to ONUSAL.

The press of new missions has in fact given the UN little choice but to purchase new goods in most cases, and to lease equipment to fill the gap between orders and deliveries. But costs sunk into leasing might better be directed toward smoothing out the acquisition of such items over the course of each year in anticipation of mission needs, even if that requires substantial enlargement of Pisa and hiring mechanics to maintain the supplies.

Although PKO and FOD can readily anticipate equipment needs, the authorizing and financial arrangements that support peacekeeping still treat it as an emergency function, and thus tend to treat each mission in fiscal and political isolation. The system does not respond to projections, only to specific mission budget requests, and the legislative arms of the UN focus on minimizing costs in each new instance. *Overall* costs might be minimized, however, with an approach that permitted total expected costs of peacekeeping to be estimated much as the regular biennial budget is estimated, and to be billed to member states just once a year, with adjustments each year to correct for over- and under-estimation.

Technology in the Field

Peacekeeping missions can make use of more than just vehicles, binoculars, and radios in their operations. Other technologies include aircraft, ground surveillance devices, and satellite communications.

Aircraft. Increasingly, air transport and air surveillance are seen as key "multipliers" of operational capabilities, especially where UN areas of operation encompass entire countries. Fixed-wing aircraft and helicopters, too expensive to purchase and maintain, are provided by governments or leased from private firms. Although civilian contractors tend to field "leaner" (and thus cheaper) units with fewer support personnel per aircraft, military units are more capable of responding to unforeseen circumstances. In Central America, for example, when ONUCA was ordered to support the redeployment and demobilization of the Nicaraguan Resistance (the Contras), and an infantry battalion showed up without transport, trucks used to support ONUCA's Canadian air unit were pressed into service as cargo-haulers; the civilian air unit had no such capacity.

The militaries of relatively few countries outside the industrialized West are equipped to provide air support to UN operations, particularly long-range transport of equipment. The US Air Force has traditionally provided most of the airlift for the initial deployment of UN peacekeepers. From the first Sinai mission in 1956 through the deployment of UNIFIL in 1978, the United States waived reimbursement for initial airlift. The US flew more than 2,000 sorties in support of the Congo operation and waived reimbursement completely for almost one-third of them.[11] When peacekeeping revived in 1988, the US government's deficit problems (and undoubtedly a certain lapse in institutional memory over the ten year gap between new missions) contributed to a decision to seek reimbursement from the UN for the cost of non-emergency airlifts. Emergency transport, as in the case of nine C-5 *Galaxy* missions to fly Finnish peacekeepers to Namibia in April 1989, has still been provided to the UN at no cost to the Organization. Such capabilities, which involve more than just aircraft—air traffic control personnel, as well as communications gear, spare parts, and repair capabilities must be distributed along the flight path—remain a predominantly American contribution.

For regional air transport, however, the UN has benefitted from the loan of aircraft from several countries, most recently from countries with emerging market economies in Eastern Europe that are interested in earning hard currency. The aircraft provided may not have the latest in instrument navigation equipment, but they cost less to lease, and to the cash-starved UN, cost is becoming a paramount concern (over and above flight safety concerns on the rise among some field personnel).

Air support is not new to UN operations, and neither is aerial surveillance, although its role has been low-key to date. Both of the Sinai peacekeeping missions benefitted from aerial surveillance capabilities, as have their non-UN successors. Moreover, US reconnaissance flights continue to be made over Sinai and the Golan Heights on a highly structured, predictable basis as part of an operation known as "Olive Harvest" that began after the October 1973 War.[12] In another case, though not strictly one of peacekeeping, Baghdad allowed the UN Special Commission in Iraq to use its own helicopters for weapons inspections after some sabre-rattling by the US.[13]

The Special Commission also marked the first time that a high-altitude reconnaissance aircraft (an American U-2) was placed under UN operational control. The aircraft's sensors, along with satellite intelligence data made available to the UN by the United States, have aided the Commission's ground inspections.[14] Other airborne technologies of potential utility would include synthetic aperture radars (SARs) able to peer beneath desert sands (and, potentially, some jungle canopies) to detect the stronger radar returns of weapons caches. Searching for such caches is a task of the UN Transitional Authority in Cambodia.[15]

Where unsettled border zones must be monitored, UN forces could put other overhead surveillance capabilities to good use. A former Commander of UNIFIL, General Gustav Hägglund of Finland, has written of the potential utility of low-altitude reconnaissance drones for peacekeeping operations.[16] A drone poses no risk to a pilot and can be very hard to see or track on radar. *Pioneer* drones, for example, operated successfully with US forces during the Gulf War, providing real time television pictures to ground controllers at ranges up to 185 kilometers. A *Pioneer* unit could maintain surveillance of a border zone up to 400 km long with overflights every two hours. To maintain politically important contact with the local populace while limiting risks at night, a peacekeeping force could routinely use human patrols during the daytime, supplemented by drones to provide additional information quickly on reported hot spots. At night, a combination of passive ground sensors to detect movement and infrared-equipped drones to verify its source would permit the proportion of human and drone patrolling to be reversed.[17]

Ground Surveillance Technology. For many years, the UN has had to operate in dangerous situations with fewer arms than the parties it is keeping apart. In many cases, it has also operated with lower-capability surveillance technologies than have been available to the parties. This was particularly true for the two missions on Israel's northern borders, UNIFIL and UNDOF, but was also the case for UNIIMOG, where observers were limited not only in the technologies they could use, but the places they could look. Thus politics plays a key limiting role and is sometimes a decisive barrier to higher-technology UN operations. However, in situations where local political support for an operation is strong enough, and the peacekeepers are perceived as even-handed, political barriers can be lowered. The region of Israel's southern border with Egypt, for example, is monitored by the independent Multinational Force and Observers (MFO), deployed in the Sinai in support of the Egyptian-Israeli Peace Treaty. That force uses a wide variety of electronic devices to assist it in monitoring a wide expanse of territory. Surveillance results are summarized and reported to the parties.[18] That a large part of the force is American helps, not only with political acceptability, but with the availability and operation of the technology.

Among potentially useful ground-based technologies are seismic ground sensors to detect movement of vehicles and (at relatively close range) people; passive night vision devices (image intensifiers and thermal imagers); and ground radars. Seismic sensors were used with success by the US Sinai Field Mission, starting in the mid-1970s.[19] Image intensifiers, which magnify ambient visible light to useful levels, enable observers to see in the dark when the air is clear (they have limited utility where ground haze is prevalent, as along the Iraq-Kuwait border). The UN has purchased image intensifiers for use in Lebanon, Kuwait, and Western Sahara. Not cheap, a pair of basic night vision binoculars may cost $3,000, and a telescope with nine or ten power magnification may cost $10,000.[20] But without such equipment, UN forces are vulnerable to local armed elements every time the sun sets.

Thermal imagers, which detect infrared emissions and translate them into images visible to the human eye, can see through haze, dust, and smoke, in daylight or at night. Advanced models were the key to coalition tank gunners' success against Iraqi armor in the Gulf War. As a result, thermal imaging technology tends to be militarily more sensitive and more liable to export restriction. It is also harder to maintain, requiring some means of keeping the imager cool (where "cool" can mean the temperature of liquid air). But for observers who need to be able to spot movement at night, the technology can be indispensable.

Problems of local politics, military sensitivity, and cost notwithstanding, high technology requires a level of skill to operate and maintain it that is found in relatively few troop contributing countries. As military technologies diffuse around the globe, general familiarity with them can be expected to rise. But the UN, for the time being, will need to rely on member states who own the more sophisticated equipment to contribute the people who will operate it in the field. Over time, and with sufficient funds, the UN could develop its own cadre of maintenance technicians based, perhaps, at an improved Pisa facility, to perform depot and field maintenance.

Training and Competence

Because the Secretariat must consider "geographic distribution" as well as military competence in requesting a government's participation in a mission or in weighing its offer of assistance, the quality and technical competence of UN troop contingents and observers tends to vary widely. Such disparities could be reduced by standardized training that included opportunities for military officers, police officials, and senior election officials to work together in simulated operational settings. The International Peace Academy has run small seminars annually, in New York and Geneva, for senior national personnel, using interpersonal simulation and role-playing to give participants a feel for the problems they are likely to encounter in the field, and some states have UN-oriented training centers. The Nordic countries, for example, take pride in the system that they have established for training participants in peacekeeping missions: Denmark trains military police; Finland trains observers; Norway provides logistics and transport training; and Sweden trains staff officers. In addition, each country trains its own infantry battalions in peacekeeping and observation techniques. The Nordics encourage other countries to visit their facilities and participate in their programs (which are conducted in English, peacekeeping's "trade language"). Partly in consequence, training programs for peacekeepers have been established in Austria, Canada, Malaysia, Poland, and Switzerland (for observers). The Austrian center also trains Hungarian officers. In the spring of 1991, the UN issued its first training manual, as well as its first compendium of standard operating procedures for peacekeeping.

The cost of specialized training for UN operations is beyond most of the individual developing states who contribute troops and observers.[21] The Organization needs a system that would give it advance assurance of the ability of a given country's troops or personnel to shoulder successfully the mandated tasks of a new mission, yet without narrowing the pool of countries from which it selects its people. The existing pool of troop contributors (and especially contributors of specialized units) is already, if anything, too small, too white, and too Western. If the UN is to maintain its image as a truly impartial, international organization, then the traditional emphasis on representative geographic distribution in its forces must also be maintained, not by lowering the Organization's standards, for that is a recipe for disaster in critical situations, but by raising standards among member states. One way to do that would be UN "certification" of national or regional training programs, and a requirement that reimbursement for troop contributions in excess of actual costs be invested in such UN-certified training and in the purchase of UN-standard equipment.

SUMMARY AND CONCLUSIONS

For decades, the UN managed peacekeeping operations with a skeleton staff and ad hoc approaches that served it quite well until the late 1980s. However, to meet the demands of peacekeeping in coming years, the UN needs to continue structural reforms begun in 1992 to rationalize its bureaucracy and enable it to plan ahead. Bringing all peacekeeping-related functions under the aegis of Peacekeeping Operations would be one way to do that, as would a stockpile of critical equipment needed routinely by new operations. Member states could enhance the UN's readiness by training their personnel to UN standards, and by earmarking people and units for contribution to UN operations on short notice. In certain cases, surveillance technology can make an impressive contribution to the operational effectiveness of a UN operation, but issues of politics, training, and support, as much as acquisition costs, determine whether and where it is used.

Notes

1. There were exceptions, of course. The SRSG for the Central American peace process conducted the mediation effort. Once a political settlement was hammered out for El Salvador, his deputy became the head of the peacekeeping operation there. But in the case of Western Sahara, even the SRSG was kept in the dark about the progress of negotiations.

2. The Congo crisis did lead to the creation of the post of Military Advisor to the Secretary General in late 1960. The first advisor, then-Brigadier General Indar Rikhye of India, served until 1969. Rikhye's replacement rose from Lieutenant Colonel to Major General over an eight-year assignment, while his successor was appointed as a Major in 1977 and also rose to Major General, without benefit of field command

3. Just over half of FOD's 90-odd New York staff are permanent UN employees. A small number (fewer than ten) are military specialists on loan from governments, and the remainder are temporary "overload" staff paid out of peacekeeping mission budgets. Several hundred FOD personnel manage logistics in the field, as well as communications between the missions and New York (Interview 93, January 21, 1992).

4. Backstoppers give the requests, demands, and pleadings from a field operation a human face and vocal advocacy back at Headquarters, lest they be lost in the continuing chorus of demands for decision-makers' time and resources.

5. Organization theory calls this the "span of control" problem. As the number of subordinates grows, a supervisor has less time to devote to each, authority is increasingly decentralized, and coordination among the disparate power centers may become increasingly difficult. To reduce span of control to manageable proportions, an organization must either add new layers of supervision, eliminate or consolidate functions, or do both at once. Adding layers makes the organization "taller," that is, raises the level to which a conflict must rise for resolution. Cutting functions wounds one or more constituencies that like or rely on those functions. In the case of the UN, policy flow is already quite vertical, but there has been no layer of management able either to halt or resolve policy conflicts before they reach the executive office of the Secretary General, or to enforce better horizontal coordination efforts amongst the Organization's various departments and offices.

Two classic treatments of public administration and organizational structure are Herbert A. Simon, *Administrative Behavior*, 3rd ed. (New York: The Free Press, 1976), and Anthony Downs, *Inside Bureaucracy* (Boston: Little, Brown, and Company, 1967), especially 49 ff.

6. United Nations, "Secretary General announces changes in the Secretariat," Press Release SG/A/479, February 7, 1992; and *An Agenda for Peace*, United Nations Document A/47/277, June 17, 1992.

7. Traditional military thinking and traditional UN philosophy differ sharply on how best to respond to military provocation. Militaries train their people in the escalating use of force to achieve field objectives, while peacekeeping emphasizes non-violent responses to provocation, and

deescalation of conflictual situations. If deescalatory responses tend to make local armed elements less, rather than more, respectful of UN operations, as seems, for example, to have been the case with some groups and some contingents in Lebanon, then UN leaders will face some unpalatable choices.

8. For further detailed recommendations, see Durch and Blechman, *Keeping the Peace: The United Nations in the Emerging World Order* (Washington, D.C.: The Henry L. Stimson Center, March 1992), especially 100-101, 104-105.

9. *Requirements for United Nations Peacekeeping*, United Nations Document A/45/217, May 8, 1990, 4.

10. "The feasibility and cost-effectiveness of a reserve stock of equipment," United Nations Document A/45/493/Add.1, October 30, 1990.

11. US Air Force, Military Airlift Command, Office of the Historian, "MATS Participation in United Nations Peace-Keeping Missions," *MATS/MAC Chronologies, 1960, 1989*, Scott Air Force Base, Illinois, 1960, 1989; David W. Wainhouse, *International Peacekeeping at the Crossroads* (Baltimore, Md.: The Johns Hopkins University Press, 1973), 547.

12. For details on the Middle East operations, see Amy Smithson, "Multilateral Aerial Inspections," in Michael Krepon and Amy Smithson, eds., *Open Skies, Arms Control, and Cooperative Security* (New York: St. Martin's Press, 1992), 113-134, and Smithson, "Open Skies Ready for Takeoff," *Bulletin of the Atomic Scientists* (January–February 1992): 17-21.

13. Hon. Les Aspin, "Winning the War and Losing the Peace in Saddam Hussein's Iraq," mimeograph text of a speech given in New York City, December 12, 1991, 7 (available from the House Armed Services Committee). See also, David Fulghum, "Protecting UN Inspectors in Iraq Would Require Many US Aircraft," *Aviation Week* (September 30, 1991): 71.

14. R. Jeffrey Smith and John M. Goshko, "US Lends Spy Plane to UN to View Iraq," *Washington Post*, August 13, 1991, 12.

15. See the *Final Act of the Paris Peace Conference on Cambodia, Annex 1: UNTAC Mandate*, section C.1.d. of UN General Assembly document A/46/608, October 30, 1991, 24. On the capabilities and operations of synthetic aperture radar, see Eli Brookner, "Radar Imaging for Arms Control," in Kosta Tsipis, David Hafemeister, and Penny Janeway, eds., *Arms Control Verification* (Washington, D.C.: Pergamon-Brassey's, 1986), 135-165, especially 136. Radar frequencies of 1.25 GHz or less are needed to reduce signal attenuation by foliage and, even then, only caches located above-ground would have any probability of detection.

16. Lieutenant General Gustav Hägglund, "Peacekeeping in a Modern War Zone," *Survival* (May–June 1990): 235.

17. The example assumes a control unit positioned in the middle of the border area to be patrolled. Built under Israeli license by a Maryland-based company, the *Pioneer* has five hours endurance and carries either a daylight TV camera or an imaging infrared camera for use at night

(AAI Corporation, *"Pioneer* RPV," Company Factsheet [Hunt Valley, MD: AAI Corp., 1987]). In Operation Desert Storm, *Pioneer* sorties averaged three hours apiece (*Aerospace Daily*, February 13, 1991, 264).

Forward-looking infrared sensors, as deployed on *Pioneer* and other drones, have a relatively narrow field of view (generally 20 degrees or less), so they are not as useful for wide-area surveillance at night as for quick follow-up investigations of events with known locations. A unit with four to six drones would cost about $10 million to acquire, and probably another million dollars a year to operate.

18. Smithson, "Multilateral Aerial Inspections," 113-134. Also, Brian S. Mandell, *The Sinai Experience: Lessons in Multinational Arms Control Verification and Risk Management*, Arms Control Verification Studies No. 3, prepared for the Arms Control and Disarmament Division, Department of External Affairs, Ottawa, Canada, September 1987.

19. Mandell, *The Sinai Experience*, 9-12.

20. Representative cost numbers provided by Ron Clayton, Electro-Optical Systems Division, IMO Industries, Inc., Garland, Texas, telephone interview, January 2, 1992.

21. Perhaps it is more correct to say that *sustaining* a trained capability over time is the problem. Soldiers rotate into and out of units, and not every country that trains troops for UN duty is called to send them into the field before their tours of duty expire. A country could spend years "marching in place," waiting for a call from the Organization, and consider its investment in New York soldiering a waste of resources. One way to recoup that investment would be to recruit peacekeeping units, as Sweden does, from the pool of citizens with military experience. The individual battalions disband upon rotation home.

5 United Nations Special Committee On The Balkans

by Karl Th. Birgisson

The United Nations Special Committee on the Balkans, established in 1947, was the first attempt by the UN to deploy an observation mission in the midst of armed conflict. It was sent to ascertain whether Greek Communist guerrillas were receiving outside support in their insurgency against the government, and to make its assistance available to restore normal relations among Greece, Albania, Bulgaria, and Yugoslavia. UNSCOB had no great impact on the Greek Civil War, but did teach the UN the importance of obtaining the consent of all local parties before deploying an operation, as well as the necessity for politically impartial conduct once deployed.

ORIGINS

In 1941, the Axis powers occupied Greece, driving King George into exile in London. An underground resistance movement known as the National Liberation Front (EAM) fought the occupation under the leadership of the Communist Party. During the war, Britain supported EAM, but later shifted its support to a rival noncommunist movement.

The two rival groups formed a Government of National Unity in 1944. Before long, however, the Communists left the coalition, and the remnants of the Communist guerrilla movement moved to the north of Greece, where they fought against the Greek government and received support from newly installed Communist regimes in Albania, Yugoslavia, and Bulgaria.[1]

In early January 1946, the USSR accused Britain, which supported the Greek government and had troops in the country, of interfering in Greek internal affairs. The British countered that they were in Greece at the request of the government, which had sought protection from Communist insurgents.[2] Greece was fast becoming one of the first battlegrounds of the Cold War.

Initiatives for UN Involvement

On August 24, 1946, the Ukrainian representative to the Security Council raised the issue of violent incidents on the border between Greece and Albania. The United States suggested that an investigative commission be established to look into incidents along the whole northern border of Greece.[3] That proposal was vetoed by the Soviet Union.

On December 3, 1946, the Greek government brought complaints before the Security Council of Albanian, Yugoslavian, and Bulgarian assistance to Communist guerrillas in northern Greece. The United States repeated its proposal, and this time the Soviet Union decided to go along. The result was a Commission of Investigation, which went to the Balkans in early 1947. In its reports, the Commission confirmed that Greek guerrillas were receiving support from the three Communist governments to the north. The Soviet Union, however, disagreed with the reports and repeatedly vetoed Security Council resolutions based on them.[4]

In a parliamentary maneuver based on a veto-proof procedural vote, the United States succeeded in removing the issue from the Council's agenda and placed it before the General Assembly, where the West was in firm control.[5] The General Assembly established the United Nations Special Committee on the Balkans (UNSCOB) on October 21, 1947, to be composed of representatives of the then-eleven members of the Security Council. The Soviet Union and Poland, however, declined to serve, leaving a Committee of nine: Australia, Brazil, China (Taiwan), France, Mexico, the Netherlands, Pakistan, the United Kingdom, and the United States.[6]

POLITICAL SUPPORT

UNSCOB was the first UN mission created directly as an instrument of Cold War competition. Its principal supporters were the United States and Britain, who saw it as a valuable opportunity to expose Communist subversion and provide political support for the recently enunciated Truman Doctrine. The Soviet Union, on the other hand, opposed the mission for obvious reasons. It agreed to the establishment of the initial Commission of Investigation probably only because it was able to have "a finger in the pie" as a member of the mission; it could at least produce a minority report that would spell out its view on the situation in Greece.[7] Others supported or opposed the establishment of UNSCOB based squarely on their positions within the emerging blocs of the Cold War. This meant, of course, that the three Communist states on Greece's northern border opposed the Committee's activities, a fact that hampered its operations considerably.

MANDATE

In its resolution establishing the Special Committee, the General Assembly called upon Albania, Bulgaria, and Yugoslavia not to furnish aid to the guerrillas, and called upon all four countries to settle their disputes by peaceful means, by establishing "normal diplomatic and good neighbourly relations." The Assembly further called for the establishment of frontier conventions and for cooperation on refugee problems. The Committee's mandate was to "observe the compliance by the four Governments concerned with the foregoing recommendations [and] be available to assist the four Governments concerned in the implementation of such recommendations."[8]

When the Committee interpreted its mandate, it decided to concentrate on the first part, namely the observation of compliance with the recommendations. The latter part was given secondary attention and its implementation was referred to three subcommittees.[9]

FUNDING

UNSCOB was funded from the UN's regular budget under provisions dealing with Investigations and Inquiries. The total cost of the operation from 1947-1951 was about $3 million. UN inexperience in establishing peacekeeping missions at the time was reflected in the fact that the only real financial controversy concerned the propriety of granting allowances for travel and subsistence (eventually set at $20 a day).[10]

PLANNING AND IMPLEMENTATION

The Committee members had a good idea of what to expect in Greece given the reports of the earlier Commission of Investigation. That Commission had concluded that the three surrounding countries had assisted, trained, and supplied the Greek Communist guerrillas in their fight against the government.[11] UNSCOB members also knew that the three Communist governments had largely refused to cooperate with the Commission and had not allowed it to enter their respective territories for investigative purposes.

When UNSCOB was established, security conditions in Greece were precarious. The new noncommunist régime was unstable and its army was not ready to meet the challenge from the guerrillas. The guerrillas controlled various areas along the northern border, where they received support and training from the three surrounding countries, particularly Yugoslavia. In addition, Bulgaria and Yugoslavia encouraged unrest among Macedonian separatists in Greece, with the purpose of incorporating Macedonia into the Yugoslav federation. Minor border incidents were frequent and, while not amounting to intentional aggression, they did contribute to very tense relations between Greece and its neighbors.

Structure and Support

A defining trait of UNSCOB was that its members represented their own states, not the UN, and therefore received instructions from their national governments. Military observers working for the Committee reported their findings directly to it, however.[12] The Committee issued its reports not to the Secretary General or the Security Council, as was usually the case later, but to the General Assembly.

Since the UN had little experience in supporting peacekeeping missions, logistics inevitably were a problem. Initally, the UN had to rely on the United States to contribute transportation, communications systems, and other necessary support items. This was not too onerous for the United States at the time, however, as it had considerable military presence in the area. Gradually, the United Nations assumed greater responsibilities for basic means of support.[13]

UNSCOB set up headquarters in Salonika, where the Secretary General provided it with "three administrative officers; four radio operators; one precis writer; three drivers; one auto mechanic; [and] one radio repairman."[14] The Committee itself consisted of delegates from the nine participating Security Council members, each of which also sent an alternate delegate. Initially, the Committee established two subcommittees, one to oversee observer groups and budgetary matters, the other to deal with the political problems and administrative matters.[15] These arrangements were modified from time to time as the situation in Greece and on the frontier changed. In 1949, a Chief Observer was appointed by the Committee to oversee the observer teams and offer them technical assistance.

Field Operations

The Committee divided its area of activities into six zones, where the observers operated in teams of two. The Committee had intended to establish a presence in all four Balkan countries, but the three Communist states refused to cooperate, forcing the Committee to establish observation points solely on the Greek side of the border. On occasion, however, Bulgarian authorities allowed UNSCOB to enter Bulgarian territory when the observers' findings were sure to embarrass the Greek government. There was no lack of activity to report in the Commission's first years, but the fighting made direct observation by UN personnel both difficult and dangerous.

UNSCOB's observers investigated complaints lodged by the Greek government. They observed traffic, examined captured weapons, and interrogated witnesses and captured guerillas, from whom they received firsthand knowledge of outside support for the Communists. In addition to observation and interrogation, the observers monitored radio broadcasts in the three Communist countries, a technique that allowed them to determine that the radio station "Free Greece" was in fact operated from Yugoslavian territory.[16]

ASSESSMENT

It is difficult to evaluate precisely UNSCOB's effect on the conditions near the Greek border. A favorable view would suggest that the Committee did indeed achieve its goals, since support for the guerrillas gradually disappeared and some normalcy was restored in state-to-state relations in the area.

However, this may not have been due as much to UNSCOB operations as to changes in the political and military environment. In a dispute with Soviet authorities, Yugoslavia left Cominform in 1948 and provided little support to the Greek Communists after that. In 1949, Yugoslavia closed its border with Greece, and shortly thereafter the two countries took steps to normalize relations.[17]

The Greek government gradually got the upper hand in its fight against the guerrillas, as its army strengthened and the country's economic situation improved markedly. By mid-1950, guerrilla activity in the north had virtually ceased, and the General Assembly decided, on Greek initiative, to terminate UNSCOB in late 1951. Thereafter, the UN decided to keep an eye on the situation through the Peace Observation Commission, whose Balkan Subcommission dispatched observers to the area in 1952. The observers reported only one incident and ceased their operation at the end of 1953.[18]

CONCLUSIONS

Compared to later peacekeeping missions, UNSCOB was, relatively speaking, operationally primitive and politically unbalanced. Nonetheless, it did provide some valuable lessons for future missions. The refusal of the three Communist governments to cooperate with the mission illustrated the necessity of obtaining the consent of all parties involved in a UN deployment. Further, continued deliveries of outside assistance to the guerrillas in Greece after UNSCOB's arrival suggested the limits of its ability to deter the movement of weapons and armed personnel.

The Cold War origins of the mission were also a liability. It was not always clear whether its real purpose was to seek impartial information or to make a political point. The fact that the mission was "directed against" one bloc also hampered field operations, since the other side most often had nothing to gain by cooperating with the observers.

However, as a first attempt to establish a peace observation mission in the field, UNSCOB served the United Nations well. It illustrated that the UN could indeed fulfill some of the premises upon which it was based—something that was neither self-evident nor widely expected at the time. Moreover, barely six months after UNSCOB had been established, the UN had the opportunity in Palestine to put the valuable experience gained in this operation to good use.

Notes

1. David W. Wainhouse, *International Peace Observation: A History and Forecast* (Baltimore, Md.: The Johns Hopkins University Press, 1966), 221-222.

2. Rosalyn Higgins, *United Nations Peacekeeping: Documents and Commentary, Vol. IV: Europe* (New York: Oxford University Press, 1981), 5.

3. Wainhouse, *International Peace Observation*, 222.

4. Higgins, *United Nations Peacekeeping*, Vol. IV, 10-17.

5. Alan James, *The Politics of Peace-keeping* (New York: Frederick Praeger, 1969), 211.
6. Wainhouse, *International Peace Observation*, 224.
7. James, *The Politics of Peace-keeping*, 210.
8. United Nations General Assembly Resolution 109, October 21, 1947.
9. Higgins, *United Nations Peacekeeping*, Vol. IV, 23.
10. Higgins, *United Nations Peacekeeping*, Vol. IV, 55-57.
11. United Nations Document S/360/Rev.1, July 28, 1950.
12. Wainhouse, *International Peace Observation*, 241.
13. Wainhouse, *International Peace Observation*, 240.
14. United Nations Document A/521, January 9, 1948.
15. United Nations Document A/574, June 30, 1948.
16. Wainhouse, *International Peace Observation*, 240.
17. James, *The Politics of Peace-keeping*, 212.
18. Higgins, *United Nations Peacekeeping*, Vol. IV, 72-73.

6 United Nations Truce Supervision Organization: 1948-Present

by Mona Ghali

The United Nations Truce Supervision Organization (UNTSO) was created by the Security Council to supervise the 1948 truce in Palestine. Although UNTSO has continuously adapted to the exigencies of the Arab-Israeli conflict, it essentially remains deployed to observe and report illegal incursions across the armistice lines and to mediate disputes between the parties. Outside its headquarters in Jerusalem, UNTSO maintains observer groups in Egypt and Beirut, as well as a liaison office in Amman, and it details observers to the United Nations Interim Force in Lebanon (UNIFIL) and the United Nations Disengagement Observer Force (UNDOF) in the Golan.

UNTSO's durability corresponds to the United Nations's desire to be seen acting in the interest of peace and security. As observers, UNTSO personnel can merely report on developments in the region; they are unarmed, with only the moral suasion of their blue berets and UN insignias to protect them from hostile parties. Yet though their function is more symbolic than substantive, UNTSO provides "basic training" for military observers and a pool of experienced personnel for quick-response site surveys or limited staffing of new, time-urgent missions.

UNTSO's mission began with the Palestinian problem. As Edward Said observed, "Two things are certain: the Jews of Israel will remain; the Palestinians will also remain."[1] Given these permanent facts, we can presume that UNTSO too will remain.

ORIGINS

The origins of UNTSO are closely linked to the proclamation of an independent state of Israel on May 15, 1948, which led to the first Arab-Israeli war. The events preceding the War of Independence, as it is referred to by the Israelis, or the Palestine War, as it is known to the Arabs, are examined extensively elsewhere (these include Jewish immigration to Palestine, the McMahon promises, the Sykes-Picot Agreement, the 1917 Balfour Declaration, the 1937 British partition plan, and the White Paper of 1939). Here we need simply note that both Palestinian and Jewish settlers felt, and continue to feel, an almost transcendental communion with the land.

The concept of a homeland inspired Jews to migrate to Palestine from Europe in the late nineteenth century and then again with renewed determination following the Holocaust. The same, yet incompatible, concept of a homeland moves Palestinians to continue their resistance to Israeli occupation of the West Bank and Gaza Strip. The term itself is significant, as it embodies a sense of rootedness, birthright, permanence, and growth that admits of little neutralism. Much of the passion and emotion that has come to be associated with the question of Palestine derives from decades of personal struggle and sacrifice on both sides. Each side feels it has an absolute right to exist on the disputed, narrow tract. Each has experienced gross injustices and has been deceived by promises, so much so that there is little room left for empathy, and little breath with which to speak of compromise. UNTSO observers have had to deal with this reality on a daily basis, unchanged in its essentials since 1948.

Initiatives Leading to UN Involvement

On April 2, 1947, the British government announced its intention to terminate its mandate for Palestine and to transfer the problem to the United Nations. In response, on May 15, 1947, the General Assembly established an eleven-member committee—the United Nations Special Committee on Palestine (UNSCOP)—to examine the Palestine problem and submit proposals to the General Assembly.[2]

Only a minority of the Committee's members (Yugoslavia, Iran, and India) favored establishment of a single, binational state. The majority supported the partition of Palestine into separate Jewish and Arab states joined by an economic union, with Jerusalem under an international regime administered by the UN.[3] The partition plan was accepted by the Jewish community, but the Arab states rejected both the proposals for partition and the binational state. Since partition required less Arab cooperation than a federal state with Arab and Jewish provinces, the General Assembly was inclined to accept the former despite Arab intransigence.

On November 29, 1947, the General Assembly passed Resolution 181 adopting the partition plan and establishing a UN Palestine Commission to implement the resolution. The Commission included a representative from Bolivia, Czechoslovakia, Denmark, Panama, and the Philippines.

Before the adoption of General Assembly Resolution 181, fighting between armed Jewish and Palestinian elements had occurred; after the resolution passed, hostilities intensified. Between December 1, 1947, and February 1, 1948, the UN reported 2,778 casualties (including 1,462 Arabs, 1,106 Jews, and 181 Britons).[4] On April 1, the Security Council called for a truce. Two weeks later, it repeated its call to the Arab Higher Committee and the Jewish Agency to cease all military activities, acts of violence, terrorism, and sabotage, and to refrain from "importing or encouraging the importation or acquisition of weapons and war materials."[5]

On April 10, 1948, the Palestine Commission reported to the Secretary General that "the armed hostility of both Palestinian and non-Palestinian Arab elements, the lack of co-operation from the mandatory Power, the disintegrating security situation in Palestine, and the fact that the Security Council did not furnish the Commission with the necessary armed assistance, are the factors which have made it impossible for the Commission to implement the Assembly's resolution."[6] Less than two weeks later, the Security Council passed a resolution establishing a Truce Commission, the forerunner of UNTSO, to assist the Council in securing a truce in Palestine. The Truce Commission was directed to assist the Security Council in supervising the implementation of the April 17, 1948, cease-fire order, and to report to the President of the Council with developments on the situation. The Commission was composed of representatives from those members of the Security Council having career consular offices in Jerusalem (the United States, France, Belgium, and Syria, with the latter declining to participate).

With the implementation of the partition plan appearing more remote, the General Assembly passed Resolution 186 on May 14, 1948, relieving the Palestine Commission of its responsibilities and creating the office of a UN Mediator for Palestine. The five Permanent Members selected Count Folke Bernadotte of Sweden. As Mediator, Count Bernadotte was empowered "to use his good offices with the local and community authorities in Palestine to arrange for the operation of common services necessary to the safety and well-being of the population of Palestine; assure the protection of the Holy Places, religious buildings and sites in Palestine; and promote a peaceful adjustment of the future situation of Palestine." Bernadotte was also enjoined to cooperate with the Truce Commission for Palestine and to invite, "as seems to him advisable, with a view to the promotion of the welfare of the inhabitants of Palestine, the assistance and cooperation of appropriate specialized agencies such as the World Health Organization, of the International Red Cross, and of other governmental or non-governmental organizations of a humanitarian and non-political character."[7]

**Table 6.1. Selected Chronology
of the Creation of UNTSO**

Resolution	Function
General Assembly 106 May 15, 1947	Establishes United Nations Special Commission on Palestine to make recommendations for the area's future.
General Assembly 181 November 29, 1947	Establishes United Nations Palestine Commission to implement new plan for political partition and economic union of Palestine.
Security Council April 23, 1948	Establishes Truce Commission to assist Security Council in securing a truce in Palestine. (Progenitor of UNTSO.)
General Assembly 186 May 14, 1948	Establishes office of UN Mediator for Palestine and deactivates Palestine Commission.
General Assembly 194 December 11, 1948	Establishes UN Palestine Conciliation Commission to help achieve permanent resolution of Palestine question.
Security Council 1376 August 11, 1949	Terminates functions of UN Mediator. UNTSO continues as independent entity supervising 1949 Armistice Agreements.

Source: Rosalyn Higgins, *United Nations Peacekeeping, 1946-1967, Documents and Commentary, Vol. I: The Middle East* (London: Oxford University Press, 1969), 7-30.

The following day, May 15, the same day that Britain terminated its mandate for Palestine, the Jewish Agency declared the new state of Israel. Egypt, Jordan, Syria, Iraq, and Lebanon immediately dispatched their armed forces to Palestine. On May 22, the Security Council ordered a cease-fire and directed the Truce Commission to report to the Security Council on local compliance with its orders. The Chairman of the Truce Commission conveyed his opinion that to execute its responsibilities, the Commission would require military advisors and observers.[8]

On May 29, the Security Council called for, *inter alia*, a cease-fire, and informed the parties that the Security Council would consider taking further action in accordance with Chapter VII of the Charter should any one of the parties refuse to comply.[9] The resolution also instructed the Mediator and the Truce Commission to dispatch a sufficient number of observers. According to Rosalyn Higgins, this point marked the birth of a body for UN Truce Supervision.[10]

Although Bernadotte negotiated a four-week truce that went into effect on June 11, hostilities resumed on July 9 and lasted eight months, punctuated intermittently by UN-mediated cease-fires. Bernadotte's task was made even more difficult by the Organization's indecision. This lack of resolve led Bernadotte to write, "The United Nations showed itself from the worst side. It was depressing to have to recognize the fact that even the most trivial decisions with regard to measures designed to lend force to its words were dependent on the political calculations of the Great Powers."[11]

On September 17, 1948, Count Bernadotte and a senior French observer were assassinated in Jerusalem by the Stern gang, a Jewish terrorist organization. Dr. Ralph Bunche, then the Secretary General's personal representative, assumed the role of acting Mediator, and Brigadier General W.E. Riley of the United States was appointed Chief of Staff of the Truce Commission.

On November 16, 1948, the Security Council ordered the parties to agree to an armistice. All parties with the exception of Egypt agreed to comply with the Council's orders. On December 11, the General Assembly passed Resolution 194 establishing the UN Conciliation Commission for Palestine to help achieve a permanent settlement to the Palestine problem. The five Permanent Members of the Security Council selected France, the United States, and Turkey as members of the Commission, which set up its headquarters at the former British Mandate Government House overlooking Jerusalem.

Egypt reversed its position on January 6, 1949, and agreed to accept a cease-fire and direct negotiations, under UN chairmanship, for an armistice agreement. Armistice agreements were concluded between the provisional government of Israel and Egypt on February 24, 1949. Three separate bilateral agreements between Israel and Lebanon (March 22), Israel and Jordan (April 3), and Israel and Syria (July 20) were concluded by the end of July 1949. Each of the four separate agreements established a general armistice between the two armed forces and marked out armistice demarcation lines (ADL) that were not to be interpreted as political or territorial boundaries between Israel and the Arab states. Each state made provisions for a Mixed Armistice Commission (MAC) composed of seven members, three designated from each side plus the Chairman, who would be either the Chief of Staff of the Truce Supervision Organization or a senior officer from the observer personnel.

The separate state of Palestine conceived in the UN partition plan adopted by the General Assembly on November 1947 was never established. Instead, its territory was divided among Israel, Egypt, and Jordan after the 1948 war. Israel annexed 2,500 square miles; Jordan, 2,200 square miles; and Egypt, the 135 square mile area of the Gaza Strip. Jerusalem was divided between Israel and Jordan. The borders marking the international frontier of Palestine in the 1947 UN partition plan formed the armistice lines for Syria and Lebanon.

With an armistice arranged between Israel and the Arab states, the Security Council terminated the role of the Mediator on August 11, 1949. The Truce Commission became known as the Truce Supervision Organization. As former UNTSO Chief of Staff General Burns observed,

> UNTSO was no longer subordinated to the Mediator, but became a subsidiary organ of the United Nations with its own well-defined functions. Its machinery for supervising the cease-fire and the truce, established under previous Security Council resolutions, was made available for assisting the supervision of the General Armistice Agreements through the Mixed Armistice Commissions set up therein. The Chief of Staff was made responsible for reporting to the Security Council on the observance of the cease-fire order of July 15, 1948, which remained in force.[12]

POLITICAL SUPPORT

The Security Council resolution of April 23, 1948, effectively authorizing the dispatch of UN observers to the Middle East passed 8 to 0, with three abstentions (Colombia, Ukraine, and the Soviet Union). As did the Ukraine, the Soviet Union expressed its suspicion that both the United Kingdom and the United States were maneuvering to establish a trusteeship in Palestine, arguing that the composition of the Truce Commission (Belgium, France, and the United States) was heavily biased toward the Western powers.

The Soviet Union and the Ukraine again abstained from voting on the Security Council's August 11, 1949, resolution dissolving the post of UN Mediator and specifying tasks for UNTSO Chief of Staff under the General Armistice Agreements. The Soviet Union felt the UN observers in Palestine should be recalled and the staff disbanded.

Local support for UNTSO and the MACs was lacking. Burns writes of constant political squabbling, posturing, and political one-upmanship. Von Horn writes of constant obstructions of UN observers' freedom of movement and of continuing petty harassment.[13] Israel renounced the Egypt-Israel armistice agreement in 1956, and the remaining agreements in 1967, so UNTSO's observers now operate outside Israeli borders.

The membership of the United Nations at large has continued to support the presence of UNTSO in the region despite (or perhaps because of) its largely symbolic value, recognizing also its utility as a trained force that can be drawn upon to staff new peacekeeping operations when the Security Council authorizes their creation.

MANDATE

No single resolution established UNTSO or set forth its mandate. The Security Council's resolution of April 23, 1948, requested the Secretary General to furnish the Truce Commission with "such personnel and assistance as it may require taking into account the special urgency of the situation with respect to Palestine."[14] Since then, UNTSO's mandate and functions have evolved in concert with political and military conditions in the region. Five phases are usually identified, most of them punctuated by major wars: May 1948–August 1949; August 1949–November 1956; November 1956–June 1967; June 1967–October 1973; and from October 1973 to the present.

Once the Armistice Agreements were signed in the first half of 1949, UNTSO's functions expanded to include: (1) demarcating armistice lines; (2) mediating differences between the parties;

(3) establishing demilitarized zones in accordance with the terms of the General Armistice Agreements; (4) deterring an arms build-up; (5) facilitating the exchange of prisoners; and (6) investigating complaints of violations of the agreements.[15]

The latter responsibility fell to the four MACs. Although Israel unilaterally abrogated its Agreement with Egypt in 1956, and with the remaining three Arab states (Lebanon, Jordan, and Syria) after the 1967 June War, the Secretary General refused to recognize Israel's unilateral action. The MACs continued to meet without Israel to symbolize the UN's contention that the Armistice Agreements remained legally in force.

Since the 1970s, UNTSO personnel have been detailed to support UNIFIL and UNDOF. Its continuing presence reflects the UN's ongoing interest in the Arab-Israeli dispute, and concern that withdrawal of the mission would send a correspondingly undesirable political signal.

FUNDING

Since its creation in 1948, UNTSO has been funded through the UN regular budget, with member states contributing on the basis of the regular scale of assessments. From its inception through 1991, expenditure on UNTSO totalled $356 million.[16]

PLANNING AND IMPLEMENTATION

The withdrawal of the British from Palestine on May 15, 1948, created a power vacuum and escalated the level of conflict. Before May 15, fighting was localized, but after the declaration of an independent state of Israel, the conflict widened to include the armed forces of Arab states. All hostilities ceased on January 7, 1949, following the unconditional acceptance of a cease-fire and direct negotiations by the parties. As already noted, UNTSO evolved along with the UN's efforts to find political compromise where none was obvious. Ultimately, the observer mission outlasted all of the political mediation efforts, reflecting, like the rump armistice commissions, a certain dogged determination on the part of the UN.

To date, twenty countries have provided military observers to UNTSO, including Argentina, Australia, Austria, Belgium, Burma (Myanmar), Canada, Chile, China, Denmark, Finland, France, Ireland, Italy, the Netherlands, New Zealand, Norway, Sweden, Switzerland, the USSR (Russia), and the US. UNTSO's authorized

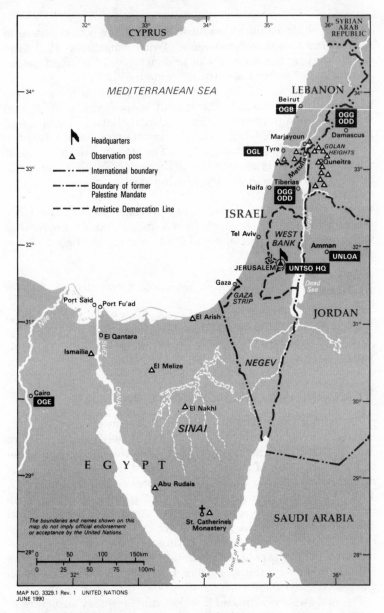

Figure 6.1. United Nations Truce Supervision Organization, Deployment as of June 1990

strength in 1990 was 298 observers. In the past, it has been as high as 572 (in 1948), and as low as 40 (in 1954).[17]

Command, Communications, and Administration

UNTSO's chain of command follows the standard UN practice wherein the Chief of Staff (equivalent to Chief Military Observer in other operations) exercises operational control of the observer group. He is appointed by, and reports to, the Secretary General. Originally, the Chief of Staff had the same legal status as other UNTSO observers, but after 1951 he was appointed as a senior official of the United Nations Secretariat with a rank of Principal Director (later Assistant-Secretary General).

UNTSO military observers detailed to UNIFIL and UNDOF come under the operational control of the Force Commanders of those operations, but remain in contact with the Chief of Staff. The Chief of Staff, in theory, has full authority over the military staff and civilian administrative officers at mission headquarters. In reality, civilian deference to the Chief of Staff's orders has not always been forthcoming.[18] The civilian component of the staff provides continuity, but it is criticized by UNTSO military observers for a disregard of the sense of urgency that may develop in a tense field situation like Lebanon, and too great a regard for strict compliance with the rules of the UN bureaucracy.[19]

Field Operations

UNTSO grew out of the first Arab-Israeli war. Each subsequent conflict through October 1973 affected its organization and operations.

The 1948 War. During the 1948 war, UNTSO was still operating as the Truce Commission, in concert with the Mediator. For the first truce mediated by Count Bernadotte, which came into effect on June 11 and expired on July 9, UN observers were dispatched to Palestine. Between June 11 and 14, the first 36 military observers of the initial 63 selected (21 each from Belgium, France and the United States) took up their positions in Palestine and the Arab states. The number was soon increased to 93 (31 each). A second truce came into effect on July 18, and required a new observer mission since the personnel and equipment from the first mission had withdrawn from the area. Again, the Mediator approached the French, American, and Belgian governments, this time asking them to contribute 100 observers each to the Truce Commission. The number was raised further, eventually to a maximum strength of 572, after the assassination of Count Bernadotte in September. Observers were designated into groups and assigned to each Arab army and each Israeli group. One observer group was made responsible for Jerusalem, one for the coast and ports of the truce area, one to monitor convoys between Tel Aviv and Jerusalem and, later, one group to supervise the airport area.[20] With the conclusion of the General Armistice Agreements in 1949, UNTSO's size was reduced. It varied between 30 and 140, depending on the political conditions, for nearly two decades.[21]

1949–1956. The four separate armistice agreements between Israel and neighboring Arab states transformed UNTSO's functions from supervising the truce to maintaining the cease-fire lines and supervising compliance with the Armistice Agreements. UNTSO observers staffed fixed observation posts, patrolled the armistice lines (ADLs), and inspected the associated demilitarized zones. These measures, along with the MAC's, were intended to reduce the frequency of infiltrations across the armistice demarcation lines and thereby to defuse tensions in the region. With the exception of Israel-Lebanon frontier, the measures taken by UN observers did not prevent incursions across the lines.

Four major controversies affected Israeli-Egyptian relations in particular: the Egyptian government's refusal to permit Israel-bound shipping through the Suez Canal after 1951 or through the Strait of Tiran after 1953; Israel's expulsion of thousands of Palestinians to the Gaza Strip; Palestinian *fedayeen* raids into Israel; and violations of the Armistice Agreements in the demilitarized zone at El Auja. Increasingly frequent fedayeen raids into Israeli territory were followed by Israeli reprisals. A February 1955 Israeli raid into Gaza resulted in the deaths of 36 Egyptian soldiers, and the wounding of 31, and made Israeli-Egyptian relations openly hostile, paving the way to the Suez crisis of 1956 (for further details, see chapter seven, on the First UN Emergency Force).

The Israel-Syria armistice demarcation line was 80 km in length. Here, as along the Israel-Egypt frontier, UNTSO military observers staffed fixed observation posts, maintained patrols, and inspected the demilitarized zones. There were few incidents of infiltrations across the Israel-Syria frontier, but two controversies obstructed the full implementation of the Israel-Syrian Armistice Agreement: (1) the status of the eastern shore of Lake

Tiberias; and (2) the demilitarized zone north and east of the lake (an area of roughly 67 square kilometers). Most of the complaints after 1950 submitted to the Israel-Syria MAC dealt with the latter and included: Israeli cultivation of the zone, an Israeli reclamation project, resettlement of Arabs living in the zone, work on a canal to divert water from the Jordan River, and the presence in the zone of Israeli frontier police.

The local parties complied with the rulings of the MAC only when such compliance served their interests. Israel claimed that the MAC had no jurisdiction on matters pertaining to sovereignty and therefore refused to suspend work on its projects pending agreement with Syria, as the Commission had ruled.

After 1951, the parties refused to attend regular sessions of the MAC, and emergency sessions were held only in exceptional circumstances. As a result, the Chairman negotiated disputes separately with the parties; the number of complaints increased; and rather than serving as a mediator, the Chairman became an envoy, a bearer of "disguised ultimatums."

1956–1967. In 1956, when Israel unilaterally abrogated the Israel-Egypt Armistice Agreement and refused to participate in the work of that MAC, UNTSO observers continued to patrol on the Egyptian side of the line in the Sinai and the Gaza Strip, and the MAC, with just UN and Egyptian representation, continued to investigate complaints although it was, in practical terms, a dead letter. The presence of UNEF, in coordination with UNTSO, reduced the frequency of incidents along the Egyptian-Israeli border and contributed to the stabilization of that frontier. The Israel-Syria MAC, on the other hand, remained whole but did not have the resources to investigate the volume of complaints submitted by the two parties. As of October 14, 1966, Syria had lodged 30,600 complaints and Israel, 35,485.[22]

The armistice agreements were initially conceived as the forerunners of a more permanent political settlement that was to be reached within 12 to 18 months. In the absence of any political headway, the armistice lines were treated increasingly with ambivalence by the parties.

1967–1973. On May 13, 1967, the Egyptian government received reports from the Soviet Union informing it (falsely) of Israeli troop concentration on the Syrian border and advising it to anticipate an Israeli invasion of Syria in coming days. On May 16, Egypt asked the United Nations Emergency Force, in place since 1956, to withdraw from the Sinai. The UN complied, and Egypt's

President Nasser closed the Gulf of Aqaba to Israeli shipping.[23] Israel, fearing a two-front attack as Syrian and Egyptian forces mobilized and moved forward, launched preemptive air and ground attacks of its own on June 5, rapidly seizing control of the Gaza Strip, the Sinai down to the Suez Canal, the Golan Heights, the rest of Jerusalem, and the West Bank of the Jordan River.

No UN observers were stationed in the Israel-Egypt sector when a cease-fire came into effect on June 8. The cease-fire line remained quiet for a month, when hostilities broke out along the Canal. Each side accused the other, but because there were no UN observers stationed in the area there could be no impartial confirmation of either side's claims. On July 9, the Security Council requested the Secretary General to work in concert with the governments of Israel and Egypt to station UN observers in the Canal area. The cease-fire lines were subsequently marked, with the exception of the Port Fouad area where the parties could not agree on a separation line.

Observation began on July 17 with personnel stationed on both the eastern and western sides of the Canal. Some of the UNTSO-drawn observers were rejected by Israel and Egypt because of their nationality. Following negotiations, six countries from which observers could be drawn were accepted.[24] The presence of observers in the Canal area contributed to stabilizing the sector until 1969 when sporadic hostilities resumed and lasted until August 1970. On the Golan Heights, UNTSO observers first demarcated the cease-fire lines on each side, as well as a buffer zone. They then staffed observation posts on both the Syrian and Israeli sides and conducted patrols of the area.

In addition to producing further territorial changes, the 1967 war radicalized the Palestinian leadership and reinforced Palestinian nationalism. The frequency of Palestinian commando raids increased, first at the Israel-Jordan frontier. No cease-fire observation was established, given the reluctance of Israel and Jordan to consent to the deployment of UN observers in the Jordan Valley. In contrast, when commando raids were staged out of Lebanon after 1970, the government of Lebanon requested UN observers, and UNTSO personnel were detached to establish three observation posts on the Lebanese side of the armistice demarcation line. These were later reinforced with two additional posts.

1973-Present. Two major conflicts, the October 1973 War and the Israeli invasion of southern Lebanon in 1978, resulted in the establishment of three new peacekeeping forces (UNEF II, UNDOF, and UNIFIL, each treated as a separate case below). All these were supported initially by personnel from UNTSO. Following the expiration of UNEF II's mandate in 1979, UNTSO observers remained in the Sinai, forming Observer Group Egypt (OGE), largely at the insistence of the Egyptian government. As of November 1990, OGE had a total strength of 50 observers, most of whom were American or Soviet nationals. OGE operates six outposts in the Sinai and maintains liaison offices in Cairo and Ismailia.[25] Before 1988, the Soviet Union prohibited its observers from patrolling the Sinai and restricted them to Cairo and Ismailia as a symbol of its opposition to the Egyptian-Israeli peace treaty. Soviet observers now have unrestricted access to the Sinai. UNTSO observers do not infringe on the area of operations of the non-UN Multinational Force and Observers (MFO) deployed in the eastern Sinai since 1982 under the terms of the 1979 Egyptian-Israeli peace treaty.

OGE observers conduct single man patrols in the Sinai. While OGE provides an added sense of security for the Egyptian government, and potentially can offer a suitable substitute for the MFO should Egypt and Israel *mutually* agree to phase out that force, UNTSO observers stationed in Egypt at present have little role to play.

On the Golan Heights, UNTSO observers seconded to UNDOF form Observer Group Golan (OGG). OGG is under the operational control of UNDOF's Force Commander; it staffs observation posts and conducts fortnightly inspections of the "area of arms and forces limitation." UNTSO observers from Permanent Five countries are prohibited from participating in UNDOF and, as a result, they form a separate unit, the Observation Detachment Damascus (ODD), providing support functions to OGG. As of June 1990, 96 UNTSO observers were assigned to OGG, 35 to ODD, and seven to staff positions at UNDOF headquarters in Damascus.[26]

In Lebanon, five UNTSO outposts were established in 1972, as noted, flanked by Lebanese army checkpoints to guarantee the safety of UN personnel. Following the outbreak of the civil war in 1975 and the dissolution of the Lebanese army, UNTSO observers relied strictly on their status as UN officers for protection. Following Israel's invasion in 1978 and the creation of UNIFIL, the functions of the military observers along the armistice lines were suspended until the termination of UNIFIL's mandate. The creation of Israel's "security zone" in the south of Lebanon further clouded UNTSO's role there. UNTSO observers were detached to assist UNIFIL and form Observer Group Lebanon (OGL). OGL is

formally under the operational control of the UNIFIL's Force
Commander, but it is more accurate to say that OGL cooperates
with UNIFIL by sharing relevant information than to say that it
takes direct orders.[27]

OGL staffs observation posts, carries out patrols, meets with the
local parties, and provides support functions at UNIFIL headquarters in Naqoura, Lebanon. OGL participants are exposed to the
same hazards, harassment, and restriction of movement as UNI-
FIL troops.[28] Neither member of its observer patrols can be
nationals of the same country. Patrols radio headquarters every
twenty minutes, indicating the high level of tension in southern
Lebanon. In UNTSO's other areas of operation like the Sinai,
observers do not strictly adhere to such a policy.

The second Israeli invasion of Lebanon resulted in the creation
of Observer Group Beirut (OGB) in August 1982 to monitor the
situation in and around the capital. Originally, ten observers
assigned to the Israel-Lebanon MAC formed OGB. This number
was raised to 50 following the massacre of Palestinian civilians
at the Sabra and Shatila refugee camps in September. OGB's
strength was reduced following the Israeli withdrawal from Beirut in 1983, and as of late 1990 consisted of just eight observers.[29]

UNTSO military observers were also detached to serve in two
small military observer groups deployed in Iran and Baghdad
between 1984 and 1988 in conjunction with UN investigations of
chemical weapons use during the Iran-Iraq War. They were also
assigned to the United Nations Good Offices Mission in Afghanistan and Pakistan, and to technical missions in Angola, Iran, and
Iraq, and the Chief of Staff headed a fact-finding mission to
Southeast Asia for the 1989 Paris Conference on Cambodia.[30]

ASSESSMENT

In terms of fulfilling its original function of maintaining the
1948 cease-fire lines and preventing incursions across the international frontiers, UNTSO unequivocally failed. Three factors
were operating against it: (1) the parties were not prepared to
cooperate with UN observers; (2) the demarcation lines were not
clearly marked; and (3) UNTSO observers were not equipped,
politically or militarily, to deal with the type of confrontations
that developed in the demilitarized zones. Had the parties cooperated, the other two problems could have been readily addressed,
and UNTSO could have functioned more smoothly and effectively.

First, the local parties refused from the start to cooperate with
UNTSO observers. Initially, the border incidents were minor,
involving private individuals or groups, but over the years both
the frequency and intensity increased as the possibility for a
permanent settlement to the conflict remained remote. Both the
Arabs and Israelis ignored repeated requests by UNTSO officials
to permit observers to conduct their activities in an unrestricted
manner and to establish either permanent or temporary observation posts where needed.

Not only did all parties disregard the principle of UN freedom
of movement, they did not employ the mechanism provided for
by the MACs to resolve disputes peacefully. As UNTSO Chief of Staff
Riley concluded: "This machinery...is only effective when both
parties are ready to use [it] to settle their difficulties, when they
willingly cooperate in an investigation with [the] assistance of
[the] Chairman and UN observers and when, in [the] absence of
agreed decision, they accept a majority decision, as provided in
[the] General Armistice Agreement."[31] By refusing to attend MAC
meetings, by restricting UNTSO personnel, and by ignoring the
decisions or requests of the Chairman and observers, the parties
undermined the machinery established to mediate the conflict
and made it virtually impossible for UNTSO to operate effectively.

Second, poorly defined armistice demarcation lines created
constant dissent among the parties. According to a later Chief of
Staff, Major General Von Horn:

> These lines had never been properly marked out on the ground and
> exact locations where heavy guns, tanks and troop concentrations
> were forbidden were hotly disputed by both sides, who based their
> claims on totally differing sets of maps. These zones which engulfed
> small villages, fields, hills, rivers, and lakes were supposed to contain
> only a minimum of troops and border police.[32]

The difficulties arising from the demarcation disputes led General Odd Bull to recommend that demarcation lines and any
boundaries supervised by observers be clearly marked on the
ground, as was the case with the 800 km cease-fire line between
India and Pakistan in Jammu and Kashmir.[33]

Third, the demilitarized zones had been created ostensibly to
reduce tension in these sensitive spots. However, disputes over
land ownership and cultivation rights made these areas the most
sensitive ones for UNTSO. Inspections rarely revealed any significant violations, most likely because the parties had enough time
prior to inspection to remove anything that could implicate them

in violating the agreements. Irregular and unannounced inspections would theoretically hinder the parties from sanitizing the area, but this option was unavailable to UNTSO. One experienced Force Commander concluded that observers could not adequately supervise demilitarized zones. This could only be done satisfactorily by military forces.[34]

Over the years, UNTSO has come to benefit from a kind of political benign neglect. Although UNTSO personnel provide no service that cannot be provided by the other peacekeeping forces stationed in the region, UNTSO remains as an assertion of the UN's right to be involved in the Arab-Israeli dispute until the belligerents sign peace treaties.

UNTSO also remains in place because of its role as a training ground and reserve pool for new peacekeeping operations. This is recognized by UN planners who have repeatedly drawn upon UNTSO staff when establishing a new peacekeeping force. Several UNTSO Chiefs of Staffs were appointed Force Commanders of new UN operations: Lieutenant General E.L.M. Burns headed UNEF I in 1956; Major General Carl von Horn headed ONUC in 1960 and UNYOM in 1963; Lieutenant General Ensio Siilasvuo headed UNEF II in 1973; and Lieutenant General Emmanuel Erskine headed UNIFIL in 1978.

CONCLUSION

Over the past forty years, UN headquarters in New York has done little to effectively change the status quo in the Middle East and has neither the influence to effect change in the attitudes of the parties concerned nor the political will to impose sanctions or other deterrent measures. UNTSO continues because it is assumed that dismantling it would do the UN and the region more political damage than good, and because of its function as a reserve of trained manpower for peacekeeping. However, in the three principal areas in which its observers are currently deployed, UNTSO is physically redundant, its contingents dwarfed by those of UNIFIL, UNDOF, and the MFO. The function of training observers could just as well be fully subordinated to those operations. However, UNTSO is UN peacekeeping's "organizational slack," its margin of flexibility. Funded from the regular UN budget, free from the hassle of annual or semi-annual renewal of budget and mandate, it provides a steadily growing pool of observers with field experience varying from the tedious (in the Sinai) to the tense (in Lebanon).

UNTSO also highlights the crucial importance of gaining the early consent and cooperation of the local parties and of establishing an operation's impartiality in its very first days of operation. UNTSO's role evolved in a period of great disorder and distrust in the Middle East and was from the very first months suspected of bias by one or both sides.

Some of these perceptions originated from a distrust of the UN. Others derived from the impressions created by individuals in their day-to-day interactions as observers or commanders. For example, the first Chief of Staff, General Riley, was regarded as pro-Israel. His successor, General Bennike, was considered pro-Arab, as was General Burns. As General Odd Bull concludes, the "head of any peacekeeping organization must be genuinely neutral and not simply objective. Privately he may make his own opinions known and may give advice, but in all negotiations he must observe the strictest neutrality."[35] Once a force's neutrality is lost it no longer stands above the conflict, but becomes a party to it.

By the same token, if consent of the local parties is lost (or never established), the mission may be roundly perceived as useless, even as a symbol of international interest in the dispute at hand. If consent of the parties is the *sine qua non* for a successful peacekeeping operation, then perhaps the UN should reconsider its presence where that consent is absent or waning. This need not imply complete disengagement by the UN; negotiations to resolve conflict should continue. But to maintain an operation that mostly suggests the powerlessness of the Organization may not be a good thing for the UN or the people in the region.

UNTSO continues to operate in an environment that has been difficult for decades. As General Von Horn conveyed in a 1958 message to General Odd Bull when the latter arrived in Beirut to assume his position as Force Commander of UNOGIL, "My job is impossible and insoluble. I dare say yours will be even more so."[36] With each war, raid and counterraid, each curfew and home demolished, local suspicions, distrust, and hatred intensify, and the utility of mere peace observation diminishes. Binoculars, maps, a compass, a radio hand set, and a jeep cannot prevent frontier violations by parties intent on pressing their claims, and moral suasion is scarcely appropriate in a community that has violated its own sense of morality.

Notes

1. Quoted in Meron Benvenisti, *Conflicts and Contradictions* (New York: Villard Books, 1986), 164.

2 UNSCOP included representatives from Australia, Canada, Czechoslovakia, Guatemala, India, Iran, the Netherlands, Peru, Sweden, Uruguay, and Yugoslavia.

3. This proposed economic union included a customs union, a joint currency system creating a single foreign exchange rate, and joint economic development (particularly with respect to irrigation, land reclamation, and soil conservation, and the operation of railways, roads, and ports, as well as postal and communication services required for trade and commerce).

4. United Nations Document A/AC.21/9, February 16, 1948, 5. Quoted in Fouad Khouri, *The Arab-Israeli Dilemma* (New York: Syracuse University Press, 1985), 59.

5. Rosalyn Higgins, *United Nations Peacekeeping, 1946-1967, Documents and Commentary, Volume I: The Middle East* (London: Oxford University Press, 1969), 12.

6. United Nations Document A/532, April 10, 1948, 36.

7. United Nations General Assembly Resolution 186, May 14, 1948. Quoted in Higgins, *United Nations Peacekeeping*, Vol. I, 14.

8. Higgins, *United Nations Peacekeeping*, Vol. I, 15.

9. Chapter VII empowers the Security Council to authorize the use of force to deal with threats to international peace and security.

10. Higgins, *United Nations Peacekeeping*, Vol. I, 16.

11. Quoted in David W. Wainhouse, *International Peacekeeping at the Crossroads* (Baltimore, Md.: The Johns Hopkins University Press, 1973), 27.

12. Lieutenant General E.L.M. Burns, *Between Arab and Israeli* (London: George G. Harrap, 1962), 27.

13. Burns, *Between Arab and Israeli*, 27-32; Carl von Horn, *Soldiering for Peace* (New York: David McKay Company, Inc., 1967), chapters 6, 9, 10.

14. United Nations Document, S/727, April 23, 1948. Quoted in Higgins, *United Nations Peacekeeping*, Vol. I, 17.

15. Wainhouse, *International Peacekeeping at the Crossroads*, 28.

16. *The Blue Helmets: A Review of United Nations Peacekeeping*, 2nd ed. (New York: United Nations Department of Public Information, 1990), 419; and United Nations Document A/46/6, Section 2, May 24, 1991, 4-7.

17. *The Blue Helmets*, 21, 420.

18. von Horn, *Soldiering for Peace*, 67.

19. UNTSO military observer who served in Lebanon, May-December, 1986, and in the Sinai, January-June 1987, interview with author, September 26, 1991.

20. *The Blue Helmets*, 19.

21. *The Blue Helmets*, 28.

22. *The Blue Helmets*, 26.

23. Abba Eban, *Abba Eban: An Autobiography* (New York: Random House, 1977), 318-21.

24. Austria, Burma (Myanmar), Chile, Finland, France, and Sweden.

25. United Nations Document S/21947, November 26, 1990, 3.

26. *The Blue Helmets*, 38.

27. UNTSO military observer who served in Lebanon, May-December, 1986, and in the Sinai, January-June 1987, interview with author, September 26, 1991.

28. In the mid-1980s, local Lebanese militias often hijacked UNTSO jeeps, which they mistook for UNIFIL vehicles, in search of weapons. Upon finding no weapons (UNTSO personnel are unarmed), they removed the radio, and friendly militias negotiated the return of the vehicle to UNTSO. In an uglier incident, on February 17, 1988, the Chief of OGL, Lieutenant Colonel William R. Higgins (United States), was kidnapped and later executed by an unidentified group.

29. United Nations Document S/21947, November 26, 1990, 3.

30. *The Blue Helmets*, 41-42.

31. United Nations Document S/3007, May 8, 1953. Quoted in Higgins, *United Nations Peacekeeping*, 168.

32. von Horn, *Soldiering for Peace*, 67.

33. General Odd Bull, *War and Peace in the Middle East* (London: Leo Cooper, 1976), 176.

34. Bull, *War and Peace in the Middle East*, 176.

35. Bull, *War and Peace in the Middle East*, 176.

36. Bull, *War and Peace in the Middle East*, 5.

7 United Nations Emergency Force I: 1956-1967

by Mona Ghali

The first United Nations Emergency Force (UNEF) was created in response to the 1956 Suez Crisis to observe the cease-fire and the withdrawal of British, French, and Israeli forces from Egyptian territory. As the first armed UN peacekeeping operation, UNEF was important not only as a precedent for other UN forces—their composition, funding, command structure, etc.— but also as a test case for the value of armed, neutral forces as conflict-dampers. At stake as UNEF deployed was the credibility of the Organization, which had to prove itself capable of transcending the diplomatic rhetoric of General Assembly sessions and of fulfilling its mandate effectively. Although UNEF helped to keep the peace in the Sinai for more than a decade, UN credibility was indeed damaged when the operation was withdrawn in the period of rising tension that culminated in the June 1967 War. Since then, the UN has been exceedingly reluctant to withdraw under pressure, even though there have been times when it would have been better to do so.

ORIGINS

The Sinai Peninsula is a triangle whose southern tip, Sharm el Sheikh, overlooks the openings of the Gulf of Suez to the west and the Gulf of Aqaba to the east. Forming the geographic transition between Asia and Africa, the Sinai covers an area of 61,000 square kilometers divided roughly into three sections. The northern region along the Mediterranean Sea is made up of sand dunes, ridges, salt flats, and palm groves, and most of the Sinai's population is found there. The central desert is mostly gravel and limestone—good tank country—except for an area of rugged terrain toward the Suez side that is accessible only by a limited number of mountain passes, the most important being Gidi and Mitla. Control of these strategically critical passes has been essential to control of the Sinai. The southernmost third of the Sinai, from the El Tih Plateau to Sharm El Sheikh, is also mountainous. Mount St. Catherine, for example, rises to 2,660 meters and Mount Sinai to 2,300 meters.

It is difficult to imagine the Suez Crisis of 1956 evolving as it did in the absence of the unique convergence of three currents in the international system during the late 1940s and 1950s—the end of European imperialism in its traditional form, nationalism and decolonization in the Third World, and the beginning of the Cold War. These three themes preoccupied the political thought and determined the motivations of the principal actors in the crisis: Egyptian President Gamal Abdel Nasser, British Prime Minister Anthony Eden and British Foreign Secretary Selwyn Lloyd, President Dwight Eisenhower and Secretary of State John Foster Dulles, French Foreign Minister Christian Pineau, and Israeli Prime Minister David Ben-Gurion.

First, European powers, particularly Great Britain and France, emerged from the Second World War militarily and politically weakened. Yet the corresponding revision in their self-image and role in the political hierarchy lagged. With the British disengagement from India in 1947, and the French loss of Indochina, it became increasingly important for these two European nations to retain their influence in the Middle East and North Africa.

British policy vis à vis the Middle East was grounded in the basic premise that had guided British foreign policy in the region for the previous century; namely, preserving its interests in the oil reserves of Iraq, Saudi Arabia and other Gulf sheikdoms, as well as its access to that oil through the Suez Canal. The French had similar interests, but they also had to counter nationalist movements in North Africa, particularly in Algeria after 1954. It became increasingly difficult for both France and Britain to sustain their interests in the Middle East and elsewhere without the kind of expenditure in blood and treasure usually required to sustain an Empire.

Second, a group of "prophet liberators" appeared, among whom were Nasser (Egypt), Ahmed Ben Bella (Algeria), Leopold Senghor (Senegal), Kwame Nkrumah (Ghana), Sukarno (Indonesia), and Pandit Nehru (India). They were the custodians of a dream of national liberation that spoke of the restoration of human dignity and freedom, and they offered their countrymen an alternative to the indignities of European imperialism.

In Egypt, although President Nasser gained wider Arab support from his nationalist ideology, he was also restricted by it. To compromise Egyptian independence by accepting some form of British domination would be to debase the principles of Arab nationalism and nonalignment and to become like Nuri al Said, Prime Minister of Iraq, whom Nasser dismissively called an "imperialist lackey." Therefore, to be faithful to the canon of Arab nationalism, it was inevitable that he would pursue policies sometimes incompatible with Western interests.

In February 1955, Iraq, Pakistan, and Turkey signed a mutual security treaty with Britain. In October, Iran joined the security arrangement then called the Baghdad Pact. The Pact was ostensibly designed to provide a "northern tier" against Soviet influence, but, more importantly, it was a foil to Nasserism. Nasser saw it as an attempt to weaken pan-Arab solidarity and denounced it, claiming that the threat to the Middle East did not originate from the Soviet Union, but from within.[1] By refusing to join the pro-Western alliance and by interpreting it as a threat to Arab political life, Nasser ran afoul of the implicit rules of the Cold War and reinforced the perception held by British and American policy-makers that the Egyptian leader was inclining alarmingly toward the Soviet sphere.

Thus, Nasser's Arab nationalism ran up against the third major international current of the period, the political competition between the Soviet Union and the United States. It was a zero-sum game, and Third World states became the pieces by which the sides kept score. Most newly independent Third World countries sought outside technology and economic aid but wished to remain politically nonaligned. During the Cold War, it was difficult to pursue both objectives simultaneously. Nasser, for example, placed himself in the rival camp by arranging a Czech arms deal in September 1955 and recognizing China in May 1956. Mohammad Heikal, then editor of *al Ahram* and confidant of Nasser, believed that Dulles interpreted the arms deal in an almost apocalyptic fashion:

> It would give the Communists a foothold in the Middle East and this would mark the beginning of a thrust aimed at denying Arab oil to the West. The arms deal had a much wider purpose than simply to oblige Egypt. It would now become impossible to ask Congress for a penny of help for Egypt, because not only the influence but the prestige of the United States was at stake. Everyone was going to say that the way to get American aid was to blackmail them.[2]

As for Eden, according to Anthony Nutting, then British Foreign Minister, the dismissal of British General Glubb from his position as Chief of Staff of the Jordanian Army by King Hussein in March 1956, after twenty-six years in service, presumably at Nasser's instigation, convinced the prime minister that Nasser should be removed, and not neutralized or isolated as his advisors recommended.[3] But the time had lapsed when Britain could control the actions of Arab governments. In the post-1945 international system, Britain's political hegemony in the Middle East required US endorsement. Until July 1956 that endorsement was forthcoming, but after July the costs of *Pax Britannica* were judged too high by the Eisenhower Administration.

Nationalization and its Aftermath

On July 19, 1956, Dulles announced the reversal of the US decision to finance the Aswan High Dam project, which was followed by a parallel statement by the British government. The British and American reversals automatically canceled the World Bank's loan to build the dam, which had been contingent upon the participation of both western countries. It is difficult to draw direct causality between Dulles' announcement and Nasser's nationalization of the Suez Canal Company one week later on July 26. Egyptian nationalists had contemplated such a move since 1909 when the Suez Canal Company concession was renewed, but as Middle East historian Albert Hourani states, "it is unlikely that Nasser would have done it without being given the opportunity presented by what appeared to Egyptians as a public humiliation by the United States and Britain".[4]

In nationalizing the Suez Canal Company, Nasser reasserted Egypt's independence of action, implying that he could not be coerced into pacts or peace treaties. If the US was not prepared to extend credit for the construction of the Aswan High Dam, then Egypt would find alternative resources. In doing so, however, Nasser had locked himself into a difficult position. To hold firm would be to risk military confrontation with the Great Powers. To give ground would be seen as betraying the trust of a population that had begun to recognize itself as belonging to a country that counted.[5]

For the British and French, the principal shareholders in the Suez Canal Company, the nationalization of the Canal provided them with the pretext to remove Nasser, by force if necessary. Certainly, Eden was disinclined to negotiate. He appropriated the images of Mussolini and Hitler by invoking the lessons of Munich to create a one-dimensional portrait of Nasser. By demonizing the Egyptian president, Eden cast British policy as higher-minded than was merited. His hard-line attitude with respect to Nasser was encouraged by his Arab allies such as Nuri Said, who said, "You must hit him. You must hit him hard, and you must hit him now."[6] Eden ordered a plan prepared for a joint Anglo-French invasion of Egypt. The attack was finally agreed upon and put into action even as discussions between UN Secretary General Dag Hammarskjöld and the foreign ministers of Britain, France and Egypt seemed close to a peaceful resolution of the crisis.[7]

Although President Eisenhower rejected the resort to force, Eden was convinced that in the absence of joint Anglo-American actions the West would forfeit its interests in the Middle East. Despite statements from the US Administration, Eden felt that in the eleventh hour the Americans would not abandon him. In contrast, Dulles felt that US intentions had been made clear.[8]

Therefore, events went forward at two levels. On the diplomatic level, the British and the French were disingenuously pursuing a negotiated settlement on the internationalization of the Canal at the first and second London Conferences in August and September; on the level of real intent, secret plans for a joint Israeli, British, and French attack were being made. On October 23, a clandestine meeting between French, British, and Israeli delegates took place at Sevres, where plans for the Israeli attack and the concomitant Anglo-French military action were coordinated. France would exercise its veto if any action were taken by the UN Security Council against Israel.

Israel cooperated with the attack plan in hopes of establishing a more secure southern frontier. The French were convinced that in neutralizing Nasser they would regain control of Algeria from militant nationalists. The plan appealed to Eden because, theoretically, it would mask Britain's real intention of eliminating the Nasser regime. With it, Eden believed he could keep both British and international opinion favorable, while at the same time avoid alienating pro-western Arab leaders.

Initiatives Leading to UN Involvement

On October 29, Israeli forces attacked Egypt, dropping a parachute battalion in central Sinai at the eastern entrance of the Mitla Pass, 70 kilometers from the Suez Canal. Later that evening, the United States immediately requested the Security Council to order an Israeli withdrawal behind the armistice lines. By going to the UN, the US was attempting to manage the crisis in such a way as to demonstrate that its policies did not necessarily coincide with those of Britain, and to preempt possible

Soviet efforts to adopt a leadership role sympathetic to smaller nations.[9]

In accordance with the preplanned design, the British and French issued an ultimatum to Egypt and Israel calling on both parties to retreat to ten miles (16 kilometers) from the Canal on October 30 and threatening to dispatch troops. Israeli forces had not yet advanced within ten miles of the Canal. Egypt, whose forces held the Canal, rejected the ultimatum, claiming that its right to defend its territorial sovereignty should not be dictated by the British or French. According to Heikal:

> News of the ultimatum was received [in Egypt] with astonishment bordering on disbelief. Britain and France's collusion had been staring us in the face, but this was a possibility which had been discounted because it was assumed that, however determined on a war Eden might be, he would have had some consideration for his friends in Iraq and other Baghdad Pact countries and for British prestige and interests in the Middle East, all of which would be irreparably damaged if he committed the one unforgivable sin—combining with Israel to attack an Arab country. Nasser found the whole situation made no sense at all—it was, in fact, quite mad.[10]

On October 31, the Anglo-French air offensive began with attacks directed against Egyptian air bases, and one week later the British landed troops at Port Said and the French at Port Fouad. On November 2, acting under the terms of the 1950 "Uniting for Peace" resolution, the UN General Assembly adopted a draft resolution proposed by Dulles urging that "all parties in the area agree to an immediate cease-fire and halt the movement of military forces and arms."[11] The resolution called for the reopening of the Canal and ordered the parties to withdraw to the 1949 armistice lines, to desist from raids across the armistice lines, and to observe the provisions of the armistice agreements. Resolution 997 was approved 64 to 5. The UK, France, Israel, New Zealand and Australia voted against, while Belgium, Canada, Laos, the Netherlands, Portugal, and South Africa abstained.[12]

The UN cease-fire order was ignored, prompting further action. The Canadian delegate to the UN submitted two draft resolutions. Resolution 998, adopted on November 4, requested the Secretary General to submit a plan within forty-eight hours to establish a United Nations force to secure and supervise the cease-fire in accordance with previous resolutions adopted with respect to the crisis. Resolution 999, adopted the same day, noted the noncompliance of the parties with Resolution 997 of November 2 and requested the Secretary General, "with the assistance of the Chief of Staff and the members of UNTSO to obtain the withdrawal of all forces behind the armistice lines." On November 5, 1956, the General Assembly adopted Resolution 1000 establishing the United Nations Emergency Force (UNEF). Under political pressure, the British government agreed to a cease-fire at midnight, November 6-7.

POLITICAL SUPPORT

The creation of UNEF was a radical departure in UN policy. The support of both the local parties and the major powers proved crucial to its success for more than a decade. When that support faltered in May 1967, Secretary General U Thant acceded to Nasser's request to withdraw UNEF troops.

Egypt

Egyptian cooperation with the UN authorities was contingent on a UN guarantee of national sovereignty.[13] A "good faith" agreement was negotiated between Nasser and Hammarskjöld, in which:

> The United Nations takes note of this declaration of the Government of Egypt [to uphold its national sovereignty] and declares that the activities of UNEF will be guided, in good faith, by the task established for the Force in the aforementioned resolutions; in particular, the United Nations, understanding this to correspond to the wishes of the Government of Egypt, reaffirms its willingness to maintain UNEF until its task is completed.

Two other memoranda were signed by Nasser and Hammarskjöld. One, relating to UNEF's area of operations, specified that the Force would not function in the Port Said or Suez Canal areas following the withdrawal of the Anglo-French forces. The second, which would later assume crucial importance, stated that UNEF's presence was contingent on continued Egyptian consent.

United States

Throughout the crisis over Suez, both Eisenhower and Dulles consistently rejected the use of force and demonstrated considerable restraint with respect to Egypt. Improved Egyptian ties with the Communist bloc were cause for alarm, but the Administration sought to avoid drawing in the Soviets and possibly prompting a superpower confrontation. The US feared that should Nasser be made to "disgorge" the Canal by force (Dulles's terminology), other Arab and developing states would be alienated, and those feelings could in turn be exploited by the Soviet Union to expand its sphere of influence.

The US therefore worked through multiple channels to defuse the crisis. Its strategy at the UN was to give the British and French a face-saving way to remove their forces from Egypt. Direct contacts by Eisenhower and Dulles with Ben-Gurion, Pineau, and Eden served to soften the Israeli and European positions and win their acceptance of General Assembly Resolution 997, as well as subsequent resolutions calling for a cease-fire and observance of the provisions of the General Armistice Agreements.

Soviet Union

While practicing some brinksmanship and threatening to intervene on the side of Egypt, the position of the Soviet Union was essentially parallel that of the United States. Anti-communist demonstrations in Hungary dominated Moscow's agenda. Students demonstrated in support of the Hungarian nationalist Imre Nagy against the country's Stalinist regime, demanded the removal of the Soviet Army and the establishment of an alternative political party to the Communists. Although Dulles had spoken of "rollback," the US Administration rejected any military response that could escalate the conflict in Hungary to the superpower level, even after Soviet tanks rolled into Budapest. In effect, the Administration was willing to tacitly accept Soviet dominance in Eastern Europe but not European colonialism in North Africa.

While the Soviet Union refused to pay its assessments for UNEF, it recognized the establishment of the Force as a means to defuse the conflict and to facilitate the withdrawal of foreign forces from Egypt.

Britain, France, and Israel

Without clearing the Suez Canal, the British and French would be dependent on the US for financial assistance in purchasing oil. Even in the event that the British were permitted to clear the Canal at Port Said, they required Egyptian cooperation in clearing sunken ships from the remainder of the Canal. Both activities were contingent on a British military withdrawal. Despite these inescapable facts, Eden refused to order anything but a symbolic

withdrawal of one British infantry battalion in response to the
arrival of an advance group of UNEF on November 21. While
officially the British government contended that it could not
withdraw until UNEF demonstrated its ability to execute its
mandate, the French pressed the British to remain in place. As
Nutting observed,

> Because of their commitments in Algeria, [the French] had them-
> selves withdrawn the equivalent of about three battalions—one-
> third of their force of 8,500 men. But they were still arguing that we
> [the British] should call the Americans' bluff and stand firm against
> an early withdrawal of all our forces. Eisenhower, they insisted,
> would never dare to allow our industries to be paralysed for lack of
> dollar credits to buy the essential supplies of oil.[14]

According to Nutting, Eden, unlike his French counterpart, was
concerned about international opinion and Britain's position at
the UN, and felt he could not dismiss the UN General Assembly
resolutions. Not only was Britain politically isolated, but its
financial and commercial interests were jeopardized. Speculation
against sterling resulted in a drawdown of foreign reserves, which
fell by $141 million in September and October, and by $279
million in November.[15]

On November 24, the General Assembly passed a resolution
calling for immediate withdrawal of Anglo-French forces. Following a meeting between Foreign Ministers Lloyd and Pineau,
Britain and France agreed to remove all troops from Egypt by
December 22.

Israel, while reluctantly complying with Assembly resolutions
under pressure from the United States, demonstrated its recalcitrance by delaying its withdrawals from the Gaza Strip and
Sharm el Sheikh (the latter to guarantee Israeli freedom of
navigation through the Strait of Tiran). Nor did Israel ever
permit UN troops to be based, or to patrol, on Israeli territory.

MANDATE

General Assembly Resolutions 998, 1000, and 1001 called for
and established UNEF. Resolution 1000 (November 5, 1956),
which set the mandate, was adopted by 57 votes to none with
19 abstentions, including Egypt, Israel, France, the UK, and the
Soviet Union and its Eastern European satellites.

Resolution 1000 gave UNEF four responsibilities: (1) to secure
and supervise a cease-fire by forming a buffer zone between

Anglo-French-Israeli and Egyptian forces; (2) to supervise the withdrawal of foreign forces from Egyptian territory and the canal clearing operations; (3) to patrol border areas and deter military incursions; and (4) to secure the provisions of the Egypt-Israel Armistice Agreements. There was considerable controversy surrounding the interpretation of UNEF's mandate. Some parties, particularly Israel, preferred to expand its functions to include the settlement of outstanding disputes such as the administration of the Gaza Strip and the question of Israel's access to the Gulf of Aqaba and the Suez Canal, which would ostensibly facilitate a more permanent improvement in the situation in the Middle East. Other nations believed that UNEF should be restricted to the manageable function of restoring the *status quo ante*.[16] The Secretary General ruled in favor of the more restricted definition stating that, while the right of innocent passage through the Straits of Tiran and the Gulf of Aqaba were significant, these were matters that fell outside the mandate established in Resolution 998.[17]

In his second and final report to the Secretary General on the plan for a UN Emergency Force, Hammarskjöld set forth the parameters of the operation:

> It would be more than an observers' corps, but in no way a military force temporarily controlling the territory in which it was stationed; nor, moreover, should the Force have military functions exceding those necessary to secure peaceful conditions....Its functions can, on this basis, be assumed to cover an area extending roughly from the Suez Canal to the armistice demarcation lines established in the armistice agreements between Egypt and Israel.[18]

Resolution 1001, adopted on November 7, established the principles for the organization and functioning of UNEF and codified the Secretary General's more modest interpretation of UNEF's mandate. The resolution requested the Chief of Command, in consultation with the Secretary General, to organize the Force; accepted Hammarskjöld's recommendation that the Force be funded from the regular UN budget; and established an Advisory Committee composed of one representative each from Brazil, Canada, Ceylon (now Sri Lanka), India, Norway, and Pakistan, and to be chaired by the Secretary General.[19]

FUNDING

UNEF was funded by assessed contributions from member countries in accordance with the regular UN budget scale of assessment. Expenses exceeding assessments were to be met by voluntary contributions credited to a Special Account for UNEF.

But from the start, certain countries opposed the Secretary General's recommendations that the expenses of UNEF, other than those provided by Governments without charge, should be borne by the Organization and apportioned among the Member States in accordance with the regular scale of assessments. The Soviet Union and its Eastern European satellites held the view that the costs of the Force should be borne by the UK, France, and Israel, the "aggressors" in the Suez crisis. After 1961, only two countries, the United States and Britain, continued to make voluntary contributions to UNEF to make up for the eastern bloc deficit.[20]

Similarly, Latin American countries such as El Salvador objected to the UN diffusing the costs of clearing the Suez Canal, and suggested that those responsible for the crisis should also be responsible for restoring the Suez Canal to operational status. On the issue of apportionment, Latin American nations such as Ecuador, Mexico, and Chile supported the principle of collective responsibility but preferred a new sliding scale assessment.[21]

Despite continuing majority support for apportionment based on regular budget assessments, in December 1959 and 1960 some concessions were made to developing countries, reducing their level of contributions. The failure of other member nations, notably France and the Soviet Union, to meet their obligations greatly aggravated a growing UN budget deficit. Of the estimated $34.6 million UN deficit in December 31, 1960, $21.6 million, or over 60 percent, was attributed to UNEF. When the costs of the newer, and larger, UN operation in the Congo were added in (see chapter 19), the Organization experienced a severe financial crisis.

The UN responded to the crisis by issuing 25-year bonds valued at $200 million, at 2 percent interest (of which $169 million were sold), and by seeking an advisory opinion from the International Court of Justice regarding the legitimacy of peacekeeping expenses. On July 20, 1962, the Court affirmed that peacekeeping costs were legitimate "expenses of the Organization" to be borne by the members as apportioned by the General Assembly.

Despite the judgment of the Court, some nations continued to ignore their financial obligations for peacekeeping. The Soviet Union and France accumulated sufficient arrears to be denied their vote in the Assembly (as allowed by Article 19 of the UN Charter). The membership remained reluctant to invoke that sanction, given the Soviet Union's threat to withdraw from the UN if Article 19 was applied to it. (Countries recalled that similar withdrawals from the League of Nations in the 1930s spelled the end of the organization's effectiveness.)

The UN's inability to enforce payment of assessments has been among its principal weaknesses and is not exclusive to the financing of UNEF. The UN's only recourse, apart from its unsuccessful efforts to generate off-budget income, was to reduce yearly expenditures for UNEF, which were cut progressively from $25 million in 1958, to $19 million in 1961, $15 million in 1966, and $14 million in 1967.

PLANNING AND IMPLEMENTATION

The Secretary General was given just forty-eight hours to submit a report on the establishment of a UN Emergency Force. He had no independent intelligence on which to base his recommendations and no military planners to assist him. Because the UN had done nothing like UNEF previously, there were no precedents as to size, structure, or makeup of the force to be deployed. Its nearest analogs were much smaller observer missions, such as UNTSO, headed at that time by Lieutant General E.L.M. Burns. Hammarskjöld asked Burns to serve as commander of UNEF and to make recommendations as to the "size, type, and equipment of troops" necessary to carry out its mandate. Burns, a former corps commander in Europe during World War Two, replied with a long telegram received during the early hours of November 5th, New York time. He recommended that the UN Force "be about the size of a division, with a brigade of tanks, and attached reconnaissance and fighter-aircraft units—the whole organized as an operational force capable of fighting."[22] Because the UN was under pressure to deploy a force as soon as possible, and because there was no military staff whatsoever at UN Headquarters, Burns's telegram represented the only advance military planning input for UNEF. His advice to deploy a combat force was, on the whole, not accepted (although UNEF troops did carry light weapons). With none of the Permanent Members of the Security Council politically neutral regarding Suez, with most of the world's industrial powers aligned with one or the other power bloc, and with Soviet suppression of revolt in Hungary taking place simultaneously, there was no politically neutral, division-sized, armored fighting force available for the Sinai. Even if there had been, it would have been unduly provocative to deploy it. Egypt would not have greeted warmly yet another heavily armed foreign force on its soil, and Israel viewed all "neutral" forces (including unarmed UNTSO observers) with suspicion, and the heavier the armament, the greater the suspicion.

As Brian Urquhart recollects, Hammarskjöld started to write his report to the General Assembly before lunch on November 5 and reviewed the text with Under-Secretary General Ralphe Bunche, Andrew Cordier, his Executive Assistant, and Constantin Stavropoulos, his Legal Counsel, later that evening. By 2:30 am, November 6, the report was completed, and was approved by Assembly Resolution 1001 the following day.[23]

Size and Composition of the Force

A group of United Nations military observers was temporarily detached from UNTSO to serve as a headquarters staff for General Burns while awaiting the arrival of contributing troop contingents. They arrived in Egypt on November 12, 1956, and established UNEF's temporary headquarters in Cairo. They organized the arrival of the first contingents and assisted with logistical and administrative tasks, including procurement and storage of supplies and equipment. As UNEF troops arrived, the observers returned to their permanent positions with UNTSO.[24]

Given the novelty of UNEF, the overwhelming international response to the creation of the Force was not surprising. Offers of troops came from twenty-four countries, of which Hammarskjöld accepted ten (Brazil, Canada, Colombia, Denmark, Finland, India, Indonesia, Norway, Sweden, and Yugoslavia). Egypt rejected Pakistan, which was a member of the pro-Western Baghdad Pact, and New Zealand, a member of the British Commonwealth.[25]

Of the ten countries contributing contingents to UNEF, Brazil, Denmark, India, Norway, and Sweden each contributed infantry battalions. Yugoslavia provided an infantry reconnaissance unit. India contributed signals and service units in addition to infantry. Canada and Poland provided logistics units.

Canadian participation initially posed a problem. Nasser at first rejected the inclusion of Canada's Queen's Own Rifles. He claimed that their titular affiliation with Britain would offend the sensibilities of Egyptians. Hammarskjöld was insistent on Canada's participation, however, because UNEF's Force Commander was Canadian, and because Canada's Foreign Minister, Lester Pearson, originated the idea for the Force. The conflict was resolved when General Burns withdrew the offer of the regiment and replaced it with a noninfantry unit that was, as expected, more amenable to the Egyptians.

The first units, from Colombia, Denmark, and Norway, arrived by air on November 15 and 16 from their home bases via Italy. Colombian troops and equipment were flown in by the US Air Force, as were Indian troops, one week later. The Italian government offered the use of Capodichino airport, Naples, as the staging area for the Force. The main elements of the Canadian and Brazilian contingents arrived at a more measured pace, in early January and February, respectively.[26]

The imperative of speed and, therefore, the reliance on airlifting troops from Naples to Egypt resulted in severe initial shortages of equipment and transport vehicles. This problem was worsened by the failure of several of the contingents to bring appropriate vehicular transport with them.[27]

During its first year in operation, UNEF maintained its authorized level of 6,000, but after 1957 the force was reduced to save money, despite the Force Commander's annual warning that further reductions would impair UNEF's capabilities. As the table below indicates, UNEF was progressively reduced in size to just under 3,400 at the time of its withdrawal in May 1967.

Table 7.1. Contributors of Military Personnel to UNEF

Country	1957	1959	1961	1963	1965	1967
Brazil	545	648	625	616	438	433
Canada	1172	983	936	940	954	795
Colombia	522					
Denmark	424	548	562	563	491	2
Finland	255					
India	957	1174	1251	1252	1269	978
Indonesia	582					
Norway	498	603	614	494	495	61
Sweden	349	659	463	529	426	530
Yugoslavia	673	719	708	708	506	579
Totals:	5,977	5,334	5,159	5,102	4,581	3,378

Source: United Nations Documents A/3694, October 10, 1957; A/4210, October 9, 1959; A/4857, August 30, 1961; A/5494, September 12, 1963; A/5919, September 27, 1965; and A/6669/Add.2, June 19, 1967.

Reductions were taken partly by attrition. As contingents were detached or repatriated, they were only patrially replaced. The Indonesian and Finnish contingents were repatriated in September and December 1957, respectively, and Colombian troops went home in December 1958. Elements of UNEF were also transferred or loaned to other UN operations. Two companies from the Swedish contingent were transferred to ONUC, the UN's Congo operation, in April 1961. Two years later, one company of approximately 115 personnel was detached from the Yugoslav reconnaissance battalion, and two of the five Royal Canadian Air Force planes assigned to UNEF were transferred, along with crews, maintenance personnel, and equipment, to support the United Nations Yemen Observation Mission.

Command, Communications, Logistics and Administration

As the first UN peacekeeping mission, UNEF established precedents upon which subsequent UN operations were loosely modelled, including the selection of participating countries and the Force Commander by the Secretary General; the recruitment of battalion-sized contingents from other than Permanent Members of the Security Council with due regard for "geographic distribution"; and rules of engagement that permit the use of force only in self-defense. While in practice there have been exceptions to the above principles (the use of French contingents in UNIFIL and British forces in UNFICYP, for example), in general they guided the composition of UN peacekeeping missions throughout the Cold War.

UNEF established the traditional chain of command for UN peacekeeping forces, running from the Secretary General or his designated representative in New York to the Force Commander, who exercised command of the national contingents. However, UNEF also retained the awkward dual chain of command established by earlier observer missions wherein a UN civilian served as Chief Administrative Officer, controlling the operation's budget, ordering its supplies, and reporting to his own superiors at UN Headquarters.

As the first UN peacekeeping force, UNEF's logistics system operated initially on an ad hoc basis. On balance, considering the unprecedented and improvisational nature of the enterprise, and the speed of its deployment, it was impossible to avert many difficulties, including shortages of equipment, spare parts, and the complications associated with nonstandardized equipment.

Inadequate vehicular transport initially impaired the functioning of the force, leaving the first groups stranded temporarily at their points of debarkation in Egypt. Some units brought no vehicles with them, and some brought equipment that was poorly adapted to the desert terrain of the Sinai. Until contractors could be engaged to service UNEF's needs through a combination of purchases and rentals, the UN procurement office had to contract with the Egyptian army to provide some vehicles, to borrow them from the UN Relief Works Agency in Gaza, or to buy them from the US Army and from British forces as they withdrew from Egypt. Vehicles were given white UN markings, and individual UN troops wore US military helmet liners painted light blue in order to be clearly recognizable. These were later supplemented by blue berets and desert caps and by UNEF badges and insignias.[28]

Field Operations

Once the cease-fire was stabilized, the deployment of UNEF occurred in five phases, the first three coinciding with the withdrawal of British and French troops from the Canal Zone between November 12 and December 22, 1956, the partial withdrawal of Israeli troops from the Sinai Peninsula between December 1956 and March 1957, and their complete withdrawal from Gaza and Sharm el Sheikh by March 12, 1957. In its fourth and longest phase, UNEF patrolled the Egypt-Israel armistice demarcation line and international frontier from mid-March 1957 to mid-May 1967. The final phase involved withdrawal of the Force at the request of the Egyptian government and in accordance with the terms of the "good faith" agreement.

Phase One: November 12–December 22, 1956. The first phase of UNEF deployment coincided with the withdrawal of Anglo-French forces from the Suez Canal area (mainly Port Said and Port Fouad) and came only after the British and French, under political and economic pressure, accepted US and UN demands to withdraw. Eden had been insisting that Anglo-French forces could not leave until UNEF had established itself in the area and salvage crews had cleared the Canal.

UNEF interposed itself between the Anglo-French and Egyptian forces, moving into position as the Anglo-French troops withdrew northwards from El Cap to Port Said. UNEF carried out the exchange of about 850 prisoners of war, detainees, and internees between the Egyptian government and the Anglo-French forces.

In addition, they cleared minefields, investigated allegations of cease-fire violations, smuggling, and missing personnel, and, after having secured the consent of Egyptian authorities for the use of British and French salvage equipment, provided protection for British and French ships engaged in clearing the Canal.

As planned, the withdrawal of Anglo-French forces was complete by December 22, 1956, with UNEF controlling the Suez Canal area. The following day, UNEF transferred all administrative and policing responsibilities of the area to the Egyptian authorities.

Phase Two: December 1956–March 1957. The second phase of UNEF's deployment centered on the pullback of Israel's forces from the Sinai peninsula. Israeli troops were obligated to withdraw behind the Egyptian-Israeli armistice demarcation line where UNEF would be stationed, as well as along the international frontier south of the Gaza Strip. Gaining Israel's consent to withdraw from the Sinai Peninsula and particularly from Sharm el Sheikh and the Gaza Strip proved more problematic than negotiations over the removal of Anglo-French forces from Canal area. Much of the problem related to the Israeli government's refusal to accept the validity of the armistice demarcation lines.

In a speech delivered to the Israeli Knesset on November 7, Ben-Gurion declared that "the armistice agreement with Egypt is dead and buried and cannot be restored to life. In consequence, the armistice lines between Israel and Egypt have no more validity. On no account will Israel agree to the stationing of a foreign force, no matter how called, in her territory or in any areas occupied by her."[29] Also, in Israeli usage, the Gulf of Suez became the Gulf of Solomon, and Sharm el Sheikh at the southern tip of Sinai became Ophira.[30] In assigning their own place names, the Israelis were trying to give these sites not just a new identity, but one derived from Israeli rather than Arab history.[31]

In a firm response to the Israeli prime minister's speech, Eisenhower wrote,

Statements attributed to your government to the effect that Israel does not intend to withdraw from Egyptian territory have been called to my attention. I must say frankly, Mr. Prime Minister, that the United States views these reports, if true, with deep concern. Any such decision...could not but bring condemnation of Israel as a violator of the principles as well as the directives of the United Nations.[32]

US pressure succeeded in bringing about a reversal of the Israeli position. Ben-Gurion cabled Eisenhower stating, "we have never planned to annex the Sinai desert," and confirmed an Israeli withdrawal "upon conclusion of satisfactory arrangements with the United Nations."[33] Beginning on December 3, 1956, and continuing through January 22, Israeli forces withdrew from the entire Sinai with the exception of the Gaza Strip and Sharm el Sheikh; the former because it was a source of frequent *fedayeen* raids and the latter because it overlooked the strategic Strait of Tiran.

Phase Three: Withdrawal of Israeli Forces from the Gaza Strip and Sharm el Sheikh. The Israeli government questioned the legal validity of Egypt's occupation of the Gaza Strip from 1948 and proposed a plan in which Israeli forces would be withdrawn and Israeli civilian administration would be established, cooperating with United Nations Relief Works Agency for Palestine Refugees, thereby eliminating the deployment of UNEF troops in the Strip.[34] Hammarskjöld rejected Israeli civilian administration of the area.

On February 2, 1957, the General Assembly passed Resolution 1124, criticizing Israel's failure to comply with previous resolutions demanding the complete withdrawal of its forces behind the armistice demarcation line. Resolution 1125, adopted by the General Assembly the same day, gave Israel the assurances that it considered essential before withdrawing its Forces from the Gaza Strip and the Sinai. Resolution 1125 "recognized that withdrawal by Israel must be followed by action which would assure progress towards the creation of peaceful conditions in the area," and affirmed that the observance of the Armistice Agreement required stationing UNEF on the Egypt-Israel armistice demarcation line (ADL).

UNEF forces assumed positions in population centers and camps in the area, controlled entry and exit points of the Strip, and with the assistance of UNRWA assumed responsibility for some essential services, including internal security functions, manning checkpoints, and patrolling with a view to contain violence and looting. The Force assumed temporary control of the prisons, guarded essential installations such as public utilities, temporarily manned the telephone switchboard in the town of Gaza, and cleared mines.[35]

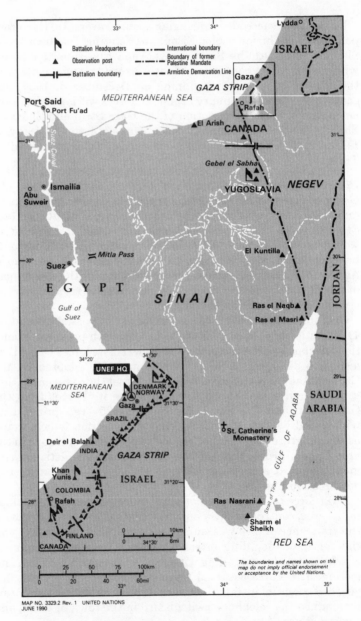

**Figure 7.1. First United Nations Emergency Force,
Deployment as of August 1957**

Phase Four: Operations Along the Armistice Line and International Frontier. By March 12, 1957, Israel had removed its forces from the Gaza Strip and Sharm el Sheikh, facilitating the fourth phase of UNEF's deployment, the patrolling of the Egyptian-Israeli armistice line and the international frontier (IF) in the south. Although Resolution 1125 had called for UNEF troops to patrol along *both* sides of the ADL and IF, Israel refused to permit UN troops on its side of the boundaries. Thus, UNEF patrolled only the Egyptian side of the international frontier to a depth of 273 kilometers.[36] Canada's 115th Air Transport Unit patrolled an additional 187 kilometers, covering the entire Sinai coast of the Gulf of Aqaba. Operating from El Arish, then the only paved airstrip in the Sinai, UNEF reconnaissance missions made daily overflights along the Egyptian-Israeli frontier and the armistice line separating the Gaza Strip from Israel. Ground patrols called upon the air unit for additional reconnaissance support when needed.[37]

UNEF patrols along the ADL and IF created overlaps between UNTSO and UNEF. While the government of Israel assumed the Egyptian-Israeli General Armistice Agreement was no longer in effect, the United Nations refused to accept unilateral abrogation of the Agreement. Instead, the Egyptian-Israeli Mixed Armistice Commission was placed under the jurisdiction of UNEF's Force Commander.

Seventy-two UNEF observations posts were positioned along the entire length of the ADL and manned in the daylight. Five- or six-man units conducted three rounds of patrols each night, concentrating on sensitive areas where infiltrations were most likely to occur. Eight outposts were established along the international frontier, from which mobile patrols were conducted. These were supplemented by air reconnaissance, at first daily, but later reduced to three per week. To deter infiltrations, the inhabitants of Gaza were prohibited from coming closer than 50 to 100 meters to the ADL by day and 500 meters at night. Although UNEF was deployed on just one side of the ADL, the Secretary General reported that the number of infiltrations across the line and firings across the international frontier were markedly reduced by the presence of UNEF. Along Israel's borders with Jordan and Lebanon, by contrast, fedayeen raids continued unabated.

Although the Suez Canal remained closed to Israeli ships during this period, freedom of navigation through the Straits of Tiran into the Gulf of Aqaba was maintained. Swedish UNEF contingents were stationed at Sharm el Sheikh until May 22, 1967, when Egypt closed the Strait to Israel-bound shipping.

Phase Five: Withdrawal of UNEF, May 1967. On May 13, the Egyptian government received reports from the Soviet Union informing it of Israeli troop concentration on the Syrian border and advising it to anticipate an Israeli invasion of Syria immediately following independence day on May 15. As Egyptian Defense Minister Shamseddin Badran stated while on trial following the 1967 war, "false Soviet reports of an imminent Israeli push to Damascus provoked a confrontational position in Sinai."[38]

On May 16, 1967, the Egyptian Chief of Staff General Mohammed Fawzi issued a request to UNEF's Force Commander, General Indar Rikhye, to withdraw UNEF troops from their positions. Rikhye refused to accede to the Egyptian request until he relayed the latest developments to Secretary General U Thant, who agreed. In the interim, Egyptian troops had occupied some UNEF observation posts.

In his letter of May 16, U Thant wrote, "A request by the U.A.R. authorities for a temporary withdrawal of UNEF from the armistice demarcation line on the international frontier, or from parts of them, would be considered by the Secretary General as tantamount to a request for the complete withdrawal of UNEF from Gaza and Sinai, since this would reduce UNEF to ineffectiveness."[39] U Thant's decision to comply with the Egyptian request, in accord with the terms of the "good faith" agreement signed between his predecessor and Nasser, set off alarms in Tel Aviv. But there is considerable controversy as to whether Nasser had requested the complete removal of all UNEF troops (including those positioned in Gaza and Sharm el Sheikh).

According to Mohammed Heikal, Foreign Minister Mahmoud Riad, and Ismail Fahmy, later Foreign Minister under Sadat, Nasser was not seeking the withdrawal of UNEF from Gaza or Sharm el Sheikh, but only from the international frontier between Sinai and the Negev, and it was U Thant's "inflexibility" that had provoked the crisis.[40] Contradicting this evidence is the testimony of UNEF Commander Rikhye, who states that the Egyptian brigadier who handed him the request specifically requested the removal of posts at Sharm el Sheikh.[41]

Regardless of Nasser's initial intent, on May 18 U Thant received a cable from Egypt's Foreign Minister explicitly stating that the government of the U.A.R. had decided to "terminate the presence of the United Nations Emergency Force from the territory of the United Arab Republic and Gaza Strip," and requested its withdrawal "as soon as possible."[42] It was clear that the UN would no longer be the guarantor of a secure Egyptian-Israeli border, and although Israel's lack of confidence in the UN apparatus would not permit it to rely to any degree on UNEF for its national security, Tel Aviv had been satisfied with its performance and results. When U Thant acceded to the Egyptian request, however, Israel's basic lack of confidence in the UN at large was reinforced. According to Abba Eban, "Here was the international peace organization being specifically invited to act as to enable 'Egyptian armed forces to go into action against Israel.' In other words, the UN was being asked to cooperate in making room for war! At the very least, we had assumed in 1957 that a broad international consultation would be held in the event that a request for the removal of UNEF was made."[43]

Once Egypt asked it to leave, UNEF's only alternative to complete disengagement was deployment on the Israeli side of the lines. Israel's delegate to the UN declared that to be an unacceptable option,[44] and the first UNEF troops began leaving the Sinai on May 29, 1967, more than ten years after the operation began. Some UNEF troops were caught in the cross fire of the Arab-Israeli war that erupted on June 5, and fifteen UN personnel were killed. The last UN troops left Egypt on June 17.

ASSESSMENT

Hammarskjöld's report to the General Assembly on UNEF dated October 1957 stated, "despite its limited authority and some unsettled questions, there would seem to be no good reason to doubt that UNEF has been effective. It has earned acceptance as a significant pioneering effort in the evolution of methods of peace-making."[45] His assessment, only one year after the deployment of UN troops in the Sinai Peninsula, is applicable to the ten and one-half year history of UNEF. In general, the Force discharged its mandate well, first, in observing the implementation of General Assembly Resolution 997's call for an immediate cease-fire, then by supervising the withdrawal of foreign forces and Suez Canal clearing operations and, finally, in monitoring the armistice demarcation line in the Gaza Strip and the international frontier in the Sinai.

UNEF's record of success is attributed to several factors: first, and most important, the consensus of the Soviet and US governments during the formative period of the crisis; second, Egyptian consent to the presence of the Force on its territory; third, Israeli satisfaction with its basic operation (including UNEF's monitoring of the Strait of Tiran); and finally, the mediation skills of Secretary General Dag Hammarskjöld.

Hammarskjöld's personal commitment to a peaceful settlement of the Suez Crisis and, more broadly, to the founding principles that guided the UN, were evident in his own version of shuttle diplomacy and his personal contact with the parties involved. Hammarskjöld, the poetic technician, used the "good faith" agreement with Egypt to reconcile the primacy of national sovereignty with the deployment of UNEF on Egyptian territory.

Although Israel did not accept a UN presence on its territory, neither did it actively restrict the Force's freedom of movement (as it was to do much later with the UN's peacekeeping force in Lebanon). UNEF troops were occasionally harassed, but these instances were not serious enough to impair the Force's operations. On the other hand, both sides watched UN air operations closely. On one occasion, Israeli fighter aircraft tried to force a UNEF Caribou transport plane to land in Israeli territory, and any UNEF flight entering Egypt had to request clearance eighteen hours in advance of takeoff. UNEF aircraft were not allowed to enter Egyptian airspace after dark, and during daylight operations pilots could not devitate from a narrow air corridor.[46]

When U Thant respected the "good faith" agreement and withdrew the Force at Egyptian government request, he was criticized for not consulting the General Assembly first. An *aide-mémoire*, written by Hammarskjöld and made public by Ernest A. Gross, a former US Ambassador to the UN, stated that Egypt was required to consult with the General Assembly before requesting the removal of UN forces from its territory. In the *aide-mémoire*, Hammarskjöld recognized the shortcomings of the "good faith" agreement and the vulnerability of the Force to the consent of the host country. Since U Thant had only consulted with the UNEF Advisory Committee and not the General Assembly, Gross concluded he had acted prematurely in agreeing to withdraw the Force.[47] Nonetheless, the "good faith" agreement was the only official UN document that controlled the stationing of UNEF on Egyptian territory.

Hammarskjöld recognized the United Nations as a place where the small powers could press their claims. The Great Powers had other more tangible means at their disposal to secure their interests, and, therefore, they tended to approach the UN or abide by its requests only when it was in their best interest. The paradox of the United Nations, as manifest in the Suez Crisis, is that a forceful UN response to the legitimate complaints of small powers, such as Egypt's protest of the Israeli invasion and subsequent Anglo-French bombing, required the political backing of the United States, and the endorsement or acquiescence of the Soviet Union. Had it not been for such superpower accord in this instance (even as Soviet tanks were crushing the Hungarian revolt), Britain and France could have continued their bombing until Nasser was forced to capitulate, and Israeli forces might have remained in the Sinai.

Finally, to judge the withdrawal of UNEF as responsible for the outbreak of hostilities in June 1967 is both facile and naive. Another UN force's experience in Lebanon in 1982 (when its positions were effortlessly overridden by the invading Israeli Defence Force) suggests that even had UNEF remained in place it would have deterred neither the Egyptian government's serious intent to initiate a war with the cooperation of its close ally, Syria, nor Israel's decision to preempt that move to avoid being overwhelmed militarily.

CONCLUSIONS

In creating UNEF, Secretary General Hammarskjöld and his staff were breaking new ground. Many of their decisions regarding the Force's command structure, logistics, composition and funding were improvised. Yet despite its ad hoc beginnings, UNEF maintained a quiescent Israeli-Egyptian front until 1967. In the intervening years, several conclusions drawn from the UNEF experience have shaped subsequent peacekeeping missions.

First, UN peacekeeping operations function most effectively when the United States is behind them. In the case of Suez, the United States exercised its political and economic power to force the British, the French, and the Israelis to withdraw their forces from Egyptian territory. Eisenhower's forceful and constant pressure was particularly important in convincing Ben-Gurion to order an Israeli pullback. In threatening to cut off American public and private aid, to impose and enforce UN sanctions, and possibly to expel Israel from the Organization, Eisenhower was able to splinter Israeli resolve. In contrast, when the United States assumes a more passive posture, as when Iraq's Saddam Hussein ordered an invasion of Iran in 1980, the UN rarely can move beyond the compulsory rhetoric.

The second lesson, and equally important for the success of a peacekeeping operation, was the need for the consent of the local parties. Although UNEF could not station its troops on both sides of the cease-fire line, both Egypt and Israel supported the Force, and it functioned satisfactorily for more than a decade. When Egyptian consent was withdrawn, the Secretary General had little choice but to withdraw the Force. Although subsequent operations may not be so vulnerable to unilateral requests for their withdrawal, loss of local consent to their presence still robs peacekeepers of their effectiveness and can make continued operations militarily dangerous as well as politically counterproductive.

Finally, the UNEF experience reveals one of the principal paradoxes of peacekeeping missions. By maintaining a status of peaceful coexistence between two or more hostile countries (or factions), and by eliminating the sense of urgency that crises impart, a peacekeeping force may subvert the search for a more permanent solution to the hostility. It may equally be argued, however, that when diplomats fail to arrive at a long-term modus vivendi between the parties, it is not the peacekeeping force that has fallen short, since it is, after all, just an interim measure to keep active hostilities in abeyance. Instead, the parties themselves, resisting political and territorial compromises in the hope that the balance of power will turn in their favor, reinforce the awkward state of no war and no peace. Settlements can be achieved only if there exists genuine desire to reach them on the part of all parties concerned. In the 1950s and 1960s in the Sinai, that desire was minimal and surely would have been no greater had UNEF not been present.

Notes

1. For Mohammad H. Heikal, this was the main difference between Nasser and Nuri al Said (*Cutting the Lion's Tail: Suez Through Egyptian Eyes* [London: Andre Deutsch, 1986], 62).

2. Heikal, *Cutting the Lion's Tail*, 82-83.

3. Eden felt that Nasser was accountable for Glubb's dismissal. According to Anthony Nutting, Eden insisted that Nasser had been hard at work trying to undermine General Glubb, a British officer commanding an Arab army, and the principal obstacle in his "ambitions" to absorb Jordan. Nasser had prevented Jordan joining the Baghdad Pact, and now he had gotten rid of Glubb. "Nasser was our Enemy No. I in the Middle East and he would not rest until he destroyed all our [Britain's] friends and eliminated the last vestiges of our influence. If he succeeded, it would be the end of Eden. Nasser must therefore be himself destroyed"

(Nutting, *No End of a Lesson: The Story of Suez* [London: Constable, 1967], 27).

4. William Roger Louis and Roger Owen, *Suez 1956: The Crisis and its Consequences* (Oxford: Clarendon Press, 1989), 401.

5. This concept is elaborated upon in Clifford Geertz, *The Interpretation of Cultures* (New York: Basic Books, 1973). Geertz writes, "once aroused, the desire to become a people rather than a population, a recognized and respected somebody in the world who counts and is attended to, is, short of its satisfaction, apparently unappeasable" (237).

6. Heikal, *Cutting the Lion's Tail*, 130.

7. Nutting, *No End of a Lesson*, 93-95.

8. Rosalyn Higgins, *United Nations Peacekeeping, 1946-1967, Documents and Commentary, Vol. I: The Middle East* (London: Oxford University Press, 1969), 222.

9. Louis and Owen, *Suez 1956*, 210.

10. Heikal, *Cutting the Lion's Tail*, 179.

11. "Uniting for Peace" (UN General Assembly Resolution A/1775, November 3, 1950) shifts jurisdiction on an issue relating to international peace and security to the majority-ruled General Assembly when the Security Council has been deadlocked by a veto.

12. Rosalyn Higgins, *United Nations Peacekeeping*, Vol. I, 228.

13. *The Blue Helmets: A Review of United Nations Peacekeeping*, 2nd ed. (New York: United Nations Department of Public Information, 1990), 53.

14. Nutting, *No End of a Lesson*, 152.

15. Nutting, *No End of a Lesson*, 134, 145.

16. Higgins, *United Nations Peacekeeping*, Vol. I, 243.

17. Higgins, *United Nations Peacekeeping*, Vol. I, 258.

18. United Nations Document A/3302, November 6, 1956. Quoted in Higgins, *United Nations Peacekeeping*, 242.

19. United Nations General Assembly Resolution 1001, November 7, 1956. Quoted in Higgins, *United Nations Peacekeeping*, 235.

20. Higgins, *United Nations Peacekeeping*, Vol. I, 434.

21. Higgins, *United Nations Peacekeeping*, Vol. I, 427-430.

22. Lieutenant General E.L.M. Burns, *Between Arab and Israeli* (London: George G. Harrap, 1962), 186-89. A division of troops may vary from 15,000 to 50,000 depending on the country of origin and the size of its logistics and other support units. A division is subdivided into three or four brigades, and each brigade in turn has three or four battalions. UN peacekeeping forces typically deploy battalions from several countries with no command echelon other than Force Headquarters above battalion level.

23. Brian Urquhart, *A Life in Peace and War* (New York: Harper & Row, 1987), 133.

24. United Nations Document A/3943, October 9, 1958. Quoted in Higgins, *United Nations Peacekeeping*, Vol. I, 282.

25. The fourteen other countries to offer troops were Afghanistan, Burma, Ceylon, Chile, Czechoslovakia, Ecuador, Ethiopia, Iran, Laos, New Zealand, Pakistan, Peru, Phillippines, and Romania.

26. US Military Air Transport Service chronologies furnished courtesy of Dr. John W. Leland, Historian, US Air Force Military Airlift Command, Scott Air Force Base, Illinois.

27. United Nations Document A/3943, October 9, 1958. Quoted in Higgins, *United Nations Peacekeeping*, Vol. I, 283.

28. United Nations Document A/3943. Quoted in Higgins, *United Nations Peacekeeping*, Vol. I, 283.

29. Donald Neff, *Warriors at Suez: Eisenhower Takes America into the Middle East* (New York: Linden Press/Simon & Schuster, 1981), 415-416.

30. Heikal, *Cutting the Lion's Tail*, 203.

31. For a sensitive discussion of "what's in a name," see Meron Benvenisti, *Conflicts and Contradictions* (New York: Villard Books, 1986), 191-202.

32. Neff, *Warriors at Suez*, 416.

33. Neff, *Warriors at Suez*, 417.

34. *The Blue Helmets*, 64.

35. United Nations Documents, A/3694 and Add. 1, October 9, 1957. Quoted in Higgins, *United Nations Peacekeeping*, 260.

36. Higgins, *United Nations Peacekeeping*, Vol. I, 258. *The Blue Helmets*, 73.

37. Amy Smithson, "Multilateral Aerial Inspections: An Abbreviated History," in Michael Krepon and Amy Smithson, eds., *Open Skies, Arms Control, and Cooperative Security* (New York: St. Martin's Press, 1992), 120.

38. Abba Eban, *Abba Eban: An Autobiography* (New York: Random House, 1977), 318.

39. Eban, *An Autobiography*, 322.

40. Sydney D. Bailey, *Four Arab-Israeli Wars and the Peace Process* (New York: St. Martin's Press, 1990), 192-193.

41. Major General Indar Jit Rikhye recalls rereading the letter of General Fawzy, Chief of the Egyptian armed forces, requesting UNEF withdrawal from the Sinai. Rikhye then asked the messenger whether withdrawal included El Sabha and Sharm el Sheikh and was given an affirmative reply (*The Sinai Blunder* [London: Frank Cass, 1980], 19).

42. United Nations Document A/6730/Add.3, June 26, 1967, paragraph 21. Quoted in Higgins, *United Nations Peacekeeping*, 347.

43. Eban, *An Autobiography*, 321.

44. Higgins, *United Nations Peacekeeping*, 347.

45. United Nations Document, A/3694, October 9, 1957.

46. Amy Smithson, "Multilateral Aerial Inspections," 120.

47. Rikhye, *The Sinai Blunder*, 173.

8   United Nations Emergency Force II: 1973-1979

by Mona Ghali

The October 1973 War, the fourth Arab-Israeli war, produced two UN peacekeeping missions: the second United Nations Emergency Force (UNEF II) in the Sinai, created on October 25, 1973, and the United Nations Disengagement Observer Force (UNDOF), established in the Israeli-occupied Golan Heights on May 31, 1974. The first is examined here, the second in chapter nine.

UNEF II performed its tasks successfully, serving between 1973 and 1979 as a buffer between Israeli and Egyptian troops, observing, investigating, and reporting violations of the Sinai Disengagement Agreements of 1974 and 1975. Its continued presence was requested in the 1979 Egypt-Israel peace treaty, but Soviet objections to that agreement prevented the Security Council from extending UNEF II's mandate, and it was eventually replaced by a non-UN force.

ORIGINS

On October 6, 1973, on the Jewish holiday of Yom Kippur, Egyptian forces launched an assault against Israeli forces entrenched on the east bank of the Suez Canal since the 1967 June War. Simultaneously, the Syrian army attacked Israeli positions in the Golan Heights seized during that same war. The dual attack took Israel by surprise. Although US and Israeli intelligence sources had monitored a Syrian and Egyptian troop build-up in early October and had reported the withdrawal of Soviet advisors, the general reading of the situation held that the Arabs would be foolish to initiate a conflict. Therefore, the signals of an impending Arab attack, while duly noted, were dismissed after serious consideration.[1] Moreover, Defense Minister Moshe Dayan stated on the second day of the war that Israel had deliberately resisted any preemptive moves so as not to be labelled the aggressor.

By October 7, the Egyptian army had broken through most of the Bar Lev line and formed bridgeheads on the eastern bank of the canal.[2] At this point, neither the Arabs nor the Israelis were prepared to discuss a cease-fire arrangement. The Egyptians and Syrians, infused with confidence by initial military success, were not about to cease their attack nor forfeit any territorial gains. For the Israelis, nothing seemed more anathema than to accept a cease-fire when the Egyptians and Syrians were beyond the lines of October 5. Israeli Prime Minister Golda Meir preferred to defer negotiations until Israel recovered militarily.[3] The United States agreed with Israel that it was not the time to seek a cease-fire arrangement at the Security Council. The US Administration, buoyed by intelligence reports projecting a quick military reversal in favor of Israel, planned to press for a return to the *status quo ante* on October 6, letting military realities soften the Arab position while avoiding the General Assembly and its "automatic pro-Arab majority."[4]

However, unlike the 1967 war, when US President Johnson was quick to publicly ascribe responsibility to Nasser even though Israel fired the first shots, President Nixon and Kissinger initially held back. As William Quandt suggests, a number of US interests dictated a balanced US approach, among them: US and European dependence on Middle East oil; the difference between an effort to recapture lost territory and an assault against internationally recognized boundaries; the belief that the frustrating condition of "no war, no peace" had prompted the Arabs to take action to break the stalemate; and the desire to maintain US-Soviet detente, the principal tool of containment during the Nixon-Kissinger years.[5]

But the quick improvement in Israel's battlefield fortunes expected by Israeli commanders and US intelligence sources had not yet come about; instead, Israeli ammunition supplies were being depleted and the Soviet-supplied Egyptian and Syrian armies, equipped with anti-tank and anti-aircraft missiles, were causing heavy Israeli plane and tank losses. Although the Israeli government initially requested only ammunition from the US, it soon became apparent that massive resupply would be needed if Israel was to regain the initiative.

While the Israeli government had refused to consider a cease-fire "in place" during the first few days of the war, its military position had weakened sufficiently after a week. Tel Aviv offered a cease-fire on October 13. According to Quandt, when it became evident that Sadat was not prepared to accept a cease-fire in place, the US Administration gave the green light for an airlift of equipment and supplies to Israel to enable it to put a quick end to the fighting.[6] After October 14, and despite Jordan entering the war, Egyptian offensive operations bogged down. The war finally began to swing in Israel's favor on October 15, bolstered by the arrival of US arms shipments.

The Israeli army reached Ismailia and Suez, virtually encircling the Egyptian Third Army. On the northern front, Israeli forces were approaching Damascus. This deterioration in the Arab military position transformed the political dynamics of the crisis. On October 20, Saudi King Faisal announced an oil embargo on the United States and the Netherlands and, for the first time, exercised the Arab economic clout derived from the "oil weapon." US Secretary of State Henry Kissinger flew to Moscow to negotiate a cease-fire resolution that would be acceptable to the Soviet Union. The two superpowers took their resolution to the UN Security Council on October 21.

Initiatives Leading to UN Action

The UN Security Council convened special sessions on October 8, 9, and 11 at the request of the United States. The majority of Council members favored a cease-fire after an Israeli withdrawal from the occupied territories. Britain favored an immediate cease-fire in place. The United States, Austria, and Australia endorsed a cease-fire and the return to the October 5 lines. China made no indication that it supported any cease-fire. Meanwhile, the fighting continued.

After delaying several days to permit their respective Middle Eastern allies to make maximum battlefield gains, the two superpowers began to press them to agree to an immediate cease-fire. Brezhnev sent his ambassador, Vladimir Vinogradov, to see Sadat in Cairo.[7] Kissinger flew to Tel Aviv from Moscow and asked Israeli Prime Minister Golda Meir to review the cease-fire document he had crafted in Moscow and to give Israel's response before the Security Council convened that evening. That is, once the United States and the Soviet Union settled upon a cease-fire in place as the most desirable option, they presented Israel and Egypt with a *fait accompli*. The Egyptian government was anxious to relieve the Third Army and was therefore prepared to accept a cease-fire in place, reversing its position of a week earlier.

Israel's approval was implicitly required for US arms shipments to continue. While Prime Minister Meir accepted the resolution, she considered that the US had run roughshod over Israel.

In the early hours of October 22, the UN Security Council adopted Resolution 338. The text reflected the agreement reached by the US and the Soviet Union in Moscow and called on the parties to "cease all firing and terminate all military activity immediately, no later than 12 hours after the passing of the resolution," and to begin immediately the implementation of Security Council Resolution 242 (which called for Israeli withdrawal from lands occupied in the 1967 war). Resolution 338 made no provision for supervision of the cease-fire.

Resolution 338 reflected the dovetailing of US and Soviet interests in expediting a cease-fire, which the UN codified and internationalized. In point of fact, noted Eban, "the United Nations had no effective role in the negotiation of the cease-fire, which, like all important security developments had to be conducted outside its walls."[8] While this suggests a fundamental flaw in the concept of UN-based collective security, at the practical level it demonstrated the incompatibility of collective security with the Cold War. Given the bipolarity of the international system at the time, plus the American view that the UN had transformed itself into the Third World's soap box, and Israel's open contempt for the Organization, it is difficult to see how the UN could have operated any differently.

When fighting continued on October 23, the Security Council passed Resolution 339, urging all parties to comply with Resolution 338 and requesting the Secretary General to dispatch UN observers "to supervise the observance of the cease-fire between the forces of Israel and the Arab Republic of Egypt, using for this purpose the personnel of the UN now in the Middle East and first of all the personnel now in Cairo."

The following day, with the Egyptian Third Army still encircled by Israeli forces and cut off from all supplies, including food and water, the Egyptian representative to the UN requested that the US and Soviet Union dispatch troops to the region to compel an Israeli withdrawal to positions occupied on October 22. The appeal was repeated by Sadat to Nixon and Brezhnev, but Kissinger strenuously opposed it as a windfall for Soviet influence in Egypt and the Middle East. However, a letter sent by Brezhnev to Nixon late in the evening of October 24 reiterated the idea of a joint US-Soviet force to implement the UN cease-fire resolutions, and threatened to intervene unilaterally if US cooperation was not forthcoming.[9]

American intelligence sources suggested that the Soviets were indeed considering military intervention and that Soviet military transport aircraft had been grounded, possibly in preparation for lifting Soviet airborne divisions to Egypt. The five-member Washington Special Action Group (WSAG) met to discuss possible US responses. In addition to Kissinger, the WSAG included the Secretary of Defense, Director of Central Intelligence, Chairman of the Joint Chiefs of Staff, and the White House Chief of Staff. They decided to place US military forces on a higher state of alert. Just before midnight on October 24, about two hours after receipt of Brezhnev's letter, all American military forces were placed at Defense Condition Three.[10] On October 25, WSAG sent a letter to Sadat warning that it would pull out of peace talks with Israel if Soviet forces deployed. The Egyptian government responded by changing its request from US-Soviet forces to a UN peacekeeping force. This reversal in Sadat's position greatly reduced the likelihood of Soviet intervention.[11]

While the US Administration's decision to place its nuclear forces on alert was directed at influencing Soviet behavior, the United States also continued to press Israel to respect the cease-fire. As Blechman and Hart observe,

> If the United States simply had countered the Soviet threat, and done nothing about Israeli efforts to dismember the Egyptian army, Sadat's regime would have been imperiled and the chances for a negotiated settlement in the Middle East destroyed. Moreover, had Washington put its forces on alert without pressing Israel to comply with the cease-fire, Russian suspicions of a double-cross would have been confirmed and the situation could easily have gotten out of control.[12]

In New York, nonaligned members of the Security Council submitted a draft proposal calling for an increase in the number of UNTSO observers as an interim step in the creation of a new peacekeeping force (a force that would *not* exclude the five Permanent Members). On October 25, the Council passed Resolution 340, regretting the noncompliance with its two prior resolutions; reiterating its demand for an immediate and complete cease-fire and the return of the parties to positions occupied on October 22; increasing the number of UNTSO observers; and creating a UN peacekeeping force (*excluding* permament members of the Security Council) to act as a buffer between the belligerents.

Resolution 340 requested the Secretary General to report back to the Council within 24 hours.

Secretary General Kurt Waldheim, who had succeeded U Thant on January 1, 1972, reported that he had ordered 900 Austrian, Finnish, and Swedish troops serving with the UN force in Cyprus (UNFICYP) to proceed immediately to Egypt. He also appointed Major General Ensio Siilasvuo of Finland, the Chief of Staff of UNTSO, as interim Commander of the new Force and established its temporary headquarters at Cairo.

Although a cease-fire resolution was in place, the absence of a disengagement agreement continued to render the situation volatile. The Egyptian and Israeli negotiating positions coincided sufficiently for Kissinger to envisage such an agreement. Two issues in particular absorbed the two parties. The Egyptian government was concerned about its Third Army, encircled by the Israelis on the east bank of the Suez Canal, and the Israelis were interested in expediting the exchange of prisoners of war.

Sadat had little more room to maneuver than his Army. With Syrian military help, he had been able to restore much of the Arab world's sense of honor, which had been violated in the first six days of June six years earlier. But he still lacked Nasser's stature among the Arabs, shared none of his charisma, and could not risk appearing to forfeit the war's precious political gains in a disadvantageous disengagement agreement. Yet he had to rescue his Army. Kissinger's approach was to persuade Sadat that immediate concern for a return to the October 22 cease-fire lines should not divert attention from a more comprehensive disengagement agreement. Although the latter would require more time to negotiate, arrangements could be made to resupply the Third Army in place while talks continued.[13]

Naturally, Golda Meir approached the situation from a different perspective. Principal Israeli concerns were the return of prisoners of war and the end of the naval blockade of Bab el Mandeb, the strait affording access to the Red Sea from the Indian Ocean. Ultimately, Kissinger's shuttle diplomacy did produce successive force disengagement agreements (detailed in the discussion of UNEF II's mandate).

POLITICAL SUPPORT

UNEF II was created after the Soviet Union and the United States agreed on the basic modalities of a cease-fire. Both countries were interested in containing the conflict and regarded a UN force as the most appropriate mechanism to facilitate the end of hostilities and the maintenance of a cease-fire. The United States was not prepared to contribute troops to a joint buffer force for the region, and the Soviet Union backed away from the idea after its rejection by the US. Thereafter, both countries backed UNEF II. The Soviet Union even paid its share of assessed expenses for the operation, reversing a nearly twenty-year policy of refusing to pay. China opposed the creation of a UN force and refused to pay its assessments, but did not use its Security Council veto.

Egypt accepted Security Council resolution 340 in order to relieve its beleaguered Third Army. Cairo also came under considerable pressure from Moscow, just as Israel came under pressure from Washington, to accept a renewed UN presence in the Sinai. Both countries came to appreciate the UN presence, which monitored successive force disengagements with assistance from US civilian observers. Thus, when Anwar Sadat courageously sought and achieved peace with Israel, helped along by the mediation efforts of US President Jimmy Carter, the resulting accords called for continuing UN presence in the Sinai. The Soviet Union, cut out of the peace process, threatened to veto an extension of UNEF II's mandate, which ran out in mid-1979.

MANDATE

The mandate of UNEF II was twice revised during its six-year presence. Its original terms of reference were: (1) to supervise the implementation of Resolution 340, which called for an immediate and complete cease-fire in positions occupied by the respective forces on October 22, 1973; (2) to prevent the recurrence of the fighting and cooperate with the International Committee of the Red Cross (ICRC) in its humanitarian activities; and (3) to operate with the cooperation of UNTSO.[14] The Force was subsequently tasked to supervise implementation of the disengagment agreements of January 1974 and September 1975.

First Force Disengagement Agreement (Sinai I)

Egypt and Israel signed their first disengagement agreement at Kilometer 101 on the Suez-Cairo road on January 18, 1974. The agreement made provision for the redeployment of forces, the establishment of a buffer zone occupied by UN forces, and zones of limited arms and forces. The details of the designated troop and arms limitations in each of the zones were spelled out in an exchange of letters between Nixon, Sadat, and Meir.

According to the terms of the agreement, Israel was to withdraw from its bridgehead on the west bank of the Suez Canal and pull back its forces on the east bank 23-32 kilometers from the waterway. In the southern sector the Israelis would be deployed west of the Mitla and Gidi Passes. The Egyptians would remain on the east bank of the Canal in a zone 8-12 kilometers deep. UN troops would be deployed in a buffer zone separating the two forces.

In the force-limited zones, the two sides were permitted a maximum of eight reinforced battalions, 30 tanks, and a maximum of 7,000 troops. No artillery larger than 122 mm was permitted and numbers were limited to six batteries. Weapons capable of interfering with reconnaissance flights, such as anti-aircraft missiles, and weapons capable of reaching the other side's positions were prohibited in these zones. The United States was responsible for performing reconnaissance flights at regular intervals to monitor supervision of the agreement.[15]

Second Force Disengagement Agreement (Sinai II)

A second agreement signed September 4, 1975, at Geneva, provided for a further Israeli withdrawal eastward and a US ground surveillance operation by US civilians known as the Sinai Field Mission (SFM). UNEF II would continue to operate the buffer zone between the arms- and forces-limited zones. The agreement called for:

- an Israeli withdrawal returning control of the Mitla and Gidi passes and the Abu Rudeis oilfield to Egypt;

- the unobstructed transit of non-military, Israel-bound cargoes through the Suez Canal and freedom of navigation through Bab el Mandeb;

- the areas evacuated by Israeli forces to be taken over by UNEF II with the exception of a small strip south of Suez city where the Egyptian forces would assume control;

- limitation of forces in the Israeli and Egyptian zones contiguous to UNEF II's area of operations to eight battalions apiece, containing no more than 8,000 troops, 75 tanks and 72 artillery pieces; weapons capable of striking the other side's positions were prohibited, as were anti-aircraft missiles; and

- an early warning system around the Gidi and Mitla passes to be operated by the SFM, comprising three watch stations and three unmanned electronic sensor fields, and supplemented by Israeli and Egyptian surveillance stations (one each).[16]

FUNDING

General Assembly Resolution 3101 of December 11, 1973, established a Special Account for the operation of UNEF II for the period ending October 24, 1974. Although the US preferred that the force be financed on the regular scale of assessments, the majority of the membership preferred a special scale. The United States and other permanent members of the Security Council were obligated to pay a share of expenses fifteen percent greater than required by the regular scale of assessment. Developing countries payed 80 or 90 percent less than required by the regular scale.[17] As a result, the US and Soviet shares of UNEF II expenses were twenty-nine percent and fifteen percent, respectively. When the UN Disengagement Observer Force (UNDOF) was established on the Golan Heights in June 1974, it was funded from the same Special Account. This pattern has been followed by every subsequent UN peacekeeping operation, except for the smallest observer missions.[18]

A total of $79.8 million was initially approved for the two missions, with UNEF II accounting for over 80 percent. The rate of obligations and expenditures for UNEF II remained constant for two years. Some $94.3 million was budgeted for UNEF/UNDOF for the twelve-month period ending October 1976, supplemented by a $10 million voluntary contribution from the United States. The US contribution suggested its commitment to the second disengagement agreement and the successful redeployment of Egyptian and Israeli forces.

A subsequent reduction in the size of the force decreased its annual operating costs to roughly $76 million through October 1978. Expenditures of $80 million were authorized for the year ending October 1979, but the mandate lapsed in July. Total expenditures for UNEF II's six-year mission were $446.5 million.[19]

PLANNING AND IMPLEMENTATION

The Secretary General's report to the Security Council on the establishment of UNEF II proposed a force of 7,000 troops. UNEF II approached this level in February 1974, but from 1975 onward it was closer to 4,000. In all, thirteen countries contributed troops, as indicated in Table 8.1. Of these, three consistent contributors to UN peacekeeping missions (Canada, Ghana, and Finland) participated from inception to withdrawal. The Soviet Union and the United States each contribued observers through UNTSO.

Table 8.1. Size and Composition of UNEF II

Country	Nov. 1973	July 1974	July 1975	Sept 1976	Oct. 1977	Oct. 1978	July 1979
Australia				44	46	46	46
Austria	382						
Canada	481	1076	831	871	855	840	844
Finland	604	482	494	640	654	637	522
Ghana	5	507	499	597	597	595	595
Indonesia		548	448	510	509	509	510
Ireland	260	1					
Nepal		571	571				
Panama	39	446	444				
Peru	52						
Poland	191	1015	789	865	957	917	923
Senegal		398	400				
Sweden	552	483	458	647	679	634	591
Totals:	2566	2527	3919	4174	4297	4178	4031

Note: Figures for Canadian and Polish logistic components assigned to UNDOF excluded. The Force was assisted by up to 124 UNTSO military observers designated as "Observer Group Sinai." **Source**: S/11056, October 28, 1973; S/11056/Add.6, November 24, 1973; S/11248, April 1, 1974; S/11758, July 16, 1975; S/12212, October 18, 1976; S/12416, October 17, 1977; S/12897, October 17, 1978; S/13460, July 19, 1979.

The inclusion of Canada (NATO) and Poland (Warsaw Pact) in the operation proved initially a contentious issue. Soviet representative Jacob Malik accepted Kurt Waldheim's suggestion that Canada contribute a logistics unit but then proposed that a Warsaw Pact nation participate as well. The US at first opposed the participation of a Warsaw Pact state but later backed away from this position, as it did from Israel's policy of rejecting troop contributions from countries with which it did not have diplomatic relations. This change in position by the US, which allowed countries opposed by Israel to serve in UNEF II, later contributed to the problems faced by those countries' contingents regarding freedom of movement.

The Irish contingent was withdrawn in May 1974 at the request of its government. By June, UNEF II's total troop strength was further reduced to 5,079 with the transfer of Austrian and Peruvian contingents, and elements of the Canadian unit, to the United Nations Disengagement Observer Force (UNDOF) in the

Golan Heights. The Sinai force was augmented with about 450 additional Canadian and Polish support troops. The Nepalese and Panamanian contingents were repatriated in September and November 1974, respectively.

By July 1975 the Force's total strength had dropped to 3,919. After the second Sinai disengagement agreement and a four-fold increase in the Force's area of operations, the Secretary General estimated UNEF II required a troop strength of 4,825. However, its strength never quite reached that level despite modest reinforcements from Finland, Ghana, Indonesia, Sweden, Canada, and Poland. In July 1976, an Australian air unit (four helicopters with accompanying crew and support personnel, for a total of 44 men) joined the force. In February 1976, the Senegalese government informed the Secretary General of its intention to repatriate its contingent of 400 men. When the Force's mandate expired in July 1979, its troop strength was 4,031.

Command, Communications, Logistics, and Administration

The majority of logistical and administrative problems encountered by UNEF II were the consequence of the inherent limitations of the UN system of international tendering and procurement. The two principal problems were the shortages of equipment and supplies and the lack of standardization. In his report to the Security Council, the Secretary General attributed the shortages of spare parts for vehicles and other machinery in part to backlogs at ports of entry but mainly to the "lengthy period that elapses between the ordering of an item and its arrival."[20]

Examples of some of the difficulties encountered include the following:

- When the Force's area of operations was expanded after the second Sinai disengagement agreement in 1975, its communications equipment was inadequate to the longer distances involved. Considerable time elapsed before the appropriate equipment arrived.

- Problems associated with maintaining supplies to the operational battalions, due in part to poor prevailing road conditions. Approximately 1,600 km of roads within the area of operations had to be kept cleared of sand and repaired.

- Shortfalls in the supply of drinking water to the battalions.

- UNEF II's headquarters were transferred twice. First from Cairo to Ismailia, where the Egyptian government provided accommodations. The government later requested that UNEF II vacate the premises in favor of the Suez Canal Authority, a move that might have been preempted had UNEF II administrators agreed to a long-term leasing agreement with the Egyptian government.

As late as October 1978, five years after its establishment, the Secretary General reported that the "supply of goods and services to UNEF continues to be handicapped by the long procurement lead times."[21] To increase standardization, the purchasing program made greater efforts to purchase common items adapted to desert conditions as older vehicles and equipment were phased out and replaced.[22] To improve equipment maintenance, a Canadian unit provided support for vehicles and equipment of North American or West European origins, and a Polish maintenance unit did the same for equipment of East European origin, whenever the repair capabilities of national contingents proved inadequate.[23] A 24-hour logistics operations center at El Gala shortened the response time of the logistics units to the demands of the operational units.[24]

To increase the available quantities of drinking water to the battalions, the Force built reservoirs and replaced worn-out pipelines. For example, a new water pipeline had been installed by October 1978 from Israeli-controlled territory to El Tasa, where the Polish and Canadian contingents each had a small logistics operation, along with a 500 cubic meter reservoir. This still did not alleviate water supply problems in the buffer zone where the battalions operated, however.[25]

Field Operations

UNEF II's operations can be separated roughly into four phases. From its inception in October 1973 to January 1974, it monitored the two sides' observance of Security Council cease-fire resolutions. From January 1974 to October 1975 and from November 1975 to May 1979, it supervised the provisions and monitored the implementation of the first and second Sinai disengagement agreements, respectively. From May to July 1979, it withdrew.

Phase One: October 1973–January 1974. The first UN troops to reach the area of operations were detached from existing UN peacekeeping missions, as noted earlier, and the Chief of Staff of UNTSO, Major General Siilasvuo, became interim Commander of the new force. His provisional headquarters staff consisted of UNTSO personnel.

Constant violations of the initial cease-fire by both the Israelis and Egyptians, and particularly Israel's continuing operations against the entrapped Egyptian Third Army, seriously hampered the Force's effectiveness and for a day or two even threatened to revert to a full-scale war involving the major powers. UNEF II began to deploy effectively only after the superpowers, and particularly the United States, weighed in heavily to stop the fighting.[26]

With the movement of contingents to the mission area, negotiations began to effect the redeployment of Egyptian and Israeli forces to the October 22 battle lines and to establish a buffer zone. On October 27, at kilometer 101 on the Cairo-Suez road, military representatives of Egypt and Israel, and General Siilasvuo, met to discuss the observance of the cease-fire and other humanitarian issues. The parties agreed to the delivery of non-military supplies to Suez City and to the Egyptian Third Army by UNEF II personnel, in coordination with the International Committee of the Red Cross (ICRC).

On October 29 and 30, General Siilasvuo met with Israeli Defence Minister Dayan to request Israeli compliance with Resolution 340. In his memoirs, Dayan states,

> After the Soviet Union and the United States had failed to secure our withdrawal to the lines of October 22, I did not think anyone would seriously think we would do so upon this UN request. But apparently, if not on the battlefield, at least in the files of the Security Council, there had to be order. On the whole, I thought one could live with the [UN]. It might not be as much help, but it could do no harm.[27]

At the meeting, Dayan agreed to the stationing and deployment of UNEF II troops in the Sinai and other Israeli-held areas and offered the use of Israeli airfields.[28] General Siilasvuo then met with the Egyptian Defence Minister, Mr. Ismail, to discuss the deployment of UNEF II. Successive meetings were held, but ultimately it was US mediation and pressure that produced an agreement that facilitated implementation of Resolution 340 and the full and effective deployment of UNEF II.

On November 11, the Egyptian and Israeli governments agreed to discussions on the questions of returning to the October 22 positions; on daily deliveries of food, water, and medicine to the town of Suez; on the evacuation of all wounded civilians in the town; on the unrestricted movement of non-military supplies to the east bank of the Canal; and on the replacement of Israeli checkpoints on the Cairo-Suez road by United Nations checkpoints, to be followed by a prisoner exchange, including wounded.[29]

On November 15, Israel transferred its checkpoints on the Cairo-Suez road to UN control, and UNEF II personnel delivered food supplies, water, and medicine to Suez city and the Egyptian Third Army in accord with the November 11 agreement. The POW exchange took place with the assistance of the ICRC. Despite these positive developments, there was uneven movement on the issue of the return to the October 22 positions. This final provision of the November 11 agreement was not implemented until the conclusion of the Sinai disengagement agreement in January 1974.

Phase Two: January 1974–October 1975. Withdrawal operations under the disengagement agreement began on January 25, 1974, and proceeded step by step. Israeli-held areas were transferred to UNEF II and in turn handed over to Egyptian forces. UNTSO military observers under the operational control of UNEF II marked the lines of disengagement with the aid of Egyptian and Israeli army surveyors.[30]

Disengagement had produced a calmer operational environment for the Force by March 4. UNEF II established observation posts and checkpoints in the zone of disengagement, patrolled between posts, and, with the assistance of UNTSO observers, conducted weekly and biweekly inspections of Egyptian and Israeli areas of limitations.[31] In addition to these operations, UNEF II continued to provide humanitarian assistance to the parties in the form of prisoner exchanges and the recovery of war dead, the latter task being officially completed in July 1974.

Phase Three: November 1975–May 1979. UNEF II's buffer zone expanded more than four times as a result of the second Sinai disengagement agreement (September 1975). UNEF II transferred its headquarters from Cairo to Ismailia in order to be closer to the area of operations.

In October 1975, new disengagement lines were drawn by a group of Swedish surveyors. The following month, UNEF II began to assist the parties in the redeployment of their forces. Once the new positions were established, UNEF II assumed its long-term functions of supervising the cease-fire and implementing the terms of Sinai II and its Protocol. The Force supervised the use of the common road sections by the parties and conducted biweekly inspections of the areas of "forces and arms limitations" as specified in the Agreement and Protocol.

As the map below illustrates, the Force was deployed as follows:

- The Swedish contingent manned three forward command posts, and up to 22 positions in buffer zone one, an area that stretched from the Mediterranean Sea to a line south-east of Ismailia. Base camp was set up at Baluza.

- The Ghanaian battalion manned two to four forward command posts and up to 18 positions in buffer zone, from the southern limit of the Swedish sector to a line south of Mitla, the site of Ghana's base camp.

- The Indonesian contingent manned one forward command post in Ras Sudr, ten positions in buffer zone one, and up to eight positions along the Gulf of Suez from the southern boundary of the Ghanaian sector to a line south-east of Ras Sudr. Base camp was at Suez.

- The Finnish battalion manned three forward command posts and up to 22 positions along the Gulf of Suez in buffer zones 2A and 2B, from the southern limit of the Indonesian sector to Abu Durba (base camp) in the south.

- The Canadian and Polish logistics contingents were based at El Gala Camp, Ismailia, with a small group deployed at a forward logistics base at El Tasa. The Polish contingent deployed one transport unit at Suez.

- The Australian air unit, which arrived in July 1976, was located at Ismailia.

Once the new lines had been established, UNEF II settled into a routine of observation and inspection that continued for nearly four years. Meanwhile, peace negotiations between Egypt and Israel were energized by Anwar Sadat's dramatic visit to Israel in November 1977 and by the subsequent bilateral talks at the US presidential retreat at Camp David, Maryland, mediated by President Jimmy Carter. The September 1978 Camp David Accords led to an Egypt-Israel Peace Treaty in March 1979.

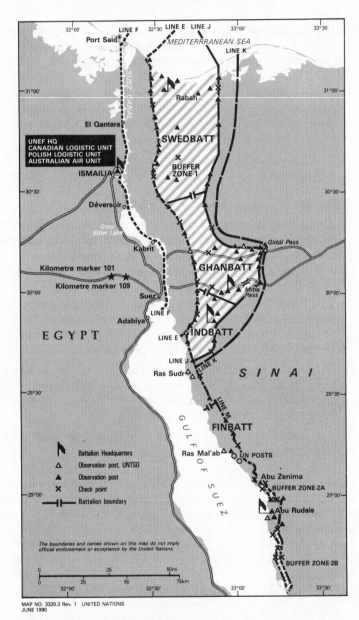

**Figure 8.1. Second United Nations Emergency Force,
Deployment as of July 1979**

Phase Four: May 1979–July 1979. The peace treaty came into effect on April 25. The treaty and an adjoining protocol made provisions for a UN force (essentially, UNEF II) to supervise implementation of the security arrangements contained in the agreement. However, the likelihood of a Soviet veto dissuaded the Security Council from taking up the issue. Thus, UNEF II's mandate was allowed to expire when it came up for renewal on July 24, 1979.[32]

On May 25, 1979, in accord with the peace treaty, Israeli forces withdrew from the northern Sinai to the east of El Arish, handing control of the area to Egyptian forces. The transfer was executed without the assistance of UNEF II, except to provide escorts to the parties. As the UN Force withdrew from its area of operations, control of the territory transferred to Egypt. UN contingents were rapidly repatriated after July 1979, when the Force's mandate expired.[33]

January 26, 1980, was the specified date for the deployment of a UN force to supervise the peace treaty, coinciding with Israel's withdrawal to the El Arish-Ras Mohammad line. While Israel would not accept UNTSO observers as a substitute for UNEF II, both parties did agree to accept the unarmed civilian observers of the US Sinai Field Mission (created by the second Sinai Disengagement Agreement of September 1975) as a substitute monitoring force until new arrangements could be made. The Field Mission performed successfully for two years, when it was merged into the new Multinational Force and Observers.[34]

ASSESSMENT

That UNEF II did its job well is undeniable given that there was no recurrence of fighting. It had a high level of political support, and it had technical support from the Sinai Field Mission, whose electronic sensor nets maintained a watch over the Sinai passes. UNEF II also received the cooperation of the local parties, although incursions into the buffer zone by both Israelis and Egyptians were reported. On the downside, there were occasional shootings in the area of UNEF II outposts and patrols that would provoke official protests, and the Secretary General's reports on UNEF II consistently, but circumspectly and without censure, referred to restrictions being placed on "certain contingents" whose governments did not have diplomatic relations with Tel Aviv.

Overall, however, UNEF II enjoyed particularly favorable conditions for a peacekeeping operation. Political relations between

Egypt and Israel improved throughout the 1970s with US help. Cairo and Tel Aviv were in firm control of their armed forces, and Palestinian fedayeen no longer were the threat to Israel's southern borders that they had been in the 1950s. Moreover, Israel was, in this case, willing to trade land for peace. Still, UNEF's presence was sufficiently useful in helping to build and maintain confidence on both sides so that their cautious steps toward peace could not easily be undone by random border incidents or unseen buildups of military force.

CONCLUSIONS

A peacekeeping force that helps to preserve a cease-fire can give diplomats the time to find settlements that address the political problems that underpin a conflict. In order to succeed, however, not only must the deployment of UN forces and observers be accepted by the conflicting parties, but there also must be a willingness on their parts to attempt to bridge the gap that separates them. In 1967, after the June War, these two factors were not present, and years of low-level conflict followed, culminating in the October 1973 attempt to force Israel from the territories it had occupied six years earlier. Both factors were present, however, after the October War. Whereas the 1967 defeat had boxed Nasser in, the October War had freed Sadat. As Ajami writes, "The men who made Egypt's difficult decision in 1973 did not intend that war to be the beginning of a new, sustained war with Israel or another captivity in inter-Arab politics. Just as Nasser's war of attrition had been a way of regaining initiative in Arab politics, so too was the October War."[35]

The international climate also made a difference. In 1967, the United States was mired in the Vietnam War as well as a nuclear arms race with the Soviet Union. In 1973, that war was over for the United States. The two superpowers had recently ratified two Strategic Arms Limitation agreements and détente was in the air. Because détente was also a strategy for containing Soviet influence, another smashing Israeli military victory over its neighbors would only make them more dependent on Moscow for arms, as it had in 1967. Therefore, Washington turned up the heat on Tel Aviv to cease firing once the Egyptian and Syrian ground offensives had been blunted; it did not wish to see Israeli armored forces bearing down on Damascus or Cairo, nor did it wish to see Soviet forces deployed to block their way. Kissinger's intensive shuttle diplomacy produced force disengagement agreements that helped Egypt to regain territory without further fighting and led to improved Egyptian-Israeli relations that eventually gave Israel its most secure frontier. UNEF II monitored that frontier and in doing so served Israeli interests and garnered Israeli support. Such local consensus in support of a peacekeeping mission is crucial to its success. In its absence, a peacekeeping force may be politically marginalized or actively harassed. Yet a supporting consensus may take time to develop. In the interim, a more grudging consent might be compelled by external pressure, but external pressure has its limits and must be accompanied by a genuine change in local political perceptions about the erstwhile enemy and about the utility of the peacekeeping force. In the case of UNEF II, this evolution took place.

However, it took place at the expense (or more accurately, without the help) of the Soviet Union, as détente was replaced by rapidly deteriorating East-West relations in the latter half of the 1970s. Because Egypt, over the same period, had been drawn into the Western orbit by a generous combination of economic, political, and military support, Moscow could do little more than block the use of UN troops to implement the Egyptian-Israeli peace. Because the United States was close to both signatories, alternative arrangements could be made.

It is only rarely the case, however, that conditions unfavorable to UN peacekeeping would be so favorable to a non-UN force, particularly since the end of the Cold War and the emergence of greater political consensus (for the moment) among the permanent members of the Security Council. Indeed, as the experience of peacekeepers in nearby Lebanon attests, chaotic internal conditions offer equal opportunities for failure of UN and non-UN forces alike.

Notes

1. Abba Eban, *Abba Eban: An Autobiography* (New York: Random House, 1977), 508. According to Eban, on Wednesday October 3, four ministers—Golda Meir, Yigal Allon, Moshe Dayan and Israel Galili—met with senior military officers to discuss the Syrian and Egyptian troop build-up for over two hours. The general conclusion, influenced heavily by a precedent the previous May when the armed forces had been mobilized in response to similar Egyptian concentrations, was that the new troop movements were similarly innocuous. Israeli intelligence reports rated the probability of war as minimal.

2. For a detailed description of the military dimension of the October 1973 War, see Anthony Cordesman and Abraham R. Wagner, *The Lessons of Modern War, Volume I: The Arab-Israeli Conflicts, 1973-1989* (Boulder, Co.: Westview Press, 1990).

3. Eban, *An Autobiography*, 506.

4. William B. Quandt, *Decade of Decisions: American Policy Toward the Arab-Israeli Conflict, 1967–1976* (Berkeley and Los Angeles: University of California Press, 1977), 171-172.

5. Quandt, *Decade of Decisions*, 171.

6. Quandt, *Decade of Decision*, 183-184.

7. Eban, *An Autobiography*, 528.

8. Eban, *An Autobiography*, 530.

9. Raymond Garthoff, *Détente and Confrontation* (Washington, D.C.: The Brookings Institution, 1985), 376-77. Kissinger played such a major role in US policy during this period because President Nixon was enmeshed in the Watergate crisis. As Kissinger negotiated the cease-fire in Moscow, Nixon staged the "Saturday Night Massacre," firing the Watergate Special Prosecutor, the Attorney General, and the deputy Attorney General (371).

10. Garthoff, *Détente and Confrontation*, 377-380; see also, Scott D. Sagan, "Nuclear Alerts and Crisis Management," *International Security* 9, no. 4 (Spring 1985): 122-128.

11. Sagan, "Nuclear Alerts," 127.

12. Barry Blechman and Douglas Hart, "The Political Utility of Nuclear Weapons," *International Security* 7, no. 1 (Summer 1982): 147.

13. Quandt, *Decade of Decisions*, 217.

14. United Nations Document S/11052/Rev.1, October 27, 1973.

15. Quandt, *Decade of Decisions*, 228. For the text of the Agreement, see Henry Kissinger, *Years of Upheaval* (Boston: Little, Brown and Co., 1982), 1250-51. On the arrangements for US aerial reconnaissance, see Amy Smithson, "Multilateral Aerial Inspections," in Michael Krepon and Amy Smithson, eds., *Open Skies, Arms Control, and Cooperative Security* (New York: St. Martin's Press, 1992), 113-134.

16. Quandt, *Decade of Decisions*, 274-75.

17. House Committee on Foreign Affairs, *United Nations Peacekeeping in the Middle East*, 93rd Congress, December 5 and 6, 1973, 8. UNEF II was the first time the Soviet Union helped finance a UN peacekeeping operation.

18. House Committee on Foreign Affairs, *United Nations Peacekeeping in the Middle East*, 21. If the contributions of Byelorussia and the Ukraine are added in the calculations, the total percentage of UNEF II costs contributed by the three countries would be less than 17 percent.

19. *The Blue Helmets: A Review of United Nations Peacekeeping*, 2nd ed. (New York: United Nations Department of Public Information, 1990), 423.

20. United Nations Document S/11758, July 16, 1975, 17.

21. United Nations Document S/12897, October 17, 1978, 33.

22. United Nations Document S/12416, October 17, 1977.

23. United Nations Document S/11056/Add.6, November 24, 1973, Annex.

24. United Nations Document S/12416.

25. United Nations Document S/12897.

26. Garthoff discusses US maneuvering to cut off the fighting and cut out the Soviets (*Détente and Confrontation*, 382-85); also, see Quandt for Israeli accounts of US pressure (*Decade of Decisions*, 197-98).

27. Moshe Dayan, *Moshe Dayan: Story of My Life* (New York: William Morrow and Co., 1976), 545.

28. United Nations Document S/11056/Add. 1, October 30, 1973.

29. United Nations Document S/11056/Add.3, November 11, 1973, Annex.

30. *The Blue Helmets*, 93.

31. *The Blue Helmets*, 94.

32. As a result, an alternative to the UN mission was needed, and the two parties, Egypt and Israel, invoked President Carter's written guarantees to provide an alternative should deployment of a UN force prove impracticable. For a further discussion of what became the Multinational Force and Observers, see Mona Ghali, *The Multinational Forces: Non-UN Peacekeeping in the Middle East*, Occasional Paper No. 12 (Washington, D.C.: The Henry L. Stimson Center, October 1992).

33. *The Blue Helmets*, 98.

34. Ghali, *The Multinational Forces*, 4.

35. Fouad Ajami, *The Arab Predicament* (Cambridge: Cambridge University Press, 1985), 99.

9 United Nations Disengagement Observer Force

by Mona Ghali

The United Nations Disengagement Observer Force (UNDOF) was the second peacekeeping operation to result from the October 1973 Arab-Israeli War, growing out of a disengagement agreement signed by Syria and Israel on May 31, 1974. The agreement created three zones—a UN area of separation flanked by Syrian and Israeli zones of restricted forces and arms—on the strategic Golan Heights. Shuttle diplomacy by US Secretary of State Henry Kissinger and a step-by-step approach produced an accord that facilitated a stable cease-fire and the redeployment of Israeli forces from the area east of the 1967 cease-fire line. Although UNDOF secured the provisions of the disengagement agreement with unequivocal success, the political stalemate between Israel and Syria stands out in stark contrast to relations between Israel and Egypt. Still, for 18 years, its mandate has been renewed every six months with the support of both parties.

ORIGINS

The Golan Heights, Syrian territory occupied by Israel since the 1967 war, rise from less than 200 meters above Israel's Yarmak Valley at their southern end, to more than 2,700 meters at the northern end, at the summit of Mount Hermon. Guns placed on the Heights behind the old armistice demarcation line could dominate much of northern Israel. On the other hand, Syria's capital, Damascus, is just 75 kilometers of good tank country northeast of the Heights. Neither Syria nor Israel, in short, can afford to allow the other side exclusive control of this land as long as the two countries view one another as enemies.

The southern part of the Heights is more accessible than the northern and contains numerous volcanic hills known as *tels*, which provide local high ground for observation posts. A line of tels from the Rafid junction to Quneitra and north to Mount Hermon demarcates the post-1967 line of Israeli and Syrian control. [1]

On October 6, 1973, Egypt and Syria simultaneously attacked Israel. The surprise assault permitted Syria some initial territorial gains along the southern Golan, but Israeli forces counterattacked after October 10 and rapidly pushed toward the town of Sasa, southwest of Damascus, in what became known as the Sasa salient. On October 22, the Security Council adopted Resolution 338, ordering the parties to cease hostilities. A cease-fire was in place by October 24, but provided only a pause in the hostilities. The Syrians refused to participate in a peace Conference convened in Geneva in December 1973, and from March 1974 to the end of May the field situation deteriorated, with increasing casualties on both sides. In April, Syrian and Israeli ground forces fought over Mount Hermon, resulting in some of Israel's heaviest casualties since the October 24 cease-fire.[2]

Between the outbreak of war and the end of May 1974, and particularly after completion of an interim disengagement agreement between Israel and Egypt in January, Henry Kissinger shuttled between Damascus and Jerusalem, received Israeli and Syrian representatives in Washington, exchanged proposals for a cease-fire, and negotiated the terms of disengagement. He sometimes chose selectively to withhold from the parties proposals that he considered unacceptable and that might work against a final agreement. By April 29, 1974, Kissinger's shuttle diplomacy produced consensus among the parties on the principle of a three-zone disengagement plan. However, the specifics of the plan, the positions of the forward lines, the size of the UN force in the buffer zone, and control of the town of Quneitra remained contentious issues.[3] Gradually, however, the two sides' differences were narrowed. Syrian President Hafez Assad gave assurances that he would not permit Palestinian *fedayeen* to enter the area of separation, and Israel agreed to withdraw from the Sasa salient and from a narrow strip of territory surrounding Quneitra. Although Quneitra would be within UNDOF's buffer zone, it would remain under Syrian civilian administration.

On May 31, Israeli and Syrian military representatives signed in Geneva the Disengagement Agreement that the two governments had accepted on May 29. The Agreement called on Syria and Israel to observe a cease-fire on land, sea and air; and to:

- be separated in accordance with the three-zone disengagement plan creating a demilitarized area of separation occupied by a UN force, and two equal areas of limitation of arms and forces;
- arrange through the military representatives of Israel and Syria in the Egyptian-Israeli Military Working Group of the Geneva Peace Conference the delineation of the areas of separation and limitation (with work to be initiated 24 hours after the signing of the Agreement and completed within five days, and with disengagement to follow within 24 hours and to be completed within 20 days); and
- exchange prisoners of war and return war dead.

At Syria's insistence, the Agreement made specific mention that this was not a peace treaty, but "only a step towards a just and durable peace on the basis of Security Council Resolution 338." The Agreement and Protocol called for the creation of UNDOF, with the Protocol spelling out the Force's role and functions. On the day of signature, the Security Council passed Resolution 350, which recognized the disengagement agreement and "the arms and force limitation zones," and requested Secretary General Waldheim to establish UNDOF with an authorized troop strength of 1,250. The Force was authorized for six months, subject to renewal by the Security Council.[4]

POLITICAL SUPPORT

Resolution 350 was jointly sponsored by the United States and the Soviet Union and was adopted 13 votes to 0, with China and Iraq abstaining. Faced with disaster in the war, Syria was only too glad to regain ground it had lost by agreeing to disengage, and Israel was interested in the improved military position that an internationally monitored buffer zone on the Heights would provide. According to John Mackinlay:

> The Syrian attitude to the agreement was, and still is, that it was just a cease-fire and that one day the nation's territorial prerogative will be resumed in the Golan....It lay in [the Israelis'] interests to secure the situation by encouraging the whole panoply of peace agreements and large, elaborate peacekeeping forces which would all serve to protect the status quo and its benefits to them for as long as possible until the original arguments of the situation became blurred by the passage of time and demographic redistribution.[5]

The Chinese representative charged the US and the Soviet Union with having hegemonic designs in the region, claiming that it was imperative to "eliminate all their interference in Middle East affairs" and demanding the withdrawal of Israel from occupied Arab territories. Iraq abstained to symbolize its opposition to Israel's occupation of Arab territory.

MANDATE

UNDOF's mandate was set forth in two documents: the Agreement on Disengagement and the Protocol to the Agreement. The product of lengthy negotiations, they were carefully constructed. The Agreement on Disengagement described above ordered a cease-fire, delineated areas of separation, and authorized a UN force, while the Protocol specified UNDOF's functions. They were:

- to ensure the observance of the cease-fire;
- to supervise the implementation of the terms of the agreement with respect to the absence of military forces in the area of separation and the restriction of arms and personnel in the Syrian and Israeli areas of limitation; and
- to facilitate the implementation of resolution 338.

Accordingly, UNDOF was to occupy the area of separation between Israeli and Syrian forces extending from Mount Hermon in the north to the Jordan River in the south. On each side of the area of separation are three zones of limited armaments extending 10, 20, and 25 kilometers from the area of separation. In the 10 kilometer zone, the parties were permitted to station a maximum of 6,000 personnel, 75 tanks, and 36 pieces of short range artillery (122 mm or smaller bore). In the adjacent zone, the parties were allowed arms not to exceed 162 artillery pieces (with a range less than 20 km) and 450 tanks. In the 25 kilometer zone, surface-to-air missiles were prohibited.

The Force was authorized to inspect and report to the parties fortnightly and was obligated to investigate alleged violations by either side. UNDOF's area of separation would be under Syrian civilian administration, and Syrian civilians would be permitted access to the area so as not to compromise Syria's sovereignty over its territory. The Force was to enjoy freedom of movement and communication and be provided with personal weapons for defensive purposes.[6]

FUNDING

UNDOF's budget was financed from the account appropriated for UNEF II. Following the expiration of UNEF II's mandate in July 1979, the account was used exclusively for UNDOF. Monthly expenditures for the maintenance of the force on the Golan have increased only incrementally since 1974. UNDOF's annual costs for 1991 were just over $41 million.

PLANNING AND IMPLEMENTATION

The presence of other UN peacekeeping missions in the Middle East facilitated the setup of UNDOF by providing an available pool of observers, both armed and unarmed. Austria, Peru, Canada, and Poland agreed to transfer some of their contingents from UNEF II to the newly established Golan force, and about 90 military observers from UNTSO were transferred to UNDOF's operational control. As the product of long negotiations rather than an urgent crisis, UNDOF could be carefully planned.

Size and Composition of the Force

Israel and Syria initially disagreed on the size of the force. Israel preferred a large, well-defended force that could enforce the cease-fire if necessary and guarantee Tel Aviv's security interests. In contrast, Syria pressed for a small force of observers. UNDOF's authorized troop strength of 1,250 was therefore a compromise. Since 1974 its strength has fluctuated by less than 10 percent up or down. Of the original four national contingents drawn from UNEF II (Austria, Canada, Peru, and Poland), all but Peru continue to provide troops to UNDOF. Contingents from permanent members of the Security Council were precluded by the Disengagement Agreement from participating in UNDOF, as were UNTSO observers from those countries.

The table below indicates the composition of UNDOF since 1975. Peru's contingent, withdrawn at the end of July 1975, was replaced by one from Iran. In March 1979, Iranian troops (largely Kurds) were repatriated at the request of the new Islamic fundamentalist government and were replaced by Finnish forces. The Finns, initially seconded from UNEF II, remain on the Golan at present. Austria and Finland provide infantry battalions of three and two companies, respectively. The Canadian and the Polish units provide logistics support as they did in UNEF.

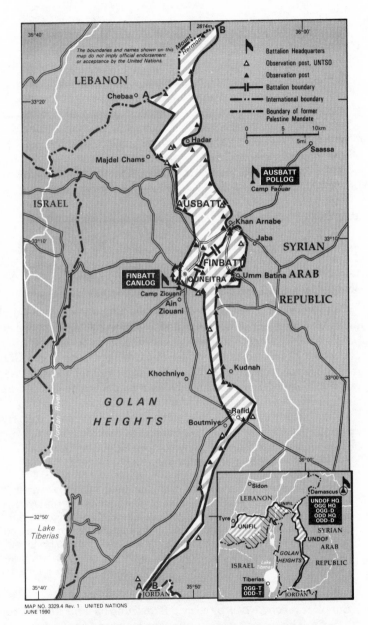

Figure 9.1. United Nations Disengagement Observer Force, Deployment as of June 1990

Table 9.1 UNDOF Personnel and Contingents

Country	May 1975	May 1978	May 1980	May 1985	May 1991
Austria	518	523	532	533	533
Canada	152	161	220	226	225
Finland			388	411	410
Iran		385			
Peru	348				
Poland	85	91	129	153	156
HQ staff from UNEF II	6				
Observers from UNTSO	89	85	20	8	7
Totals:	1198	1245	1289	1331	1331

Note: UNTSO figures do not include personnel assigned to the Israel-Syria Mixed Armistice Commission. Source: United Nations Documents S/11694, May 21, 1975; S/12710, May 17, 1978; S/13957, May 23, 1980; S/17177, May 13, 1985, and S/22631, May 21, 1991.

Command Structure, Communications, Logistics, and Administration

UNDOF's modest authorized troop strength makes it a simple force to command. The command structure follows the usual practice for UN peacekeeping missions. Two infantry battalions and the logistics units are under the control of the Force Commander, who reports to the Secretary General. The UN-appointed Chief Administrative Officer controls the budget and reports separately to the Field Operations Division in New York.

UNDOF headquarters in Damascus facilitates contact with Syrian officials. Contact with the Israelis is facilitated by a liaison officer located in Tiberias. However, as Brigadier General Yuill, a former UNDOF Chief of Staff, has noted,

> communications directly to Israel from Damascus, other than through UN agencies, are non-existent. This not only inhibits day-to-day contact with one of the host nations, but could be a critical factor in time of increased tension. It would probably be impossible to command the force effectively from Damascus if hostilities were to break out and for that reason, a hardened Force Command Post has been developed in Quneitra as an emergency location from which to exercise command.[7]

Supplies reach UNDOF by sea via Israel, and by land from Europe via Syria. The majority of supplies are transported overland. The two logistics units deliver water, fuel, rations, stores, and mail to the base camps. The two units are responsible for the operations and maintenance of the Force's vehicles and equipment, and the Polish logistics unit provides mine clearing teams.

Field Operations

UNDOF's field operations included the immediate tasks associated with the redeployment of forces to their respective zones and long-term tasks associated with supervising the cease-fire in the Golan.

Immediate Tasks. As of 1109 hours Greenwich Mean Time on May 31, 1974, the Chief of Staff of UNTSO reported that all firing in the Syrian-Israeli sector had ceased in accord with the terms of the Disengagement Agreement. The Egyptian-Israeli Military Working Group of the Geneva Peace Conference, presided over by Lieutenant General Ensio Siilasvuo, Commander of UNEF II, held six meetings between May 31 and June 5, 1974, with Syrian representatives. The Military Working Group reached agreement on a four-stage disengagement plan and timetable that UNDOF was mandated to supervise. The plan called for the redeployment of Israeli forces from the area east of the 1967 ceasefire line, for Israeli withdrawal from Quneitra and Rafid, and for the demilitarization of the area west of Quneitra still held by Israel. By June 27, the separation of forces was complete, with UNDOF observers occupying an 80-kilometer buffer zone.

UNDOF's other short-term tasks included:

- establishing a forward headquarters in the area of separation dividing the forces at each phase of the disengagement operation;
- inspecting the redeployment of Israeli and Syrian forces after each phase in accordance with the agreed timetable;
- denying access to military forces attempting to reenter the vacated separation zones; and
- carrying out inspections of the limitation areas on either side of the separation area once the redeployment was completed.[8]

As specified in the Disengagement Agreement, UNDOF also facilitated the repatriation of prisoners of war and the exchange of war dead by June 6 with the aid of the International Committee of the Red Cross.

Long-Term Tasks. UNDOF personnel occupy static observation posts 24-hours a day and conduct mobile patrols to ensure the absence of non-UN military forces in the UN area of separation (AOS). The Austrian battalion occupies 19 permanent positions and seven outposts in the area of separation north of the Damascus-Quneitra road and conducts about two dozen daily patrols at irregular intervals on predetermined routes, including the Damascus-Quneitra road. It shares base camp near Wadi Faouar, eight kilometers east of the AOS, with the Polish logistic unit. The Finnish battalion staffs 16 positions and six outposts in the AOS south of the Damascus-Quneitra road and conducts a similar number of daily patrols, also at irregular intervals. It shares base camp with the Canadian logistic unit near the village of Ziouani, west of the AOS.[9]

Observers, assisted by liaison officers of the respective host countries, carry out fortnightly inspections of the Israeli and Syrian areas of limitation of armaments and forces (AOL). In accord with the Disengagement Agreement, the conclusions of the inspection teams are made available to the liaison officers. Military observers seconded from UNTSO operate out of Tiberias, Israel, and Damascus, Syria. They staff 11 observation posts in the area of separation, monitor the area, and report violations of the Disengagement Agreement. Each post is manned by two officers for a period of seven days. The Tiberias and Damascus locations play an important diplomatic role in resolving alleged violations such as unauthorized crossings.

Apart from these functions, UNDOF also engages in such humanitarian activities as facilitating the exchange of parcels and mail and supervising the reunion of Syrian families separated by the disengagement zones. The presence of UNDOF in the Golan has contributed to stability in the Israel-Syrian sector by encouraging the return of civilians to the area of separation. Since 1974, the population of this area has doubled.[10]

ASSESSMENT

Two principal factors underlay UNDOF's success in maintaining peace on the Golan Heights since 1974: the political support of both Israel and Syria and a clear, limited mandate derived from the Disengagement Agreement and Protocol.

First, UNDOF provided a mechanism whereby the two parties could step back from military conflict. Since the 1974 cease-fire, both sides have been satisfied with the performance of UNDOF personnel and the security that its presence imparts, although the status quo remains less than ideal. As John Mackinlay has observed, UNDOF suits both the Israelis and the Syrians in that it remains an impartial force, does not threaten the sovereignty of either party, and would set off an alarm if either attempted to seize exclusive control of the Golan.[11] Israeli-occupied Golan imparts a sense of security in Tel Aviv, and the UN-patrolled buffer zone reinforces it. The Syrians intensely desire to recover the Golan, but with a military solution out of reach, they await a territorial compromise.

Second, UNDOF's unambiguous mandate has not imposed unrealistic demands on the force. Its functions are important, but relatively simple, and detached from higher politics. The task of negotiating a political settlement has been prudently left to diplomats.

Although both parties have cooperated with UNDOF personnel during inspections of the area of limitations, the Secretary General's reports on UNDOF consistently conveyed concern about restrictions on the Force's freedom of movement, particularly by Israel, until 1990. Although not nearly as severe as the restrictions experienced by UNIFIL personnel in Lebanon, Israel nonetheless hampered operations by UNDOF's Polish and Iranian contingents when both countries had poor relations with Israel. Iran withdrew from the Force in 1979; the remaining restrictions on Poland were lifted when it officially recognized the state of Israel in 1990. Although the area of separation is under Syrian civilian administration, this arrangement has not impaired UNDOF's functioning, principally because of good relations and open communication between UNDOF personnel, Syrian authorities, and the civilian population in the area.

CONCLUSION

In arriving at a Syrian-Israeli Disengagement Agreement in 1974, Kissinger persuaded President Assad that the accord was part of a process that would ultimately culminate in the recovery of Syrian territory lost in 1967. UNDOF helps to buy time for the two parties to reach a happier modus vivendi. So far, however, the impulse toward a permanent solution has been weak at best. Until both parties are genuinely prepared to compromise, the status of UNDOF will likely remain unchanged.

The prospects for change improved after the 1991 Persian Gulf War and the United States's recognition of Syria as an integral player in a permanent settlement, a goal Hafez Assad has ardently pursued. No longer seeking to isolate Assad, the US Administration has actively engaged him in its bid to break the deadlock at the Arab-Israeli interface. The first round of direct Arab-Israeli talks at the Madrid Conference in October 1991 were the preliminary soundings of a possible change in the territorial lines now held in the Golan.

Israel remains cautious about returning the Golan to Syrian control. But, obviously, a state of no war/no peace is not equivalent to peace, and although the security advantages provided by occupation of the Golan Heights are a disincentive for further disengagement, Israel's long-term security hinges on political and territorial adjustment. If and when such adjustments are made, UNDOF may continue to play a role in overseeing their implementation.

Notes

1. Anthony H. Cordesman and Abraham R. Wagner, *The Lessons of Modern War, Volume I: The Arab-Israeli Conflicts, 1973-1989* (Boulder, Co.: Westview Press, 1990), 43.

2. John Mackinlay, *The Peacekeepers: An Assessment of Peacekeeping Operations at the Arab-Israel Interface* (London: Unwin Hyman, 1989), 123-24.

3. Patrick Seale, *Asad of Syria: The Struggle for the Middle East* (London: I.B. Tauris, 1988), 245.

4. United Nations Documents S/11302 and 2/11302/Add.1, May 29-30, 1974. See also, Henry Kissinger, *Years of Upheaval* (Boston: Little, Brown, and Co., 1982), 1253-54.

5. Mackinlay, *The Peacekeepers*, 131.

6. United Nations Documents S/11302 and Add.1-2, May 29-30, 1974; and June 6, 1974.

7. Brigadier General W.A. Douglas Yuill, "UNDOF: A Success Story," *Peacekeeping and International Relations* (May-June 1991): 5.

8. Mackinlay, *The Peacekeepers*, 133.

9. United Nations Document S/21950, November 19, 1990, 4.

10. United Nations Document S/21950, 5.

11. Mackinlay, *The Peacekeepers*, 151-152.

10 United Nations Observation Group in Lebanon: 1958

by Mona Ghali

The United Nations Observation Group in Lebanon (UNOGIL) was established in June 1958 following allegations by the Lebanese government, during a period of civic turmoil, that the United Arab Republic or UAR (a union of Egypt and Syria formed in February 1958) was interfering in its domestic affairs. The government accused the UAR of inciting and arming Lebanese opposition factions and illegally infiltrating personnel across the border. In response, the Security Council dispatched UNOGIL to observe and report on the situation. It verified no infiltration, was politically overshadowed by the landing of US Marine units in Lebanon a month after it commenced operation, and departed within six months after the situation in Lebanon had cooled.

UNOGIL was the first of several peacekeeping operations in Lebanon. The second, United Nations Interim Force in Lebanon, is the subject of chapter 11. Two non-UN missions, Multinational Force I & II, are treated separately. Of the four operations, only the first Multinational Force can claim unqualified success.[1]

This unsatisfactory record is closely linked to the nature of the Lebanese conflict. Its duration and intensity are derived from both internal and external factors. Regional powers such as Syria and Israel have intervened on the side of their Lebanese clients, widening the conflict to an Arab-Israeli concern. What was needed before the deployment of a peacekeeping force was both an explicit recognition of Lebanon's territorial sovereignty by neighboring states and some firm basis for political reconciliation among its different communities. Short of this, any peacekeeping force would find itself in an impossible situation. It would be caught between militias not yet prepared to accept a political compromise and states ready to resort to force to uphold their national interests.

A thorough examination of the historical, economic, and socio-political determinants of Lebanon's several civil wars is beyond the scope of this study, and the reader is encouraged to refer to the extensive literature on the subject.[2] A brief discussion of the conflict follows, however, in order to place the discussion of peacekeeping in Lebanon in political context.

LEBANON: CROSSROADS AND BATTLEGROUND

Lebanon is a small country bordered by Syria to the east and north, Israel to the south, and the Mediterranean to the west. From west to east its topography is one of alternating lowlands and highlands. The coastal plateau is flanked by the Lebanon Mountains, also called Mount Lebanon. The eastern-most mountain range is the Anti-Lebanon. Running between the two ranges is the Bekaa Valley, Lebanon's principal agricultural area.

The state of Lebanon was created only after World War I, when France was entrusted with the mandate for the area under Article 22 of the Covenant of the League of Nations. In 1920, France expanded the territory of Mount Lebanon, which was dominated by the Druzes and Maronites, to include the coastal cities of Beirut, Tripoli, and Sidon, the Bekaa Valley, Jebal Amal in the south, and the Akkar plain in the north. In yielding to the request of their Christian co-religionists to create *Grand Liban* (Greater Lebanon), the French transformed both Lebanon's demographics and its identity.

According to the 1921 census, which was partially boycotted by Muslims, the population of Greater Lebanon was 608,000, of which Christians numbered 428,000, or about 70 percent of the total population. The more accurate 1932 census, the last official census taken, indicated a changing balance between the Christian and Muslim population.[3] The Christians comprised only 51 percent of the population. Of the three main religious sects, Maronites comprised 29 percent, Sunni Muslims about 23 percent, and Shi'a Muslims 20 percent. Rough demographic estimates have established the present (1991) Christian-Muslim ratio at 40:60, with the Shi'a constituting about 30 percent of the total population.

The expanded territory of Mount Lebanon also brought into question the Lebanese identity. The Maronites perceived themselves as the custodians of a Christian Lebanon with a decidedly Western orientation. Lebanese Muslims, in contrast, found greater affinity with the Arab heartland. The Sunni population of Tripoli, Beirut, and Sidon, for example, was heir to the political culture of the Ottoman Empire, and that inheritance included a different attitude not only toward the relationship of Lebanon with the outside world, but also towards the relationship of spiritual and temporal, government and society, leaders and masses.[4] Kamal Salibi eloquently describes this conflict between "Arabism" and "Lebanism":

> In Lebanon, from the very beginning, a force called Arabism, acting from outside and inside the country, stood face to face with another exclusively parochial social force called Lebanism; and the two forces collided on every fundamental issue, impeding the normal development of the state and keeping its political legitimacy and ultimate viability continuously in question.[5]

It should not be altogether surprising that the conservative Maronites, as the claimants to Lebanese political power, would resist forfeiting their privileged position and abandoning their vision of Lebanon, or that the Muslims would accept the position of inferiority which that role implied. Two conditions were necessary to govern these two incompatible parochial forces of Lebanism and Arabism: a political consensus among the different communities, and balanced socio-economic development. These two conditions failed to materialize.

The Maronites did not accept their Muslim compatriots as political equals and with a jealous watchfulness were skeptical of their motives. The Maronites argued that the Muslims were susceptible to the divisive appeals of Arab nationalist leaders and could not be trusted with sensitive political and administrative positions. Moreover, certain political formulas reinforced sectarianism. For example, the unwritten National Pact of 1943 reserved the presidency for a Christian, assigned a Sunni Muslim as prime minister and a Shi'a Muslim as speaker of parliament, and set the ratio of Christian and Muslim deputies in parliament at six to five.

Economic development favored Christian-dominated areas over others. Of the four major communities (Maronite, Druze, Sunni, and Shi'a), the Shi'a were the most economically deprived. While the alliance between the Sunni urban notables and the Maronite elite guaranteed the development of the Sunni coastal towns of Tripoli, Sidon, and Tyre, the political marginalization of the Shi'a left the south underdeveloped. After the 1970s, and particularly under the tutelage of Imam Musa al Sadr, the Shi'a community became politicized and was prepared to press its claim to a share of the goverment's political and economic power commensurate with its numbers.

As Hourani writes,

> For Lebanon to maintain its separate existence, there had to be some kind of authority which, whatever its origins, stood above the interests of particular communities; an agreement on the sharing of power between them; and some measure of agreement also on the purposes for which that power should be used, in particular in relation to the surrounding states.[6]

Only recently, with the acceptance of the Ta'if Accord in October 1989, has such an arrangement been accepted. The accord was mediated by an Arab League Tripartite Committee consisting of King Fahd of Saudi Arabia, President Chadli Bendjedid of Algeria, and King Hassan II of Morocco. The document recognized Lebanon as an independent country with an Arab identity. It set forth a political reform program not unlike those of the past. Although the agreement anticipated the end of political arrangements based on sectarian affiliation, it implicitly accepted confessional politics, with membership in the Lebanese parliament distributed equally between Christians and Muslims.[7]

After more than 15 years of war, there are indications that Lebanon's communities have accepted the need for compromise and political consensus as an undeniable fact. The Ta'if document is the first step in the development of the country's national identity and the restoration of its sovereignty and independence.

ORIGINS OF UNOGIL

During the 1950s, Arab nationalism intensified the confrontation between Christian and Muslim political leaders in Lebanon. As Fouad Ajami writes in a semi-autobiographical essay,

> There was the shadow of the Egyptian Gamal Abdel Nasser that lay over the Muslims of Lebanon. There was the drama of the struggle over Palestine—between Arab and Jew—and the pull of the Palestinian cause. The Egyptian leader who came to dominate our world in West Beirut—really in Muslim Lebanon as a whole—had made the cause of Palestine his rallying cry. The towns and villages of Mandatory Palestine were a veritable extension of my ancestral land in south Lebanon. For my elders a fight had taken place between *Arab Filastin* (the Arabs of Palestine) and *al Yahud* (the Jews).[8]

There was increasing dissension among the Lebanese political elite on how to respond to Nasserism. Some leaders favored a more conciliatory posture. Others, headed by President Camille Chamoun, preferred to favor Lebanon's western allies and the conservative Arab monarchies and to take a hardline position against Arab nationalist states. Chamoun's pro-western inclination was particularly evident during the 1956 Suez crisis when he refused to support Nasser and resisted Arab pressure to suspend diplomatic relations with Great Britain and France. To contain the strength of opposition Muslim leaders, Chamoun initiated electoral reforms that facilitated the election of anti-Nasser parliamentarians during the 1957 elections. The situation came to a head in 1958 when Chamoun sought to amend the constitution to permit himself to be reelected as President for a second term.

The ensuing civil unrest after May 1958 should not be interpreted solely as a response to President Chamoun's bid to achieve reelection. It was more accurately a reflection of cumulative resentment of the political and economic inequities in the country. Arab nationalism had raised a new political consciousness among the Lebanese Muslim community. Political notables such as the Druze leader Kamal Jumblatt sought to redress the inequalities with a call to arms. On the other hand, there is no evidence to suggest that Muslim leaders ever planned to overthrow the existing political arrangements or to reunite Lebanon with Syria. Indeed, once the crisis ended following the election of a new President in July, a Muslim political leader from Tripoli, Rashid Karami, agreed to become prime minister.[9]

Initiatives Leading to UN Involvement

In early May 1958, the murder of a dissident Christian newspaper editor led to the outbreak of civil war between Chamoun's backers and his mostly Muslim opponents. Because the army commander, General Fuad Chehab, hesitated to use his 9,000-man, half-Christian, half-Muslim force against the rebels lest it fracture along sectarian lines, the rebels soon controlled part of Beirut and all but a few kilometers of the Lebanese-Syrian frontier.[10] On May 13, President Chamoun asked Washington about the prospects for US military intervention in Lebanon. President Eisenhower replied that he could agree to send troops if they were requested, but not for the purpose of supporting a second Chamoun term in office; rather, they would be sent to support the current, legal government and to protect American lives and property. Moreover, Eisenhower wanted at least one other Arab state to agree to US intervention.[11]

On May 22, Lebanon's representative to the United Nations requested that the Security Council take up the issue of UAR intervention in the internal affairs of Lebanon. He claimed there was:

> infiltration of armed bands from Syria into Lebanon, the destruction of Lebanese life and property by such bands, the participation of United Arab Republic nations in acts of terrorism and rebellion against the established authorities in Lebanon, the supply of arms from Syria to individuals and bands in Lebanon rebelling against the established authorities, and the waging of a violent radio and press campaign in the United Arab Republic calling for strikes, demonstrations and the overthrow of the established authorities in Lebanon, and through other provocative acts.[12]

The UAR representative to the UN denied these allegations and noted that Lebanon had approached the Security Council only after its domestic situation had deteriorated. He asserted that the Lebanese government was attempting to internationalize a domestic conflict in order to persuade the West to intervene and rejected outright the allegation that the UAR had intervened in Lebanon's domestic affairs.

The Security Council postponed action on Lebanon's complaint until it became apparent that the Arab League could not devise a response to the situation that was satisfactory to the Lebanese government. The matter was first taken up by the Council on June 6; on the 10th, the Swedish delegate, Dr. Gunnar Jarring, submitted a draft resolution calling for the establishment of an observation group to investigate the charges of illegal infiltration of personnel and materiel from Syria. His resolution was adopted the following day and UNOGIL was launched.

POLITICAL SUPPORT

The Swedish resolution was adopted by a vote of 10 to 0, with the USSR abstaining.[13] The Soviet spokesman claimed that the Lebanese government had failed to provide convincing evidence of UAR intervention. Given the Soviet Union's alignment with Egypt and Syria, its position vis à vis Lebanon was to be expected, since any other action would have alienated its Arab allies. It did not veto the resolution, however, recognizing that the issue would only be shifted to the Western-dominated General Assembly.

Once UNOGIL was established, Eisenhower continued to defer the deployment of American forces, wanting to give it a chance to work. Secretary General Hammarskjöld, determined to prevent unilateral intervention in Lebanon, visited both Lebanon and Egypt on June 17-19. According to General Odd Bull, his visit convinced the US that the situation in Lebanon did not merit US intervention at that time.[14]

However, on July 14, the pro-Western government of King Faisal of Iraq was overthrown in a bloody military coup. President Chamoun immediately requested American military help, seeing in the Iraqi coup a threat to all moderate Arab regimes, including his own. King Hussein of Jordan thought likewise and requested British aid.[15] US Marines landed in Beirut on July 15, and British troops were flown into Jordan two days later. A July 17 US proposal to transform UNOGIL into an armed peacekeeping force was vetoed by the Soviet Union.[16]

Deadlocked, the Security Council adjourned, and after a three-week hiatus the issue was taken up in the General Assembly. By that time, however, the situation in Lebanon had calmed down considerably, General Chehab had been elected President, and the new government of Iraq had begun to make sufficiently moderate noises that it had been granted diplomatic recognition by both the United States and the United Kingdom. Thus, the main issue for the UN now became how best to facilitate the withdrawal of US forces from Lebanon and British forces from Jordan. On August 18, the US and Britain sent identical letters to the President of the Assembly offering to withdraw their forces if the General Assembly determined them to be "unncessary for the maintenance of international peace and security." On the 21st, the Assembly decided to leave that determination to Hammarskjöld, requesting that he make "such practical arrangements" as might be needed to "facilitate the early withdrawal of foreign troops" from Lebanon and Jordan. This resolution, sponsored by all of the UN's Arab member states, passed unanimously.[17]

MANDATE

UNOGIL was mandated "to proceed to Lebanon so as to ensure there is no illegal infiltration of personnel, [or] supply of arms or other materiel across the Lebanese borders."[18] Although the passage of General Assembly Resolution 1237 provided a tacit understanding that UNOGIL was to help stabilize the situation so as to allow for the withdrawal of foreign forces from the country, at no time was UNOGIL mandated to facilitate an end to the civil war itself. Indeed, UN resolutions for a stronger mandate had already been vetoed in the Security Council by the USSR. It was deployed in Lebanon only to observe and report.[19]

FUNDING

UNOGIL was not funded a special account, as was the case with such peacekeeping missions as UNEF I but from that part of the regular UN budget allocated to "special missions and related activities." For the fiscal year 1958, $3.7 million was appropriated for UNOGIL out of a total "special missions" budget of $6.8 million.

PLANNING AND IMPLEMENTATION

As there was little time for advance planning or purchasing, this operation made heavy use of UN facilities and personnel already deployed in the region. UN Relief Works Agency facilities in Beirut served as UNOGIL's initial headquarters; UNTSO provided the first 15 military observers and a dozen jeeps; and UNEF loaned it communications equipment.

Size and Composition of the Force

Twenty-one countries eventually contributed military personnel to UNOGIL.[20] By June 26, 94 military observers from eleven countries had arrived. By July 15, there were 113 ground observers and 20 air operations personnel.[21]

Soon after US troops landed in Lebanon, UNOGIL gained access to areas previously restricted by opposition leaders and required more people and equipment. In his second interim report on UNOGIL dated July 17, the Secretary General recommended that the group be expanded to 200. By by late September, the number of ground observers had grown to 214, while air operations personnel increased to 73.[22]

The growth of UNOGIL seemed somewhat paradoxical: the better the political situation in Lebanon, the more observers the Secretary General requested. But as Higgins observed, the better the situation, the better UNOGIL's access to more remote sections of the country, and the more observation posts it considered necessary.[23] By November 17, the number of ground observers had risen to 501, and the number of air observers to 90. By that time, however, the operation's work was about to end, and by mid-December fewer than 30 UNOGIL personnel remained in Lebanon.

Command, Communications, Logistics, and Administration

The Observation Group formally consisted of three senior members: Mr. Galo Plaza of Ecuador, Chairman of the Group, who dealt with the Lebanese government; Mr. Rajeshwar Dayal of India, liaison to the Lebanese opposition; and Major General Odd Bull of Norway, who was appointed executive member in charge of the military personnel assisting the Observation Group.[24] Observers assigned to assist the Group operated in six areas (Tripoli, Baalbek, Chtaura, Marjayoun, Sidon, and Beirut).

The government of Lebanon established a commission of liaison with UNOGIL, to supply the Group with information about the infiltration of armed men and materiel across the Lebanese border. Most of the information supplied by the government could not be independently confirmed.

As an observer mission responsible for surveying the entire country, UNOGIL needed a good deal of transport and communications equipment. As of June 26, there were 74 vehicles for 94 observers; by November, there were 290 vehicles for the 501 ground observers, and the five field stations outside Beirut maintained continuous radio communications with headquarters, observer outstations, and patrols.[25]

Aerial surveillance was an important component of UNOGIL operations. In his second interim report (July 17) the Secretary General transmitted the Group's request for:

An adequate number of planes and trained personnel capable of providing continuous air patrols on all sections of the frontier. The Group estimates that 18 reconnaissance planes and 4 helicopters with air crews supported by sufficient ground personnel and equipment would be required. Additional helicopters would be required to maintain contact and to insure rapid communications within the expanded network of outstations and observation posts.[26]

By mid-August, UNOGIL was outfitted with 12 small Cessna and four old Harvard fixed-wing aircraft, and four Bell helicopters whose use was limited for lack of spare parts. Although the number of air sorties had risen from 160 in July to 210 in August, to 221 for the first 20 days of September, this operating tempo still amounted to less than one sortie per aircraft per day.

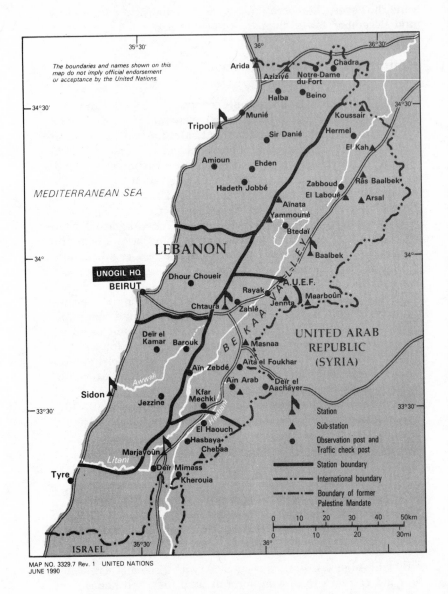

MAP NO. 3329.7 Rev. 1   UNITED NATIONS
JUNE 1990

**Figure 10.1. United Nations Observation Group
in Lebanon, Deployment as of July 1958**

Although UNOGIL reported that this sufficed to maintain continuous surveillance over the whole of Lebanon, the Group had no night photo-reconnaissance capability.[27]

Field Operations

UNOGIL operations concentrated on Lebanon's rugged border districts but in theory covered all potential infiltration routes. These included the Akkar plain, which extends from Tripoli north and east to the Syrian border (more than 500 square kilometers); the Bekaa Valley, along the eastern frontier; south-east Lebanon including Marjayoun; and south-west Lebanon, including Sidon and Jezzine. UNTSO observers were responsible for the southern border with Israel, and the Lebanese government patrolled the coast.

Initial Deployments. Permanent observation posts were staffed by military observers and maintained continuous radio communications with UNOGIL headquarters in Beirut and with one another. UN teams composed of two observers, each with a radio-equipped vehicle, and one radio officer with a communications jeep, patrolled most main roads and access routes. They operated in convoys and maintained constant communication with one another.[28] Light aircraft together with helicopters conducted aerial reconnaissance missions. An emergency reserve of military observers was stationed at headquarters in Beirut, as was an evaluation team responsible for analyzing information from the field and for coordinating the activities of the observers. The Lebanese government provided information about suspected infiltration sites, which the observer group then investigated.[29]

Initially, the Group encountered considerable resistance in establishing positions and patrolling much of the mission area controlled by the Lebanese opposition. Nor was the government in a position to guarantee the Group's safe conduct or its freedom of movement. Finally, given the lack of suitable alternatives early on, observation posts were located in hotels or other public facilities, that is, in places where infiltration was unlikely to occur. It was only with the arrival of supplies in mid-July that tented camps were established closer to the frontier and UNOGIL was able to report that it had gained full freedom of access to all sections of the Lebanese frontier.[30]

US Military Intervention and UNOGIL. Following the coup in Iraq, the Lebanese and Jordanian governments invoked Article 51 of the UN Charter—the self-defense clause—and sought US and British military assistance, respectively. Invoking the Eisenhower Doctrine, which endorsed US intervention in the Middle East whenever a legitimate government believed itself threatened by Communism and requested American aid, the US landed troops in Lebanon on July 15.[31]

US intervention dealt UNOGIL a temporary setback by affecting local perceptions of its independence and impartiality. There were rumors, for example, that the UN force had acted as an advance party for the Americans.[32] To distance itself from the US operations, the Group issued the following communiqué on July 16, the day after the US landing:

> The United Nations Observation Group in Lebanon wishes to clarify its position in regard to its relationship with the foreign forces on Lebanon soil. The United Nations Observation Group alone is in Lebanon in pursuance of the mandate contained in the Security Council resolution of 11 June 1958 (S/4023). The United Nations Observation Group represents the only action taken by the Security Council. There is, therefore, no basis for establishing any contact or working relationship, formal or informal, between the United Nations Observation Group and any non-Lebanese forces in Lebanon beyond what may be strictly required for the independent fulfillment of its mandate from the United Nations Security Council, which cannot be altered without further action by the Council.[33]

The United States conveyed its preference for UN-US coordination, but UNOGIL commander General Odd Bull quickly dismissed such an arrangement. An agreement was reached, however, whereby American troops would restrict their activities to the Beirut area, and UNOGIL military observers would operate in the rest of the country.[34] By dissociating itself from the US military action, UNOGIL sought and to a large degree succeeded in restoring its image of impartiality .

Two weeks after the US intervention, the election of General Chehab as President of Lebanon stemmed the political disintegration of the country and helped to restore the government's legitimacy. Following the election, pressure for US troop withdrawal intensified. To expedite the withdrawal, Hammarskjöld, acting under authority given him by the General Assembly, raised the authorized number of military observers to 888. Although never reaching its authorized strength, UNOGIL more than tripled in size between July and November.

By the end of October, the US and Britain had withdrawn their forces from Lebanon and Jordan. On November 16, the Lebanese representative to the UN asked to rescind his complaint of May

22 that precipitated UNOGIL's deployment. The restoration of government authority over all Lebanese territory removed the original justification for that deployment. In a letter to the President of the Security Council, Secretary General Hammarskjöld reported that the task of UNOGIL had been completed and he had instructed the Group to terminate operations. The last personnel departed Beirut on December 9, when UNOGIL's operations officially ceased.

ASSESSMENT

UNOGIL was not capable of fulfilling its mandate to assess the extent of illegal infiltration of arms and personnel into Lebanon. Four factors undermined its effectiveness: its size, the area and the nature of the terrain in which it operated, restrictions on its movement, and inadequate equipment.

In his reports to the Security Council on the deployment of UNOGIL, the Secretary General consistently requested an increase in the number of personnel, the number of fully manned observation posts, and the amount of equipment. The system's response to these requests was slow, and the time-lag diminished the Group's capacity to execute its mission effectively. This inevitably affected its credibility. Given the large area that UNOGIL was responsible for monitoring, and the dangers of patrolling at night, it was unrealistic to expect that the Group could adequately observe and report illegal infiltration.

Its task was made more difficult by the nature of the terrain, which obstructed mobile patrols. UNOGIL personnel were concerned mainly with Lebanon's eastern and northern borders since UNTSO military observers were responsible for the southern frontier with Israel. The eastern frontier is characterized by mountain formations that reach heights of 2,400 to 2,800 meters. Roads run from northeast to south-west in the Bekaa Valley, parallel to the mountains, with the exception of the Beirut-Damascus highway, which cuts across the 10 to 25 kilometer-wide Bekaa.

The physical nature of the northern frontier similarly frustrated UNOGIL's monitoring of potential infiltration sites. No road linked this area with the northern Bekaa valley, access to it being limited to the coastal highway running northeast from Tripoli towards Homs in Syria. And since the area north of Tripoli was initially held by opposition forces, UNOGIL's access to the northern frontier was frustrated for at least the first month.

UNOGIL's final patrol area included the approximately 220 kilometers of Lebanon's sea coast. Here, air patrols were conducted to supplement mobile ground patrols. Sea patrols had been considered, but the Group concluded they were the obligation of the Lebanese authorities.[35]

Although the Lebanese government assured the Group that it would have freedom of movement, the limited amount of territory under effective government control when UNOGIL deployed, and General Chehab's unwillingness to use force to extend that control, left the UN with access merely to the five percent of the border that lay in government hands. In the first month, not only were observers obstructed from entering opposition-held areas, they were on occasion fired upon and their movements limited by the mining of roads and the destruction of bridges.[36] The Lebanese opposition viewed their quarrel with the government as an internal matter that was beyond UN purview; they formed an important local party whose consent to UN operations had not been obtained in advance.

Thus, during a politically sensitive period the Observation Group was not able to function fully. As a result, despite its best efforts, the information it compiled may not have accurately reflected actual conditions on the ground. Even after it had obtained access to most of Lebanon, however, the Group reported that,

> In no case have United Nations observers, who have been vigilantly patrolling the opposition-held areas and have frequently observed the armed bands there, been able to detect the presence of persons who have indubitably entered from across the border for the purpose of fighting....There is no evidence of the existence of radio contact between the opposition forces scattered over different parts of the country nor of any co-ordinated military planning and control.[37]

As for the issue of the UAR arming Lebanese opposition groups, UNOGIL reported that the arms held by those groups were of French or British make and could not be conclusively traced in origin.

Such conclusions were understandably frustrating, even embarrassing, to President Chamoun, who had asked for observers to substantiate his claims of UAR interference and to support his power base. He is not the only head of state for whom a UN field operation has not behaved as expected, and that is to the UN's credit.

On the other hand, the fact that the US sent troops into Lebanon despite UNOGIL's failure to find external interference in Lebanon's affairs suggests US disregard for the Group's findings. It would have been more convenient for the US, as for the Lebanese government, had the Group found extensive illegal infiltration. The US chose to believe, and to support, Chamoun.

CONCLUSION

The United Nations sent an observer mission into Lebanon at a time of rising Arab nationalism and rising Cold War tensions in the region, and the events that followed suggest how peacekeeping during the Cold War was closely tied to East-West as well as regional politics, and how it complemented US foreign policy. When the pro-Western government of Iraq was overthrown in mid-July 1958, the United States moved quickly to avert (in its view) a similar fate for Lebanon. The US military presence overshadowed UNOGIL militarily and politically. But once the Marines stormed ashore and found that they had little to do, the UN presence in the country gave the United States political cover for a speedy and reasonably graceful exit by allowing it to hand over its stabilizing mission (implicitly) to UNOGIL.[38] This tacit role explains why UNOGIL continued to grow all through the fall, even as the conflict in Lebanon abated. The growth reflected a determined effort on the part of the Group to demonstrate that the situation in Lebanon was sufficiently stable that it could safely fold its tents and go home.

Notes

1. For the non-UN missions, see Mona Ghali, *Multinational Forces: Non-UN Peacekeeping in the Middle East*, Occasional Paper No. 12 (Washington, D.C.: The Henry L. Stimson Center, October 1992). The first Multinational Force (MNF I), composed of French, Italian, and American troops, secured the withdrawal from Lebanon of Palestinian fighters cornered in Beirut by the 1982 Israeli invasion of Lebanon. It departed Lebanon only to return rapidly after massacres of Palestinian civilians who remained behind in refugee camps south of Beirut. French and American contingents of MNF II became increasingly identified with one Christian faction and were drawn into Lebanon's civil war. In October 1983, both suffered heavy loss of life from car bomb attacks on their respective barracks and soon withdrew from Lebanon.

2. The literature on Lebanon is abundant, and much of it excellent. Particular attention should be given to Kamal Salibi, *House of Many Mansions* (Berkeley and Los Angeles: University of California Press,

1988); Albert Hourani, *Syria and Lebanon* (London: Oxford University Press, 1946); Helena Cobban, *The Making of Modern Lebanon* (Boulder, Co.: Westview Press, 1985); David Gilmour, *A Fractured Country* (New York: St. Martin's Press, 1983); Itmar Rabinovitch, *The War for Lebanon: 1970–1985* (Ithaca: Cornell University Press, 1985); Walid Khalidi, *Conflict and Violence in Lebanon: Confrontation in the Middle East* (Cambridge, Mass.: Center for International Affairs, Harvard University, 1979); and two contributions from journalists, Thomas Friedman, *From Beirut to Jerusalem* (New York: Farrar Straus Giroux, 1989) and Robert Fisk, *Pity the Nation* (New York: Atheneum, 1990).

3. Successive Lebanese governments have published only unofficial population figures, fearing that formal recognition of the new numbers would strengthen demands for the redistribution of political power and economic resources in line with demographic changes.

4. Albert Hourani, *The Emergence of the Modern Middle East* (Berkeley and Los Angeles: University of California Press, 1981), 147.

5. Salibi, *House of Many Mansions*, 37.

6. Albert Hourani, "Ideologies of the Mountain and the City," in Roger Owen, *Essays on the Crisis in Lebanon* (London: Ithaca Press, 1976), 23.

7. The Ta'if agreement gives Christians and Muslims each 54 seats in the Lebanese Parliament. The Maronite community is allocated 30 seats, the Sunni, 22, the Shi'a, 22, and the Druze, 8. The balance is distributed among the remaining Christian communities and the Alawi.

8. Fouad Ajami, "The End of Arab Nationalism," *The New Republic*, August 12, 1991, 24.

9. Roger Owen, *The Crisis in Lebanon* (London: Ithaca Press, 1976), 29.

10. David W. Wainhouse, *International Peacekeeping at the Crossroads* (Baltimore, Md.: The Johns Hopkins University Press, 1973), 103. Chehab's fears about potential disintegration of the Army were well founded, as events following the 1975 civil war would prove.

11. Dwight D. Eisenhower, *White House Years: Waging Peace* (Garden City, NY: Doubleday & Co., 1965), 267. Preparing to intervene, US amphibious forces were moved into the Eastern Mediterranean, and airborne units based in Europe were placed on alert. But when the fighting subsided, the US held back.

12. United Nations Document S/4007, May 23, 1958.

13. In 1958, there were only 11 members of the Security Council.

14. General Odd Bull, *War and Peace in the Middle East* (London: Leo Cooper, 1976), 6.

15. Eisenhower, *White House Years*, 269-270.

16. *The Blue Helmets: A Review of United Nations Peacekeeping*, 2nd ed. (New York: United Nations Department of Public Information, 1990), 180.

17. General Assembly Resolution 1237, August 21, 1958. Quoted in Rosalyn Higgins, *United Nations Peacekeeping, 1946–1967, Documents*

and Commentary, Vol. I: The Middle East (London: Oxford University Press, 1969), 543, 545.

18. United Nations Document S/4023, June 11, 1958, 47.

19. Higgins, *United Nations Peacekeeping*, 568.

20. These included Afghanistan, Argentina, Burma, Canada, Chile, Denmark, Ecuador, Finland, India, Indonesia, Ireland, Italy, Nepal, the Netherlands, New Zealand, Norway, Peru, Portugal, Sweden, Sri Lanka and Thailand (Wainhouse, *International Peacekeeping at the Crossroads*, 133).

21. United Nations Document S/4038, June 28, 1958.

22. United Nations Document S/4085, August 12, 1958.

23. Higgins, *United Nations Peacekeeping*, 557-58.

24. Major General Carl von Horn, *Soldiering for Peace* (New York: David McKay Co., Inc., 1967), 102.

25. United Nations Document S/4038, June 28, 1958, 121.

26. United Nations Document S/4052, July 17, 1958.

27. It did, however, fly at night, and stocked a quantity of illumination flares (Wainhouse, *International Peacekeeping at the Crossroads*, 116).

28. United Nations Document S/4029, June 16, 1958, 70.

29. United Nations Document S/4040, July 1, 1958. UNOGIL's first report, which failed to confirm Lebanese government allegations of weapons infiltration, was severely criticized by the government partly because it was based on daylight-only observations. In its second report, UNOGIL acknowledged the problem, but "in view of the harassments suffered by its observers...even by day, it reluctantly came to the conclusion that night patrols would involve a degree of risk to the observers which it could not accept." In a thinly veiled return volley, the report went on to note that since "well-armed Lebanese forces have established no control along the routes in question," its own unarmed patrols shouldn't be expected to do better (United Nations Document S/4069, July 30, 1958, para. 8; quoted in Higgins, *United Nations Peacekeeping*, 578).

30. United Nations Document S/4051, July 15, 1958.

31. The doctrine had been approved by the Congress in January 1957, three months after the Suez Crisis (for a discussion of Suez, see chapter seven).

32. Bull, *War and Peace in the Middle East*, 12.

33. United Nations Document S/4085, August 12, 1958.

34. Bull, *War and Peace in the Middle East*, 12.

35. United Nations Document S/4069, July 1, 1958.

36. United Nations Document S/4040, July 1, 1958.

37. United Nations Document S/4069, July 25, 1958.

38. As Higgins puts it, "once it had been decided to continue UNOGIL's work in spite of the changed circumstances of the United States landings, it was tacitly hoped that the stabilizing influence of an enlarged UNOGIL would facilitate the speedy withdrawal of United States troops. Indeed, the United States (and the British *viz a viz* Jordan) had made it clear that if the UN could in some sense protect the governments, they

themselves would withdraw their troops" (Higgins, *United Nations Peacekeeping*, 548).

11 United Nations Interim Force in Lebanon: 1978-Present

by Mona Ghali

Since 1978, the United Nations Security Council has repeatedly accepted both the recommendations of the Secretary General and the requests of the Lebanese government to renew the mandate of the United Nations Interim Force in Lebanon (UNIFIL), despite UNIFIL's failure to implement key elements of its mandate. Many consider the force ineffectual and point in particular to its failure to deter the 1982 Israeli invasion; others, while acknowledging UNIFIL's problems, plead mitigating circumstances.[1] The latter contend that UNIFIL was given an impossible mandate. The government that it was deployed to support had lost its authority in southern Lebanon to such a degree its restoration (UNIFIL's putative task) was for many years unthinkable. The regime in Beirut neither controlled the country's territory nor could it influence the actions of opposition groups, and together with them had abandoned the slogan of the 1958 civil war, "no victors, no vanquished."

Lebanon's factions sought a military settlement but in the end acquiesced to a program of national reconciliation through the externally brokered Ta'if Agreement of 1989. This acceptance came reluctantly, and only after more than fifteen years of civil war, two invasions by Israel, and the failure of General Michel Aoun's bid to restore Christian Maronite hegemony in 1989–90. UNIFIL remained in place through it all and suffered more than 150 casualties, a force largely invisible to the outside world.

ORIGINS

Some observers claim that had external agents not intervened, Lebanon's communities would have been able to arrive at an acceptable political formula much sooner. There is no doubt that the intervention of non-Lebanese actors, whether directly (with forces) or indirectly (with financial assistance for their respective Lebanese clients), expanded the intra-Lebanese conflict to the regional level and made the conflict more intractable. The PLO, Syria, Israel, Iraq, Iran, and Saudi Arabia each have some interest at stake. Table 11.1 summarizes the principal militia groups and their sponsors as of mid-1991.

Table 11.1. Lebanese and Non-Lebanese Militias in Lebanon, 1991

Group & Leader	Area of Operations	Number	Sponsor
Lebanese Army Gen. Emile Lahhud	Expanding from Beirut area	40, 000	Govt. of Lebanon
Amal Nabih Berri	Southern Lebanon	6, 500	Syria
Hezballah	Beirut suburbs and southern Lebanon	3, 500*	Iran
Progressive Socialist Party (Druze) Walid Jumblatt	Shouf	3, 000	
Lebanese Forces Samir Jaja	Beirut	3, 000	Iraq
South Lebanon Army Gen. Antoine Lahd	Southern Lebanon	<6, 000	Israel
Syrian Forces	Bekaa Valley	40, 000	Syria
Israeli Defense Force	Southern Lebanon		Israel
Iranian Revolutionary Forces	Baalbek	2, 000	Iran
Palestine Liberation Organization	Refugee camps south of Beirut	10,000	

*Estimated at 2,500 by Lebanese Embassy, Washington, September 1991. **Source**: Augustus Richard Norton, "Lebanon After Ta'if: Is the Civil War Over?" *The Middle East Journal* 45, no. 3 (Summer 1991): 468.

The PLO

Following the Arab defeat in 1967, it became obvious that Egyptian President Nasser would not be the Moses who would lead the Palestinians to the promised land. There arose a new militant Palestinian nationalism intent on expressing its moral purpose through the barrel of a gun. Following the Israeli occupation of the West Bank and Gaza Strip in 1967, Palestinian commandos based themselves in Jordan and launched attacks into Israeli territory.

By 1969, King Hussein was no longer willing to permit his kingdom to be a proxy for Palestine. He violently asserted Jordan's sovereignty and deployed the army against the Palestinian fighters. While Arab leaders were quick to verbally reassert their fidelity to the Palestinian cause, their actions betrayed a desire to abandon it altogether and go on with business as usual. The Cairo Agreement allowed them this luxury.

The Cairo Agreement, signed by Yasser Arafat and the Lebanese Army's Chief of Staff on November 3, 1969, was designed to regulate and control the Palestinian armed presence in Lebanon. In practice, however, it shifted the Palestine problem away from the Arab world in general and onto the Lebanese, since the PLO used the Agreement as a license to mount military raids against Israel from Lebanese territory.

Lebanon's political fragmentation and weak army permitted the Palestinians to act with relative impunity. The problem of reconciling the PLO's freedom of action in Lebanon, as codified in the Cairo Agreement, with Lebanon's sovereignty, independence, and territorial integrity deepened sectarian divisions in Lebanese society. The Maronite community, and particularly the Phalange, resented the PLO's virtual license to create a state-within-a-state in the south.

On April 13, 1975, Phalangist gunmen ambushed a bus at Ain el Roumaneh, killing 27 Palestinians. This incident is often considered to have triggered Lebanon's 1975 civil war, but the real antecedents of the Ain el Roumaneh massacre are to be found in the distribution of political and economic power among Lebanon's fractious communities, which is, and has always been, the country's fundamental problem. As Itmar Rabinovitch writes, the Christian forces were, "defending not so much the violated authority of the Lebanese state as the pattern of life in Christian neighborhoods of Beirut. Their Palestinian rivals were protecting not merely the position and privileges they had seized in recent years but also the political environment that had facilitated their acquisition."[2] The Palestinian presence in Lebanon asked the Lebanese to choose between sides. At least initially, support for the Palestinians was a test of an individual's Arab identity. As Kamal Salibi wrote, "To the ordinary Muslim in Lebanon...to let down the Palestinians was tantamount to letting down the Muslim Lebanese cause."[3]

The PLO did manage to wear out its welcome among many Lebanese groups over time, but despite efforts by the Maronites, Syria, Israel, and others to rout the PLO from Lebanon, about

10,000 fighters were still concentrated in the refugee camps south of Beirut in 1991. They continued to launch rocket attacks against Israeli forces in the south and to clash with the Israeli-sponsored South Lebanon Army (see below).

Syria

On June 1, 1976, Syrian forces crossed the Lebanese frontier after tacit agreement with Israel that they would not advance south of the "red line" defined roughly by the Litani River. Syria's President Hafez Assad recognized the implications of Lebanon's insecurity: if the Christian Maronites partitioned Lebanon, the Israelis would become their protectors; if the Palestinians managed to defeat the Christians, the Israelis would be forced to intervene. Assad's fundamental intent, therefore, was to preempt these two possibilities and bring Lebanon into Syria's sphere of influence. He first deployed Syrian troops in 1976 on the side of the Maronites, but later, with the endorsement of the Arab League and under the legitimate cover of the Arab Deterrent Force established in October 1976, he used them to stabilize the situation in Lebanon.

Assad's policy in Lebanon was aimed at consolidating Syria's position as a regional power. He supported Nabih Berri's Shi'a Amal militia in southern Lebanon against Iranian-backed Hezballah during the "turf war" of 1988–90; and he backed Elias Hrawi, the Sunni prime minister, against the Maronite leader General Michel Aoun when the latter, with the support of Iraq, initiated his "war of liberation" in 1989 to eliminate the Syrian presence from Lebanon.

Assad is dependent on Saudi financial backing. Syria's backing of the Coalition during the 1991 Gulf War reinforced and rehabilitated Damascus's relations with Riyadh and Washington, respectively. In contrast, Saddam Hussein's invasion of Kuwait cost him the Gulf's financial backing and indirectly helped consolidate Syria's position in Lebanon.

Israel

Even with the Arab-negotiated cease-fire in 1976, the PLO retained its freedom of action and continued its raids into northern Israel from southern Lebanon. On March 11, 1978, PLO forces seized an Israeli bus south of Haifa. In the ensuing confrontation with Israeli security forces, nine guerrillas and 37 Israelis were killed. Consistent with Israel's policy vis-à-vis Palestinian terrorism, Prime Minister Menachem Begin promised retaliation. It came on March 14–15, when the Israeli Defense Force (IDF) initiated its first invasion of southern Lebanon, codenamed Operation Litani. The IDF deployment was designed to disrupt the PLO's main infiltration routes and lines of supply and to uncover its potential base camps for attacks against Israel. The United Nations Security Council responded to the situation by creating UNIFIL.

The failure of Operation Litani (and, for that matter, UNIFIL) to stop Palestinian attacks into northern Israel prompted a second IDF invasion of Lebanon in June 1982, which this time advanced north to Beirut. In 1984, the Israeli government decided to redeploy its forces south to the international frontier, but did not completely withdraw from Lebanese territory. Since 1985, the Israelis have maintained a self-declared "security zone" in southern Lebanon. Israel also maintains control of areas outside its zone in southern Lebanon through its Lebanese proxy, the South Lebanon Army (SLA), the successor to General Saad Haddad's De Facto Forces (DFF), which were established after the first invasion in 1978.

The SLA, led by General Antoine Lahd, has a troop strength of 2,500 and is trained and supplied by Israel. Should Israel decide to discontinue its support of the SLA, the militia would cease to exist.

Iran

Iran sponsors two groups in Lebanon: Hezballah, and the non-Lebanese group, the Iranian Revolutionary Forces. With the death of Ayatollah Khomeini in June 1989 and the consolidation of power of his successor, Hashemi Rafsanjani, Iranian support for Hezballah was reduced.[5]

The interaction in Lebanon of all these groups means that any permanent political formula for Lebanon must accommodate both intra-Lebanese and inter-state interests. UNIFIL has been caught in the middle of this political drama, having to operate within the constraints imposed by the numerous local militias and government forces in southern Lebanon.

Initiatives Leading to UN Involvement

US President Jimmy Carter was particularly concerned about the impact of Israel's 1978 invasion on the historic peace negotiations then underway between Egypt and Israel. The invasion was a serious embarrassment for Egyptian President Sadat, and any inaction on the part of the Carter Administration might have been perceived as de facto complicity with Israel. Because the Cold War was still very real and close at hand (the USSR had several thousand air defense and associated troops deployed in neighboring Syria), the United States turned, as it had in the past, to the United Nations.

US Representative to the UN Andrew Young sponsored a draft Security Council resolution calling for: (1) an immediate cease-fire, (2) the withdrawal of Israeli forces from all Lebanese terri-tory, and (3) the introduction of a peacekeeping force to supervise the withdrawal of Israeli forces from Lebanon in order to reaffirm Lebanon's territorial integrity, sovereignty, and political inde-pendence. The draft proposal was adopted as UN Security Council Resolution 425 on March 19, 1978.

Resolution 425 also requested a report from the Secretary General on the implementation of the resolution. In response to that report, UN Security Council Resolution 426 (March 19, 1978) approved the establishment of a UN force with a total strength of 4,000 for an initial six-month period. Thus UNIFIL was born.

POLITICAL SUPPORT

The resolution sponsored by the US was adopted by the Security Council by 12 votes in favor with two abstentions (Soviet Union and Czechoslovakia) and one member not participating (China). The United States supported a UN peacekeeping force both to assist with the withdrawal of the IDF and to avert a direct Israeli-Syrian confrontation.

The Soviet representative, Mr. Troyanovsky, condemned what he described as Israel's bid to occupy southern Lebanon and destroy the Palestinian resistance movement, and he asked the UN to demand the immediate and unconditional withdrawal of Israeli troops from Lebanon. He emphasized that UNIFIL's costs should be borne singularly by Israel. In support of that position, the USSR and its Warsaw Pact allies withheld their share of the cost of UNIFIL until April 1986, when Moscow changed its mind under the influence of Soviet President Mikhail Gorbachev's "new thinking."[6]

Historical political and personal ties between Beirut and Paris have made Lebanon's affairs the reflexive concern of France. As such, the French representative to the UN supported the adop-tion of a cease-fire, the withdrawal of Israeli forces, and the establishment of a peacekeeping force. Indeed, France contrib-uted the first infantry batallion to UNIFIL.

Israel, consistent with its general lack of confidence in the UN, opposed the adoption of any resolution that would place a peacekeeping force in southern Lebanon. During the debate preceding the adoption of Resolutions 425 and 426, the Israeli representative to the UN, Mr. Herzog, argued that the restoration of the Lebanese government could be achieved by Israel and Lebanon working together without the interference of outside parties. He asserted that the buildup of PLO bases in southern Lebanon and Israel's national security interests left it no alternative but to intervene militarily in Lebanese affairs. He denied Israel's actions were motivated by retaliation or the desire to occupy Lebanese territory. Reluctantly, and only after the United States exercised its political leverage, did Israel agree to cooperate with UNIFIL.

Arab states including Syria were vocal in their condemnation of the Israeli invasion and supported the UN initiative. Lebanon's opposition parties similarly supported the deployment of a UN peacekeeping force, believing that it would expedite the removal of Israeli forces from Lebanese territory.

Since its creation in 1978, UNIFIL's mandate has been renewed without much discussion in the Security Council. While the members of the Council acknowledge that the Force has not fulfilled its mandate, its humanitarian activities in southern Lebanon are considered sufficient grounds for keeping it in place.

MANDATE

UNIFIL's mandate, phrased in equivocal vocabulary so as to accommodate the local parties and Security Council members and thus ensure the adoption of resolution 425, called for UNIFIL to: (1) confirm an immediate Israeli cease-fire and withdrawal from Lebanese territory; (2) restore international peace and security; and (3) ensure the restoration of Lebanese governmental authority and its territorial integrity, sovereignty, and territorial independence.

By explicitly assigning UNIFIL the task of ensuring the restoration of the government's effective authority, the mandate disregarded or downplayed the disintegration of both the Lebanese state and its national army. In its ambiguity, it left the local parties to read into it what they willed.

While the Secretary General preferred a well-defined perimeter for UNIFIL's area of operation, Security Council members could not reach a consensus on the subject. Moreover, the Israeli and

Lebanese governments and the PLO held incompatible interpretations of the Force's area of operations. Israel wanted UNIFIL to control the entire area south of the Litani River (with the exception of its border enclave), including Tyre and the Kasmiya Bridge, two Palestinian strongholds. North of the Litani, UNIFIL was encouraged by Israel to incorporate Nabatiya and Hasbaya in its area of operations.

The PLO opposed UNIFIL deployment in Tyre and at the Kasmiya Bridge, arguing that the IDF had not occupied either. The Lebanese, on the other hand, gave UNIFIL carte blanche. Following negotiations with the PLO and the IDF, the UN Secretariat defined UNIFIL's area of operations as all areas then in the control of the IDF (all areas south of the Litani except the Tyre pocket).

Not only were there distinctive views of the appropriate area of operation for the Force, there were differences of opinion regarding UNIFIL's responsibilities. The IDF assumed that UNIFIL would clear the entire area of Palestinians, and the failure of the force to deter Palestinian forays into northern Israel was used to justify Israel's continuing presence in the South. PLO Chairman Arafat, on the other hand, maintained that the 1969 Cairo Agreement legitimized the Palestinian presence in southern Lebanon. He claimed that the UN force should therefore not restrict Palestinian movement and that Palestinian fighters should be permitted access to the Force's area of operations.

After the second Israeli invasion of Lebanon in 1982, Security Council Resolution 511 of June 1982 gave UNIFIL the additional "interim" tasks of extending its protection and providing humanitarian assistance to the local population in its area of operations. That task continues.

FUNDING

Funds for UNIFIL are assessed as expenses of the Organization and, as such, are the collective responsibility of the members. However, several members have, for political reasons, refused to submit their contributions, resulting in a widening deficit in the UNIFIL Special Account. The annual costs for maintaining UNIFIL for the 1991 calendar year were estimated at $153.5 million, assuming an average strength of 5,850. This represented over 45 percent of the total costs of UN peacekeeping operations in 1991.[7]

The Soviet Union and its then-Warsaw Pact allies withheld financial support from UNIFIL for eight years. In the mid-to-late 1980s, the United States made only partial contributions to the operation in line with its policy of squeezing the UN to induce administrative and fiscal reform. Together, these countries were responsible for 85 percent of the $264 million in outstanding payments for UNIFIL at the end of 1991. They were joined by "rejection front" Arab states and a number of smaller Latin and African states who were at least five years in arrears in their contributions.[8] As a result, the Organization has fallen several years behind in its reimbursements to troop-contributing governments. UNIFIL's experience illustrates the inherent danger of the longstanding custom of separate assessments for each UN peacekeeping mission instead of a single annual peacekeeping assessment from which all missions draw.

PLANNING AND IMPLEMENTATION

All planning for UNIFIL was done in a traditional rush. Unlike most peacekeeping operations, which are deployed only with the consent of the local parties, UNIFIL was established in southern Lebanon with neither the PLO's nor Israel's full consent. The Lebanese government had lost virtually all authority in the country and thus could not guarantee the Force's freedom of movement or its safe conduct. Negotiations with the local parties to define the Force's area of operations were, as noted, unsatisfactory for the PLO, Israel, and UNIFIL.

Political-military conditions in southern Lebanon remained tense and highly volatile as UNIFIL prepared to deploy. The IDF occupied most of southern Lebanon to the Litani River; the PLO were concentrated in the Tyre pocket and in bases north of the Litani. On March 27, 1978, the Secretary General appealed to all parties to respect the general cease-fire. On April 8, Lieutenant General Emanuel Erskine, UNIFIL Force Commander, reported that the situation in the field was generally quiet except for intermittent exchanges of fire in the Tyre area, the eastern sector, and the PLO base at Chateau de Beaufort north of the Litani.

Size and Composition of the Force

The deployment of UN troops to southern Lebanon was simplified by the presence of other UN missions in the Middle East. Military observers from UNTSO were transferred to southern Lebanon, as were an Iranian and a Swedish rifle company from UNDOF and UNEF II, respectively, after the UN obtained permission from the governments involved. Canadian and Swedish logistics and signals units from UNEF II were also reassigned to southern Lebanon until they were replaced by the more permanent force.

On the recommendation of the Secretary General, the size of the force was increased from 4,000 to 6,000 by Resolution 427 of May 3, 1978. By September 13, eight countries had contributed contingents. Fiji, France, Iran, Nepal, Nigeria, Norway, and Senegal each provided infantry battalions of about 600 troops each; Canada, France, and Norway also provided logistics units, collectively creating a force of 5,931. The inclusion of France as one of UNIFIL's troop-contributing states was an exception to the principle of the nonparticipation of Permanent Members of the Security Council (the only other case before 1978 was British participation in the United Nations Force in Cyprus).

In February 1982, on the recommendation of the Secretary General, UNIFIL's total troop ceiling was raised to about 7,000. By mid-August, two months after the Israeli invasion, its total strength peaked at 6,975. France redeployed 482 troops assigned to UNIFIL to Beirut in September 1982 to participate in the non-UN Multinational Force. These troops returned to southern Lebanon in February 1984.[9]

As of July 1991, nine countries provide contingents to UNIFIL, making up a force with a total strength of 5,848.

Command Structure, Communications, Logistics, and Administration

In accord with UN practice, the chain of command for UNIFIL runs from the UN Secretary General, through the Office of Peacekeeping Operations, to the Force Commander.[10] While UNIFIL HQ at Naqoura is responsible for the coordination and integration of Force activities, national contingents retain considerable autonomy. The interpretation of UNIFIL's standard operating procedures varies with the temperament and dispositions of the national units and the nature of their respective areas of operations.[11]

Naqoura Headquarters. The selection of Naqoura as the site of UNIFIL Headquarters raised serious security considerations and restricted UN movement as it was completely surrounded by the Christian enclave controlled by Major Haddad on the west coast south of Tyre. Initially, an informal agreement regulating UNIFIL's movement was reached with Haddad's DFF whereby UNIFIL troops would be given free access on the main roads in its enclave five days per week to facilitate the rotation of personnel and resupply, and UNIFIL helicopters could use the enclave's airspace with prior approval. However, Haddad could restrict UNIFIL's freedom of movement at will.

Although there were two alternative Headquarters locations, one in Tyre and another, more suitable location at the Zaharani refinery south of Sidon, both were rejected, the former on the grounds that it was in territory occupied by the PLO and the latter on the grounds that its location was partially controlled by the Syrians. Moreover, despite the intervention of the UN Secretary General and Lebanese President Sarkis, the Syrians refused to leave. The UN opted for Naqoura, where UNTSO observers of the Israel-Lebanon Mixed Armistice Commission were already established and had communication links to Jerusalem.

The imprudence of this choice was manifest when, on April 19, 1979, Haddad ordered the shelling of all UNIFIL areas as the Lebanese Army attempted to push into inside the DDF's enclave. This attack resulted in damage to buildings and helicopters; six Irish soldiers and two Dutch officers were injured. This incident not only exposed Naqoura's vulnerability to Haddad's impulsiveness, it reaffirmed the confusion at UNIFIL HQ.

This vulnerability continues to impair the Force's ability to function as an integrated unit. The Norwegian battalion, for example, has been located in Israeli-controlled territory since 1982 and has had great difficulty communicating with Force Headquarters. Partly as a result, Norbatt has become rather independent in its actions. Other battalions also developed characteristic approaches to dealing with the various armed elements in the early days of the operation before UNIFIL Headquarters was in effective contact with its own operational units. These often-inconsistent policies continued into the mid-1980s, a situation made worse, suggests Mackinlay, by the evident lack of mission-wide standard operating procedures on how to deal with armed confrontations.[12]

System of Rotations. With the exception of Fijibatt and Finbatt, battalion contingents are rotated at six-month intervals.[13] That is, once troops have reached a stage where they can be effective, the continuity and consistency of field operations are disrupted. When troops are rotated, the initial phase is critical. This is the period often accompanied by increased violence, when local militias try to challenge the incoming troops and watch to see who blinks. While there are exceptions, units where rotation is not staggered tend to perform less effectively in this initial period.

Training and Equipment. Differences in training among the national contingents have affected the integration of the Force. Most contributors send regular infantry battalions without formal training in peacekeeping. The Norwegians and Finns do train their battalions for UN service. Sweden also provides training, but its people are all volunteers in units specially raised for peacekeeping. France provided well-trained soldiers and officers who were more inclined to engage local militias agressively and to define various groups, in effect, as the enemy. They suffered higher than average casualties in return.[14]

Differences in equipment also contribute to the non-uniform performance of the national contingents. Contingents from poor countries may bring with them only personal weapons and uniforms. The Nepalese contingent arrived in 1978 without sleeping bags or vehicles. The vehicles were provided by West Germany and the United States, as were five-hour driving lessons. At the other end of the economic spectrum, Sweden has its own special communication system enabling it to locate all of its people in the country and has experimented with moving-target-indicator ground surveillance radars. The UN has introduced limited quantities of night vision devices into UNIFIL, a capability that is sorely needed.

The Force's equipment and the kind of national units provided were not always appropriate for the task. Peacekeeping forces such as UNIFIL do not possess heavy mortars and artilley, but more precise weapons can enhance a unit's credibility. For example, when the Dutch contingent emplaced TOWs (wire-guided anti-tank missiles), all incursions in their sector ceased.[15]

Field Operations

The infantry companies initially seconded from UNDOF were deployed at the Akiya Bridge in the central sector on March 24, 1978. The Swedish contingents from UNEF occupied the Khardala bridge and the environs of Ibil as-Saqy in the eastern sector on the same day. The French contingent arrived on March 23 and the Norwegian contingent on March 25. Initially, the French battalion was to be deployed in the Tyre pocket and at Kasmiya bridge. However, the PLO was unyielding, and it became quickly obvious that UNIFIL would have to confront the PLO militarily if it was to assume these forward positions. Meanwhile, the Arab states expressed solidarity with the Palestinian position. Given the UN's emphasis on the nonuse of force (and UNIFIL's light armament), the Secretary General could not exercise any military leverage to bring about a change in the PLO's position. Under these circumstances, the Secretary General decided to exclude the Tyre pocket and Kasmiya bridge from UNIFIL's area of operations. The French established headquarters outside of the Tyre pocket, manned checkpoints, and conducted patrols on the coastal road from Zaharani to Tyre.[16] The Norwegian battalion was deployed in the northeastern sector, replacing the Swedes. By deploying professional and well-trained forces in these two sensitive sectors, the UN hoped to mitigate Palestinian infiltration into UNIFIL's area of operations. The Tyre pocket was the principal infiltration route of the PLO from the western sector. The northeastern sector, in addition to providing a main infiltration route, also was the site of large PLO base camps.

IDF Withdrawal. The first IDF withdrawal from southern Lebanon was completed on April 11, 1978, when the northeastern sector and part of the eastern sector were transferred to UNIFIL. The second IDF withdrawal from the area southeast of the Litani River followed on April 14. The third withdrawal on April 30 from the western and eastern areas gave control of the area to the Senegalese battalion. On the same day, the Nepalese battalion assumed its position at Ett Taibe and the surrounding area as the IDF withdrew. By April 30, UNIFIL controlled an area of about 650 square kilometers, or about 45 percent of the total area occupied by the IDF.[17]

The deployment of UNIFIL battalions was as much a matter of coincidence as design. The Senegalese battalion assumed responsibility in the western and eastern areas because it had arrived as the IDF withdrew from those areas. Had its arrival been delayed, control of the area might have been lost to any of a number of Lebanese militias.[18]

On June 13, 1978 the IDF withdrew from its remaining positions in southern Lebanon. However, rather than handing over the final areas to UNIFIL as it had in April, the IDF transferred them to the command of Majors Saad Haddad and Sami Chidiak of the DFF. As a result, UNIFIL was forced to negotiate with the DFF to seek control of an area which constituted about 30 percent of its expected area of operation.

A year after UNIFIL's deployment, two incidents reinforced local perceptions of UNIFIL's weakness. First, while General Erskine was on leave in Accra in April 1979, UNIFIL headquarters at Naqoura was shelled. He only learned of events at Naqoura after the third day of shelling, and he only returned to South Lebanon upon the urging of a colleague. As Force Commander, Erskine should have been apprised of what was happening on the ground at all times. That he was not indicates serious failings in communications.[19]

Second, the shooting of a DFF soldier during the April 1979 DFF shelling of Ghanbatt prompted Major Haddad, with the implicit support of the IDF's General Ben Gal, to demand that UNIFIL pay about $8,000 in compensation to the soldier's family. In the absence of Force Commander Erskine, acting Force Commander Brigadier Martin Vadset refused the request for compensation, denying that the soldier had been deliberately shot. The situation came to a head when three Dutch soldiers were abducted on May 9. At the request of Major Haddad, Erskine met with him at Metulla, the headquarters for IDF liaison officers attached to Haddad. Upon entering the room, Erskine was assaulted by a crowd of Lebanese, whom Haddad ostensibly attempted to pacify. After the room was cleared and order reestablished, Haddad agreed to release the Dutch soldiers if compensation was made. Erskine yielded to the conditions and departed.[20]

The import of these events may have been lost at the time, but they reinforced the tone already set wherein the DFF, the IDF, and the Palestinians could obstruct many of UNIFIL's operations with virtual impunity. The Force's vulnerability to external obstruction and its capitulation to Haddad's demands compromised its authority and credibility.

Deployment of the Lebanese Army South. In April 1979, DFF forces obstructed the deployment of the Lebanese army to the south. A Lebanese battalion of 500 men was deployed in the UNIFIL area. Despite DFF shelling of UNIFIL positions, including its headquarters at Naqoura, between April 15 and 18, the Lebanese army established a headquarters at Arzun in the Nigerian sector. This was the second time the DFF had tried to prevent the Lebanese army from deploying its forces in the south. On July 31, 1978, the army dispatched a task force of about 700 men to Tibnin. It was to travel through the Bekaa Valley, past Kaoukaba and Marjayoun, the headquarters of the DFF. Haddad ordered his troops to fire on the task force when it reached Kaoukaba, provoking its withdrawal. At that time, the Secretary General approached the Israeli government for assistance, but the Israelis maintained that this was purely an internal Lebanese affair.

The IDF also carried out searches for armed Palestinian elements inside UNIFIL's area, often leading to UNIFIL-IDF confrontations.

After June 1980, Israeli violations of Lebanon's waters and air-space increased. In late 1980, the IDF continued its effort to improve access to the area from Israel by laying asphalt roads and dirt tracks. The IDF also laid minefields, established observation posts, and manned checkpoints.

Most clashes between the IDF and the PLO took place outside UNIFIL's perimeter and, as a result, the Force's efforts had to be restricted to arranging cease-fires and to bringing more serious incidents to the attention of the Security Council. IDF-DFF clashes with the PLO in July 1981 resulted in six dead and 59 wounded. On July 17, 1981, the President of the UN Security Council issued an appeal to all parties to observe a cease-fire. Four days later, the Council adopted Resolution 490 calling for an immediate end to all hostilities and the reinstitution of Lebanon's sovereignty, territorial integrity, and independence.

Diplomatic efforts in bringing about a cease-fire were not re-stricted to the UN Security Council. Philip Habib, the personal representative of the US President, mediated a cease-fire ar-rangement that took effect on July 24, 1981. Both the Israelis and the PLO gave assurances they would observe the cease-fire, which held until April 1982. However, infiltrations into UNIFIL areas by the PLO and Lebanese militias continued, as did DFF harassment. The DFF attempted to establish a position near At Tiri in the Irishbatt sector.

In this period, the Shi'a militia, Amal, emerged. The Shi'a comprised the least developed community in Lebanon. During the 1970s, they awoke from political quiescence to press their claim to a share of power. Their spiritual leader, Imam Musa al Sadr, helped articulate a new political and social consciousness. Israeli retaliation against the PLO in the south promoted an exodus of Shi'a to Beirut, where they lived largely in shantytowns at the perimeter of the capital. As a result, they felt a great deal of resentment against the Palestinians, so that when the Israelis invaded in 1982, they were received by Shi'a villagers more as saviors than as villains.

Israeli Invasion, June 1982–1985. Early on June 6, 1982, UNIFIL Force Commander Lieutenant General William Callaghan was informed by IDF Chief of Staff Rafael Eitan of Israel's inten-tions to launch its second invasion into Lebanon (Operation Peace for Galilee). In the preceding months there had been attacks on Israeli diplomats abroad and an escalation of Israeli retaliatory air attacks against PLO targets in Lebanon. On June 5, the

Security Council adopted Resolution 508, charging all parties to discontinue armed military activities in Lebanon no later that 0600 hours local time on June 6. Shortly after the cease-fire deadline expired, Israeli forces invaded Lebanon.

Force Commander Callaghan issued orders to all UNIFIL troops to block the advancing IDF, adopt defensive measures, and remain in position unless their safety was "seriously imperilled."[21] UNIFIL units were more an inconvenience than a serious obstacle to the advancing forces, however. The description offered by Israeli military correspondents Schiff and Ya'ari virtually caricatures the Force:

> The UN peacekeeping troops appeared to be stunned by the number of tanks rumbling toward them in two columns. They made no attempt to stop the armor; on the contrary, after regaining their wits some of the UN soldiers began to wave amiably, and one soldier even flashed a V with his fingers. The tank crews assumed that such goodwill was motivated more by an instinct for self-preservation than true support for their cause. The UNIFIL troops had no sane choice but to stand aside. Their commanders had ordered them not to oppose the Israeli forces, and although some dutifully tried to keep tally of the number of vehicles passing by their positions, they soon grew tired of counting. Yet despite their studied neutrality, not all the peacekeepers emerged unscathed. Soon after the Israelis had crossed the frontier, a UN jeep was caught in the cross-fire between the Israelis and Palestinians and all four of its passengers were injured.[22]

Israel's Partial Withdrawal and the Creation of a "Security Zone." The IDF withdrew from the environs of Beirut in September 1983 and began a further withdrawal from Lebanon on February 16, 1985, starting with the Sidon area. The redeployment was accompanied by an escalation in Shi'a-IDF confrontations, which increasingly took place in UNIFIL's area of operations. UNIFIL could neither frustrate Shi'a resistance nor deter IDF counteraction.

A further phase of Israel's withdrawal followed in March and April 1985. Despite efforts by the Secretary General and the Lebanese government, the Israeli government refused to withdraw completely from Lebanese territory. Israel continued to hold positions in southern Lebanon, creating a "security zone" controlled by the IDF and the SLA.

Since 1986, UNIFIL has divided its area of deployment into four parts: the northwestern area; the central area; the Israeli controled area (ICA); and the Norbatt sector, separated from the other deployment areas and, since 1982, located entirely within the ICA.

The northwestern area surrounding Tyre includes about half of Ghanbatt. Given the volume of traffic in this area, it is impractical to conduct a check on all vehicles. The central area borders the northwestern sector and the ICA, and includes Fijibatt, Nepbatt, the western part of Finbatt and the northern half of Irishbatt. Located within the ICA are the eastern half of Finbatt and southern part of Irishbatt. These battalions maintain observation posts to report and verify incidents and, where permitted, they conduct patrols and block incursions into villages under UNIFIL protection, thereby giving the local population a degree of security. The movement of Norbatt is the most restricted among the national contingents as a result of its location completely within the ICA.

As of 1991, Israel continued to control areas in southern Lebanon held by the SLA and the IDF. Despite the Israeli government's assertions that it has no desires to annex Lebanese territory, road construction has continued, making areas more accessible, and it has strengthened its civilian administration in local towns and villages.

ASSESSMENT

UNIFIL can be judged on two levels, as a peacekeeping force and as a humanitarian organization. On the first level, its record is dismal. But even here, judgment must be qualified.

First, its mandate was impracticable from the start. In entrusting the force with restoring the authority of the Lebanese government, the Security Council did not give adequate consideration to the fact that the government had lost all effective authority. The Security Council, in effect, called for UNIFIL to raise a Lazarus. Second, the consent of all local parties, particularly Israel, was not assured prior to deployment.

In order for UNIFIL to act as a buffer between Lebanese and Israeli forces, the consent of all parties was required. The Israelis felt the United States had pressured the UN Security Council to adopt its draft proposal as Resolution 425 without adequately considering Israel's national security interests. From the beginning, they were not prepared to cooperate fully with UNIFIL, being skeptical about the Force's ability to contain PLO incursions in its area of operations. As Force Commander Erskine wrote, "It became clear that the concept of the so-called Christian enclave

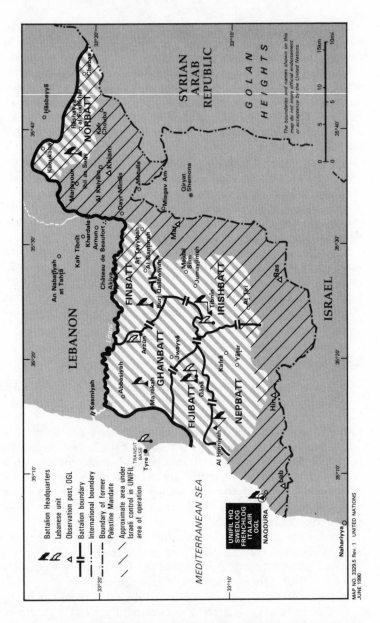

**Figure 11.1. United Nations Interim Force in Lebanon,
Deployment as of June 1990**

(security zone) was the strategic basis for the invasion of South Lebanon on 14-15 March [1978]. Little did the Security Council, meeting on 19 March to decide the establishment of UNIFIL, realize that Israel was in South Lebanon to stay."[23] And as the Secretary General reported in January 1991,

> The Israeli authorities continue to state that they have no territorial ambitions in Lebanon, that the "security zone" is a temporary arrangement necessitated by the security of northern Israel so long as the Lebanese Government is not able to exercise effective authority and prevent its territory from being used to launch attacks against Israel. They do not consider that UNIFIL, as a peacekeeping force, can assume this responsibility. They continue to build up DFF and to improve their ability to reinforce IDF's strength inside Lebanon quickly. A consequence of this policy is that the Israeli-controlled area is becoming increasingly separated from the rest of Lebanon.[24]

From the start, the Palestinians considered the Israeli invasion a permanent arrangement.[25] Several factions of the Palestinian resistance impaired UNIFIL's ability to contain armed hostilities. By 1981, the number of Palestinian "armed elements" within UNIFIL's territory was estimated at 450, up from about 140 during the initial deployment of the Force.

Apart from IDF/DFF harassment and PLO infiltration into its area of operations, UNIFIL has had to operate alongside other armed elements, both Lebanese and non-Lebanese, such as the militias of Amal and Hezballah. The Force's freedom of movement was, and remains, dependent on its relations with all these groups operating in southern Lebanon. Since the "Lebanese government" had neither the support of its armed forces nor the support of the majority of Lebanese from the beginning of the civil war in 1975 through 1990, it could not control the actions of the militias, guarantee the freedom of movement of the UN force, or ensure its safe conduct. This left UNIFIL to foster independent relations with each of the parties operating in southern Lebanon, some of whom were intransigent.

Although UNIFIL failed to execute its original mandate, its interim tasks of providing humanitarian support and protecting the local population helped to restore the sense of security and physical safety of the civilian population and to strengthen the local economy in the UN's area of operations. The practical significance of these minor successes for the daily lives of Lebanese should not be devalued. About 250,000-300,000 people, depending on the degree of violence north of the Litani River, are estimated to live in UNIFIL-controlled areas. The Force provides water, food, fuel, electricity, and medicine; it escorts farmers and provides equipment or services to schools; and UNIFIL's hospital at Naqoura treats approximately 3,000 civilian patients per month.[26] This contribution should be assessed in light of the otherwise demoralized state of Lebanon's public life since 1975.

CONCLUSION

The politics of Lebanon are changing rapidly, but in general there are four potential futures for UNIFIL: (1) withdrawal without replacement; (2) replacement with a non-UN force; (3) redefinition of the mandate by dropping "restoration of Lebanon's sovereignty and territorial integrity"; and (4) maintaining the status quo.

Withdrawal without Replacement

After 14 years in southern Lebanon, there are both psychological and political components to UNIFIL's presence. On the psychological level, the local population considers UNIFIL essential to its security and physical safety. This being the case, a precipitate UNIFIL withdrawal could stimulate an exodus from southern Lebanon to areas north of the Litani River now under government control. Such a displacement of population could destabilize the country's new political consensus. On a political level, withdrawal has the potential to create a power vacuum and to cause the local militias—Hezballah, Amal, the SLA—and the IDF to move forcibly to increase the areas of control in the south. On the other hand, the presence of UNIFIL has not dissuaded Israel from hot pursuit of hostile militias within and beyond UN-controlled areas of Lebanon, and some might argue that removing this permeable UN presence would merely leave the local parties to do what they do anyway, while saving the hard-pressed United Nations more than $100 million a year. Humanitarian aid, in this view, is best left to humanitarian agencies.

A Non-UN Force in the South

With the end of the Cold War and the redefinition of NATO's role in international security, some have suggested that UNIFIL should be reconfigured with NATO and former Warsaw Pact troops. A more credible military force, in this view, could deter infiltrations across the Lebanese-Israeli border and expedite a withdrawal of other foreign (Syrian and Israeli) troops from Lebanon.[27]

One of the first problems likely to be encountered in replacing UNIFIL with a non-UN force is a scarcity of volunteers. While France may be prepared to assume some role, most Western nations would probably prefer not to shoulder such responsibility. As for the United States, it has still not recovered from the "Lebanon syndrome" induced by the bombing of the Marine compound at Beirut airport in October 1983. The record of US involvement in Lebanon inspires confusion and regret—not the kind of emotions a US President can utilize to secure public support. The urgency with which President Bush called back US troops from the Gulf War in 1991 suggests that US leaders believe there is low public tolerance for an extended US ground presence in the region.

Another problem in proposing a peacekeeping force of NATO troops is the unresolved debate on NATO's role in the new era. Historically, NATO deployment has been premised on East-West security issues. The organization's involvement in the 1991 Gulf War was defended on the grounds of ensuring the security of a NATO member (Turkey). It has not been able to agree on the deployment of forces much closer to home, in Yugoslavia. A peacekeeping force for Lebanon would be even farther afield, politically as well as geographically.

Another alternative might be a bilateral US-Russian force with Lebanese, Israeli and Syrian approval. However, improved Russo-Israeli relations have not advanced sufficiently that Tel Aviv would have enough confidence to entrust its security to such a joint enterprise. Although Syria's relations with Washington have also improved since its support of the coalition during the 1991 Gulf War, it prefers a UN force in the region.

Redefinition of Mandate

A reinterpretation of UNIFIL's mandate and functions has often been suggested. One variant pressed by the Lebanese government would be to strengthen the Force and give it greater enforcement powers. To date, the United Nations has rejected such a rein-terpretation. The Organization has also rejected reinterpreting UNIFIL's mandate to recognize formally the Force's interim humanitarian activities and to rescind its original tasks of confirming the withdrawal of Israeli forces and assist the government of Lebanon to restore its effective authority. However, relatively sanguine political developments in Lebanon would seem to support the preservation of the status quo as Lebanon works its way back to political stability.

Maintaining the Status Quo

The 1989 Ta'if agreement provides the most optimistic signs for the future implementation of UN Security Council Resolution 425. The restoration of the government's authority remains attendant on political reform, on disarming and rehabilitating Lebanon's militias, and on securing control over *all* Lebanese territory. The latter is contingent on arriving at a workable consensus among the forces now operating in the south: the PLO, the IDF, the SLA, and such Lebanese militias resisting Israeli occupation as the pro-Iranian Hezballah and the Shi'a Amal movement. But, after fourteen years, the political and military conditions in Lebanon may finally be working in concert with UNIFIL.

As Elie Salem, former Lebanese Deputy Prime Minister and Foreign Affairs Minister said,

> The liberation of the South is the key to peace in Lebanon, for all the problems that triggered the Lebanese war converged in the South. The South has become the microcosm of the Great Historical Drama amongst Jews, Christians, and Muslims, a drama which has been played for over a century in a passionate political context and in a spirit alien to the deepest messages of these three monotheistic religions.[28]

In order to convince Israel that it should remove its presence from the south, the Lebanese government will first have to provide security guarantees for Israel's northern border. An armed Palestinian presence and Israel's security interests are used to justify its de facto occupation of southern Lebanon. The Lebanese army's successful disarming of the PLO would delegitimize Israel's rationale. As for the SLA, it would cease to exist without Israeli financing, equipment, and training. Whether Israel would press for some role in the government for the SLA's General Antoine Lahd is uncertain.[29]

Israel will also demand guarantees of Syrian disengagement from Lebanon. Both the Ta'if agreement, which describes Lebanon's relations with Syria as "distinctive," and the bilateral treaty of brotherliness, cooperation, and coordination signed by Syria and Lebanon on May 22, 1991, reinforce the Israeli claim that Damascus and not Beirut is in control of Lebanon.

The best-case scenario would include an agreement between the parties and the Lebanese government eventually leading to a PLO, Syrian, and Israeli military disengagement from Lebanon. The Lebanese government would be the guarantor of Israel's northern border, and thereby terminate the utility of the SLA.

History suggests, however, that best-case scenarios are unlikely to materialize in Lebanon. If one of the above elements failed to materialize, the entire process of restoring government authority in the South, as well as the country's territorial integrity and sovereignty, could be jeapordized.

UNIFIL has a role to play in reducing the likelihood of hostilities during the period of adjustment. First, it could continue to provide humanitarian assistance to the civilian population. Second, it could provide low-level military mediation to keep implementation of disputes localized; supervise the disarming of militias; and oversee the withdrawal of foreign forces. All of these are tasks that the UN has performed successfully elsewhere in recent years.

Many years of war have reinforced one lesson that was only recently (and reluctantly) accepted with the Ta'if Agreement in 1989—that no single party could impose its will in Lebanon.[30] Syria could not defeat the PLO in 1976 or the Phalange in 1978. The Israelis could not crush the PLO in either 1978 or 1982. Phalangist President-elect Bashir Gemayel and his successor and brother Amin could not restore Maronite hegemony in 1982, even with the endorsement of Israeli prime minister Menachem Begin, and General Michel Aoun failed in his bid to expel the Syrians from Lebanon in 1989–90. History since 1975 has demonstrated that there is no place for the military combatant in Lebanese politics. The reluctant acceptance of this fact by the local and regional parties may eventually allow UNIFIL to act as the Security Council originally intended, as a peacekeeper rather than a humanitarian agency.

Notes

1. Alan James, "Painful Peacekeeping: the United Nations in Lebanon: 1978–82," *International Journal* (October 1983): 630.

2. Itmar Rabinovitch, *The War for Lebanon: 1970–1985* (Ithaca: Cornell University Press, 1985), 44.

3. Kamal Salibi, *House of Many Mansions* (Berkeley and Los Angeles: University of California Press, 1988), 54.

4. Patrick Seale, *Asad of Syria: The Struggle for the Middle East* (London: I.B. Tauris, 1988), 276.

5. Augustus Richard Norton, "Lebanon After Ta'if: Is the Civil War Over?" *The Middle East Journal* 45 (Summer 1991): 471.

6. K. Skjelsbaek and A. McDermott, eds., "Introduction," in *A Thankless Task: The Role of* UNIFIL *in Southern Lebanon*, NUPI Report 123 (Oslo, Norway: Norwegian Institute of International Affairs, December 1988), 10.

7. United Nations Document S/22129/Add. 1, January 23, 1991.

8. United Nations Documents S/22129, 7, and *Status of Contributions as at 31 December 1991*, ST/ADM/SER.B/364, January 8, 1992, 15.

9. For a discussion of the Multinational Force in Beirut, see Mona Ghali, *Multinational Forces: Non-UN Peacekeeping in the Middle East*, Occasional Paper No. 12 (Washington, D.C.: The Henry L. Stimson Center, October 1992).

10. Until February 1992, Peacekeeping Operations was called the Office of Special Political Affairs.

11. Marianne Heiberg has differentiated between passive and aggressive battalions. The latter category include Fijibatt and Norbatt, who pursue a policy contrary to official norms in preventing by all means available the establishment of non-UNIFIL forces in their areas of operation. In contrast, the IDF, until its withdrawal from Lebanon in 1985, maintained positions in the area of operations "controlled" by Irishbatt, classified by Heiberg as a passive battalion. See Marianne Heiberg, "Observations on UN Peace Keeping in Lebanon," NUPI Note 305 (Oslo, Norway: Norwegian Institute of International Affairs, September 1984), 34.

12. John Mackinlay, *The Peacekeepers: Peacekeeping Operations at the Arab-Israeli Interface* (London: Unwin Hyman, 1989), 59, 65.

13. In Fijibatt the rotation period for individuals is one year, with half rotated in June, and the remainder in November. Since Fiji's three battalions rotate service in Lebanon, about half of the troops stationed have had at least six months of prior experience. Finbatt's period of rotation is one year, but only one-third of the troops are changed at a time, so that the two-thirds who remain are familiar with operations.

14. Although contributors receive periodic reimbursements from the United Nations for their Lebanon operations, they receive no reimbursement for training.

15. Interview 12, October 12, 1990.

16. *The Blue Helmets: A Review of United Nations Peacekeeping*, 2nd ed. (New York: United Nations Department of Public Information, 1990), 120.

17. *The Blue Helmets*, 121.

18. Lieutenant General Emmanuel Erskine, *Mission with* UNIFIL (New York: St. Martin's Press, 1989), 27.

19. Erskine, *Mission with* UNIFIL, 66.

20. Erskine, *Mission with* UNIFIL, 68-69.

21. *The Blue Helmets*, 142.

22. Ze'ev Schiff & Ehud Ya'ari, *Israel's Lebanon War* (New York: Simon & Shuster, 1984), 119-120.

23. Erskine, *Mission with* UNIFIL, 25.

24. United Nations Document S/22129, January 23, 1991, 8.

25. Erskine, *Mission with* UNIFIL, 26.

26. United Nations Document S/22129, 6.

27. Interview 11, October 12, 1990.

28. Elie A. Salem. Paper presented to the American Task Force on Lebanon at the Conference on Lebanon, Washington, D.C., June 27-30, 1991, 11.

29. In a discussion between Israeli Prime Minister Menachem Begin and Lebanese President Bashir Gemayel in 1982, in which the latter recognized Israel's permanent interests in a secure northern border, Gemayel offered to deploy the Lebanese Forces in the south to serve as a buffer. Begin asked about Major Haddad, adding "We will not abandon our allies. Haddad should be given a command position in the new hierarchy—commander of the southern region, for example, if it proves impossible to appoint him chief of staff or commander of the army" (Schiff & Ya'ari, *Israel's Lebanon War*, 235).

30. According to the Ta'if Agreement, Syria will redeploy its troops to the Bekaa Valley within two years after the formation of a government of national reconciliation and the enactment of political reforms—a deadline now reported as September 1992—after which "an agreement will be signed defining the size of the Syrian forces and the duration of their presence in these areas" (*Middle East Economic Survey* [June 3, 1991]: C3).

12 United Nations Yemen Observation Mission

by Karl Th. Birgisson

In the civil war in Yemen (1962–70), the forces of Arab nationalism and traditionalism clashed, both locally, in the form of Republican and Royalist factions, and regionally, in the form of Egyptian support for the former and Saudi Arabian support for the latter. US-inspired mediation efforts produced a disengagement agreement less than one year into the conflict. The agreement was premature, lacking key elements of local support. In addition, the United Nations Yemen Observation Mission (UN-YOM) sent to monitor Saudi and Egyptian compliance with the accord was short on the operational basics—personnel, equipment, and funding—that every peacekeeping mission requires. UNYOM floundered for 14 months under very adverse conditions and was withdrawn. The civil war continued for six more years, eventually winding down to a compromise settlement among the local parties themselves.

ORIGINS

The Republic of Yemen lies at the southwestern tip of the Arabian Peninsula at the mouth of the Red Sea. Until 1990, it was two separate political entities. Northern Yemen, the subject of this chapter, was ruled for a thousand years by the Zeidi Imams, of the Shi'a sect of Islam. The Zeidis's power base lay in the tribes of the central and northern highlands, an isolating topography of 3,000-meter mountains and fertile valleys that sustained an atomized, feudal, warlike society that had changed very little since the 10th century. The southern reaches of the Zeidis's realm were populated by the Shaffeis, who were Sunni Muslims. The Ottoman Empire extended its influence over both in the 16th and 17th centuries, and again from the mid-19th century until its breakup after World War I, ruling through the Zeidis.[1]

Although the Zeidi Imams did their best to keep out foreign influences, Imam Yahya (1904–48) sought to modernize his military after losing a border war with Saudi Arabia in 1934 and to that end sent his Army officers to train in Iraq and Egypt. Many Yemenis also worked in the Aden Proctectorate, observing alternatives to Yemen's existing political order. Dissatisfaction culminated in the Imam's assassination in 1948, but his son, Ahmed, managed to restore the old order. Following an abortive coup attempt seven years later, he appointed his son, Crown Prince Mohammed al Badr, head of government. Al Badr, extensively travelled in the West as well as in the Arab world, invited Egyptian doctors, teachers, and military advisors into Yemen. Uninvited but impossible to keep out was Radio Cairo, which preached secular, pan-Arab nationalism to all within range of its signal. Although the regime had long banned possession of radios, battery-powered transistor technology made the ban impossible to enforce by the late 1950s, and made Yemen's isolation increasingly difficult to sustain.[2]

By the time Ahmed died (of natural causes) on September 19, 1962, the detribalized and urbanized bits of his kingdom, and those army officers schooled on the outside or trained by the Egyptians, were ready to jettison feudalism. Apparently so was the new Imam, al Badr, but reform from above was cut short when, barely a week into his reign, army tanks shelled the palace in Sana'a with Badr inside. He managed to evade his assassins, however, and fled north to form the core of Zeidi tribal resistance to the newly proclaimed Yemen Arab Republic (YAR).[3]

Royalist (to use a convenient shorthand) and Republican factions received immediate support from Saudi Arabia and Egypt, respectively, which threatened escalation of the conflict beyond Yemen's borders.[4] The Saudis sent arms to the Royalists across Yemen's porous northern border, and the Egyptians sent troops and aircraft, supplying them through the Red Sea port of Hodeida, recently connected to Sana'a by a Chinese-built, hard-surface road. Partly because the Royalists retained the loyalty of the fiercest of Yemen's tribes, most of the Republicans' fighting was done for them (at least initially) by the Egyptian expeditionary force.

In mid-November, US President John Kennedy proposed a peace plan that entailed phased withdrawal of Egyptian forces, an end to Saudi and Jordanian support for the Royalists, a phased withdrawal of all military forces from the Saudi-Yemeni border, third-party oversight of these measures, and US recognition of the YAR. Nasser answered that Saudi aid should cease first, while the Saudis wanted restoration of the old regime. Neither was prepared for compromise. The US pulled back for the moment and recognized the YAR on December 19th.[5]

Nasser expected to rout the "reactionaries" in a few months and, indeed, during a late winter 1963 offensive, his forces pushed out from Sana'a and seized the country's few urban centers.[6] Outside mediation resumed at this high-water mark for Egyptian operations.

Initiatives toward UN Involvement

The United Nations first became involved in the Yemen conflict when the Yemeni mission in New York, still staffed by Royalists, wrote a letter to Secretary General U Thant on November 27, 1962, asking the UN to establish whether or not the September coup had been fostered in Cairo. The letter was not put on the UN agenda but was informally circulated to UN members. In early December, a delegation from the YAR showed up at the UN with credentials from the new government. The question of who really represented Yemen was taken up by the Credentials Committee, which found in favor of the new mission on December 20, and the new delegation was seated by the General Assembly the same day.[7]

Since the US's good offices had been rejected, Washington encouraged U Thant to send a UN mission to Yemen. In late February 1963, he sent Under-Secretary General for Special Political Affairs Ralph Bunche on a fact-finding trip to the region. Bunche arrived in Sana'a as the Egyptians were finishing their big offensive, noted that the YAR seemed to be in control of the country, and declared that it was within its rights to have Egyptian assistance. But because he did not speak with Imam al Badr or his representatives during the visit, Bunche was unwelcome in Saudi Arabia and was thus unable to close the diplomatic circle.[8]

While Bunche flew between Cairo and Sana'a, US Ambassador Ellsworth Bunker shuttled between Cairo and Riyadh, keeping the Secretary General informed of his activities. Bunker eventually worked out a disengagement agreement between Egypt and Saudi Arabia that bore a close resemblance to Kennedy's November proposals.[9]

Political Support

The conflict in Yemen was a contest between ancient and modern, between traditional theocratic monarchy, represented by Saudi Arabia, and the forces of secular pan-Arab nationalism led by Egypt. Seen from Washington's perspective, however, the conflict gave the Soviet Union an opportunity for further inroads into Arabia, a development that potentially threatened Western access to the Red Sea and the Suez Canal, as well as to Persian Gulf oil. A nationalist regime on the northern border of the Aden Protectorate also threatened Britain's position there, hastening the development of radical anti-colonial movements and leading Britain to slip convoys of arms and supplies to Royalist forces.[10]

When the UN-backed disengagement agreement was signed, Egypt and the Republicans controlled more than half of Yemeni territory. The Republicans were pleased enough to see fighting stop at that point, but a complete pullout of Egyptian forces would leave their still weak army vulnerable to attack by Royalist tribesmen. Imam al Badr and his loose coalition of forces were not party to the disengagement accord and had no particular reason to support it, being in a relatively weak bargaining position. Their prospects for defeating YAR forces would have been much better absent the Egyptians, but Egyptian forces withdrawn at their moment of triumph might well be reintroduced later. It was better that Cairo first learn the limits of its military power; then it would never come back.

Egypt, whose forces already had been in Yemen longer than anticipated, had an interest in shortening what might otherwise turn into a costly, long-term deployment. In fact, Nasser had pushed the Royalists back about as far as he could with his conventional military. As the Soviet Army would learn twenty years later in Afghanistan, a conventional army has difficulty coping with guerrillas based in mountain caves who refuse to give up.[11] But at the time of the disengagement agreement, Egypt appeared to have the upper hand. Moreover, Egyptian commanders assured UN officials soon after the agreement was signed that they were not about to leave the YAR vulnerable to a Royalist attack.

The Saudis, having just witnessed the rout of their Royalist allies from all of Yemen's major towns, may have been concerned that Egyptian forces might try to capture Saudi border areas long claimed by Yemen. Those areas already had been subject to periodic Egyptian air attack. The disengagement agreement would halt the northward march of Egyptian forces. On the other hand, if Egypt wasn't leaving, the Saudis were not about to squeeze off the Imam's supply line.

In short, although it looked good on paper, the disengagement agreement was dead before the ink was dry.

Being a godparent of the agreement, and having a generalized interest in political stability in the region, the United States supported both the agreement and UNYOM, though not enough to sink money into it. The United Kingdom strongly favored a UN-observed cease-fire and disengagement in north Yemen, particularly if it meant the withdrawal of Egyptian troops from Yemeni soil, and thus removal of a military threat to Aden. The Soviets did not initially favor the UN mission, but once it was clear that the YAR favored UNYOM's deployment, Moscow settled for an abstention on the Security Council's enabling resolution.[12]

MANDATE

Secretary General U Thant announced on April 29, 1963, that Yemen, Saudi Arabia, and Egypt had asked for UN assistance in carrying out their disengagement agreement in Yemen. On June 7th, he announced his intention to dispatch a small UN advance team to Yemen without further delay. The Soviet Union thereupon requested a meeting of the Security Council, which adopted Resolution 179 on June 11th, establishing UNYOM.[13]

The operation's mandate as set out in the Security Council resolution was very brief. The Council requested "the Secretary-General to establish the observation operation as defined by him." The basic definition of UNYOM's responsibilities was to be found in the disengagement agreement itself, under which Saudi Arabia agreed to cease all support for the Royalists, and Egypt agreed to withdraw all its troops from Yemeni territory. A demilitarized zone of 20 kilometers width was to be established on either side of the Saudi-Yemeni border. UN observers were to verify Egyptian withdrawals and the cessation of Saudi arms aid.[14] The Secretary General reminded the Council that,

> by the provisions of the agreement on disengagement, UNYOM's functions are limited to observing, certifying and reporting. This operation has no peace-keeping role beyond this....It bears emphasis, also, that the agreement on disengagement involves only Saudi Arabia and the United Arab Republic....UNYOM, therefore, is not concerned with Yemen's internal affairs generally, with the actions of the Government of Yemen, or with that Government's relations with other Governments and bordering territories.[15]

In short, the civil war would continue without support from Saudi Arabia and Egypt while UNYOM went about its business. [16]

The Secretary General's caveats on the limited nature of the operation are a recurrent theme in his regular reports. Over time, he realized that UNYOM was too small to carry out its original mandate and that the parties to the disengagement agreement were simply not going to live up to its terms.

FUNDING

In his report to the Security Council on May 27, 1963, U Thant estimated the total cost of the Yemen Observation Mission to be less than $1,000,000 for a mission of four months' duration. He had received oral assurances from Saudi Arabia and Egypt that they would equally share the financial burdens of the operation. In the end, this fourteen-month operation cost the two countries $1,828,042. [17]

UNYOM deployed at the time of the UN's "funding crisis," caused largely by the refusal of the Soviet Union and France to pay their share of assessments for the large peacekeeping operations in the Sinai and the Congo (see the chapters 7 and 19 on UNEF I and ONUC). U Thant, probably realizing that UNYOM would be doomed were he to ask the UN to fund it, didn't even raise the issue.

PLANNING AND IMPLEMENTATION

U Thant selected Major General Carl von Horn, Chief of Staff of UNTSO, as Chief Military Observer for UNYOM and immediately sent him on a fact-finding mission to the region. Von Horn received conflicting estimates on requirements for the mission in Riyadh and Cairo, and he subsequently conducted both ground and aerial reconnaissance of both sides of the Saudi-Yemeni border, visited Qizan, Najran, Sada, and Hodeida, and covered the 15,000 square kilometers of the proposed buffer zone. [18]

The situation in the field as UNYOM moved toward deployment remained unsettled. The Saudis complained of repeated Egyptian air raids on their territory and threatened retaliatory action. The Egyptians, on the other hand, citing Saudi "aggression" against the Yemen Arab Republic, vowed to continue assistance to the YAR until the Saudis stopped providing money, arms, and training inside Saudi Arabia to "mercenaries" destined for Yemen. The YAR, meanwhile, accused Britain of infiltrating Yemen from Aden

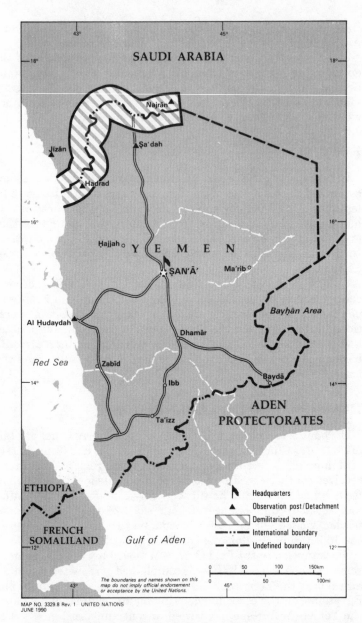

Figure 12.1. United Nations Yemen Observation Mission, Deployment as of October 1963

and attacking Yemeni forces with artillery fire and aerial bombing. The British, in return, said the actions were designed to evict Yemeni forces from South Arabian Federal territory and were measures of last resort.[19]

Size and Composition of the Force

The Secretary General had initally suggested 50 observers for UNYOM, but he revised that figure upward to about 200 after receiving von Horn's recommendation in May calling for 240. The deployed force consisted of just six observers, a Yugoslav reconnaissance unit of 114 men redeployed from UNEF I, 50 Canadians from ONUC flying two Caribou and six Otter fixed-wing aircraft, and a few H-19 helicopters. There was a small military headquarters staff based in Sana'a, and a civilian staff of 28 UN employees and 20 local recruits.[20]

The small force was spread among bases in Yemen and Saudi Arabia. Inside the YAR, the main port of Hodeida was allocated one observer and a logistics detachment, and Sada, the northernmost town, was allocated one section of the Yugoslav company. At Harad, on the Yemeni side of the demilitarized zone, there were two observers and one platoon of the Yugoslav company. At Jizan, Saudi Arabia, near the demilitarized zone, there were two observers and one detachment of the Canadian force with two Otter aircraft. At Najran, on Saudi territory within the zone, there were roughly two platoons of the Yugoslav company, four observers, and a detachment of Canadians with a pair of Otters. There were no UN detachments along the country's eastern or southern borders.[21]

Field Operations

When UNYOM first deployed, it was allowed to contact the parties to the disengagement agreement (the Saudis and Egyptians) and the government, but not the Royalists. This made some legal sense, but it meant that UNYOM could not accept complaints from the Royalist side and thus diminished the sense of impartiality that successful UN peacekeeping missions need to maintain. These orders were countermanded within a month of deployment, however, after allegations of Egyptian use of poison gas reached the outside world.[22]

The location of UNYOM's observation posts inside Yemen made it likely that any Egyptian troops on the move would be observed. They followed the roads and the roads were few, and Hodeida was the only one useful port for embarking and debarking troops. The situation on the Saudi border was very different, however. The border ran for 650 kilometers through very rugged territory, much of which was not clearly demarcated. Physical conditions were very harsh, and supplies and facilities were meagre given the operation's threadbare funding situation. The two observation posts inside the demilitarized zone and the available aerial reconnaissance were inadequate to watch traffic across the border, especially since the UN's aircraft were not equipped for night observation. Moreover, the helicopters borrowed from ONUC did not operate satisfactorily at the high altitudes required in the mountainous north and were quickly taken out of service. Ground observers were periodically stationed at checkpoints "for 40 hours or more" to maintain surveillance through the night, but the numerous tracks crossing the demilitarized zone far exceeded the number of UN checkpoints. The Yugoslav reconnaissance unit was also constrained in its operations by backchannel instructions from its national government.[23]

Von Horn resigned on August 20, 1963, citing inadequate staffing and equipment and the lack of administrative support from UN headquarters, all of which were in his view crippling liabilities for the mission. He was succeeded ad interim by his second in command, Colonel Branko Pavlovic of Yugoslavia, and formally on September 12 by Lieutenant General P.S. Gyani of India, temporarily detailed from his post as commander of UNEF. On November 4, 1963, UN civilian official Pier Spinelli was given a joint appointment as Special Representative and head of UNYOM, and Gyani returned to UNEF.[24]

About the same time, the Yugoslav company began a gradual withdrawal and the number of Canadian Otters was reduced. The aerial inspection operation was replaced by 25 military observers from Denmark, Ghana, India, Italy, the Netherlands, Norway, Pakistan, Sweden, and Yugoslavia. When informal UN consultations with the two governments indicated that the original disengagement agreement would not be kept and that a new one was not in sight, the Secretary General concluded that the time had come to terminate the mission. The mission ended on September 4, 1964, at which time the Royalists were as strong as ever and Egyptian troop presence in Yemen was estimated at 40,000 and growing.[25]

ASSESSMENT AND CONCLUSIONS

UNYOM lacked nearly all the components of successful peacekeeping: local consent and support; active Great Power support; adequate resources; and a feasible mandate. Each can be summarized briefly.

Viewed from a political-military level, the disengagement agreement and UNYOM were both premature. The United States pushed for an agreement when conditions were not ripe for one. The field situation was not yet seen as stalemated by the local parties, and an unexhausted opposition remained ready to fight; moreover, their regional backers were testing one another's political will and respective claims to leadership in the Arab world, and neither was willing as yet to compromise those claims. Each was willing to earn points with the US by signing the disengagement accord but very likely assumed that nonfeasance by the other party would assure its rapid demise and relieve them of compliance obligations.

The United States, having launched the agreement and pressed for a UN force, did not follow through with the sort of material support that was forthcoming (and crucial) for contemporary operations in the Sinai and the Congo. The improving state of US-Soviet relations in mid-1963 (negotiation of the partial nuclear test ban treaty, for example) may have contributed to a more relaxed US approach to the question of political instability (and thus opportunities for Soviet influence) in Yemen.

The lack of resources severely constrained UNYOM's operations, but very different conceptions of UNYOM's real purpose at UN Headquarters in New York and in the field led to different conclusions about what should be done. New York, extremely short of cash and insistent that UNYOM not exceed its donated budget, kept the mission on a very short leash at the administrative level. At its highest political levels, New York likely viewed the mission more as a face-saving gesture for the Secretary General than as a real effort at verification.[26] Von Horn, on the other hand, strove to make his mission operationally effective. From New York's perspective, Von Horn didn't "get it." From Von Horn's perspective, New York was hanging good men out to dry.[27]

However, with local and regional support for the disengagement agreement temporary and marginal at best, and with one very active local party not involved in it at all, there was little compliance for UNYOM to monitor. Along the Saudi border, arms flowed whenever or wherever the UN was not looking, and, with its very limited resources, it was not looking in lots of places most of the time. More observers and better technology might have helped, but without the cooperation of the Royalists and their suppliers, UNYOM's task was fundamentally impossible.[28]

Notes

1. The region to the south and east of the Zeidi kingdom, including the great deepwater port at Aden on the southern coast, fell under British control in the 18th century and remained a British protectorate until 1968. When the British withdrew, southern Yemen became a independent state until its merger with the north in 1990 (Dana Adams Schmidt, *Yemen, the Unknown War* [New York: Holt, Rinehart and Winston, 1968], 42-43).

2. Edgar O'Ballance, *The War in the Yemen* (Hamden, Conn.: Archon Books, 1971), 51, 62; Ali Abdel Rahman Rahmy, *The Egyptian Policy in the Arab World: Intervention in Yemen, 1962–67* (Washington, D.C.: University Press of America, 1983), 80; Saeed M. Badeeb, *The Saudi-Egyptian Conflict over North Yemen, 1962–1970* (Boulder, Co. and Washington, D.C.: Westview Press and the Arab-American Affairs Council, 1986), 3, 9.

3. Badeeb, *The Saudi-Egyptian Conflict over North Yemen*, 71-72, 82.

4. The United States and Soviet Union had just stepped back from the nuclear precipice of the Cuban Missile Crisis and into a period of "mini-détente," and both recognized the Republican government, reducing the Royalists to insurrectionist rebels. Still, the US felt constrained to make a tangible demonstration of support for Saudi Arabia, stationing a partial squadron of jet fighters at Jedda in the second half of 1963 (Schmidt, *Yemen, the Unknown War*, 168, 186; Badeeb, *The Saudi-Egyptian Conflict over North Yemen*, 64).

5. Badeeb, *The Saudi-Egyptian Conflict over North Yemen*, 61-62.

6. Egyptian troops began to arrive in the YAR to support the new government within days of the coup. Saudi aid to the Royalists commenced just as quickly, as evidenced by the defection of several arms-laden Saudi aircraft to Egypt in early October (Badeeb, *The Saudi-Egyptian Conflict over North Yemen*, 96, 101, 106, 147-49; O'Ballance, *The War in the Yemen*, 79, 84-85, 87). Nasser eventually characterized the Yemen intervention as "my Vietnam" (Rahmy, *Egyptian Policy in the Arab World*, 195).

7. Rosalyn Higgins, *United Nations Peacekeeping 1946-1967: Documents and Commentary, Vol. I* (London: Oxford University Press, 1970), 611-612; *The Blue Helmets: A Review of United Nations Peacekeeping*, 2nd ed. (New York: United Nations Department of Public Information, 1990), 188.

8. Badeeb, *The Saudi-Egyptian Conflict over North Yemen*, 75.

9. United Nations, *Report of the Secretary General on the terms of the disengagement in Yemen*, Security Council Document S/5298, April 29, 1963.

10. O'Ballance, *The War in the Yemen*, 127-28, 130.

11. And who cannot be intimidated by the bombing of civilians. In 1963, and more extensively in 1967, the Egyptian air force used lethal chemical agents on mountain villages. The guerrillas themselves were prone to make wholesale examples of villages caught cooperating with the Republican government (O'Ballance, *The War in the Yemen*, 106, 174; and Schmidt, *Yemen, the Unknown War*, 260 ff.

12. Alan James, *The Politics of Peace-keeping* (New York: Frederick A. Praeger, 1969), 109-10.

13. United Nations, *Report of the Secretary General on Maj. Gen. Carl Von Horn's report on exploratory talks concerning UN observers for Yemen*, Security Council Document S/5321, May 27, 1963; and *Report of the Secretary General on the organization of an observer mission for Yemen*, Security Council Document S/5325, June 7, 1963.

14. United Nations Document S/5298, April 29, 1963.

15. United Nations, *Report of the Secretary General on the functioning to date of the Yemen Observation Mission*, Security Council Document S/5412, September 4, 1963.

16. Several authors note that UNYOM's presence did seem, however, to encourage a series of tacit truces and that fighting died down for six months after signature of the disengagement agreement (Schmidt, *Yemen, the Unknown War*, 170-72; Rahmy, *Egyptian Policy in the Arab World*, 151).

The UN has operated other observer missions fairly successfully under similar conditions, monitoring Cuban withdrawal from Angola (UNAVEM I) in 1988 and Soviet withdrawal from Afghanistan (UNGOMAP) in 1989, but the Cubans and Soviets really wanted to end their commitments and wanted international certification of their departures, whereas the Egyptians, in 1963, did not.

17. United Nations Document S/5321.

18. Major General Carl von Horn, *Soldiering for Peace* (New York: David McKay Co., Inc., 1966), 316-22. The Egyptian military suggested a UN expeditionary force equivalent to their own that would be able to protect the Sana'a regime. The Saudis told von Horn that the buffer zone was an exclusively Saudi-Egyptian concern, as they did not recognize the YAR, but that they would accord the UN full freedom of movement. Beyond that they had no operational recommendations.

19. The Saudis paid a number of British and other guerrilla war experts to advise Royalist forces (Rahmy, *Egyptian Policy in the Arab World*, 152-53, 197). Letters to the Secretary General from the governments of the YAR and UK were circulated as UN Security Council Documents S/5333, June 17, 1963, and S/5336, June 21, 1963.

20. United Nations Documents S/5298, S/5321, and S/5412; von Horn, *Soldiering for Peace*, 335.

21. In reality, there was no eastern border since the terrain trailed off into the vast Empty Quarter (United Nations, *Report of the Secretary General on the functioning to date of the Yemen Observation Mission*, Security Council Document S/5447, October 28, 1963).

22. von Horn, *Soldiering for Peace*, 370-71.

23. *The Blue Helmets*, 193; von Horn, *Soldiering for Peace*, 372-73. Any order received from the UN command was first checked with Belgrade, whose first priority was preventing its troops from engaging in any risky operations. This proved quite frustrating for von Horn, but discretion probably was the better part of valor given the political and operational realities in which UNYOM operated.

24. *The Blue Helmets*, 192, 433.

25. *The Blue Helmets*, 192; James, *The Politics of Peacekeeping*, 112. Fighting continued, however. Saudi and Iranian financial support, and mercenary training of Royalist forces, had impressive results beginning in late 1964 when the Royalists started a six-month offensive, attacking mostly at night to avoid Egyptian air attacks. Egypt and Saudi Arabia reached a bilateral peace accord in August 1965 without consulting the Yemenis. Saudi aid to the Royalists was suspended and Egypt withdrew 30-50,000 of its 70,000 troops. The remainder were moved to Yemen's coastal plain, away from Saudi borders, by April 1966. The force was back to 60,000 troops by year's end, however, and Egypt resumed gas attacks on Yemeni villages. Its ground involvement in Yemen was finally ended by the demands of the June 1967 Middle East War. Nasser reached a final mutual disengagement agreement with Saudi Arabia at an Arab summit at Khartoum, Sudan, on August 31st. In October, YAR supporters protesting Egyptian withdrawals attacked departing troops at the port of Hodeida, and 100 soldiers were killed. The last Egyptian troops left in December, as Royalist fighters besieged Sana'a, but the government held out. Following a Soviet arms airlift to Sana'a in October 1968, fighting gradually died down. In May 1970, 30 Royalist leaders made separate peace with the government. In July, Saudi Arabia and the UK finally recognized the YAR (Rahmy, *Egyptian Policy in the Arab World*, 224-240; O'Ballance, *The War in the Yemen*, 185-7).

26. Since the US had originally proposed UN monitoring in Yemen and U Thant had agreed to provide it, some sort of field operation had to be mounted to close the loop, politically.

27. Shortages of money, and a Headquarters attitude that military men, trained to survive on short rations, can just make do with them, still combine to leave field missions scrambling for resources (see the case on Central America), or drying in the desert (see Western Sahara).

28. Thus it joined the list of UN missions sent to monitor cross-border arms flows that could not fulfill their mandates satisfactorily. Others include the 1947 mission to the Balkans, the 1958 mission to Lebanon and, many years later, the 1989-91 mission to Central America.

13 United Nations Peacekeeping Force in Cyprus

by Karl Th. Birgisson

A civil war broke out in Cyprus in 1963 between the island's Greek and Turkish communities. The United Nations Peacekeeping Force in Cyprus (UNFICYP) was established in an effort to prevent further escalation and restore normal conditions. Thereafter UNFICYP kept an uneasy peace on the island, but the underlying political conflict has proved to be one of the most intractable ones in recent times.

ORIGINS

The large island of Cyprus is located at the eastern end of the Mediterranean, just 70 kilometers south of Turkey. Its population of about 700,000 is 80 percent Greek and 18 percent Turkish origin. Historically, Cyprus has enjoyed strong ties with Greece, which continued when the two countries became part of the Ottoman Empire in 1571. As was often the case in Ottoman colonies, the Turks ruled through local religious institutions, in the case of Cyprus through the Greek Orthodox Church. In this role it became the most powerful political force on the island, sustaining the hellenic orientation of its population and establishing the archbishop as its political leader. In the nineteenth century, the idea of *enosis*, or union, with Greece emerged as a unifying force within the Greek Cypriot community, a sentiment that was further intensified when Cyprus came under British rule in 1878 and the British sought to secularize authority on the island.[1]

The first sixty years of the twentieth century saw *enosis* become the central theme of Cypriot politics and one that led to a brutal campaign of violence against the colonial authorities. The campaign began in 1955 with the formation of EOKA, a paramilitary group led by Colonel George Grivas, and continued until 1959, when representatives of the United Kingdom, Greece, and Turkey met in Zurich to negotiate the future status of Cyprus.[2]

The result of the Zurich negotiations was an independent Republic of Cyprus, formally established on August 16, 1960. The agreement took the form of four documents: a Treaty of Establishment (signed by the United Kingdom, Cyprus, Greece, and Turkey), a Treaty of Guarantee (with the same signatories), a Treaty of Alliance (between Cyprus, Greece, and Turkey), and a Constitution for the new Republic. Under the Treaty of Guarantee, the three signatories were to consult each other in case of breach, but retained the right to intervene unilaterally to reestablish the political status quo specified by the Treaty. The Treaty of Alliance allowed Britain to retain two Sovereign Base Areas, and Greece and Turkey to station armed contigents on the island, numbering 950 and 650, respectively. The constitution, meanwhile, expressly forbade the partitioning of Cyprus as well as its union with any other State.[3]

The constitutional arrangements were designed to promote a peaceful coexistence between the Greek and Turkish Cypriot communities, recognizing the predominance of Greek Cypriots while safeguarding the rights of Turkish Cypriots. Thus, the President was to be Greek Cypriot and the Vice-President Turkish Cypriot, with both having veto power over certain legislation, including budget and taxes. Turkish Cypriots were to choose three out of ten Cabinet members and 15 of 50 members of the legislature. The armed forces were similary divided, as was the civil service.[4]

Contrary to the intentions of the Guarantor Powers, these elaborate provisions only created further divisions between the two communities. Certainly, Greek Cypriot leaders disliked the arrangements from the start, having been forced to accept them as a *fait accompli* and give up the goal of *enosis*. For their part, Turkish Cypriots never trusted their Greek compatriots, jealously guarding their rights and testing the strength of the constitutional framework in various ways. The result was further estrangement and mutual suspicion, a growing apart rather than consolidation of the two groups.

Following a series of political and constitutional crises, Archbishop Makarios, President of Cyprus, proposed amendments to the constitution on November 30, 1963, which would have eliminated the special status of Turkish Cypriots. The President's proclaimed aim was to unite the two communities by removing the obstacles that had kept them apart. Turkish Cypriots, on the other hand, suspected that this was part of a larger plan to consolidate Greek Cypriot authority, the ultimate aim being union with Greece. They rejected the proposals out of hand and heated rhetoric followed.

Mutual recriminations turned violent on December 21, when fighting broke out in the northern part of Nicosia and reports ensued of disturbances elsewhere. The Turkish government sent its national military contingent to the aid of Turkish Cypriots and had military aircraft fly over the island in a show of strength. Naval concentrations were also reported on the south coast of Turkey.

On December 24, the governments of Britain, Greece, and Turkey jointly offered to form a peacekeeping force under British command, consisting of contingents already stationed on the island. The government of Cyprus accepted the offer, a truce was arranged between the warring factions, and a "green line" of cease-fire was drawn through Nicosia to be patrolled by British troops. This delicate and unstable arrangement was to be maintained until a conference was held in January 1964.

The five parties met in London in January to negotiate a peaceful solution to the conflict. The British representative proposed that the current peacekeeping force be strengthened with forces from other NATO countries. The neutral government of Cyprus vehemently rejected the idea of NATO intervention, preferring to bring the matter to the United Nations. Eventually, this was agreed upon, in large part because the situation in Cyprus was deteriorating rapidly and Britain feared unilateral action if a solution was not found.[5]

Initiatives toward UN Involvement

On December 26, Cyprus requested a United Nations Security Council meeting to discuss its complaints over Turkish military activity. The meeting took place the following day. Subsequently, the four governments asked the Secretary General to appoint a special representative to observe the peacekeeping operations in Cyprus. On January 17, Secretary General U Thant appointed Lieutenant General P.S. Gyani of India to this post.[6]

The ad hoc peacekeeping arrangement made in December proved insufficient to contain the volatile mood in Cyprus. Sporadic violence was reported throughout the country, reaching a peak in February. On February 15, Britain and Cyprus asked for a Security Council meeting to discuss the establishment of an international force. The Secretary General urged all parties involved to show restraint and immediately began negotiations for the organization of the prospective force.

On March 4, the Security Council recommended the creation of a United Nations force "to prevent a recurrence of fighting and, as necessary, to contribute to the maintenance and restoration of law and order and a return to normal conditions."[7] This remained UNFICYP's purpose until a drastic change in conditions in 1974.

On July 15, 1974, on the initiative of the seven-year-old military dictatorship in Greece, a group of officers in the Cypriot National Guard staged a coup d'état against the government of Archbishop Makarios. Five days later, Turkey intervened militarily, citing its rights under the 1960 Treaty of Guarantees. The new military regime in Cyprus collapsed, as did the junta in Greece. A new government was formed in Cyprus under the leadership of Glafcos Clerides, the Speaker of the House, but it was unable to stop the advance of the Turkish military, which had by that time occupied large parts of northern Cyprus, including Kyrenia, and had established links with the Turkish enclave in Nicosia.[8]

Upon the request of Cyprus and the Secretary General, the Security Council met on July 16 and 19 and called for a cease-fire commencing July 22. When fighting continued, especially around Nicosia International Airport, the Council reaffirmed its earlier positions and fighting was finally halted on July 24.[9]

The foreign ministers of the United Kingdom, Greece, and Turkey met in Geneva on July 25–30 and agreed to establish a security zone under UNFICYP control between the front lines of the Cypriot National Guard and Turkish forces, and to entrust UNFICYP with the protection of Turkish enclaves. Further talks broke down, however, on August 14, and the Turkish army moved forward still. By the time a cease-fire was arranged two days later, the Turks controlled the northern forty percent of Cyprus.

POLITICAL SUPPORT

Of the five permanent members of the Security Council, Britain and the United States have been the strongest supporters of UNFICYP. Initially, however, both had similar ideas about how to address the problem without involving the United Nations. Britain had particular responsibilities towards Cyprus as its former colonial master and one of the Guarantor Powers of the treaties of 1960. When its initial peacekeeping and peacemaking efforts of December 1963 and January 1964 proved fruitless, Britain approached the United States with the suggestion that a NATO force be sent to Cyprus. This was only logical since the conflict in Cyprus had the potential for war between Greece and Turkey, both members of NATO. The United States government was not ready to send its forces to Cyprus, although it certainly did appreciate the possible nuisance and embarrassment resulting from an intra-NATO conflict. The Americans, therefore, accepted the idea, on the condition that the forces be under British command and come from a number of NATO countries. The idea was further elaborated, only to be dismissed by the strongly neutralist President Archbishop Makarios of Cyprus. In the face of Makarios's adamant refusal to accept a NATO force, the United States and Britain saw no alternative but to embrace the concept of a United Nations force for Cyprus.[10]

The Soviet Union had little at stake in the Cyprus conflict, but viewed the situation as an opportunity for NATO to extend its influence and issued a public warning against NATO interference when the idea first arose. The Soviet Union saw UNFICYP as a potential barrier against a NATO takeover of a newly established nonaligned government. But although the Soviets supported the establishment of UNFICYP, they did have serious doubts about the powers handed to the Secretary General in its mandate, a concern shared at the time by France. Both countries objected to a provision leaving the size and composition of the force up to the Secretary General, arguing that too much power was being delegated to his office. This concern was somewhat alleviated by the short-term nature of the mandate, three months, but both France and the Soviet Union abstained in the vote on this particular paragraph of the resolution.[11]

The countries most directly affected by the Cyprus crisis, of course, were Greece and Turkey. Both countries had a very special relationship with Cyprus, but neither was at the time willing to solve the matter militarily. Greece was considered militarily weaker and preferred to use diplomatic means to reach a settlement between the two communities in Cyprus. Turkey was much more belligerent, as evidenced by its show of military strength and subsequent threats of unilateral action, but pressure from its NATO allies kept Turkey at bay, at least until 1974.[12] The Turkish invasion, it should be noted, came at a time when the United States government was undergoing a constitutional crisis, only five days after President Richard Nixon resigned.

Turkey's invasion of Cyprus was universally condemned at the time and no government other than Turkey has recognized the

Turkish Republic of Northern Cyprus established in 1983. No one has been able effectively to challenge the Turkish occupation, however, and its NATO allies have continued to play the role of impartial mediators.

MANDATE

In its basic form the Security Council mandate for UNFICYP is contained in Security Council Resolution 186 of March 4, 1964. The Council advised UNFICYP to "use its best efforts to prevent a recurrence of fighting and, as necessary, to contribute to the maintenance and restoration of law and order and a return to normal conditions."[13]

This formulation was relevant to the conditions that prevailed in Cyprus at the time, that is sporadic intercommunal fighting and a gradual disintegration of regular governmental functions. The events of 1974 changed the situation drastically, however, and the mandate was modified to take the new circumstances into account. In particular, UNFICYP was asked to take on various humanitarian functions resulting from the partitioning of the country and now has four major tasks on its hands:

- Maintaining the cease-fire;
- Maintaining the status quo;
- Restoring law and order, and a return to normal conditions; and
- Humanitarian functions.[14]

The mandate, originally intended for three months, has been extended regularly for six months at a time. Despite modifications over time, it is still vague and subject to various interpretations. The "restoration of law and order and a return to normal conditions," for example, do not have the same meaning in 1991 as they did in 1964. Before the island was partitioned, normal conditions referred to economic and social life and governmental authority as it was before fighting broke out in late 1963. But now the words can mean anything from seeking to maintain a tolerable situation considering the political circumstances, on the one hand, to the restoration of Greek Cypriot authority over the northern part of the country on the other. This vagueness has advantages as well as drawbacks: it allows the UN force considerable leeway in dealing with particular situations, but it also highlights the force's lack of political direction and its inability to substantially affect change in the political vacuum in which it operates.

FUNDING

UNFICYP is unique among United Nations peacekeeping operations in that it is funded voluntarily. When the force was created in 1964, the UN was experiencing a crisis over funding, having accumulated substantial debts in its operations in the Congo (ONUC) and along the Egyptian-Israeli frontier (UNEF I). In particular, the Soviet Union and France refused to take on financial commitments for UNFICYP, as they refused such commitments for ONUC and UNEF. Consequently, the Security Council decided that the costs of the operation would be borne primarily by the countries contributing the military contingents and would be defrayed by voluntary contributions.

The troop-contributing countries provide their troops' regular pay, allowances, and normal expenses. They can claim reimbursements from the UN for other costs they incur; in many instances, however, they have chosen not to do so. These expenditures have been in the range of 70-75% of the total cost of UNFICYP operations.[15]

The costs incurred by the United Nations stem from operations that fall outside regular troop expenditures, as well as from reimbursements the troop-contributing members decide to claim. However, the voluntary contributions forwarded to the UN have come largely from these same troop-contributing countries and various NATO countries. Moreover, contributions have never equalled actual expenditures, one consequence being that reimbursements to troop-contributing countries are running far behind schedule. As of May 31 1991, the UN had only reimbursed for expenditures incurred through December 1980. At that time, the UNIFICYP special account was running a deficit of $178.7 million.[16]

This method of funding has resulted in a very inequitable distribution of burdens and has been a serious constraint on the force's operations. Since 1964, a total of 78 countries have made contributions for the UN-incurred costs in Cyprus. The following table illustrates the cumulative distribution of burdens among the 78. It provides a stark contrast to the distribution that would result were members of the United Nations to undertake financial responsibilities according to the UN peacekeeping scale of assessments.

Table 13.1. Contributions Paid or Pledged to the UNFICYP Special Account as of 31 July 1991

Country	Amount (mn. US$)	Percent of Total	Usual UN Assessment	Difference (mn. US$)
United States	212.6	47.1%	30.690%	+ 74.1
United Kingdom	86.3	19.1%	5.965%	+59.4
Germany	32.6	7.2%	8.080%	-3.8
Greece	25.7	5.7%	0.080%	+25.3
Switzerland	15.4	3.4%	1.080%	+10.5
Norway	12.6	2.8%	0.550%	+10.1
Italy	10.9	2.4%	3.990%	-7.1
Cyprus	9.8	2.2%	0.004%	+9.8
Sweden	8.6	1.9%	1.210%	+3.1
Japan	7.2	1.6%	1.380%	-44.1
Denmark	6.3	1.4%	0.690%	+3.2
Belgium	5.9	1.3%	1.170%	+0.6
Austria	5.4	1.2%	0.740%	+2.1
Australia	3.4	0.8%	1.570%	-3.7
Netherlands	2.5	0.6%	1.650%	-4.9
Turkey	1.8	0.4%	0.064%	+1.5
Finland	1.1	0.2%	0.510%	-1.2
France	0.3	0.1%	7.672%	-34.3
Soviet Union	0.0	0.0%	12.266%	-55.3
China	0.0	0.0%	0.962%	-4.3
Others	2.4	0.5%	1.870%	-6.0
Totals:	450.8	99.9%	92.193%	

Source: UN Budget Office

The eight troop-contributing countries provide around 25 percent of the voluntary contributions, whereas their total UN peacekeeping assessment for other operations is just 14 percent. NATO countries have provided about 88 percent of the voluntary contributions, while their cumulative UN assessment for other UN peacekeeping is about 64 percent. Notably absent from the list of contributors is the Soviet Union, which has a UN assessment of 12.27 percent, but has contributed nothing to the UNFICYP operation. Of the other permanent members of the Security Council, France, with a UN assessment of 7.67 percent, contributed $340,937 from mid-1989 to the end of 1990 (0.07 percent of the total contributions). China, with a UN assessment of 0.96 percent, has contributed nothing.

Financial strains on the contributing countries have in some cases led them to withdraw from UNFICYP. Sweden reduced its contingent to a token force in 1988, and Finland's similar troop reduction in 1977 may also have been for financial reasons. In the spring of 1992, Canada and Denmark threatened to leave the Force by the end of the year, and Austria was reported to be reassessing its participation. No countries stepped forward offering to replace them.[17]

Several countries, the UK and Canada prominent among them, have argued for a change in UNFICYP funding from the current voluntary arrangement to funding based on assessments. These proposals have met with little positive reaction, as have repeated suggestions by the Secretary General that UNFICYP be put on a stronger financial footing.

PLANNING AND IMPLEMENTATION

UNFICYP faced one set of circumstances when it started in 1964, but very different circumstances after Turkey's invasion of Cyprus in 1974. When UNFICYP began its operations, there were no defined front lines or particular points of conflict to which the force could direct its attention, nor was there a cease-fire agreement which the force could try to enforce. The violence was sporadic and widely dispersed throughout the country's 700 towns and villages. In many cases, however, the Turkish population was concentrated in enclaves (or had moved there after fighting began), which were often the targets of attack by Greek Cypriots. The two sides were well armed, particularly the Greek Cypriots who had been part of EOKA some years before.

The initial planning at the United Nations headquarters in 1964 was done under great pressure. In the several weeks it took to conclude arrangments for the establishment of the force, the situation in Cyprus remained very unstable. The small British contingent on the ground was only able to contain a small portion of the escalating conflict. The operation became even more urgent when the Turkish government threatened publicly to take unilateral action to protect Turkish Cypriots until the United Nations could deploy sufficient forces in the area.

In addition, several constraints were put on the composition of the force. The government of Cyprus demanded that there be a balance between NATO and non-NATO forces, while at the same time refusing to allow any troops of color onto her territory. The only certain contributor of troops was Britain, although the

Secretary General soon received positive reactions to his inquiries from others. All had reservations, however, about the nature of the operation and the financial uncertainties pertaining to it.[18]

A small Canadian advance party arrived in Cyprus on March 17, and, ten days later, a multinational force of 6,200 became operational under the command of Lieutenant General Gyani of India. The contingents came from Austria, Canada, Denmark, Finland, Ireland, Sweden, and the United Kingdom. In addition, Australia, Austria, Denmark, New Zealand, and Sweden contributed to a civilian police force (UNCIVPOL) which became operational in late April.[19]

The UN force was deployed throughout the island. Two contingents under Canadian command were stationed along the "green line" in Nicosia in an observation role. Another took up position between defense lines in the district of Kyrenia, observing and patrolling the area, while a fourth covered the district of Lafka. Two contingents were assigned to cover the remaining districts of Larnaca, Limassol, and Paphos. They were generally deployed where situations were unstable and violence likely to erupt. All contingents consisted of observation squads and mobile units that were sent into areas to interpose themselves between warring factions.

UNFICYP soon established a very strong system of liaison with the two sides at all levels of command. This enabled the force to react swiftly to dangerous situations and resolve problems at the local level. In addition, UNCIVPOL established liaison with the local Cypriot police, observed them when they conducted searches of vehicles, manned police posts in certain sensitive areas, and conducted investigations into incidents which involved members of the two opposing communities.

The Secretary General and the government on Cyprus reached an agreement establishing freedom of movement for UNFICYP throughout Cyprus. The force was entitled to use roads, bridges, and airfields as it saw necessary, although some qualifications were made concerning large troop movements.[20]

After the invasion of 1974, however, the situation looked more like a traditional stand-off between two regular armies. The Turkish army had occupied the northern part of the island, and most Greek Cypriots had fled south into Greek-controlled territory. A new security zone was established along the front lines that still remains in mid-1991; it reaches some 180 kilometers across the island and ranges in width from a few meters in parts of Nicosia to seven kilometers at its widest. The zone is divided into four operational sectors, each under the control of one national contingent: Danish, British, Canadian, and Austrian. There are 143 observation posts along the zone, 56 of which are permanently manned, and there is only one major crossing point between the two communities. As of June 14, 1991, the force was composed as indicated in table 13.2.

Table 13.2. Composition of UNFICYP as of June 1991

Country	Military personnel	Number	National Totals
Austria	HQ UNFICYP	12	
	Infantry Battalion	388	
	Military police	10	410
Canada	HQ UNFICYP	7	
	HQ CANCON	5	
	Light infantry btln	538	
	Signal squadron	14	
	Military police	11	575
Denmark	HQ UNFICYP	5	
	Infantry battalion	323	
	Military police	13	341
Finland	HQ UNFICYP	4	
	Military police	3	7
Ireland	HQ UNFICYP	6	
	Military police	2	8
Sweden	HQ UNFICYP	4	
	Military police	3	7
United Kingdom	HQ UNFICYP	19	
	HQ UNFICYP support regt.	45	
	HQ BRITCON	6	
	Scout car squadron	109	
	Infantry battalion	349	
	Engineer detachment	8	
	Signal squadron	53	
	Army aviation flight	18	
	Transport squadron	103	
	Medical centre	5	
	Ordnance detachment	11	
	Workshops	30	
	Military police	9	765
Subtotal		2113	
	Civilian police		
Australia		20	
Sweden		18	38
Total UNFICYP		2151	

Source: UN Document S/22665, June 14, 1991.

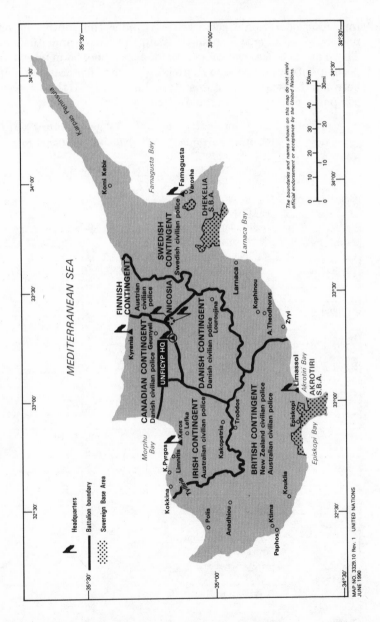

**Figure 13.1. United Nations Peacekeeping Force in Cyprus,
Deployment as of December 1965**

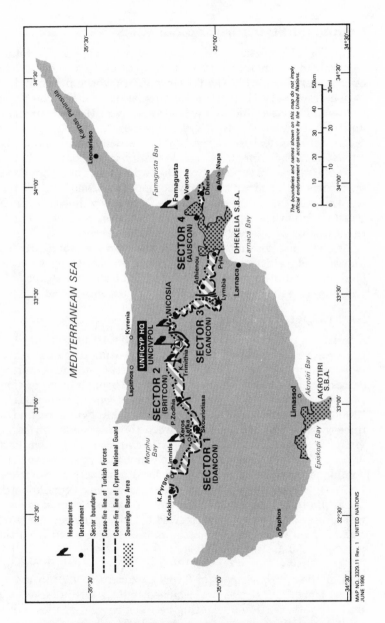

Figure 13.2. United Nations Peacekeeping Force in Cyprus, Deployment as of June 1990

Command Structure and Logistics

The Force Commander of UNFICYP is appointed by the Secretary General and responsible to him. His status is parallel to the Special Representative, the political officer whose function is to aid the Secretary General in his mediation efforts. The Force Commander has a Chief of Staff (alternately British or Canadian) and a Police Adviser, who oversees UNCIVPOL.

The defining feature of the UNFICYP mission (and one of the principal reasons for its operational success) is that it receives most of its logistics support from the two British Sovereign Bases on the island. The bases are fully equipped and well stocked, and were already capable of supporting a force many times the size of UNFICYP when the operation began.[21] These were ideal conditions, and ones not likely to be reproduced elsewhere.

The national contingents provide their own weapons, radios, and combat vehicles, while the British provide troop vehicles, food, fuel, maintenance organization, and ordnance stores.[22] In addition, various goods and services are purchased locally.

Field Operations

In the first phase of the operation, UNFICYP had primarily a preventive role to play. It did so by interposing its forces where violence erupted, negotiating with the parties, and maintaining a presence in areas of continuing unrest. Through interposition, negotiation, persuasion, observation, and extensive consultation, UNFICYP managed to prevent major outbreaks of violence, and an uneasy truce was maintained between the two communities. By virtue of these circumstances, settlements of particular local crises had an ad hoc quality to them, which in turn served to build confidence between the force and local authorities. Moreover, UNFICYP played an important part in restoring economic and social life to normal conditions. With a few exceptions, relative peacefulness and calm characterized life in Cyprus, and UNFICYP was reduced in strength to 2,200 men in 1974, down from the peak of 6,200 in August of 1964.[23]

The abortive coup d'état and the subsequent Turkish occupation of the northern part of Cyprus placed UNFICYP in a very difficult position. It was not designed to deal with a large-scale military intervention or fighting between regular armies. While reinforcements started to arrive on July 24, placing the Force at 4,400 by mid-August, it could not substantially affect the general military situation. It did manage to negotiate local cease-fires, safeguard some of the civilian population, and protect several villages, as well as assist in the evacuation of foreign missions from Nicosia to the British base at Dhekelia.[24]

Subsequently, UNFICYP took up positions along the new security zone created after the advance of the Turkish military. This "no man's land" separating the (Greek) Republic of Cyprus and the self-proclaimed Turkish Republic of Northern Cyprus remains to this day the main area of UNFICYP's operations.

In addition to the regular tasks of a peacekeeping force, UNFICYP has taken on a variety of other functions in its administration of the buffer zone. These include maintaining water and electrical facilities in the zone and safeguarding agricultural use of the very productive land that falls therein. UNFICYP also administers the transfer of mail and medical supplies through the one major crossing point between the two communities and performs such additional tasks of local governments as firefighting, controlling rabid animals, and eradicating mosquitoes.

ASSESSMENT

UNFICYP has performed its assigned functions well in a difficult and volatile environment. Between 1964 and 1974, the Force managed to create the necessary conditions for a truce, albeit an uneasy one, between the Greek and Turkish Cypriot communities. The force was sufficiently strong to prevent major outbreaks of violence and to protect the Turkish enclaves that were most frequently the focal points of friction. These enclaves eventually came to resemble defensive fortifications, however, prompting in turn the creation of siege-like camps around them. UNFICYP achieved little in terms of dismantling the forts, although on occasion the force was able to persuade troops to leave and thus create more distance between the opposing sides.[25]

Furthermore, the Force succeeded in its purpose of restoring life to somewhat normal conditions in its early years in Cyprus. Government services resumed, as did regular economic activity and commercial and civilian traffic. This degree of normalcy could not have been achieved had it not been for the stabilizing presence of the UN force.

The experience has not been without its dark moments, however. UNFICYP did not prevent crisis situations from developing nor did it disarm the opposing sides. The UN force has found itself in situations where it was fired upon by both sides and had to return fire. Serious fighting broke out in 1967, when the Cypriot

National Guard moved into the Kophinou area in an attempt to "normalize" conditions. Violence spread quickly in what amounted to a breakdown of the cease-fire, with the National Guard occupying Turkish areas and the Turkish Air Force responding to this incursion.[26]

These and other incidents of violence, obstruction, and harassment were at times apparently meant to test the resolve and capabilities of the UN force. UNFICYP has withstood those tests and gradually has come to command the respect and confidence necessary to fulfill its mandate in these difficult circumstances. Since 1974, the ground situation has been relatively calmer, partly because the UN force is concentrated within a well-defined area between the two sides, and partly because both parties have come to accept the force as their best guarantee against surprise attacks. As in several other instances, the UN force in Cyprus has played the important role of building confidence and raising the threshold of violence in a volatile situation.

CONCLUSIONS

While UNFICYP has successfully fulfilled its basic mandate, there has been little progress on the diplomatic front toward a long-term solution of the underlying political problem. Its maintenance of the status quo, it can be argued, may even weaken the chance of a meaningful settlement between the two Cypriot communities. Everyday life in the two communities appears to be adjusting to the de facto partitioning of the country. "Normalization" has in many cases come to mean division, whether in terms of infrastructure, economics, education, or governmental services. UNFICYP has managed to foster a semblance of calm and normalcy about the current situation that may indeed discourage dialogue between the two communities and, thus, a lasting political settlement.

UNFICYP's experience underlines the importance of combining peacekeeping with a continued search for a durable political settlement. The UN Secretary General's Special Representative, Mr. Oscar Camilión, continues to work with the two sides at achieving a settlement, but the few glimpses of hope don't often last longer than a few weeks. If the initial conflict between the two communities was difficult to solve, the events of 1974 made it almost intractable. The northern part of the country remains occupied by some 30,000 Turkish troops; Turkish immigrants have taken over the homes of Greek Cypriots who fled in 1974;

and population transfers have resulted in a serious refugee problem and widespread property losses. Several thousand Greek Cypriots are still "missing" since the war of 1974.

The international community has tended to look at Cyprus as a problem under control and not urgently in need of attention. In July 1991, President George Bush visited Greece and Turkey—the first time an American President had done so in decades. The visit raised hopes that a settlement might be reached, and Washington signed up all four local parties for a conference in Washington that September, but the initiative soon stalled, perhaps overshadowed by the much greater effort by the US to reenergize the Middle East peace process, launched with a joint Arab-Israeli meeting in Madrid that fall.[27]

In April 1992, energized by news that Austria, Canada, and Denmark might withdraw from UNFICYP, and by a pressing need to shift diplomatic and military resources to new and critical mission areas like the Balkans, Somalia, and Cambodia, the Security Council directed the new Secretary General, Mr. Boutros-Ghali, to press Greek and Turkish leaders to reach an accord on Cyprus. Boutros-Ghali issued a thinly-veiled warning that the UN may pull out of Cyprus if Cypriots continued to refuse to confront and resolve their differences.

Notes

1. Augustus Richard Norton, "The roots of the conflict in Cyprus," in Kjell Skjellsbaek, ed., *The Cyprus Conflict and the Role of the United Nations*, NUPI Report 122 (Oslo: Norwegian Institute of International Affairs, 1988), 5-6.

2. Norton, "The roots of the conflict in Cyprus," 7-9.

3. *The Blue Helmets: A Review of United Nations Peace-keeping*, 2nd ed. (New York: United Nations Department of Public Information, 1990), 281.

4. Colonel Robert Mitchell, "Peacekeeping and Peacemaking in Cyprus," Background Paper 23 (Ottawa: Canadian Institute for International Peace and Security, October 1988), 2.

5. Alan James, *The Politics of Peace-keeping* (New York: Frederick A. Praeger, 1969), 320-323.

6. *The Blue Helmets*, 283-284.

7. United Nations Document S/5575, March 4, 1964.

8. Mitchell, "Peacekeeping and Peacemaking in Cyprus," 4.

9. *The Blue Helmets*, 301-303. UNFICYP suffered several dozen combat casualties, most of them during the Force's defense of Nicosia Airport in 1974.

10. James, *The Politics of Peace-keeping*, 322-323.

11. James, *The Politics of Peace-keeping*, 323-324.

12. James H. Wolfe, "United States policy and the Cyprus conflict," in *The Cyprus Conflict and the Role of the United Nations*, 46-50.

13. United Nations Document S/5575.

14. United Nations, Security Council, *Report by the Secretary-General on the United Nations Operation in Cyprus*, S/18491, December 2, 1986. Humanitarian functions include facilitating visits south of the buffer zone for Greek Cypriots living in the northern part of the island; support for the refugee assistance efforts of the UN High Commissioner for Refugees, including delivery of foodstuffs; and cooperation with the UN Development Program, World Health Organization, and other agencies working on Cyprus.

15. United Nations Document S/18431, Annex, October 29, 1986.

16. United Nations, *Report of the Secretary-General on the UN Operation in Cyprus for the period 1 December 1990–31 May 1991*, Document S/22665, May 31, 1991.

17. Alan James, "The UN Force in Cyprus," *International Affairs* 65, no. 3 (Summer 1989): 489; Paul Lewis, "UN Warns that Time is Running Out on Cyprus," *New York Times*, April 12, 1992, 13; Tony Banks, "Canada 'Should quit UN force,'" *Jane's Defence Weekly* (June 20, 1992): 1061.

18. James, *The Politics of Peace-keeping*, 325-326.

19. *The Blue Helmets*, 287.

20. *The Blue Helmets*, 290-293.

21. David W. Wainhouse, *International Peacekeeping at the Crossroads* (Baltimore: The Johns Hopkins University Press, 1973), 351.

22. Indar Jit Rikhye, et al., *The Thin Blue Line: International Peacekeeping and Its Future* (New Haven: Yale University Press, 1977), 116.

23. Mitchell, "Peacekeeping and Peacemaking in Cyprus," 4.

24. *The Blue Helmets*, 302.

25. Mitchell, "Peacekeeping and Peacemaking in Cyprus," 4.

26. *The Blue Helmets*, 297.

27. Dita Smith, "Cyprus Talks Gain Tentative Approval," *Washington Post*, August 3, 1991; Marlise Simons, "With New Talks Near, Cypriots Wonder How the Divide Can Be Bridged," *New York Times*, August 19, 1991, A3.

14 United Nations Iran-Iraq Military Observer Group

by Brian D. Smith

The Iran-Iraq Military Observer Group (UNIIMOG) was a traditional-type peace observation mission. UNIIMOG demonstrated the ability of the United Nations, through the offices of the Secretary General and Security Council, to help bring an end to an ongoing conflict and to encourage movement toward normalization of relations between the warring parties. However, it also showed how difficult it is for the UN to resolve conflicts that are stoked by Great Power arms sales—both open and covert, direct, and via third parties—and the importance of the belligerents' support and cooperation if an observer mission is to succeed. Because that cooperation was sharply limited in this case, UNIIMOG's impact was limited as well. Peace negotiations made real progress only after Iraq's August 1990 invasion of Kuwait gave Baghdad an urgent reason to pacify its border with Iran. UNIIMOG was decreased in size throughout the fall of 1990 and was officially terminated as UN-authorized, US-led armored forces sliced into Iraq in late February 1991.

ORIGINS

Border disputes between Iran and Iraq have a long history, and have been particularly acute with respect to the Shatt al-Arab, the waterway that separates the two countries as it connects the Persian Gulf with the inland river systems of the Tigris and Euphrates. The port of Basra, on the Shatt, provides Iraq's only direct access to the Persian Gulf and thence to the open ocean. On the opposite bank, the Iranian city of Abadan is a major petroleum refining center and shipping terminus.[1]

The two states signed a treaty in 1937 that ceded a large amount of control over the Shatt al-Arab to the new Iraqi state (which emerged from a British-administered League of Nations mandate in 1932). Iraqi control of the waterway extended to the Iranian bank, except at at Abadan, where jurisdiction split at the thalweg line (the mid-point of the navigable waters). This agreement lasted until the 1950s, when deteriorating relations between Iran and Iraq were punctuated by sporadic border clashes. Relations between the two continued to sour until the early 1970s when Iraq emerged from a period of self-induced isolation and began to make overtures to its neighbors. In March 1975, the Shah of Iran and Iraqi Vice President Saddam Hussein signed an agreement, the Algiers Treaty, that settled several border disputes and granted the Iranians a navigable border along the entire length of the Shatt. In return, the Shah withdrew support for Kurdish insurgents in northern Iraq. Between 1975 and 1979 relations between the two states improved steadily.[2]

The fall of the Shah on February 11, 1979, produced another change in Iran-Iraq relations. The Iraqis were initially encouraged by the downfall of the powerful Shah, and relations between the parties were cordial for a time. Indeed, Iraq extended diplomatic recognition when the Islamic Republic of Iran was just two days' old. But the relationship did not retain its cordiality for long. The growing fundamentalist movement in Iran, fueled by the return of the Ayatollah Ruhollah Khomeini, threatened to stir up the Shi'a living in southern Iraq. Khomeini had lived among them for 13 years, in the Iraqi holy city of Najaf, but was deported to France in 1978 as a gesture of good faith to the Shah.

Khomeini held Hussein personally responsible for his demeaning expulsion, and his radical brand of Shi'a Islam posed a significant political threat to the secular, socialist Ba'ath regime in Baghdad. Moreover, to the extent that it had religious ties, the Ba'athist regime represented Iraq's minority population of Sunni Moslems, not the Shi'a.[3]

Already concerned about the potential for a new Kurdish uprising in the north, Iraq was very sensitive to potential internal disruptions brought on by the activities of other states. Iraq exchanged insults and threats with Iran throughout much of the period between its recognition of the new regime and the outbreak of general hostilities a year and a half later. Each side encouraged the other's dissidents and engaged in border skirmishes and sporadic artillery duels, most notably in the areas near the Shatt-al-Arab.[4]

One of these areas was Iran's Khuzistan province, an oil producing region. Certain areas of Khuzistan (known as Arabistan to Iraqis) were to have been ceded to Iraq under the Algiers Treaty. However, at the time of the overthrow of the Shah, they were still held by Iran and used, according to Baghdad, to launch attacks against Iraqi settlements.[5]

On September 7, 1980, Iraq lodged a formal complaint with Iran regarding Tehran's slow withdrawal from these territories. On September 10, Iraqi forces moved into them, and, on the 17th, Iraq abrogated the Algiers Treaty. This decision was communicated to UN Secretary General Kurt Waldheim on September 21. The next day, Iraq launched air strikes against all Iranian air bases within range of the border and followed up with a full-scale ground invasion. Other rationales were given for the attack, but Iraq was most interested in redrawing its border at what appeared to be an opportune time, given Iran's political instability and evident military vulnerability.[6]

However, the result was just the opposite of Iraqi expectations. The invasion helped to consolidate the Khomeini regime behind a wave of nationalism and accelerated the rebuilding of an effective military machine in harmony with the interests of the Iranian revolution. Internal dissent was suppressed and opposition groups crushed under the weight of Iranian nationalism and revolutionary fervor. During the same time period, Moscow cut off supplies of arms to Baghdad, reducing Saddam Hussein's ability to exploit early battlefield gains.

Within a year, Iraq's early successes were reversed as Iran made use of its great advantage in population. Outnumbering the Iraqis nearly three to one in total population, the Iranians were able to amass up to four and one-half times as many troops on the battlefield. By July 1982, Iran was able to push into Iraqi territory using human wave tactics, which produced high casualties but succeeded in changing the character of the war from one of maneuver to one of attrition, where Iran's superior numbers gave it an advantage.

The Gulf Arabs, energized by the threat of possible Iranian victory and the subsequent spread of Islamic fundamentalism, began to support Iraq in earnest. In the West, France extended several billion dollars in loans to Iraq, and by 1983 over 40 percent of French arms exports were Baghdad-bound. Moscow, too, concerned about the potential impact of Iranian fundamentalism on its heavily Islamic Central Asian republics, resumed major arms sales to Baghdad. Britain maintained neutrality. Washington, uncomfortable with the thought of either side winning the war, allowed American-made arms to reach Baghdad from other countries in the region and supplied Baghdad with crucial military intelligence, including data from Saudi Airborne Warning and Control System aircraft.[7]

The conflict settled into the kind of horrific, stalemated attrition warfare that typified the Western Front in World War I, even down to the use of poison gas by Iraq in 1983 to break up Iranian human wave assaults. As stalemate overtook the war on the ground, conflict spread into the Gulf itself. Iraq began earnestly to attack Iranian tankers and shore facilities in an effort to cripple Iranian oil exports. Since Iraq exported its oil by pipeline, not tanker, Iran opted to retaliate against the shipping of Iraq's Gulf Arab allies, especially Kuwait.[8]

By November 1984, Washington had resumed diplomatic relations with Baghdad and was leading a public bid to cut international arms shipments to Iran. Within a year, however, it launched a second effort to supply arms covertly to Tehran, again with Israel's help, to buy the freedom of American hostages taken by pro-Iranian groups in Lebanon. This effort surfaced as part of the Iran-Contra scandal, in which proceeds of the sales to Iran were used to buy Congressionally prohibited military supplies for the Nicaraguan Resistance (the "Contras"). This US aid, which included several thousand lethal TOW anti-tank missiles, was complemented by large amounts of military hardware from China (often exchanged for oil and funnelled through North Korea). Effectively resupplied, Iran launched a new offensive in early 1986 that carried its forces to the Fao Peninsula, a spit of Iraqi territory at the mouth of the Shatt al-Arab opposite Kuwait.[9]

The "tanker war" also escalated sharply and Kuwait invited both the United States and the Soviet Union to help protect its shipping. The Soviet Union immediately accepted and chartered three of its tankers to the Kuwaitis. The twin specters of an increased threat to shipping in the Gulf and increased Soviet influence in the region spurred the US to agree to hoist the American flag over eleven Kuwaiti-owned tankers, thus bringing them under the protection of the US Navy.[10]

The tanker escort operation in turn produced several sharp exchanges with Iranian forces. In April 1988, after the frigate *Samuel Roberts* struck a mine, US naval forces retaliated against Iranian offshore platforms, sank two Iranian patrol craft and a frigate, and damaged another.[11] As this battle was underway in the southern reaches of the Persian Gulf, Iraq launched an offensive to recover the Fao Peninsula and succeeded. Thereafter, it began pushing Iranian forces back toward the border. On July 3, the US cruiser *Vincennes* misidentified an Iranian Airbus as hostile and shot it out of the sky, killing 290 passengers and crew. Despite the magnitude of this tragedy, Iran was unable to rouse sufficient support in the UN to condemn the US. The ground war was also going increasingly badly. These losses, and the recognition of its ultimate international isolation, led Iran finally to accept a cease-fire.[12]

Initiatives toward UN Involvement

Secretary General Waldheim moved quickly to seek an end to the war. From the first day of fighting, he offered his good offices to help reach a peaceful solution. When the fighting continued, he moved to call an emergency meeting of the Security Council. On September 28, 1980, the Security Council adopted Resolution 479, which called for an immediate end to the use of force and for a peaceful process of conflict resolution. Iraq, whose offensive was not nearly as effective as it had hoped, agreed. Iran, however, rejected the resolution because it lacked a clause requiring the withdrawal of troops to internationally recognized borders and failed to name Iraq as the aggressor.[13]

Iran at that time was disregarding international norms of conduct by holding US diplomats hostage (seized in November 1979, they were not released until January 1981). As a result it was diplomatically isolated and few nations were willing to go to bat for it. Tehran returned the disfavor, viewing Resolution 479 as evidence of pro-Iraqi bias on the Security Council's part. This perception did not extend to the Secretary General, however, who proved to be a more successful arbiter of the war for the UN.[14]

After the passage of 479, the Security Council did not meet formally again to discuss the war until July 1982, by which time the situation had changed greatly, as noted above. The Council passed two resolutions calling for an immediate cease-fire. The following year, Resolution 540 called again for a cease-fire and asked the Secretary General to consider dispatching UN observers, in consultation with the parties, to monitor that cease-fire. Iraq accepted Resolution 540 but Iran rejected it, again demanding that Iraq be branded the aggressor and required to pay compensation for war damages. Iran's stance helped generate international support for Baghdad and further isolated Tehran.[15] For nearly four years following passage of Resolution 540, the Security Council took no further action on the conflict itself.

On July 20, 1987, the Security Council passed Resolution 598, which called for the immediate cessation of hostilities, withdrawal of forces behind internationally recognized boundaries, implementation of a cease-fire accord, and the observation of such an accord by a UN force.[16] The United States and the United Kingdom both pushed hard for passage of the resolution, the US in particular seeking a cease-fire before attacks on non-belligerent shipping disrupted the flow of oil from the Gulf. Included in Resolution 598 was a key clause that provided for establishment of a board to determine which party was responsible for initiating hostilities. The clause was included at the insistence of West Germany to balance some of the resolution's harsh language directed at Iran. The resolution received unanimous support in the Security Council and was immediately accepted by Iraq. Iran, on the other hand, agreed to accept it only if Iraq were named the aggressor. The United States treated this conditional acceptance as a rejection and pushed for an arms embargo on Iran.[17] The Soviet Union preferred to give Iran more time to complete negotiations with the Secretary General on implementing the resolution. In late February 1988, Iran informed the Secretary General that it accepted his ten-point plan for implementation, but not the resolution as a whole. Five months later, on July 18, 1988, Iran came before the Security Council to protest the downing of Iran Air flight 655 by the US Navy. When other countries failed to rally behind it, Iran decided to accept Resolution 598. The Ayatollah Khomeini described the action as being "more bitter than taking poison."[18]

On August 8, 1988, the Security Council unanimously approved the implementation plan for Resolution 598. The cease-fire came into effect on August 20, and peace negotiations under the auspices of the Secretary General commenced five days later.[19]

POLITICAL SUPPORT

Great Power political and material involvement in the Iran-Iraq War complicated efforts to end it and may have helped prolong it. Rising tensions between Moscow and Washington in the early- to mid-1980s also meant that each step taken by the one was scrutinized by the other, initially for its impact on the global competition for influence, and only secondarily for its utility in ending the war. Of the two local powers, Iraq, unable to finish what it started, consistently supported UN calls for a cease-fire, whereas Iran did not. Aggrieved that the UN refused to label Iraq the aggressor, and seeing itself as the standard-bearer of a new Islamic revolution, Iran continued its effort to punish Iraq and oust Saddam Hussein until further fighting was clearly counterproductive. Its attitude toward the subsequent deployment of UN peacekeepers was at best ambivalent.

The Great Powers

US policy in the Persian Gulf operated on several levels. Washington sought to forestall Iranian hegemony, to support the Gulf Arabs, to limit Soviet influence, and to maintain freedom of navigation and the free flow of petroleum.[20] The US officially supported the immediate cessation of hostilities from the outset of the conflict, and thus it supported Resolution 479, passed one week after fighting broke out. The US had little sympathy for revolutionary Iran, but neither could it appear to condone Iraqi aggression. Moreover, Iraq was no friend of Israel. But Iran's refusal to heed Security Council resolutions calling for a cease-fire shifted the onus for the war sufficiently that, beginning in 1983, the United States could move away publicly from its policy of "interested" neutrality and make overtures to Iraq, and finally restore diplomatic relations after the 1984 presidential elections.[21]

The United States supported Resolution 598 as "a comprehesive approach to the conclusion of hostilities," and lobbied other members of the Security Council to back the inclusion of a clause that would impose sanctions on any party failing to comply with the resolution. The US was unable to garner sufficient support for the sanctions clause, and so sponsored a follow-up resolution to 598 that would accomplish the same objective. It was withdrawn in the face of Soviet and Chinese opposition.[22]

The USSR initially welcomed the Iranian revolution and the collapse of US influence that accompanied it. During the debate over Resolution 479 in September 1980, the Soviets expressed their support for resolution of the conflict but qualified that support with calls for an airing of grievances by both parties. The war further complicated Soviet foreign policy in the region, which aimed to maintain a friendly relationship with Iraq that entailed substantial arms sales revenues while cultivating relations with Iran's new Islamic Republic. The Soviet invasion of Afghanistan in late 1979 had hurt Soviet-Iranian relations. Moreover, Moscow had begun to worry about Islamic fundamentalism's potential to generate unrest in predominantly Muslim Soviet Central Asia. As Iran began to urge Islamic peoples to rise in opposition to the secular modernity of the superpowers, Soviet concerns grew, leading to its resumption of arms sales to Iraq.[23]

When Mikhail Gorbachev came to power in 1985, Soviet foreign policy began to change. With respect to the Gulf War, Moscow continued to tilt toward Iraq in practical terms, selling arms and escorting oil tankers chartered by Kuwait, then a major supporter of Iraq. At the same time, the USSR made diplomatic gestures in Tehran's direction, counselling against a UN arms embargo on Iran when it did not immediately and unconditionally accept Resolution 598. [24]

Britain worked behind the scenes in the Security Council to generate support for the resolution, and it joined the United States in pressing for a follow-up arms embargo when Iran initially failed to accept the resolution. France, while supporting UN resolutions, shipped substantial quantities of arms to Iraq. China did much the same, but for Iran. [25]

Iran

Throughout the conflict, Iran viewed the Security Council as a "dishonest broker," but international sympathy for Iran declined further with each successive resolution passed by the Security Council that Iran refused to support. [26] Its heavy-handed efforts to coerce the Gulf States into cutting aid to Iraq also proved counterproductive. Iranian pilgrims disrupted the Haj, the holy pilgrimage to Mecca, in 1987. Tehran also threatened shipping in the Gulf, taking a page from Iraq's playbook and backing its threat by purchasing Silkworm cruise missiles from China and positioning them near the Strait of Hormuz, at the mouth of the Gulf. Iranian attacks on third-country, and particularly Kuwaiti, ships eroded its remaining international support and provoked the superpower reactions that it had hoped to avoid. The US, USSR, and several European NATO navies escorted tankers, and Iranian actions prompted several violent encounters with the US Navy, of which the Airbus incident caused the greatest loss of life.

The domestic situation in Iran also influenced the government's attitude toward the discontinuation of the war and the acceptance of a UN peacekeeping force. Sharp drops in Iranian oil revenues—from plummeting oil prices and damage to its production facilities—together with increasing military expenditures produced a financial and political crisis in Tehran. Iraq's extensive, and demoralizing, use of battlefield chemical weapons and SCUD missile attacks on Tehran also disposed Iran to seek peace. Iran decided, reluctantly, to accept Resolution 598, but it proved to be much less cooperative than Iraq in implementing the resolution, and much more suspicious of the UN presence. Its attitude severely constrained UNIIMOG operations on the Iranian side of the cease-fire line, as described below, and thus circumscribed its effectiveness.[27]

Iraq

Baghdad used the Security Council's dislike for the Khomeini regime to lever political support from the international community. By supporting the early UN resolutions and by accepting the UN as mediator of the conflict, Iraq bolstered its international position at a time when its military situation was precarious. The political and material support that flowed in from abroad allowed Iraq to purchase advanced military equipment at a time when Iran's superiority in numbers was making itself felt in the field. It must be recognized, however, that Iraq was not using the UN resolutions and the good offices of the Secretary General to find an equitable solution to the conflict. Even after it accepted Resolution 598 in July 1988, Iraq continued to fight, and continued its illegal use of chemical weapons, in an effort to improve its field position. By so doing, Baghdad demonstrated the expediency of its support for Security Council injunctions.[28]

MANDATE

Security Council Resolution 598 called for an unarmed military observer force on the Iran-Iraq border, and Resolution 619 of August 9, 1988, approved its mandate. UNIIMOG was to monitor and maintain a cease-fire between the two parties and to monitor the withdrawal of the respective forces, until such time as a more permanent solution to the conflict could be worked out between Iran and Iraq in talks that followed the acceptance of the cease-fire.[29] The mandate stipulated that UNIIMOG was to:

- establish with the parties agreed cease-fire lines on the basis of the forward defended localities occupied by the two sides on D-day but adjusting these, as may be agreed, when the positions of the two sides are judged to be dangerously close to each other;

- monitor compliance with the cease-fire; investigate any alleged violations of the cease-fire and restore the situation if a violation has taken place;

- prevent, through negotiation, any other change in the status quo, pending withdrawal of all forces to the internationally recognized boundaries;

- supervise, verify and confirm the withdrawal of all forces to the internationally recognized boundaries; thereafter,

- monitor the cease-fire on the internationally recognized boundaries, investigate alleged violations, oversee exchanges of prisoners of war, and prevent, through negotiations, any other change in the status quo, pending negotiation of a comprehensive settlement; and

- obtain the agreement of the parties to other arrangements which, pending negotiation of a comprehensive settlement, could help to reduce tension and build confidence between them, such as the establishment of areas of separation of forces on either side of the international border, limitations on the number and calibre of weapons to be deployed in areas close to the international border and patrolling by United Nations naval personnel of certain sensitive areas in or near the Shatt-al-Arab.

Its mandate gave UNIIMOG tasks that were beyond its power to perform, one being the "restoration" of the situation after ceasefire violations. Iraq took several hundred Iranian prisoners only days after UNIIMOG deployed and held them for two years. Iran flooded the lowlands of the southern border region in September 1988. Not until Iraq invaded Kuwait in August 1990 and had to contend with much more pressing military problems did the two sides sit down in earnest to iron out their remaining differences.

FUNDING

The General Assembly financed UNIIMOG by means of a special assessment and separate expense account. The total assessment for the operation, from August 9, 1988, to March 31, 1991, was about $235 million. Although five to fifteen percent of assessments for UNIIMOG were always unpaid, the operation did not run at a deficit. Operational savings resulted from reductions in personnel (at the Iranians' request), from cancellation of maritime patrols in the Shatt al-Arab, and from non-deployment of UN helicopter units. The operation was further reduced in size following the invasion of Kuwait and the subsequent build-up of coalition forces.

Some nations made voluntary contributions to UNIIMOG. Kuwait, New Zealand, South Korea, Switzerland, and the Soviet Union made contributions in equipment, supplies, and services worth about $11 million. Voluntary contributions were automatically deducted from country assessments. The Swiss contributed a Jetstream 31 aircraft for use as an air ambulance, while the Soviets airlifted a Canadian communications unit to and from the mission area. They also transshipped other troops and equipment to Tehran that were initially airlifted by the United States to Incirlik, Turkey, and to Baghdad, because Tehran refused to allow US aircraft to land in Iran.[31]

PLANNING AND IMPLEMENTATION

When Iran accepted Resolution 598 on July 18, 1988, after nearly eight years of temporizing on UN Security Council resolutions, it came as a surprise to most of the world. Between July 25 and August 2, the Secretary General sent an advance team of political, logistics, and military advisors, under the leadership of UNTSO Chief of Staff, Lieutenant General Martin Vadset of Norway, to assess the area of operations and to obtain sufficient information for a detailed implementation plan. On August 10, one day after Security Council authorization, advance elements of UNIIMOG (a dozen people for each side, including nine observers borrowed from UNTSO) deployed to establish liaison with Iran and Iraq and to reconnoiter forward sites where observers would be deployed. The actual cease-fire was established ten days later. The small UN offices that had been set up in the two capitals in 1984 to investigate chemical weapon use against civilians helped the new mission to quickly establish its system for resolving cease-fire disputes.[32]

The belligerents agreed to use the internationally recognized boundary as the cease-fire line, but, when fighting stopped, the two armies were in very close proximity, in some places as close as ten meters. Each held small amounts of captured territory as well as large numbers of prisoners.[33]

Size and Composition of the Force

The 350 observers in UNIIMOG came from 26 countries (see table 14.1). None came from Middle Eastern countries, as most of those had supported one side or the other in the recent war. The UN initially planned on having 174 international civilian staff, 150 locally recruited staff, and 240 other military personnel to provide support and to operate and maintain three fixed-wing aircraft, twelve UN-operated helicopters, and two marine patrol vessels. Following consultation with the belligerents, the numbers of non-observers were reduced significantly, to 105 international and 93 local civilian staff, and 53 military support staff. The UN-controlled helicopters and marine vessels were never deployed. The recruitment of specialists and local staff in Iran was hampered by the difficulty of obtaining hiring permission from Iranian authorities and by the harrassment and arrest of locals who did work for the UN.[34]

Table 14.1. UNIIMOG Observers and Specialized Unit Personnel

Country	Sept. 1989	Nov. 1990	Jan. 1991	Feb. 1991
Argentina	10			
Australia	15	8		
Austria	6	9	7	1
Medical Section	4	4	4	2
Bangladesh	15	5	1	1
Canada	15	8	4	4
Signals Unit[1]	525			
Denmark	15	6	4	3
Finland	15	9	9	9
Ghana	15	2		
Hungary	15	15	15	15
India	15	11	11	11
Indonesia	15	5		
Ireland	14	2	1	1
Military Police	36	25	17	16
Italy	15	11	11	9
Kenya	15	2		
Malaysia	15	15	15	10
New Zealand	10	1	1	1
Air Unit	17	17		
Nigeria	16	16		
Norway	15	8	3	1
Peru	7			
Poland	15	9	4	1
Senegal	15	4		
Sweden	16	9	7	7
Turkey	15	3	1	1
Uruguay	12	9	9	9
Yugoslavia	11	11	11	11
Zambia	9	6	5	1

Note 1: Signals unit withdrew at the end of 1988. **Sources:** United Nations Documents S/20862, September 22, 1989; S/21960, November 23, 1990; S/22148, January 29, 1991; and S/22263, February 26, 1991.

After the Iraqi invasion of Kuwait, and on the recommendation of the Secretary General, UNIIMOG began to decrease its staff and observers by rotation without replacement. By late 1990, just 60 observers remained on the Iranian side and 56 on the Iraqi side. On January 16, 1991, when coalition air strikes on Iraq began, UNIIMOG moved the bulk of its forces out of Baghdad to Iran. The UN had some concern about bomb damage (although no UN positions were damaged) but greater concern about hostile reactions among the Iraqi populace to the sight of blue berets at a time of UN-sanctioned military action. Thus, by January 18, only three UNIIMOG personnel remained in Baghdad as part of the UN Offices of the Secretary General in Iran and Iraq (UNOSGII). They continued to investigate and, to the extent feasible, to mediate border incidents. As the ground invasion of Iraq began, remaining personnel were evacuated to Cyprus.[35]

Command Structure, Communications and Logistics

The Chief Military Observer (CMO) reported as usual to the Office of Special Political Affairs in New York. The CMO and his small personal staff of political and legal advisers and a press liaison shuttled weekly between Baghdad and Tehran. Below his level, however, observers operated exclusively in one country or the other. Assistant Chief Military Observers (ACMOs) were stationed in Baghdad and Tehran with headquarters staffs that included a chief of staff and deputies for operations, local liaison, personnel, and aviation. The ACMOs directly commanded UNIIMOG operations in their respective countries. ACMO-Baghdad commanded three sectors—northern, central and southern. ACMO-Tehran commanded four—Saqqez (northern), Bakhtaran (north central), Dezful (south central), and Ahwaz (south). Sector boundaries matched except in the south, where the Dezful and Ahwaz sectors in Iran were just half the size of the southern sector in Iraq. Each sector contained a number of permanently staffed observer-team sites that divided up the task of monitoring the cease-fire lines within the sector.[36]

The mission's Chief Administrative Officer reported to the CMO and maintained liaison with the ACMOS in Baghdad and Tehran, but, as is standard for such UN operations, he also reported to the Field Operations Division in New York. The Division, and not the CMO, had final say over money questions (also standard), and its civilian technicians controlled communications for the operation after the initial period.

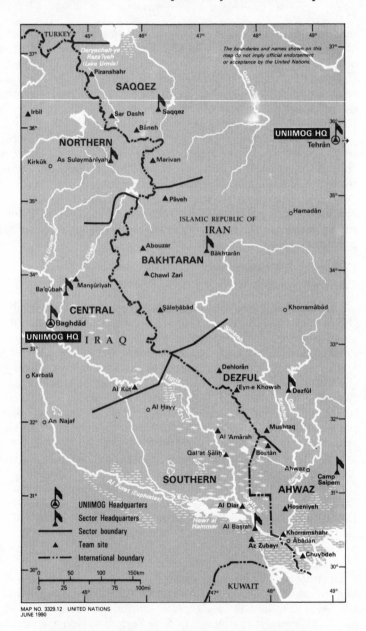

**Figure 14. 1. United Nations Iran-Iraq Military
Observer Group, Deployment as of June 1990**

Initial links between New York and UNIIMOG headquarters were established by a Canadian signals unit using large-dish satellite communications equipment.[37] This arrangement continued until the UN was able to establish its own direct link, which was partly interrupted again when the UN's dish in Tehran was impounded by Iranian authorities. Difficult terrain also posed problems for the setup of UNIIMOG's intra-theater UHF radio net. The communications link between the two national capitals originally used small-dish INMARSAT terminals, but this link was terminated in the face of Iranian objections. Intercapital communications were temporarily conducted through the satellite links to New York, but eventually they used local land lines and encrypted Telex. Iran also initially held up the deployment of radio-equipped UN ground vehicles, making communications with the mobile units very difficult for a time. Eventually, the vehicles were deployed and allowed to use their radio sets.[38]

Field Operations

UNIIMOG patrolled a 1,400-kilometer border using patrol sectors that varied from 250 kilometers in the mountainous north to 70 kilometers among the marshes of the southern sectors. Operating procedures emphasized conflict prevention and timely response to cease-fire violations, so as to contain disputes at a low level and keep them from spreading.

Quick responses were believed to have limited the escalation of border incidents, but early incidents were serious nonetheless, as noted earlier. Both sides also reinforced their field positions and edged them forward; such minor incidents accounted for 80 percent of the first year's 1,435 reported cease-fire violations.[39]

UNIIMOG developed dispute settlement procedures with both sides but failed to work out settlement criteria that both sides would accept. Efforts to establish a Mixed Military Working Group were unsuccessful. The Working Group almost met once, at the end of October 1990, but the meeting was cancelled at the last minute for political reasons.[40]

Occasionally, UN observers were denied access to parts of the cease-fire zone and their movements were restricted. Access denial and impediments to freedom of movement were immediately protested to the host government, but with mixed results.

UNIIMOG's operations were particularly constrained on the Iranian side of the border. In addition to the communications restrictions already noted, the Group was unable to deploy all of its vehicles on that side of the cease-fire line, and had true freedom of movement only within Tehran, within the southernmost patrol sector, and along the narrow ceasefire line. All other movement required frequently unavailable liaison officers. (Iran's liaison unit was specifically created to escort UNIIMOG observers, and consisted of personnel with military training who could speak English but were not regular military.) Iranian commanders continually sought direction from Tehran and frequently would not permit UN activities even after having received instruction to do so. Although no place was perpetually beyond the observers' purview, such denials were frequent, and doubtless affected UNI-IMOG's ability to respond quickly to outbreaks of violence on Iran's side of the border.

In Iraq, on the other hand, UNIIMOG was entirely self-sufficient in land transportation and had freedom of movement throughout its area of operations. Iraqi liaison officers were regular military.

The plan for UNIIMOG had originally envisioned the use of twelve UN helicopters for cease-fire observation, six on each side of the border. But because Iran objected, the UN had to rely upon six helicopters provided and piloted by Iran and Iraq. Since the helicopters remained under the control of the local parties, they could not cross the internationally recognized border to conduct inspections.

Under the best of circumstances, these restrictions would have limited the UN's ability to respond rapidly to violations in progress. But Iran often failed to make the helicopters available when needed, except for medical evacuations, and used its UN-designated helicopters, without UN observers aboard, to conduct some intelligence and reconnaissance missions of its own. Because Iran painted only the removable doors of its helicopters "UN White," they could easily revert to military operations when not in UN service. The UN brought a halt to this practice after two or three such flights. Iraq was not enthusiastic about providing helicopters if Iran refused to do so, but complied fully with UN requests for helicopter support, nonetheless.[41]

Helicopter patrols were extremely valuable in the northern patrol sectors because of the terrain was otherwise accessible only on foot. The mountainous regions were also politically sensitive, as each side sought to supply Kurdish dissidents in the other's country. Moreover, the borders of northern Iran were garrisoned largely by militant Revolutionary Guards, which complicated liaison.

To better coordinate its operations, UNIIMOG asked for three border crossing points, but Iran did not agree to open any of these points in practice. As a compromise, the parties did agree to allow UN "flag meetings" at border points, but only the ACMO and his headquarters assistants from either side could actually cross.[42]

UNIIMOG organized and attended, when appropriate, a series of low-level technical military meetings between the parties to expedite the maintenance of the cease-fire line. Higher level mediation efforts were the responsibility of the Special Representative of the Secretary General, Jan Eliasson of Sweden. The Special Representative and UNIIMOG maintained contact through New York. The separation of the mediation effort from the ground forces insulated UNIIMOG from the politics of conflict resolution, although peacekeepers contributed valuable military advice to the negotiators. As the operation came to a close in late 1990 and early 1991, Iran and Iraq were able to agree upon a one-kilometer-wide area of separation along the border, and to begin the process of exchanging information on the location of minefields. By February 28, both sides were to indicate that all territory had been returned and that they had established joint teams to survey the boundary. As of mid-1991, there had been no implementation of this agreement.

After stabilization of the cease-fire line and a significant reduction in violations, UNIIMOG participated in a series of confidence-building measures at the direction of the Secretary General. UNIIMOG supervised the removal of bodies from the one-kilometer buffer zone and oversaw repatriation of war dead to both sides.[43]

ASSESSMENT

UNIIMOG helped to keep the peace on the Iran-Iraq border for two and one-half years. Except for the final six months of that period, the border was a volatile and violence-prone place, and the presence of UN observers more than likely kept the war from flaring up anew in the face of mutual provocations. It is ironic, given subsequent history, that Iraq was something of a model host. Some of that was due to the briefing of Iraqi officials by Egyptian counterparts who had long experience in dealing with peacekeepers, so Iraq knew what to expect. Iran had no such crash course in peacekeeping protocol, but its obstructionism had far deeper roots than unfamiliarity.

The UN worked under severe operational handicaps imposed by Iran's suspicious, xenophobic rulers, who had accepted a cease-fire only under duress. UNIIMOG was a foreign element in the revolution's body politic, and Iran tried hard to limit the contamination while seeing to it that the UN learned no more about Iranian military dispositions than was absolutely necessary. The UN's communications gear was impounded, its helicopters were prohibited, and its every move subject to restriction and surveillance. Its local employees were hounded and its field personnel were forbidden to look in the wrong direction or to cross the border in the course of their work. Under the circumstances, it is impressive that UNIIMOG managed to do its job as well as it did.

Its experience only reemphasizes the basic notion that local consent and cooperation are key to successful peacekeeping. Peacekeepers can dispel misperceptions, bridge the mistrust that has built up between combatants, and help to contain outbreaks of violence by their accurate reporting (which helps to quash rumors) and by active mediation. They cannot do much more than that. Like other buffer forces, UNIIMOG could treat the symptoms of conflict but not its underlying political causes. That was and is the task of diplomacy. Ultimately, diplomacy was accelerated by the outbreak of war on another front. The Iraqi invasion of Kuwait and the UN response to it led Iraq to speed the process of negotiations and eliminate potential obstacles to mending its relations with Iran.

CONCLUSIONS

The United Nations was involved in trying to end the Iran-Iraq War from the first week of hostilities. But the efforts of the Secretary General to end the war, and the Security Council's calls for a cease-fire, were drowned out by the din of battle, by Iran's insistence that Iraq be formally labelled the aggressor, and by its determined efforts to destroy Iraq as payback for that agression. They were muffled as well by the ringing of cash registers in capitals around the world, as the war's demand for weapons and ammunition drew billions of dollars in armaments into the Persian Gulf, openly and covertly.

Although neither belligerent was seen as a model regime, either by the world's major powers or by the other Gulf states, Saddam Hussein was at the time considered the lesser evil. Iraq, in fending off massive and costly Iranian ground assaults, was acting out many states' desires to stop the Iranian revolution before it could spread; that Saddam used poison gas to do it caused a few second thoughts, but not enough to affect fundamentally the judgment of all those powers who supported a thug to contain a pariah.

As the bloodshed in the Gulf came to an end, the UN moved in to help sustain a shaky peace. What is to be hoped is that it will, before too long, be capable of rising to the occasion at the start of a war, rather than its finish.

Notes

1. S. H. Amin, "The Iran-Iraq War: Legal Implications," *Marine Policy* 6, no. 3 (July 1982): 193, 199. Iran, however, does have alternative access to the sea from several other deep water ports along its Persian Gulf coast.

2. Amin, "Legal Implications," 200; Gary Sick, "Trial by Error: Reflections on the Iran-Iraq War," *Middle East Journal* 43, no. 2 (Spring 1989): 231.

3. Behrouz Souresrafil, *The Iran-Iraq War* (Plainview, New York: Guinan Lithographic Co., 1989), 23; Sick, "Trial by Error," 232.

4. Souresrafil, *The Iran-Iraq War*, 23; Brian Urquhart and Gary Sick, eds., *The United Nations and the Iran-Iraq War* (New York: Ford Foundation Conference Report, 1987), 7.

5. Amin, "Legal Implications," 203.

6. Urquhart and Sick, *The United Nations and the Iran-Iraq War*, 8; Sick, "Trial by Error," 230.

7. David Segal, "The Iran-Iraq War: A Military Analysis," *Foreign Affairs* 66 (Summer 1988): 955; Shahram Chubin and Charles Tripp, *Iran and Iraq at War* (London: I.B. Tauris and Co., Ltd., 1988), 190, 209; Judith Miller and Laurie Mylroie, *Saddam Hussein and the Crisis in the Gulf* (New York: Random House, Times Books, 1990), 109-123.

8. Chemical use was reciprocated by Iran beginning in 1987. Syria shut down Iraq's pipeline in 1982, cutting its exports in half. Iraq built new ones through Saudi Arabia by 1986, and doubled the capacity of the lines through Turkey by early 1987 (*Strategic Survey, 1987-88* [London: International Institute for Strategic Studies, 1988], 126-27; United States, *Department of State Bulletin* [hereafter, *DOS Bulletin*], October 1987, 39-41; Miller and Mylroie, *Saddam Hussein*, 146; Segal, "A Military Analysis," 955-56, 959-60; Chubin and Tripp, *Iran and Iraq at War*, 142).

9. Seymour M. Hersh, "US Secretly Gave Aid to Iraq Early in Its War Against Iran," *New York Times*, January 26, 1992, A1.

10. David C. Martin and John Walcott, *Best Laid Plans* (New York: Simon & Schuster, 1988), 327 ff.

11. Captain Bud Langston and Lieutenant Commander Don Bringle, "The Air View: Operation Praying Mantis," and Captain J. B. Perkins, "The Surface View: Operation Praying Mantis," *US Naval Institute Proceedings* (May 1989) 54-59, 66-70.

12. Perkins, "The Surface View," 70. A US Navy report issued in August 1988 attributed the event to crew stress rather than faulty equipment. However, the International Civil Aviation Organization

criticized the Navy for having had no equipment aboard *Vincennes* able to monitor and communicate on civil aviation channels (*New York Times*, December 4, 1988, 3).

13. Urquhart and Sick, *The United Nations and the Iran-Iraq War*, 9, 10, 15.

14. Urquhart and Sick, *The United Nations and the Iran-Iraq War*, 17, 22.

15. D.D. Lincoff, ed., *Annual Review of United Nations Affairs* (Dobbs Ferry, New York: Oceana Publications, Inc., 1983), 99-100; Ibid., 1985, 123.

The Council did, however, approve several resolutions dealing with other issues related to the war, such as free passage through the Persian Gulf and the Strait of Hormuz, and it investigated, and condemned, the use of chemical weapons by both parties (Urquhart and Sick, *The United Nations and the Iran-Iraq War*, 10).

16. Sick, "Trial by Error," 240.

17. Dilip Hiro, *The Longest War: The Iran-Iraq Military Conflict* (London: Grafton Books, 1989), 232, 228-9.

18. Sick, "Trial by Error," 242; Souresrafil, *The Iran-Iraq War*, 150.

19. Sick, "Trial by Error," 243. Direct negotiations did not take place, however, for two years following the cease fire. Chronology, *Middle East Journal* 44, no. 4 (Autumn 1990), 680.

20. *DOS Bulletin*, February 1987, 23 and August 1987, 78.

21. *DOS Bulletin*, December 1980, 2; Chubin and Tripp, *Iran and Iraq at War*, 190, 209.

22. Sick notes that this effort came just days after US Assistant Secretary of State Richard Murphy met with Iraq's President Saddam Hussein. Within a week of the meeting, the US frigate *Stark* was attacked in the Gulf and 37 of its crew were killed by Iraqi cruise missiles, evidently fired by accident or misdirection, but nonetheless part of a campaign of terror against high seas shipping that evoked no US military response, as it then was focused on Iranian shipping (*DOS Bulletin*, August 1987, 75-77; May 1988, 67; October 1988, 61-62; Sick, "Trial by Error," 240).

23. United Nations, *UN Monthly Chonicle*, September 1980, 7; Hiro, *The Longest War*, 122.

24. Hiro, *The Longest War*, 228-29.

25. Hiro, *The Longest War*, 228-229.

26. Chubin and Tripp, *Iran and Iraq at War*, 203.

27. Hiro, *The Longest War*, 199; Chubin and Tripp, *Iran and Iraq at War*, 203, 217.

28. Sick, "Trial by Error," 243; Souresrafil, *The Iran-Iraq War*, 150-53.

29. United Nations Document S/20862, September 22, 1989, 1-2.

30. United Nations Document A/44/874, December 14, 1989, 10.

31. United Nations Document A/44/874, 8.

32. *The Blue Helmets: A Review of United Nations Peacekeeping*, 2nd ed. (New York: United Nations Department of Public Information, 1990), 324, 329-330.

33. United Nations Document S/20862, 4-5; Alan James, *Peacekeeping in International Politics* (New York: St. Martin's Press, 1990), 173.

34. *The Blue Helmets*, 415; United Nations Documents S/20862, 4, and A/44/874, 3; Interview 72, June 20, 1991.

35. United Nations Document S/22148, January 29, 1991, 2, 4, 5.

36. *The Blue Helmets*, 415; and United Nations Documents S/20862, 4, S/21960, and S/22148. Major General Slavko Jovic served as CMO through November 1990. The first two ACMOs were Brigadier General J. Kelly of Ireland in Tehran, and Brigadier General V. M. Patil of India in Baghdad. Kelly was replaced in September 1989 by Brigadier General P. Kallstrom of Sweden, who was replaced in turn one year later by Colonel H. Purola of Finland. Brigadier General Patil was replaced by Brigadier General S. Anam Khan of Bangladesh; Khan became Acting CMO in November 1990, and his former duties were assumed by Colonel P. Grabner of Austria. Thus, as the mission was reduced in size through the fall of 1990, it was also reduced in rank.

37. US Air Force transport aircraft flew the Canadian unit into Baghdad. Since US military aircraft were unwelcome in Tehran, elements headed there were flown into the region and then transferred to Soviet aircraft for the final leg of their trip. The Soviets flew the entire unit home in December 1988.

38. United Nations Document S/20862, 7; Interview 72, June 20, 1991.

39. United Nations Document S/21960, 5; Interview 72, June 20, 1991.

40. Interview 72, June 20, 1991.

41. Interview 72, June 20, 1991.

42. United Nations Document S/20862, 7.

43. United Nations Documents S/20862, S/21960, and S/22148; Interview 72.

15 The Iraq-Kuwait Observation Mission

by William J. Durch

The United Nations Iraq-Kuwait Observation Mission (UNIKOM) is one year old at this writing. It grew out of the Security Council's 1990–1991 Chapter VII enforcement action against Iraq and thus can claim unique parentage among peacekeeping operations. Of the three UN missions impinging on Iraqi territory after the second Gulf War, only UNIKOM can be characterized as a peacekeeping mission. The other two operations were the punitive Special Commission, set up to dismantle Iraqi mass destruction weapon capacity, and the relief efforts in northern Iraq on behalf of the Kurdish population, which were adorned with a symbolic UN constabulary and backed by substantial military forces. And even UNIKOM, which enjoys only grudging support from Iraq, its nominal host country, relies more than most UN operations on the implicit threat of Great Power military backup to maintain stability in its area of operations.

ORIGINS

With conflict endemic to the Middle East and Persian Gulf, Iraq's August 1990 invasion of Kuwait was, from the perspective of the previous decade of regional history, tantamount to business as usual. What was not usual was the reaction of the industrialized world, since, for most of the previous decade, the Great Powers actively manipulated the bloody war between Iraq and Iran for their own benefit and did not intervene decisively on either side.[1] What transformed Saddam Hussein's 1990 land grab into a major international crisis, complete with references to World War Two and Adolph Hitler, was a quick policy pirouette by the American government, which decided to challenge Baghdad after tilting toward it throughout the 1980s.

Initiatives toward UN Involvement

To its credit, once the United States decided to challenge the invasion of Kuwait, it turned to the United Nations, seeking sanctions under Chapter VII of the Charter and bringing along much of the rest of the international community. The Security Council took action by degrees through a series of resolutions. It first demanded Iraqi withdrawal from Kuwait (Resolution 660), then established an embargo and froze Iraqi and Kuwaiti funds overseas (Resolution 661), condemned and rejected Iraq's "annexation" of Kuwait (Resolution 662), demanded the release of diplomatic and consular officials and other foreign nationals held hostage by Iraqi forces (Resolutions 664, 667, 674), authorized naval enforcement of its embargo (Resolution 665), explicitly extended the embargo to air traffic (Resolution 670), and, finally, authorized "Member States cooperating with the Government of Kuwait,"

> unless Iraq on or before 15 January 1991 fully implements...the foregoing resolutions, to use all necessary means to uphold and implement resolution 660 (1990) and all subsequent relevant resolutions and to restore international peace and security in the area.[2]

As the Security Council was taking these actions, often at US initiative, the United States was deploying land, sea, and air forces in and near the Persian Gulf to enforce the UN embargo and deter further Iraqi military action. It was also assembling a coalition of like-minded European, Arab, and other states to join in that task. Immediately following US Congressional elections in early November, and two weeks before passage of Resolution 678, President Bush ordered US forces in the Gulf to be reinforced considerably, giving them the capability of forcibly evicting Iraqi forces from Kuwait.[3]

On January 16, 1991, coalition forces launched six weeks of air attacks on Iraq, its forces, and its strategic infrastructure. On February 24th, armored ground units swept into southern Iraq and Kuwait, capturing much of what remained of Iraqi forces there. However, a US decision to halt the ground war after 100 hours, before Iraq's army was fully surrounded, allowed several divisions of Republican Guard troops and armored personnel carriers to escape northward.[4] These forces were used subsequently to suppress postwar rebellions in the Shi'a-majority southern part of Iraq and in the Kurdish-majority north, where a mass exodus toward the border with Turkey and Iran first created a humanitarian crisis, then triggered a Western military response. Ground and air forces intervened to form a buffer between Kurdish refugees and the pursuing Iraqi army. There was no similar response in the south; indeed, Iraqi helicopters strafed Shi'a positions within sight of US tank crews in the coalition-occupied part of Iraq.[5]

Five weeks after the US-declared cease-fire in the coalition ground war, the Security Council passed Resolution 687, a watershed in collective security that mandated the destruction of all Iraqi chemical, biological, and nuclear weapons, materials, and production facilities, as well as all ballistic missiles with a range greater than 150 kilometers. Resolution 687 established a Special Commission to deal with inspection and destruction of the non-nuclear weapons and facilities, and delegated responsibility for nuclear elements to the International Atomic Energy Agency. Resolution 687 also reaffirmed economic sanctions against Iraq, including an arms embargo, offered a formal cease-fire upon Iraq's acceptance of its terms, and established a UN observer force and buffer zone along the Iraq-Kuwait border. Iraq accepted on April 6.[6]

POLITICAL SUPPORT

UNIKOM is unique for being part of a package developed by the Security Council to end a war that was sanctioned under Chapter VII of the UN Charter. As such it also enjoys perhaps a unique level of international political support. There is, for example, broad agreement that some sort of buffer and monitoring effort is needed between Iraq and Kuwait for the indefinite future.

The scope of that support, and the seriousness with which the Council views the mission and its context, are reflected in the contribution of military observers by all five permanent members of the Security Council, a first for UN peacekeeping.

Regional and local support for UNIKOM are less certain, on the other hand. No Persian Gulf states, and no other Arab states, contributed personnel to the operation. Moreover, its presence has but the grudging acquiescence of Iraq.[7]

MANDATE

Resolution 687 asked the Secretary General to submit to the Security Council

> a plan for the immediate deployment of a United Nations observer unit to monitor the Khor Abdullah [waterway] and a demilitarized zone, which is hereby established, extending ten kilometers into Iraq and five kilometers into Kuwait from the boundary referred to in the Agreed Minutes between the State of Kuwait and the Republic of Iraq regarding the Restoration of Friendly Relations, Recognition and Related Matters of 4 October 1963.

Deployment of the observer unit in this demilitarized zone (DMZ) was intended to allow coalition ground forces to withdraw from Iraq.

The Secretary General responded to Resolution 687 on April 5, 1991, with a report that proposed the following additional functions for UNIKOM:

- To deter violations of the boundary through its presence in and surveillance of the demilitarized zone; and

- To observe any hostile or potentially hostile action mounted from the territory of one State to the other.[8]

The report was approved, and UNIKOM formally authorized, by Security Council Resolution 689 of April 9.

As an observer unit, UNIKOM was not authorized to take any physical action to stop or interfere with incursions or other "hostile actions" in the zone that it patrols. Moreover, the Secretary General interpreted its mandate to be limited to observing and reporting only those activities that could be seen from the DMZ. Nor was UNIKOM given any civil administrative or humanitarian functions; basic services and law and order inside the DMZ remained the responsibility of the two local parties. Refugee relief was to be the joint responsibility of the UN High Commissioner for Refugees (UNHCR) and the Red Cross. The Secretariat did not want UNIKOM to devolve, like UNIFIL, into a largely humanitarian effort, with the supply train and costs which that would entail.[9]

Finally, unlike most UN peacekeeping operations, UNIKOM has an open-ended mandate. Although its finances are reauthorized every six months, the mandate is merely "reviewed." It will continue until terminated by action of the Security Council.

FUNDING

UNIKOM was financed in the manner usual for peacekeeping forces since 1973, as an expense of the Organization to be funded by a special assessment on member states. Given the press of time and limited number of experts available to draw up the initial budget for the operation, the Secretariat fell back on "full cost" estimates—the cost to the UN if no host nation support were provided, and all vehicles and equipment had to be purchased new. The initial estimate for the first six months of the operation was $83 million. By the time it reached the Advisory Committee on Administrative and Budgetary Questions (ACABQ), the request had been pared to $74 million. Allowing for host nation support and reuse of equipment from UNIIMOG (the disbanded Iran-Iraq Military Observer Group) and other missions, the ACABQ reduced UNIKOM's initial budget to $60 million, cautioning against acquisition of "equipment that is more sophisticated and expensive" than necessary to fulfill its mandate.[10] The impact of this skeptical attitude toward "sophisticated" equipment was felt in the field, where UNIKOM's kit was singularly unsophisticated by comparison to US Army units whose presence it displaced.

UNIKOM's budget was not approved by the General Assembly until May. The ACABQ meanwhile allowed the Secretariat nearly $7 million in "unforeseen and extraordinary expenditures" to facilitate contracting for goods and services and deploying UN field personnel.

PLANNING AND IMPLEMENTATION

Contingency planning for a peacekeeping mission in Kuwait was said to be underway in February 1991 as the air war in the Persian Gulf continued. By April 3rd, five weeks after the fighting subsided, the Secretariat should have been able to scope out the requirements for a peacekeeping mission in the region, devise its budget, and line up troop contributors. The Secretary General did report back to the Security Council within the three days stipulated by Resolution 687, but the logistical and budgetary details of the operation required another two weeks to work out, suggesting that detailed planning did not begin until late March at the earliest.[11]

Size and Composition of the Force

UNIKOM peaked at 1,440 personnel in June 1991. The 300-strong military observer force was backed up, initially, by five companies of infantry (680 troops in all) on temporary reassignment from UN missions in Cyprus and Lebanon, plus various small support units, and a cadre of UN civilian administrators and communications experts. Table 15.1 shows force composition as of October 1991.

Table 15.1. Composition and Strength of UNIKOM, October 1991

Military Observers		Military Observers, cont.	
Country	**Number**	**Country**	**Number**
Argentina	7	Pakistan	9
Austria	7	Poland	7
Bangladesh	7	Romania	7
Canada	1	Senegal	7
China	20	Singapore	7
Denmark	7	Sweden	8
Fiji	8	Thailand	7
Finland	7	Turkey	7
France	20	USSR/Russia	20
Ghana	8	UK	20
Greece	7	USA	20
Hungary	7	Uruguay	8
India	8	Venezuela	7
Indonesia	7	**Administration and Logistics**	
Ireland	8	Canada (engineers)	300
Italy	6	Chile (helicopters)	50
Kenya	8	Denmark (movement control, postal)	19
Malaysia	8	Norway (medical)	50
Nigeria	7	Sweden (logistics)	30
Norway	8	Other Staff	177
		Total Force:	**913**

Source: United Nations, *Report of the Secretary-General on the United Nations Iraq-Kuwait Observation Mission*, Security Council document S/23106, October 2, 1991, 2.

Command, Communications, and Logistics

General Günther Greindl (Austria) was appointed Commander of UNIKOM on April 10th. General Greindl, a veteran of several previous UN operations, including tours as Force Commander on the Golan Heights and Cyprus, arrived in the mission area three

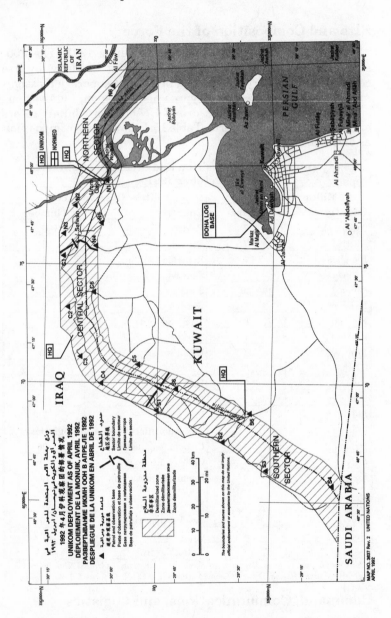

Figure 15.1. United Nations Iraq-Kuwait Observation Mission, Deployment as of October 1991

days later with a dozen temporary headquarters staff borrowed from UNTSO. This nucleus drew up the operation's structural deployment plan. On April 24, deployment of UNIKOM began with a symbolic raising of the UN flag at Safwan, Iraq, inside the demilitarized zone. A handful of UN observers took to the field west of Safwan and in Umm Qasr, the eventual site of the operation's headquarters. Small liaison offices were established in Baghdad (using former UNIIMOG offices) and at Doha, Kuwait (also the site of the operation's logistics base).

Logistics were initially quite rocky, and UNIKOM was wholly dependent upon US Army support in its first weeks. Troops and equipment arrived in Kuwait before the UN's civilian communications and movement control people. Two US military observers (seconded from US Air Force Headquarters staff) became impromptu transport and movement control planners, and another worked up initial patrol plans. The first observers sent into the field had little more than tents to mark their observation posts. The US Army provided generators, created earth berms, and strung concertina wire around the posts to give them an appearance of permanence and defensibility. For the first five months of the operation, however, also the hottest months of the year, non-air-conditioned tents were the only accommodations for observers in the field. Air-conditioned trailers became available in September. In general, members of the observer group arrived in Kuwait sooner than UNIKOM's equipment, even though much of the operation's rolling stock and communications gear was transferred from UNIIMOG, the operation on the Iraq-Iran border that was terminated at the end of February 1991.[13]

Mine clearing and disposal of other unexploded ordnance was another major hurdle. Many mines in the DMZ were cleared by American forces before their departure, but a 300-strong Canadian engineer company was assigned to UNIKOM to complete the task. In its first six months of operation, it cleared 7,000 pieces of ordnance.[14]

Five infantry battalions were loaned to UNIKOM from other UN missions to provide initial security: three companies from the Fijian, Ghanaian, and Nepalese battalions of UNIFIL (in Lebanon), and two companies from the Austrian and Danish battalions of UNFICYP (on Cyprus). All returned to their parent battalions by the end of June, as did a Swedish logistics company borrowed from UNIFIL.[15]

UNIKOM was declared operational on May 6th. The last US Army unit to leave Iraq, the 1st Brigade, 3rd Armored Division, departed Safwan May 7th, and the demilitarized zone was officially established on the 8th. However, the UN was not effectively deployed throughout the DMZ for another two to three weeks.[16]

UNIKOM's area of operations is divided into three roughly equal sectors (North, Central, and South). Each sector has a headquarters and six observation posts, which double as patrol bases. The Force undertakes mobile patrols, but the danger of unexploded ordnance limits their forays to those tracks cleared by the engineers. (Full operations in south Sector were delayed for months by the density of unexploded ordnance.) Ground patrols are supplemented by the operation's six Chilean helicopters and two small fixed-wing aircraft (donated, together with crews, by Switzerland).[17]

Field Operations

After the departure of its infantry units, UNIKOM became a standard unarmed UN observer force. By August 1991, bands of Iraqis in civilian dress were venturing regularly into the DMZ to raid weapons caches and dig up land mines, for which the Baghdad government offered cash payments, and for which there was a thriving black market among the local Bedouin population. Numerous casualties and 16 deaths among the scavengers were recorded by UNIKOM, which was often asked to evacuate the injured to hospitals.

In mid-September 1991, 80 Iraqis who claimed to be fishermen were intercepted by Kuwaiti patrols on or near Bubiyan Island, on Kuwait's side of the Khor Abdullah waterway, alledgedly after firing on the Kuwaitis. Only the northeast coast of Bubiyan is within the DMZ, and UNIKOM observation posts did not see this event. In mid-October, Iraq promised to stem the incursions.[18]

Iraqi citizens were not the only ones to violate the DMZ, however. Indeed, in terms of sheer numbers, ground violations from the Kuwaiti side of the border, especially in the first month after the war, were ten times more frequent than violations in the other direction. And allied aircraft appear initially to have overflown the zone quite frequently in the first two months (see Table 15.2). This may have reflected a sense on the part of coalition forces that the DMZ and UNIKOM functioned as adjuncts to their operations, as but another constraint on Iraq, whereas the UN as usual made every effort to run its operation impartially.

The border violations highlighted the small size and limited reach of the UN operation, as well as its relative lack of equipment. UNIKOM must cover a porous, 200-kilometer land and water border that runs through a DMZ 15 kilometers deep with only one observer for every ten square kilometers. Moreover, its observers have only the most basic of equipment: binoculars and one passive night vision device for each fixed observation post. They have no thermal imaging equipment and no ground surveillance radars to spot incursions and cue patrols. In the sandy, humid, hazy (and, for the first six months, smoky) atmosphere of the Iraq-Kuwait DMZ, binoculars do not see very far in the daytime, and image intensifier scopes only brighten the haze at night.[19]

Table 15.2. Violations of the Demilitarized Zone Observed by UNIKOM

	IRAQ				KUWAIT/Allied Forces			
	Ground	Air	Police Weapons	Total	Ground	Air	Police Weapons	Total
May 10–June 9	8	0	0	8	57	29	0	86
June 10–July 9	4	0	0	4	29	28	0	57
July 10–Aug. 9	1	0	6	7	9	9	6	24
Aug. 10–Sept. 9	5	0	4	9	13	13	1	27
Sept. 10–Oct. 2	0	0	1	1	6	7	3	16
Totals:	18	0	11	29	114	86	10	210

Source: UN Document S/23106, October 2, 1991, 5.

ASSESSMENT

UNIKOM is doing the job it was sent out to do, but its early weeks were far more disorganized than they needed to be. Operational plans were drawn up in the field, as observers and initial equipment began to arrive and stack up, reflecting the basic lack of planning capacity at UN Headquarters. The delays in establishing habitable field accommodations illustrate an outmoded supply system that has no reserves and no stockpiles, as well as a seemingly counterproductive requirement for committee approval of any novel expenditure over $40,000.[20]

UNIKOM's task (to observe and report) and its capabilities (quite basic) are classic UN. In the wake of an operation as sweeping and hi-tech as the second Gulf War, however, that may no longer suffice. The Force Commander reported that in the early weeks of the operation UNIKOM was referred to locally as "the UN forces" and was expected to take control of the DMZ as a kind of occupying power.[21] Once it became clear that the UN would not be exercising effective control over the zone, Iraq began the sort of salami-slicing tactics in the DMZ that it employed elsewhere to delay and discourage the work of the UN Special Commission sent to dismantle its weapons of mass destruction. In addition to the weapon-gathering forays, Iraq refused to move five police posts apparently on Kuwaiti territory until the UN Border Demarcation Commission completed its task. As of March 1992, it still maintained posts closer to the border than the 1,000 meters minimum separation distance requested by the UN.[22]

UNIKOM's task is simpler than the Special Commission's. Still, one or two battalions of infantry might have made a stronger impression on a heavily armed local population and a cynical Baghdad government, and might have inspired more confidence among Kuwaitis, than do unarmed Blue Berets. Historically, unarmed observer forces have been used in places where the presence of armed troops would be too sensitive politically (as in Kashmir, Central America, or between Iran and Iraq). But in this instance, peacekeepers deployed in the wake of a UN-sanctioned military action to repel a declared aggressor. There was, in other words, sufficient political headroom to deploy an armed force, one with responsibility to maintain order in the DMZ at least until the border between Iraq and Kuwait had been demarcated in accord with Resolution 687.[23]

On the other hand, the UN Secretariat did not wish to make UNIKOM a magnet for political refugees. A UN-controlled DMZ would have been an attractive haven to thousands of unhappy Iraqis of various stripes, unwelcome in their homeland and equally unwelcome in Kuwait, a new population of UN dependents. Although UN peacekeeping is not usually thought of in such hard-edged terms, UNIKOM's mandate was carefully limited to avoid humanitarian entanglements and to tightly constrain the operation's geographic scope. In his interpretation of the mandate, the Secretary General confined UNIKOM's responsibilities to reporting on border threats originating in the DMZ. Detecting threats to Kuwait that might originate outside the DMZ was, by implication, the responsibility of the Great Powers.

Resolution 687 did one other thing that looks sensible on paper, but proved dubious in practice and was likely honored largely in the breach. The resolution enjoined Kuwaiti and Iraqi police from carrying anything heavier than sidearms into the DMZ in order to prevent large-scale armed clashes and to keep Iraq from building up military forces near the border. However, given UNIKOM's hands-off mandate, the injunction has meant that bandits, scavengers, and gun-runners are more heavily armed than the forces responsible for law and order in the zone. Instances in which police are seen carrying more than sidearms are noted as violations of 687 by UN observers.

CONCLUSION

UNIKOM is playing a traditional role in a most untraditional drama that pits the will and resources of the Security Council against the will and resourcefulness of Saddam Hussein and the government of Iraq, not just in UNIKOM's domain but in the northern Kurdish areas, and in the game of hide and seek that Baghdad plays with the Special Commission as it waits for the world to tire of the chase.[24] As part of the endgame of a rare Chapter VII enforcement action, UNIKOM has unusual parentage and an unusual degree of implicit military backup. In terms of its very narrow mandate, it is thus likely to succeed. But the UN is accustomed to sending relatively threadbare forces on important but primarily symbolic missions that few countries, much less global news media, have followed on a routine basis. As the UN assumes greater responsibility for peacekeeping in many parts of the world, and the costs of operations escalate, it will encounter growing international scrutiny. Its operations will need to be better planned and more cost effective, with more labor at the front end, more technology in the field, and a real supply system in between.

Notes

1. For synopses of the Arab-Israeli dispute, the civil wars in Lebanon, and the eight-year war between Iraq and Iran, refer to the Middle East cases, and the case of UNIIMOG.

2. United Nations, Security Council, S/Res/678, 29 November 1991. For reprints of the complete text of these resolutions, see Micah Sifry and Christopher Cerf, eds., *The Gulf War Reader* (New York and Toronto: Random House, Times Books, 1991), 137-156.

3. For a summary of US decision-making in the months leading up to the war, see Thomas L. Friedman and Patrick E. Tyler, "From the First, US Resolve to Fight," *New York Times*, March 3, 1991, A1. The fall troop buildup was decided in a two-hour White House meeting on October 30, 1990, but not announced until two days after the election.

4. US General Norman Schwartzkopf believed that the "gate" had been closed on the Iraqi army by the time the cease-fire took hold. See Michael R. Gordon with Eric Schmitt, "Much More Armor than US Believed Fled Back to Iraq," *New York Times*, March 25, 1991, A1.

5. Nora Boustany, "US Troops Witness Iraqi Attack on Town," *Washington Post*, March 31, 1991, A1; Michael Gordon, "GI's in Iraq, Hands Tied, Try to Aid the Refugees," *New York Times*, April 2, 1991, A1.

6. For the complete text, see United Nations Document S/Res/687, April 3, 1991, and the *New York Times*, April 3, 1991, 13. Also, John M. Goshko, "Iraq Accepts UN Terms to End Gulf War," *Washington Post*, April 7, 1991, 1.

7. Patrick Tyler, "Baghdad Formally Agrees to 'Unjust' UN Conditions for Permanent Cease-fire," *New York Times*, April 7, 1991, A1. A year later, the US still maintained about 10,000 Army, Air Force, and Marine Corps personnel ashore, and 12,500 Navy personnel in the Persian Gulf region (*European Stars and Stripes*, April 7, 1992, 1).

8. United Nations, *Report of the Secretary-General on the Implementation of Paragraph 5 of Security Council Resolution 687 (1991)*, Security Council Document S/22452, April 5, 1991, 1.

9. Iraqis in the DMZ who were fleeing Saddam Hussein's security forces were technically "displaced persons" and not "refugees" under international law, but UNHCR agreed to help them. However, the displaced Iraqis were a potentially explosive issue. They had accepted food, water, and medical attention from American forces. As the DMZ returned to Iraqi jurisdiction, Iraqi police would regain full legal control over camps on the Iraqi side of the border, raising the prospect of summary arrests and executions, about which the UN could do little, occurring under its very nose.

The situation was defused when Saudi Arabia offered to house up to 40,000 refugees/displaced persons at a camp near Rahfa, on the Saudi-Iraq border. Some 17,000 people were flown to Rahfa by US transport aircraft through the first week in May. Once the exodus was complete, the last US ground units withdrew from Iraq. See Paul Lewis, "Big Refugee Role for UN," *New York Times*, April 9, 1991, A14; Edward Gargan, "UN Says its Forces Can't Care for Iraqi Refugees in Southern Zone," *New York Times*, April 20, 1991, 4; and Gargan, "Last GI's Leave a Major Iraq-Kuwait Border Post," *New York Times*, May 8, 1991, A16.

10. United Nations, *Financing of the Activities Arising from Security Council Resolution 687 (1991): United Nations Iraq-Kuwait Observation Mission*, General Assembly Document A/45/1005, April 29, 1991, 2,5.

11. The ACABQ's report referred to "the short notice for preparation of the Secretary-General's report and the insufficient lead-time for the operational plan" which led to "a number of uncertainties with regard to the estimates" (General Assembly Document A/45/1005, 2).

12. Interview 83, October 15, 1991.

13. Interview 65, May 15, 1991.

14. United Nations Document S/23106, October 2, 1991, 3.

15. United Nations, *Reports of the Secretary-General on the United Nations Iraq-Kuwait Observation Mission*, Security Council Document S/22580, May 9, 1991 and S/23106, 4.

16. Edward Gargan, "Last GIs Leave a Major Iraq-Kuwait Border Post," *New York Times*, May 8, 1991, A16; Security Council Document S/23106, 2; Interview 83, October 15, 1991.

17. United Nations, *Financing of the Activities Arising from Security Council Resolution 687 (1991)*, General Assembly Document A/45/240/Add.1, April 22, 1991, 5-6, 18.

18. United Nations Document S/23106, 9; Caryle Murphy, "Iraqis Roam Kuwait's DMZ," *Washington Post*, September 19, 1991, A36.

19. Thermal imagers use the infrared radiation emitted by all warm bodies and equipment and see through haze that blocks visible light. Radars emit their own signals and detect objects from the signals they reflect.

20. *Financial Regulations and Rules of the United Nations (Series 100)*, United Nations Document ST/SGB/Financial Rules/Rev.3 (1985), 32 (Rule 110.17, Committee on Contracts).

21. United Nations Document S/23106, 9.

22. United Nations Document S/23106, 6; UN, *Note by the President of the Security Council*, Document S/23699, March 11, 1992, 3.

23. Because of differences in the way the UN pays for observers, as opposed to "formed military units," armed units would not have been more costly than unarmed observers. The five infantry companies borrowed from other UN operations (some 680 troops) cost UNIKOM just 10 percent more per month, on average, than its 300 military observers, including reimbursements for wear and tear on the infantry units' equipment. Costs would have been higher, of course, if the UN had been given actual control of the DMZ. See General Assembly Document A/45/240/Add.1, 8.

24. See Rep. Les Aspin, "Winning the War and Losing the Peace in Saddam Hussein's Iraq," mimeograph of a speech given in New York, December 12, 1991 (transcript available from US House of Representatives, Committee on Armed Services, Washington, D.C.).

Part Three:

Peacekeeping in
South and Southeast Asia

16   United Nations Military Observer Group in India and Pakistan

by Karl Th. Birgisson

The United Nations Military Observer Group in India and Pakistan (UNMOGIP) is over forty years old, established in 1949 and still in operation. Its original purpose was to oversee a cease-fire between India and Pakistan in the disputed state of Kashmir, where the two countries had been at war. In this, UNMOGIP was initially very successful, but Indian authorities have not involved themselves in UNMOGIP's operations in recent years, making its mission ineffective and of little practical import. UN presence in the area, however, does serve a useful political purpose by signalling continued UN interest in the Kashmir dispute and is not likely to end anytime soon.

ORIGINS

The State of Jammu and Kashmir (hereafter referred to as Kashmir) is a very mountainous region of the northwestern Indian subcontinent. India lies to its south, Pakistan to the west, and China to the north and east. Its population of roughly 8 million is predominantly Muslim, but about one-third are Hindus. Kashmir has been divided since the late 1940s along a line extending southwest to northeast; territory west of the line is under Pakistani control, while territory east of it is ruled by India.

The division dates from shortly after Great Britain's decision to relinquish control of British India to local governments. The Indian Independence Act, passed in July 1947, provided for the creation of two independent countries: Pakistan, comprised of the predominantly Muslim provinces, and India, covering the predominantly Hindu provinces. In addition, the Act technically and legally made independent some 584 princely states with a combined population of 99 million people.[1]

Most of the princely states were quite small and the majority were Hindu. Considering economic and geographic realities, most of them decided to join either Pakistan or India. By the time those two countries became independent on August 15, 1947, all but three of the principalities—Hyderabad, Junagadh, and Kashmir—had made this choice. Hyderabad, one of the largest states, had a population of almost 17 million and was the size of Germany. It was predominantly Hindu, but ruled by a Muslim. He intended for his state to remain independent, but India invaded in 1948 and forced Hyderabad into its Union. A similar fate awaited Junagadh; it, too, was predominantly Hindu and ruled by a Muslim who sought to join Pakistan. An Indian invasion and a subsequent plebiscite led to its incorporation into India.[2]

Kashmir, on the other hand, remained undecided. The Hindu Maharaja Sir Hari Singh ruled over a mostly Muslim population of four million. His government was unpopular and autocratic, and it faced strong domestic opposition from Muslim leaders who sought to join their religious brethren in newly formed Pakistan. He was also under pressure from the British Viceroy of India, Lord Mountbatten, to join one of the two states.[3] No decision, however, was forthcoming from the Maharaja. In August 1947, revolt broke out in Poonch, near the border with Pakistan.

When the Maharaja sent his state troops into Poonch to quell the uprising, many of his Muslim soldiers deserted and formed the Azad (Free) Kashmir movement. Further unrest followed in the weeks to come and culminated in the invasion of Kashmir by some 5,000 Pathan tribesmen on October 22. They captured the outpost of Domel in the northwest and moved on in the direction of the capital, Srinagar. In addition, raiders advanced from Gilgit in the north and came within 50 kilometers of the capital by late October.[4] Fighting in these encounters was fierce, and the tribesmen looted, burned, raped, and pillaged wherever they went.

The Maharaja suspected Pakistani complicity in the invasion and decided to ask India for military assistance. Such assistance, however, was only available if Kashmir joined India first. On October 24, the Maharaja signed an Instrument of Accession to India, although with the important mutual understanding that the final question of accession should be "settled by a reference to the people" once peace had been restored. India now sent its troops to Kashmir, where they encountered well-organized tribesmen equipped with machine guns and mortars.[5]

Initially, the Indian troops managed quite well against the tribesmen, evicting them from various important posts. In the long run, however, a permanent military solution proved impossible, and the stage was set for full-scale war between India and Pakistan. Lord Mountbatten attempted to find a political solution acceptable to both parties, but mutual recriminations and suspicion thwarted any effort in that direction.

Initiatives For UN Involvement

On January 1, 1948, India brought the matter before the UN Security Council, claiming that Pakistan was assisting and participating in the invasion of Kashmir and thus threatening international peace.[6] Pakistan denied the charges and countered that Kashmir's accession to India was illegal and that the question should be decided in a plebiscite held under UN supervision.[7] India accepted the idea of a plebiscite, but insisted that it be administered by the Kashmiri government once peace had been restored.

After extensive consultations between the Security Council and the two governments, the Council resolved on January 20 to establish the United Nations Commission on India and Pakistan (UNCIP).[8] The resolution was passed 9-0, with the Soviet Union and the Ukraine abstaining. UNCIP was to be composed of three member states, one chosen by each side and the third by the two other members of the Commission. Its purpose was to "investigate the facts pursuant to Article 34 of the Charter of the United Nations...to exercise...any mediatory influence likely to smooth away difficulties...and to report how far the advice and directions, if any, of the Security Council have been carried out."[9]

India nominated Czechoslovakia to the Commission and Pakistan chose Argentina. Disagreements arose, however, about the selection of the third country, as the respective positions of India and Pakistan on Kashmir grew still further apart. UNCIP, therefore, although instructed to "proceed to the spot as quickly as possible," didn't arrive in Kashmir until July 1948. By that time, its membership had grown to five: Belgium and Colombia had been appointed as additional members, and the United States was appointed as the "third" member in the absence of an agreement between Czechoslovakia and Argentina.[10]

Upon so enlarging the Commission, the Security Council instructed it to "proceed at once to the Indian subcontinent and there place its good offices and mediation at the disposal of the Governments of India and Pakistan...with respect to the restoration of peace and order and to the holding of a plebiscite." It further provided that the Commission should establish in Kashmir "such observers as it may require."[11] The resolution contained extensive language on a Plebiscite Administrator, appointed by the UN although formally an officer of the State of Kashmir, but a plebiscite was contingent upon the withdrawal of Pakistani troops from Kashmir and a cease-fire agreement between the two parties. Such an agreement was reached in August 1948, to take effect on January 1, 1949. It included provisions for the appointment of military observers "who under the authority of the Commission and with the co-operation of both Commands will supervise the observance of the cease-fire order."[12]

Accordingly, the Secretary General appointed a Belgian officer, Lieutenant General Maurice Delvoie, as Military Adviser to the Commission. He arrived in the area on January 2, 1949. One month later a group of twenty UN military observers was in place to oversee the cease-fire.[13] This was the beginning of the United Nations Military Observer Group in India and Pakistan, UNMOGIP.

UNCIP did not achieve its intended purpose of assisting in negotiations between the two governments and overseeing a plebiscite on the future of Kashmir. After several months of attempts at mediation, the Security Council came to the conclusion that UNCIP had outlived its usefulness and decided on March 14, 1950, to terminate the Commission. Yet UNMOGIP remained in place and is still there today.[14]

POLITICAL SUPPORT

Of the five permanent members of the Security Council, Great Britain obviously had the most at stake in the dispute over Kashmir. Britain's overriding concern was that the matter be settled peacefully and according to the arrangements set up when it relinquished control of the Indian subcontinent. Certainly, the very sudden loss of the Indian empire was embarrassment enough for Britain, and it exercised its utmost influence to make the transition a peaceful one. Although it had pressured the Kashmiri Maharaja to join in a union with Pakistan or India, Britain did not take sides with either party. It accepted the Kashmiri Instrument of Accession to India with the important caveat that a plebiscite be held to determine the future status of the state.

The two superpowers did not involve themselves greatly in the Kashmir conflict. They probably saw the dispute for what it was, primarily a religious and nationalistic one, and could not make much use of it in a Cold War context. However, the Soviet Union, as a supporter of anti-imperial movements, enjoyed good relations with the new Indian government. Similarly, Pakistan was seen as leaning more towards the West, although certainly not to the extent it was later. Both "affiliations," however, were fragile and did not entail important commitments, much less an alliance in the usual sense of the word.

Both India and Pakistan supported United Nations involvement in their dispute, especially as it pertained to observing a cease-fire. The idea of a UN-administered plebiscite also had their support initially, although India realized that it would almost certainly result in Kashmir joining Pakistan. After the 1965 outbreak of hostilities, India publicly opposed the idea of a plebiscite, a stance it has reiterated many times since. Since 1971, moreover, India has not been involved in UNMOGIP activities.

MANDATE

Initially, UNMOGIP received its mandate indirectly. When it decided to enlarge UNCIP in April 1948, the Security Council said that the Commission should establish in Kashmir "such observers as it may require." Pursuant to this, a Military Adviser to the Commission was appointed to organize and oversee the work of UN observers.

When UNCIP was terminated in March 1950 and a UN Representative appointed in its place, the Security Council decided to divorce the responsibilities of UNMOGIP from the political duties of the Representative. The Military Adviser was made Chief Military Observer (CMO), with no duties towards the Representative.[15]

As the initial UNMOGIP mandate was both vague and indirect, its real duties were spelled out in the Karachi Agreement, a bilateral instrument between India and Pakistan. The Agreement and subsequent elaborations on it established the UNMOGIP functions as being:

- Observation of the cease-fire line
- Investigation of alleged breaches
- Adjudication of conflicting claims
- Recording the nature and disposition of the forces

These have been and still are the functions of UNMOGIP, derived not from a UN mandate but from bilateral national agreements. It was not until March 1951 that the Security Council formally "authorized" UNMOGIP when it decided that "the Military Observer Group shall continue to supervise the cease-fire in the state." Such decisions have been made periodically since.[16]

Because UNMOGIP's responsibilities devolved mostly from the Karachi Agreement, the UN found it necessary to establish UNIPOM as a separate mission when hostilities broke out in 1965. The function of UNIPOM was to observe a cease-fire along the India-Pakistan border, as distinguished from the Kashmir cease-fire line.

FUNDING

UNMOGIP has been financed from the UN's regular budget under the heading "Special Missions and Inquiries." It has not generated much controversy, although on occasion the Soviet Union has objected to UNMOGIP expenditures on the grounds that they were decided by the Secretary General contrary to the UN Charter.[17] Since its inception, UNMOGIP has received approximately $76 million from the UN budget. Current annual expenditures are around $4.3 million.[18]

PLANNING AND IMPLEMENTATION

UNMOGIP had excellent field information at its disposal when it began its operations. Its head, Lieutenant General Delvoie, had in early February closely inspected both the Pakistani and Indian fronts from "low-flying planes, as well as by car and by jeep."[19] However, from his descriptions and recommendations it is clear that the General had no illusions about the difficulties that his observer group would confront on the ground.

There was a truce in effect but no agreed cease-fire line when UNMOGIP arrived on the subcontinent in early 1949, and the Group played an instrumental role in working out its details. Over a period of several months, Lieutenant General Delvoie worked in close consultation with the two High Commands to establish as precisely as possible the positions of their forces. When an agreement on those positions had been reached, "the observers...called meetings of the opposing commanders and surveyed with them the line on the ground, making a written description of the natural boundaries and establishing signs such as marks on trees or stone cairns."[20] In some cases, Delvoie, in his capacity as Military Adviser to UNCIP, was called upon to adjudicate conflicting claims. The final arrangements on a cease-fire line were confirmed in the Karachi Agreement of July 27, 1949.

The Agreement de facto partitioned Kashmir; it left the northern and western parts under Pakistani control, while India controlled the south and east, including the Vale of Kashmir and Srinagar, the capital. The line was nearly 800 kilometers long and extended over mountainous areas that were extremely difficult to negotiate. Indian and Pakistani troops were stationed all along the cease-fire line, in many instances in close proximity. There was, however, a 500 meter "no-man's land" into which troops could not enter without breaching the agreement.

Size, Composition, Command, and Control

The Secretary General bears final responsibility for UNMOGIP. He appoints the Chief Military Observer (CMO), who heads the mission and reports back directly to him. The CMO's reports are not laid before the Security Council, nor does the Secretary General give the Council an annual progress report.[21] This is a reflection of the indirect mandate and authorization of UNMOGIP and constitutes considerable delegation of authority by the Security Council.

The size of the operation normally ranges from 32-36 people. The initial contributing countries were Belgium, Canada, Mexico, Norway, and the United States. The mission's current strength is 36 observers from Belgium, Chile, Denmark, Finland, Italy, Norway, Sweden, and Uruguay.[22]

The observers are divided into two groups, one attached to each army, although they are rotated periodically lest they develop too close ties to one side. Two control headquarters were established, one in Rawalpindi on the Pakistani side, the other in Srinagar on the Indian side. Both groups work in close liaison with the respective field commanders of the national armies and are under the direct command of the CMO, whose headquarters rotate between the two cities twice a year. A Chief of Military Staff acts as liaison with the two groups and coordinates their activities, while another assistant, the Operations Officer, oversees the location of Field Observation Teams.[23]

Field Operations

The observers operate in groups of two and are attached to various units as deemed necessary by the circumstances. The armies provide the observers with necessary transportation as well as food and lodging, making the units highly mobile, but

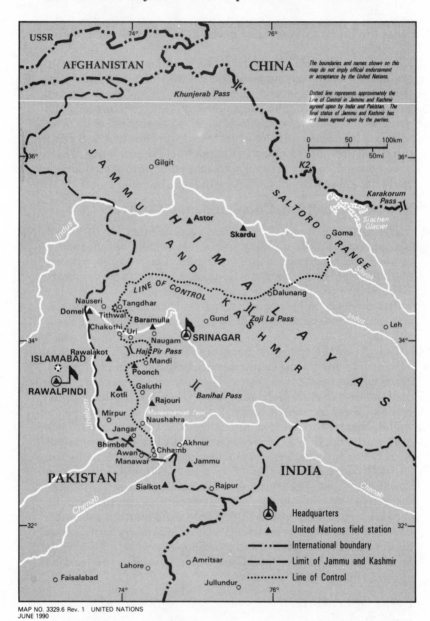

Figure 16.1. United Nations Military Observer Group in India and Pakistan, Deployment as of June 1990

dependent. The number and location of the Field Observation Teams varies greatly according to need. Most are located along the cease-fire line, although teams have been established elsewhere upon the request of the armies.

In cooperation with the two armies, the CMO worked out a detailed list of acts that were considered breaches of the cease-fire, and UNMOGIP investigated virtually hundreds of complaints from 1949–1971. In most cases, problems were resolved on location. However, when a satisfactory solution was not found in cooperation with local commanders, the CMO was able to take up the issue with the two High Commands. In many such instances, the CMO played not only the role of observer and investigator but that of adjudicator. Having concluded investigations of particular incidents, the CMO repeatedly validated complaints raised by either side and issued citations to that effect. For obvious political reasons, this adjudicative function was not the subject of public discussion (until the parties decided to make it so in 1965).[24] It was an important one, however, both as a means of resolving otherwise intractable disputes and as a confidence-building measure illustrating the effectiveness and impartiality of the UN force.

The outbreak of hostilities in 1965 temporarily changed the scope and magnitude of UNMOGIP operations. After extensive and serious fighting, the two sides agreed in January 1966 to withdraw their troops to the positions they had held before the fighting broke out. When withdrawal was completed and UNIPOM had been terminated, UNMOGIP was able to function roughly as it had since 1949.

It took a much smaller conflict to undermine the effectiveness of UNMOGIP seriously. For two weeks in December 1971, the Indian and Pakistani armies exhanged fire in various locations in Kashmir as well as along their own borders. By the time a cease-fire went into effect, the Indian army had made significant advances beyond the original 1949 cease-fire line. Indian authorities informed the United Nations that they intended to reach a settlement on the territory in direct negotiations with Pakistan without United Nations participation. In addition, India reiterated its claim that Kashmir was an integral part of India. Shortly thereafter, India stopped reporting alleged cease-fire violations by Pakistan to UNMOGIP, although Pakistan continued to do so.[25]

ASSESSMENT AND CONCLUSIONS

UNMOGIP has successfully fulfilled its original task of observing the cease-fire spelled out in the Karachi Agreement. Although there was no shortage of alleged and actual violations of the cease-fire, most of the incidents were minor and constituted no threat to the general military situation.

This situation changed after the 1971 war. For two decades, Pakistan has continued to report incidents to UNMOGIP while India has all but ignored its presence, thereby undermining its military significance and effectiveness. With only one side reporting incidents, UNMOGIP's observations and investigations appear to contribute little directly to the maintainance of peace. Moreover, the Kashmir conflict increasingly has become a civil one. Fighting has flared and moved into cities and villages; it is no longer a conflict between two armies, but between police, army, and civilians. By its very nature, UNMOGIP can do little to quell civil strife of that kind.

Indeed, in some respects, UNMOGIP seems to have long outlived its usefulness. When it was established, there remained an active possibility of resolving the Kashmir dispute peacefully under international supervision. In those circumstances, UNMOGIP served the important purpose of reducing the prospect of armed conflict and assuring both parties of impartial observation of each other's activities. It was an effective peacekeeping mission, keeping the lid on military conflict while a political solution was sought. But UN mediation proved fruitless, and today the dispute seems further from resolution than ever before. India remains adamant in its claim to Kashmir as Indian territory, and the idea of a plebiscite is no longer on its agenda.

The Secretary General has taken the position that explicit Security Council action is required to terminate UNMOGIP. Such a decision has not been forthcoming, and there are important reasons to continue UNMOGIP's operation despite all the negatives. Its situation is parallel to that of UNTSO in the Middle East, another observer mission begun a year before UNMOGIP that the UN also doggedly maintains. The Mixed Armistice Commissions that UNTSO is supposed to support have been ignored by Israel for decades, much as India ignores UNMOGIP. Still, the machinery continues to turn.

One argument for such determination is that a UN presence, however small, in such highly volatile situations cannot but have a benevolent effect, if only because any international presence and reportage may discourage or contain irresponsible behavior by bringing it to light. There are, however, other reasons for the United Nations to stay involved in the dispute.

The United Nations has invested considerable political capital to ensure that peace is kept between the armies in Kashmir. In the absence of a request by one party that it leave (as distinguished from mostly ignoring it, as India now does), the UN cannot leave its duties behind without suffering a loss in political and moral authority. The conditions that created the need for UNMOGIP still exist, even if they have changed drastically, and the departure of UN peacekeeping forces would constitute an unnecessary admission of failure when the forces still serve a useful political purpose.

UN presence in the area serves to keep the Kashmir dispute alive as an international issue. India has sought to define Kashmir as an internal matter, arguing that the territory is an integral part of India. However, in its early resolutions (and subsequent ones) the United Nations has endorsed the idea of a plebiscite to determine the fate of Kashmir. Admittedly, there is not much likelihood that this will happen in the near future, but this international commitment and recognition of Kashmiri rights to self-determination is not to be abandoned lightly. UN departure without progress on this issue could be seen as abandonment of an important principle of international relations—indeed, one of the primary principles the United Nations was created to uphold.

Notes

1. Rosalyn Higgins, *United Nations Peacekeeping 1946-1967: Documents and Commentary, Vol. II: Asia* (London: Oxford University Press, 1970), 315.

2. Higgins, *United Nations Peacekeeping*, 316.

3. Sydney D. Bailey, *How Wars End: The United Nations and the Termination of Armed Conflict 1946-1964, Vol. II* (Oxford: Clarendon Press, 1982), 61.

4. Bailey, *How Wars End*, 63.

5. Alan James, *The Politics of Peace-keeping* (New York: Frederick A. Praeger, 1969), 24; Bailey, *How Wars End*, 66.

6. United Nations Document S/628, January 2, 1948.

7. United Nations Document S/646, January 15, 1948.

8. United Nations Document S/654, January 20, 1948.

9. United Nations Document S/654.

10. Higgins, *United Nations Peacekeeping*, Vol. II, 323.

11. United Nations Document S/726, April 21, 1948.

12. Higgins, *United Nations Peacekeeping*, Vol. II, 323-325.

13. *The Blue Helmets: A Review of United Nations Peace-keeping*, 2nd ed. (United Nations: Department of Public Information, 1990), 157.

14. United Nations Document S/1469, March 14, 1950. In 1965, hostilities broke out between India and Pakistan over Kashmir and extended to the regular border of the two countries. Rather than enlarge the mission of UNMOGIP, the United Nations chose to create a separate mission, the United Nations India-Pakistan Observation Mission (UNIPOM). However, the two missions were administered jointly and under the same Chief Military Observer command. UNIPOM was operational from September 1965 to March 1966 (*The Blue Helmets*, 163-66, 431).

15. *The Blue Helmets*, 339.

16. United Nations Document S/2017, March 30, 1951.

17. David W. Wainhouse, *International Peacekeeping at the Crossroads: National Support—Experience and Prospects* (Baltimore: The Johns Hopkins University Press, 1973), 79.

18. *The Blue Helmets*, 170.

19. Higgins, *United Nations Peacekeeping*, Vol. II, 378.

20. Higgins, *United Nations Peacekeeping*, Vol. II, 342.

21. Higgins, *United Nations Peacekeeping*, Vol. II, 352.

22. *The Blue Helmets*, 430. During the crisis of 1965, however, 89 observers were on duty, in addition to those who were assigned to UNIPOM.

23. Higgins, *United Nations Peacekeeping*, Vol. II, 356.

24. Higgins, *United Nations Peacekeeping*, Vol. II, 333-345.

25. *The Blue Helmets*, 168-169.

17 UN Temporary Executive Authority

by William J. Durch

The United Nations Temporary Executive Authority (UNTEA) was one of the more ambitious and successful peacekeeping operations carried out by the Organization in its first twenty years, overseeing the transition of western New Guinea from Dutch colonial rule to Indonesian administration. Importantly, the operation was limited in duration from the outset and had the support of both these countries, who also paid for it. Not until the UN contemplated administering Cambodia in the 1990s would it come as close to having full administrative authority in a territory during the course of a political-military mission. On the other hand, the Organization didn't do that well by the local population, whose eventual "vote" to join Indonesia rather than be independent was carefully orchestrated by Indonesian authorities and took place six years after UN forces left.

ORIGINS

New Guinea, in the Southwest Pacific just north of Australia, is the second-largest island in the world, a land of dense jungle and forbidding mountains whose peaks, rising to 5,000 meters, form the jagged east-west spine of the island. In the nineteenth century, the island was divided into three zones of colonial administration by Great Britain (which thereafter governed the southeast quadrant), Imperial Germany (the northeast quadrant), and the Netherlands (the western half). Dutch New Guinea became the eastern anchor of the Netherlands East Indies, which included all of the large archipelago that is now Indonesia.

In World War Two, the Dutch were overwhelmed by Japanese forces. Days after Japan's surrender in 1945, resistance leader Sukarno declared Indonesia's independence. The Netherlands moved to reassert control over the territory and a struggle ensued. A threatened cutoff of US aid to the Netherlands under the

Marshall Plan gave the Dutch an incentive to relinquish the colony, which they did in 1949, except for West New Guinea. The Netherlands argued that the Papuans of West New Guinea were an ethnically and culturally distinct people who had a right to self-determination, but Indonesia claimed the territory as an "integral" part of its new nation. The two parties agreed to a cooling-off period of one year, but the Dutch then refused to resume negotiations. Indonesia brought the issue before the UN General Assembly from 1954 through 1957 but failed to dislodge the Dutch by that route. (The Security Council was a dead end because it was clear that France or Britain would veto any mandate favoring Indonesia.) In 1958, now-President Sukarno changed tactics, confiscating Dutch property worth billions of dollars and expelling Dutch nationals from Indonesia. In 1960, Indonesia broke diplomatic relations with the Netherlands and embarked on a military build-up, which the Dutch in West New Guinea reciprocated. In January 1961, Indonesia signed a billion-dollar arms deal with the Soviet Union, and the USSR and China both endorsed its claims to West New Guinea.

Initiatives toward UN Involvement

In October 1961, the Netherlands tried and failed to get the General Assembly to assume temporary administrative control over West New Guinea, as a transition to its independence. The UN was in some disarray at that time due to the recent death of Secretary General Dag Hammarskjöld.[1] Although this particular proposal was not accepted, the concept of a transitional UN regime emerged as a central feature of the ultimate settlement, but only after long and difficult negotiations.

In December 1961, Sukarno "mobilized" his country for a new military struggle, began to infiltrate Indonesian forces into West New Guinea, and proclaimed that "West Irian," as he called the territory, would be part of Indonesia before the end of 1962.[2] The United States, which had reasonably good relations with Indonesia, did not wish to see yet another war erupt in Southeast Asia, as it had enough to do at the time in Laos and Vietnam. Nor did Washington wish to see the Netherlands, an important NATO ally, embroiled in a colonial war that it could not win but into which the US might be drawn. Sentiment in the State Department, however, supported a policy of studied neutrality, which favored the status quo and thus the Dutch. This changed when President Kennedy asked Ambassador Averell Harriman to take the post of Assistant Secretary of State for the Far East. Harriman, who dismissed his predecessors' critical views of Sukarno, was decidedly more sympathetic to Indonesian aspirations and embarked on an active effort to break the diplomatic logjam before it erupted into war.[3]

Independently, Acting UN Secretary General U Thant urged Indonesia and the Netherlands to reach a negotiated settlement under UN auspices. But each side's preconditions amounted to demands that the other concede the outcome before talks began; the Hague wanted guarantees of Papuan self-determination, whereas Jakarta wanted the territory transferred immediately to Indonesian control. The issue for Sukarno was one of completing Indonesia's national identity by removing the last Dutch foothold in the region.[4]

A February 1962 overseas trip by Robert Kennedy, the president's closest adviser, included stops in Indonesia and the Netherlands. The upshot was a series of secret "pre-negotiations" between Dutch and Indonesian officials, outside Washington, that began in March. To facilitate agreement, retired US Ambassador Ellsworth Bunker mediated the talks. Officially, Bunker represented U Thant; unofficially, he represented the US government and its interest in a peaceful settlement of the dispute.[5]

Through five months of frustrating talks, punctuated ultimately by renewed Indonesian threats of war, US warnings to Sukarno that such a move could have grave consequences, and parallel warnings to the Dutch not to expect US support, the two sides reached agreement on a transitional regime, suggested by Bunker, to be run by the UN. Sukarno had by far the stronger negotiating position in these talks, and it was US pressure and the availability of a UN buffer that allowed the Dutch to retreat with a modicum of face saved. The Hague was able to claim force majeure, on the one hand, in the form of a lack of US support, and good faith, on the other, by having retained in the transition agreement the principle of a Papuan "vote" on affiliation with Indonesia at a future date.[6]

The talks were made public in New York on August 13, 1962, and, after some last-minute wrangling over the symbolically important issue of whose flag should fly where, and when, the talks were completed on August 15, in time for Indonesian independence day (August 17).

POLITICAL SUPPORT

Since UNTEA grew directly out of the bilateral agreement between Indonesia and the Netherlands, it had their formal support, but both sides made life more difficult for UNTEA than it needed to be once the mission deployed. Indonesia constantly pressured the UN to speed up the process of transition to Indonesian control. (In response, U Thant's *chef de cabinet*, C. V. Narasimhan, visited the territory in February 1963, but concluded that the original transition schedule would be maintained.) The Netherlands supported the agreement because it had no choice, but rapidly (one might say petulantly) withdrew its civilian administrators once the transition period began, leaving the UN to scramble for competent people to administer the territory.[7]

Because UNTEA did not involve the Security Council, it lacked the public Cold War drama of its larger contemporary, the operation in the Congo. And whereas the chief rivals of the Cold War were on opposite sides much of the time in the Congo crisis, they both backed Indonesia in this case, although for different reasons. Soviet arms shipments to Indonesia gave Sukarno bargaining leverage and an edge in firepower. The USSR had perhaps as much to gain from a successful Indonesian "anti-imperialist" military campaign as from a peaceful settlement. The United States, on the other hand, had nothing to gain from a Dutch-Indonesian conflict and worked actively to prevent it. Besides instigating and shepherding the mediated negotiations, the US also furnished aircraft and helicopters for use by UN observers and for supply flights and troop deployments in the theater.

MANDATE

Unlike other UN peacekeeping operations, UNTEA had no formal UN mandate. It operated on the basis of the General Assembly's September 21, 1962, endorsement of the August 15 Dutch-Indonesian accord. The Assembly acted one day after the two parties exchanged instruments of ratification of that accord, which served, in effect, as the UN mission's mandate.

There were to be three phases to the UN operation following implementation of a cease-fire: provision of overall administration and security for the territory during a seven-month transition period (October 1962 through April 1963); transfer of administration to Indonesia "at the discretion of the [UN]

Administrator" anytime after May 1; and UN assistance and participation in the Papuans' exercise of "freedom of choice" regarding affiliation with Indonesia by the end of 1969.

A Dutch-Indonesian memorandum of understanding that accompanied the August 15 agreement asked for immediate UN assistance in implementing a cease-fire, including observation, protection for Dutch and Indonesian forces, restoration of the peace after any breaches of the cease-fire, and the notification and resupply of Indonesian forces scattered across the Papuan landscape. Because UNTEA was geared to a specific objective and timetable, its marching orders were clear. Because funding was available, it was immediately implementable without financial stress.

FUNDING

UNTEA is not unique in having been funded by the parties directly involved (the same was true for the UN's operation in Yemen a year later). However, it is unique in having received sufficient funds under such an arrangement to support an effective operation. Rather than specify a fixed amount to be contributed toward UN expenses, the Dutch-Indonesian agreement specified that "The Parties...will reimburse the Secretary-General for all costs incurred by the United Nations under the present Agreement." The parties also agreed to split the costs evenly and to advance the UN what it needed to do the job. Each side gave the Secretary General one million dollars by early September 1962 and advanced another five million dollars apiece in early November. The UN earned $300,000 in interest on its advances and managed to collect another $6.3 million in taxes, customs duties, and other revenues while administering the territory, so that the operation came in nearly $6 million under budget, and some of the parties' contributions could therefore be refunded. Through 1963, the total bill came to $26.4 million, and little cost was incurred by the UN in monitoring the Papuans' later exercise of "free choice." Thus, in the net, Indonesia and the Netherlands each contributed about $13 million to the operation.[8]

PLANNING AND IMPLEMENTATION

Because the UN's role in UNTEA had been mapped out in advance by the parties' transition agreement, the operation required less UN staff planning than most peacekeeping ventures.

The UN assumed control of an intact civil administration, plus military bases and equipment turned over by the Dutch. However, detailed information on the incountry supply situation and on logistics and transport requirements were not that good, necessitating calls back to New York by UN officials upon arrival in West New Guinea to hastily arrange substantial additional measures of support.

Size and Composition of the Force

There were two separate UN military operations in West New Guinea. To implement the cease-fire, the Secretary General sent his military adviser, then-Brigadier General Indar Rikhye, to head a 21-man observer group drawn largely from existing UN operations. Nine observers came from ONUC, eight from UNEF, two from UNTSO, and two were contributed independently by Ceylon (now Sri Lanka). U Thant dispatched the force without prior authority from the General Assembly or the Security Council, a first.

Rikhye arrived in West New Guinea on August 20, two days after the Netherlands Military Command had ordered a cease-fire. He was followed by the rest of the observers: eight Swedes, five Indians, and two observers each from Brazil, Ireland, Nigeria, and Sri Lanka. The observer mission finished its work in a month and withdrew on September 24.

The longer-term UN Security Force (UNSF) for UNTEA was drawn primarily from the army and navy of Pakistan, which had agreed in late August to provide 1,000 troops (see Table 17.1). As an Asian and Muslim country, Pakistan was acceptable to Indonesia, and as a Western alliance partner (a member of CENTO) it was acceptable to the Netherlands. In addition to infantry, Pakistan sent engineers, supply, signals, and other support units. UNSF's air contingents, however, were Canadian and American, and both countries' units served as part of the UN force. This was another first achieved by UNTEA—the subordination of an American military unit to operational UN command.[9]

Command Structure and Communications

UNTEA's leadership phased in along with its forces. Brigadier General Rikhye was in charge for the first month, as Chief Military Observer. As one of his first actions, he sought to establish a direct radio link between UN field headquarters at Hollandia (now Jayapura) on the north New Guinea coast and Indonesia's capital, Jakarta, four thousand kilometers away, where the observer group sent two liaison officers. The link was not established until January 1963, however, well after the observer mission had left.

Table 17.1. UN Security Force, West New Guinea

Personnel	November 1962	February 1963
Pakistan		
HQ Staff	22	23
Ground	1357	1408
Naval	106	106
United States Air Force	99	59
Canada Air Force	12	11
Totals:	1596	1608

Source: David W. Wainhouse, *International Peacekeeping at the Crossroads* (Baltimore: The Johns Hopkins University Press, 1973), 144.

Given West New Guinea's limited road network (only nine hundred kilometers altogether), its large size (a half-million square kilometers), and the limited number of UN personnel available to oversee the cease-fire, Rikhye asked New York for aircraft. The US Air Force brought in four DC-3s and six light helicopters. The Canadian armed forces contributed two Twin Otters. These aircraft formed the air detachment that later supported UNSF.[10]

On September 4, UNSF's Force Commander, Major General Said Uddin Khan of Pakistan, arrived in West New Guinea to scope out the requirements for his force. He asked for a six-company battalion, one company for each major administrative area. The USAF airlifted some advance parties of this force into position by October 7, one week after UNTEA formally assumed control of administration. By the end of November, all six military units had been deployed. They remained in their garrisons, on call for emergencies, and were not dispersed over the countryside.[11]

Technically, UNTEA's structure violated the principle of unity of command, as the Force Commander (Major General Khan) did not have control over the various indigenous forces in the theater;

these reported to the civilian UN Administrator (see below). However, accounts of the transition suggest that the Administrator used his control over these units largely to keep them out of each other's way, and that folding them into UNSF would not have appreciably improved the transition.

Logistics

UNTEA's logistical requirements were eased by the fact that its ground forces were drawn from a single country, Pakistan, but they were made difficult nonetheless by the remoteness of the locale and the difficulty of the topography. West New Guinea's port towns (and UNSF's major deployment locations) were scattered along a coastline some three thousand kilometers long. The distance from Force headquarters at Hollandia, in the northeast, to the southernmost UN garrison at Merauke was seven hundred kilometers across a towering mountain range. The distance from Headquarters to the westernmost UN garrison at Sorong was a thousand kilometers. Coastal locations did facilitate resupply by sea, which was done by Pakistani naval crews operating ex-Dutch amphibious vessels. However, as most of the southern coast is stormy from October to May, resupply of the three southern garrisons had to be done largely by air.

The air detachment was headquartered on Biak, an island off the northwestern coast of New Guinea, roughly equidistant from Hollandia and Sorong. The detachment's Otters and DC-3s distributed the Force initially from Biak to the other garrisons, a platoon at a time, and then did the same for perishable supplies.

Although UNSF inherited equipment from the departing Dutch, including radio transmitters, trucks, and the like, the unfamiliar equipment had to be mastered without the benefit of manuals written in Punjabi. The Pakistani maintenance and engineering forces seem to have managed the task well enough, but with a dwindling supply of spare parts, UNSF might have been in significant trouble had the mission lasted any longer than it did, falling back further on US-supplied equipment and air transport.

Administration

The Secretary General's deputy *chef de cabinet*, José Rolz-Bennet, was appointed Special Representative for West New Guinea on September 7 and on October 1 became temporary Administrator of UNTEA. The "permanent" Administrator, Djalal Abdoh of Iran, was not appointed until late October and arrived at his post in mid-November.

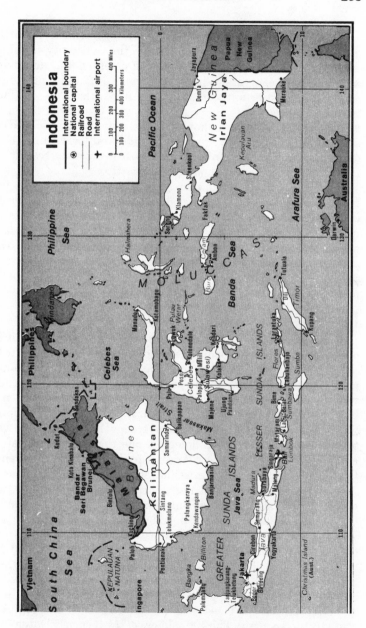

**Figure 17.1. New Guinea and the
Indonesian Archipelago**

UNTEA's administrative tasks included appointing heads of 18 governmental departments to maintain the continuity of public services. Administrators had to be competent non-Indonesian, non-Dutch bureaucrats willing to cope with unfamiliar problems in a distant and primitive land for seven months. The solution, frequently repeated for later missions, was to draw these individuals primarily from "in house" ranks, namely, the Secretariat and the UN Specialized Agencies. In addition to running their departments, these administrators were to oversee the transition from Dutch to Indonesian policy and practice.

The UN's job was made more difficult by the departure, between September and November 1962, of 90 percent of the Dutch officials in the territory, leaving the UN to fill vacant slots in middle management ranks, which it did largely with Indonesian administrators. Partially in response to Indonesian requests, the placement of Indonesian administrators was accelerated so that by March 1, the number two people in all administrative departments were Indonesian.

Field Operations

Indonesian troops present in Western New Guinea when UN operations began had been airdropped or otherwise clandestinely deployed. Their locations at the time of the cease-fire were not precisely known. Moreover, in many cases they were out of touch with Jakarta. By late August, many Indonesian units had not been resupplied for some time. The first task for the UN, therefore, was to locate and convince these troops that the struggle was over, a cease-fire had been accepted, and that they could safely assemble in designated areas for resupply by the UN. To that end, the UN used broadcasts over radio Jakarta and airdropped large numbers of leaflets. Nonetheless, during the first month or two of the UN operation, clashes continued between Indonesian infiltrators and the local forces trained by the Dutch to fight them.

Dutch forces in West New Guinea, about 4,500 troops, were placed under UN control after October 1 and repatriated by mid-November. The roughly 1,200 Indonesian troops there when the UN first deployed were rotated out by December, replaced by a like-sized group of fresh troops (who, as Wainhouse notes, had a "better attitude"). These also were placed under the UN Administrator's control. The 400 soldiers of the formerly Dutch-led, anti-Indonesian "Papuan Volunteer Corps" were placed under UN authority and transitioned to Indonesian officers by January 1963. Finally, the 1,600-strong Papuan Police Force, geared to fight Indonesian infiltrators, was given a British commander and police command ranks from the Philippines replaced departing Dutch officers; transition to Indonesian officers was completed in March.[12]

ASSESSMENT

UNTEA did its job and went home on schedule and under budget. The Dutch flag was furled and the Indonesian flag unfurled as stipulated in the implementing agreement. Within the terms of its mandate, UNTEA was a successful operation, the more remarkable for its relative complexity and for the generally tense international political climate of the period. It demonstrated the utility of a single-nation security force for peacekeeping, although the formula would not be duplicated for 30 years (in the agreement for the referendum in Western Sahara).

UNTEA also demonstrated the need for adequate logistical preparations for operations in physically remote areas with marginal infrastructures, including arrangements for air transport and resupply. UNSF arrived in West New Guinea with three months of basic stores and all resupply for such a small force could in theory have been done by sea. Most men and supplies were indeed brought into the area of operations by ship, but weather and geography often mandated the use of air transport to distribute them further. UNTEA benefitted in this respect from the American forward presence in the Philippines. Aircraft and spare parts could be shipped from Clark Air Force Base far more readily than from North American bases. This is one reason, perhaps, why the Canadian air detachment operated in conjunction with the US contingent; the two countries differed not in competence (the UNTEA air adviser at Force Headquarters was, after all, Canadian) but in logistical capacity.

In terms of its second political objective—the oversight of the Papuans' exercise of free choice regarding their association with Indonesia—UNTEA was less successful. Between 1963 and 1969, Indonesia took steps to suppress, by force, any stirrings of Papuan nationalism or organized resistance to ultimate *anschluss* with Indonesia. In 1968, the Secretary General appointed a representative to monitor the act of choice required by the August 1962 Dutch-Indonesian agreement, but he had no powers to guide or to intervene in the process.

The act of choice unfolded in a series of tribal council meetings where most of the participants were hand-picked by the Indonesian government. Meeting without benefit of secret ballot, the councils reported unanimous consensus to join Indonesia, a result announced in August 1969 by Indonesia's foreign minister. The Secretary General's representative, Fernando Ortiz-Sanz, reported that, although the process had been carried out under tight political control, an "act of free choice" by "the representatives of the population" had taken place "in accordance with Indonesian practice." On November 19, 1969, the General Assembly noted that the tasks assigned to the Secretary General under the August 1962 agreement had been fulfilled.[13]

CONCLUSIONS

The United Nations played an important role on several levels in the transition of West New Guinea from colonial rule, from the negotiation of the agreement to its implementation. First, the UN gave the United States a fig leaf of neutrality behind which Ellsworth Bunker could mediate the talks between Indonesia and the Netherlands. The talks provided a channel for introducing new concepts for settlement—including UNTEA itself—and gave interested third parties greater leverage for avoiding conflict. Second, UN administration of the territory buffered the transfer of control between the two antagonistic powers, so that their forces and administrators did not have to deal directly with one another; for the Dutch, UNTEA coated a rather bitter pill. Third, the UN role kept the dispute from escalating into a conflict in which the two major antagonists of the Cold War could have been arrayed on opposite sides.

If UNTEA highlighted the valuable role of the UN as a buffer, it also highlighted the importance of Great Power interest in peaceful crisis resolution. Not until the United States decided to intervene actively to help settle the dispute were direct negotiations begun. Moreover, without periodic US arm-twisting, the talks still might have been overtaken by war, one into which the US might have been dragged to protect its NATO ally even though it disagreed with Dutch policy. Thus, the US urged Indonesia to wait, while it urged the Dutch to move. This pressure allowed the parties, especially the Netherlands, to change their positions with less loss of face than would have been the case for similar concessions made in unmediated talks.

On an operational level, UNTEA suggests the importance of gauging sustainability, as well as initial capacity, when the UN is weighing a new mission. Deliberations of the Security Council preceding a mandate should be informed by the Secretariat's analyses of the mission's long-term operational requirements and possible bottlenecks in meeting those requirements. When lead times are measured in months, ad hoc fact-finding missions may be sufficient to develop such data; when lead times are short, in a fast-moving crisis, initial actions must be based on the data at hand. UNTEA, in fact, was an in-between situation, where fact-finding for UNSF was done in the month before its deployment. For operations involving more than one battalion, that amount of time is unlikely to be enough (as UNTAG's initial deployment in Namibia later showed).

UNTEA was also unusual in that significant funds for the operation were directly available in advance and were ample as the operation took place; most UN peacekeeping operations are months to years in arrears in their financing, with general revenues and troop contributors taking up the slack. The Secretariat should have the right to refuse to undertake peacekeeping missions that lack such advance funding.

Finally, by contemporary standards, the act of choice in the case of West New Guinea/Irian Jaya was neither free nor, practically speaking, a choice, although it did conform to the realities of political power. Having threatened war to push the Dutch out, the Indonesian Government was not about to let the territory slip away because it was not loved by the local inhabitants. Moreover, the alternative to the relatively peaceful, orchestrated endorsement of Indonesian rule provided by the 1962 accord was the sort of bloody war of conquest by which Indonesia ousted the Portuguese governors of East Timor in 1975 and annexed the area in 1976. Not until the international community, through UN action or by other means, is willing to address itself consistently to issues of human rights will the menu of political alternatives expand.

Notes

1. See chapter 19 on the UN Operation in the Congo.
2. Christopher J. McMullen, *Mediation of the West New Guinea Dispute, 1962, A Case Study* (Washington, D.C.: Institute for the Study of Diplomacy, Georgetown University, 1981), 7-9.
3. Roger Hilsman, *To Move A Nation* (New York: Doubleday, 1967), 376-77.
4. Hilsman, *To Move A Nation*, 371.
5. McMullen, *Mediation of the West New Guinea Dispute*, 10-13.
6. David W. Wainhouse, *International Peacekeeping at the Crossroads* (Baltimore, Md.: The Johns Hopkins University Press, 1973), 137-8.

7. Wainhouse, *International Peacekeeping at the Crossroads*, 142; *The Blue Helmets*, 273.

8. Wainhouse, *International Peacekeeping at the Crossroads*, 140.

9. American units fighting in the Korean War were nominally under UN command but operational command was American.

10. Wainhouse, *International Peacekeeping at the Crossroads*, 141-45.

11. Wainhouse, *International Peacekeeping at the Crossroads*, 145.

12. *The Blue Helmets*, 271.

13. McMullen, *Mediation of the West New Guinea Dispute*, 73; *The Blue Helmets*, 276-77; and Wainhouse, *International Peacekeeping at the Crossroads*, 139. Brian May notes that educated Papuans derisively called it the "act free of choice" (*Indonesian Tragedy* [London and Boston: Routledge and Kegan Paul, 1978], chapter five). From a militant Papuan perspective, the land traded one colonial power for another. See *West Papua: The Obliteration of a People* (London: TAPOL, 1983).

18 United Nations Good Offices Mission in Afghanistan and Pakistan

by Karl Th. Birgisson

In 1988, the Soviet Union decided to withdraw its military forces from Afghanistan, where they had been fighting Afghan guerrillas since the Soviet invasion of December 1979. The United Nations was asked to provide observers to monitor the withdrawal, which it did via the UN Good Offices Mission in Afghanistan and Pakistan (UNGOMAP). This was one of the few occasions when the United Nations sent its forces into a full-fledged war without a cease-fire being in effect. It was also the first time that the UN sent a mission into a conflict where the forces of either superpower were directly involved.

ORIGINS

The Central Asian republic of Afghanistan is landlocked between Iran on the west, Pakistan to the south and east, and the republics of Turkmenistan, Uzbekistan, and Tadzhikistan in the north. Its estimated population of 15 million includes three to five million refugees from the civil war, located mainly in Pakistan. Only ten to fifteen percent live in the country's four principal cities (Kabul, the capital, Kandahar, Herat, and Mazari-sharif), and control of these widely separated urban areas is not to be confused with control of the country, as the Soviet Union eventually learned.

Afghanistan's high-altitude terrain is rugged and well-suited to both guerrilla warfare and long-standing ethnic divisions. The Hindu Kush mountain range, part of the Himalayas, runs through the country from northeast to southwest, dividing it into three distinct regions. The Central Highlands include the mountains and several key passes of great strategic importance. They are populated by the Hazara people, who are Shi'a Muslims with close ties to Iran. The relatively narrow Northern Plains are part of the Central Asian steppe, and Afghanis who live there, just over a third of the population, are Uzbeks or Tajiks, both with ethnic kin across the country's northern border. The Southwestern Plateau is a region of barren highlands, sandy deserts, and the occasional fertile valley. The Pathans (or Pashtuns) who live there constitute about half of Afghanistan's population and are its traditionally dominant group, politically.

With this geography and social make-up, Afghanistan historically has been a collection of principalities, sometimes partly united under strong warlords. Periodically, foreign powers conquered parts of the country, and the British regarded Afghanistan as a vital link to their Indian empire, fighting three wars between 1839 and 1919 to preserve their influence there. In 1893, the British and the Russians established Afghanistan's current boundaries.

Following the last Anglo-Afghan war in 1919, Afghanistan gained relative independence as a kingdom. Modernization and secularization prompted religious conflicts, which were compounded by ethnic and tribal rivalries. The kingdom survived until 1973, when a republic was created in a bloodless coup d'état. Five years later, however, the marxist People's Democratic Party of Afghanistan (PDPA) seized power.

The new government introduced reform programs that threatened old religious and social institutions and met with strong resistance in the countryside, leading to spontaneous revolts throughout the country. By the fall of 1979, the government had lost control of two-thirds of the country to Islamic insurgents. The citizens of Herat rioted, and when Prime Minister Hafizullah Amin had the President murdered, prompting intra-party violence, the Soviet Union decided to intervene.[1] The Soviet Army invaded on December 27, 1979, and upon their arrival in the capital installed Babrak Karmal, the leader of one of the PDPA's two main factions, as prime minister.

Resistance to the new regime proved strong, and the 100,000 Soviet troops found themselves fighting small groups of guerrillas all over the country. The guerrillas, collectively known as the *mujahideen*, controlled most of the countryside, including strategically important mountain areas, while the Soviet and Afghan armies held all major cities and towns. The mujahideen were not well organized, however. Attempts at unifying the various groups were thwarted by divided ethnic, religious, and regional loyalties, and no organized liberation alliance was formed. Many resistance leaders moved their bases to Pakistan, from which they managed the campaign and channeled American and other western support to the guerrillas.

Gradually, the Soviet and Afghan forces managed to inflict damage on the resistance groups, particularly because of Soviet air supremacy. In the spring of 1985, increasing Soviet use of *Spetznaz* special forces added to the toll. Soon after, the United States decided to increase substantially the quality and quantity of weapons provided to the resistance, and the guerrillas began receiving large amounts of Western weaponry, such as surface-to-surface rockets, mortars, guided anti-tank missiles, and Stinger anti-aircraft missiles. Subsequently, the Soviet forces began sustaining considerable casualties.[2]

Initiatives for UN Involvement

The United Nations Security Council debated Afghanistan in January 1980 but, not surprisingly, failed to agree on a resolution, whereupon the issue was shifted to the General Assembly under the "Uniting for Peace" procedure. By a vote of 104 to 18, with 18 abstentions, the General Assembly on January 14 approved a resolution strongly condemning the invasion and calling for the "immediate, unconditional and total withdrawal of the foreign troops from Afghanistan."[3] However, in a somewhat contradictory move, the Assembly first approved the credentials of the delegation of the Karmal regime, which then provided one of the 18 votes against the General Assembly resolution. This recognition of the new Afghan regime was to shape the character of the subsequent UN-sponsored negotiations over Afghanistan.[4]

On May 14, 1980, the government in Kabul issued a statement directed to the governments of Pakistan and Iran, outlining ideas for a political solution to the "tension that has come about in this region." It contained the four points that came to be the foundation of the eventual Geneva Accords: the withdrawal of foreign troops, noninterference in domestic affairs, international guarantees, and the voluntary return of refugees to Afghanistan.[5]

These initial overtures were rejected by the governments of Pakistan and Iran, which did not want to extend any semblance of recognition to the Kabul regime by way of negotiation. This obstacle was overcome when Secretary General Kurt Waldheim appointed Javier Pérez de Cuéllar, Under-Secretary-General for Special Political Affairs, as his Personal Representative on the Situation Relating to Afghanistan.[6] On visits to the region in April and August 1981, Pérez de Cuéllar gained the acceptance of the governments of Aghanistan and Pakistan to a four-point agenda for subsequent talks that mirrored the statement issued a year earlier by Kabul. The mujahideen were not part of this process, and, in sympathy, the government of Iran declined to participate.

Javier Pérez de Cuéllar became Secretary General in January 1982 and appointed Diego Cordovez as his successor in the Afghanistan negotiations. From his headquarters in Geneva, Cordovez conducted talks that eventually produced the Geneva Accords of 1988. Representatives of the Afghan and Pakistani governments never actually met at the same table, but Cordovez acted as an intermediary.

The Geneva Accords, signed on April 14, 1988, were in fact four instruments. The first three dealt with noninterference and nonintervention, international guarantees by the USSR and the USA, and the voluntary return of refugees. The fourth contained provisions for the phased withdrawal of Soviet troops and arrangements for the smooth implementation of all four instruments, including assistance provided by the Secretary General as requested by the parties. Accordingly, the Secretary General dispatched a group of 50 military observers to Afghanistan and Pakistan, to be operational by the time the agreements entered into force on May 15. They comprised the UN Good Offices Mission to Afghanistan and Pakistan, whose job was to monitor the withdrawal of Soviet troops, nonintervention and noninterference by the two countries in one another's internal affairs, and the return of refugees from Pakistan to Afghanistan.[7]

POLITICAL SUPPORT

The Geneva Accords had the full support of the international community. This was particularly true regarding the withdrawal of Soviet troops from Afghanistan. Some states, mostly smaller and medium-sized, wanted the accords to encompass an agreement on Afghan self-determination, that is, to make the mujahideen a part of the arrangement. This was never a very likely possibility, partly because the Afghan resistance was never a single entity, and partly because the nature of the accords was governed by larger interests.

As far as the superpowers were concerned, the conflict was part of their larger geopolitical competition and was dealt with primarily in that light. The United States did not support the mujahideen for reasons of self-determination or ideological affinity. The Afghan resistance was primarily valuable as an ally in containing perceived Soviet expansion.[8] The Soviet Union's decision to withdraw its troops was a political victory as far as the United States was concerned, regardless of the outcome of the Afghan national struggle.

The pivotal role in this geopolitical drama was that of the Soviet Union. When the UN representative began his efforts to find a solution to the Afghanistan question, the Soviet Union held a very hard-line position on the issue. General Secretary Brezhnev had no intention of suffering defeat at the hands of Afghan guerrillas, nor did his successor, Yuri Andropov. The war was, after all, not going badly; the regime in Kabul was secure, had received some international recognition, and Soviet forces were not sustaining heavy casualties in the fighting.

In the early years of Mikhail Gorbachev's rule, however, several things changed. Gorbachev launched a foreign policy based on "new political thinking," attempting to redefine the geopolitical goals of the Soviet Union. Better relations with the United States and Western Europe were essential to his scheme, and the war in Afghanistan was a nuisance that stood in the way of other, more important, achievements.

The domestic political cost of the war was growing. The Afghan adventure was increasingly unpopular in the Soviet Union, particularly in the Central Asian republics. In 1985, the year that Gorbachev came to power, the Afghan guerrillas began receiving hi-tech Western weaponry, including anti-aircraft weapons that proved to be highly effective. Rising casualty rates further increased political pressure on the Soviet leadership to find an acceptable solution to the Afghan conflict.[9]

The 1988 decision to withdraw from Afghanistan, then, was a logical reaction to international and domestic political realities. By this time, most of the old guard in the Politburo either had died or had been "retired" and replaced by others not responsible for the initial involvement in Afghanistan.

Despite the prohibitions of the Geneva accords, both sides in the civil war continued to receive outside aid. The government of Pakistan provided the guerrillas with training, weapons, logistics, and bases from which they conducted raids into Afghanistan. In addition, the governments of Iran and Saudi Arabia have been sources of support for some guerrilla factions. The Soviet Union and the United States, moreover, had reached an informal agreement that each would continue to assist their protegés as long as the other one did, meaning that American and other western assistance continued to flow to the guerrillas. (In September 1991, however, with Soviet forces long gone, the two countries decided jointly to terminate all assistance to the combatants in Afghanistan.)

MANDATE

The substantive mandate for the UN operation is contained in the four instruments signed in Geneva. On April 14, 1988, the Secretary General informed the Security Council of the agreements' requests for UN assistance and asked for its concurrence in providing that assistance once the accords had been signed. The Security Council agreed provisionally, emphasizing that its exchange of letters with the Secretary General on the subject not be regarded as a precedent for the establishment of future UN commitments.[10]

The first of the Geneva documents was a *Bilateral Agreement Between the Republic of Afghanistan and the Islamic Republic of Pakistan on the Principles of Mutual Relations, in particular on Non-Interference and Non-Intervention*. It defined, inter alia, the obligations of each party "to ensure that its territory is not used in any manner which would violate the sovereignty, political independence, territorial integrity and national unity or disrupt the political, economic and social stabililty of the other High Contracting Party"; and to "refrain from the promotion, encouragement or support, direct or indirect, of rebellious or secessionist activities...or from any other action which seeks to disrupt the unity or to undermine or subvert the political order of the other High Contracting Party." In addition, each signatory was obliged to "prevent within its territory the presence, harbouring, in camps and bases or otherwise, organising, training, financing, equipping and arming of individuals and political, ethnic and any other groups for the purpose of creating subversion, disorder or unrest in the territory of the other High Contracting Party."[11]

The second Geneva accord was the *Declaration on International Guarantees*, signed by the US and USSR. In it, the superpowers undertook to "refrain from any form of interference and intervention in the internal affairs of the Republic of Afghanistan and the Islamic Republic of Pakistan." The third instrument was a *Bilateral Agreement between the Republic of Afghanistan and the Islamic Republic of Pakistan on the Voluntary Return of Refugees*, providing that all Afghan refugees in Pakistan be given the opportunity to return to their homes.[12]

The fourth and final instrument, *Agreement on the Interrelationships for the Settlements of the Situation relating to Afghanistan*, was signed by Afghanistan and Pakistan and witnessed by the US and the USSR as States-Guarantors. It provided for the withdrawal of half of the Soviet troops by August 15 and the remainder before February 15, 1989. An appendix to the agreement stipulated that the Secretary General and his personnel "shall investigate any possible violations of any of the instruments and prepare reports thereon." UN personnel were to "receive all the necessary co-operation from the Parties, including all freedom of movement within their respective territories required for effective investigation."[13]

FUNDING

From its inception, UNGOMAP was financed from the regular budget of the United Nations, initially by means of ACABQ approval of the necessary "extraordinary and unforeseen expenses" for the mission. The operation lasted until March 1990 and cost the United Nations about $14 million.[14]

PLANNING AND IMPLEMENTATION

There was not much information available on the ground situation when the UN observers arrived in Afghanistan. The observers were redeployed rather hastily from other operations, and the United Nations appears not to have given them much information beforehand. According to one officer, national embassies in Pakistan and Iran had to be used to obtain such elementary materials as maps.[15]

The battlefield situation in Afghanistan in May 1988 was volatile at best. The Soviet Union had 103,000 troops in 18 garrisons in 17 of Afghanistan's 30 provinces. In cooperation with the 50,000-strong Afghan army, they held all major cities and towns in the country.

The mujahideen were scattered in smallish bands all over the countryside, controlling major highways and mountain passes, and constantly attacking Soviet and Afghan forces in classic guerrilla operations. The mujahideen were not party to the Geneva Accords. Although some guerrilla leaders held back while Soviet forces were preparing for their departure, and even cooperated in letting them travel through guerrilla-held territory on their way out, others saw no reason to let up on a successful campaign, particularly since in many cases the guerillas were able

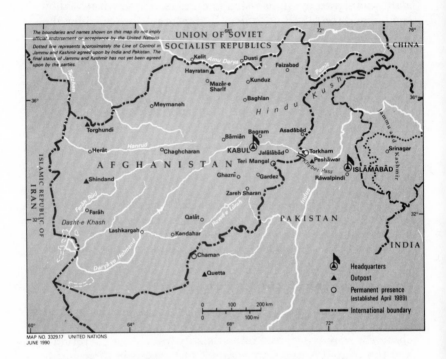

Figure 18.1. United Nations Good Offices Mission in Afghanistan and Pakistan, Deployment as of February 1989

to capture Soviet weapons in raids on Soviet and Afghan positions.[16]

Size and Composition of the Force

UNGOMAP personnel numbered 50 at the beginning of the operation. Forty of these were military officers temporarily redeployed from existing UN operations: UNTSO, UNDOF, and UNIFIL. They came from ten countries: Austria (2), Canada (3), Denmark (4), Fiji (5), Finland (2), Ghana (6), Ireland (5), Nepal (6), Poland (4), and Sweden (3).[17] Diego Cordovez continued to serve as the

Secretary General's Personal Representative, assisted by Major General Rauli Helminen of Finland as Deputy to the Representative. General Helminen was succeeded by Colonel Heikki Happonen in May 1989 after the Soviet withdrawal had been completed.[18] Mr. Cordovez established firm control over the UNGOMAP mission, which created friction between him and the UN office in New York, and probably contributed to his being replaced in January 1990 by Mr. Benon Sevan of Cyprus. UNGOMAP set up headquarters in Kabul and Islamabad. In addition, three permanent outposts were set up in Afghanistan: at Hayratan and Torghundi on the Soviet-Afghan border and at Shindand air base. According to the Soviet military representative in Afghanistan, these were the posts through which the Soviet Union intended to withdraw its troops. Each UNGOMAP post was normally manned by two officers.[19]

Field Operations

During the first phase of the Soviet withdrawal, UNGOMAP was present during or immediately after the evacuation of only four of ten garrisons evacuated. UN observers had been invited by the Soviets to be present wherever they wished, but unpredictable guerrilla activity did not always allow it. By August 15, just over fifty thousand Soviet troops had been withdrawn, leaving a similar number behind in eight garrisons in Kabul and the northwestern part of Afghanistan.[20]

After the initial withdrawal of troops, the Soviet representative informed UNGOMAP that the second phase would begin by mid-November. By that time, however, the mujahideen appeared to have gained such strategic superiority that the Soviets decided to postpone further withdrawal. It was not until late January 1989 that they announced their intention to resume the withdrawal, having brought in reinforcements of heavy weaponry and some 30 MiG aircraft and having satisfied themselves that the Kabul regime could withstand an expected guerrilla offensive.[21]

Then, within a few days in early February, the remaining fifty thousand Soviet troops left Afghanistan. The Commander-in-Chief, Lieutenant General Boris Gromov, was the last Russian out of Afghanistan when he crossed the river Oxus on February 15.[22] General Gromov later assumed the second-highest office at the Soviet Ministry of the Interior, a post he held until after the coup attempt in August 1991.

UNGOMAP also had the responsibility to investigate alleged violations of the first Geneva Accord, relating to "non-intervention and non-interference." By the end of its mandate, the UN mission had received 7,545 specific complaints from Afghanistan alleging Pakistani violations, and a total of 1,317 complaints from the Pakistani side. UNGOMAP officers said they made every effort to investigate such complaints, and by March 1990 they had submitted 102 reports on such investigations to the parties and held 15 joint meetings with them. UNGOMAP's efforts, however, were hampered by the small number of personnel at its disposal and by logistical difficulties, in addition to the ever-present "security conditions" that made their whole operation difficult to execute.[23]

As to the refugees, they did not show much interest in returning home while the fighting continued. Their numbers in Pakistan increased periodically as fighting escalated after the Soviet withdrawal. Since then, however, some have also returned under a repatriation program implemented by the UN High Commissioner for Refugees (UNHCR) and the government of Pakistan.[24]

ASSESSMENT

That UNGOMAP successfully observed the withdrawal of Soviet forces from Afghanistan was due not so much to its extraordinary efforts as to the Soviets' determination to abide by the Geneva Accords. The Soviets cooperated very well with the UN, which was not in a position to record all troop movements and possible violations of the withdrawal agreement. UNGOMAP's 50 people simply did not have the resources to follow their mandate to the letter, even if security conditions in the country had been significantly better. As it was, the mujahideen both controlled strategically significant areas, such as the Salang highway from Kabul to the northwest, and continued attacking various positions where Soviet forces were concentrated. While UNGOMAP was in the country, Kabul was besieged by several guerrilla groups which, according to one report, were firing up to 100 rockets a day at the capital. One Soviet reporter recalled the withdrawal of the first Soviet column in May 1988 under constant rocket attacks from surrounding guerilla groups.[25]

Security conditions particularly hampered investigations of complaints of violations of the Geneva agreements. The alleged incidents took place all over the country and were naturally most prevalent where the fighting was heaviest. In addition, Soviet forces had established over 2,000 minefields in the country since their arrival. Although all but 613 of them had been cleared by

August 15, 1988, these remained active and under the control of the Afghan military after final Soviet withdrawal. Under such conditions, UNGOMAP was unable to venture effectively into the field.

CONCLUSIONS

UNGOMAP placed a UN stamp of approval on the Soviet withdrawal from Afghanistan. The Soviet Union would have withdrawn its forces with or without UN observation; it was simply politically necessary for it to do so. Nonetheless, the withdrawal of Soviet forces was of great geopolitical importance. It was an important and necessary step in the restructuring of Soviet foreign policy, and it removed a significant stumbling block in East-West relations. The presence of UN observers gave Soviet policy a degree of legitimacy in the eyes of world public opinion, a contribution that certainly was valuable to the Soviet Union. Thus UNGOMAP was, in a sense, of global significance. On the other hand, the operation did not affect the situation in Afghanistan or the surrounding region significantly, which made UN-GOMAP an unusual mission.

The civil war continued unabated after UNGOMAP completed its work. The mujahideen went on the offensive, as expected, but remained unable to dislodge the Afghan armed forces from any towns or cities for three years. Attempts at unifying the guerrillas as a political force also failed as the regime in Kabul continued to withstand offensives, supported by up to $300 million per month in Soviet economic and military aid.[26]

Upon the termination of UNGOMAP, the UN Secretary General established the Office of the Secretary General in Afghanistan and Pakistan (OSGAP) in order to continue pursuit of a political settlement in the conflict. OSGAP was headed by Special Representative Benon Sevan, who had in his service a Military Advisory Unit consisting of ten military officers. It was the first of a new class of UN field missions established for purposes of maintaining UN political contacts after peacekeeping operations depart. These quasi-diplomatic missions have generated some controversy, partly because of the costs involved and partly because they serve as an autonomous source of information for the Secretary General, a function that some members of the UN do not appreciate.[27]

Through OSGAP, the Secretary General continued his search for a peaceful settlement in Afghanistan. Several events in the latter half of 1991 and early 1992 altered the prospects for settlement for the better. First, in the aftermath of the abortive hard-line coup in the Soviet Union, Washington and Moscow reached agreement to suspend military aid to their respective clients in Afghanistan, effective January 1, 1992. The United States announced an end to its assistance in mid-October; it had previously ended aid to three fundamentalist Afghan rebel factions whose leaders had supported Iraq in the recent Gulf War.[28]

Second, Pakistan saw considerable opportunity in the new Central Asian republics. Its government decided that it wanted the war to end so that it could establish routine access to those markets. In January 1992, it joined the US and Russia in shutting off the arms spigot.[29]

Third, it seemed increasingly clear that neither side was going to win a clear military victory. The factions fighting the Kabul government were if anything even less united three years after Soviet military withdrawal from their country. Factions comprised primarily of Tajik, Uzbek, and other minority groups consolidated their hold over the northern part of the country, while the Pathan-dominated groups controlled their traditional areas to the south.[30]

OSGAP took advantage of these changed political circumstances to win agreement of all but the three most hard-line factions to contribute delegates to a 150-person meeting in Vienna, slated for April, which was to choose a group of 30-35 persons who would then canvass all major groupings in Afghanistan in preparation for a *Loya Jirga*, or Grand Assembly of the tribes. The Assembly would determine the shape of a new government and set the stage for nationwide elections. Prospects for progress were improved in mid-March when President Najibullah announced his intention to resign, meeting a longstanding demand of the mujahideen.[31]

As the UN pressed for a settlement, however, events in the hinterland took their own course. The Afghan Army began to fragment along ethnic lines. Minority generals in the north, particularly General Rashid Dostam, split with Kabul's Pathan-dominated government and allied with Ahmad Shah Massoud's predominantly Tajik and Uzbek Islamic Army. While Sevan continued to meet with various factional leaders, government resistance began to dissolve; Najibullah attempted to flee the country in mid-April, failed, and sought asylum at UN offices in Kabul. In late April, mujahideen forces converged on Kabul; its Tajik garrison commander struck a deal with Massoud's predominantly Tajik forces, which moved into the city from the north, unopposed, as fighters of Gulbuddin Hekmatyar's Pathan-based, fundamentalist, Hizbe-Islami faction converged on the capital from the south. Artillery duels and small arms clashes broke out but were silenced for two months by a power-sharing accord reached by the major factional leaders.[32]

In late June, the ten-member ruling council oversaw the peaceful transfer of the office of interim Prime Minister to Burnhanuddin Rabbani, leader of Jamiat-i-Islami, Massoud's faction.[33] Strife in Kabul resumed, however, causing hundreds of casualties. The coalition government's effective authority was limited. At the same time, refugee flows back into Afghanistan from Pakistan reached 80,000 a week as the camps in Pakistan (and, presumably, Iran) began to empty.[34]

As of this writing, the UN peace process for Afghanistan has been superceded and the country is taking its own course. The efforts by the new powers in Kabul to create a government of national consensus are up against ethnic and regional forces that threaten the "Lebanization" of the country (the disintegration of a polity into ever smaller and more ferocious pieces). Whether the country falls into that trap depends on the willingness of its heavily armed factions to seek reasonable political compromise, and on the interests of its neighbors in seeking to stabilize what has become, by dint of the breakup of the Soviet Union, the new political fulcrum of the region. Should the spirit of compromise win out, the UN may once again have a role to play.

Notes

1. Olivier Roy, *The Lessons of the Soviet/Afghan War*, Adelphi Paper 259 (London: International Institute for International Studies, Summer 1991), 12-13.

2. Roy, *The Lessons of the Soviet/Afghan War*, 23; and Steve Coll, "Anatomy of a Victory: The CIA's Covert Afghan War," *Washington Post*, July 19, 1992, A1, A24. US supplies to the *mujahideen* increased from ten thousand tons per year in the early 1980s, under a program begun by President Jimmy Carter, to sixty-five thousand tons a year by 1987. Altogether, the US poured $2 billion into the Afghan covert action program.

3. United Nations General Assembly Resolution A/Res/ES-6/2, January 15, 1980.

4. William Maley, "The Geneva Accords of April 1988," in A. Saikal and W. Maley, eds., *The Soviet Withdrawal from Afghanistan* (Cambridge: Cambridge University Press, 1989), 14-15.

5. Maley, "The Geneva Accords," 15.

6. *The Blue Helmets: A Review of United Nations Peace-keeping*, 2nd ed. (New York: United Nations Department of Public Information, 1990), 316.

7. *The Blue Helmets*, 316-317; United Nations Document S/19834, April 26, 1988.

8. Richard A. Falk, "The Afghanistan 'Settlement' and the Future of World Politics," in *The Soviet Withdrawal from Afghanistan*, 157.

9. Maley, "The Geneva Accords," 15.

10. United Nations Document S/19836, April 26, 1988.

11. Maley, "The Geneva Accords," 18.

12. Maley, "The Geneva Accords," 18-19.

13. United Nations Document S/19835, April 26, 1988.

14. *The Blue Helmets*, 321-322. The ACABQ is the General Assembly's Advisory Committee on Administrative and Budgetary Questions, which has the power to authorize expenditures by the Secretary General up to $10 million when the Assembly is out of session.

15. Interview 76, August 1991.

16. *The Economist*, August 20, 1988, 28.

17. United Nations Document S/21879, October 17, 1990.

18. *The Blue Helmets*, 318.

19. United Nations Document S/20465, February 15, 1989.

20. United Nations Document S/20465.

21. *The Economist*, November 12, 1988, 36.

22. *The Economist*, February 18, 1989, 31.

23. United Nations Document S/21879.

24. Donatella Lorch, "Afghan Refugees Prepare to Go Home," *New York Times*, April 23, 1992, A6.

25. *The Economist*, February 11, 1989, 29; Gennady Bocharov, *Russian Roulette: Afghanistan Through Russian Eyes* (New York: Harper Collins Publishers, 1990), 177.

26. Paul Lewis, "UN Chief Taking his Afghan Plan to Moscow," *New York Times*, January 14, 1990, 15.

27. Interview 67, May 1991.

28. The three factions supporting Iraq were those led by Gulbuddin Hekmatyar, Abdul Rasul Sayyaf, and Burhannuddin Rabbani. The Gulf War was otherwise a source of booty for the mujahideen. The United States, Saudi Arabia, and Pakistan are said to have shipped some 7,000 tons of captured Iraqi weapons, including tanks and artillery, to Afghanistan in the spring and summer of 1991 (Robin Wright and John M. Broder, "US will Send Iraqi Arms to Afghan Rebels," *Los Angeles Times*, May 19, 1991, 1; Thomas L. Friedman, "US and Soviet to End Arms Sales to Afghan Rivals," *New York Times*, September 14, 1991, A1; Steve Coll, "Afghan Rebels Said to Use Iraqi Tanks," *Washington Post*, October 1, 1991, 12).

29. *The Economist*, February 1, 1992, 40; *Jane's Defence Weekly*, February 8, 1992, 201; Edward Gargan, "Fiscal and Political Forces Move Pakistan to Seek Afghan Peace," *New York Times*, February 16, 1992, A1.

30. *The Economist*, January 11, 1992, 33.

31. Edward Gargan, "A Few Grains of Hope Flavor Political Stew in Afghanistan," *Washington Post*, March 13, 1992, A1; and "Afghan President Agrees to Step Down," *Washington Post*, March 19, 1992, A3.

32. Ahmed Rashid, "Peace with Pitfalls," *Far Eastern Economic Review*, May 7, 1992, 10-13; *The Economist*, June 20, 1992, 33, and June 27, 1992, 35-36.

33. *New York Times*, June 29, 1992, A5.

34. Edward Gargan, "Afghan Refugees Trek Home to a Bleak, Uncertain Future," *New York Times*, July 22, 1992, A1. UNHCR sought to give each returning refugee allotments of cash and wheat, but of the needed $180 million for the program, just $30 million had been raised in the face of competing demands from like programs for Cambodia (330,000 refugees) and Angola (250,000). Afghanistan's refugee problem was ten to twenty times larger.

Part Four:

Peacekeeping in Africa

19 The UN Operation in the Congo: 1960–1964

by *William J. Durch*

The UN Operation (known by its French initials, ONUC) in the former Belgian Congo, now Zaire, was the UN's second armed peacekeeping operation and for thirty years by far the largest, involving 20,000 troops and civilians. Undertaken during a frosty period in US-Soviet relations that spanned the Berlin Wall and Cuban missile crises, it sent peacekeepers where none had gone before. Accustomed to monitoring tense border zones in the Middle East, the UN faced in the Congo a much less structured, and much more rapidly changing situation. ONUC was sent to save a failing decolonization effort that was rapidly spawning separatist civil wars and great civilian hardship. Its mission, and how it unfolded over many months, are not easily summarized. In essence, ONUC's job was to buy time for the Congo until the Congolese could sort out their political affairs, and to prevent, in the interim, a direct clash of superpower military forces. Operating on unfamiliar ground, the UN often improvised its policies, always under a torrent of criticism from countries who did not understand, or who understood but did not appreciate, Secretary General Hammarskjöld's policy of strict political neutrality. In war, partisans often look upon "neutrals" as covert members of the opposition, and UN leaders had to cope with the suspicions of both cold warriors and tribal warriors, together with the ambivalence, and sometimes the opposition, of European powers, whose own colonies bordering the Congo were also in a state of transition.

In the end, ONUC held the Congo together, but at a high cost. It took a long time to acquire what would now be considered basic prerequisites for a peacekeeping force: a solid operational plan with sustained, high-level political backing; assured funding; a clear, strong mandate; and effective transport, logistics, and administration. As ONUC slowly did so, the operation created an acute political and financial crisis that scarred the Organization for a long time, and among its casualties was the UN's remarkable poet-diplomat, Secretary General Dag Hammarskjöld. All in all, ONUC was an operation that a generation of UN officials wanted to forget, or, if not forget, then never to repeat.

ORIGINS

In the 1950s, pressure for independence from European colonial dominance swept through much of Africa, producing outright rebellion in rough proportion to the tenacity with which the metropolitan powers sought not only to maintain their colonies, but to keep political and economic control in strictly European hands. In the case of the Congo (now the Republic of Zaire), the colonial power, Belgium, maintained just such a strangle hold until early 1960, doing little to train a Congolese elite to whom power might be passed upon independence. Of an indigenous population of 14 million, perhaps half were literate (a high rate for the region at the time), but fewer than 20 had college educations. The senior civil service, and all military officers, were Belgian. The colony comprised 70 major ethnic groups, subdivided into several hundred tribes, who were spread over an area equivalent in size to all of Western Europe.[1] For all its size, however, the Congo was and is nearly landlocked, its access to the sea limited to a narrow stretch of land on either side of the Congo River estuary. Its major port is Matadi, 200 kilometers upstream from the river's mouth.

The country's resources are unevenly distributed, with the bulk of exploitable minerals found in the southern highlands, and especially in Katanga (now Shaba) Province, which covers one fifth of the country. Katanga generated 80 percent of the Congo's export revenue and half of its total income. In 1906, the Belgian company *Union Minière du Haut Katanga* was given exclusive mining rights in the province until 1999.[2]

Riots broke out in Léopoldville (Kinshasa), the capital city on the lower Congo River, in January 1959, and in Stanleyville (Kisangani) in November. The unrest led Belgium to call a Round Table Conference on the Congo in Brussels in January 1960, where it proposed a four-year timetable for complete independence. Congolese leaders in attendance pressed for and unexpectedly won a compressed, six month timetable.[3] The prevailing Belgian view, however, was that given the acute shortage of technically trained Congolese, Belgian nationals would be needed as much after independence as before to run the country, thus cushioning the transition to full autonomy and preserving Belgian economic interests.

In March 1960, an "Executive College" of six Congolese political leaders, including Joseph Kasavubu, Patrice Lumumba, and Moise Tshombé, formed to advise the colony's Governor-General, to serve as a transitional regime, and to draft a constitution. These rivals worked in uneasy alliance. Kasavubu led the political party of the Bakongo people, whose traditional territory spilled across three colonial boundaries near the Atlantic coast and included the national capital. He commanded little political loyalty beyond his ethnic and territorial base. Lumumba's political base was a leftist, nationalist party, the *Mouvement Nationale Congolaise* (MNC). His territorial base was in the northeast, around Stanleyville (Kisangani). Tshombé headed a coalition party of southern Katangan tribes and was interested in greater financial autonomy for that rich province.

Elections to provincial assemblies and a national parliament were held in late May 1960 by "universal male suffrage." Lumumba's MNC won majorities in both houses, and, after some indecision, he was invited by the King of Belgium to form a government, which he accomplished one week before independence. Parliament in turn elected the Head of State, choosing Kasavubu. Tshombé, whose party won a bare majority of seats in Katanga's provincial assembly, was elected provincial president.

Public order in the Congo was maintained by the 25,000-man *Force Publique*, known after independence as the *Armée Nationale Congolaise* (ANC). Brussels assumed that the renamed force, with its 1,000 Belgian officers, would continue to function as a well-disciplined army-cum-constabulary. This proved to be a great misjudgment. Under the colonial administration, troops were regularly assigned outside their own tribal areas to reduce the risk of their acting on behalf of local, rather than colonial, interests. This divide and rule deployment scheme helped to ensure that ANC garrisons in the newly independent country would have scant regard for either local or larger national interests. On July 5th, the garrisons nearest the capital ousted their Belgian officers and "ceased to exist as...cohesive and disciplined" units. From there, the mutiny spread.[4]

Roughly 100,000 Belgian citizens lived and worked in the Congo on independence day. As civil order dissolved, many began to flee the country, adding to the breakdown in public services and to the government's general inability to function. Others called for

Belgian help as attacks against Europeans increased. Three thousand Belgian paratroops, who remained in the country under terms of an unratified Belgium-Congo Treaty of Friendship signed shortly before independence, were quartered at two bases at Kitona, near the Atlantic coast, and Kamina, in northern Katanga province. On July 9th, Belgium began to reinforce these garrisons; on the 10th, against the wishes of the Congo government, the troops moved first into Katanga's capital, Elisabethville (now Lubumbashi), then to the port of Matadi, and then into Léopoldville, where they secured the European quarter. By July 19th, the Belgian presence had roughly tripled, to 10,000 troops, a small number relative to the size of the country, but politically explosive nonetheless.[5] Although Belgium justified its military moves as humanitarian intervention to safeguard European lives, others saw less altruistic motives.

On July 11th, one day after Belgian troops deployed, Moise Tshombé declared the secession of Katanga. Considered "pro-Western" by many Western politicians, Tshombé appointed Belgian citizens to lead Katanga's civil administration and later appointed seconded Belgian officers to lead his provincial army, or *gendarmerie*. Many eastern-bloc and nonaligned countries viewed the Belgian military intervention and Tshombé's declaration, in a province dominated by Belgian mining interests, as a joint effort to circumvent Congolese independence and to preserve European control of its principal sources of wealth.

Tshombé's decision was not universally acclaimed in the province, whose northern population was a separate tribal federation, the Baluba. A second group of Baluba lived in neighboring Kasai Province, which produced 80 percent of the world's industrial diamonds. An educated and entrepreneurial group, the Kasai Baluba provided manpower for basic technical services throughout the country. One month after Tshombé's announcement, South Kasai proclaimed its own secession, setting the stage for a chain of events that would soon sow misery in the region and bring down the Central Government.[6]

Tshombé's move was not opposed by those in control of most of the lands that bordered the Congo, however. Portugal controlled Angola to the southwest (whose own insurrection would begin in 1961). The British colony of Northern Rhodesia lay to the south and southeast; due east were the British colonies of Tanganyika and Uganda and the Belgian-administered UN Trust Territory of Ruanda-Urundi. Although most of these lands would shortly gain independence (Tanganyika in December 1961; Rwanda and Burundi in July 1962; Uganda in October 1962; and Zambia in October 1964), colonial interests added to ONUC's initial political complexity.

Finally, Western perceptions of both the Congo's intrinsic value, stemming from its mineral wealth, and the country's vulnerability to Communist pressure made the country both an open and covert Cold War battleground. This affected political support for ONUC, placed Secretary General Hammarskjöld in a political cross-fire, and helped to generate a funding crisis that brought the UN to the brink of insolvency.

Initiatives Toward UN Involvement

On July 10th, as the military mutiny spread throughout the Congo, Belgian troops entered Congolese cities, and fighting ensued with the ANC, contradictory appeals for assistance were launched in several political directions by various Congolese officials. Contributing to the confusion were the divided nature of the Congolese leadership, the disappearance of mid-level government administration, and the resulting marginal state of communications in the country.[7]

The first call for assistance was made by Lumumba on July 10th to Under Secretary General Ralph Bunche (who was in the Congo to oversee other UN aid programs). Lumumba asked the UN for assistance in training the ANC. In New York, the Secretary General approached the President of the Security Council to arrange a briefing in the SG's office regarding the Congo situation for Council members. As the situation continued to deteriorate, Hammarskjöld took the (historically rare) initiative of formally notifying the Security Council of an emerging "threat to international peace and security," as he is authorized to do by Article 99 of the Charter.[8]

The second call for assistance was made the next day by three Congolese Central Government ministers, who asked the US ambassador in Léopoldville for American troops to help restore internal order. They repeated their request in a cable to Washington but were referred to the UN. Most chroniclers agree that they and the top leadership of the country knew very little about the international body at that time. This contributed to later frustration about just whose interests ONUC was to serve.

The requests for aid continued on July 12th. Kasavubu and Lumumba, who were upcountry trying to reach Katanga, cabled the UN directly for military assistance against "external aggression," that is, against Belgian intervention. On the 13th, hearing finally of their ministers' appeal for US aid, they cabled the UN again, reiterating that the assistance requested was *not* to restore internal order, and stating that only neutral-country military personnel were acceptable. On the 14th, they asked the Soviet Union to stand by to render assistance, and Premier Nikita Khrushchev expressed his willingness to do so. By then, however, the Security Council had authorized Hammarskjöld "to provide... such military assistance as may be necessary."[9]

POLITICAL SUPPORT

Support for ONUC depended upon how well the Force served the observer's national, regional, or personal political interests. This section looks at the United States, Soviet Union, France, Britain, Belgium, the nonaligned states, and the local parties.

Local Parties

Kasavubu and Lumumba invited UN assistance on the assumption that the Organization would act as an ally of the government. Upon learning that ONUC had a palliative rather than curative mission, that it could take actions contrary to their desires in the course of fulfilling its mandate, and that it could not be removed by decree from Léopoldville (since its mandate came from the Security Council), both leaders regarded ONUC with ambivalence and, eventually, hostility: Lumumba because ONUC refused to fight in Katanga; Kasavubu because ONUC protected Lumumba and refused to recognize any faction as sovereign for the six months in which the Congo teetered on the brink of civil war.

Once it was clear to Lumumba that ONUC had not come to reign in Katanga, he took it upon himself to do so. One hundred trucks, 30 jeeps, one to two dozen IL-14 transport aircraft, and 200 technicians were put at his disposal at Stanleyville by the USSR, a move that caused great concern among Western embassies.[10] On August 23rd, Lumumba used his Soviet equipment to ferry ANC troops loyal to him from Stanleyville to Luluaborg in Kasai province. The ANC troops and fighters of the Bena-Lulua tribe attacked secessionist South Kasai, proceeding to massacre upwards of 1,000 Baluba tribespeople in a Sherman-like march toward Katanga. This action soon led to Lumumba's ouster from office by President Kasavubu.[11]

A constitutional crisis and eleven months of further political disarray were triggered on the night of September 5, 1960, when President Kasavubu went on radio to announce the dismissal of

Lumumba as prime minister, blaming him for the Kasai massacres. Lumumba in turn claimed to fire Kasavubu—a legally untenable but potentially enforceable proposition because of Lumumba's Russian logistic support. Concerned that Lumumba might try to fly his troops from Kasai or Stanleyville into the capital, UN officials on the scene closed the Congo's airports to all but UN traffic and shut down the Léopoldville radio station. These actions stayed in effect for a week, keeping Lumumba off the airwaves and preventing his allies from reaching the capital.

In mid-September, the ANC's chief of staff, Colonel Joseph Mobutu, declared all government factions "neutralized" in what was, in effect, a coup d'état. He also expelled Soviet and other eastern bloc personnel. Their transport aircraft and trucks left with them.[12] Because Mobutu had only tenuous control over the ANC, Kasavubu continued to function as the nominal president, and in November his delegation won the right to represent the Congo in the UN General Assembly, giving de facto recognition to his regime.

During this turmoil, however, Hammarskjöld decreed a policy of equidistance from all political factions to maintain the UN's neutrality, a policy that did not sit well with either Kasavubu or Western embassies, as it implicitly kept Lumumba in the game when those countries wanted him out. ONUC offered physical protection to all the players in this political drama through the fall of 1960, although the effort arguably benefitted Lumumba the most, as the UN guards surrounding his residence were in turn besieged by ANC troops seeking Lumumba's arrest. He was also a target for reprisals by Baluba soldiers in the ANC, who held him responsible for the deaths of their fellows in Kasai.

In late November, Lumumba slipped away from his residence in a thunderstorm and travelled upcountry. Had he reached Stanleyville, where his followers had been gathering since the UN vote to seat Kasavubu, the Congo could have plunged into civil war with overt Great Power backing. Instead, a seemingly leisurely pace of travel led to his arrest. He was jailed in the ANC garrison at Thysville, outside the capital. His supporters, including his former deputy, Antoine Gizenga, declared a new "central" government in Stanleyville in his name, and its influence soon spread into adjoining provinces, events which Kasavubu blamed on UN passivity.[13]

When a pro-Lumumba mutiny wracked the Thysville garrison in mid-January, Kasavubu shipped his prisoner and two compatriots to Katanga on a chartered Belgian airliner. Severely beaten enroute and upon arrival at Elisabethville airport by his Baluba escorts (the latter action observed at a distance by Swedish troops), all three prisoners died the same day at the hands of Tshombé's colleagues, according to the UN report on the subject, although the announcement of their deaths "while escaping" was made only four weeks later. The bodies were never recovered.[14]

In the aftermath of Lumumba's death, an upsurge of violence against UN personnel (encouraged by Léopoldville), and a campaign by Tshombé's forces to subjugate north Katanga through terror, led Hammarskjöld to seek a tougher mandate that would better permit ONUC to defend itself as well as Congolese civilians. Kasavubu and Mobutu, meanwhile, declared war on a supposedly "pro-Lumumba" UN Command, repeatedly (and ultimately successfully) demanding the replacement of the SG's Special Representative, Rajeshwar Dayal. Accomplishing that goal in April 1961, Kasavubu warmed to the UN once again, suggesting the degree to which local personal pique affected the UN's ability to carry out its mission.

Katanga's Tshombé was never supportive of ONUC, which he viewed with suspicion at best. Hammarskjöld himself led a contingent of Swedish peacekeepers into Katanga in August 1960, and other units followed, but the relationship remained uneasy, for good reason from Tshombé's perspective: ONUC first arranged the removal of Belgian forces from Katanga, then the removal of Tshombé's Belgian officer corps, then his mercenaries, and, finally, it forcibly ended his secession in January 1963.

United States

The domino theory figured prominently in US policy towards the Congo. In the words of Assistant Secretary of State for African Affairs, G. Mennen Williams, testifying before a closed hearing of the Senate Foreign Relations Committee in early 1961, "[I]f we pulled out completely and the Russians could fill this vacuum in the center of Africa, we would soon lose much, if not all, of Africa." With the Cold War in full swing, the United States wished to avoid involvement on the ground, fearing commensurate Soviet action. But it also wished to forestall a Soviet military initiative. The United States thus supported UN intervention, providing half of the money and most of the airlift, even as it worked to "manipulate the rival Congolese factions, their outside supporters, and the UN itself." In addition to public diplomacy, the US mounted covert operations, and was not alone in doing so, making Congolese politics even more complex and fluid.[15]

US policy was itself a matter of contention between liberals and conservatives who took very different views of African nationalism, the role of Communist influence in the region, and the relative importance of good relations with Third World countries when that goal clashed with traditional relations with the NATO allies, several of whom retained colonial empires. These tensions existed within the State Department, within the Congress, and among the media's many shapers of public opinion. They reduced the Kennedy Administration's flexibility and made it reluctant to endorse the use of force by the UN until it was eminently clear, in late 1962, that force was the only remaining option. By that time, of course, Kennedy himself had endured the Cuban Missile Crisis (October 1962), from which he emerged with a much stronger international and domestic political image.[16]

Soviet Union

Seeing support of forcible decolonization ("wars of national liberation") as its ticket to influence in the Third World, the USSR supported the initial Security Council actions of July 14th and August 9th, 1960, to deploy a large force to the Congo, but did so in the expectation that ONUC would be used to push out Belgian forces and put down secession in Katanga.

Following the collapse of the Congolese government, the Soviet Union attacked Hammarskjöld for the UN's actions that seemed to support Lumumba's ouster (for example, the seizure of broadcast facilities and the closing of Léopoldville airport, as well as Hammarskjöld's subsequent policy of equidistance from the contending factions). Moscow demanded his resignation and deadlocked the Security Council. At US initiative, the Council then decided to place the issue of the Congo on the agenda of the General Assembly under the 1950 "Uniting for Peace" resolution (veto-proof because it was a procedural motion). On September 20th, the Assembly handed Moscow a stiff rebuff when it reaffirmed Council actions 70-0, with 11 abstentions (the Soviet bloc, France, and South Africa). On September 23rd, when Khrushchev addressed the Assembly, he demanded that Hammarskjöld resign, and that the office of Secretary General be replaced by a *troika* of pro-Western, neutralist, and pro-Soviet bloc officials (effectively extending the veto power into the Secretariat).[17]

In early 1961, after Lumumba's murder, the USSR introduced resolutions calling for Hammarskjöld's dismissal and withdrawal of UN forces, which failed to garner majority support. Moscow then abstained on Security Council actions that gave ONUC authority to use force, but supported an April 1961 GA resolution condemning the continued Belgian military presence in Katanga—in part because it made no reference to the Secretary General. The following November, two months after Hammarskjöld's death (discussed below), the USSR supported a Security Council resolution that condemned the Katanga seccession and authorized the new Secretary General, U Thant, to use force to expel non-UN military personnel from the Congo.

Throughout this period, the USSR refused to pay its assessment for ONUC, as it had refused to pay for UNEF I.

France and Great Britain

As in the case of Suez in 1956, British and French interests did not quite coincide with those of the United States or the United Nations. France, under de Gaulle, sympathized with Belgium and opposed ONUC, refusing to pay its assessment, although it did not use its veto. Influential with the newly independent Francophone states of Central Africa, Paris persuaded them to deny overflight rights to US military aircraft ferrying UN troops to the Congo, just as it denied such rights over French territory. France also permitted the recruitment, on its territory, of mercenaries for Katanga.[18]

Britain had direct interests in the situation because of its colonial holdings in eastern and southern Africa and because of its financial stake in *Union Minière*. After civil disorder disrupted rail links between Katanga and the Congo River port of Matadi, most of Katanga's mineral exports were sent by rail through Angola and Northern Rhodesia. The latter's (British colonial) prime minister denounced UN actions to expel mercenaries from Katanga and gave shelter to Tshombé when the new Central Government first tried to arrest him in September 1961. Similarly, British colonial authorities in Uganda were slow to grant overflight and refueling rights to Ethiopian fighters assigned to protect UN troops against the small Katangan air force. However, Britain paid its assessments and purchased UN bonds to finance ONUC, and British officers seconded to Ghana and Nigeria served in ONUC with those countries' contingents.[19]

Belgium

Belgium stressed the humanitarian objectives of its initial intervention and strongly objected to being told by the UN to withdraw those forces. Nonetheless, most of its troops were withdrawn within two months of ONUC's deployment, except for

231 officers and non-coms who remained in Katanga for a year, seconded to Tshombé's regime. Belgian civilian technicians and other advisors began returning to the Congo in the fall of 1960. Since their initial exodus had been a contributing factor in the country's slide into chaos, the return of non-military personnel might have been welcomed by the UN as beneficial. But under the terms of UN resolutions, beginning with the General Assembly's action of September 20, any such advisers were to be withdrawn "immediately." This reflected the views of Afro-Asian states, among others, that the Belgian presence was a destabilizing factor, indeed, the "central factor" in Congolese unrest.[20] The Special Representative of the Secretary General, Rajeshwar Dayal of India, also argued that Belgian civilian advisors to Congolese ministries hampered implementation of UN programs in health, telecommunications, and air traffic control.

Belgian attitudes toward ONUC and compliance with UN mandates began to improve after April 1961, when a new coalition government came to power in Brussels, but five more months would pass before Belgian officers left Katanga (only to be replaced by mercenary troops from Rhodesia, South Africa, and France).

Exchanges between U Thant and the new Belgian Foreign Minister, Paul-Henri Spaak, indicate the degree to which misinformation at the center may have contributed to tension between New York and Brussels. After fighting broke out in December 1961 between UN and Katangan forces, Spaak complained that mortar fire from UN forces severely damaged a "new hospital" and wounded medical personnel. He denied that *Union Minière* had supplied Katangan forces with the armored vehicles and bombs used against ONUC. Thant replied that the "hospital" had never been used as such, had no medical personnel, and was in fact a "mercenary stronghold" with an observation post on the roof; he suggested that Spaak relied too much upon the pro-forma protestations of *Union Minière* officials in Brussels, since company officials in Katanga had "boasted" of their military support for Tshombé. Not until Katanga's secession was ended did tension between Brussels and the UN subside.[21]

Neutral and Nonaligned States

The growing nonaligned bloc of developing countries in the United Nations mostly supported ONUC, tended to be "Lumumbist" in their political preferences, and sought a greater role for UN forces in suppressing the Katangan secession. (An exception was the Brazzaville Group of newly independent Francophone African states, which opposed the operation, echoing the line from Paris.[22]) Resolutions drafted or sponsored by the Afro-Asian group were often the only politically acceptable basis on which to build majority support for UN action. Moreover, the major troop contingents in the Congo were drawn largely from nonaligned states in Africa and Asia (Ireland and Sweden excepted).

The troop-contributing nonaligned countries varied in their views of ONUC's proper role. Some, such as India, conditioned their agreement to send troops on their being used actively and constructively to restore order and the authority of the central government. Others were most concerned not to incur any casualties, or they supported the operation only so long as a favored Congolese political faction continued to benefit from it. For example, countries that supported Lumumba's faction—including Guinea, Indonesia, Mali, Morocco, the United Arab Republic, and Yugoslavia—removed their contingents in protest after his detention and death, temporarily reducing UN force levels by one third in a critical period.[23]

MANDATE

In a case involving so many competing political interests—local, regional, and Great Power—it would have been unrealistic to expect a mandate for the peacekeeping force that laid out precise objectives. The mandate initially passed by the Security Council on July 14, 1960, was clear on one point: it called for the withdrawal of Belgian troops. But it set no timetable for their withdrawal and made no mention of "aggression" (the term Kasavubu and Lumumba used in their first letter to Hammarskjöld). This tactic successfully skirted questions about Chapter VII and formal sanctions that would arise once a state is labeled an aggressor. The resolution read, in part,

> The Security Council...[d]ecides to authorize the Secretary General to take the necessary steps, in consultation with the Government of the Republic of the Congo, to provide the Government with such military assistance as may be necessary until, through the efforts of the Congolese Government with the technical assistance of the United Nations, the national security forces may be able, in the opinion of the Government, to fully meet their tasks.[24]

Of the permanent members, the US and USSR voted for the resolution. Britain, France, and China (Taiwan) abstained.

The resolution gave Hammarskjöld a great deal of flexibility, but it did not authorize use of force, did not set objectives for the operation, and did not define what "tasks" were to be met by indigenous security forces that would allow the UN to consider its work complete. Congolese leaders may be forgiven for interpreting the resolution to mean that the UN was coming in as the Government's good right arm; that is what they had requested, and the resolution seemed to offer UN assistance as a substitute for the national army. Lumumba in particular wanted help in suppressing Katanga's secession; when he didn't get it, he launched the Kasai expedition, with disastrous results for the local population, his political position, and ultimately his life.

Lumumba's trials, in turn, triggered revolt in Stanleyville. Within days after his death was announced, Gizenga's Stanleyville regime had received diplomatic recognition from Ghana, Guinea, Mali, Morocco, the United Arab Republic, the National Liberation Front of Algeria, East Germany and other Soviet bloc states, and China (Beijing). The African countries listed above were at the time contributing more than one-third of ONUC's military manpower. All but Ghana withdrew their forces from ONUC by mid-March 1961, and Ghana scaled back its contribution by two-thirds.[25]

Eventually, ONUC took active steps to put down the Katanga revolt and produced the results that Lumumba had sought, but only after two and one-half years in the field and several upgrades of its mandate. For its first eight months, ONUC found itself in an impossible situation: reluctant to withdraw, for the the sake of the civilian populace; reluctant to take sides, to preserve a semblance of impartiality; and unable to take significant military initiatives, because the mandate was interpreted to forbid such actions, particularly by Hammarskjöld, who was strongly averse to violence. ONUC therefore marched in place, taking such steps as it could to maintain order locally and to protect UN and civilian lives. It guarded national leaders and set up and guarded camps and food distribution centers for displaced civilians.

In February 1961, as attacks on UN personnel continued, as Stanleyville's rebellion spread, and as Tshombé's forces moved against Baluba tribespeople in north Katanga, ONUC won a revised and far stronger mandate.[26] In it, the Security Council,

1. Urges that the United Nations take immediately all appropriate measures to prevent the occurrence of civil war in the Congo, including arrangements for ceasefires, the halting of all military

operations, the prevention of clashes, and the use of force, if necessary, in the last resort;

2. Urges that measures be taken for the immediate withdrawal and
evacuation from the Congo of all Belgian and other foreign military
and paramilitary personnel and political advisors not under the
United Nations Command, and mercenaries.

All Council members supported the resolution, save France and
the USSR (who both abstained).

After Lumumba's death, the USSR settled for its second-best
scenario: the UN wresting Katanga from Western control on
behalf of the central government. The United States was also
disposed to help the "moderate" new government consolidate its
power, which also entailed ending Tshombé's secession. Thus,
on November 24, 1961, the Security Council further expanded
ONUC's mandate by declaring its "full and firm support for the
Central Government of the Republic of the Congo" and condemning and demanding the end of "secessionist activities illegally
carried out by the provincial administration of Katanga." It
authorized the new Secretary General to "take vigorous action,
including the use of the requisite measure of force, if necessary,"
to expel foreign mercenaries from the Congo, and to "take all
necessary measures" to prevent their return or the influx of arms
to support Katanga's revolt. Both the United States and the
Soviet Union voted in favor of the resolution. France and the UK
abstained.[27]

This final mandate was more forceful than the previous ones in
part because the country's political situation had changed, in part
because the international climate had changed, and in part because the UN's leadership had changed. Congolese leaders had
formed a new government, with UN assistance, in August 1961.
It presented a moderate face to the world, which appealed to the
West, and it sought to unify the country and to expel from
Katanga the die-hard Europeans supporting Tshombé, which
appeased the East. Not until the end of 1962, however, after the
Berlin and Cuban crises had ended, was the international situation such that the UN might be assured of the necessary support
if it acted decisively. Moscow and Washington had stepped to the
brink of nuclear war over the Cuban Missile Crisis and had even
more quickly stepped back. Thereafter, there was a period of
détente.[28]

The UN itself was in no shape to take decisive action in the
Congo in the months following Hammarskjöld's death. His

successor, although less averse to intervention in Katanga and less averse to using force than was Hammarskjöld, awaited the international backing needed for forceful action. That backing, especially from Belgium and the United States, became available in late 1962 for the reasons already noted. Until then, U Thant relied on diplomatic initiatives, with one sharp exception in response to harassment by the Katangan gendarmerie after passage of the November 1961 mandate (see below).[29]

FUNDING

At its peak, ONUC cost the United Nations $120 million a year, that is, more in one year than UNEF spent in six, at a time when the basic UN budget was about $75 million a year. By UN standards, then, ONUC was a monumental undertaking that would have been hard to finance even if it were noncontroversial. As it was, the political fights over the character and mandate of ONUC spilled over into the budget arena, as some states withheld funds to protest UN policy and others worked to reduce their share to a minimum. The result was a financial emergency for the Organization. By late 1962, arrears for peacekeeping (ONUC and UNEF combined) totalled $117 million (equal to more than $600 million at 1991 prices), and only one fourth of the membership had paid their assessments for ONUC.

Initially, the Fifth Committee of the General Assembly, its budgetary and administrative body, proposed in December 1960 that the expenses of ONUC be considered expenses "of the Organization" and thus subject to mandatory assessments under Article 17(2) of the Charter. In approving a draft resolution to this effect, the Committee was heavily divided: 46 votes for, 17 against, 24 abstentions. The Soviet Union opposed mandatory assessments, holding that the whole operation in the Congo was Western-inspired and "biased," and thus should be supported by voluntary contributions from those countries with a direct interest in it, much as it had earlier insisted that the costs of UNEF be borne "by the aggressors." Moreover, the USSR insisted that the GA, in voting funds for a military operation such as ONUC, had usurped the role of the Security Council (where the USSR had a veto).

On December 20th, by a similarly split vote, the General Assembly authorized $48.5 million for ONUC's 1960 expenditures. Unlike more recent peacekeeping operations, ONUC had been sent into the field on the Security Council's authorization, without prior approval of funding by the Assembly. The Congo experience would ensure a change in that procedure.

As it voted the 1960 money, the Assembly also authorized expenditures of $8 million a month for ONUC in the first quarter of 1961, "pending action by the GA at its resumed fifteenth session" that spring, but did not specify how the money was to be raised. In April, the resumed GA authorized another $100 million to cover January through October 1961. That authorization was billed to member states using the standard scale of assessments, except that levies on the poorest member states were reduced by 80 percent, and richer countries were asked to make up the shortfall with voluntary contributions. Through 1962, only the United States made such contributions, worth $30.6 million. The shortfall was made worse by the refusal of France and the USSR to pay any ONUC assessments at all. The Soviet example was followed by the rest of the eastern bloc.

In December 1961, one month after the Security Council approved the final "use of force" mandate for ONUC, and as UN forces engaged in combat in Katanga, the GA authorized another $80 million for the operation through June 1962, and further authorized the Secretary General to issue $200 million in UN bonds to cover expenses for ONUC and UNEF. Voting against the bond issue were the Soviet bloc, Belgium, and France; 24 largely developing states abstained. The bonds were to be repaid over 25 years through regular UN assessments. Subscriptions to the bond issue funded UN peacekeeping operations from July 1962 to June 1963.

The US Congress, in authorizing purchase of the bonds, stipulated that US purchases could match, but not exceed, bond purchases by other countries, and that the principal and interest due the United States each year was to be deducted from its annual assessment due the UN, to ensure repayment. Other countries purchasing at least $2 million worth of bonds included Sweden, West Germany, the UK, Italy, Canada, Denmark, Norway, Japan, Australia, India, and the Netherlands (in descending order).[30]

Also in December 1961, the GA requested an Advisory Opinion from the International Court of Justice. In July 1962, the Court affirmed that peacekeeping expenses were legitimate "expenses of the Organization" which member states could be obligated to pay. The Soviet Union and France continued to withhold payments; indeed, from roughly mid-1962 through mid-1963, ONUC was funded by the bond issue alone.[31]

In mid-1963, the GA managed to pass another funding resolution that authorized $33 million for ONUC through the end of the calendar year. Once again, a novel scale of assessments was used, with $3 million of the total apportioned according to the regular scale of assessments, and the rest billed to developed countries at their regular rate of assessment and to "economically less developed" countries at 45 percent of the regular rate. Developed countries were again asked to make up the difference with a voluntary contribution. In October 1963, ONUC's mandate was extended through June 1964, and $18.2 million was authorized and similarly assessed.[32]

Voluntary contributions for ONUC totalled $2.8 million in 1963 (of which 63 percent came from the US).[33] Contributions in 1964 totalled $1.2 million (61 percent from the US). By late 1963, the USSR owed $37 million to the UN, France $16 million, and Belgium $3 million. As the GA convened in the fall of 1965, the USSR and France owed the UN more than the equivalent of two years of regular assessments, and according to Article 19 of the Charter should have been deprived of their votes in the Assembly. Rather than press the issue and create a greater crisis for the Organization, and perhaps a Soviet withdrawal (akin to Japan's from the League of Nations in the 1930s), the US agreed to go along with the consensus view that the Assembly proceed without voting during its 1965 session.[34]

The gross cost of the UN Operation in the Congo came to $408 million or roughly $2 billion at 1991 prices. Of that amount, the US waived $10.3 million in initial airlift costs, the USSR waived $1.5 million, Canada $650,000, and the UK $520,000, and roughly $40 million was recouped through the disposal of surplus stores and equipment. Including the cost of bonds purchased, the US contribution to ONUC's military operations totalled nearly 48 percent. In addition, the US funded about 71 percent of the cost of the UN's civilian operation in the Congo.[35]

The cost of the operation would have been much higher had the UN reimbursed its forces for basic pay. Troop contributors covered those costs, while the UN provided a $1.30 per diem in local currency (50 percent convertible to hard currency at the end of a tour) and paid for overseas allowances (for example, $8 a month for Indian soldiers; $120 a month for Swedish soldiers). In addition, the UN accommodated other national demands: India required the UN to pay the cost of reserves mobilized to replace troops sent to the Congo, while Sweden insisted that the UN pay the full salary of its troops, all volunteers, at $390 a month.[36]

ONUC's financial troubles derived partly from the highly charged politics of the time, when Cold War tensions as well as pressures for decolonization were both at their peak, and partly from the size and ambition of the operation itself. It demonstrated the inadequacy of the UN's system of funding for peacekeeping, and the unwillingness of developing states to pay their regular share for such costly operations, which were seen as serving the interests of the Great Powers as much or more than their own. The bond issue that kept the Organization going for a year was a novel idea that has not since been repeated.

PLANNING AND IMPLEMENTATION

Lacking formal intelligence on the evolution of the political situation in the Congo, the UN relied on the reports of UN staffers on the scene in Léopoldville, on member states' missions in New York, and on the Congo's political leadership, which was inexperienced, insecure, and suspicious of foreigners. Moreover, both the situation in the country and what the world learned about it were subject to manipulation by those powers that had intelligence assets and interests at stake in the Congo.

An earlier appreciation of the Congo's internal problems might have dissuaded the UN from military involvement. But the UN was and is not an independent entity. Great Power political relations being what they were at the time, the operation would have been pressed upon the Secretariat by the United States, and perhaps by the Soviet Union, even if the Organization had had much better information available to it (and was, consequently, more reluctant to become involved). Indeed, Hammarsjköld is quoted by ONUC's first military commander as saying that he had "no other choice" but to go ahead.[37]

Knowing more of the field situation, however, or having better military advice, he might have sought a stronger, more specific mandate early on, and might have better provided for the Force's initial communications and transport needs. On the other hand, the Security Council was probably too divided to agree on a strong, specific mandate in the early weeks of the crisis, and it seems clear that the Secretariat in July 1960 was neither organizationally nor psychologically prepared to orchestrate a deliberate, division-sized military operation half a world away.

Most important, however, sketchy information permitted the leadership in New York to ignore, avoid, or downplay the importance of the ANC as a key source of disorder in the Congo. Had initial information been more detailed, New York might have been willing to seek Council approval to disarm the ANC and to press this condition upon the Congo government as a price of ONUC's deployment. On the other hand, stripping the government of its nominal monopoly on armed force would have made the UN a de facto occupying power and the Congo a de facto trusteeship. At no time in ONUC's four-year history was the Security Council disposed to such drastic action, and no politician in the Congo would have willingly ceded such power to an organization beyond his control. In fact, the ANC *was* partially disarmed early in ONUC's tenure, on the initiative of UN military commanders in the field, but once UN political leaders learned of the policy, they reversed it.

Character of the Situation in the Field

Most UN peacekeeping forces deploy after conflict or after political agreement in order to guarantee a peace that the parties cannot easily maintain for themselves. In this instance, the parties who called in the UN wanted it to make peace on their behalf, something that the Organization was not prepared to do. Moreover, in July 1960 when ONUC first deployed, the country was undergoing political and administrative collapse. Public order, already unstable, was being actively undermined by the country's nominal security force, the ANC. Local animosity toward the former colonial power, Belgium, often led to the misidentification of any European-looking person, including UN officers, as "Belgian," with dangerous and occasionally fatal consequences. Intertribal fighting and secessionist campaigns produced a sequence of massacres and reprisals.

At one time or another, every political faction in the Congo was hostile to the UN presence thinly scattered throughout the country, especially during the period of central government paralysis that began shortly after ONUC deployed and continued for 11 months. During this period, ONUC found itself in a kind of tropical Wonderland in which scheming political leaders changed their views as often as they changed their suits, and competence had virtually nothing to do with government appointments. ONUC focused on protecting the innocent from those who vied for power, somewhat as UNIFIL in Lebanon functions today, but over an area the size of Central Europe. Once government was reestablished in Léopoldville in August 1961, ONUC shifted its focus and dealt with Katanga's secession in an increasingly direct and forceful manner. The Congo remained short on public order, but from

August 1961 the UN was at least operating as an ally of the central government.

Initial Planning

Dag Hammarskjöld took personal charge of recruiting the forces that would comprise ONUC and rarely delegated authority beyond a small, trusted circle of UN staff. In this recruitment drive he had to start "from scratch," using personal contacts with heads of government of likely troop-contributing countries. Hammarskjöld worked without a master plan; and with scant details about the field situation he began his calls in the predawn hours of July 14, immediately following passage of the initial mandate for ONUC.[38] The initial forces arrived in the country before the initial command staff could be brought down from UNTSO in Jerusalem; indeed, the UNTSO contingent was delayed five days by a lack of air transport. The troop contingents had not worked together before, and their commanders did not know one another. Their supplies and communications were rudimentary. Hammarskjöld initially wished to rely upon African forces exclusively and received offers of troops from Ghana, Guinea, Morocco, and Tunisia even before the Security Council had acted. Ethiopia also offered and was invited to send troops. For a second-phase buildup, Hammarskjöld appealed to "three European, one Asian, and one Latin American" country. He asked Ralphe Bunche, his chief aide in this process, to clear these choices with the Congolese government.[39] Other countries were asked to provide logistics support, aircraft, and communications.

The initial choice of Force Commander appears to have been influenced largely by availability. Major General Carl von Horn, UNTSO's Chief of Staff, was already serving under UN command, and that mission's settled, if at times trying, routine meant that staff could be borrowed to establish a headquarters for ONUC quickly without jeopardizing the older operation's basic mission. However, turning reflexively to UNTSO entailed certain risks. Perhaps most important, it short-circuited the talent search. ONUC needed a command staff urgently. However, if the UN had spent a bit more time pulling such a staff together from a somewhat larger pool of talent, and had delayed the dispatch of ground force contingents for a day or two as a result, ONUC might have been more effective in the critical first month of the operation.

Even as the UN poured thousands of troops into the country, Hammarskjöld's philosophical aversion to "interference" in the Congo, the UN's non-existent intelligence capabilities, and ONUC's vague initial mandate conspired to prevent the Secretariat and the Force itself from planning and taking certain actions early on that could have averted much later bloodshed. Foremost among those early actions should have been the disarming of the ANC preparatory to its reorganization and retraining. If that force had been disarmed, Lumumba would have been unable to undertake his Kasai expedition, which directly precipitated his ouster and the year-long constitutional crisis.[40]

The ad hoc approach to appointments for ONUC continued long past the first weeks. In mid-1961, Hammarskjöld discovered at the last moment that the UN official he had chosen to be the new UN representative in Katanga had been Defense Minister in Republican Spain in the 1930s, which could have placed him at risk from some of the extreme rightist mercenaries then in Tshombé's employ. In a hurry to appoint a replacement, Hammarskjöld invited Conor Cruise O'Brien, then a member of Ireland's mission to the UN whom he did not know well, to take the position. This would have momentous consequences, as O'Brien was not steeped in the Secretariat's pacifist ethos.

Size and Composition of the Force

Within 48 hours of passage of the mandate for ONUC, the first troop contingents began to arrive in the Congo, most of them aboard American transport aircraft. For the first month's build-up, the principal combat troop contributions came from the countries indicated in Table 19.1. In addition, support units in place or en route included an Indian supply and dispatch unit, a Pakistani ordnance unit, a Canadian signals company, and miscellaneous smaller support detachments from Denmark, Norway, and the Netherlands. Crews, mechanics and aircraft for the internal supply lift were provided by Argentina, Brazil, Ethiopia, India, Norway, Sweden, Yugoslavia, and later Italy.

Over the course of the operation, the entire Nigerian and Ghanaian armies, and up to two-thirds of the Ethiopian and Malaysian armies, cycled through the Congo. India's brigade formed one-fourth to one-third of ONUC in the critical period from May 1961 through March 1963, and in terms of man-years in the field, India contributed most to the operation. Indian generals were also the UN commanders in Katanga for all three major engagements there. After India, the heaviest contributors of manpower to ONUC included Ethiopia, Nigeria, Tunisia, Ghana, Sweden, Malaysia, Ireland, Indonesia, Pakistan, Morocco, Canada, and (technically) the Congo itself, since a battalion of ANC was placed under UN command from December 1961. Each of these nations contributed more than 1,000 person-years to the ground operation.[41]

Table 19.1. Sources of Troops for ONUC
During the First Month's Build-up

Contributing Country	Number of Troops				
	July 18	July 20	July 26	July 31	Aug 19
Ethiopia	460	460	1,160	1,860	2,547
Ghana	770	770	2,340	2,412	2,389
Guinea		700	741	741	744
Ireland				678	1,317
Liberia			225	225	225
Mali					574
Morocco	1,250	1,250	2,320	2,465	3,250
Sudan					390
Sweden		635	623	623	628
Tunisia	1,020	1,020	2,087	2,151	2,427
Totals:	3,500	4,835	9,496	11,155	14,491

Source: Rosalyn Higgins, *United Nations Peacekeeping, 1946-1967, Documents and Commentary, Vol III: Africa* (Oxford: Oxford Univ. Press, 1980), 87-89.

ONUC reached its peak strength in July 1961, with 19,825 troops. It acquired a small international air force in the fall of 1961 after the first fighting in Katanga, with four jet fighters from Sweden, four from Ethiopia, and six Canberra light bombers from India. By December of that year, when fighting broke out in Katanga, withdrawals of brigades from Tunisia and Ghana had reduced the Force by 4,000; after that clash, ONUC slowly rebuilt to nearly 20,000 troops.[42]

When the military phase of the operation ended in January 1963, ONUC once again totalled more than 19,400 troops and had an air force of ten to twelve Swedish fighters, plus four Iranian and five Italian jets. The Indian brigade withdrew in March 1963, followed by a steady reduction in other nations' forces. By mid-1963, ONUC had 8,000 troops in the Congo; by early 1964, 5,500. All together, 34 countries contributed ground force or support troops to the operation, as many as 28 countries at once (in December 1960) and 20 on average from mid-1961 to spring 1963.[43]

Command Structure and Communications

ONUC's command structure was civilian dominated, the first UN field operation to combine civil and military functions in what would now be called a "multicomponent" operation. This structure resulted in sustained civilian-military friction evident from the very first days of the operation. The initial delay in establishing a UN military command staff in Léopoldville led newly arrived General Henry Alexander, the seconded British commander of Ghana's contingent to ONUC, to proclaim himself temporary Force Commander. Reading of this on the Associated Press wire, Hammarskjöld hastily gave Bunche control of UN military matters.[44] Perceptions of rapid decay in social order led Bunche to dispatch troop contingents to the far corners of the country before the UN had the communications equipment to remain in touch with them, leaving brigade and battalion commanders to fend for themselves in often volatile situations. Special Representative Dayal's first report emphasized that in some cases a single brigade had been given responsibility for policing an area "the size of France." The Force's dispersion also affected communications within units, since the designers of field radios for infantry companies usually assume that they will operate well within 100 kilometers of their parent battalions.[45]

Responsibility for communications soon devolved upon Canada. Its 57th Signal Squadron, headquartered in Léopoldville from August 9th, initially sent detachments to seven regional UN headquarters upcountry, and eventually to all major UN deployments, using American-supplied Army radios with barely enough range to reach the farthest outposts. The network began operations about four weeks after the first UN ground units deployed. In other words, for the first month, ONUC had to rely upon commercial telephone and cable, such as it was, or upon air transport, to communicate with its far-flung troops.[46]

UN civilians involved in making ONUC operational were harshly critical of the first Force Commander, Major General von Horn, and the recriminations were mutual. Von Horn was appalled at the utter chaos of the operation, and objected on military grounds to certain decisions of the political leadership, threatening to resign on three occasions within a month of his arrival in Léopoldville: once after Hammarskjöld rebuffed his request for a force more realistically sized to the task of pacifying so large a country; a second time upon ferreting out that all of his communications to and from New York were subject to civilian screening; and a

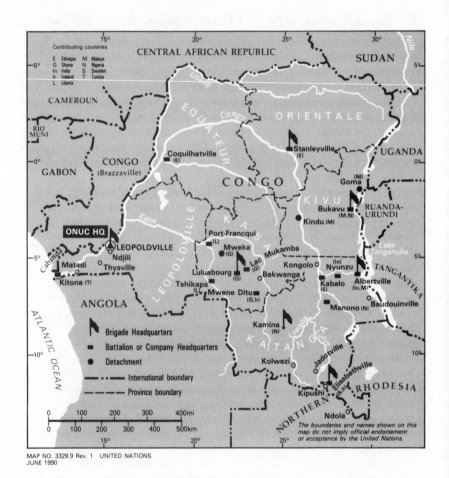

Figure 19.1. United Nations Operation in the Congo, Deployment as of June 1961

third time after refusing to implement an order from Bunche, in the third week of August, to release arms confiscated from the ANC. [47]

These and other clashes earned von Horn the enmity of UN civilians, who dismiss him in their memoirs as "orthodox" and "easily ruffled," and dismiss his UNTSO adjutants as "mostly useless." Von Horn, on the other hand, saw his staff as good military people given an impossible job with the most grudging and marginal logistical support.[48] In December 1960, as the Congo slid toward civil war, von Horn resigned for reasons of health, returning to UNTSO, and was replaced by the Irish Army's Chief of Staff, General Sean McKeown.

Command and control in ONUC remained tenuous, however, in part because the Force Commander had an impossibly broad span of control, with dozens of units scattered across the Congolese landscape reporting directly to Léopoldville. Less than half of ONUC's ground forces reported to a brigade headquarters, the normal intervening level of command between a battalion—the standard UN operating unit—and a division, and ONUC was roughly division size. That ONUC was able to conduct its business in any reasonable manner is a tribute to its logistics and transport personnel but, more importantly, is also indicative of the disorganized nature of the opposition it encountered and, in the case of Katanga, the inability or unwillingness of the opposition to bring its full firepower to bear against UN forces.[49]

A second source of ONUC's command and control difficulties was a chain of command that reached from New York to Katanga, beginning with the Secretary General, who retained ultimate authority over the operation. Reporting to him was Ralph Bunche, the Under-Secretary General for Special Political Affairs, who had returned to New York from the Congo in late August 1960.[50] Reporting to Bunche were the Special Representative (later Officer-in-Charge) in Léopoldville, and the Force Commander. The Chief Administrative Officer in ONUC, representing the UN Field Service and responsible for administering money and supplies for all UN forces, reported to the Director of the Office of General Services in New York, nominally through the Officer-in-Charge in Léopoldville. In fact, Field Services retained considerable autonomy. There were also subordinate UN civilian and military authorities in Elisabethville, Katanga, where a growing fraction of ONUC's forces were sent. In 1962, 70 percent of the force fell under this "subordinate" command.

As is often the case, field people felt the press of events on the ground most keenly, and the forces of international politics seemed remote and abstract. The reverse was true for the Secretariat in New York, and UN officials in Léopoldville felt pressure from both directions. These differing perceptions, the multi-tiered chain of command, the physical distances and their impact on the quality and timeliness of telecommunications, help to explain the breakdowns in command and control involving ONUC's activities in Katanga.

The mercenary problem in Katanga had been growing since early 1961 and, with it, harassment of UN forces and of largely Baluba civilian populations in north Katanga, who had resisted Tshombé's regime. From mid-1961 on, the leadership of Tshombé's gendarmerie increasingly included members of the French OAS, led by Colonel René Falques. This "secret army" of disaffected extreme rightists opposed to de Gaulle's policy of independence for Algeria had attempted a coup in France in April 1961. The remnants who found their way to Katanga were viewed as white supremacists far more dangerous than Tshombé himself, with their own designs for Katanga.[51]

The February 1961 mandate for ONUC called for expulsion of foreign military forces and mercenaries, but did not directly condemn the secession of Katanga. ONUC had authority to move against the foreign fighters supporting Tshombé, but not against Tshombé's regime; authority to detain but not to deport the fighters that it encountered, and no explicit authority to use force in doing so (its authority to use forceful measures extended only to preventing civil war). Under this mandate, in late August 1961, UN forces in Katanga conducted a surprise, peaceful, but unfortunately partial roundup of 338 non-Congolese members of the Katangan gendarmerie in an operation dubbed "Rumpunch." The Belgian consul in Elisabethville promised to see to the detainees' repatriation if the roundup operation were suspended, but then professed to lack authority to deport the private citizens among them whom the local authorities wished to keep around. Some of the mercenaries were repatriated; others were given shelter by their respective consulates. After the failure of this operation, Baluba tribespeople in the Elisabethville area fled to UN protected camps whose population quickly swelled from 700 to 35,000.[52]

On September 11th, the new Government in Léopoldville presented warrants for the arrest of Katangan officials to the UN's chief civilian in Katanga, Conor Cruise O'Brien. O'Brien interpreted ONUC's mandate as encompassing both the forcible roundup of mercenaries and the termination of Katanga's secession, viewing both actions as consistent with "prevention of civil war." Acting upon instructions from Mahmoud Khiary, the forceful head of UN civilian operations in the Congo (which itself says much about ONUC's tangled lines of civilian and military authority), O'Brien ordered a new operation, in the early hours of September 13, 1961. Code-named "Operation Morthor" (Hindi for "Smash"), it duplicated the earlier "Rumpunch" but this time failed to achieve surprise and led to eight days of fighting between UN forces and the gendarmerie (a label that obscures the fact that its units outgunned and outnumbered UN troops in Katanga by roughly two to one). Hammarskjöld did not authorize Morthor, and neither did ONUC's top civilian or military leadership. Its timing may have been influenced by the Secretary General's imminent visit to Léopoldville, and by the desires of at least some officials on the scene to finish the uncompleted August roundup of mercenaries before he arrived. In the event, with fighting flaring in Katanga and with Western governments vigorously protesting O'Brien's actions, Hammarskjöld decided to meet with Tshombé, who meanwhile had fled to the border town of Ndola in Northern Rhodesia. Flying a circuitous route at night to avoid Katanga's lone fighter aircraft, Hammarskjöld's plane crashed on approach to Ndola, killing all on board. The UN negotiated an uneasy truce with Katanga four days later, which Tshombé treated as a victory.[53]

Morthor was not the last lapse in command and control for ONUC, but in its ramifications it was the most serious. The UN fell into temporary disarray at the sudden loss of Hammarskjöld, whose stature, already larger than life in the minds of many supporters, assumed mythic proportions after his death. O'Brien, though not publicly reprimanded for his actions, was replaced as UN representative in Katanga in November 1961 and resigned from UN service on December 1st.[54]

Logistics and Administration

Keeping such a large multinational force supplied was a complex task that the UN had not undertaken before on such a scale. However, the UN's Office of General Services did have working arrangements with the US government to supply UNEF, in the Sinai, and those arrangements were adapted to ONUC's needs. The Secretary General phoned US Secretary of State Christian Herter on July 13, 1960, and was assured of airlift support for the operation. The United States subsequently drew down US Army stocks in Europe for ONUC and provided significant amounts of air- and sealift. In the first two weeks of the operation, 41 US Air Force C-130 sorties into Léopoldville established the airlift and its ground support, and over the next four years the US flew over 76,000 troops and 14,000 tons of cargo into and out of the Congo. In addition, it moved 44,000 troops and eight thousand tons of cargo by sea.[55]

The United States did not provide routine airlift inside the country. Nor did US personnel see to the distribution of supplies. Airlift within the Congo was undertaken by a composite group of Italian, Indian, Brazilian, Argentinian, Swedish, Norwegian, and Canadian aircraft and crews, flying a comparably mixed group of aircraft. Logistics support was the responsibility of Indian and Pakistani units.[56] The US did fly troops and supplies into Katanga in support of UN combat operations there. In December 1961, the USAF flew in Swedish, Irish, and Ethiopian battalions, and Swedish armored cars. That role was repeated in December 1962.[57]

The United States waived the $10 million cost of the initial airlift for ONUC, but billed the UN $25 million for subsequent air support, plus $8 million in sealift costs. In no instance did the US charge the UN for base pay or allowances for the Air Force, Navy, or Military Sea Transport Service personnel involved in the lift. US logistical capabilities and personnel were given the highest accolades by participants and chroniclers alike.

When there were complaints, they tended to be directed at the UN's Office of General Services and its Field Operations Service. It is traditional for military commanders to knock civilians and vice versa, but the problems experienced by ONUC in dealing with the UN supply system, its rules and its civilian administrators, tend to be echoed in later peacekeeping missions as well. The basic difficulties lie in the UN's traditional dual chain of authority for its field operations, where military officers have ostensible command of an operation, but UN civilians retain tight control over budgets and requisitions. Generally speaking, the problems that arose in ONUC remain relevant thirty years later.

Field Operations

Initially tasked by the Security Council to oversee the withdrawal of Belgian paratroops and to serve as an impartial force for public order, ONUC largely accomplished the first task within two months, except in Katanga, but it was woefully ill equipped to provide internal security until its mandate had been successively expanded. The first expansion, in February 1961, shortly after Lumumba's murder had been revealed, called for, among other things, reorganization of the ANC, which the ANC and some Congolese leaders interpreted as a new call for its disarmament by ONUC. Attacks on the Force worsened throughout the Congo.[58]

Perversely, general hostility toward ONUC in the first quarter of 1961 served to push a number of political factions together. As a result of two conferences in the spring of 1961, a political agreement in June, and a convocation of the Congolese Parliament in July, which was heavily guarded by UN forces, there emerged in early August a new Central Government headed by Cyril Adoula (with Kasavubu continuing as head of state) that had the backing of all local players except Tshombé. Thereafter, ONUC's most difficult field operations, and most of its casualties, involved attempts to end the secession of Katanga, first with Rumpunch, then with the ill-fated Morthor, and finally with two major military actions in December 1961 and 1962.

ONUC had built up its forces in Elisabethville through the fall of 1961, including a small air force, while central government troops had waged a desultory campaign against Katanga notable only for causing civilian casualties. In late November 1961, the Security Council had voted new authority for ONUC to use force, and within two weeks battle had been joined once again, as harassment and physical abuse of non-African UN officials in Katanga escalated. In early December, the gendarmerie had moved to isolate various components of ONUC in and around Elisabethville. After several days of fruitless warnings, and in the face of mounting evidence that the gendarmerie were not under effective political control and were planning assaults on UN forces, ONUC attacked Katangese roadblocks to restore its freedom of movement, and substantial casualties ensued on both sides. When it became clear that *Union Minière* buildings were sheltering snipers, anti-aircraft guns, and mortar emplacements, air strikes were called in on those facilities.[59]

At the instigation of the US government, Tshombé and Adoula met on December 20, and the next day announced an accord in which Tshombé appeared to capitulate. The UN held its fire while the talks were underway and, indeed, for most of the succeeding year, while representatives from the two factions thrashed out the details of Katanga's reintegration. After eight months of deadlock, U Thant offered the parties a Plan of National Reconciliation in August 1962, the greater part drafted by the United States. The Plan called for a federal constitution, shared revenues, government and army reorganization, and economic sanctions if deadlines for achieving several of the objectives were not met. Adoula accepted immediately on behalf of the central government, and Katanga followed suit ten days later.[60]

Great Power attention was diverted in October and November as the US and USSR worked through the Cuban Missile Crisis. But with the crisis resolved, U Thant notified Tshombé, on

December 10th, that sanctions would be applied to Katanga. The next day, Adoula asked foreign governments to embargo imports of Katangan copper, and shortly thereafter both Belgium and the United States demonstrated their willingness to see Katanga's secession ended by force—a key turning point.[61]

ONUC, meanwhile, had continued to build up its forces in Katanga and by December 1962 had roughly 13,500 troops deployed there. Katanga continued to build up as well, acquiring jet aircraft and 300-500 additional mercenaries. UN Katanga commander Major General Dewan Prem Chand (who, 12 years later, would face down Turkish forces at Nicosia airport, and later still, would command UN troops in Namibia) drew up contingency plans for Grandslam, ONUC's final military push. UN leaders had an incentive to bring matters to a head as the Indian Brigade of nearly 6,000 troops was to be sent home in March 1963 to help fight India's border war with China.[62]

ONUC positions in Elisabethville were attacked by gendarmerie December 24th. The UN held its fire for four days, then retaliated, disabling the modest Katangese air force and moving to secure Elisabethville and other towns in Katanga against relatively little resistance. The operation's official rationale was not ending Katangan secession but restoring full UN freedom of movement. Nonetheless, in the course of executing Grandslam, ONUC disarmed or dispersed the gendarmerie, including its mercenary elements, and Moise Tshombé announced an end to secession.

ONUC began a gradual withdrawal from the Congo thereafter, and the operation officially terminated at the end of June 1964. Although its four-year presence arguably prevented even worse disintegration of civil order, ONUC did not by any means put an end to civil and political unrest in the country. Indeed, in the fall of 1964, the taking of European hostages by rebels in the Stanleyville region led the United States to airlift Belgian paratroops into the Congo to effect a rescue.[63] Nor did civilian constitutional government long survive ONUC's departure, as the ANC's Mobutu seized power in October 1965. Mobutu remained in power for a quarter of a century, but pressure continued to build for democratic reform, and his government lost much of its Western aid due to its poor human rights record.[64]

ASSESSMENT

The UN Operation in the Congo lacked every element that history now says is necessary for a successful peacekeeping mission; namely, effective support from the Great Powers, consistent support of all local parties, a clear mandate, stable and adequate funding, and sufficiently good command, control, communications and logistics. Evaluated by these criteria, the operation was a muddle from start to finish. And yet, soon after ONUC had brought the secession of Katanga to an end, Harlan Cleveland, then-US Assistant Secretary of State for International Organization Affairs, could say that, because of the UN's Congo operation, "there are no uninvited foreign troops, no Communist enclaves, no 'army of liberation,' no reason for a single American soldier to die there, no excuse for a Soviet soldier to live there."[65] In short, while perhaps not a textbook peacekeeping operation, ONUC was, at least from the US perspective, better than the alternatives. However, the US perspective was not the only one.

Political Support

Great Power attitudes toward ONUC ranged all the way from supportive (United States) to tepid (United Kingdom), to obstructionist (France), and hostile (Soviet Union). This fission among the permanent members of the Security Council was faithfully reflected by their embassies in Léopoldville, their consulates in Katanga, and the respective local and regional factions they supported. Thus, ONUC's fundamental problem was that, outside the Secretariat, there were no disinterested parties. All of the rivalries of the Cold War, and all of the tensions of African decolonization (political, economic, social, and racial), tugged at the operation and distorted it. Moreover, the partisans didn't believe the Secretariat's own protestations of neutrality. Congolese politicians of all stripes, each of whom seemed to have close ties to one or another outside power, were hard put to believe that ONUC was not itself a proxy for the United States, its battalions sent to a place too dangerous, politically, for American troops. (US material and political support for the operation was indeed impressive from start to finish.)

Given all of the international and internal struggles for power, it is perhaps not surprising that at one point or another every Congolese political faction considered ONUC the enemy. Hammarskjöld adopted a policy of political equidistance following the September 1960 collapse of the central government. But while

UN leaders in New York may have convinced themselves that the Organization could deploy 20,000 troops and still be seen as neutral with respect to those affairs, preventing massacres of civilians did in fact constitute intervention, as did closing the Léopoldville airport when Lumumba wanted to fly in loyal troops, protecting him from vengeance-minded Baluba, or rounding up mercenaries. It was, as Special Representative Dayal concluded, "massive intervention in the guise of non-intervention."[66]

Once central government was more or less restored in August 1961, the fiction of nonintervention was pretty much dropped, and ONUC supported the central government's efforts to promote national unity. Still, the UN never added "ending the secession of Katanga" to the formal objectives of the Force. Even its most forceful actions against Tshombé's regime were taken, officially, to preserve its own freedom of movement.[67]

Mandate

Upon first reaching the Congo, the Force as a whole lacked the political and legal authority to deal with the situation they found there, and when the more enterprising of UN officials on the scene tried to take effective action, they were invariably brought up short by the outraged objections of one or another outside party pressuring the Secretariat on behalf of local clients. ONUC's initial mandate was to help the central government, but during its first year there were up to four "governments," contending factions backed (to some degree) by outside powers who were equally at odds. Hammarskjöld had to ride the tiger as best he could, unable to dismount and equally unable to rein the beast in. He waged a war of words, in New York and Léopoldville, to maintain the image and moral authority of the UN and the integrity of its forces in the field. There being no historical precedent for what ONUC was doing, he was forced continually to improvise, politically, legally, and operationally. Ultimately, however, good example and moral suasion proved inadequate to keep order in a situation where standards of public order had already broken down. Indeed, the Congo was probably beyond the reach of good example when the Force first deployed. Hammarskjöld was loath to use force, even when limited authority to do so was given him, but his successor found the judicious use of force to be the only way to face down the thugs who ran secessionist Katanga and to be the only method that offered the UN any prospect of an honorable exit from the Congo morass. Making no pretext of settling all of the country's political problems, the UN withdrew once its mandate in Katanga was fulfilled.

Funding

ONUC deployed without a budget or a source of funds, and its deployment brought to a head a long-simmering argument over how to pay for such peacekeeping operations, then a less than five-year-old concept that was already costing much more than the rest of the UN combined. Gaps in funding were bridged by voluntary US contributions and by a one-time issuance of long-term bonds, but it was clear that, without greater agreement on the politics of peacekeeping and who was to pay for it, peacekeeping would not evolve into a normal function of the Organization. And indeed, for a quarter-century it did not.

Command and Control

ONUC deployed on the spur of the moment, without advance planning or a full appreciation of what lay ahead of it in the field. Its military units were flung to the far corners of a country in chaos without command, control, communications, or authority to act. That chaos was the rationale for rapid deployment, yet battalion commanders without ties to higher levels, and thus without instructions or backup, had little chance of restoring order even had they the mandate to do so, which, initially, they did not. Nor could they effectively call upon the moral authority of the United Nations to aid them in their task, since few local people knew what it was, what it stood for, or what it was trying to do in their country. As near as one can tell from contemporary accounts and memoirs, there was little in the way of a public information campaign to raise the level of awareness. Among people both illiterate and accustomed to foreign domination, it is not easy to spread the word, nor have it accepted at face value. Rather, the worth of a UN operation must be demonstrated, effectively, on a daily basis.

That the UN was ultimately successful in Katanga owes much to the fact that both military commanders and the bulk of the troops were from one country, India, which supplied a brigade-level command structure for a brigade-level force. Moreover, the November 1961 expansion of its mandate specifically authorized ONUC to use force as needed to expel foreign mercenaries from the country and to curb the flow of arms into Katanga.

CONCLUSIONS

The use of force by UN troops and the great struggles that accompanied ONUC's deployment left their marks on the Organization and helped to ensure that the UN funded no new peacekeeping operation for a decade. The small missions to Yemen and West New Guinea were funded by the contending parties, and the mission on Cyprus was (and is) funded voluntarily.

ONUC was also a trauma for sub–Saharan Africa, which did not host another UN peacekeeping operation until UNTAG deployed in Namibia in 1989. That operation was not undertaken until all the local parties within and around Namibia supported it. UNTAG also benefitted from its being associated with decolonization and the struggle against apartheid.

The hesitation has been mutual. The UN has studiously avoided reinvolving itself in Africa's still-frequent civil wars. The Organization of African Unity informally sounded out the UN for material help in dealing with civil war in Chad in 1981, for example, but came away empty-handed, as did the Economic Community of West African States regarding the civil war in Liberia, in 1990.

After ONUC, and Hammarskjöld, no Secretary General exhibited the same degree of initiative with respect to peace and security issues. Indeed, no Secretary General from U Thant through Javier Pérez de Cuéllar was encouraged to take such initiative. With the new-found cooperative spirit among the five permanent members of the Security Council, that may change. Indeed, the Council encouraged the new Secretary General, Boutros Boutros-Ghali of Egypt, to take greater initiative in this area. But a side effect of greater cooperation among Council members may be less freedom of action for the Secretary General. That freedom can be circumscribed just as readily by a Council that knows precisely what it wants as by one that can reach no decision at all.

Some administrative lessons learned in the Congo were applied to subsequent operations. The financial lessons seem to have been learned well; for UNEF II and subsequent peacekeeping missions funded as "expenses of the Organization," a new scale of assessments was established that shifted the bulk of developing countries' peacekeeping assessments to the five permanent members of the Security Council. Uniform rates of reimbursement were established for troop contributors, and approval of funds by the General Assembly before deployment was made a general requirement, which slows down the Secretariat's ability to respond to crises, but assures that money will be allocated in advance to cover a mission's expenses.

ONUC also showed the need for better training and coordination of UN operations, from planning and deployment through logistics and communications. Civil-military relations were rocky to begin with and improved only slowly. The studies cited in this case history were replete with recommendations for change. But in the aftermath of the Congo operation, the Secretariat and member states were more interested in forgetting than in learning, more interested in avoiding future ONUCs than in doing them better. The missions to Yemen and West New Guinea passed quickly, Cyprus soon settled into familiar, if frustrating, routine, and UNEF II was old, if important, territory. Not until the late 1980s was the UN confronted with the need to do things any differently than it did them a quarter century before. Thus, until then, it didn't.

Notes

1. Fred E. Wagoner, *Dragon Rouge: The Rescue of Hostages in the Congo* (Washington, D.C.: National Defense University, Research Directorate, 1980), 6-7; Ernst Lefever, *Crisis in the Congo, A UN Force in Action* (Washington, D.C.: The Brookings Institution, 1965), 6-7, 9.

2. Wagoner, *Dragon Rouge*, 9; Major General Carl von Horn, *Soldiering for Peace* (New York: David McKay Company, Inc., 1967), 145; Rosalyn Higgins, *United Nations Peacekeeping, 1946-1967, Documents and Commentary, Vol. III: Africa* (Oxford: Oxford Univ. Press, 1980), 8.

3. Lefever, *Crisis in the Congo*, 8-9; Higgins, *United Nations Peacekeeping*, 8-9.

4. Lefever, *Crisis in the Congo*, 12.

5. Higgins, *United Nations Peacekeeping*, 12; Georges Abi-Saab, *The United Nations Operation in the Congo 1960-1964* (Oxford: Oxford University Press, 1978), 8.

6. Catherine Hoskyns, *The Congo Since Independence January 1960-December 1961* (New York: Oxford University Press, 1965), 7; Senate Foreign Relations Committee, *Executive Sessions of the Senate Foreign Relations Committee*, 87th Cong., 1st Sess., February 6, 1961, *History Series*, Vol. 13, Part 1, testimony of Claire H. Timberlake, US Ambassador to the Congo, 107 (hereafter, *ESFRC* 13:1).

7. Brian Urquhart, *Hammarskjöld* (New York: Alfred A. Knopf, 1972), 394-396.

8. Lefever, *Crisis in the Congo*, 13-14; Abi-Saab, *The United Nations Operation in the Congo*, 9.

9. UN Secretariat Document S/4387, July 14, 1960, cited in Abi-Saab, *The United Nations Operation in the Congo*, 14.

10. Timberlake, *ESFRC* 13:1, 101; Wagoner, *Dragon Rouge*, 11; Lefever, *Crisis in the Congo*, 40.

11. Higgins, *United Nations Peacekeeping*, 140; Wagoner, *Dragon Rouge*, 11; von Horn, *Soldiering for Peace*, 205-6.

12. Senate Foreign Relations Committee, *Executive Sessions of the Senate Foreign Relations Committee*, 87th Cong., 2nd Sess., January 18, 1962, *History Series*, Vol. 14, April 1986, testimony of Secretary of State Dean Rusk, 113 (hereafter, *ESFRC* 14).

13. Lefever, *Crisis in the Congo*, 51; Rajeshwar Dayal, *Mission for Hammarskjöld* (Princeton: Princeton University Press, 1976), 158.

14. Dayal, *Mission for Hammarskjöld*, 190-98.

15. *ESFRC* 13:1, 116 (testimony of Hon. G. Mennen Williams, Assistant Secretary of State for African Affairs); Roger Hilsman, *To Move a Nation* (Garden City, New York Doubleday & Co., 1967), 245; Wagoner, *Dragon Rouge*, 78-80; Dayal, *Mission for Hammarskjöld*, 65-66; John Stockwell, *In Search of Enemies, A CIA Story* (New York: W.W. Norton & Co., 1978), 137; Victor Marchetti and John D. Marks, *The CIA and the Cult of Intelligence* (New York: Dell Publishing Co., 1974), 131.

16. Hilsman, *To Move a Nation*, 245-48, 253-55.

17. Hilsman, *To Move a Nation*, 240.

18. Higgins, *United Nations Peacekeeping*, 270-71.

19. Higgins, *United Nations Peacekeeping*, 268-70; Lefever, *Crisis in the Congo*, 81.

20. General Assembly Resolution 1599 (XV), April 15, 1961, on which 33 states, including the US, abstained (Higgins, *United Nations Peacekeeping*, 27, 33-34, 222).

21. Higgins, *United Nations Peacekeeping*, 238-39.

22. Dayal, *Mission for Hammarskjöld*, 187.

23. Lefever, *Crisis in the Congo*, 50-51.

24. United Nations Document S/4387, July 14, 1960. Quoted in Higgins, *United Nations Peacekeeping*, 15.

25. Ernest W. Lefever and Wynfred Joshua, *United Nations Peacekeeping in the Congo: 1960–1964, An Analysis of Political, Executive, and Military Control, Vol. 3: Appendices*, a report prepared for the US Arms Control and Disarmament Agency (Washington, D.C.: The Brookings Institution, 1964), Appendix H, Chart E; Hilsman; *To Move a Nation*, 235.

26. Higgins, *United Nations Peacekeeping*, 30.

27. Higgins, *United Nations Peacekeeping*, 37-38.

28. The fruits of this period included the Limited Nuclear Test Ban Treaty.

29. Dayal, *Mission for Hammarskjöld*, 220, 234, 237, 267; Higgins, *United Nations Peacekeeping*, 424-5, 435-36.

30. David W. Wainhouse, *International Peacekeeping at the Crossroads* (Baltimore, Md.: The Johns Hopkins University Press, 1973), 305-31, 340-41; John G. Stoessinger, *Financing the United Nations System* (Washington, D.C.: The Brookings Institution, 1964), 126-130.

31. Higgins, *United Nations Peacekeeping*, 295.

32. Higgins, *United Nations Peacekeeping*, 282-97.

33. Lefever and Joshua, *United Nations Peacekeeping in the Congo*, Appendix Z.

34. Higgins, *United Nations Peacekeeping*, 298-300.

35. Wainhouse, *International Peacekeeping at the Crossroads*, 340-41.

36. Lefever, *Crisis in the Congo*, 147-48.

37. von Horn, *Soldiering for Peace*, 180.

38. Lefever, *Crisis in the Congo*, 32; Brian Urquhart, *A Life in Peace and War* (New York: Harper and Row, 1987), 147.

39. Ghana had received a bilateral request for aid from Congolese authorities, but wished to respond under a UN umbrella (Urquhart, *Hammarskjöld*, 398-99; Higgins, *United Nations Peacekeeping*, 86).

40. Lefever, *Crisis in the Congo*, 36-38.

41. Lefever and Joshua, *United Nations Peacekeeping in the Congo*, Appendix H.

42. Wainhouse, *International Peacekeeping at the Crossroads*, 297.

43. Lefever and Joshua, *United Nations Peacekeeping in the Congo*, Appendix H, Chart E.

44. Urquhart, *Hammarskjöld*, 400.

45. Higgins, *United Nations Peacekeeping*, 90.

46. Fred Gaffen, *In the Eye of the Storm, A History of Canadian Peacekeeping* (Toronto: Deneau and Wayne, 1987), 221-22.

47. Bunche subsequently issued the release order directly to brigade and battalion commanders. Within a week, Lumumba launched his Kasai campaign (von Horn, *Soldiering for Peace*, 198-201).

48. Urquhart, *Hammarskjöld*, 148, 155; Dayal, *Mission for Hammarskjöld*, 23; von Horn, *Soldiering for Peace*, 153-55, 175-78, 199-201.

49. Wainhouse discusses command and control issues at some length in his *International Peacekeeping at the Crossroads* (331-334).

50. Bunche was given the title in 1961, but had functional responsibility for military affairs in the Congo from this time.

51. Urquhart describes them as "the rifraff of declining colonial empires" (*Hammarskjöld*, 551).

52. Lefever, *Crisis in the Congo*, 77-79.

53. Higgins, *United Nations Peacekeeping*, 397-407.

54. Conor Cruise O'Brien. *To Katanga and Back* (New York: Grosset and Dunlap, 1966), 246-69.

55. Wainhouse, *International Peacekeeping at the Crossroads*, 281-303, 332n.

56. Wainhouse, *International Peacekeeping at the Crossroads*, 291.

57. Wainhouse, *International Peacekeeping at the Crossroads*, 297.

58. Dayal, *Mission for Hammarskjöld*, 21-26; Lefever, *Crisis in the Congo*, 34.

59. Higgins, *United Nations Peacekeeping*, 425-34.

60. Higgins, *United Nations Peacekeeping*, 435-38; Lefever, *Crisis in the Congo*, 103-4.

61. On December 11, Belgium dubbed Tshombé a "rebel" and declared its support "for armed force by the United Nations or Léopoldville to end

secession." The US dispatched a military aid mission to the Congo on December 20, headed by Lieutenant General Louis Truman to determine what additional aid the US could give to the UN to "maintain peace in the Congo." The Truman mission grew out of a policy reappraisal by the Kennedy Administration begun in late November (Lefever, *Crisis in the Congo*, 106-107).

62. Lefever, *Crisis in the Congo*, 105-07

63. Wagoner, *Dragon Rouge*, especially 130 ff. As a fitting postscript to its mission, Moise Tshombé was named prime minister of the Congo one week after the last of ONUC departed. Soon he was once again recruiting mercenary assistance, this time to put down rather than support secession. Tshombé was ousted in the coup that put Mobutu in power in October 1965 and died in exile.

64. *New York Times*, November 13, 1991, A6, and December 9, 1991, A3.

65. Address, January 17, 1963 (US Department of State Press Release No. 34, 1963, 2); cited in Lefever, *Crisis in the Congo*, 112. Ironically, even tragically, as the UN was extricating itself from the Congo, the United States was becoming more deeply involved in Vietnam. Having used the UN to avoid direct military involvement in one nightmarish conflict, the US turned and plunged headlong into another.

66. Dayal, *Mission for Hammarskjöld*, 116.

67. Against more formidable opposition it would not have been able to do even that. More recently, for example, in Lebanon, UNIFIL has faced just such opposition from all sides and has been greatly hampered in its operations as a result.

20 United Nations Transition Assistance Group

by Virginia Page Fortna

The United Nations Transition Assistance Group (UNTAG) was conceived in 1978 and implemented between April 1989 and April 1990 as part of a political settlement to a longstanding and complicated conflict. UNTAG assisted and monitored the transition of Africa's last colony, South West Africa, from South African control to independence as the new state of Namibia, enabling a war-torn people to hold free and fair elections and establish a multiparty democracy. As the first of a series of post–Cold War "multicomponent" UN peacekeeping operations, UNTAG broke new ground and emboldened UN mediation efforts in other long-running conflicts in Cambodia, El Salvador, and elsewhere.

ORIGINS

Namibia is a vast, sparsely populated land situated on the Atlantic coast just to the north of South Africa. Its other neighbors are Angola to the north, Botswana to the east, and Zambia (at the end of the narrow Caprivi Strip) to the northeast. The Namib desert runs along the coast; the land rises to a rugged plateau that tails off into the Kalahari Desert. Over half of Namibia's population of one million or so live in the better-watered northern one-third of the country.[1]

Namibia had been an area of concern for the UN since the Organization's creation, when it inherited responsibility for League of Nations mandates. South Africa had occupied German South West Africa during World War I and then was given responsibility for the territory under a class "C" League mandate. After World War II, South Africa refused to accept UN authority over South West Africa as successor to the League and attempted to annex the territory. The international community's reaction to this move marked the beginning of its efforts to promote Namibian independence. The issue became more important to the

UN as Europe's African colonies gained independence and joined the Organization in the 1950s and 1960s. Namibians and other individuals interested in their plight petitioned the UN for assistance during these years, reinforcing its interest in working for Namibian independence. Meanwhile, South Africa continued to move toward outright annexation by extending South African apartheid laws to the territory. These actions prompted the UN General Assembly in 1966 to revoke South Africa's mandate to administer the territory and caused the International Court of Justice in 1971 to rule South African occupation illegal.

Meanwhile, the territory's inhabitants began to take matters into their own hands. In 1960, the Ovambo People's Organization broadened its ethnic base and became the South West African People's Organization (SWAPO), with Namibian independence as its goal. Six years later, SWAPO began to use military means and its People's Liberation Army of Namibia (PLAN) began operations against South African occupation.

After the fall of the Caetano regime in Portugal in 1974, indigenous Marxist governments came to power in Portugal's former colonies of Angola and Mozambique. In the South African view this meant the fall of the *cordon sanitaire* that had protected it from Communism and black Africa, making Namibia all the more important to retain as a buffer territory.

The civil war that erupted in Angola in 1975 as Portugal withdrew became one of many regional conflicts in which the superpowers played out their Cold War rivalry. Cuba and the Soviet Union gave military aid to the regime of the MPLA (*Movimento Popular de Libertação de Angola*) while the United States and South Africa aided the MPLA's rivals, UNITA (*União Nacionale para a Independência Total de Angola*) and FNLA (*Frente Nacionale de Libertação de Angola*).[2]

In September 1975, South Africa held a Constitutional Conference in the Turnhalle building in Windhoek, Namibia. The Turnhalle initiative was an attempt on South Africa's part to lead Namibia to independence on its own terms, that is, with an apartheid system of separate administrations for each ethnic group and a friendly, non-Marxist, non-SWAPO government. This was not acceptable to the international community, however. In January 1976, the Western nations then on the Security Council (Canada, France, Great Britain, the United States, and West Germany) formed the Contact Group (also known as the Western Five), which operated under UN auspices to mediate a peaceful settlement of the Namibia conflict. The Contact Group members feared that a violent liberation struggle would foster further Soviet influence in the region. They were also concerned that if South Africa went ahead with its unilateral plan for independence (the Turnhalle initiative) the UN General Assembly would call for sanctions, a measure Western nations wanted neither to impose nor to veto.

The Contact Group proposed a settlement plan in a letter to the Security Council on April 10, 1978.[3] The plan called for the creation of a United Nations Transition Assistance Group (UN-TAG) to assist a Special Representative appointed by the Secretary General in supervising free and fair elections of a Constituent Assembly that would adopt a constitution for an independent Namibia. The plan, which envisioned independence within the year, was approved by Security Council Resolution 435 (1978). Mutual consent to the independence plan took a decade of difficult mediation and negotiation, however. The Namibia Accords, consisting of a trilateral agreement among Cuba, Angola, and South Africa allowing implementation of Resolution 435 linked with a bilateral agreement on the withdrawal of Cuban troops from Angola, were not signed until December 22, 1988. During the course of the negotiations both the international and regional situations changed significantly, and the Resolution 435 peace plan was expanded and modified.[4]

Political settlement was feasible in part because the low-level bush war in Namibia and Angola had been stalemated for some time. Angola could not prevent losses from South African raids and SWAPO could not drive South Africa out of Namibia, but neither could South Africa defeat SWAPO or the Angolan army. Moreover, the war was costly for South Africa, as was the administration of Namibia.[5] These costs became unbearable as South Africa's economy worsened under the pressure of international economic sanctions and a global recession. Reform at home and maintaining domestic order became higher priorities than control of Namibia, especially when Namibian independence would reduce some of the international animus that had led to the imposition of sanctions in the first place. Militarily, South Africa found itself more and more bogged down in the war and slowly came to the realization that superior weapons and training would not bring a decisive victory in the guerilla war without unacceptable escalation.

Two military events influenced a decisive shift in South African thinking on the war. One was a major increase in the number of Cuban troops in Angola and their movement to within 30 miles of the Namibian border in early 1988, raising the stakes of the war significantly.[6] The second was the costly battle at Cuito Cuanavale between November 1987 and March 1988, which shattered South Africa's assumption that its superior army was undefeatable. The prospect of white South African boys dying abroad hit home, and public sentiment began to turn against the war. Cuito Cuanavale became a symbol of the disaster that the war was becoming. At the same time, changes in Soviet foreign policy and inclusion of Cuban troop withdrawal in the settlement package diminished South Africa's overall sense of external threat. Gloomy military prospects and the reduced threat made settlement an increasingly preferred option.

For Angola, the mounting costs of the war, both financially and in terms of the social disruption it was causing in the country, made the stalemate increasingly painful. Recognition of the need to end the war peacefully, as well as other changes described in the next section, made the conflict ripe for resolution by the end of the 1980s.[7]

POLITICAL SUPPORT

Because UNTAG was part of a negotiated settlement, seen as beneficial by all involved, it was blessed with high levels of political support from both international and regional parties. This proved crucial to its success.

International

On the international level, Namibia was very much tied up in the Cold War. Until the late 1980s, each superpower was more concerned with minimizing its rival's influence than with promoting a peaceful solution to the conflict.[8] Since 1975, when the West "lost" Angola to Soviet influence, southern Africa had been a region of conflict in US-Soviet relations. With the election of Ronald Reagan came the new American policy of constructive engagement led by Assistant Secretary for African Affairs, Chester A. Crocker. The United States broke away from the Contact Group and began a unilateral effort to mediate change in southern Africa.[9] With the new policy, Namibian independence and South African reform continued to be American goals, but removal of Cuban troops from Angola was inserted as a priority. The United States proposed linking Cuban troop withdrawal to South African acceptance of UN Resolution 435 and Namibian independence. Eventually this linkage provided an important trade-off that facilitated settlement, but for many years the issue was used by South Africa to stall at the negotiating table. In the late 1980s, as relations between the superpowers improved dramatically, Namibia went from an issue that the US and the USSR used in playing out their zero-sum rivalry, to a positive-sum opportunity for cooperation. Both countries, but especially the Soviet Union with its de-ideologized, "new political thinking" and its ailing economy, were looking for ways to reduce regional competition and the high cost of funding third parties in regional conflicts.[10] The new cooperation between the US and the USSR in mediating a solution to the conflict and in encouraging their respective allies in the region to accept that solution was a major reason a settlement became possible in 1988. The successful resolution of the Namibia conflict lent prestige to the United States as a successful mediator. It also quieted domestic critics of the policy of constructive engagement. For the Soviet Union it provided a way out of the costly rivalry in southern Africa.

Involved Parties

As relations improved between the superpowers, regional changes were also creating more favorable conditions for a settlement to the conflict in southern Africa. These changes were most important for their effect on South African policy. The other regional players, both SWAPO and the Angolan government, basically agreed to the Resolution 435 settlement plan from the beginning. SWAPO had never believed it could win militarily and was willing to accept any proposal that gave it a legitimate political role in the independence process. SWAPO occasionally objected to details of the plan and broke off the negotiations, but the problems were never so serious that the Frontline states could not convince SWAPO to come back to the table.[11] Angola was in favor of Resolution 435 but initially preferred to wait rather than concede to US and South African demands for linkage of Cuban troop withdrawal to the Namibian settlement. Angola objected on principle to the United States and South Africa using its internal affairs as an excuse to delay the progress of the negotiations on Namibia, but the Cuban troops cost Angola $20 million a year, which it could no longer afford to pay.[12] They were there to protect Angola from South African raids, but the peace package that called for their withdrawal also removed the South African threat, so it was not difficult for Angola to accept linkage in the end. Given Angola's acceptance of Cuban troop withdrawal, Cuba voiced no objections. It was able to save face by claiming victory in protecting Angola from South Africa.

South Africa, on the other hand, had serious objections to allowing Namibian independence in 1978 when Resolution 435 was passed. But the economic and military downturns described earlier, as well as domestic political events, had by 1988 changed the South African view of the costs and benefits of holding on to "South West."

A general shift to the left in South African public opinion in the 1980s weakened the hold of the far-right or *verkrampte* sector, which was deeply opposed to giving up South-West Africa. Inclusion in the settlement package of constitutional principles protecting minorities reduced fears about treatment of white Namibians after independence. Securing the withdrawal of Cuban troops allowed the South African government to save face with its conservative constituents when it agreed to settle. Among the growing ranks of liberal white South Africans, anti-war sentiment, including support for an End Conscription Campaign, was strong. South Africa was in many ways going through what the United States went through in the Civil Rights movement and Vietnam, with heightened domestic racial unrest and increasing unwillingness to let South African boys fight what was beginning to be seen as an unnecessary and unjust war. By 1988 a shift within the South African government giving more influence to the diplomacy-minded Department of Foreign Affairs, and less to the military-minded "securicrats" in the Defense Department made the government more willing to settle than fight. This shift was related to P.W. Botha's loss of influence and the coming to power of the more liberal F.W. de Klerk.[13] All of these political developments coincided with the economic and military reasons to end the war peacefully and allow Namibian independence.

At the negotiating table, the Resolution 435 peace plan and Cuban troop withdrawal had gained acceptance and the details were being successfully cleared up. After US-mediated meetings between Angola, Cuba, and South Africa in London and Cairo, discussions in New York in mid-July 1988 led to agreement on "Principles for a Peaceful Settlement in South-Western Africa." After agreement on preliminary steps and on the text of the trilateral agreement in Geneva in early August, a de facto cease-fire came into effect.[14] By the end of 1988, therefore, the international and regional situations were conducive to settlement, and the negotiations had produced a package acceptable to all. With the signing of the Namibia Accords the process of political transition got under way. Cuban troops began to withdraw from Angola according to the negotiated timetable. Their withdrawal was monitored by the United Nations Angola Verification Mission (UNAVEM I).

Before UNTAG deployed to Namibia, therefore, South Africa, Cuba, and Angola had formalized their political support for the plan. South Africa was less enthusiastic about UNTAG than about other aspects of the plan, because it doubted the UN's impartiality. But the South African Defense Forces (SADF) cooperated with UNTAG in resolving problems to a greater degree than many had expected. [15] There were a series of problems that the UN brought up with South Africa, for example the fact that two-thirds of the infamous *Koevoet* ("crowbar" in Afrikaans) counterinsurgency unit, known and feared for its violent tactics, had been absorbed into the police force rather than disbanded, and in that capacity was still intimidating the public. Eventually, South African authorities gave way on this and other issues because of their support for the peace process. [16] Without this support, UNTAG would have had serious trouble in carrying outs its mission. For Angola, and even more so for SWAPO and other Namibians, UNTAG was the vehicle through which Namibian independence would be achieved and therefore had their full support.

At the very beginning of the operation an incursion of SWAPO guerrillas across the border from Angola nearly derailed the peace process (see below for details). The eventual solution to this crisis proved that the regional powers, the USSR, and the West were committed to the peace. This political support was absolutely crucial to UNTAG's success, and the resolution of this early crisis built confidence in the rest of the operation.

MANDATE

The official mandate was Resolution 435, which established a United Nations Transition Assistance Group "for a period of up to 12 months in order to assist [the Secretary General's] Special Representative...to ensure the early independence of Namibia through free and fair elections under the supervision and control of the United Nations." However, the original details of the plan are spelled out in the Contact Group letter of April 10, 1978. [17] The UNTAG plan changed somewhat from its original form with the addition of several informal understandings and protocols (for example, an understanding on impartiality, and Principles for the Constituent Assembly and the Constitution, both of which were agreed to in 1982). The term "Resolution 435" is often used as shorthand for this more complex settlement plan, but the UNTAG mandate is not set down clearly in any one place.[18] In general, UNTAG had three roles: election monitoring, police monitoring, and supervision of the cease-fire.

Monitoring of Free and Fair Elections

UNTAG's civilian component was responsible for ensuring that conditions were established for free and fair election of a Constituent Assembly that would draw up the Constitution for the new state. The Special Representative was to verify that specific requirements had been met before elections took place, including the repeal of any discriminatory or restrictive laws, regulations, or administrative measures that would interfere with free and fair elections; the release of political prisoners and detainees; the return of refugees; and the prevention of intimidation. Elections were run by South Africa's Administrator General for the territory but they were held "under UN supervision and control."

Monitoring of South African Police

Primary responsibility for maintaining law and order lay with the existing, South African-controlled South West African Police (SWAPOL) under the Administrator General. The Special Representative was to monitor SWAPOL and to take necessary actions to ensure the suitability of SWAPOL procedures, and specifically to ensure that the police were not being used for political intimidation. SWAPOL was South Africa's only active security force in Namibia once its troops and other forces were demobilized or restricted to base. It was feared that SWAPOL would be used to undermine conditions for free and fair elections. UNTAG's civilian police monitors, known as CIVPOL, therefore monitored SWAPOL's conduct very closely.[19]

Monitoring the Cease-fire

The military component of UNTAG was responsible for monitoring the cessation of all hostile acts; the restriction of South African troops to base and their phased withdrawal from the territory; the conduct of those South African military personnel who continued to perform civilian duties during the transition; the dismantling of command structures of citizen forces, commando units, and ethnic forces, and confinement of their arms; the disarming of SWAPO guerrillas before their repatriation; and the restriction of remaining SWAPO troops to bases in Angola and

Zambia. The military component was also responsible for preventing infiltration and for border surveillance. Lastly, the military component was responsible for assisting the civilian component, protecting entry points and reception centers for returning refugees, and providing security at polling stations. UNTAG was given the authority to use force in self-defense and its military observers were authorized to carry defensive weapons at the Force Commander's discretion, but the force was not intended to have any combat role to compel adherence to the peace plan.[20]

The transition to independence was to proceed along a negotiated timetable for the withdrawal of troops. South West African security forces were to be disbanded, and South African troop strength was to be reduced to 12,000 by May 14, 1989, and to 1,500 by July 1, with remaining troops to leave by November 8, one week after the elections. (Meanwhile, half of Cuba's 50,000 troops were to leave Angola, and the rest were to withdraw north of the 13th Parallel by November 1, 1989, and all Cuban troops were to leave Angola by July 1, 1991.)[21]

Although not set down completely in one UN document, UNTAG's general objectives were clear enough, but several issues were consciously left unsettled or unmentioned by negotiators so as not to derail the negotiation process. For example, the peace plan called for elections in the "whole of Namibia as one political entity" but did not specify whether this included the port of Walvis Bay, territory which is still disputed. Any express inclusion or exclusion would have been rejected by South Africa or SWAPO, respectively. Several issues were left rather hazy to get the settlement through the negotiation process: the border security mandate, the "status of informal understandings" on UN impartiality, the projected independence date, and the question of changed security conditions permitting a smaller military component, all were left unclear.[22]

On other issues, however, gaps and ambiguities were inadvertent. How the constitution was to be ratified was never specified, and while the repeal of discriminatory measures was called for, it was not made clear whether this requirement applied to all such measures or just those that would affect elections. South Africa's Administrator General interpreted this requirement quite narrowly.[23]

UNTAG was not a peacekeeping operation in the classic sense. Moreover, its most important roles, and the ones in which it was most successful, lay beyond the specifics of the mandate. UNTAG was to serve as a counterweight to South Africa's presence, to behave impartially, and to monitor and reinforce a climate of security.[24] But most important, it was to build confidence in and to legitimize the peace process, the elections, and the result of the transition: the new state of Namibia.

FUNDING

A debate over the size and cost of the Force broke out within the UN just prior to UNTAG's deployment. The permanent members of the Security Council, especially the United States, wanted to cut the cost of the operation from $650 million to $450 million by cutting the number of infantry battalions deployed from seven to three. The five permanent members of the Security Council shoulder 57 percent of the cost of a peacekeeping operation and felt they should not pay for troop levels that had been planned to prevent SWAPO incursions before SWAPO seemed willing to cooperate. The General Assembly, and especially the African nations, opposed the cuts for fear that they would reduce UNTAG's ability to prevent South African misbehavior.[25]

In the end, Secretary General Javier Pérez de Cuéllar called for an official upper limit of 7,500 troops to be left on the books, but for just 4,650 to be deployed initially, the rest to be held as a reserve force. This compromise, which brought the estimated cost down to $416 million, was approved unanimously by the Security Council in mid-February 1989.[26]

Repatriation of 45,000 Namibians by the United Nations High Commission for Refugees (UNHCR) was originally intended to be funded entirely through voluntary contributions and from UN bodies and funds for southern Africa and Namibia. Almost $32 million was contributed, but the repatriation actually cost over $35 million. The Secretary General proposed (over US objections) charging the shortfall to the UNTAG special account.[27]

As of March 31, 1991, the UN had received about $386 million of the total amount assessed to member states for UNTAG. Since the total cost of the entire operation was $368 million, $48 million under the budget estimates, the operation ran comfortably on the resources available to it. However, those resources were not always available on time, particularly at the start of the operation.[28]

Tight funds before the operation began precluded preparations for deployment as the settlement neared. The budget was not approved by the General Assembly until March 1, 1989, delaying deployment by two weeks as well as the advance work necessary for a smooth operation.[29] The difficulties with funding contributed directly to the problems UNTAG experienced with logistics, planning, and initial field operations.

PLANNING AND IMPLEMENTATION

Because of the long period of time between the conception of UNTAG in 1978 and actual implementation, the UN had fairly thorough information on Namibia. Between 1978 and 1988 the UN was in frequent contact with South Africa and the Frontline states discussing details of the UNTAG operation. The Secretary General, his Special Representative (UN Under-Secretary General Martti Ahtisaari), the designated Force Commander (Lieutenant General Dewan Prem Chand of India), and other officials traveled to southern Africa, and fact-finding teams and technical missions were sent to gather information. In October 1988, as the settlement neared, a technical mission was sent to review the ground situation, speak to South African counterparts, and collect technical data and information. Because the UN had a longstanding interest in and responsibility for Namibia, UN agencies such as the Council for Namibia had substantial background information on the situation there.[30]

UNTAG went into Namibia with plenty of good information. The staff was particularly aware of political sensitivities and was therefore able to maneuver through them successfully. The UN did not always put its information to good use operationally, however. Organizational and logistical mistakes were made that could have been avoided given the quality and extent of available information.

Indeed, advance operational planning was one of the weakest aspects of UNTAG. The UN spent a decade working hard for the political settlement, but did not develop operational plans sufficiently during that period to be ready when the settlement suddenly came through. Although Lieutenant General Prem Chand had been involved in logistical and technical discussions since his appointment, very few other military officers were involved in the planning of the operation.[31] The relative lack of attention to the operational plans made for UNTAG until very late in the game caused some rough edges when it first deployed. For example, UNTAG arrived in Ovamboland in northern Namibia with very few people who knew the local language and with few accompanying interpreters; and South Africa expressed concern that UNTAG would be unable to patrol the northern border without proper engines and tires adapted for the Namibian climate and terrain.[32]

Much of the ten-year-old operational plan was stale by the time the operation began. The size and composition of the Force had not been substantially reevaluated for several years, despite changing political and military circumstances, leading to the debate over size and cost that delayed UNTAG's deployment. The Permanent Five argued that the military component, planned during the border war in 1979–80, was far too large considering the high level of local support for the settlement.

To compensate partially for the cut in troop strength from 7,500 to 4,650, the number of military observers was raised from 200 to 300 and they were given some of the infantry's tasks (for example, monitoring the cease-fire, the demobilization of some local forces, and the confinement to base of remaining forces). The number of police monitors was raised from 360 to 500 as it became clear that the police, especially the *Koevoet* element, were perhaps the greatest threat to the plan, a "loaded revolver pointed at UNTAG." These last-minute adjustments still left too many troops and not enough monitors, however, and the police monitor force was subsequently increased to 1,000 and then to 1,500 because of complaints about police conduct in the north, and especially the conduct of ex-*Koevoet* members, validating concerns expressed by African nations during the General Assembly budget debate.[33]

The troop contributing countries for UNTAG were not reevaluated, either, as the settlement grew near. Originally the Swedes were to send a battalion to Namibia, but because they had shifted their policy in favor of SWAPO and the African National Congress in South Africa, South Africa rejected their participation as the operation started.[34]

Size and Composition of the Force

In the end, the military component of UNTAG was made up of three battalions of 850 troops each from Finland, Kenya, and Malaysia (the four reserve battalions, never used, were from Bangladesh, Togo, Venezuela, and Yugoslavia); 300 mobile military observers and monitors from Bangladesh, Czechoslovakia, Finland, India, Ireland, Kenya, Malaysia, Pakistan, Panama, Peru, Poland, Sudan, Togo, Venezuela, and Yugoslavia; and a 100-strong Force Headquarters staff. Logistics troops totalled 1,700 and included engineers from Australia, a Signal Corps unit from the United Kingdom, airplane and helicopter pilots from Spain and Italy, respectively, logistics units from Canada, Denmark, and Poland, and a medical unit from Switzerland (the first time Switzerland had played an integral role in a peacekeeping operation).[35]

The civilian component included 1,500 police monitors under the leadership of Steven Fanning (Ireland) from the following countries: Austria, Bangladesh, Barbados, Belgium, Cameroon, Canada, Egypt, Fiji, German Democratic Republic, Federal Republic of Germany, Ghana, Guyana, Hungary, India; Indonesia, Ireland, Jamaica, Kenya, Netherlands, New Zealand, Nigeria, Norway, Pakistan, Singapore, Sweden, and Tunisia.[36] The other elements of the civilian component included the electoral division, the Special Representative's office, the office of the Independent Jurist (Professor Carl Nörgaard of Denmark), and an administrative division. UNHCR's operations were run independently, but in cooperation with UNTAG.[37]

During the elections, most of the UN's civilian police monitors were assigned to election-related duties such as monitoring political gatherings, voter registration and polling stations, and guarding ballot boxes together with local police. Approximately 800 UN troops from the military component, as well as nearly 900 people from 27 member states, acted as election supervisors, working with approximately 2,500 counterparts appointed by the South African Administrator-General. Electoral supervisors were trained in four-day seminars at four training centers in Namibia. Senior officials attended seminars in Geneva and New York.[38] A relatively high percentage of UNTAG's civilian professionals were women, a matter of great pride to the operation.

Command, Communications, and Logistics

The entire operation was under the authority of the Special Representative, Martti Ahtisaari, who reported to the Secretary General. The chair of the Task Force for Namibia, Marrack Goulding, Under-Secretary for Special Political Affairs, acted as backstopper. Occasionally, as during the April crisis, the Secretary General himself would chair the Task Force. Its membership included Military Adviser Major General Timothy Dibuama, representatives from the Secretary General's executive office, legal experts, and all Under-Secretary Generals with some responsibility for the region.[39] The Deputy Special Representative was Mr.

L. Joseph Legwaila. The military component, as noted, was under Lieutenant General Prem Chand.

Apparently there was some problem with ambiguity in the chain of command, specifically over the issue of whether the military Force Commander was to report to the Special Representative or directly to New York on military matters. The original plans for UNTAG, drawn up ten years before deployment, envisioned it as primarily a military operation with the Force Commander as the top authority. By the time the mission came into being, however, it had become much more political and civilian in nature. In practice, the Force Commander reported to the Office of Special Political Affairs in New York on technical matters. On the more political matters, such as regrouping or departure of forces, he theoretically reported to Ahtisaari, but there was some friction between them over the proper role of the military component, and three months into the operation a civilian Deputy Special Representative was appointed to supplant the Force Commander as number two in the operation and to coordinate the civilian and military components. Communication and cooperation between the civilian and military components were not helped by the fact that the Force Commander's headquarters were on the other side of Windhoek from UNTAG's main headquarters. Moreover, gaps in logistics led to requests for equipment from the field going outside of established UN channels.[40]

Communication is difficult in an area as vast as Namibia, especially when many areas lack telephone service. UNTAG therefore used fixed, mobile, and transportable radios (VHF and HF), radio teletype, encryption devices, transportable satellite telephones, and a satellite earth station to communicate. Because of the war in Angola, South Africa had kept the north-south roads very well maintained, but the east-west roads were not as good. In general, while roads and communications were thin in Namibia, where they existed they were at least functional.[41]

Logistical planning does not seem to have been extensive. An average of two people at UN headquarters (ranging from zero to four over the course of the operation) planned the deployment, sustainment, and redeployment of UNTAG. When the budget dispute was finally settled, there was very little lead time available for the acquisition of equipment. During the April 1989 crisis, the US provided free airlift on C-5 aircraft for the Finnish battalion (the US billed the UN for airlifts that were planned in advance). The UN was able to have 1,000 vehicles manufactured in Japan in only six weeks but shipping them to Namibia took another six weeks. The cost of shipping them by air was prohibitive; transport by C-5 costs $15,000 per hour, each way. In the original plans, almost all of UNTAG's equipment was to be shipped by air, but at the last minute two US military transport specialists detailed to UN Headquarters chartered a cargo fleet to ship most of the equipment by sea, cutting the transport bill by several million dollars. With enough lead time, shipping time would have been no problem—as it was, UNTAG had to deal with a lack of equipment on top of its other problems as the operation got under way.[42]

Lesser logistical oversights posed potentially large obstacles as well. UNTAG personnel had no maps for the first two months of the operation, for example, so they bought them in bookstores. The Finnish battalion brought its own equipment, but the other troops were badly equipped. Operational officers worked together for only a week before UNTAG began when in reality they needed a month.[43]

A final, political problem complicated equipment acquisition. The General Assembly objected to UNTAG's purchase of South African goods because this would violate UN sanctions, but such goods were often much cheaper than any alternatives. This problem was resolved with a statement that UNTAG would make an effort to use the widest possible sources of procurement, but would still buy South African goods when they were cheapest. Because of long lead times required to buy buses and other heavy vehicles, including mine-resistant vehicles (see the Field Operations section), they were leased locally and some Jeep-type vehicles were acquired from Botswana and Zimbabwe.[44]

Because the territory was large, UNTAG was very spread out, operating from forty-two political offices. The civilian police monitors responsible for accompanying South African police forces operated out of approximately 50 district and subdistrict stations. The electoral supervisors operated out of 358 polling stations, of which 215 were fixed and 143 were mobile. The electoral offices corresponded with South Africa's existing administrative districts, but UNTAG's political offices unfortunately did not. A unitary structure would have been more conducive to smooth operations.[45]

At the end of the operation, rather than auction off equipment publicly or sell it to UN personnel, UNTAG equipment (valued at $14.5 million) potentially useful for future missions was kept in reserve. A further lot worth $374,000 was sold to UN agencies or other organizations remaining in Namibia, and about $26 million

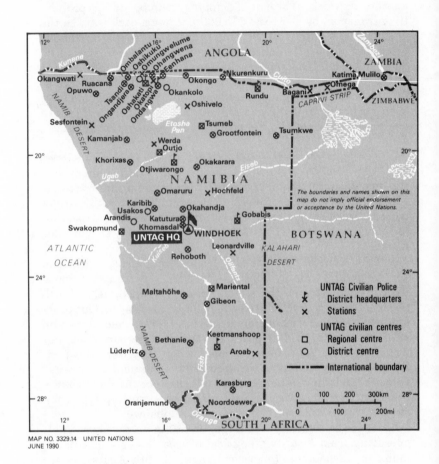

MAP NO. 3329.14   UNITED NATIONS
JUNE 1990

**Figure 20.1. United Nations Transition Assistance Group,
Civilian Deployment as of November 1989**

worth was donated to the new Namibian government. Most of the
vehicles, other than large trucks, were right hand drive, limiting their usefulness in other areas.[46]

Field Operations

Just prior to UNTAG's deployment in April 1989, South African
security forces in Namibia numbered 30,743 men. Of these, 9,895
were South African Defense Force (SADF) troops; 5,450 were

citizen forces; 6,128 were in commando units; and 9,270 were ethnic forces, also known as the South West African Territorial Force (SWATF). The *Koevoet* counterinsurgency unit was estimated at 3,000 members.[47] SWAPO and its PLAN army were stationed in Angola and Zambia in accordance with the cease-fire. The de facto cease-fire had been in effect since August of 1988 but was made official on April 1, 1989, with the start of the UNTAG operation.

UNTAG almost failed before it even began. On March 31 and April 1, 1989, according to South African reports, 1,500-1,800 SWAPO guerrillas crossed the border from Angola into northern Namibia in violation of the cease-fire agreement, and fighting broke out between SWAPO and the South African-controlled territorial police. South Africa wanted to unleash its defense forces, which had been confined to base. After a six hour meeting between South African Foreign Minister R.F. Botha, Administrator General Louis Pienaar, UN Special Representative Ahtisaari, and Force Commander Prem Chand, South Africa released its forces under a UN "fig leaf." In the ensuing clashes there were approximately 230 casualties, almost entirely SWAPO.

While South African forces contained the incursion, the Joint Commission, a product of the 1988 tripartite agreement that provided for regular meetings between Angola, Cuba and South Africa (with the United States and the Soviet Union as observers), held an emergency meeting at Mount Etjo near Windhoek.[48] The Commission declared that SWAPO guerrillas would have safe passage north of the 16th parallel in Angola. The original April 15 deadline for SWAPO to complete its withdrawal was extended to May 15 because of the difficulty in verifying how many fighters had crossed back. Many SWAPO troops feared ambushes by South Africa near the UN pickup points and therefore crossed on their own.

The reason for the SWAPO incursion is not clear; it cost the organization considerable credibility. It may have reflected a misunderstanding of where the guerrillas were supposed to go after the cease-fire, or it may have been an ill-conceived attempt to take advantage of the vacuum caused by confinement to base of South African forces before UN troops, delayed by the budget wrangling, were deployed. Only 100 UN staff and 921 troops had arrived when the incursion began.[49] Ironically, part of the argument made for cutting the troop strength during the budget delay was that a SWAPO incursion was unlikely.

Whether UNTAG's presence would have prevented the infiltration, and how the UN would have handled the situation had it been fully deployed, are open questions. If UNTAG had tried to intervene militarily between SWAPO and SADF during the April crisis, the results could have been disastrous. If they had been in place during that event, according to one source, they would have withdrawn rather than become caught in the crossfire. On the other hand, if UNTAG forces had been in northern Namibia before April 1, SWAPO might never have attempted the border crossing. Even if SWAPO did cross, the presence of UN troops already in place between SWAPO and SADF forces might have persuaded South Africa to let the UN handle the incursion, preventing the clashes and bloodshed. Fortunately, the crisis was eventually solved politically, and this solution's proof of the parties' commitment to peace lent greater strength to UNTAG. Unfortunately, it also delayed UNTAG's preparations for the elections and it revived mistrust in Namibia.[50]

More than the potential to use military force, UNTAG's real power was its effective use of the spotlight of international attention to bring UN prestige to bear on South Africa and, through it, on the South West African authorities to change policies inimical to the UN's vision of the transition process. This power was limited, however. In an extreme case Ahtisaari could have threatened to suspend the peace process, but this was not a very credible threat. There was no formal mechanism for resolving conflict between the Special Representative and the Administrator General. Several times UNTAG could do nothing to stop territorial police from firing on unarmed crowds. In general, however, when problems arose, as when demobilized militia forces remained on the South African payroll, or when UNTAG received complaints of intimidation by former members of the *Koevoet* counterinsurgency unit, discussions at which the Secretary General raised the problems with South African authorities were successful at changing South African behavior.[51]

UNTAG was able to curb outright intimidation but it was not able to prevent South Africa from trying to influence the elections, sometimes through covert means. South Africa has admitted that it gave over $35 million to political parties opposing SWAPO in the elections. Busloads of white South Africans arrived in Namibia to vote and then return home to South Africa. About 10,000 were eligible to vote by virtue of having lived in Namibia or having had a parent born there, but many found it inappropriate that South Africans who could afford the trip could vote even though they did not live in Namibia.[52]

There were also allegations of a more subversive role played by the South African government. The Civil Cooperation Bureau of the South African army was accused of assassinating Anton Lubowski (the only white member of SWAPO's leadership) and of attempts to discredit SWAPO and prevent its winning a two-thirds majority in the elections.[53] As expected, SWAPO won a majority, but it needed a two-thirds majority to impose its own constitution. South African actions helped prevent that.

UNTAG's police monitors conducted their own patrols and accompanied the local police on its patrols. They had some difficulty following South African police forces until UNTAG leased or bought approximately 40 mine-resistant vehicles. In addition to the physical effect of being able to follow South African vehicles, there was an important psychological effect. The South African mine-resistant vehicles, known as *casspirs*, were infamous symbols of South African intimidation, and the sight of white UN casspirs or "friendly ghosts" gave the populace confidence that the UN could monitor South Africa effectively.

After the crisis in early April, security was not a major problem for UNTAG. Other than leftover mine fields, the biggest danger for UN personnel was remembering to drive on the left side of the road. (The UN lost ten people to traffic accidents.) By October, the military component of the operation was largely unnecessary.[54]

UNTAG curbed intimidation by local police (especially after the number of police monitors rose to 1500) and, with the exception of the events of early April, maintained the cease-fire. UNTAG also assisted UNHCR with the repatriation of approximately 58,000 refugees.

The UN found that it needed to sell the electoral process to Namibians by explaining its legitimacy and usefulness. UNTAG used radio, television, newspapers, visual aids and other means of explanation as part of its voter education program, and printed 600,000 pieces of electoral material. United Nations supervision of the registration of voters and close monitoring of the entire electoral process ensured free and fair elections, and dampened political violence associated with the election campaiging. Voter turnout was extraordinarily high—96 percent of those eligible to vote did so.[55]

ASSESSMENT AND CONCLUSIONS

The high level of support for the UN from all of the parties to the conflict enabled UNTAG to carry out its responsibilities well, especially as the operation overcame the initial mistrust of Namibians as to its effectiveness and of South Africa as to its impartiality. UNTAG lent legitimacy to the democratic political process, and to its results—the Constituent Assembly and the government of independent Namibia—and the presence of the UN aided the reconciliation of groups previously at war, thus leaving a strong framework for democratic processes in the future. In accomplishing all this the operation also gained legitimacy for and confidence in the UN to perform other operations of a similar nature: "the practicability of physically putting a solution in place through the management of the UN, given the requisite support of member states, need no longer be in question."[56]

In many ways UNTAG was the first operation of its kind. It was a large composite mission, with a substantial non-military component. UNTAG involved more police work than had previous operations and was the first mission charged with preparing a nation for elections and independence.

Namibia is one of the few examples of highly successful peaceful solutions to conflict. UNTAG's success was made possible by the strength of the political settlement, but it also reinforced that settlement and Namibia's peaceful transition to independence.

UNTAG was primarily a political operation and was highly effective as such. Its weaknesses were on the technical side, with problems, for example, with the chain of command, timely deployment, and lead time for start up of the operation. With the exception of not being ready to deal with the SWAPO incursion, these shortcomings appear not to have overly hampered the operation.

UNTAG enjoyed more than grudging support from the parties to the conflict, as the resolution of the April crisis showed. It was embedded in a political solution that was the result of a long and difficult process of peacemaking by the UN, the Contact Group under UN auspices, and by the United States. Peacekeeping and implementation of the settlement took place only when the situation was ripe for resolution. It became ripe with the end of the Cold War, and as a result of American pressure to settle and provision of US good offices, a jointly recognized military stalemate, and the availability of face-saving compromises on the mutual withdrawal of Cuban and South African troops. Waiting for the ripe moment was the key to UNTAG's success and the success of the conflict resolution process in Namibia.

Notes

1. I. William Zartman, *Ripe For Resolution: Conflict and Intervention in Africa* (New York: Oxford University Press, 1989), 173; and *Africa South of the Sahara 1991*, 20th ed. (London: Europa Publications Ltd., 1990), 738.

2. For further discussion see chapters 21 and 22 on the UN missions in Angola, UNAVEM I and II.

3. United Nations Document S/12636, April 10, 1978.

4. Robert Jaster, *The 1988 Peace Accords and the Future of South-Western Africa*, Adelphi Paper 253 (London: International Institute for Strategic Studies, Autumn 1990), 33-35; Chester Crocker, "Southern African Peace Making," *Survival* 32, no. 3 (May–June 1990): 224-25.

5. The cost of the war and the administration of the territory was estimated to be approximately $44.5 million a year in 1985 (Colin Legum, ed., *The Battlefronts of Southern Africa* [New York: Africana Publishing Co., 1988], 344). South Africa's defense budget was $2.012 billion in 1986–1987, excluding intelligence and internal security forces (Colin Legum, ed., *African Contemporary Record 1986–1987* [New York: Africana Publishing Co., 1988], B791, B820-21).

6. Zartman, *Ripe For Resolution*, 227.

7. Zartman, *Ripe For Resolution*, 227.

8. Zartman, *Ripe For Resolution*, 7.

9. John Marcum, "Africa: A Continent Adrift," *Foreign Affairs* 68, no. 1, (American and the World, 1988-89): 161, 164.

10. Allen Lynch, "Gorbachev's International Outlook," Institute for East-West Security Studies Occasional Paper Series, no. 9, 1989; Kurt Campbell and Neil MacFarlane, eds., *Gorbachev's Third World Dilemmas* (New York: Routledge, 1989).

11. The Frontline states at that time consisted of Angola, Botswana, Mozambique, Zambia, and Zimbabwe.

12. Jaster, *The 1988 Peace Accords*, 29.

13. Interviews with Peter Rousseau, Office of the Administrator General, January 18, 1990; and Gerhard Erasmus, drafter of the Namibian Constitution, January 17, 1990, Windhoek.

14. United Nations Document S/20412, January 23, 1989, 3.

15. Interview 10, October 11, 1990.

16. All ex-*Koevoet* members had been removed from the South West African Police, under UNTAG monitoring, by late October 1989 (United Nations Document S/20943, November 31, 1989, 4).

17. United Nations Document S/12636.

18. Jaster, *The 1988 Peace Accords*, 33. Most of the details of the mandate and the implementation plan can be found in United Nations Document S/20412.

19. United Nations Document S/20883, October 6, 1989, 7-8.

20. United Nations Documents S/20457, February 9, 1989; S/12636; S/20412, 12-15.

21. United Nations Document 2/20345, December 22, 1988, 4; *Los Angeles Times*, April 2, 1989, 1, 12.

22. Jaster, *The 1988 Peace Accords*, 34; Crocker, "Southern African Peace Making," 231.

23. Jaster, *The 1988 Peace Accords*, 34.

24. Crocker, "Southern African Peace Making," 223-4.

25. Troop size had been an issue in the negotiations. South Africa was inclined to see UN troops as SWAPO allies rather than as potential preventers of SWAPO border crossings. In 1981 they proposed that UNTAG have no military component at all (Crocker, "Southern African Peace Making," 224-5; *New York Times*, December 20, 1988, A3; January 1, 1989, 9; March 30, 1990, A5).

26. Jaster, *The 1988 Peace Accords*, 35; *New York Times*, February 17, 1989, A10.

27. *United Nations Chronicle*, June 1989, 15; United Nations Document A/45/997, April 16, 1991, 28; and John Fox, "United States Delegation Performance Report on UNTAG," mimeograph of a speech delivered April 29, 1991 (Washington, D.C.: US Department of State).

28. United Nations Document A/45/997, 4.

29. Interviews 1 and 13, October 8, 1990 and November 14, 1990; *The Blue Helmets: A Review of United Nations Peace-keeping*, 2nd ed. (New York: United Nations Department of Public Information, 1990), 352.

30. "Namibia: Chronology 1: Informal Chronology of Contacts of the Secretary-General and his Special Representative for Namibia with Southern African Leaders following the Adoption of Resolution 431 in 1978" (New York: United Nations, 1988); United Nations Document S/20412, 6.

31. Interview 10, October 11, 1990; United Nations, "Namibia: Chronology 2, Informal Chronology of Security Council Decisions, Secretary General's Reports to the Council and Other Communications" (New York: United Nations, 1988); and "Namibia: Chronology 1."

32. Jaster, *The 1988 Peace Accords*, 35-6.

33. United Nations Document S/20412, 14-15; Interviews 7 and 63, October 10, 1990 and May 14, 1991; *United Nations Chronicle*, March 1989, 35, and September 1989, 5-6; *The Blue Helmets*, 360.

34. Interview 10, October 11, 1990.

35. In the event, the actual number deployed was 4,493 as fewer air support personnel were needed than planned (*The Blue Helmets*, 359-360; *UNTAG in Namibia: A New Nation is Born*, UN Sales No. E.90.I.10 [Windhoek: United Nations, 1990]; United Nations Document S/20412, 13-15; *United Nations Chronicle*, March 1989, 35).

36. The Blue Helmets, 358; United Nations Document S/20883, 8.

37. *The Blue Helmets*, 355-7.

38. United Nations Document S/20967, November 14, 1989, 1; S/20883, 7-9; S/20943, 3; Alan James, *Peacekeeping in International Politics* (New York: St. Martin's Press, 1990), 260-61.

39. Interviews 25 and 26, both December 10, 1990.

40. Interviews 29, 37, and 63, December 10, 1990, January 23, 1991, and May 14, 1991; *The Blue Helmets*, 359.

41. United Nations Documents A/45/997, 29; A/44/856, December 11, 1989, 14; Interviews 27 and 32, December 10, 1991, January 23, 1991.

42. Interviews 15 and 19, November 14, 1990 and November 19, 1990.

43. Interview 10, October 11, 1990.

44. *New York Times*, March 1, 1989, A3; United Nations Document A/44/856, 12.

45. Interview 73, July 3, 1991; United Nations Document S/20967; *The Blue Helmets*, 358.

46. Interviews 13 and 32, November 14, 1990, and January 23, 1991; United Nations Documents A/45/997, 32, and A/45/1003, April 26, 1991, 2; John Fox, April 29, 1991 speech. Liquidation of the operation was complete by September 30, 1990.

47. United Nations Document S/20883, 3, 5.

48. For more on the Joint Commission, see James, *Peacekeeping in International Politics*, 253-55.

49. Jaster, *The 1988 Peace Accords*, 36-9; *New York Times*, April 4, 1989, A1, A6; *United Nations Chronicle*, June 1989, 6.

50. Crocker, "Southern African Peace Making," 229; *The Blue Helmets*, 367; Interview 7, October 10, 1990.

51. Jaster, *The 1988 Peace Accords*, 34-35, 42.

52. *New York Times* July 25, 1991, A3; and November 12, 1989, 3.

53. *New York Times*, July 1, 1991, A7.

54. Interviews 27 and 73, December 10, 1990, and July 3, 1991.

55. United Nations Documents S/20943, 3 and S/20967, 2. For future operations of this nature, interviews suggested that people trained specifically as information officers should do the media work and confidence building associated with an election (Interview 29, December 10, 1990).

56. United Nations Document A/45/1, September 16, 1990, 4.

21 United Nations Angola Verification Mission I

by Virginia Page Fortna

The first United Nations Angola Verification Mission (UNAVEM I) was created as part of the political settlement that led to Namibia's independence. It was not, as its successor would be, the result of a political settlement between the parties to Angola's long civil war (see next chapter). UNAVEM I was a small and straightforward mission charged with verifying Cuban troop withdrawal from Angola. As such, it provided political balance to UNTAG, which primarily monitored South African compliance with the settlement plan for Namibia described in the previous chapter.[1] The mission began with the signing of peace accords among South Africa, Angola, and Cuba on December 22, 1988, and was mandated to run 31 months, to conclude in July 1991, after the last Cuban troops were to be withdrawn. The mission ended two months early when Cuban withdrawals were completed ahead of schedule.

ORIGINS

The People's Republic of Angola is a large, sparsely populated, and war torn country on the western coast of Africa, north of Namibia and south and west of Zaire. An estimated ten million people live in Angola's 1.2 million square kilometers, predominantly in rural areas. Fewer than one in four live in towns of more than 2,000 people. Angola is home to eight major ethnic groupings, and it has fractured politically along ethnic lines.[2]

Three nationalist groups emerged in the fight for independence from Portuguese colonial rule in the 1950s and 1960s: the *Movimento Popular de Libertação de Angola* (MPLA), the *Frente Nacional de Libertação de Angola* (FNLA), and the *União Nacional para a Independência Total de Angola* (UNITA).[3] Relations among the three were not good during the struggle for independence, and armed conflict broke out as

independence neared. The leftist Portuguese government that
came to power in a coup in April 1974 beat a hasty retreat from
Angola, while most of the white population fled, devastating the
modern sector of the economy. The Portuguese tried briefly to
reconcile the three warring groups by mediating the Alvor Accord,
signed in January 1975, which set up a transitional government
and set independence for November 11, 1975. Renewed fighting
broke out, however, and the transitional government collapsed
by August. With Cuban support, the MPLA took control of most of
the country including the capital, Luanda, before independence
day.

Even before official independence the civil war had become part
of the cold war. The MPLA had longstanding ties with the Soviet
Union and Cuba. In 1973, China began sending arms and advisers
to the FNLA. In 1974 the United States, through the CIA, began
funding the FNLA and UNITA to prevent an easy MPLA victory and
to contain Soviet and Cuban influence in the region. The Soviet
Union resumed its aid to the MPLA (temporarily halted during a
leadership fight within the organization) shortly thereafter. In
1975, Cuban troops arrived to back up the MPLA, while South
African forces intervened in favor of a loose alliance between FNLA
and UNITA.[4]

Long after the MPLA became the recognized government of
Angola, South Africa conducted raids into the country, ostensibly
pursuing guerrillas of the South West African People's Organization who were fighting South African rule in Namibia and given
harbor by the MPLA government. Fighting also continued between
the Cuban-backed government and UNITA, supported by South
Africa.[5]

In the early 1980s, the war began to escalate as South Africa
increased its raids into Angola, nominally against SWAPO positions but with the additional aim of destabilizing the country.
Meanwhile, the Reagan administration proposed linking Cuban
troop withdrawal to Namibian independence. Renewed US support for UNITA was intended to force Angola to concede on the
issue. In August 1985, Congress repealed the ten-year-old Clark
Amendment, which had prohibited US military aid to UNITA. In
February 1986, the Reagan administration announced a $15
million military aid program. The organization received Stinger
surface-to-air missiles and TOW anti-tank weapons, among other
things. Deliveries of Soviet arms to the Angolan army and the
arrival of more Cuban troops continued the deadlock at an escalated level.[6]

Initiatives for UN Involvement

In response to South Africa's increasingly aggressive actions in southern Angola, the United Nations Security Council passed Resolution 602 in November 1987, condemning South Africa and demanding its immediate withdrawal from Angolan territory. The Secretary General sent a mission to Angola in mid-December to monitor South Africa's troop withdrawal. Discussions with the Angolan government and a visit to Xangongo in Cunene province, near the fighting, showed that South Africa had not begun to remove its troops. The South Africans claimed to be withdrawing but would not be more specific, maintaining that troops being withdrawn under "operational conditions" would be in danger if details were given. The pullout was not completed.[7]

A major military defeat for Angola at the Lomba River in 1987 and the stand-off at Cuito Cuanavale in late 1987 and early 1988 caused Angola and South Africa, respectively, to reevaluate significantly the price of a decisive victory. By 1988, the military stalemate had finally become painful for the participants. Changing political and economic factors, new superpower cooperation, domestic political conditions in South Africa, and the ever mounting human and financial cost of the war led both sides to conclude that a political settlement was a better option than continuing the stalemate. Angola's economy was in ruins despite rich oil resources and its infrastructure had been badly damaged, especially since roads and the Benguela railway—the country's major east-west artery—had been targets favored by UNITA. The local currency, the Kwanza, was so worthless that Angola largely moved to the "beer standard"—foreign companies paid local employees with consumer goods, usually imported beer, which could then be traded on the black market.[8] Drought compounded the normal horrors of war, causing widespread suffering.

By early August 1988, when Cuba, Angola, and South Africa met in Geneva as part of the on-going US-backed peace negotiations, enough agreement had been reached for the declaration of an immediate, de facto cease-fire. South Africa withdrew all of its forces by the end of August, and the 50,000 Cuban troops stationed in Angola moved to positions at least 50 kilometers north of the Namibian border. SWAPO accepted the cease-fire and agreed to deploy 160 kilometers north of the border. UNITA, however, did not accept the cease-fire.[9]

The diplomatic process that led to withdrawal of foreign troops from Angola, the end of South African aid to UNITA, and its relinquishing of Namibia, came to fruition on December 22, 1988, at a signing ceremony at UN headquarters. The trilateral agreement among South Africa, Cuba, and Angola allowing Namibian independence was accompanied by a bilateral agreement between Cuba and Angola for the "phased and total withdrawal" of the Cuban troops from Angola. As part of the latter agreement, both parties requested "the Security Council to carry out verification of the redeployment and the phased and total withdrawal of the Cuban troops from the territory of the People's Republic of Angola." Formal letters of request to that effect were sent to the Secretary General from the permanent representatives of Angola and Cuba to the United Nations just prior to the signing of the accords.[10]

POLITICAL SUPPORT

The high level of political support, both international and local, for the overall settlement plan that created UNTAG and UNAVEM I has been discussed in the previous chapter. Support for UNAVEM I was even higher than for UNTAG, however, as it was the least controversial aspect of the plan and was to the benefit of those interested in Cuban withdrawal—the West and, especially, South Africa. The US put some pressure on UNAVEM I when it considered that the UN operation was being unduly trusting of the Cubans, but it was otherwise supportive. South Africa was capable of verifying the Cuban withdrawal with its own technology, but charges of Cuban noncompliance would carry very little weight coming from South Africa alone.[11] South Africa was uncomfortable about the UN's impartiality but trusted UN monitors to report what they saw.[12] Angola and Cuba wanted verification of their compliance with the peace plan to be indisputable to ensure that they were not blamed for any attempt by South Africa to back away from the plan. UNITA had not been part of the negotiations and did not sign the peace accords. Its actions (discussed further, below) temporarily halted the Cuban withdrawal, but the rebels wanted that withdrawal completed and verified at least as much as South Africa did, and they never interfered with the UN observers. In short, it was in everyone's interest to cooperate so that UNAVEM I could do its job effectively.

MANDATE

Security Council Resolution 626 of December 20, 1988, created UNAVEM I based on recommendations of the Secretary General. The mandate was clear and straightforward. The group of unarmed observers was to "verify the redeployment northwards and the phased and total withdrawal of Cuban troops from the territory of Angola in accordance with the timetable agreed between Angola and Cuba." In addition to watching ports and airports and inspecting declared bases out of which Cubans had been deployed, UNAVEM was also mandated to make ad hoc inspections, on the Chief Military Observer's initiative or at the request of a member of the Security Council, if Cuban troops were suspected to be present where they should not have been.[13]

The 27-month timetable for the redeployment northwards and withdrawal of the 50,000 Cuban troops is shown in Table 21.1. (For actual withdrawals see Field Operations section, below.)

Table 21.1. Cuban Troop Withdrawal Schedule

Date	Redeployment Northwards and Withdrawal
April 1, 1989	3,000 troops withdrawn
August 1, 1989	Redeployment to 15th Parallel (adjusted)[a]
October 31, 1989	Redeployment to 13th Parallel (adjusted)[b]
November 1, 1989	25,000 troops withdrawn (50%)
April 1, 1990	33,000 troops withdrawn (66%)
October 1, 1990	38,000 troops withdrawn (76%)
July 1, 1991	50,000 troops withdrawn (100%)

Notes:[a] "The 'adjusted 15th parallel' is a direct line from a point on the coast 30 kilometres south of Namibe to a point on the west bank of the Cunene River, 30 kilometres south of the 15th parallel; thence northwards up the west bank of the Cunene River to the 15th parallel; and thence eastwards along the 15th parallel to the Angolan-Zambian border."

[b] "The 'adjusted 13th parallel' is a line running 30 kilometres south of the 13th parallel from the coast to the 16th meridian; thence northwards up to (sic) the 16th meridian to the 13th parallel; and thence eastwards to the Angolan-Zambian border" (Ibid).

Source: United Nations Documents S/20338, 5 and S/20345, 4.

FUNDING

In January 1989, the estimated cost of the full 31-month operation was $18.8 million, $9.0 million for the first twelve months and $9.8 million for the following nineteen. Money for the first year was not appropriated by the General Assembly until mid-February 1989, six weeks after UNAVEM's deployment. However, the Secretary General was allowed to spend up to $4.2 million to cover costs until this first appropriation. Further appropriations totalling $9.8 million were made in December 1989 and December 1990.[14]

The mission used $1 million less than anticipated in its first year, but the money was kept in the special account to offset the deficit created by members not paying their assessed contributions.[15] Costs were kept down somewhat by requiring the Angolan government to provide office and residential accommodation for UNAVEM headquarters in Luanda, and at the ports and airport for the permanent monitoring teams, as well as some land and air transport, particularly for UNAVEM inspections.[16] UNAVEM I was able to complete its job early because the last Cuban troops were withdrawn over a month ahead of schedule. UNAVEM II was getting under way by then, so the special account was kept open and the leftover funds were rolled over for use by the new mission.

PLANNING AND IMPLEMENTATION

Because of the small and straightforward nature of UNAVEM I, planning and implementation were relatively simple affairs. No significant independent information gathering was done by the UN. At the Cape Verde round of negotiations in July 1988, General Rosales of Cuba and General Geldenhuys of South Africa worked out the military problems of the withdrawals and their timetables. At the end of the year when the negotiations seemed about to yield an agreement, the UN Secretariat consulted with Cuban and Angolan delegates in New York on how verification would take place.[17] Presumably these details were based on the agreements reached with South Africa.

The technical mission sent to Angola in December 1987 after Resolution 602 provided the United Nations with background information useful in the preparations for UNAVEM I, but no other mission was sent to Angola prior to UNAVEM's deployment. UNAVEM thus did not have exact information on the number of Cuban troops in Angola or their equipment before it arrived, but this information was provided by the Cubans and Angolans once UNAVEM became operational. Despite allegations from UNITA that the estimate of 50,000 Cuban troops was too low, it proved to be accurate.[18]

The details of the UNAVEM verification plan were negotiated in November and early December 1988, just before the peace accords were signed.[19] Planning for the operation was therefore done on short notice. Discussions on the plans were held in New York between the Secretary General and delegations from Cuba and

Angola in the days leading up to the signing of the peace accords on December 22, 1988, only two or three weeks before deployment began.[20] Refinement of the procedures for verification did not take place until after the mission started, when the Chief Military Observer and his staff worked with Cuban and Angolan authorities.[21]

Size and Composition

An advance team of 18 observers arrived in Angola on January 3, 1989 to verify the departure of the first 450 Cuban soldiers on January 10. The rest of the observers arrived shortly thereafter. At its largest, UNAVEM I consisted of 70 military observers, seven each from the following countries: Algeria, Argentina, Brazil, Congo, Czechoslovakia, India, Jordan, Norway, Spain, and Yugoslavia, as well as 22 international and 15 local civilian staff members. In November 1989, after ensuring that the Cubans had redeployed north of the 13th parallel, the UNAVEM outstation at Namibe (south of the 13th parallel) was closed, and the number of military observers was reduced to 60, with one observer from each country going home.[22]

The simple job of counting troops did not in itself require military personnel, but UNAVEM I had to operate in a war zone. As UNAVEM arrived in Angola in 1989, the civil war between the MPLA government's forces and UNITA continued to plague the country, although the fighting had been significantly deescalated by the removal of South African troops. Furthermore, the need for expertise in identifying military equipment as it left with the Cubans, and the fact that UNAVEM staff had to work with Angolan and Cuban military staff, justified the choice of military rather than civilian personnel.[23]

Command, Communications, and Logistics

UNAVEM I was under the command of the Chief Military Observer (CMO), Brigadier General Péricles Ferreira Gomes of Brazil. Headquarters were in the capital city, Luanda. Teams of eight military observers were stationed permanently at the ports of Cabinda, Lobito, Luanda, Namibe (until November 1989), and the Luanda airport, where they recorded any movement of Cuban military personnel or equipment. Since rotation of Cuban troops continued during withdrawal, incoming as well as outgoing troops had to be counted. Two or three mobile inspection teams of six observers each verified Cuban redeployments.[24]

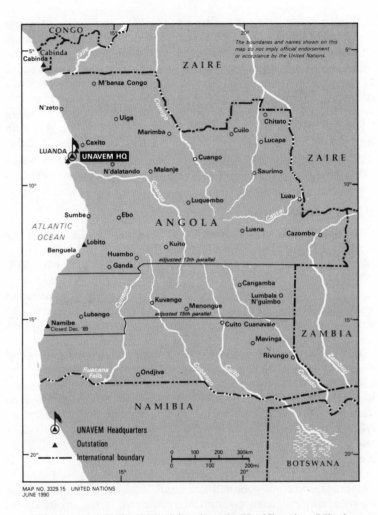

**Figure 21.1 United Nations Angola Verification Mission,
Deployment as of June 1990**

UNAVEM's counting job was made easier by the fact that Angola
and Cuba were required to give the CMO at least a week's notice
before any departure or rotation of troops or equipment. Cuban
and Angolan authorities were also required to confirm the redeployments northward and to inform the CMO of all the locations
from which troops had been withdrawn.[25]

A joint commission consisting of the CMO and a senior officer from both Angola and Cuba coordinated verification and dealt with any problems as they arose. Angolan and Cuban liaison officers also accompanied the UN inspection teams (except south of the redeployment parallels, where only the Angolan officer was allowed). Communications between Angola, Cuba, and the UN were further enhanced by a direct telephone link between UNAVEM headquarters and the headquarters of the Angolan and Cuban forces. UNAVEM's communication equipment included a portable satellite earth station, radio teletype, mobile VHF radio, crypto-fax and text cypher machines, as well as a voice encryption device donated by the Swiss.[26]

Field Operations

In the days after the August 1 and October 31 deadlines for the northward redeployments of Cuban forces, the mobile observer teams, and in some cases the CMO along with other senior UNAVEM officials, used fixed wing aircraft, helicopters, and ground transport to verify the absence of Cubans from the declared areas as well as several other areas inspected on the CMO's initiative. The Angolans provided aircraft, liaison personnel, and logistical support for these inspections.[27]

With one exception, the Cuban troop withdrawal proceeded smoothly and ahead of schedule. In response to an attack by UNITA on a water purification plant that killed four Cubans and wounded five others, the troop withdrawal was suspended on January 23, 1990. The withdrawal resumed on February 25 (partly as the result of efforts by the Secretary General to keep the withdrawal on track), but the process took until April 25 to catch up with the withdrawal schedule.[28]

In each of the other withdrawal periods, Cuba and Angola demonstrated their goodwill and confidence in the peace process by removing more troops than was required. In the initial stage, for example, in which 3,000 Cubans were to leave before April 1, 1989 (the start date for implementation of Resolution 435 in Namibia), the actual number withdrawn was 4,624. Similarly, the final pullout was completed by May 25, 1991, more than a month ahead of schedule, to facilitate implementation of a May 31 cease-fire between the Angolan Government and UNITA.[29]

ASSESSMENT

UNAVEM I had a limited job to do, but did it well. Had either Cuba or Angola wanted to evade the UN monitors it probably would have been possible. The system was set up to put an international stamp of approval on the withdrawal, not to enforce it. As such, the monitoring and verification procedures proved adequate and the mission encountered no major problems. But this success depended greatly on high levels of cooperation from both the Cuban and Angolan authorities.

CONCLUSION

While UNAVEM I was not particularly large or significant in itself, it was an important adjunct to the peace process in southern Africa. Without assurances of Cuban troop withdrawal, South Africa would not have allowed Namibian independence.

The goal of ridding southern Africa of Cuban troops was important in and of itself for the United States and South Africa, but many also hoped that removing foreign troops would deescalate the civil war in Angola and foster an internal peace process. United States mediators had been able to link the Namibia conflict to the issue of foreign troops in Angola—itself an ambitious and controversial move—but they could not include Angola's internal conflict in the peace process. A US initiative for an internal settlement, which necessarily would involve a political role in Angola for the UNITA rebels, would have unduly complicated the already tricky political balancing act in which US mediators were engaged.[30]

So the civil war in Angola continued as the December 1988 peace plan got underway. Initial assessments of the southern African peace settlement criticized it for this shortcoming. This pessimistic conclusion was premature, however. Once foreign troops and the complicating issue of Namibia's political status had been removed from the picture, negotiations between the Angolan government and UNITA, mediated by Portugal, could get underway in earnest. The talks came to fruition in May 1991, just as the Cuban withdrawal was completed. To help implement this new peace settlement, the UNAVEM mission was extended, creating a UNAVEM II with a new and much more extensive mandate.

Notes

1. Chester Crocker, "Peacemaking in Southern Africa: The Namibia-Angola Settlement of 1988," in David D. Newsom, ed., *The Diplomatic Record 1989–1990* (Boulder, Co.: Westview Press, 1991), 24.

2. Major groups include the Ovimbundu, Mbundu, Bakongo, Lunda-Chockwe, Nganguela, Nyaneka, Humbe, and Ovambo peoples (*Africa South of the Sahara 1992*, 21st ed. [London: Europa Publications Ltd., 1991], 213; *Keesing's Record of World Events, 1991*, Vol. 37 [London: Longman, 1991], 38040).

3. These three groups, divided ideologically, also were split to some extent along ethnic and regional lines. MPLA was made up primarily of *mestiços* and Mbundus in the north-central and eastern regions of Angola; FNLA's support was mostly Bakongo in northern Angola; and UNITA's base was primarily Ovimbundu (with some support among the Chockwe and Nganguela) in the southern and eastern parts of the country (Robert Jaster, *The 1988 Peace Accords and the Future of South-western Africa*, Adelphi Paper 253 [London: International Institute for Strategic Studies, Autumn 1990], 8-9; and I. William Zartman *Ripe for Resolution: Conflict and Intervention in Africa* [New York: Oxford University Press, 1989], 141-2).

4. Jaster, *The 1988 Peace Accords*, 8-11; *Africa South of the Sahara 1991*, 234-35; José Manuel Durão Barroso, "The Peace Process in Angola: Evolution and Prospects, " speech delivered to the CSIS Study Group on Angola, Washington D.C., Center for Strategic and International Studies, February 20, 1991; William J. Durch "The Cuban Military in Africa and the Middle East," *Studies in Comparative Communism 11*, nos. 1 & 2 (Spring–Summer 1978): 63-70; John Stockwell, *In Search of Enemies: a CIA Story* (New York: W.W. Norton & Co., 1978), 67-69; Donald Rothchild and Caroline Hartzell, "Great- and Medium-Power Mediations: Angola," *Annals of the American Academy of Political and Social Science 518* (November 1991): 40-41.

5. *Africa South of the Sahara 1991*, 235.

6. Jaster, *The 1988 Peace Accords*, 14-16; Zartman, *Ripe for Resolution*, 206-224.

7. United Nations Security Council Resolution 602, November 25, 1987; United Nations Document S/19359, December 18, 1987; *New York Times*, December 16, 1987, A11.

8. *New York Times*, December 29, 1987, A6.

9. Jaster, *The 1988 Peace Accords*, 25-26.

10. United Nations Documents S/20346, December 22, 1988; S/20345, December 22, 1988; S/20336 and S/20337, both December 17, 1988.

11. Interview 89, December 11, 1991.

12. Alan James, *Peacekeeping in International Politics* (New York: St. Martin's Press, 1990), 255-6.

13. United Nations Document S/20338, December 17, 1988, 1.

14. United Nations Documents A/43/249/Add.1, January 31, 1989, 3; A/45/718, November 16, 1990, 3; A/45/882, December 19, 1990, 3.

15. United Nations Document A/45/718, 6.

16. United Nations Documents S/20625, May 10, 1989, 3; A/43/249/Add.1, 4; S/20338, 3.

17. Jaster, *The 1988 Peace Accords*, 24; *The Blue Helmets: A Review of United Nations Peacekeeping*, 2nd ed. (New York: United Nations Department of Public Information, 1990), 337.

18. United Nations Document S/20338, 2; *New York Times*, November 30, 1988, A3.

19. Chester Crocker, "Peacemaking in Southern Africa," 15.

20. United Nations Documents S/20338, 1; S/20625, May 10, 1989, 3.

21. United Nations Document S/20625, 2.

22. United Nations Documents S/20351, December 23, 1988, 1; S/20625, 1-2; S/21246, April 12, 1990, 1-2; *Blue Helmets*, 338.

23. James, *Peacekeeping*, 256.

24. United Nations Documents S/20783, August 11, 1989, 2; S/20955, November 9, 1989, 1.

25. United Nations Document S/20338, 3.

26. United Nations Documents S/20338, 3-4; A/45/718, 3; A/43/249/Add.1, 11-12.

27. United Nations Documents S/20338, 3; S/20783, 3; S/20955, 2-3.

28. United Nations Document S/21246, 2. An earlier incident in which UNITA ambushed a truck and killed six Cuban soldiers in August 1989 had been met with a warning and a denunciation of continued US aid to UNITA (United Nations Document S/20799, August 21, 1989, 2).

29. United Nations Documents S/20625, 2-3; S/20783, 2; S/20955, 2; S/21246, 3 and Add.1; S/21860, October 10, 1990, 2; S/22644, May 28, 1991, 2-3.

30. Interview 84, October 16, 1991.

22 United Nations Angola Verification Mission II

by Virginia Page Fortna

The sixteen year old civil war between Angola's *Movimento Popular de Libertação de Angola* (MPLA) government and the *União Nacional para a Independência Total de Angola* (UNITA) rebels seemed to come to an end in May 1991 when the parties reached a political settlement. The mandate of UNAVEM was extended and expanded to monitor the new accord. UNAVEM II deployed in June 1991 with a seventeen month mandate. The Angolan settlement is testimony to the ability of peace to spread once successfully implemented in a region of conflict but its implementation warns of the ability of conflict to reignite without strong and sustained international support for peace.

ORIGINS

As discussed in the previous chapter, the Angolan civil war deescalated with the removal of South African troops and the staged withdrawal of Cuban troops that came about as part of the December 1988 agreements among Angola, Cuba, and South Africa. Tentative steps were taken towards peace in Angola in early 1989 when both the Angolan government and UNITA put forward peace plans. In June, eighteen African heads of state attended a summit held in Gbadolite, Zaire. President Mobutu Sese Seko of Zaire mediated by walking back and forth between the UNITA and MPLA delegations, which did not negotiate face to face. The summit yielded a cease-fire agreement and a photo of UNITA leader Jonas Savimbi and Angolan President Eduardo José dos Santos, who had never met before, shaking hands. The cease-fire did not hold, however, as the agreement had been based on Mobutu's misrepresentations to each side of the other's position.[1] At that point the conflict was not ripe for resolution; the parties were not yet committed to finding a peaceful settlement. Each side felt the withdrawal of its opponent's foreign backers would give it the upper hand and allow a definitive military solution to the conflict.[2]

At the end of 1989 and into early 1990, MPLA forces launched a major offensive against the UNITA-held town of Mavinga in southeast Angola, but fighting in February and March ended in stalemate. Government forces were not able to destroy the rebels even though UNITA now lacked the support of South African troops. On the other hand, UNITA realized that lack of Cuban troops did not leave the government entirely vulnerable, either. Having tried and failed one last time to settle the conflict militarily, both sides were ready to talk.[3] A drought, and the threat of widespread famine if the war continued, gave added impetus to finding a political solution.

Portugal took the initiative as mediator; the former colonial power had strong cultural and historical ties with Angola. Both the MPLA and UNITA were somewhat suspicious of Portugal initially. The MPLA was concerned by Portuguese President Mário Soares's support for UNITA, yet Portugal had maintained fairly good relations with the Angolan government. UNITA was worried that Portuguese business ties with the Angolan government would jeopardize Lisbon's neutrality, but as a democracy, Portugal was perceived as supporting UNITA's goal of a multiparty state. José Durão Barroso, Portugal's Secretary of State for Foreign Affairs and Cooperation, was the central mediator.[4]

The first three rounds of talks between MPLA and UNITA in Portugal (in April, June, and August 1990) began work on fundamental political principles. The original negotiating positions of the two sides were very far apart on issues as basic as recognition of each other—MPLA wanted recognition as the legitimate government, while UNITA wanted recognition as a legitimate political party, requiring a change in Angola's one-party constitution. The sides showed more flexibility as the meetings progressed, however, and the gap between them began to close.[5]

Starting with the fourth round, in September, the United States and the Soviet Union were invited to the talks as observers. The superpowers were not to act as supporters of the sides they backed; rather, they were to encourage compromise, and by working together for a solution, to lend their weight to the peace process. One of the US and Soviet contributions to the process was their agreement on a "zero-zero option." That is, they would cease to supply lethal material to their clients once a cease-fire agreement was reached.[6]

At the fourth round the negotiators began to tackle military and cease-fire issues, but these discussions were kept in a separate "basket" from the discussions on political principles. By the fifth round, in November, the parties had agreed on major parts of a cease-fire document and the document on political principles.[7] The negotiations ran into trouble in early 1991 over the issues of setting a date to sign the cease-fire agreement and establishing a time period for holding elections.[8] Differences were worked out relatively quickly, however, and on May 1, 1991, UNITA and the MPLA government initialed a peace agreement. A de facto cease-fire took effect on May 15, and became official when dos Santos and Savimbi formally signed the *Acordos de Paz para Angola* in Lisbon at the end of the month.

The principles of the peace package were threefold: (1) a cease-fire to be monitored by the United Nations and controlled by a joint monitoring commission; (2) elections under international monitoring to be held between September and November 1992; and (3) the integration of the two armies into a single national army. Integration was to start immediately and be completed before the elections.[9]

Initiatives toward UN Involvement

UNAVEM I had been stationed in Angola since January 1989 to monitor Cuban troop withdrawal, and the UN provided advisors to the negotiations to end the internal conflict. The Secretary General's Deputy Military Adviser, for example, took part in the last stages of the negotiations as a technical adviser on the cease-fire.

Once the peace accords were signed, the Angolan government formally requested that the UN participate in the verification of their implementation by keeping the UNAVEM mission in Angola until the elections. The UN was asked to monitor the cease-fire and the police, but whether or not UNAVEM would be requested to help with the elections was left open initially.[10] The UN agreed to help; although the Angolan conflict was primarily an internal one, the UN's role was justified by the extensive international dimensions of the conflict.

POLITICAL SUPPORT

Superpower rivalry fueled the civil war in Angola with money and weapons.[11] As the Cold War ended, the United States and the Soviet Union realized that their cooperation towards a peaceful solution could end what had become an expensive and largely pointless war. The Soviet Union had too many pressing problems at home to worry about the MPLA. Changes in the Soviet Union and the absence of Cuban troops from Angola also took the edge off US conservatives' support for UNITA. But neither superpower wanted simply to abandon its side by cutting off aid while the war continued, so they took an active and cooperative role in the peace process. Portugal was careful to bring the superpowers on board during the negotiations and thus ensure their backing for the agreement.

The political support of the United States and the Soviet Union did not translate into full financial support, however. Neither superpower was willing to fund a large peacekeeping operation in Angola. UNAVEM II was therefore given only a limited role in the peace plan while the parties themselves were responsible for most of the implementation.

Portugal had also kept South Africa informed during the negotiations to make sure that it would not throw a wrench into the works when the peace plan got underway. Like the United States, South Africa had domestic conservative constituents demanding that UNITA be supported. But the accords gave UNITA a legitimate political role in Angola and were therefore supported by South Africa.

The Angolan government and UNITA, having decided that a military solution was out of reach, agreed to a political settlement. Deep mutual mistrust kept both sides from complying fully with the accords, but sixteen years of civil war and stalemate encouraged them not to break with the peace plan, there being no viable alternatives to it. Pressure from Russia, the United States and Portugal also has helped keep the parties in line. On the other hand, the UN's ability to press them to resolve their disputes was hampered by the fact that Angola's situation had lost much of its international dimension. The Cubans were gone, the South Africans were gone, the Cold War was over, and other events had stolen the international spotlight. The same evolution of international politics that facilitated negotiation of the peace plan reduced outside interest in its implementation. Thus the UN's standard tactic of using publicity to pressure the parties to settle their disputes was of limited utility. The parties' own perceptions of their self-interest became critical to successful implementation of the plan.

MANDATE

The mandate of UNAVEM I to verify Cuban troop withdrawal from Angola officially applied until July 22, 1991, although the last Cubans had left by May 25. Security Council Resolution 696 extended the mission, now UNAVEM II, by seventeen months to cover Angola's internal peace plan.[12]

The Angolan peace accords created a Joint Political-Military Commission (CCPM) "to see that the peace accords are applied, thereby guaranteeing strict compliance with all political and military understandings, and to make the final decision on possible violations of those accords." The CCPM included representatives of the government and UNITA as members, and representatives of Portugal, the United States and the Soviet Union (Russia) as observers. A UN representative could be invited to participate in meetings. Reporting to this commission were a Joint Verification and Monitoring Commission (CMVF) and a Joint Commission for the Formation of the Armed Forces (CCFA).[13] The CCPM, not the United Nations, had responsibility under the accords for making the peace plan work. The original timetable for the plan is given in Table 22.1.

Table 22.1. Original Peace Plan Timetable

May 1, 1991	Peace accords initialed.
May 15, 1991	Cease-fire takes effect.
May 29–31, 1991	Accords signed.
June 15, 1991	Monitoring groups complete setup and begin to function.
June 30, 1991	UN verification system completely setup.
July 1, 1991	UNITA and government forces begin to assemble at specified areas.
August 1, 1991	Assembly of forces complete.
Elections, September–November 1992	Peace process complete; new national government and integrated armed forces created; verification and monitoring bodies end their work.

Source: United Nations Document S/22609, May 17, 1991, 7.

UNAVEM's mandate was "to verify the arrangements agreed by the two Angolan parties...for monitoring the cease-fire...and for monitoring the Angolan police during the cease-fire period."[14] UNAVEM's role was therefore to ensure that the CMVF and other monitoring groups did their jobs. United Nations military and police observers were to work with, but remain operationally distinct from, the monitoring teams made up of UNITA and government personnel. UNAVEM II observers were to report, for example, on the number of soldiers at the troop assembly areas, the conditions and morale there, and the storage conditions for weapons. Mobile observer teams also were to help the CCPM investigate and resolve cease-fire violations and other problems. In short, UNAVEM II's mandate was to watch the watchers.[15]

When the peace accords were signed, the two sides had not worked out all the details for the 1992 elections. The accords referred to the possibility of asking for UN electoral advice and of international election observation, but left open whether that was to be done by the UN, the OAU, or by others.[16] In November 1991, Angola formally asked the UN to observe and provide technical help for the elections. Election observation was therefore added to UNAVEM II's mandate. The election dates were eventually set for September 29–30, 1992. Arrangements were made for the UN Development Program to provide a team of sixteen consultants on election organization, logistics, and communication who were to give technical assistance.[17] A small electoral division was also added to UNAVEM II, modelled on the election observation missions in Nicaragua and Haiti. The UN made it clear that it would observe and verify the elections, but not run them.[18]

FUNDING

Because the parties themselves were responsible for ensuring compliance with the peace accords through the joint commissions, UNAVEM II's costs were considerably lower than they might have been. Concern over the cost of the operation, especially on the part of the United States and the Soviet Union, was the main reason for setting the plan up in this way.[19]

In July 1991, the Secretary General estimated that UNAVEM II would cost $121.4 million ($58.7 million for June through December 1991, and $62.7 million for January through October 1992). The General Assembly's Advisory Committee on Administrative and Budgetary Questions (ACABQ) estimated UNAVEM's costs to be much lower, however, for several reasons: deployment was delayed (see Field Operations section) resulting in lower staff costs; not all of the requested planes and helicopters were needed for the entire period of the mission; and UNAVEM II obtained surplus equipment, especially vehicles and communication equipment, from UNTAG and other peacekeeping operations at depreciated cost. ACABQ estimated the mission's budgetary needs to be just over $49 million for the first seven months, from June through December 1991. As UNAVEM II was treated as an extension of UNAVEM I, the $1.4 million left in the UNAVEM special account after UNAVEM I's early termination was available for UNAVEM II. The total 1991 assessment for the two operations came to $52 million.[20]

UNAVEM II's initial budget was not approved until mid-August 1991, two and a half months after the operation began, contributing to a delayed start and requiring that the mission be phased into operation more slowly than planned. The ACABQ authorized the Secretary General to spend $10 million (the limit of its discretionary spending authority) to tide the mission over until the General Assembly approved the full budget. Later, a further $42 million was assessed to cover the missions costs for January 1 through October 31, 1992. This amount was not intended to cover the cost of the electoral observation (estimated at $19 million) since the UN's role in the elections had not been settled at the time the assessment was made.[21]

PLANNING AND IMPLEMENTATION

The UN was quite familiar with Angola when UNAVEM II deployed. While the UN did not create the peace plan or the cease-fire, it was involved in the negotiations and thus had full information on the plan as it took form.[22] The UN did not know the exact troop strengths of UNITA or the MPLA, but neither did the parties themselves. Original estimates were exaggerated, and this was partially responsible for the lower than expected turnout at the assembly areas (see Field Operations section).[23] Before deploying its field units, UNAVEM II sent reconnaissance missions to look over the various troop assembly points and other mission-relevant areas. Reconnaissance at some UNITA areas was delayed until August because UNITA was slow in clearing UNAVEM's entry.[24]

Size and Composition of the Force

The UN force included 350 military observers, a military medical unit of 14, 126 police observers (raised from 89 in May 1992), 54 international civilian support personnel, and 41 locally recruited staff.[25] UNAVEM's electoral division consisted of 100 people, with 300 additional electoral observers needed for the polling itself. The military observers and civilian police monitors were contributed by the twenty-four states listed in table 22.2. These included the ten states that had contributed to UNAVEM I.[26]

Table 22.2. National Composition of UNAVEM II

Military Observers	Police Monitors	Military Observers	Police Monitors
Algeria		Malaysia	X
Argentina	X	Morocco	X
Brazil	X	Netherlands	X
Canada		New Zealand	
Congo		Nigeria	X
Czech & Slovak Republic		Norway	
Egypt		Senegal	
Guinea-Bissau		Singapore	
Hungary		Spain	
India		Sweden	X
Ireland	X	Yugoslavia	X
Jordan		Zimbabwe	

Note: Countries in italics participated in UNAVEM I as well. **Source:** United Nations Documents S/22716, June 18, 1991, 1, and S/23191, Oct. 31, 1991, 4.

Command, Communications, and Logistics

UNAVEM II military and police observers worked with the CMVF observers but were under separate UN command. Because of the UN mission's expanded role, the rank of the Chief Military Observer was raised to Major General. UNAVEM I Chief Military Observer, Brigadier General Pericles Ferreira Gomes, lay down his command on May 31, 1991. UNAVEM II was commanded by Major General Edward Ushie Unimna of Nigeria.[27] In February 1992, the new Secretary General, Boutros Boutros-Ghali, appointed Margaret Joan Anstee of the United Kingdom as his Special Representative for Angola. Ms. Anstee was the first woman appointed Special Representative for a peacekeeping mission. She took responsibility for both the civilian and military aspects of the mission, signifying the transition of UNAVEM to a multicomponent mission.

The mission's organization followed the CMVF's structure, with monitoring groups deployed into six regions: Luanda, Huambo, Lubango, Saurimo, Luena, and Mavinga. The CMVF monitoring groups were deployed on a full-time basis at eighty-two far-flung locations throughout Angola. These monitors covered fifty areas in which troops assembled after the cease-fire, twenty-three for UNITA troops and twenty-seven for government troops, as well as

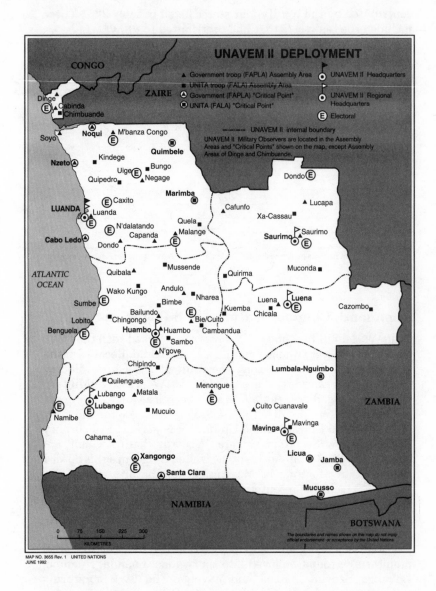

Figure 22.1. Second United Nations Angola Verification Mission, Deployment as of June 1992

thirty-two "critical points," that is, airports and ports not already covered by monitors at assembly areas. The United Nations maintained a permanent presence at sixty-two of these eighty-two locations. Military observers deployed in teams of five at each of the fifty assembly areas, and in teams of two or more at twelve of the other "critical points." Keeping watch at these entry points was important to ensure that neither the MPLA nor UNITA were receiving lethal materiel from outside sources. Observers were also deployed at six regional headquarters and at Mission Head-quarters in Luanda. Mobile rapid reaction teams were set up to monitor and defuse incidents and investigate cease-fire violations in locations where there was no resident UNAVEM presence.[28] United Nations personnel were unarmed; their security was supposed to be the responsibility of the party in control of the territory in which they were located. But a "deteriorating" secu-rity situation, including thefts and armed robberies of UNAVEM staff, prompted the misson to contract armed security guards and to request armed UN security guards.[29]

Angola's communications infrastructure was very poor, with no telephone service in much of the country. UNAVEM II used a four-channel portable earth station for satellite communication with UN Headquarters in New York. Portable and fixed HF and VHF radio links were used for text transmission and voice com-munication in-country.[30]

Logistics and transportation were also difficult. The country is vast, its few railways were badly damaged by the war, and most roads were mined. The situation improved as mines were cleared off main roads, but air transport still provided the only access to many parts of the country, especially during the rainy season. UNAVEM II's civilian air unit was equipped with one fixed-wing cargo aircraft and a dozen helicopters. A heavy cargo aircraft and a small passenger aircraft were hired as necessary. In addition, the various international organizations in Angola (for example, the International Committee of the Red Cross and the World Food Program), as well as the Angolan government, cooperated and shared flights with each other when possible.[31] Serious logistical problems and shortages of equipment plagued CCPM's attempts to implement the peace accords, and CCPM had to rely heavily on UNAVEM logistics, especially for its police monitoring and for voter registration. This put heavy strains on the UN mission.[32]

A shortage of comfortable housing was a major problem for UNAVEM, with many monitors living for the first part of the mission in grass huts or buildings damaged during the war. This was especially problematic in the rainy season. Some UNAVEM personnel were deployed in areas with little or no access to water. In one case, water had to be supplied by air. The delay in approval of the budget contributed to these problems, delaying purchase of prefabricated buildings, generators, and communications equipment.[33] Once these materials were delivered, however, UNAVEM II had rather fewer logistical problems and mishaps in its operations than might have been expected given the extreme difficulty of communication and transportation in Angola.

Field Operations

For years, Angola's territory had been split by the war, with UNITA controlling the south-eastern third of the country (approximately) and the government controlling the rest. By the time UNAVEM II deployed, the cease-fire between the government and the rebels had been in effect for two weeks, was holding despite some sporadic fighting, and Angola was beginning to rebuild itself. Particularly important was the reopening of roads long closed by mines and the threat of ambush. The country still had a very long way to go in its reconstruction, however; transportation and communication facilities were in serious disrepair, and the economy continued to operate largely on the barter system (see previous chapter).

UNAVEM II took longer than anticipated to become fully operational. In the beginning of June 1991, an advance party of 61 military observers and 32 civilians set up five of the six regional headquarters. The rest of the mission was deployed in stages as assembly areas were set up.

The first CCPM meeting was originally planned for June 1, but there were no accommodations available in Luanda for the Portuguese, US, Soviet, or UNITA members of the committee. Lack of office space and housing in the overcrowded capital was a point of contention between UNITA and the government, which was supposed to provide accommodation. The first meeting was not held until June 17, setting back the timetable for implementation of the peace accords. Deployment of UNAVEM II personnel was therefore also delayed, as there was little for them to do until implementation got under way and CCPM's monitoring groups were set up. The delay in approval of UNAVEM's budget would have made deployment on schedule difficult in any case.[34]

Verification by military observers took place primarily at the assembly points and "critical points," and consisted of counting and checking on conditions of troops and arms. There was very little verification elsewhere in the country, except in response to specific problems or allegations of cease-fire violations, in which case UNAVEM conducted on-site inspections. The process depended critically on the parties' good will, rather than on a stringent inspection regime.

Police observer teams operated using a different administrative bias. There were three CMVF police monitoring teams in each of Angola's eighteen provinces. A team of four UNAVEM II police observers was deployed in each province. They normally worked in pairs, following some but not all of the CMVF monitoring teams.[35]

Deployment of UN monitors into UNITA areas was delayed, as mentioned earlier, because UNITA did not clear UNAVEM's reconnaissance missions into its territory until August 1991. Some of UNITA's assembly areas were relocated after review by the CMVF, requiring further reconnaissance. Deployment of UNAVEM military monitors in all of the open assembly areas was not completed until September 30, 1991. UNAVEM police monitors deployed in late August and September, but CMVF police monitoring teams were not established until early 1992 and were not functioning in all 18 of Angola's provinces until mid-June. UNITA often refused to recognize the government police forces as having authority to maintain law and order in its areas.[36]

The original timetable of the peace plan called for completion of troop assembly by August 1, 1991. This was unrealistic, and failed to allow for the logistical difficulty of organizing and transporting troops to the assembly points.[37] Commanders also were reluctant to have their units be the first to assemble, as they feared a trap. Moreover, the assembly points lacked adequate food supplies. The government in particular had trouble feeding and paying its soldiers, and the threat of severe food shortages at the assembly points raised fears of broke, hungry soldiers raiding for food.

As a temporary solution, the United States flew more than 450,000 Meals-Ready-to-Eat, as well as tents and other supplies, from stockpiles in Europe and the Gulf to soldiers in Angola. In addition, a six month, $27.5 million UN special relief program began in early October 1991 to deliver food and other supplies to the assembly areas. Since a UN disaster relief program had been in Angola for several years, there was a preexisting structure that could be used to distribute food to the troops. The UN World Food Program made an exception to its rule of not supplying military forces, and agreed to take over the job of feeding Angolan troops, while UNICEF provided nonfood items. UNAVEM's logistical arm, with help from the United States, distributed most of these supplies. Special Representive Anstee helped coordinate the UN's various relief efforts.[38]

The delay in troop assembly did not pose a political problem at first, but both sides held back some troops as a hedge, and the number of troops at the assembly areas leveled off at about 60 percent of initially declared numbers. Some of the discrepancy between the expected number of troops and the number who showed up was due to the inaccuracy of the original troop strength estimates. The government also claimed that some of its soldiers had deserted, while UNITA claimed that many of its troops were now working in UNITA's political party. It became clear, however, that it was not only these explanations and difficulty with transportation, but lack of political will to comply with the accords that was preventing assembly. This posed a potentially serious risk to the peace process, as there was no mechanism set up to monitor troops outside the assembly areas. By June 1992, 85 percent of UNITA's troops were assembled, but only four percent had been demobilized; just 37 percent of the government's troops had reached assembly points, but half of those had been demobilized. Others drifted away from the camps prior to formal demobilization since, despite the emergency relief program, shortages of food, medicine, and clothing at the assembly areas continued to be a problem. Moreover, army leadership was poor, and morale was consequently terrible.[39]

Integration of the government and rebel armies was supposed to be complete before elections were held, but the process was behind schedule by early 1992, again because of shortages of food and equipment. This compounded problems at assembly areas.[40] Under the accords, the UN did not have a direct role in the demobilization process or the training of the new army. The Portuguese, French, and British were responsible for training the new army. A Joint Commission for the Formation of the Armed Forces was created in the peace accords, under the authority of the CCPM, but plans for military integration were not spelled out in the agreement. The likelihood that three armies would still exist in Angola at the time of national elections raised the possibility of violent, partisan dissent from the election results.

Although security was tenuous throughout Angola because of the number of weapons at large and the lack of control over them, problems in Cabinda province, separated from the rest of Angola by Zaire's land corridor to the sea, were especially acute due to an active secessionist movement. All aspects of the peace process in Cabinda, including troop assembly and voter registration, have been hampered or paralyzed by continuing violence.

Elsewhere there were several incidents between UNITA and the MPLA after the peace settlement that reflected the two sides' continued maneuvering for political position. The CCPM, on which UNITA sits as an equal, necessarily infringed government prerogratives and the MPLA wanted to keep its jurisdiction limited. For example, when an MPLA pilot was shot after he and some others drunkenly harassed a guard at Jonas Savimbi's residence, the government sought to handle the incident as a civil matter under its own control, whereas UNITA wanted it to be treated as a cease-fire violation under the purview of the CCPM. In the end the guard was handed over to UNAVEM.[41]

Other incidents included the killing of a UNITA soldier by a government policeman, which prompted retaliation by 40 UNITA soldiers against government buildings and the police. Monitoring teams and UN personnel were able to defuse many of these incidents, but along with the sharp rise in armed robberies and banditry they have made reconciliation more difficult. Neither these incidents nor the problems with troop assembly irrevocably upset the peace, but there is no agreement over how to handle such problems. CCPM meetings were often suspended by one side or the other or bogged down in handling them; any solutions were worked out on an ad hoc basis.[42]

Still, verification and reporting mechanisms functioned well initially, and MPLA and UNITA field personnel cooperated with the UN much better than expected. The de-mining subcommittee of the CCPM was a heartening example. Teams of MPLA and UNITA troops cleared some 300,000 mines in the first month after the accords were signed.[43] Over 40,000 Angolans were maimed by land mines; cooperation in clearing the roads and farmland of this threat was crucial to the country's recovery from the war. So while accusations flew on the political level between the government and UNITA, the two sides cooperated to a significant degree at the operational level.

ASSESSMENT AND CONCLUSIONS

The internal Angolan peace process was not a direct descendant of the peace process that led to the December 1988 tripartite agreements, which were criticized in some quarters for their failure to halt Angola's civil war. A new set of negotiations, mediated by Portugal, a third party considered more impartial in the civil conflict than the United States, had to be initiated. But the atmosphere of peaceful resolution of conflict and Namibia's transition to independence, as well as the removal of foreign troops from Angola as a result of the first peace process, certainly contributed to the second one. It seems clear in hindsight that the 1988 accords did facilitate the later Angolan settlement.

Other factors played a major role as well, particularly the continued stalemate on the battlefield; the rising costs of conflict for the participants, as their funders began to doubt the wisdom of providing aid; the emergence of Portugal as a mediator; and the participation of the US and USSR as engaged observers. The confidence and atmosphere of reconciliation created by the agreements between Angola, Cuba, and South Africa, and the process of reconciliation and nation-building in Namibia, as well as the United Nations' successful mission there, contributed to progress in the talks between the MPLA and UNITA that yielded the May 1991 accords.

Despite some misgivings on the part of the UN about merely monitoring the progress of the peace plan rather than having an active hand in implementating it, UNAVEM II plunged ahead. However, its own successes in setting up its monitoring and verification system often were not matched, or matched only after considerable delay, by the Angolans themselves in setting up the mechanisms that the UN was supposed to monitor.

Despite the cease-fire and the peace agreement, relations between MPLA and UNITA continued to be characterized by deep mistrust. The MPLA was not always willing to let UNITA exercise its rights as a political party, and UNITA was not always willing to abide by government laws. It planned, for example, to accept aid from the United States despite a law barring political parties from receiving financial or other assistance from outside the country.[44]

Although both parties professed that they did not want to go back to war, ethnic divisions between UNITA and MPLA, whose respective power bases lay in the traditionally rival Ovimbundu and Mbundu peoples, became more prominent as their ideological differences waned. The continuing fear and mistrust held the seeds of ethnic conflict if the peace plan faltered, and it did.

By mid-1992, the peace plan was running neck and neck with social and economic disintegration. When elections were held in late September 1992, UNITA retained some 30,000 men under arms and the MPLA about 10,000. When Angola's partially-monitored election results gave a near-majority to President dos

Santos and a parliamentary majority to the MPLA, Savimbi contested them. At the end of October, the civil war resumed. Government police in Luanda summarily executed suspected UNITA supporters, while UNITA hunted down and killed a reported 15,000 civilians in and around the central city of Huambo who were suspected of being "government sympathizers." Peace talks held in the Ivory Coast failed, and in May 1993 the United States recognized dos Santos' government.[45] As of this writing, the once-promising Angolan peace process is a tragic failure. It might have been otherwise with a more forceful international presence, but the ferocious killing that occurred in November 1992 suggests a leadership, if not a society, much further removed from reconciliation than international mediators had supposed.

Notes

1. Shawn McCormick, "Angola: The Road to Peace," *CSIS Africa Notes*, no. 125, June 1991, 2-4.
2. José Manuel Durão Barroso, "The Peace Process in Angola: Evolution and Prospects," text of a speech delivered to the CSIS Study Group on Angola (Washington, D.C.: Center for Strategic and International Studies, February 20, 1991); *New York Times*, April 26, 1990, A3; on the issue of ripeness of a conflict for resolution, see I. William Zartman, *Ripe for Resolution: Conflict and Intervention in Africa*, updated edition (New York: Oxford University Press, 1989).
3. Barroso, "The Peace Process in Angola," 11-12; International Institute for Strategic Studies, *Strategic Survey 1990–1991* (London: Brassey's, 1991), 235.
4. Barroso, "The Peace Process in Angola," 13-14; McCormick, "Angola: The Road to Peace," 8.
5. Barroso, "The Peace Process in Angola," 14-15; *Strategic Survey 1990-1991*, 236.
6. This was also known as the "triple-zero option," the third zero representing the fact that the two Angolan parties were not to receive lethal aid from any other outside parties either.
7. Barroso, "The Peace Process in Angola," 14-19; *Strategic Survey 1990-1991*, 236; United Nations Document S/22609, May 17, 1991, 4.
8. Barroso, "The Peace Process in Angola," 19-24.
9. Barroso, "The Peace Process in Angola," 27; *New York Times*, May 2, 1991, A1, A4.
10. United Nations Documents S/22609, 6; S/22627, May 20, 1991, 3.
11. Soviet aid to the MPLA amounted to $800 million annually in the late 1980s, while the US gave $50 million a year in aid to UNITA (*New York Times*, September 17, 1990, A3). For more background on the civil war and foreign involvement in it, see Zartman, *Ripe for Resolution*, chapter 5; Robert S. Jaster, *The 1988 Peace Accords and the Future of*

South-western Africa, Adelphi Paper 253 (London: International Institute for Strategic Studies, Autumn 1990); William J. Durch "The Cuban Military in Africa and the Middle East," *Studies in Comparative Communism* 11, nos. 1 & 2 (Spring/Summer 1978); and John Stockwell, *In Search of Enemies: a CIA Story* (New York: W.W. Norton & Co., 1978).

12. United Nations Document S/Res/696, May 30, 1991.

13. United Nations Document S/22609, May 17, 1991, 6.

14. United Nations Document S/23191, October 31, 1991, 2.

15. United Nations Documents S/22609, 6; S/22627, 4-6.

16. United Nations Documents S/22609, 42, 45-46; S/22627, 3.

17. United Nations Document S/24145, June 24, 1992, 3.

18. United Nations Document S/23671, March 3, 1992, 2,9.

19. United Nations Document S/22627, 6. Interview 89, December 11, 1991.

20. United Nations Documents A/45/1028, July 1, 1991, 4; A/45/1043, July 31, 1991, 2-6; S/23191, 4; Johannesburg Radio, August 16, 1991, cited in United States, *Foreign Broadcast Information Service, Sub-Saharan Africa* (hereafter *FBIS*), August 19, 1991, 22; and Interview 69b, June 19, 1991.

21. United Nations Documents ST/ADM/SER.B/380, June 4, 1992, 23; S/24145, 11.

22. United Nations Document S/22627, 1.

23. Interview 87, December 6, 1991.

24. United Nations Document S/23191, October 31, 1991, 4-5.

25. United Nations Documents S/23191, 3; S/24145, 2.

26. Of this 300, 100 would come from UNDP and other UN personnel in Angola, 100 from the UN Secretariat, and 100 from Member States. United Nations Documents S/23671/Add.1, March 20, 1992, 1; S/24145, 10.

27. United Nations Documents S/22627, 4; S/23191, 3.

28. United Nations Documents S/22627, 2-4; A/45/1028, 5, 13.

29. United Nations Documents A/45/1028, 5; S/24145, 12.

30. United Nations Document A/45/1028, 20-22.

31. United Nations Document S/23191, 4; and interview 88, December 9, 1991. UNAVEM II used satellite positioning systems and radio beacons to navigate on patrols in the eastern part of Angola (United Nations Document A/45/1028, 22).

32. United Nations Document S/24145, 7, 10-11.

33. United Nations Document S/23191, 6.

34. United Nations Document S/23191, 4.

35. United Nations Documents S/22627, 5; A/45/1028, 6.

36. United Nations Documents A/45/1043, 3; S/23191, 4-6, 8; S/23671, 12; S/24145, 5.

37. United Nations Document S/22672, June 4, 1991; Interview 69b, June 19, 1991; Luanda Radio, July 16, 1991, cited in *FBIS*, July 17, 1991, 15; Luanda Radio, July 29, 1991, cited in *FBIS*, July 30, 1991, 11; Luanda Radio, August 2, 1991, cited in *FBIS*, August 5, 1991, 17; and BBC World Service, July 31, 1991, cited in *FBIS*, August 1, 1991, 15.

38. United Nations, "Emergency Aid Contributions Received for De-mobilizing Troops in Angola," Document IHA/421, October 14, 1991; and United Nations Document S/24145, 3, 7. Interviews 87, December 6, 1991; 88, December 9, 1991; and 89, December 11, 1991; *Washington Post*, October 3, 1991, 35; *New York Times*, October 6, 1991, 18. The relief program was extended to aid 1.4 million displaced people and refugees, as well as to demobilized soldiers and their families. By May 1992, however, only one-fourth of the $167 million needed for this voluntarily funded program had been pledged by governments (S/24145, 7).

39. United Nations Document S/24145, 6. Interviews 87-89, December 1991.

40. United Nations Document S/24145, 6.

41. Interviews 87, December 6, 1991, and 88a, February 3, 1992.

42. United Nations Document S/24145, 5; Interview 88a, February 3, 1992; Interview 87, December 6, 1991.

43. *Jane's Defence Weekly*, August 10, 1991, 219.

44. *Washington Post*, July 12, 1991, A27. The United States Congress earmarked $30 million to help UNITA make the transition from a rebel group to a political party (*New York Times*, December 16, 1991, A9).

45. *New York Times*, October 18, 1992, 7; April 13, 1993, A1; May 20, 1993, A28; May 22, 1993, A1; and July 1, 1993, A3. *Washington Post*, November 1, 1992, A38; and November 20, 1992, A46.

23 United Nations Mission for the Referendum in Western Sahara

by William J. Durch

United Nations political involvement with the Western Sahara dates from the early 1960s, when the territory was a colony of Spain. When Spain withdrew in 1976, ceding control to Morocco and Mauritania, their claims were bitterly contested by the *Frente Popular para la Liberación de Saguia el-Hamra y de Río de Oro* (POLISARIO). UN mediation from the mid-1980s onward led to a plan to give Western Saharans (or Sahrawis) the right to choose between independence and merger with Morocco (Mauritania having long since relinquished its claim). The UN's Mission for the Referendum in Western Sahara (MINURSO) was created to implement that plan. Its history shows how marginal Great Power support and a blind eye to local political realities can undermine a field operation, threatening UN credibility and the credibility of international peacekeeping.

ORIGINS

Western Sahara lies between Morocco and Mauritania on the northwest coast of Africa. An arid coastal plain with little agriculture rises to meet the western edge of the Sahara Desert. Phosphate mines in the northwestern part of the territory are its principal economic resource. Sparsely populated, its 264,000 square kilometers are home to a largely nomadic population of 186,000; more than 60,000 are refugees, living in camps in southwestern Algeria.

The territory's basic demographics are grim: infant mortality 18 percent; life expectancy 40 years; literacy rate 15 percent; population growth rate 2.8 percent, producing a population structure with a majority under the age of 20. Grim as they are, however, these numbers are not that different from neighboring Mauritania or other countries of the Sahel.

Spain established a colony, Spanish Sahara, in 1884 and held onto it until 1976, resisting pressure from the UN and the Organization of African Unity (OAU) to permit a referendum on Saharan self-determination. In August 1974, Madrid did agree to hold a referendum under UN auspices in the first half of 1975, but that agreement was stillborn.

King Hassan II of Morocco reacted to the Spanish announcement by denying the validity of any UN referendum and promising to oppose by force any result unfavorable to Morocco. Western Sahara was seen by Moroccans as part of "Greater Morocco," a concept that included portions of Algeria and all of Mauritania until 1970, when the latter claims were relinquished. Hassan relented to the extent of proposing arbitration by the International Court of Justice (ICJ), and in December 1974 the UN General Assembly asked the ICJ for an advisory opinion on the legal status of Western Sahara. On October 16, 1975, the ICJ held that such "historic claims" as Morocco's were irrelevant to the issue of self-determination for the Saharan population, which could only be determined through a "free and genuine expression" of popular will.[1]

One day after the ICJ's ruling, King Hassan declared his intention to march several hundred thousand Moroccans into Western Sahara in early November (the "Green March"). On November 14, Morocco, Spain, and Mauritania announced the results of secret negotiations to partition Saharan territory between Morocco and Mauritania while permitting Spain to keep a large minority interest in Saharan phosphate production. Toward the end of November, Moroccan forces invaded the territory from the northeast, and Mauritanian troops invaded from the south. By February 1976, when the Spanish formally withdrew, the two armies were in control of most of Saharan territory. The de facto annexation was formalized by the Rabat Agreement of April 1976, which assigned two-thirds of the territory to Morocco and one-third to Mauritania.

The Frente POLISARIO, organized in 1973 to resist Spanish control, also resisted the new invasions, trying at first to hold key Saharan towns. Greatly outnumbered, and devastated by Moroccan control of the air, POLISARIO and some 60,000 Saharans sought refuge in neighboring Algeria. The refugees, eventually organized into a series of camps near Tindouf, remained there in 1991.[2]

In late February 1976, POLISARIO, which received financial and material support from Algeria, Libya, and Cuba, proclaimed the independent Saharan Arab Democratic Republic (SADR). Having suffered badly in conventional warfare, POLISARIO switched to hit-and-run guerrilla tactics, concentrating first on Mauritania. Strained by the cost of the war, the latter relinquished its claims and signed a peace treaty (the Algiers Agreement) with POLISARIO in August 1979; declared its neutrality regarding Western Sahara; and resumed diplomatic relations with Algeria. Its third of the territory was immediately annexed by Morocco.[3]

As a conservative Arab country and former French colony, Morocco received support from both France and the United States. But even with that support, the cost of the war for Western Sahara drained Morocco's finances and increased its foreign debt substantially. Having to protect the entire Saharan border against POLISARIO incursions taxed its military resources. Thus, in August 1980, Moroccan forces began building the first of what would eventually be an interlocking chain of fortified sand berms reaching 3,300 kilometers from the Morocco-Algeria border, south along the Saharan border with Mauritania and westward to the sea, near the coastal city of Dahkla. The sand wall was completed in April 1987. Studded with mines and electronic sensors, and defended by 100,000 Moroccan troops, it strengthened Morocco's hold over the territory.[4]

As Morocco's military position improved, political relations complicated the picture. The OAU had picked up the issue of Western Sahara in 1975, and was the main forum for its discussion for the next eight years. In 1979, the OAU summit in Monrovia called for a ceasefire and a "general and free" referendum in Western Sahara, establishing a committee to work toward that goal in cooperation with the UN. By 1980, a majority of OAU members recognized the SADR, POLISARIO's state-in-exile, as the government of independent Western Sahara. Tensions within the organization mounted when the more radical Frontline States of Southern Africa proposed membership in the organization for the SADR. When they pressed their case at a February 1982 pre-summit meeting, Morocco and 18 other pro-Western members walked out and subsequently boycotted the 1982 summit, slated for Tripoli, Libya. The following year, the scenario repeated. The SADR was elected to membership at the pre-summit, and only its graceful "withdrawal" allowed the June summit meeting to take place. At that 1983 meeting, the OAU supported a referendum in the territory under joint UN-OAU auspices, to be held in the context of a peacekeeping operation and direct negotiations between the parties.[5]

By 1985, the SADR won a seat in the OAU, and Morocco resigned from the organization in protest. On the other hand, a 1984 treaty of "union" between Morocco and Libya required Libya to end support to the POLISARIO, which it did, leaving Algeria as the SADR's sole source of material support. After a year of little military action, Hassan, through his Foreign Minister, declared a unilateral cease-fire in October 1985.[6]

A 1986 visit to Morocco by then-Prime Minister Shimon Peres of Israel led Libya to suspend the treaty of union in December of that year. Fighting in Western Sahara resumed in early 1987 and continued into the spring, as Morocco finished the final southern section of its defensive wall. But even as its military fortunes waned, POLISARIO continued to score small political victories. In April 1987, it was invited to address a session of the PLO's Palestine National Council, held in Algeria. Moroccan representatives walked out of the meeting, but one month later, following personal shuttle diplomacy by King Fahd of Saudi Arabia, Moroccan-Algerian relations began to improve, and King Hassan and Algeria's President Benjedid held their first face-to-face meeting in four years. Further improvements in relations were impelled by a combination of Moroccan military success, Algerian economic troubles, and two looming regional concerns: the anticipated impact on North Africa of growing European economic integration and, more immediate, the agricultural devastation threatened by the worst plague of locusts to infest the Mahgreb in 30 years.[7] In late May 1988, Morocco and Algeria resumed diplomatic ties.

In the interim, Morocco and POLISARIO began to talk. Morocco soon reiterated its support for a referendum on Western Saharan self-determination, a position first espoused at the OAU summit of 1981. At the same time, Algeria increased pressure on the POLISARIO to reach a peaceful settlement of the conflict, suggesting, to knowledgeable analysts, that a deal was struck at POLISARIO's expense to use the referendum as a vehicle for legitimizing Moroccan rule. Relations between the two countries had improved sufficiently by February 1989 to facilitate the founding of the Arab Mahgreb Union, modelled on Europe's common market.[8]

Initiatives toward UN Involvement

The General Assembly adopted its first resolution on self-determination for then-Spanish Sahara in December 1965, and one year later endorsed the concept of a UN-supervised referendum there. A further six resolutions were passed through 1973, the last two also affirming Western Sahara's right to independence. After the SADR took its seat in the OAU, prompting Morocco to withdraw from the organization, UN involvement in settling the conflict became more active. In July 1985, the Secretary General paid a visit to Morocco. However, Pérez de Cuéllar ruled out UN mediation of the conflict so long as there were no direct talks between the adversaries. In October, when King Hassan declared his unilateral ceasefire, Morocco also declared its willingness to have the UN supervise a referendum on Western Sahara's future, but still refused to deal directly with POLISARIO. In November, POLISARIO advanced a proposal for direct UN administration of the territory with the support of a joint UN-African security force, pending the outcome of a UN-supervised referendum. POLISARIO also proposed direct talks with Morocco and withdrawal of Moroccan forces and 100,000 Moroccan settlers before the referendum took place.[9]

After Morocco and POLISARIO started to talk, the UN sent a technical fact-finding mission, which included OAU observers, to Morocco, Algeria, and Western Sahara. The mission also contacted POLISARIO leaders. Its findings were reported to the Secretary General in early 1988. That May, the Secretary General paid a second visit to Morocco, went on to Mauritania and Algeria, and spoke with POLISARIO leaders. In July, King Fahd invited Moroccan and POLISARIO leaders to meet privately in Ta'if, Saudi Arabia. Although Morocco still publicly refused to talk directly with POLISARIO, this meeting apparently cleared a path for more direct UN mediation.[10]

The Secretary General subsequently met separately in Geneva with delegates from the two sides, and in New York, on August 11, 1988, presented to them a joint UN-OAU plan for a ceasefire and referendum to be conducted under UN auspices. Both sides accepted the plan in principle on August 30th, and on September 20th the Security Council passed Resolution 621 (1988), which asked for a more detailed implementation report and authorized the appointment of a Special Representative of the Secretary General (SRSG) for Western Sahara. Hector Gros Espiell of Uruguay was appointed in October, and served until his resignation in late 1989. His replacement was Johannes Manz, of Switzerland. Neither appears to have played a large role in the pre-deployment mediation effort. That role was reserved for the "peacemakers" in the Executive Office of the Secretary General.[11]

POLITICAL SUPPORT

Although the two local parties agreed in principle to a UN-supervised referendum in 1988, they remained far apart on important details right up to and after MINURSO's initial deployment. For POLISARIO the operation represented its last, best hope for political victory, whereas Morocco's support for MINURSO was calculated at best.

POLISARIO

After release of the UN peace plan, POLISARIO continued to insist on face-to-face talks with Moroccan authorities (much as Israel has insisted on direct talks with its Arab neighbors, because they convey symbolically important, de facto recognition of political status). POLISARIO also continued to insist upon complete withdrawal of Moroccan forces from Western Sahara before the vote, as well as the return of its own supporters to participate in the referendum. To add emphasis, POLISARIO increased its attacks on Moroccan interests in September 1988, but declared a unilateral truce late in the year after King Hassan agreed to meet with POLISARIO leaders in Marrakesh. This meeting took place January 4-5, 1989. POLISARIO supported the UN referendum as its best chance to win control of Western Sahara in one double-or-nothing role of the dice. Although its self-appointed government-in-exile had been recognized by roughly 70 countries, its military effort had been stymied by Morocco. A win in the referendum would, in practice, allow POLISARIO to set up its government of choice; a loss would require it to disarm and go out of business. Any fighters who had voted in the referendum would have already been disarmed and demobilized under MINURSO supervision. POLISARIO's supporters, especially Algeria, would be unlikely to back a return to the old guerrilla war, particularly if the referendum were declared "free and fair" by the UN. Moreover, POLISARIO would no longer have a political and popular base among the Tindouf refugee population on which to base a new campaign. Most of them would have been repatriated by MINURSO.

Morocco

King Hassan remained unbending toward POLISARIO throughout. In June 1990, he instructed Morocco's delegates to a UN voter identification commission meeting in Geneva to pass along his "fatherly greetings" to his "subjects," the POLISARIO representatives. In a November 1990 speech on the fifteenth anniversary of the "Green March," Hassan referred to his "sons and subjects living beyond the...frontiers of Morocco," and offered them a choice: returning to Morocco before the referendum, or voting in favor of Moroccan sovereignty, which would produce "neither winner nor loser." The following August, one month before the UN-supervised ceasefire in Western Sahara was to take effect, Hassan warned the Secretary General that MINURSO would not be allowed to proceed until outstanding differences over voter eligibility were resolved (see below). Finally, in his November 1991 "Green March" anniversary address, he spoke of "this confirmatory referendum [which] can only give us satisfaction."[12]

In short, even as the referendum approached, Hassan and Morocco were not reconciled to the possibility that they might have to give up the last remnant of "Greater Morocco." Moroccan participation in the UN referendum presupposed victory, and Rabat was doubtless chagrined in spring 1991 to find the UN truly expecting to conduct an open vote. It responded, that summer, with a list of 120,000 new names for the voting rolls, long-lost Sahrawis found to be living in southern Morocco. They were, in fact, far more numerous than the entire population of 74,000 counted in the final Spanish census of 1974, which had been the agreed basis for eligibility to vote. The UN's acceptance of the additional voters would give Rabat a lock on the election, and disagreement on this score stalled MINURSO for months.[13]

The Great Powers

France and the United States are the two permanent members of the Security Council most closely associated with Morocco and the two with the most interest in the outcome of the referendum. France is the former metropole, and the United States has long supported Morocco's moderate stance on East-West issues and on the Arab-Israeli dispute. On the other hand, the dispute over Western Sahara has not sufficiently engaged Perm Five interests to induce the sort of involvement that benefitted other recent conflict mediation efforts (for example, Namibia, Ethiopia, Cambodia, and Angola).

The Permanent Five objected to the cost of MINURSO (see the discussion on finances, below), but once that cost had been reduced, all five agreed to provide members of the mission's military observer group. The initiative to participate came from the Soviet Union, with initial support from the United States and reluctance on the part of the other three. When the US then hesitated, Morocco refused to accept any Perm Five observers unless all five participated, so in early July 1991 the US relented. Since that time, however, Washington's attention (or more to the point, that of President Bush, Secretary of State Baker, and the two men's closest advisors) has been focused elsewhere: on the Middle East peace process, on the status of nuclear weapons in the former Soviet Union, on the civil war in Yugoslavia, on the shaky peace in Cambodia, on the rise of Islamic fundamentalism (in, among other places, Algeria), and on the standoff between the UN and Iraq. Washington has not focused on the UN's other standoff, with Morocco, in the Western Sahara. This combination of local resistance and tepid international interest left MINURSO spinning its wheels in the desert for more than a year.

MANDATE

The long evolution of MINURSO's mandate suggested the political difficulty of the operation. Seeing what it was supposed to do, and comparing that with what it has been able to do, suggests the degree to which the operation was carried forward by a kind of collective wishful thinking on the part of an organization unwilling to admit the limits of international moral authority in a confrontation with nationalism. The UN looked for last-minute compromises although the agreement that it was supposed to implement presumed none. It presumed, instead, a binary choice.

The agreement in principle reached in August 1988 with PO-LISARIO and the government of Morocco gave the Special Representative of the Secretary General unusually broad authority over all matters in the territory relating to the referendum, including power to suspend local laws and regulations that could impede the conduct of a free and equitable vote. This principle carried through to the final mandate and, on paper, marked a watershed in UN peacekeeping. In the previous ground-breaking operation, in Namibia, the UN monitored and certified the election but did not conduct it, and could request the suspension of invidious statutes, but not demand it. In Western Sahara, the referendum was to be a UN operation from start to finish and the SRSG was to have final say over all relevant laws and regulations.

The 1988 Proposals

The 1988 settlement proposals called for a transitional period of unspecified length, starting with a formal ceasefire between Morocco and POLISARIO that was known in later plans, unfelicitously, as "D-Day." An Identification Commission would start work on D-Day to establish a list of eligible voters based on the 1974 Spanish census of the territory. Eligible voters were to be free to return to the territory and to vote without intimidation. The plan called for unspecified Moroccan troop withdrawals over a 12-week period following D-Day. Forces remaining in the territory were to be confined to their bases. When Moroccan withdrawals were complete, a UN military observer group would deploy to monitor remaining forces, oversee release of political prisoners, and "neutralize" Moroccan paramilitary forces. The loser of the referendum would quit the territory (Morocco by removing its forces, POLISARIO by disarming) within 24 hours of learning the results of the vote.

The 1988 proposals left some large gaps. Moroccan forces were given free run of the territory, unmonitored, for 12 weeks *after* the ceasefire, and their draw down would not have been monitored by the UN. Saharan refugees were allowed to return and vote, but no UN assistance was specified to help them do so, nor did an amnesty guarantee returnees' safety after the vote. The time frame for the losers' withdrawal (24 hours) betrayed a lack of appreciation for elemental military logistics and seemed to reflect the mediators' lack of familiarity with such operational matters.[14] Finally, the proposals did not specify what would happen in the territory if the referendum endorsed independence; there was no provision for a transitional regime or a constitutional conference. The UN would declare the results, monitor the loser's retirement, pack up, and go home.

The 1990 Plan

In June 1989, after a difficult year in which the parties held just one, brief, face-to-face meeting, the Secretary General once again traveled to meet King Hassan in Morocco and to visit POLISARIO camps in the region. He continued on to Mauritania, Mali, Senegal, and Algeria, looking without success to set a date for the referendum.[15] When talks dragged into the fall of 1989, POLISARIO demonstrated its impatience with the process by launching its first attacks against Morocco's Saharan sand wall in October and November. King Hassan used the attacks as a reason to abort further face-to-face talks with POLISARIO. Although the UN General Assembly called again for such talks in a December 1989 resolution, none were held. However, on February 21, 1990, in response to a request from the Secretary General and corresponding to the first visit of SRSG Manz to the region, King Hassan declared a unilateral truce. At the end of March, the Secretary General returned to the region in an effort to restart direct talks between Morocco and POLISARIO, again without success.[16]

Nonetheless, the Secretariat managed to draft a more detailed implementation plan for Western Sahara and present it to the Security Council in June 1990. The revised plan allocated more time to voter identification, starting the ID Commission's work 14 weeks before D-Day and relying heavily on the soundness of the existing, informal ceasefire to protect UN field staff. D-Day came to mean that point at which both sides would agree to confine their forces to barracks under UN supervision.

The 1990 plan also provided for MINURSO's military unit to be "effectively deployed throughout its area of operations" by D-Day, not differentiating among infantry, observers, and support elements. This envisaged deployment of the full force helped to drive up the cost of the mission. Uncertainty about field conditions helped to drive it up even more.[17]

The 1991 Plan

The final operational plan that emerged in April 1991 filled in some more gaps. It specified the type and number of Moroccan troops to remain in Western Sahara after draw down, and the size and composition of the civilian and military components of MINURSO. Reflecting fiscal concerns, it moved up the date of the referendum by four weeks, reduced the period of political campaigning from six weeks to three, and lopped a week off Morocco's withdrawal schedule. The resulting squeeze on the process of voter registration was addressed by letting the Identification Commission begin its work as soon as the Security Council approved the plan and before the General Assembly approved the overall budget. The rest of the mission timetable was keyed to budget approval, a procedure that reflected the UN's experience with its Namibia operation in 1989, where a fixed starting date ran afoul of unexpected delays in budget approval. The delays nearly wrecked that mission in its first week.[18] The complex mission timetable approved by the Security Council for MINURSO is given in Table 23.1.

In a change from the 1990 plan, deployment of the infantry unit was delayed until ten weeks after the ceasefire, near the end of Morocco's troop reduction and the beginning of voter repatriation, for which the infantry unit would provide security. Military observers and support elements, deployed by D-Day, would monitor the confinement of forces and the pullout of Moroccan units.

Table 23.1. Mission Timetable for MINURSO

Timeline	Related Mission Activity
D-Day minus 18	Security Council authorizes MINURSO and the Identification Commission begins work.
D-Day minus 16	General Assembly approves the budget. SG appoints Referendum Commission and Independent Jurist.
D-Day minus 12	The local parties accept SG's proposed date and time for D-Day ceasefire. Initial administrative units and logistics battalion deploy. ID Commission publishes revised census list.
D-Day minus 9	First ID Commission mobile team arrives in the territory.
D-Day minus 8	Deadline to apply for inclusion on voter lists. Bulk of air support unit is deployed.
D-Day minus 4	Signals and medical units, and advance party of military observers, deployed. Deputy Special Representative arrives in mission area.
D-Day minus 2	Remainder of civilian administrative and support staff deploy.
D-Day minus 1	Special Representative arrives in mission area. Remainder of military observers deploy. Parties inform MINURSO of the strengths and locations of their forces.
D-Day and "as soon as possible" thereafter.	Publication of consolidated voter lists; voter registration begins. Ceasefire comes into effect, transitional period begins, combatants are confined to UN-designated locations. Exchanges of prisoners of war, proclamations of general amnesty, release of political prisoners and detainees.
D+10	Infantry battalion arrives. Remaining civilian police arrive.
D+11	Draw down of Moroccan forces completed. Local laws contrary to a free and fair election are suspended by the UN. Voter registration is complete and final voter list is published. Repatriation program begins. "Paramilitary units in existing police forces are neutralized," their arms held by the UN.
D+17	Repatriation completed. Referendum campaign begins.
D+18	Additional polling officers deploy to the territory.
D+20	Referendum. Proclamation of results. MINURSO begins to withdraw. Morocco begins withdrawal, if it loses; POLISARIO disbands under UN oversight, if it loses. No rules as to what either side does if it wins.
D+24/26	Loser's withdrawal/disbandment complete. MINURSO responsibilities at an end.
"Thereafter"	Operation is shut down, equipment is disposed of, and remaining MINURSO personnel withdraw from Western Sahara.

Source: UN Document A/22464, April 19, 1991.

Neither side was obliged to reveal the strength or locations of its forces until one week before the ceasefire. Moroccan forces were to be confined to "static or defensive positions along the sand wall," and reduced in size to 65,000 troops, with reductions to be made in "intervention forces," air interdiction capability, and "offensive operations" units. UN military observers would disarm and confine to barracks all local paramilitary units (reflecting another lesson from Namibia, where paramilitary police forces initially roamed at will). POLISARIO units were to be confined to locations near but outside the sand wall, a solution that caused some discomfort on the Moroccan side, which preferred to have no POLISARIO bivouacs within the borders of Western Sahara. POLISARIO fighters who wished to vote in the referendum were to go to Tindouf to be registered, disarmed, and repatriated along with other refugees.[19]

The Identification Commission really began its work, in low-key fashion, in 1989, but it was formally established along with the rest of MINURSO by vote of the Security Council on April 29, 1991. The Commission's revised census list was to be published in late June 1991. Saharans who believed themselves eligible to vote but whose names did not appear on the list would then have four weeks (until late July) to file appeals with the Commission. A final list of eligible voters was to be published before D-Day, by mutual agreement of the UN and the parties, after which the transition would begin.

After D-Day, the process of voter registration—contacting individuals, verifying their identities, and giving them ID cards—was to take another eleven weeks. Registration of Saharan refugees would take place in the Algerian camps. Movement (repatriation) of voters and their immediate families who had been registered would then begin under the auspices of the UN High Commissioner for Refugees and the protection of MINURSO's infantry unit. Returnees would be processed through UN checkpoints over a six-week period, and would have the benefit of a general political amnesty that applied to combatants and noncombatants alike. (How the amnesty was to be promulgated proved a political sticking point, as POLISARIO did not seek, nor would it accept, "amnesty" from King Hassan for having fought, in its view, for Saharans' rights to self-determination.)

The main problem facing MINURSO at this stage proved to be the correlation of names on the census list with living individuals. Because Western Sahara was historically a nomadic, pastoral society that lacked such basic written evidence of citizenship as birth certificates, MINURSO was forced to fall back on the personal memories of the society's numerous tribal chiefs, whose honest cooperation became the linchpin of the registration effort.

As the Identification Commission completed its work, most of its staff were to transition to the Referendum Commission, the unit responsible for running the vote. During the three-week "referendum campaign," the UN would publicize the free and fair nature of the referendum while the two local parties conducted their own partisan campaigns. The Referendum Commission would recommend to the SRSG changes in or suspensions of local laws or regulations not in harmony with the proper conduct of the referendum. The referendum itself was to take place twenty weeks after the ceasefire, in late January 1992; or later if the Special Representative determined that conditions were not yet conducive to a free and fair election.

Following the UN's announcements of the referendum results, the loser would withdraw (or demobilize) as described earlier. But the plan remained silent as to the nature of an independent Saharan government, and as to the status of Moroccan settlers, more than 100,000 of whom had come into the territory by 1991. Thus MINURSO's mandate left open the possibility of a post-vote "purge" of settlers by a victorious POLISARIO, not unlike the forced exodus of guest-workers from Nigeria in the late 1980s, to make room in the economy for the tens of thousands of returned refugees. Nor did the plan preclude a similar crackdown on returnees by Morocco, amnesty notwithstanding, if POLISARIO lost. In the words of one official close to the planning process, "In this place [traditionally], if you lose, they hang you."[20]

All UN peacekeeping operations depend on the cooperation of the local parties, but the character of the situation in Western Sahara imposed special burdens on the implementation plan. In Namibia, South Africa was committed to withdrawal from the territory before UNTAG deployed. Morocco made no such prior decision to vacate Western Sahara. Indeed, its announced expectations of victory were more than the usual upbeat sloganeering one expects from political campaigns. Morocco both expected to win and took unsubtle steps to insure it, including the belated "discovery," noted earlier, of more long-lost voters than there were names on the census that had served, since at least 1988, as the agreed basis of voter eligibility. Seeing in MINURSO's mandate a more or less ironclad guarantee of a free and fair election, Morocco used the eligibility issue to guarantee a favorable outcome. If the UN accepted the proposed new names, Morocco would be assured of winning the vote; if it did not, then Morocco could use its sovereign powers to throw MINURSO into stasis and wait until the UN ran out of patience, money, or both.

FUNDING

The three-year delay in pulling together the implementation plan for MINURSO meant that, by the time its budget came before the Fifth (Financial) Committee of the General Assembly, and its Advisory Committee on Administrative and Budgetary Questions (ACABQ), the UN was deep into its second surge of peacekeeping since the end of the Cold War, with new missions underway or about to start in Kuwait, Angola, and El Salvador, and the largest operation in history, for Cambodia, just over the horizon. Moreover, the Organization's finances were still deeply in arrears. In mid-1991, the UN was about $200 million in the red on peacekeeping alone (a significant amount, since total assessments for peacekeeping that year totaled just $490 million). Thus it was an inauspicious time to bring a large new mission before the UN's funding bodies.

The mission's complex and ambitious mandate at first generated an estimated budget of $260 million for a 36-week operation. Its annualized rate of spending was equivalent to that of the operation in Namibia for one-tenth as many voters. MINURSO had greater operational responsibilities, including the actual conduct of the referendum, but that did not keep member states from balking at the cost.

The Western Sahara Task Force (discussed below) tried twice without success to produce satisfactory budgets in the fall of 1990. In late April 1991, its working group met in a marathon session to reduce projected spending by at least 30 percent. The budget was first reduced to $200 million and then to $177 million, partly by the simple expedient of excising the money for repatriation of refugees. Although the Secretary General's planning reports continued to talk of their "integral" role in the mission, the UN's refugee people gained a seat on the working group relatively late in the game. Moreover, the ability of the Geneva-based office of the UN High Commissioner for Refugees (UNHCR) to protect its position was hampered by the six time zones and 5,000 kilometers that separated its decision makers from the New York planning process.[21]

Aware that the permanent members of the Security Council were growing resistant to the rising cost of peacekeeping, the Secretary General assured an informal session of the Council that he would review MINURSO's plan with an eye toward reducing its actual expenditures. On April 29, the Council authorized the mission, and on May 6, the ACABQ agreed to release roughly $600,000 to fund the operation of MINURSO's Identification

Commission. It had earlier approved about $300,000 to operate the office of the Special Representative. Both amounts were drawn against the Secretary General's small ($10 million) annual fund for "unforeseen and extraordinary" expenses.

The ACABQ then spent a week assessing that budget, and its unusually critical report to the Fifth Committee reflected member states' (and particularly US) concerns about MINURSO planning. The report took the Secretariat to task about the cost of air transport; about housing for staff, per diem rates, and vehicle purchases; and about the number of high-ranking posts associated with the mission. Adding, in some sense, insult to injury, it also demanded a detailed budget for the voluntarily financed UNHCR repatriation effort.[22]

The ACABQ took particular umbrage at the plan's top-heavy personnel roster, which included two Under-Secretaries General and three Assistant-Secretaries General. However, its recommended fix (one USG, the Special Representative, and only one ASG, the Force Commander) triggered an immediate and angry reaction from the Secretariat. Particularly exercised was the office of the Under-Secretary for Administration and Management, Martti Ahtisaari, who as head of the UN's operation in Namibia experienced great frustration with a military deputy. The ACABQ's action seemed, moreover, to endorse a traditional, "Middle East" model of peacekeeping—a military operation with political overtones—whereas multicomponent operations like MINURSO are viewed in the Secretariat as fundamentally political operations conducted with military support. For the status-conscious (and military-averse) Secretariat, then, a military deputy for MINURSO would not do. Following Ahtisaari's personal intervention, the Fifth Committee approved a budget with one USG and two ASGs, giving the Deputy Special Representative and the Force Commander equal rank.[23]

To encourage greater austerity, the United States pressed for a "two-step budget" that would appropriate only part of the amount requested for the operation, pending later review of actual spending rates. UN officials viewed this proposal with concern bordering on indignation, as it both second-guessed their competence (and integrity) in mission planning, and could leave a time-limited mission short of funds at a critical stage. In the case of MINURSO, six months coincided, in the original plans, with the start of voter repatriation, a critical phase of the mission. However, the General Assembly concurred, appropriating $140 million for the first six months of the operation, with the remainder subject to a separate vote in the fall 1991 session.[24]

PLANNING AND IMPLEMENTATION

The UN has been dealing with the Saharan situation for some years and has had the opportunity to become thoroughly familiar with it. The UN's first investigative mission was sent to the region in late 1975. UNHCR has funded relief to the Saharan refugee camps from its General Fund since 1980 and is familiar with their situation.[25] A second fact-finding mission visited the region in late 1987. The Identification Commission began work in 1989 to prepare a roster of eligible voters. Two further field missions were dispatched in July and December 1990 to scout out the terrain. Yet for all this preliminary work, planning for MINURSO was singularly disjointed, in part because of the organizational and informational gap between political mediators and mission planners, a gap widened in 1988 by the formal withdrawal of all "peacemaking" functions into the Executive Office of the Secretary General.[26]

Detailed mission planning also depended on the shape of the supporting political arrangements, and important parts of those arrangements remained unsettled through 1990. POLISARIO wanted Moroccan troops to vacate Western Sahara before the vote and wanted the UN to take over administration of the territory. Morocco resisted both of these proposals, successfully, even as it continued to resist direct talks with POLISARIO. The SRSG was, oddly enough, not closely involved in the mediation effort. Indeed, in the final year before deployment, the SRSG's office often remained in the dark about negotiating results having a direct bearing on the mission that it was supposed to run.

MINURSO planning also suffered from a lack of stability at the top. Of the high-level peacekeeping Task Forces set up by Secretary General Pérez de Cuéllar following administrative reforms in 1987-88, only the one for Western Sahara was not chaired by the Undersecretary for Special Political Affairs (SPA), Marrack Goulding. Western Sahara was instead the purview of the USG for Special Political Questions, Regional Cooperation, Decolonization and Trusteeship, Abdulrahim Farah. Other members of the Task Force included Goulding and the Under-Secretaries for Legal Affairs (Carl-August Fleishchauer) and Administration and Management (Ahtisaari), the Special Representative (Manz, who held the rank of USG), the Controller (then Kofi Annan, an ASG), and the chief mediator from the SG's Executive Office (Issa Diallo).[27]

When Farah retired in late 1990, his post was assumed by James Jonah, a career official who has a long association with UN peacekeeping. However, dissatisfaction with the new arrangement quickly led the SG, in January 1991, to give responsibility for the Task Force to Goulding. But he and SPA were by this time watching the Second Persian Gulf War unfold and preparing contingency plans for expected UN involvement in its aftermath. At the same time, SPA's handful of political and military officers were involved in advance planning for expected operations in Cambodia, El Salvador, and Angola, where diplomatic initiatives looked to be on the verge of producing political settlements incorporating extensive UN peacekeeping operations. As a result, MINURSO drifted for several months.[28]

Shaping the Mission Plan

A few weeks after the Security Council gave the 1990 plan its interim approval, a 32-person technical mission went to Western Sahara for three weeks to gather data to be used in crafting the operation's budget. Headed by mediator Diallo, rather than Special Representative Manz, the large mission included an official from Manz's small New York office, a team from the UN's Field Operations Division (which does logistics), a civilian UN communications specialist (UN civilians manage communications with New York), and a military group headed by UN Military Advisor Timothy Dibuama. The latter group included a Polish logistics specialist, Canadian infantry and air transport officers, Swiss medical officers, and an Australian signals officer (all representatives of the national units that would be selected for the mission one year later, indicating that a large degree of selection had already been done by mid-1990). Also involved were a repatriation team from UNHCR and representatives from the World Food Program, the UN Department of Public Information, and the OAU.[29]

Although there were expectations in mid-1990 that MINURSO might be able to go ahead later in the year, the technical mission reportedly recommended a "radical" restructuring of the implementation plan in ways that, inadvertently or not, favored Morocco. Meetings of the Task Force continued through the fall of 1990, as the implementation date receded. Another fact-finding mission visited the region in December 1990, but by this point communications within the Secretariat regarding MINURSO were sufficiently fragmentary that its report was not seen by key officials in SPA until July, when the mission was already underway. Because of the unknowns about voter identification and the uncertainty about the level of cooperation to be expected from the local parties, especially Morocco, even the final mission plan was considered by some close to the operation to be nearly unworkable.[30]

Size and Composition of the Operation

MINURSO plans called for 1,695 military and 1,600 civilian personnel. Some 580 civilians were to come from member states and 459 were to be recruited locally. Table 23.2 shows the maximum size, and source, of each field component.

Table 23.2. Components of MINURSO

Component	No./Source of Personnel			
	UN	Govts.	Local	Total
Office of the Special Representative	49	0	16	65
Identification Commission and staff	89	75	70	234
Referendum Commission and staff	18	15	0	33
Staff shared with ID Commission	25	0	10	35
Office of the Independent Jurist	5	0	0	5
Administrative staff	275	0	225	500
Information service	9	0	4	13
Other support staff	11	0	39	50
Polling officers (D+20 to D+23 only)	80	190	95	365
Civilian police (300 deployed thru D+10; 300 in reserve)	0	300	0	300
Military police	0	40	0	40
Infantry battalion (from D+10)	0	700	0	700
Military observers	0	550	0	550
Logistics battalion	0	200	0	200
Air support unit	0	110	0	110
Medical unit	0	50	0	50
Signals unit	0	45	0	45
Totals:	561	2275	459	3295

Source: UN Secretariat.

More than 50 countries agreed to contribute personnel or units to MINURSO. Canada provided the Force Commander, Major General Armand Roy, and Peru the Deputy Commander, Brigadier General Luis Block Urban. Australia agreed to send a signals unit, Poland a logistics unit, and Switzerland a medical team. Canada was the source of one infantry battalion and an air unit, both components of its UN standby force. The operation's heavy technical demands led to the use of military units predominantly from Western industrial countries. This often happens because most developing states' militaries lack the necessary long-range communications, logistics, and mobility required by a mission like MINURSO. Moreover, developed countries can better afford the wait for reimbursement from the financially strapped UN.[31]

In MINURSO, the principle of "equitable geographic distribution" was made good in the staffing of other components. Thirty-one countries (21 of them nominally developing) offered to contribute military observers and 25 (17 developing) to contribute civilian police. In addition, Cuba, Egypt, Japan, Jordan, Namibia, New Zealand, Pakistan, Singapore, and Tunisia pledged to send election observers. Countries contributing military observers or civilian police are listed in Table 23.3.

Table 23.3. Countries Contributing Military Observers or Civilian Police to MINURSO

Country	Military Observers	Civilian Police	Country	Military Observers	Civilian Police
Argentina	X	X	Indonesia	X	
Austria	X	X	Ireland	X	X
Bangladesh	X		Italy	X	
Belgium		X	Kenya	X	
Benin		X	Malaysia	X	X
Bulgaria	X	X	Mauritius		X
Cameroon		X	Nepal	X	
Canada		X	Nigeria	X	X
Chile		X	Norway		X
China	X		Pakistan	X	
Congo	X		Peru	X	X
Costa Rica		X	Singapore	X	X
Czech / Slovak Rep.	X	X	Togo	X	X
Egypt	X		Tunisia	X	X
Finland	X		Turkey	X	
France	X		USSR	X	
Germany		X	Uruguay		X
Ghana	X	X	UK	X	
Greece	X		United States	X	
Guinea			Vanuatu		X
Honduras	X		Venezuela	X	X
India	X	X	**Total countries:**	31	25

Source: UN Secretariat.

Command, Communications, and Logistics

MINURSO was designed as an integrated operation with the Special Representative in overall charge and a Deputy Special Representative to run things in his absence. The military Force Commander, the Police Commissioner, the Chief Administrative Officer, and the heads of the Identification and Referendum Commissions all were to report to the SRSG. The military logistics unit was to provide support for the entire operation, along with UN civilian logisticians co-located with that unit. The mission plan called for MINURSO's military unit to render assistance as needed to the operation's civilian police, especially for polling place security (another lesson learned from Namibia, where such assistance was hard to come by).[32]

The size of the area of operations, which included both Western Sahara and adjacent locations that were home to Saharan refugees (near Tindouf, Algeria), as well as the paucity of paved roads, dictated a decentralized operation with heavy reliance on air transport and surveillance to supplement the usual fleet of white UN four-wheel-drive vehicles, and extensive use of satellite communications. For communications to New York, the mission purchased a trailer-mounted Intelsat earth station. For communications between the eight field offices and mission headquarters, MINURSO was to use smaller, portable INMARSAT terminals, radio teletype, and encrypted radio-facsimile machines. MINURSO was also one of the first UN missions slated to give its personnel handheld NAVSTAR Global Positioning System receivers able to calculate the user's location within 100 meters. Ground vehicles were to be equipped with shortwave radios and individual observers with line-of-sight very-high-frequency (VHF) walkie-talkies. Each of the mission's 24 remote team sites would have a VHF repeater to boost radio signals transmitted over the territory's large expanses of desert.[33]

Aircraft were to be used heavily for monitoring and logistical support, with observers using four light, fixed-wing aircraft. Eight helicopters would provide lift and surveillance capabilities for sectors without airstrips and a chartered C-130 cargo aircraft —an unusual acquisition—would provide heavy lift capability. Facilitating the use of these units, MINURSO was to have freedom of movement over its area of operations. Moroccan air traffic controllers were permitted by the mission plan to interrupt the movements of UN air units only for legitimate technical reasons,

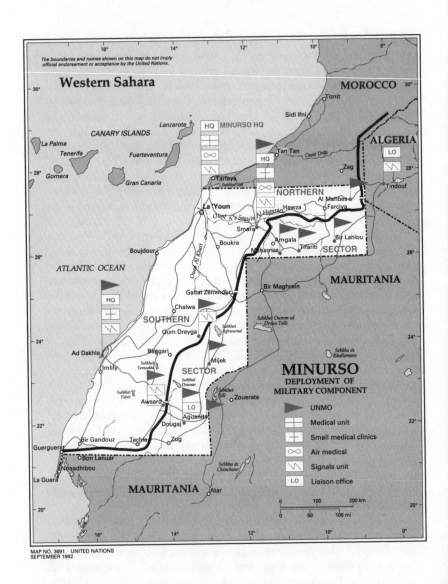

Figure 23.1. United Nations Mission for the Referendum in Western Sahara, Deployment as of May 1992

and UN experts were to be on hand in or near the control towers to verify the validity of any such requests.[35]

In its review of MINURSO's budget, the ACABQ complained about the cost of all of these items. Some of the communications gear may indeed have been redundant under normal circumstances, and the UN has traditionally been reluctant to pay for any redundancy in its field missions, lest it be charged with wasting member states' money. But such a stringently cost-conscious approach can prove disastrously short-sighted if conditions in the field turn nasty or the mission's one secure line to New York breaks down. A time-limited mission, in particular, has but one chance to do its job; it hasn't the endless, if boring, luxury of fine-tuning its operations through years of trial and error.[35]

Field Operations

In Western Sahara, the UN faced a military situation in which Morocco deployed 130,000 well-equipped troops, mostly along the sand wall, backed by air power. POLISARIO had a few thousand well-organized guerrilla fighters, most of whom were based outside the sand wall. The sides were observing an informal ceasefire at the time MINURSO began to deploy.

Given the nature of the situation, only the total cooperation of both sides with the objectives and procedures specified in MINURSO's mandate would permit the referendum to be carried out peacefully and successfully. As the operation began, neither side showed any expectation of losing, yet the success of the mission depended upon the loser's willingness to withdraw gracefully from the field. Absent such willingness, the UN's credibility as a guarantor of political transitions stood to be damaged, with implications for future operations, particularly in Africa, a continent whose people appear increasingly impatient with nondemocratic forms of rule.

The portents were ominous approaching September 6, 1991, the agreed date for the cease-fire. The Identification Commission had been working since the spring to edit the 1974 census list of 74,000 names that was to be the basis of voter eligibility. Morocco, having anticipated for several years that the vote would go its way, became worried when neighbor Algeria, and the UN, both seemed to be insisting that the referendum really be conducted in a free and fair manner. In mid-summer 1991, Morocco moved to shore up its position with the list of new names noted earlier, requiring that the Identification Commission take valuable time to track down the names, associate them with individuals, and accept or reject them as voters. This amounted to an added processing requirement of 1,000 names per day if the original timetable was to be kept, an impossible task. The revised list of eligible voters, originally planned for release in September 1991, had not been published as of late 1992.

Delaying the referendum worked in Morocco's favor. As the prospective date for the vote receded into 1992, the 1974 census became increasingly invalid, as Saharans born since the old census turned 18 and became eligible to vote. Should a new census be necessary, it would be very difficult to prove that Moroccans who have settled in the country since 1976 are not, indeed, "Saharans" of longer standing with a right to vote.

Although King Hassan warned the Secretary General in August 1991 that he would not let MINURSO deploy until the issue of voter eligibility had been settled, the UN hewed to the agreed date of September 6 for the cease-fire and deployed 200 military observers (the most allowed by Morocco) into Western Sahara. They established ten austere field sites, five on Morocco's side of the sand wall, and five across the wall, with POLISARIO. Morocco would not allow deployment of UN logistics, communications, or medical units, and held up other UN equipment at Agadir (the sole official port of entry). Although Morocco assumed responsibility for support of the 200 UN observers, that support was marginal, forcing the observers to tend more to survival and housekeeping than to their appointed tasks.[36]

The freedom of movement granted MINURSO in its mandate failed to materialize. Moroccan units obstructed UN patrols, sometimes at gunpoint. Part of the difficulty could be traced to the lack of a Status of Forces Agreement, which the UN normally signs with the host country at an early point in every mission.[37]

By contrast, POLISARIO was very cooperative and supportive of UN units to the extent of its abilities. Since the referendum represented its last, best shot at political power, it was of course in POLISARIO's interest to be supportive of the UN.

The Secretary General issued three reports on MINURSO through May 1992. The first report stretched the definition of voter eligibility to anyone whose father had been born in Western Sahara, as well as to their immediate family. This was a step toward Morocco's position that there were indeed Saharans outside the territory when the 1974 census was taken, but not a big enough step to suit Morocco.[38]

After the turn of the year, Morocco did allow entry to MINURSO's air unit, medical unit, and signals unit (although perhaps not its communications equipment). To save money, all nonessential personnel were being repatriated from the operation. As of late May, there had been 102 cease-fire violations reported, 97 attributed to Morocco and five to POLISARIO. The continued laying of minefields posed the greatest hazard to UN personnel.[39]

Reflecting in part the frustrations of his assignment, Special Representative Manz resigned effective the first of the year. His Deputy was appointed acting SRSG, but was in turn asked to resign at the end of February, having performed unsatisfactorily. In late March, Morocco and POLISARIO finally agreed on Sahabzada Yaqub-Khan of Pakistan as the new Special Representative.

In his February report to the Security Council, the Secretary General promised to keep working on behalf of the Saharan referendum, but stressed frequently the need for full cooperation from the parties, which in practice means the full cooperation of Morocco. He noted, however, that the patience and the resources of the international community are finite, and warned that continued lack of progress would force a reassessment of the entire situation. His report in May stressed that, while MINURSO's military observers were helping to maintain the cease-fire, the referendum plan remained in abeyance.[40] The peace process remained deadlocked through the summer and into the fall of 1992.

ASSESSMENT AND CONCLUSIONS

By spring 1991, MINURSO and its gestational troubles had become Exhibit A for those who believed that the formal separation of peacemaking and peacekeeping by the Secretary General in 1988 was a potential disaster in the making. The lack of formal lines of communication and authority between the mediators and the operational planners (the Western Sahara Task Force notwithstanding) hampered both mission planning and effective negotiation. Politics is the art of the possible, and with neither experience in operational peacekeeping nor direct lines to the UN's operational people, the mediators were in a poor position to sift the possible from the fanciful. Such reality checks were doubly important in the kind of indirect mediation effort that Moroccan policies made necessary, and they were evidently lacking until very late in the game. The close hold on what was discussed and concluded in the negotiations allowed the parties, in certain instances, to contradict UN understandings about what had been agreed on key points (for example, the location of UN-supervised security zones for POLISARIO fighters). It also encouraged the floating of dark rumors of a pro-Moroccan bias on the part of the UN negotiating team.

The operation was carried forward, some contend, by the wave of euphoria that followed the formal cease-fire in the Second Gulf War. MINURSO was sent over the top with UNIKOM, the mission to monitor Kuwait's borders, despite ongoing difficulties in nailing down the details of the referendum. Voter eligibility, long highlighted as a likely bone of contention in the best of circumstances, became the issue used, successfully, by Morocco to bring the referendum process to a dead halt without having to pull out of it entirely.

MINURSO suffered from some very basic problems. The operation did not enjoy the consent of all local parties. Morocco really only consented to host a successful referendum that would destroy POLISARIO's claim to political legitimacy, and for all practical purposes withdrew its consent when the outcome of the referendum could not be assured. With time on its side, Morocco was content to outwait the UN, knowing that its members would not wish to finance indefinitely a mission that was dead in the water.

Second, although MINURSO was perceived as impartial, to a partisan local party like Morocco that is still bent on victory, the operation's impartiality was a liability, not an asset.

Third, the operation did not enjoy the close and continuing political support of the Great Powers. Rather, the United States was preoccupied with the Middle East peace process, in which Morocco was seen as a valuable "Arab moderate." Morocco was also shrewd enough to keep itself on the good side of international lending institutions, who represented a further potential source of external pressure on the government. Finally, other, larger peacekeeping missions in Yugoslavia and Cambodia were growing rapidly and diverting UN money and attention from the Western Sahara, which is much further off the beaten track of international politics. MINURSO was orphaned by a political system unable or unwilling to give it needed support.

Barring some dramatic turnaround at the political level, as of fall 1992 it appeared that MINURSO would fail to implement its mandate. Morocco had slated nation-wide elections for late in the year that encompassed Western Sahara. POLISARIO, having lost its major foreign patrons and its bid for political power through the UN referendum plan, was reported to be fading away. The refugee population remained in Tindouf, its fate uncertain. Its best hope lay in the prospect that Morocco might support its return to a Western Sahara that could be given a tangible degree of autonomy within the Moroccan state.

Notes

1. Thomas Franck, "Theory and Practice of Decolonization: the Western Sahara Case," in Richard Lawless and Laila Monahan, eds., *War and Refugees, The Western Sahara Conflict* (London and New York: Printer Publishers, 1987), 10-12; United Nations, "Western Sahara Peace Proposal is Made by UN Secretary General," *UN Backgrounder*, September 1988.

Iraq's 1990 invasion of Kuwait was based on historic claims similar to Morocco's, and was rejected by the international community through the actions of the Security Council. In the case of the Western Sahara, 15 years earlier, the Security Council did not act.

2. Franck, "Theory and Practice of Decolonization," 10-12; David Seddon, "Morocco at War," 100-101; *Africa Research Bulletin*, July 1990, 9715.

3. Seddon, "Morocco at War," 102-3. Also I. William Zartman, *Ripe for Resolution: Conflict and Intervention in Africa*, updated ed. (New York and Oxford: Oxford University Press, 1989).

4. Seddon, "Morocco at War," 105-8; *New York Times*, August 15, 1985, I,1; *Facts on File, 1987* (New York: Facts on File, Inc., 1987), 344.

5. Henry Wiseman, "The OAU: Peacekeeping and Conflict Resolution," in Yassin El-Ayouty and I. William Zartman, eds., *The OAU after Twenty Years* (New York: Praeger Publishers, 1984), 136-37; Seddon, "Morocco at War," 110-111; and OAU Resolution AHG/104, June 1983.

6. *Facts on File, 1985*, 825-26.

7. The locusts bred, fittingly enough, in the Sahara-Mauritania border region, in the wake of unusually heavy rains in 1986. From there, the disturbance spread north and east (*Facts on File, 1988*, 359).

8. Zartman, *Ripe for Resolution*, 46; International Institute for Strategic Studies, *Strategic Survey 1988–89* (London: Brassey's, 1989), 186-87, 189, 193.

9. *New York Times*, July 1, 1985, 1; *Facts on File, 1985*, 825; Seddon, "Morocco at War," 111.

10. *Strategic Survey*, 1988–89, 192-93; *Facts on File, 1988*, 359.

11. *Strategic Survey, 1988–89*, 193; *Keesing's Record of World Events, 1989* (London: Longman, 1989), 37014-15. For the preliminary implementation plan, see the September 1988 proposals of the Secretary General, contained in United Nations Document S/21360, June 18, 1990, 5-12.

12. *Financial Times*, November 8, 1991, 8.

13. *Keesing's Record of World Events, 1990* (London: Longman), 37221; *Africa Research Bulletin*, February 1990, 9561, July 1990, 9715, and November 1990, 9890. Also *Financial Times*, November 6, 1991, 4, and November 8, 1991, 8.

14. United Nations, *The Situation Concerning Western Sahara: Report of the Secretary General*, Security Council Document S/21360, June 18, 1990, 6-12.

15. *Keesing's, 1989*, 36748.

16. *Keesing's 1990*, 37221; *Africa Research Bulletin*, March 1990, 9597, and April 1990, 9634; and United Nations Document S/21360, 7.

17. United Nations Document S/21360, 16.

18. United Nations, *The Situation Concerning Western Sahara: Report of the Secretary General*, Security Council document S/22464, April 19, 1991, and Corr. 1, April 22, 1991. UN infantry battalions were delayed in deploying to Namibia in early 1989. In early April, forces of the Southwest Africa People's Organization (SWAPO), which were to have remained in their encampments in Angola while the UN supervised voting for Namibia's first constituent assembly, poured across Angola's southern border into Namibia. The director of the UN's Transition Assistance Group in Namibia authorized South African Defense Force elements to leave their barracks to confront SWAPO and, in the fighting that followed, several hundred people died (*New York Times*, April 4 1989 A1, A6; *United Nations Chronicle*, June 1989, 6).

19. United Nations Documents S/21360, 16; S/22464, 5. The numbers and locations of these POLISARIO encampments, to be established by MINURSO at Aquamite, Tifani, and Majit Mal, had been agreed to by both parties. At the last minute, reference to this fact disappeared from the draft of United Nations Document S/22464, and Morocco subsequently refused to allow any POLISARIO encampments on Saharan territory.

20. Interview 37, January 1991.

21. Interview 70, June 1991.

22. United Nations, General Assembly, *Financing of the United Nations Mission for the Referendum in Western Sahara: Report of the Advisory Committee on Administrative and Budgetary Questions*, A/45/1011, May 13, 1991, 3-5. UN and government-provided personnel on mission, other than those in military units, are provided a "mission subsistence allowance," in effect a per diem. The rate for Western Sahara was set at $85, or $65 if the UN provided housing. Although housing was budgeted for virtually the entire international mission (military and civilian), the Secretariat's per diem budget assumed that only 30 percent of the civilians would be UN-housed. The ACABQ urged the SG to "pursue every effort to obtain premises for the operation and accommodation of the staff without cost to MINURSO," that is, Morocco should pay.

23. Interview 63, May 1991; United Nations Document A/45/1011, May 13, 1991; and United Nations, General Assembly, Financing of the United Nations Mission for the Referendum in Western Sahara: Report of the Fifth Committee, A/45/1013, May 16, 1991.

24. See United Nations Document A/45/1013 for the results of three days of Fifth Committee debate on the MINURSO budget. In actuality, the amount initially appropriated was more than enough to fund the truncated deployment of MINURSO through the end of 1991.

25. James Firebrace, "The Sahrawi Refugees: Lessons and Prospects," in *War and Refugees*, 173.

26. William J. Durch and Barry M. Blechman, *Keeping the Peace: The United Nations in the Emerging World Order* (Washington, D.C.: The Henry L. Stimson Center, March 1992), 69.

27. Interviews 25, December 1990; 37, January 1991; and 60, 68, 70, May-June, 1991.

28. Interview 47, February 27, 1991, and 68, May, 15, 1991. As MINURSO prepared to deploy, chief mediator Diallo took a new, unrelated job as Executive Secretary of the Economic Commission for Africa, headquartered in Nairobi. His replacement, Mr. Rizvi, was appointed in June 1991 with the title of Deputy Special Representative.

29. Interviews 37, January 1991; 68, May 1991; 71, June 1991. Morocco considered the OAU partial to POLISARIO and accordingly restricted the movement of the UN team's OAU representative. The friction between Morocco and the OAU led the UN to downplay the extent of coordination between the two organizations with respect to MINURSO, but the OAU expected to have teams of observers with the operation, and provision was made for them in MINURSO's budget.

30. Interviews 60, 68, May 1991. As late as January 1991, people close to the planning effort still expected MINURSO to deploy by May (Interview 37).

31. Countries contributing forces to the UN operations in Cyprus and Lebanon have waited, sometimes for years, for reimbursement (the Cyprus operation is voluntarily funded and the one in Lebanon was subject to politically motivated withholdings of contributions by the governments of the former Warsaw Pact, and by the United States). For a listing of arrearages in peacekeeping contributions, see United Nations, *Status of Contributions as at 31 December 1991*, Document ST/ADM/SER.B/364, January 8, 1992.

32. Interviews 63 and 64, May 1991; United Nations Document S/21360, June 18, 1990, 20.

33. United Nations Document A/45/241/Add.1, May 8, 1991, 33.

34. United Nations Document A/45/241/Add.1, 33; and interview 64, May 1991.

35. If the UN, including the ACABQ, gets serious about an equipment stockpile for peacekeeping operations, then some of the necessary mission redundancy can be had at a discount. It may well be that UN mission planners saw a chance to initiate a stockpile, using MINURSO as a cash cow. Member states have been singularly reluctant to fund equipment with no immediate mission application.

36. See Senate Committee on Foreign Relations, *The Western Sahara: The Referendum Process is in Danger*, 102d Cong., 2d sess., January 1992, S.Prt. 102-75, 5-7.

37. *The Western Sahara*, 8-9.

38. See *Report of the Secretary General on the United Nations Mission for the Referendum in Western Sahara*, S/23299, December 19, 1991,

annex; and United Nations Documents S/23662, February 28, 1992, 7, and S/24040, May 29, 1992.

39. United Nations Document S/24040, 3.

40. United Nations Document S/24040, 4.

Part Five:

Peacekeeping in the Western Hemisphere

24   UN Observer Group in Central America

by Brian D. Smith and William J. Durch

The United Nations Observer Group in Central America (ONUCA) was the first UN peacekeeping operation in the Western Hemisphere, once the exclusive security preserve of the United States. Its deployment marked the end of the Cold War in Central America, and it supported regional peace accords intended to replace a decades-long cycle of repression and violence with a process of democratic change and respect for human rights. ONUCA began as an observer mission, grew into a security force that helped manage the demobilization of the Nicaraguan Resistance (the "Contras"), and finished its two-year mission by supporting the establishment of a new, even more ambitious UN operation in El Salvador.

ORIGINS

The popular uprisings and insurgencies in Central America of the 1970s and 1980s grew out of long-term economic and political disparities in those countries that were cast in sharp relief by the global competition for influence between Washington and Moscow. Considered objectively, the conflicts and upheaval in Central America posed no serious threat to the postwar balance of power, but their links to the larger ideological contest, at a time when American politics was reacting sharply to a perceived rise in Soviet power, made them a focal point of US foreign policy in the 1980s.

The maldistribution of wealth and political power in Central America has roots that date to colonial times and a small settler class that ruled a much larger general populace. As the nations of Central America gained their independence in the 19th century, the social structure persisted, and with it the historically inequitable distribution of wealth.[1]

Following the Second World War, Europe's remaining colonies gained their independence. Although the states in Central America had been nominally independent for the better part of a century, the ideology of the new independence movements resonated within Central America, whose people were subject not so much to foreign domination (although US influence was strong) as to home-grown repression. Although Central America had known its share of earlier uprisings, those of the postwar era were of a different kind, charged with new ideas about the redistribution of wealth and the ownership of property and capital.[2]

Washington, historically suspicious of independent-minded Latin countries (lest they give European powers a toe-hold in the hemisphere), viewed political deviation in Central and South America with a jaundiced eye, never moreso than during the Cold War. The Eisenhower Adminstration took pride in having foiled (as it saw it) a Communist coup in Guatemala, in 1954, but "lost" Cuba in 1959 to Fidel Castro, who not only survived many US attempts to oust him, but occasioned the deepest US-Soviet nuclear crisis of the period, and sought to spread the gospel of revolution throughout the region.[3]

Economic expansion enabled the several oligarchic regimes in Central America to stave off unrest in the 1960s, but the global economic downturn of the 1970s encouraged new efforts to oust the powerful ruling families of El Salvador and Nicaragua. The *Frente Faribundo Marti para la Liberacion Nacional* (FMLN) in El Salvador and the *Frente Sandinista* in Nicaragua drew inspiration and support from socialist movements in other countries, the Sandinistas from the Soviet Union and Cuba, and the FMLN from the Sandinistas.[4]

The United States supported the Somoza regime in Nicaragua until very near the end, but Somoza was otherwise isolated internationally. As a Sandinista victory came closer, the Carter Administration also withdrew its support with a view towards improving its prospects with the new government. The cessation of US aid speeded Somoza's downfall and the Sandinistas took power on July 19, 1979. Although not opposed initially by the Carter Administration, the Sandinistas' movement toward single-party rule and their growing involvement with Cuba and the Soviet Union caused growing unease in Washington.[5]

Soon after taking office in 1981, the Reagan Administration prepared to roll back Soviet influence globally, and Central America became a test case for the new Administration's policies. The domestic political environment in the US was averse to direct military intervention, and because there was no organized indigenous counter-revolutionary movement to support in Nicaragua, the United States undertook to develop and supply a rebel force that would seek the Sandinistas' ouster.[6]

By early 1982, the US had established, trained, and deployed the counterrevolutionary forces that began to attack the Sandinistas from bases in Honduras.[7] The Contra war in Nicaragua added yet another insurgency with complicating extra-regional dimensions to Central America's stormy politics. A bloody civil war in neighboring El Salvador escalated in parallel, with army-guerrilla clashes in the countryside and right-wing death squads operating in the cities. The Reagan Administration sent US military advisors to El Salvador, determined not to "lose" it, which helps account for the failure of the FMLN to gain control as the Sandinistas did in 1979. Nonetheless, the FMLN grew rapidly in the early 1980s, and peaked at perhaps 12,000 fighters in 1983.[8]

The Regional Peace Process

As fighting flared in both of these countries, as well as in Guatemala, the threat of continuous regional instability and fear of active US military intervention led Mexico, Panama, Colombia, and Venezuela to form the Contadora Group to seek a negotiated peace for the entire region.[9] After consultations with the presidents of Nicaragua, Honduras, Costa Rica, El Salvador, and Guatemala, the Group issued the Contadora Act of September 7, 1984. The Act included provisions for the settlement of internal and regional disputes and for the verification of such settlements by an international body. Nicaragua announced its readiness to sign the accord without revisions on September 21, and the other four Central American states indicated similar intentions.

After Nicaragua's announcement, the United States objected to the agreement's verification provisions and lobbied the other states in the region not to sign it.[10] A visit by US Secretary of State Shultz to Costa Rica, Honduras, Guatemala, and El Salvador in October 1984 resulted in a meeting of foreign ministers from those countries, and those ministers agreed, with Guatemala abstaining, to issue a number of revisions to the original Contadora Act without the participation of Nicaragua or the Contadora countries. Nicaragua objected to the proposed revisions and the Contadora process was temporarily stalemated. However, on July 27, 1985, it received support from Argentina, Brazil, Peru, and Uruguay, which pledged to support the establishment of regional peace in Central America through the

Contadora process, and who were known thereafter as the Contadora Support Group.

In September 1985, a second draft of the Contadora Act addressed some of the concerns of Honduras, Costa Rica, and El Salvador by strengthening the verification provisions (allowing a verification commission to inspect suspicious sites on its own initiative, for example). The new draft was rejected by Nicaragua, however, as it allowed continued "international military maneuvers" in the region (particularly US maneuvers in neighboring Honduras) and did not require an end to US support for the Contras.[11]

In February 1986, foreign ministers of the Contadora and Support Group states tried unsucessfully to convince Secretary Shultz to delay a $100 million aid package to the Contras, arguing that the US aid hindered rather than helped the peace process. The following May, the foreign ministers of the five Central American countries met in Esquipulas, Guatemala, and agreed to sign a new, "final" peace accord by June 6. The new draft (which became known as Esquipulas I) was duly drawn, agreed to by Nicaragua, but criticized by El Salvador, Honduras and Costa Rica, and soon died.[12]

In early 1987, Costa Rican President Oscar Arias put forward his own plan in conjunction with the presidents of El Salvador, Honduras, and Guatemala. The "Arias Plan" drew heavily on the older draft accords, but placed greater emphasis on democratization. Arias received support from the new Democratic leadership in the US Senate, but failed in another attempt to convince the White House that its policy of support for the Contras was hurting more than helping. The Reagan Administration (by this time deep into the Iran-Contra scandal)[13] believed that its support for the Contras would coerce concessions from the Sandinistas.[14]

On August 7, 1987, a new agreement based on the Arias plan was signed by the five Central American presidents. In this agreement, known as "Esquipulas II," the five states committed themselves to take steps toward terminating conflicts in the region. Specifically, they would,

- grant amnesty to political prisoners and establish national reconciliation commissions;

- negotiate an end to hostilities and take the necessary steps to achieve ceasefires;

- support a democratic and effectively pluralistic political process, and hold free and fair elections;

- end support for irregular and insurrectionist forces and prevent the use of their territory for attacks on other states;
- resume negotiations on the outstanding security provisions of the Contadora framework, including voluntary disarming of irregular forces;
- provide support to refugees and displaced persons;
- promote economic development and seek development assistance; and
- support the establishment and work of an International Commission for Verification and Follow-Up (CIVS).[15]

CIVS consisted of the Secretaries-General of the OAS and the UN (or their representatives), the foreign ministers of the Central American countries, the Contadora Group, and the Contadora Support Group, for a total of fifteen members. The Central American countries were thus heavily outnumbered on the Commission, and this had important operational consequences.[16]

CIVS teams visited the five Central American countries in early January 1988, talking extensively with representatives of human rights groups as well as representatives of governments. The resulting report was uncharacteristically blunt on human rights issues, and El Salvador, Guatemala, and Honduras took strong exception to it, while Nicaragua (which fared better) supported it. The report also noted that continued US support for the contras violated Esquipulas II, resulting in an exchange of accusations between El Salvador and Nicaragua over Nicaraguan support for the FMLN, and between Nicaragua and its immediate neighbors relating to the use of foreign territory by the Contras.[17]

The large consensus-based CIVS proved to be too cumbersome a mechanism to function effectively. When El Salvador strongly challenged the impartiality of the Commission's report (meaning, its politically embarrassing frankness) at the Central American presidents' January 1988 summit meeting, the Commission's work was effectively ended. Its dissolution also amounted to rejection by the Central Americans, for the time being, of impartial international verification of Esquipulas II, and put the regional peace process on hold for the better part of a year.[18]

While Esquipulas languished, a promising bilateral initiative gave brief hope of new progress. Following a sharp border clash in March 1988 that saw Sandinista forces pursue Contra bands into Honduras, Honduran aircraft attack Nicaraguan targets, and the United States airlift a brigade of Army troops into

Honduras, the Nicaraguan government and Resistance leaders sat down for their first direct talks. The Sapoá Accord of March 23, 1988, that resulted from those talks established an interim ceasefire and specified further talks toward a permanent ceasefire, the gradual implementation of a general amnesty for political prisoners, humanitarian aid to the Contras (who would concentrate their forces in agreed areas), and unrestricted freedom of expression. However, the talks produced a leadership crisis among the Contras by late April in which hardliners ousted their more conciliatory colleagues. By June, escalating Contra demands had deadlocked the talks. However, the ceasefire continued on a month to month basis.[19]

For the rest of 1988, the players in Central America's multiple, deadly dramas mostly awaited the results of the US presidential elections. Those elections, although returning the Republican party to the White House, marked a new, pragmatic turn in US policy toward Central America. Less ideologically motivated than its predecessor, the Bush Administration set out to find workable compromises, first with the US Congress, and then with the nations of the region. As a result, the peace process could move ahead once again.[20]

Initiatives for UN Involvement

In their efforts to find a practical means of verifying regional compliance with Esquipulas II, the Central American nations turned increasingly to the United Nations, and the UN in turn supported the peace process, first rhetorically and later operationally. In Resolution 42/1 of October 7, 1987, two months after the signing of Esquipulas II, the General Assembly expressed its "firmest support" for the agreement and requested that the Secretary General provide the fullest support possible to achieve peace. A joint UN/OAS team was sent to Central America to appraise the requirements for on-site inspections under Esquipulas II. It concluded that the accord was too vague on what was to be verified and that asking inspectors to work amidst ongoing conflicts was too risky.[21]

Regional disagreements and lack of clarity on operational matters hampered the Central Americans' search for international help in implementing Esquipulas II for another two years. In April 1988, the Executive Commission of Central American foreign ministers that replaced CIVS prepared to extend invitations to Canada, West Germany, and Spain to create a Technical Auxiliary Group under UN auspices to advise it on new verification mechanisms for Esquipulas II.[22] Opposition from El Salvador and Honduras delayed the invitations until November, however, and then channeled them through UN Secretary General Javier Pérez de Cuéllar, followed closely by a request from the Central American presidents for a UN peacekeeping mission. But Pérez de Cuéllar would not move ahead until the Central Americans were more specific about just what they wanted the UN to do.[23]

In an effort to reinvigorate the peace process, the Executive Commission met in New York in February 1989, followed immediately by a meeting of the five presidents at Tesoro Beach, El Salvador. In the agreement that emerged from that meeting, Nicaragua agreed to advance its general elections from November to February 1990, to open them to international observation, and to open the election campaign to opposition parties. The other states agreed in turn to develop a plan within 90 days for the voluntary demobilization, repatriation, or relocation of the Nicaraguan Resistance (RN) and their families.[24]

In mid-March, the Executive Commission met in New York with UN representatives to discuss a working paper on the UN's role in Esquipulas II. Two weeks later, the Commission formally requested ONUCA's activation. The Secretary General again demurred, however, because of a formal reservation by Honduras. The Honduran government wanted Nicaragua to withdraw a case that it had lodged with the International Court of Justice (ICJ) in 1986, charging Honduras with harboring the Contras; unless that case was withdrawn, Honduras was unwilling to implement Esquipulas. This glitch delayed implementation for another four months.

In early August 1989, the Sandinistas and Nicaragua's internal opposition parties signed an accord that established agreed terms for the conduct of national elections and called for demobilization of the Contras. At a meeting of the five Central American presidents in Tela, Honduras, on August 7, Nicaragua agreed to defer its case before the ICJ for 90 days, in return for the others' agreement to a joint plan calling for the voluntary demobilization, repatriation, or relocation of the Contras in the same time frame, a plan that the United States vigorously opposed. The plan was to be implemented by a new, joint, UN-OAS International Commission of Support and Verification (CIAV) to be established within 30 days. That was done, and on October 11, Pérez de Cuéllar submitted his report to the Security Council requesting the establishment of ONUCA. [25]

A deteriorating field situation temporarily blocked ONUCA's deployment, however. The Contras were not party to the regional accords and did not support the Tela timetable.[26] At about the same time, 2,000 Contra fighters located in Nicaragua began staging attacks to interrupt election registration. The killing of 18 army reservists while enroute to register on October 21 led the government of Nicaragua to lift the 19-month ceasefire a week later. Meanwhile, the FMLN in El Salvador launched a major urban offensive. On November 25, El Salvador suspended relations with Nicaragua when a Nicaraguan-registered plane, flying from that country, crashed and was found to be carrying surface-to-air missiles bound for the FMLN.[27]

The Tela deadline passed without movement toward demobilization, and the Central American presidents met once more in an effort to salvage the peace process. The San Isidro Declaration of December 12 was a mix of carrots and sticks that condemned "armed action and terrorism being waged by irregular forces in the region," and urged the FMLN to "immediately and effectively...cease hostilities" and "publicly renounce any type of violent action that may directly or indirectly affect the civilian population." The five also urged accelerated deployment of ONUCA and a role for it in demobilizing the Contras. The Sandinistas agreed to a further 6–12 month deferral of their case before the ICJ, and offered Contras who demobilized by February 5 the right to vote in the February 25 national election. Finally, they requested that $67 million in US humanitarian aid earmarked for the Contras be given to CIAV instead so as to expedite the demobilization process. (CIAV at the time had approximately $3 million, also provided by the US; Washington agreed to shift the funds.) The San Isidro document contained sufficient concessions by the hard-pressed Sandinistas to allow the peace process to resume, and effective deployment of ONUCA to begin.[28]

POLITICAL SUPPORT

As the verification mechanism of a regional political settlement agreement, ONUCA had unusual depth of political support. But that support (and the UN's willingness to mount the operation) evolved slowly, along with the Central American peace process, the larger process of democratization in Latin America, and the global relationship of the United States and the Soviet Union. Moreover, each of these factors evolved at its own pace, and none had evolved very far in the first half of the 1980s.

In the second half of the decade, however, significant changes occurred. Mikhail Gorbachev consolidated his power in Moscow, and by late 1988 it was clear that Soviet foreign policy had changed a great deal, as Moscow pulled out of regional conflicts in Asia and Africa and promoted their settlement, and moved to end the long-running military confrontation in Central Europe. The change of Administrations in Washington over the winter of 1988–89 also brought a new pragmatism to US foreign policy, and thus a new flexibility. The domestic compromise reached by the White House and the Congress in March 1989 spelled an end to US military aid to the Contras. On the other hand, the Bush Administration retained its predecessor's willingness to use military force unilaterally, and the US invasion of Panama in late December 1989, justified in part to return a stolen election to the actual winners, may have given Sandinista leaders further incentive to keep Nicaragua's own electoral process free and fair.

At the same time, UN peacekeeping was proving its worth in new places as disparate as Afghanistan, Angola, Iran, and Namibia. This new track record of achievements gave the states of Central America confidence that UN participation would take their halting peace process over the top. It was that process itself, however, that slowly built a new model of governance for Central America, so that when combat arms finally lost favor as the principal agent of change in the region, an alternative had been worked out and enjoyed wide support.

Regional political phasing remained uneven, however. A settlement in El Salvador would require two more years, to the end of 1991. The FMLN's large offensive just as ONUCA was set to deploy, and its hostility to the UN operation, forced ONUCA's observers to steer clear of FMLN-controlled territory. The eventual UN-mediated settlement in El Salvador would require a new peacekeeping operation. In the interim, however, ONUCA enjoyed valuable political support from the five Central American governments, the larger regional states, and the Great Powers. With political support assured, the greater challenge proved to be implementing its mandate effectively.

MANDATE

ONUCA's mandate derived from Esquipulas II and from the subsequent declarations of the five Central American presidents, especially Tesoro Beach (which called for an "effective mechanism" to verify Esquipulas II), and the Tela summit (which called for establishment of CIAV). After examining CIAV's mandate, Secretary General Pérez de Cuéllar noted that elements of its mission involving collection and custody of weaponry were best done by armed peacekeepers rather than CIAV's civilians, but he did not seek such a mandate for ONUCA initially, as the Contras had not yet expressed willingness to demobilize. Until they did, ONUCA would monitor the five Central American governments' commitment to

- cease all forms of military assistance to irregular and insurrectionist movements;
- prevent acts of aggression against other states in the region from or through their territories, air space, or territorial seas;
- prevent third parties from using their territory or air space to support irregular or insurrectionist movements within any of the five countries' territories; and
- prevent establishment of "radio or television transmissions for the specific purpose of directing or assisting" such movements.

After the San Isidro Declaration requested help from ONUCA in demobilizing the Contras, and following the Nicaraguan elections, when the Contras themselves showed some willingness to disarm, the Secretary General sought a larger mandate from the Security Council. The Council agreed to authorize deployment of an infantry battalion to provide security for demobilization centers and oversee weapons disposal.[29]

A second expansion of the mandate grew out of talks between the Contras and the government of Nicaragua to allow demobilization in Nicaragua. The Contras did not wish to disarm outside Nicaraguan territory and risk being stuck there without recourse should the government somehow decide not to let them and their families return. The government did not relish the prospect of having the entire Contra army inside Nicaragua, fully armed, but the Contras unilaterally moved a number of troops across Nicaragua's borders after the election (in March and early April 1990), resulting in some armed clashes with the Army, which remained Sandinista-controlled.[30]

At first, Contra leaders discussed demobilization plans with ONUCA officials in Tegucigalpa. They were encouraged to undertake talks with the government, for which the UN offered transportation. In mid-April, the Northern Front *commandantes*, out of uniform and unarmed, were flown to Managua in a UN aircraft for negotiations with the Ortega government. The face-to-face talks started out predictably tense, but soon produced the Managua Agreements, signed April 19, which called for:

- a formal ceasefire to be monitored by ONUCA and Cardinal Obando y Bravo;
- the establishment of five security zones of 550-600 square kilometers each to which Contra forces were to move by April 25;
- withdrawal of government forces by April 21 from those zones and from 20-kilometer-wide "demilitarized zones" surrounding them, also to be monitored by ONUCA and the Cardinal;
- provision of humanitarian aid by CIAV to Resistance members in the security zones; and
- an agreed timetable for complete demobilization of the Resistance, between April 25 and June 10.[31]

ONUCA was to monitor these withdrawals, provide security within the assembly areas via ground and air patrols, and receive and destroy each demobilizing fighter's personal weaponry. The Secretary General requested a second mandate enlargement for ONUCA on the same day that the parties in Nicaragua signed their accord, and the Council approved the new mandate on April 20. Once demobilization of the Contras was complete, ONUCA reverted to its original mandate.[32]

FUNDING

As usual for peacekeeping operations since 1973, ONUCA was declared an "expense of the Organization," member states were billed for their share of its cost according to an established scale of assessment, and a special account was established to receive their payments. The budget for the first six months of operation was $40.8 million. Subsequent six-month periods were successively cheaper, both because major communications and transportation equipment needed to get the mission going were bought in the initial period and because ONUCA was steadily reduced in size over its final year.[33]

When ONUCA's mandate was expanded in the spring of 1990, and a 700-strong infantry battalion was added to it, its budget was not increased. Officers in the field complained of being made to stretch a "marginal" budget even further, but diplomats in New York averred that the initial budget had been constructed with demobilization of the Contras in mind.[34] The initial (October 1989) budget anticipated an operation of 675 persons (up to 475 military, 118 international civilians, and 82 locally hired civilians). While UN peace observation missions like this one usually cost about $90,000 per person per year in the field, ONUCA was budgeted at $126,000 per person-year for its first six months. And indeed, ONUCA underspent its first year's budget by roughly 44 percent, even with the expanded mandate.[35]

By budgeting for a larger civilian staff and more military observers than were actually deployed through mid-1990, the UN retained a capacity to respond rapidly to political events, avoiding the start-up delays that nearly sank the UN operation in Namibia the previous year. Member states criticize such "balloon budgeting," and it can backfire, causing the General Assembly's advisory committee on budget matters to carve chunks out of funding proposals, and causing member states to be less than prompt and less than complete with their dues payments, since "everbody knows" that the Secretariat asks for much more than it needs. The Secretariat did, however, refund most of the excess assessments on a semi-annual basis (which, we might note, domestic government agencies almost never do). Given the uncertainties that UN mission planners face in devising new operations in developing countries, usually where peacekeeping missions have never been mounted before, and the relative handful of people involved in such planning, the Secretariat would rather ask for too much and give some back than run risks in the field and face delays while going back to member states with yet another dun for money.[36]

Altogether, from November 1989 through its termination in mid-January 1992, ONUCA cost about $87 million, after deducting roughly $19 million in unspent assessments credited back to UN member states. At termination, however, member states technically still owed the UN nearly $9 million in unpaid assessments for ONUCA.[37]

PLANNING AND IMPLEMENTATION

In September 1989, the Secretary General sent an 18-member survey mission to Central America led by the Chief Military Observer (CMO) of the UN observation mission in Angola, Brigadier General Péricles Ferreira Gomes. Its job was to flesh out the working paper on ONUCA drawn up six months earlier by UN staffers and the Central Americans' Executive Commission. Its three-week reconnaissance formed the basis for Pérez de Cuéllar's October 11 report to the Security Council requesting establishment of ONUCA.[38]

Recruitment of military and civilian staff also began in October, and senior military staff were brought to New York one month later for two days of mission familiarization, as soon as the Security Council authorized the operation. The Secretariat's Field Operations Division (FOD), which does logistics and communications support for UN peacekeeping, did not participate in the briefings, however; military and civilian staffers, and operational and support planning, followed separate, parallel tracks that did not meet until all parties deployed to Central America, where ONUCA's military chief of staff met his civilian administrative counterparts on December 2. At that point, the military side of the operation also had its first exposure to the FOD "standard operations document" that detailed basic UN field procedures and determined that much of the initial operational planning had to be scrapped to meet evolving field conditions. New plans were drawn up by mid-January, but deployment of the observer teams was delayed.[39]

Although a possible role for ONUCA in demobilizing the Nicaraguan Resistance had been in the air since October, and the Central American heads of state requested such assistance in December, the military side of ONUCA did not receive word of this likely new mission until late January. Operational plans began to be drawn up two weeks later.

Size and Composition of the Force

As originally conceived, ONUCA at full deployment was to consist of 260 unarmed military observers, 115 personnel for operations and maintenance of one fixed-wing aircraft and 12 helicopters, 50 crew and support personnel for a naval unit of eight vessels, 14 medical personnel and staff, 104 international civilian staff, and 82 locally recruited civilians. Deployment was to occur in four phases, with the final phase, and complete deployment, dependent on political circumstances. The fourth phase was underway by May 1990.

Table 24.1. ONUCA Personnel, 1990-91

	Initial Plan	April 1990	Oct. 1990	April 1991	Oct. 1991
Military Observers	260	169	254	158	132
Argentina				(1)	(1)
Brazil			(21)	(14)	(11)
Canada		(34)	(45)	(29)	(24)
Colombia		(12)	(12)	(8)	(7)
Ecuador		(21)	(21)	(12)	(10)
India			(21)	(12)	(10)
Ireland		(31)	(31)	(19)	(18)
Spain		(49)	(59)	(37)	(30)
Sweden			(21)	(12)	(10)
Venezuela		(22)	(23)	(14)	(11)
Infantry					
(Venezuela)		702			
Naval Squadron					
(Argentina)	50		29	29	32
Military Air Unit					
(Canada)	115	124	130		
Commercial Aviation Unit		10	12	21	20
Fixed-Wing Aircraft					
(Germany; voluntary)		3	4	4	4
Civilian Medical Unit					
(Germany; voluntary)	14	13	10	10	8
International Civilian Staff	104	85	90	65	56
Local Civilian Staff	82	89	93	82	86
Totals:	625[a]	1,195	538	369	338

Note: [a] A military communications unit of 50 persons was also planned initially.
Source: United Nations Documents S/20895, October 11, 1989; S/21274, April 27, 1990; S/21909, October 26, 1990; S/22543, April 21, 1991; and S/23171, October 28, 1991.

ONUCA drew participants from twelve nations representing four continents, with five from Latin America, four from Europe, two from North America and one from Asia. Table 24.1 shows the distribution of personnel over time.[40]

Air transport and surveillance capabilities were important to this relatively far-flung operation. Germany donated the operation's fixed-wing VIP aircraft and crew, while helicopters of the Canadian military air unit, supplemented by commercially chartered helicopters, performed the routine transport and aerial surveillance tasks. The forested terrain in ONUCA's main patrol area on the Honduras-Nicaragua border was extremely rugged and the rainy season rendered many unpaved roads nearly impassable, often making access by air the only viable option.

Initial plans called for an air unit with a dozen helicopters (four light observation and eight medium cargo). In early 1990, Canada sent a unit with eight light observation helicopters. ONUCA's military asked the UN for another four cargo aircraft, but instead received four light Allouette IIIs commercially chartered from US-based Evergreen Aviation. The relatively high patrol altitudes in the mountainous border areas of Central America proved a challenge for all of the light choppers, and Canada swapped out four in exchange for four heavier UH-1s ("Hueys") that had recently returned from service with the Multinational Force and Observers in the Sinai. Once Contra demobilization began in May 1990, ONUCA was able to get Evergreen's contribution changed to commercial Hueys, and in June convinced UN Headquarters to add four more Hueys, for a total fleet of 16.[41] The helicopters were heavily used to supply the Contras' "security zones" in Nicaragua, and to transport staff and supplies for CIAV.

ONUCA's naval component, which was to patrol the Gulf of Fonseca on the Pacific coast, did not deploy until the end of June 1990. Argentina provided four fast patrol boats and 29 naval personnel. Originally planned to be based in El Salvador, it was shifted to the politically calmer waters of San Lorenzo, Honduras.

For the first UN peacekeeping operation in Latin America, Spain and Venezuela, in particular, put their very best foot forward, selecting officers to participate in the operation who were top graduates of their respective military academies and bilingual in Spanish and English. Venezuela also sent its best airborne battalion to assist in demobilizing the Nicaraguan Resistance. Some traditional troop-contributing nations were said to have been less selective in their choice of observers. Moreover, these troops, used to using English as the working language of UN peacekeeping, were surprised and nonplussed when the CMO declared that Spanish would be ONUCA's official working language. Many had to work through interpreters.[42]

Command, Communications and Logistics

ONUCA was commanded for the first year by Major General Agustin Quesada Gomez of Spain. From ONUCA headquarters in Tegucigalpa, Honduras, he and Deputy CMO Brigadier General Ian Douglas of Canada, who functioned as operational chief of staff, directed an operation with five liaison offices (one in each of the five capitals of the Esquipulas signatory countries), up to

18 verification centers (five in capitals and 13 in smaller towns—
one in Costa Rica and El Salvador, three in Guatemala and
Nicaragua, and five in Honduras), and three or four upcountry
observation posts. The verification centers, with the exception of
those in Costa Rica, were positioned on main roads in a crescent
around El Salvador.

On December 20, 1990, Major General Quesada, who carried
the UN rank of Assistant Secretary General, completed his tour
with ONUCA. The UN used the transition to downgrade the UN
and military rank of the CMO, corresponding to the decreasing
size and responsibilities of the operation. Brigadier General
Douglas having finished his tour and returned to Canada in
October, DCMO Brigadier General Lewis MacKenzie (also of Canada) became CMO *ad interim*. He was replaced in turn by Brigadier
General Victor Suanzes Pardo of Spain on May 13, 1991.[43]

To communicate with New York, ONUCA headquarters used
portable, suitcase-sized INMARSAT terminals that provided secure
voice and fax communications. Although early plans included a
small Canadian signals unit to establish initial communications
(much as a Canadian unit established communications for the
UN's Iran-Iraq observer mission one year earlier), the relatively
slow pace of ONUCA's deployment allowed communications to be
handled entirely by civilian UN Field Service technicians.[44]

Logistical planning for the operation assumed that the battalion sent to help demobilize the Contras would deploy with their
own transport, as the UN requested. However, the Venezuelan
battalion arrived with none. As a result, ONUCA had to scramble
to find whatever large trucks it could rent or charter locally to
move personnel and material. It also borrowed transport from the
support company deployed with Canada's air unit.[45]

Field Operations

ONUCA's members had several jobs to do. Their basic task was
verification of Esquipulas II. Their most important single task
was demobilizing the Contras.

Basic Verification. ONUCA's basic job was to verify that no
signatory of Esquipulas II was aiding irregular military forces in
the region or permitting its territory to be used for cross-border
attacks. In his first report to the Security Council, the Secretary
General noted,

[T]he nature of the terrain is such that it is very difficult for the local
authorities to prevent, and for international observers to detect,

clandestine movement of armed personnel and military supplies across borders. Vegetation is dense, metalled [sic] roads are few and far between...and many of the border areas are believed to be mined. While specific breaches of...Esquipulas II have not been directly observed by ONUCA patrols, cross-border movements have undoubtedly taken place..., especially a major movement of members of the Nicaraguan Resistance from Honduras into Nicaragua during March and early April [1990].[46]

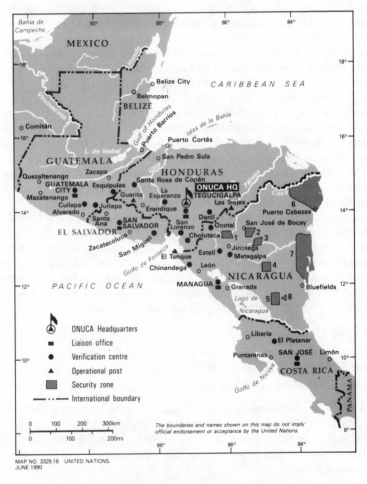

Figure 24.1. United Nations Observer Group in Central America, Deployment as of June 1990

This particular troop movement involved an estimated three to five *thousand* Contras. Indeed, when the first-deployed company of the Venezuelan battalion reached the Contras' main base camp at Yamales, Honduras, in mid-April, there were no combatants to be found.[47]

Nor did ONUCA succeed in spotting arms flows from the Sandinistas to the FMLN, although evidence of such support turned up periodically (even after Nicaragua's new president assumed office). UN observers investigated complaints lodged by governments, but often seemed to take weeks to follow up, leaving ample time for reported transmitters to be dismantled or hideouts to be vacated.[48] Naval patrols in the Gulf of Fonseca were no more successful in spotting violations. Combined air and sea patrols, using helicopters as long-range eyes for the boats, were introduced in October 1990. In the first six months of naval operations, patrols were limited to daylight hours, but night patrols were introduced in early 1991. The Naval Verification Center at San Lorenzo compiled a database of regular traffic patterns to facilitate identification of deviations that would suggest a violation of the Esquipulas agreements, but none was ever detected.[49]

From the spring of 1991, ONUCA changed its major mode of operating from border patrolling to liaison with the armed forces and national police of the five Central American governments, verifying how well those forces were patrolling their own borders to prevent violations of Esquipulas II. This change made the best use of ONUCA's diminishing resources, and may well have nudged the five governments to do a better job of monitoring their own national borders.[50]

ONUCA continued to patrol, however, not so much in expectation of spotting violations, but as a confidence-building measure. In Nicaragua, in particular, relations among ex-Contras, ex-Sandinista soldiers, and the active Army remained tense, occasionally flaring into violence. The UN observers' periodic presence showed that the outside world continued to monitor what happened in the region, and in the country, making political backsliding just a bit harder.

Demobilizing the Contras. The United Nations had never before taken on the task of disarming and demobilizing a guerrilla army. Although the voluntary demobilization of the Contras went smoothly enough once it had gained momentum, it proved quite difficult to get started. Contra *commandantes* remained suspicious of the Sandinistas; although they had lost the presidential election, the Sandinistas still controlled the Nicaraguan Army. On the other hand, the Contras' days as a fighting force were numbered. They were running out of funds, and support from Washington all but dried up following the opposition's election victory. Moreover, Honduras was anxious that it not be left with a hungry, heavily armed refugee population on its hands, and all five Central American countries wanted the Contras demobilized peacefully but effectively, as an example to the contending parties in El Salvador. This combination of pressures led to the Managua Agreements of April 19, 1990.

Although demobilization was to commence on April 25, delays continued into May. The rainy season (which would make it much harder to supply the Contras' new camps) was due within weeks. Continued reluctance on the part of Contra field commanders was the major contributing factor in the delay.[51] On May 25, Northern Front commanders suspended demobilization (then only four to five percent complete), accusing Nicaraguan forces of gross cease-fire violations. ONUCA demonstrated its value by investigating the charges and finding no evidence to support them. What could have escalated into violence instead resulted in a new accord on May 30. The Resistance, the Chamorro government, and the Cardinal agreed to add a Protocol to the Managua Agreements. In it, the government agreed to establish "development areas" for demobilized Contras and their families, to provide economic assistance, to create a police force for those areas that included former Resistance members, and to take other measures to help reintegrate the Resistance into national life. In return, the Contra leaders pledged to demobilize "at least 100 combatants each day in each zone," aiming to finish by June 10. Actual rates of demobilization fell 25 percent short of what was needed to meet that objective, and the Secretary General asked for a three-week extension for ONUCA's infantry battalion, to the end of June.[52]

Each fighter who presented him or herself for demobilization handed over (to ONUCA) their weapon, uniform, and any ammunition in their possession; these were destroyed on the spot. In exchange, each received a demobilization certificate, a shirt, "designer jeans," and a food ration (from CIAV). Ultimately, there were many more Contras demobilized than the UN and OAS had estimated (over 22,000, versus estimates of 12,000). As the process gathered steam (nearly 1,900 Contras presented themselves for demobilization on June 12 alone, for example), CIAV's supplies were stretched thin. Delays in US congressional funding of $139 million in assistance for CIAV did not help matters.[53]

Table 24.2. Demobilization of the Nicaraguan Resistance

Personnel Demobilized			
Status	Honduras	Nicaragua	Total
Armed	217	16,361	16,578
Unarmed	2,542	3,253	5,795
Total	2,759	19,614	22,373
Weapons Destroyed			
Type	Honduras	Nicaragua	Total
Small arms (assault rifles, light machine guns)	512	14,632	15,144
Heavy machine guns	2	2	4
Mortars	28	109	137
Grenade launchers (including anti-tank)	83	1,199	1,282
Grenades	570	763	1,333
Mines	4	142	146
Surface-to-air missiles	37	82	119

Source: *United Nations Observer Group in Central America, Report of the Secretary General*, Security Council Document S/21909, October 26, 1990, 10-13.

Toward the end of June, the Contras turned in their best weapons—shoulder-fired surface-to-air missiles (119 altogether). The UN's involvement in demobilization ended and the security zones were abolished on June 28, and Venezuela's battalion returned home. The 500 or so fighters who showed up for processing after that turned in their weapons to Nicaraguan authorities and received humanitarian support from CIAV, which continued to operate. Through September, ONUCA did keep observers in areas of Nicaragua where large numbers of former Resistance were living, "so as to help to encourage a sense of security and confidence among the population."[54] After that, they were withdrawn.

Since watching for aid and arms flows to the Contras had been one of ONUCA's principal tasks, after their demobilization its original mandate could be met with fewer observers. The Secretary General sent 94 home and, as noted earlier, appointed a less senior general officer as chief military observer. As 1991 drew to a close, agreement was reached to end the conflict in El Salvador. Many of ONUCA's remaining resources were transferred to the separate UN Operation in El Salvador, and ONUCA was officially terminated on January 17.[55]

ASSESSMENT

ONUCA had two jobs, each with operational and symbolic components. The first job, verifying compliance with Esquipulas II, was similar to mandates given other UN operations (in Greece, 1947–51; in Lebanon, 1958; and in North Yemen, in 1963), none of which directly detected contraband activity. Neither did ONUCA, which was a source of great frustration both to its field commanders and to New York. As the Secretary General's fall 1990 report noted,

> It was originally thought that ONUCA might have some capacity to detect violations of the security undertakings....In practice, however, it quickly became clear that ONUCA's detective capacity is very limited...mainly due to the fact that an international peacekeeping operation cannot undertake the detection of clandestine activities without assuming functions that properly belong to the security forces of the country or countries concerned, not least because they require armed personnel to carry them out.

Nonetheless, ONUCA soldiered ahead because the first job had a secondary component—confidence building, a contribution to regional security that the local parties could not easily make themselves.

Demobilizing the Resistance, its second job, had a large political-psychological component. ONUCA provided an atmosphere that encouraged Contra fighters to participate in a rite of passage. Each one handed over the symbols of military rebellion and received back symbols of civilian reintegration. The importance of such authoritative ritual (especially when observed and supported by the dominant Catholic Church, as represented by Cardinal Obando y Bravo) should not be underestimated. Since the UN had no illusion that it destroyed all of the Contras' armaments, the political-psychological value of formal demobilization—its dissolving of the Resistance as a movement—was the greater one.

Although disorder continued to flare in Nicaragua as the country struggled to rebuild its economy, rearmed former Contras (or "re-contras") who gained visibility in 1991 numbered fewer than 1,000. The most confrontational re-contras demobilized again in early 1992, as the government pursued a policy of negotiation rather than force. Old military opponents were sometimes brought together by a new common enemy, economic want, to noisily draw the government's attention to past-due promises of land and housing.[56]

ONUCA's experience did highlight some deficiencies in UN field operations that need to be addressed. Inadequate advance planning was a hindrance, as was the assemblage of the full team for the first time only when they reached the field. While ONUCA field personnel were able to improvise, the logistical problems encountered when the operation's mandate changed were indicative of deeper problems with the UN's antiquated supply system and its lack of either material or personnel reserves.

CONCLUSIONS

This first phase implementation of the Central American political settlement showed several things. It showed the importance of positive support by interested Great Powers. Political changes in the world outside set the context for change within the region, and the drying-up of external support for the two principal conflicts in Nicaragua and El Salvador gave the peace process a boost in the late 1980s. But without the continuing efforts of President Arias of Costa Rica, the other regional presidents, and the newly democratic governments of the Contadora and Contadora Support Groups, there would have been no "peace process." Regional involvement and persistence was crucial. On the other hand, without the assistance of international organizations, there might have been no implementation. ONUCA showed how impartial international entities can give crucial material support to a regional settlement; its peacekeepers visibly represented all of the changed political circumstances that made peace posssible. Without their presence, the support of the OAS, and the work of UN mediators, the fighting in Central America might merely have tailed off into persistent low-level conflict and banditry as "Contras without a country" struggled to survive.

The experience in demobilizing armed factions that the UN gained in ONUCA was subsequently put to use on a much larger scale in Cambodia, where ten to fifteen times as many fighters and twice as many factions had to be disarmed. Its experience in mediating direct talks between the Contras and Sandinistas was put to good use immediately in mediating the conflicts in neighboring El Salvador and Guatemala. And its final operational emphasis on monitoring local government performance should serve as a model for future operations where cross-border arms flows are a subject of concern.

Above all, the presence of international peacekeepers in situations like Central America's can help reinforce local confidence that a peace settlement will be fairly and faithfully implemented, allaying suspicions and reducing tensions. The peacekeepers' role, like that of the UN's peacemakers (or mediators) is to facilitate nonviolent change, and in that role, their presence can be vital.

Notes

1. J. M. Roberts, *The Pelican History of the World* (Harmondsworth, Middlesex: Penguin Books, Ltd., 1986), 610-15, 751-2.

2. Roy C. Macridis, *Contemporary Political Ideologies: Movements and Regimes*, 4th ed. (Glenview, Il: Scott, Foresman & Co., 1989), 256, 261-64; Edward Best, *US Policy and Regional Security in Central America* (London: Gower and the International Institute for Strategic Studies, 1987), 9; Roberts, *The Pelican History of the World*, 751.

3. See, for example, F. Parkinson, *Latin America, the Cold War, and the World Powers, 1945-1973* (Beverly Hills: Sage Publications, 1974), and Edward Gonzalez, *Cuba Under Castro: The Limits of Charisma* (Boston: Houghton Mifflin, 1974).

4. Roberts, *The Pelican History of the World*, 979-980.

5. Lisa North, *Between War and Peace in Central America: Choices for Canada* (Toronto: CAPA, 1990), 172.

6. William M. Leogrande, "From Reagan to Bush: The Transition in US Policy Towards Central America," *Journal of Latin American Studies* 22, no. 3 (October 1990): 595.

7. These fighters were known colloquially as the "Contras," and more formally, especially to their supporters, as the Nicaraguan Resistance. The terms will be used here interchangeably.

8. The government and the FMLN fought each other to a standstill by the late 1980s, by which time the larger Cold War was over. In October 1989, the FMLN and the government of Alfredo Cristiani signed an accord in Mexico City that launched talks aimed at ending the war. In April 1990, after the Sandinistas lost control of the Nicaraguan presidency in an internationally observed election, representatives of the two Salvadoran sides met in Geneva and established a framework for a Salvadoran peace process mediated by the United Nations. That process bore initial fruit in July 1990. The San José Agreement called for national guarantees for basic human rights, with UN oversight. Continued negotiations produced an April 1991 agreement on constitutional reform, with emphasis on the armed services, the judicial system, human rights, and the electoral system. In May 1991, the UN Security Council authorized establishment of the UN Observer Mission in El Salvador (ONUSAL), whose first task was active surveillance and promotion of human rights in the country and investigation of rights abuses. On January 16, 1992, after further arduous negotiation, the FMLN and the government signed

a Peace Agreement to end the civil war, reduce and reform the army, and disarm guerrilla forces and reintegrate their members into civil society. As of mid-1992, however, the implementation process was going slowly (United Nations, Department of Public Information, *The Peace Process in El Salvador and the United Nations*, ONUSAL Fact Sheet One [July 1991]; UN Security Council, *United Nations Observer Mission in El Salvador: Report of the Secretary General*, United Nations Document S/23642, February 25, 1992, 1; "UN Operations in El Salvador," *International Defense Review* 3/1992, 218).

9. Contadora was named for the location of its original meeting in January 1983.

10. US policy had presumed that Nicaragua would reject the Contadora Act; the Sandinista regime was supposed to be averse to serious negotiations (*Strategic Survey, 1984–85* [London: International Institute for Strategic Studies, 1985], 36; Wayne S. Smith, "Lies About Nicaragua," *Foreign Policy* 67 [Summer 1987], 97-98).

11. Jack Child, *The Central American Peace Process, 1983–1991* (Boulder, Co: Lynne Reinner, 1992), 35. Child emphasizes the behind-the-scenes role of Canada in helping craft the verification provisions of the various Central American peace accords.

12. North, *Between War and Peace in Central America*, 181.

13. For details on this elaborate covert operation *cum* private foreign policy initiative, see *The Tower Commission Report* (New York: Times Books, 1987).

14. Child, *The Central American Peace Process*, 64.

15. North, *Between War and Peace in Central America*, 179.

16. *The Blue Helmets: A Review of United Nations Peacekeeping*, 2nd ed. (New York: United Nations Department of Public Information, 1990), 390.

17. *The Blue Helmets*, 72-74; North, *Between War and Peace in Central America*, 185.

18. North, *Between War and Peace in Central America*, 185, and Interview 80, August 23, 1991.

19. *Strategic Survey, 1988-89* (London: International Institute for Strategic Studies, 1989), 208-210.

20. Secretary of State James Baker negotiated the so-called "treaty of Washington," in which the Administration backed away from the Reagan goal of overthrowing the Sandinistas by force in favor of a combination of diplomatic and economic pressure, in return for Congress's continuing non-military aid to the Resistance pending elections in Nicaragua. In turn, the Contras were to stand down during the period leading up to the those elections. The Congress's refusal to fund military aid left support for Esquipulas, with its ban on support of regional insurgencies and call for free elections, as the only realistic policy for the Administration (Leogrande, "From Reagan to Bush," 598-99).

21. Child, *The Central American Peace Process*, 68-69.

22. Canada, with long experience at peacekeeping, had been quietly advising the Contadora/Esquipulas process on issues of verification for

several years. Spain was the cultural motherland. Germany was a less obvious choice, but had been active politically in the region, had technical and financial resources, and involved a major power in the peace process other than the United States. Added later to the advisory group was Venezuela, which would eventually contribute the infantry battalion to ONUCA (Child, *The Central American Peace Process,* 78-80, 89).

23. Child, *The Central American Peace Process,* 65

24. Leogrande, "From Reagan to Bush," 599-600. Neither side in the Nicaraguan conflict was doing very well at this point. US military aid for the Contras was ended and military victory was out of the question. On the other hand, Contra camps were beyond reach of the Sandinista army, and the March 1988 flareup of fighting had demonstrated the escalatory danger of hot pursuit into Honduras. Meanwhile, the Nicaraguan economy was growing worse by the month. Gross domestic product shrank by nine percent in 1988 and hyper-inflation of several thousand percent per year leeched the value of the *córdoba* (*Strategic Survey, 1988–89,* 209).

Nicaragua made its formal request for UN election verification in early March 1989. The Secretary General sent several small survey missions to Nicaragua through the spring, and in July, after acting under his "good offices" authority and a General Assembly resolution (United Nations Document A/Res/43/24 of November 15, 1988) that urged "fullest possible support to the Central American Governments in their efforts to achieve peace," Pérez de Cuéllar agreed to establish the United Nations Mission to Verify the Electoral process in Nicaragua (ONUVEN). The UN Security Council, in Resolution 637 of July 27, 1989, took approving notice of the plan (a helpful political gesture, even though ONUVEN did not operate under the Council's authority). The mission began its work on August 25, 1989, six months prior to the election. It was the UN's first mission to observe elections in an independent state, and was justified by the Secretary General in terms of its origins in the multilateral Esquipulas process. ONUVEN was funded from the regular UN budget (see United Nations Documents A/44/210, April 5 1989; A/44/304, June 6, 1989; and A/44/375, July 7, 1989). Other observers of the election included the OAS and teams from the Carter Center at Emory University. All observers concluded that the election process was freely and fairly conducted, both at the polls and in the months leading up to the vote. Two hundred seven UN observers monitored the election, visiting 2,155 polling stations (United Nations, Department of Public Information, *The United Nations Role in the Central American Peace Process* [New York: UN, May 1990]).

25. For the text of the Tela Declaration and Joint Plan for Contra demobilization, see United Nations Document A/44/451, August 9, 1989. See also Leogrande, "From Reagan to Bush," 601; North, *Between War and Peace in Central America,* 187; *Strategic Survey, 1989-90,* 187.

26. Leogrande, "From Reagan to Bush," 602. Two members of CIAV (one from the UN and one from OAS) visited Contra border camps near Yamales, Honduras in mid-October, urging battalion commanders to

support Tela and abandon an "anachronistic" crusade before their chief supporter abandoned them. A week later, US Secretary of State Baker denounced the visit (Mark Uhlig, "Nicaraguans at Rebel Camp Are Asked to Disband," *New York Times*, October 15, 1989, 22; and Uhlig, "Dispute Highlights Difficulty of Disarming Contras," *New York Times*, October 21, 1989).

27. *Strategic Survey, 1989-90*, 187.

28. However, the availability of funds did not appreciably affect the pace of negotiations aimed at demobilizing the Contras (Interview 80, August 23, 1991); for the text of the San Isidro Declaration, see United Nations Document A/44/872, December 12, 1989.

29. United Nations Document S/21194, March 15, 1990; United Nations Security Council Resolution, S/Res/650, March 27, 1990.

30. United Nations Document S/21274, April 27, 1990, 5.

31. Interview 75, July 11, 1991. United Nations Document S/21259, April 20, 1990, 2-3. Elements of the Venezuelan battalion patrolled the security zones, assisted by up to 122 of ONUCA's unarmed military observers.

32. United Nations Document S/21259, April 20, 1990, annex; United Nations Security Council Resolution, S/Res/653, April 20, 1990; United Nations Document S/21274/Add.1, May 2, 1990.

33. United Nations Document A/44/246/Add.1, November 13, 1989.

34. Interview 62, May 14, 1991, and interview 75, July 11, 1991.

35. Data on average costs of peace observation missions is from William Durch and Barry Blechman, *Keeping the Peace* (Washington, D.C.: The Henry L. Stimson Center, March 1992), 54, based on UN cost data. For initial cost estimates for ONUCA, see United Nations Document A/44/246/Add.1, November 13, 1989.

36. For further discussion, see chapter 20 on the UN's Transition Assistance Group, UNTAG.

37. The majority of the arrearage (roughly $5 million) was owed by the USSR (United Nations Document ST/ADM/SER.B/364, January 8, 1992, 28-31).

38. United Nations Document A/44/344/Add. 1, October 9, 1989, 3. The Venezuelan Air Force donated the airlift for the reconnaissance mission (United Nations Document A/45/833, December 10, 1990, 5).

39. Interview 75, July 11, 1991.

40. UN Security Council Document S/20895, October 11, 1989, 6-7.

41. A loan of several US heavy-lift Chinoook helicopters, which routinely trained at Palmerola air base in Honduras, was the preferred option of ONUCA's military staff. The extra Evergreen Hueys were a fallback.

42. Interview 75, July 11, 1991.

43. United Nations Document S/22543, April 29, 1991, 2.

44. Accustomed to using very high frequency (VHF) radios for inter-unit communications in the field, the UN in this instance had to acquire ultra high frequency (UHF) equipment because the Central American states

used VHF for their own governmental communications (Interview 75, July 11, 1991).

45. Interview 75, July 11, 1991.

46. United Nations Document S/21274, 5.

47. Child, *Central American Peace Process*, 131; United Nations Document S/21274, 7.

48. For example, on March 15, 1990, the Salvadoran government complained to ONUCA of an FMLN transmitter, command post, and garage for the outfitting of smugglers' vehicles. ONUCA listened to the radio for three weeks, then forwarded the complaint to Nicaraguan authorities and was allowed to inspect the facilities in question three days later (United Nations Document 21274, 6-7).

In January and May 1991, the Salvadoran government asked ONUCA to investigate the origins of Soviet-origin shoulder-fired anti-aircraft missiles possessed by the FMLN. In the first instance, the government of Nicaragua confirmed that a quantity of SAM-7 and SAM-16 missiles had been "illicitly removed from Nicaraguan army arsenals" in October 1990. The FMLN returned 17, having fired 11 (and caused serious problems for the Salvadoran military). In the second instance, a serial number check appeared to account for all Nicaraguan SAM-16s, the type of missile in question, and the UN let the matter drop (Mark Uhlig, "Managua Defends Army Chief in Missile Uproar," *New York Times*, January 10, 1991, A6; United Nations Documents S/22543, 5; and S/23171, 6).

49. United Nations Document S/22543, 4.

50. United Nations Document S/22543; Interview 86, December 6, 1991.

51. Remaining leaders were, by this time, mostly less-educated men of rural origin who were suspicious of government intentions regardless of who was nominally in charge (Child, *Central American Peace Process*, 130).

52. The agreement covered forces previously based in Honduras, that is, the "Northern Front" of the Resistance, but not the "Southern Front," which operated out of Costa Rica. As of early June, the latter still had no demobilization accord with the government, but one was reached on June 8-9 that included a separate security zone. Two large additional security zones were established in the northeast part of the country to demobilize fighters of the Miskito Indians, who formed the "Atlantic Front" of the Resistance (United Nations Documents S/21341, June 4, 1990, 3-5; and S/21379, June 29, 1990, 1-2).

53. Interview 75, July 11, 1991; United Nations Document S/21379, 2; Child, *Central American Peace Process*, 146.

54. United Nations Document S/21909, October 26, 1990, 4.

55. United Nations Document, S/23421, January 14, 1992, 2-3.

56. *New York Times*, November 10, 1991, 10 and February 11, 1992, A10; and *Washington Post*, March 7, 1992, A17.

Epilogue: Peacekeeping in Uncharted Territory

by William J. Durch

The four-fold expansion of UN peacekeeping operations in 1992 and the continued growth in demand for peacekeepers in 1993 outstripped the UN Secretariat's cottage industry approach to planning, financing, command, and control. Although the Secretariat made efforts to reform itself in 1993—expanding the staff of the Military Advisor's office and bringing the Field Operations Division into a consolidated Department of Peace Operations—it continues to face severe shortages of money, troops, and other resources needed to cope with the complex and dangerous new operations thrust upon it by the Security Council. Four of these are sketched briefly here, chosen for the precedents they set and, in the case of operations in former Yugoslavia and Somalia, for the difficult questions they raise about the proper role of international peacekeeping—and enforcement—in the post–cold war world.

EL SALVADOR

The civil war in El Salvador, whose origins are outlined in the chapter on ONUCA, continued to burn through 1989. Although the new government of President Alfredo Cristiani and the *Frente Faribundo Marti para la Liberacion Nacional* (FMLN) had begun a tentative "dialog aimed at ending the armed conflict... by political means," in November the FMLN launched their largest offensive of the war against the capital city, San Salvador.[1] The guerrillas failed to ignite a popular insurrection but demonstrated that they could bring the war to the doorsteps of the country's elite. The government, on the other hand, outraged US public opinion when air force planes bombed city neighborhoods suspected of harboring FMLN guerrillas and army troops murdered six Jesuit scholars considered rebel sympathizers because they advocated a negotiated peace.[2]

Stalemated militarily, both sides accepted UN mediation in January 1990. The following April, they agreed to the framework of a settlement. The first formal agreement signed under this framework in July 1990 called on the United Nations to verify the observance of fundamental rights and freedoms in El Salvador. The UN would have free run of the country, authority to speak with any individual or group and to visit "any place or establishment freely and without prior notice." Although agreement on the rest of the peace package went slowly, a small UN office opened in San Salvador in January 1991 and the Security Council authorized a larger United Nations Mission in El Salvador (ONUSAL) in May 1991. The lack of a formal cease-fire made ONUSAL's work more dangerous, but the two Salvadoran parties' agreement the previous month to a sweeping series of constitutional reforms, including reform of the military, appeared to more than justify the UN deployment as an important confidence-building measure.[3]

Fighting continued along with the peace talks. The FMLN acquired and used shoulder-fired Soviet surface-to-air missiles against the Salvadoran air force, grounding it for a time and eliminating a key government advantage over the guerrillas.[4]

On September 25, 1991, the two sides reached agreement on most remaining issues, but three more months would pass before the last details were ironed out in the final hours of Javier Pérez de Cuéllar's tenure as Secretary General. The final treaty of peace was signed January 16, 1992, and a formal cease-fire took effect on February 1.[5]

The Security Council increased the size of ONUSAL to 1,098 on January 14. Military observers began arriving in El Salvador in time to oversee the initial separation of forces and their assembly in designated cantonment areas. The peace agreement called for demobilization of the FMLN; for a smaller, "purified" army; and for a complete restructuring of the Salvadoran security apparatus, including the creation of a National Civil Police that would relieve the armed forces of all responsibility for internal security—a crucial reform.[6]

Demobilization of the FMLN ran late and the sides traded charges of foot-dragging but there were no significant cease-fire violations. On the other hand, elements of the FMLN withheld significant quantities of arms from the UN as a hedge against government non-compliance. Their existence was revealed when a garage in Managua, Nicaragua, exploded in late May 1993. Not wanting to further complicate the peace process, the FMLN promised full cooperation with the UN and all arms had reportedly been handed over to ONUSAL for disposal by mid-August 1993. The government, for its part, was slow to enact land reforms and to dismiss military officers cited by a UN commission for severe human rights violations during the long civil war. However, under international pressure (including a suspension of US military aid) President Cristiani ultimately complied. Such pressure, a substantial UN presence, and a fundamental desire on all sides to leave the war behind, helped to keep the Salvadoran peace accords on track.[7]

CAMBODIA

Cambodia avoided the worst of the Indochina War for a quarter century, only to fall victim to the most genocidal regime to take power since the fall of Nazi Germany in 1945. The Communist Khmer Rouge killed more than a million Cambodians (about one in seven) between 1975 and 1979, and more than 200,000 Cambodians fled the country as refugees (of these, 140,000 were resettled permanently in the United States). Vietnam invaded Cambodia in 1979, drove the Khmer Rouge into the bush, and installed a new government. In 1983, former Cambodian leader Prince Norodom Sihanouk formed the "Cambodian National Resistance," which joined two noncommunist guerrilla armies— Sihanouk's National Army of Independent Kampuchea and the Khmer People's National Liberation Front—in an unlikely alliance with the Khmer Rouge to fight the Vietnam-backed State of Cambodia (SOC). The new fighting caused still more Cambodians to flee their homes.[8]

It became clear by the late 1980s that neither the SOC nor the Resistance had sufficient strength to win militarily. In February 1989, the Resistance called for a UN peacekeeping force to supervise withdrawal of Vietnamese forces from the country, to oversee national elections, and to supervise the creation of a new, integrated national military. Six months later, under pressure from Congress, the Bush Administration agreed to stop seeking military aid for the Resistance and to seek a political solution to the conflict. The five Permanent Members of the Security Council, who were also the major external funders of Cambodia's various factions, published the outline of a plan for a UN peacekeeping force and UN-supervised elections in January 1990. Eight months later, a fleshed-out version of the plan was endorsed by all four

Cambodian factions, under pressure from their respective donors.[9]

For the next year, the Cambodian parties wrangled over important details while their patrons were distracted by the crisis and war in the Persian Gulf. When that distraction ended, progress resumed, and the four factions reached agreement on a cease-fire in June 1991. In September, they asked for a small UN peace mission to oversee the cease-fire. On October 23, they signed a "Comprehensive Political Settlement of the Cambodia Conflict," a settlement that called for a remarkable makeover of the country's political system.[10]

For the United Nations, the hard part was just beginning. The UN did not have access to detailed information on the size, equipment, or disposition of each faction's forces. Such data was crucial to decisions about the number and location of troop cantonment areas and the number of peacekeepers needed to guard them, but it was not in hand until December 1991. Meanwhile, the observer mission requested by the parties in September began to deploy.

The small UN Advance Mission in Cambodia (UNAMIC) established communications amongst the headquarters of all four factions, tried to resolve violations of the cease-fire, and trained civilians to avoid and report land mines and booby-traps. But the scale of the mine problem led the UN quickly to emphasize de-mining operations and to add a thousand ordnance disposal experts to the UNAMIC staff.[11]

The larger UN Transitional Authority in Cambodia (UNTAC) remained in the planning stage, however, as 1992 began. In late January, the Secretary General asked the General Assembly for $200 million to support early deployment and equipment purchases, lest the operation be even further delayed. The mission plan for UNTAC, completed in February, called for twelve battalions of infantry (10,200 troops) plus 12,000 other military and civilian personnel (logistics, communications, and transport troops, police monitors, election officials, and civil administrators). The total budget came to $2.1 billion.[12]

The first UN troops arrived in Phnom Penh in mid-March 1992, just two weeks after the Security Council approved the plan for UNTAC but nearly five months after signature of the Paris Accords. The troops were followed by the Special Representative of the Secretary General, Yasushi Akashi, a long-time UN official and the first Japanese to head a UN peacekeeping mission.

Akashi's arrival in Cambodia was punctuated by Khmer Rouge attacks on SOC forces in the north-central part of the country. Although the Khmer Rouge soon allowed UN forces into areas that they controlled, they refused to move their troops into UN cantonment areas or to cooperate in preparations for nationwide elections set for May 1993. Unable to physically dislodge the Khmer Rouge, who were roundly suspected of hiding large amounts of arms for later use, the UN opted to work around them, hoping that, as normal conditions returned in the rest of the country, Khmer Rouge cadres and their families would vote with their feet and slip away to UN/government territory.[13]

Only two months before the elections, violence on the part of government supporters against opposition politicians and the detention of UN peacekeepers (and killing of other UN officials) in Khmer Rouge–held areas produced a crisis within UNTAC. Indeed, the violence and intimidation continued until the eve of the vote. However, outside pressure, UN perseverance, and the determination of the average Cambodian led in the end to elections in which 89 percent of registered voters cast ballots. The royalist opposition party known as FUNCINPEC (the French acronym for United Front for an Independent, Neutral, Peaceful and Cooperative Cambodia), founded by Prince Sihanouk, won an unexpected 45 percent of the vote to the government party's 38 percent. (Eighteen other parties shared the remaining 17 percent.) The mixed results produced a flurry of Sihanouk-led coalition-building and astonished the Khmer Rouge, whose propaganda was predicated on a steamroller win by the SOC. After weighing the results for a time, they offered to join the process they had been threatening, if they were given some role in the new coalition government. As of mid-summer 1993, their offer had not been accepted; indeed, the new government appeared ready to take on the Khmer Rouge militarily as UNTAC prepared to fold its tents and go home.[14]

Cambodia was far from healed by mid-1993, but the peace accords gave the country a new start. Although their country remained poor and riddled with mines, many Cambodians were able to go home for the first time in a decade and they had the makings of a government widely recognized as legitimate for the first time in two decades. For all of its troubles, UNTAC made that possible.

THE FORMER YUGOSLAVIA

The state of Yugoslavia was a patchwork of nations created by the victors of World War I from the ashes of the Austro-Hungarian Empire and the Balkan provinces of the former Ottoman Empire. Age-old animosities were not resolved by this political marriage, merely suppressed beneath one or another political structure: Serbian royalty before World War II, Nazi occupation during the war, and Marshall Tito's Communist federation afterward. During the occupation at least a million Yugoslavs died, either fighting in resistance groups, as victims of Nazi reprisals, or in concentration camps. Many of the latter were Jews or Serbs targeted by a collaborationist Croat regime, the Ustashe, who gave the Serbs another reason to hate their Croat neighbors.[15]

Still, Tito managed to keep his fractious country together and, at least in urban areas, its peoples mingled peaceably. After his death in 1980, however, the tenuous nature of national unity was clear. The country's presidency rotated among its several component republics. When the demise of the Warsaw Pact ended the major external threat to the country, Yugoslavia's peoples could focus more single-mindedly on their differences. The northernmost republic, Slovenia, which is ethnically homogeneous, declared independence on June 25, 1991 and fought off a brief Yugoslav Army effort to bring it back into the fold. Thereafter, it was left alone.[16]

Croatia, its neighbor to the south, declared its independence at the same time but was less well-prepared to defend itself, having long and difficult borders and a large Serbian minority that sought to create its own "republic" with help from the Serb-dominated Yugoslav Army and Air Force. Fighting began in late summer 1991 and continued through the end of the year.[17]

Former US Secretary of State Cyrus Vance, serving as UN mediator for the conflict, negotiated a series of short-lived cease-fires. In late February 1992, when Vance's 15th cease-fire accord had been holding for six weeks, the Security Council agreed to deploy a 14,000-strong peacekeeping force—the sadly-misnamed UN Protection Force (UNPROFOR)— into Serb-controlled areas and to place militia weapons under lock and key.[18]

The leaders of the operation reached Croatia in early March. They soon decided to establish Force Headquarters in Sarajevo, capital of neighboring Bosnia-Herzegovina, which had remained relatively free of violence.[19] However, Bosnia-Herzegovina's population in early 1992 was about 17 percent Croat, 30 percent

Serb, and 44 percent Muslim (descendants of Slavs who converted to Islam under the Ottoman Empire). There were no clear ethnic enclaves, although Serbs tended to dominate the countryside while urban areas were mixed.[20]

Germany recognized the independence of Slovenia and Croatia in December 1991 and the European Community followed suit in January. No sooner had Germany recognized these republics, however, than Bosnia applied for recognition as well, prompting Serbian nationalists within Bosnia to seize what land they could before the government could build up its armed forces. The Bosnian Serbs tapped into rural arms depots and their military ranks swelled with soldiers "released" from national service as the Yugoslav Army withdrew from Bosnia under international pressure.[21] The Serbs were, as a result, far better armed than the Bosnian government itself when fighting broke out in early April 1992, one day after the EC and the United States recognized Bosnian independence.

Serbian gunners began to shell Sarajevo, and militia bands elsewhere in the country began the infamous campaign of "ethnic cleansing" designed to drive non-Serbs from their homes and create a "pure" Serb territory. The campaign ultimately displaced more than two million people and killed thousands.[22]

Units of UNPROFOR were sent to Sarajevo in June to help secure food shipments to the beleaguered city. At about the same time, casualty estimates for the country as a whole began to climb rapidly as outsiders (primarily relief agencies and the press) learned more about the systematic brutality of the ethnic cleansing campaign.[23] On August 13, the UN Security Council authorized the use of force to facilitate delivery of humanitarian assistance within Bosnia. But a situation unsuited to peacekeeping looked to be equally unsuited to outside military intervention. Securing aid to Sarajevo alone was estimated to require 100,000 troops.[24]

As an alternative to forceful intervention, starting in September 1992, NATO countries and Ukraine contributed several thousand troops to escort humanitarian relief convoys under peacekeeping-type rules of engagement. That is, they fired only when fired upon, and then sparingly, and tried to negotiate their way past military obstacles, turning back when negotiation failed. They probably helped get supplies into isolated towns when unescorted convoys would have failed to do so but they also became hostages to the good behavior of the United States and

NATO, which periodically seemed on the verge of forceful intervention.

By early 1993, negotiations conducted by Cyrus Vance and EC mediator Lord Owen had produced the Vance-Owen peace plan for ten semi-autonomous provinces within the existing borders of Bosnia. Most of these were to have a dominant ethnic group.[25]

The Bosnian Croats accepted the plan immediately and the Muslim-led government accepted it within a few months but the Bosnian Serbs refused, partly because the plan required that they give back much of what they had conquered and partly because it assumed that a fair apportionment of land and resources was what the parties to this conflict wanted. It was not. The expatriate Serbs in both Bosnia and Croatia looked to join a Greater Serbia and were materially supported in their ambitions by Serbia's nationalist President Slobodan Milosevic. The Bosnian Croats, in turn, looked toward anschluss with Croatia, and its President, Franjo Tudjman, was happy to oblige. Military help from Zagreb was increasingly visible by the summer of 1993, and fighting in central Bosnia between Croats and Muslims became as vicious as earlier fighting between Muslims and Serbs, as partition loomed and each group clawed for territory.[26]

The three-cornered war further complicated any notion of outside military intervention, including military support for the "safe areas" established by the Security Council around six Bosnian cities with large Muslim refugee populations. The United States and NATO made motions to intervene several times through late summer 1993. Each threat seemed to bring progress in negotiations and each default more fighting, as Serbs and Croats came to believe that anything they wished to do could be done with little risk of reprisal from the international community.

The breakup of Yugoslavia illustrates one of the wrenching dilemmas of the emerging world of ethnic conflict that seems to be succeeding the Cold War. If Western countries, and the United States in particular, wish to maintain a position of moral and political leadership in the world, they cannot afford to ignore these internecine battles, especially when states and peoples who support the rule of law have been set upon by those who do not. But if they become directly involved in settling strife by force, Western states may find themselves committed to endless struggle in every corner of the globe, with waning political support from their publics, who have their own valid claims to national resources.

The international response to the Yugoslav conflict and others like it in the Caucasus, Afghanistan, and Africa suggest that states are not eager to embark on such a campaign. If a region as wealthy and powerful as Europe is unwilling to commit more than food relief and mediators to conflict situations, poorer and less well-organized regions are unlikely to do more. Yet the tug of human tragedy, made stronger by live television images of chaos and death, cannot always be ignored. Thus it was that, in late 1992, the United States and the United Nations sent troops into the territory that had once been the state of Somalia.

SOMALIA

During the Cold War, Somalia was a valuable piece of strategic real estate to the superpowers. Occupying the tip of the Horn of Africa, Somalia borders sealanes used by shipping bound for Israel and the Suez Canal. In the 1970s, the port and air strip at Berbera in northern Somalia were used by the Soviet Navy and, from 1978 to 1988, by the US Navy. Both countries bought the allegiance of Somalia's leader, Mohammed Siad Barre, with economic and military aid. By the time the Cold War was over, Somalia was awash in weapons.

Although Somalis share a single ethnic background, a single language, and a single religion (Sunni Islam), they are divided by clan, subclan, and family. To keep himself in power for more than two decades, Siad Barre recruited government officials from his own Marehan subclan, which represents just one percent of Somalia's population, played other clans against one another, and ruthlessly suppressed opposition.[27]

Separate clan-based resistance movements sprang up nonetheless in the central and southern regions, and by late 1990, fighters of the Hawiye-based United Somali Congress (USC) were closing in on the capital, Mogadishu. As the city collapsed into gunfire and looting, the expansive grounds of the American Embassy became a last refuge for the 250 foreigners remaining in the city, including Soviet diplomats. The US mounted a brief rescue operation that swept them all to safety.[28]

Siad Barre fled Mogadishu at the end of January 1991. Although Ali Mahdi Mohamed of the USC was sworn in as interim president, the country settled into a long night of armed anarchy. Although confirmed as interim president by most of the country's factions meeting in nearby Djibouti the following July, Mohamed controlled little more than the northern half of Mogadishu. He soon faced opposition from the military leader of the USC, General Mohamed Farah Aidid, who controlled the southern half. Serious fighting broke out in November 1991. Both sides' forces consisted largely of teenaged gunmen high on *qat*, a local narcotic, who roved the city in land cruisers armed with anti-aircraft cannon or recoilless rifles, which they fired at anything that moved and most things that didn't. The city in which they fought had no public administration, no police, no courts, no power, and little of value that had not long since been looted.[29]

The fighting interrupted Red Cross food shipments (UN relief agencies had long since pulled out of the country) and without food aid, the city began to starve. Some aid still reached the countryside, but the fighting displaced farmers and kept them from sowing new crops, while hunger led others to eat their seed stocks. By early spring, while the UN attempted to broker a cease-fire between the two warlords, the entire country verged on starvation as the gangs fought over relief supplies, some at the behest of merchants who then offered the food for resale.

Cease-fire pledges signed in March 1992 did have some effect. Mohamed and Aidid agreed to a UN "monitoring mechanism" to oversee the cease-fire and distribution of food in the city. However, of the estimated 20,000 fighters roaming Mogadishu, perhaps one in five was under the nominal control of either leader, leading some to argue that a cease-fire would only arise from a massive infusion of foodstuffs and not vice-versa.[30]

In late April 1992, the Security Council approved deployment of 50 unarmed military observers to Mogadishu to mind food shipments, after the United States objected to the cost of an armed force of 500. The State Department's argument—that the Congress would not countenance yet another peacekeeping mission that year—was undercut by Senator Nancy Kassebaum's visit to the region and subsequent public advocacy of an armed force to protect UN workers and food shipments. In August, the UN started relief flights into Somalia's wasted interior, joining the Red Cross in doing so. As the first UN aircraft took off, Washington announced an independent US airlift of supplies.[31]

Without security on the ground, however, foodstuffs were either pinned in dockside warheouses or looted en route to distribution centers. One-third of Somalia's population approached starvation.

In August, the Security Council authorized a 4,200-member peacekeeping mission, dubbed the UN Operation in Somalia (UNOSOM), to escort food supplies. But only Pakistan contributed troops and its 500-strong contingent was too small and too lightly-equipped to deal with the heavily-armed gangs ruling Mogadishu's streets.[32]

As the security situation in southern Somalia continued to deteriorate, relief ships approaching Mogadishu harbor were shelled and little relief was reaching refugees. In late November, the United States offered US ground forces to protect relief shipments, and the Security Council accepted with alacrity. In short order, some 34 other countries volunteered to send troop contingents to Somalia under US command. The first contingents of US Marines arrived in Mogadishu December 9, followed closely by French Legionnaires, units of the US Army's 10th Mountain division, and Saudi, Belgian, and other forces. Over a period of three weeks, as adequate forces built up, the "Unified Task Force" (UNITAF) secured food delivery and distribution throughout southern Somalia.[33]

It soon became clear, however, that UNITAF would need to do more than simply deter the gangs and return fire when fired upon. By late December, it began to round up heavy weapons and in early January began to raid arms markets and weapons caches, particularly those of Gen. Aidid, the least cooperative local leader, who had arranged angry mobs to greet Secretary General Boutros-Ghali when he visited Somalia. When Somali factional leaders meeting in Addis Ababa agreed to a cease-fire, UNITAF began to enforce it. On February 25, however, Gen. Aidid's supporters launched two days of destructive rioting in Mogadishu, reminding the international force that he remained a force to be reckoned with.[34]

That reckoning was postponed until after the United States handed over its responsibilities in Somalia to the United Nations. In early June, one month after the transition, Aidid's forces ambushed Pakistani peacekeepers, killing 24 and wounding 59. UN forces retaliated against compounds held by Aidid in a series of operations, both ground and air, some of which caused substantial Somali casualties. By late summer 1993, Gen. Aidid remained at large. Although the rest of southern Somalia was returning to a semblance of order, Mogadishu remained a tense and costly place for the UN, and the operation had no clearly defined end in sight.[35]

♦   ♦   ♦   ♦

Protecting individual human rights while sustaining or rebuilding war torn countries may be the UN's new calling, although, as both Yugoslavia and Somalia demonstrate, it is neither cheap nor easy. Moreover, as we tried to make clear in the introduction to this book, peacekeeping is just one of many tools for containing or reducing conflict. The world is going through a tempestuous period whose end result is not within view and may only be a continuing tempest. The UN hasn't the capacity to deal with all of it, or even most of it, nor is it clear that it should have the responsibility. But if member states and regional organizations continue to give the issues that are "too hard" to the world body, then provided it does not fail ignominiously, the added exertion may yet produce some muscle. To be effective, that muscle must still be used with the consent of those it is to benefit, but the consent may emanate from peoples rather than governments—from the new source of sovereignty rather than the old. Like peacekeeping itself, which was devised to untangle warring states and has evolved to assist suffering peoples, the United Nations, with its growing programs of support for human rights and democratic political process, may yet evolve, not into world government but into a global overwatch on government. *Quis custodiet ipsos custodes?* [Who will guard the guardians?] We may be seeing, after many centuries, a glimmer of an answer.

Notes

1. "ONUSAL: The Peace Process in El Salvador and the United Nations," United Nations Document DPI/1149A, July 1991, 1.
2. Joel Millman, "A Force Unto Itself: El Salvador's Army," *The New York Times Magazine*, December 10, 1989, 47, 95. Most of the 75,000 who died in the Salvadoran civil war were civilians, and most of those died at the hands of extra-legal death squads associated with the government's security forces.
3. "ONUSAL," 2, and *New York Times*, April 29, 1991, A3. For the text of the July 1990 agreement, see United Nations Document A/44/971, August 16, 1991. This phase of ONUSAL was authorized by Security Council Resolution 693, May 20, 1991.
4. *New York Times*, July 24, 1991, A2, and August 23, 1991, A5.
5. Shirley Christian, "Salvadoran Chief and Rebels Reach Broad Agreement," *New York Times*, September 26, 1991, A1.
6. United Nations Security Council, press release, SC/5345, January 14, 1992, and *International Defense Review*, 3/1992, 218. For the text of the agreement, see United Nations Document A/46/864, January 30, 1992.

7. United Nations, *Further Report of the Secretary-General on the United Nations Observer Mission in El Salvador* (S/26005), June 29, 1993, 1–5. *Washington Post*, March 16, 1993, A1. *New York Times*, July 2, 1993, A5. *Los Angeles Times*, August 19, 1993, 2.

8. Most of the nearly 350,000 people who fled the fighting in the 1980s got no further than a series of camps set up along the Thailand-Cambodia border, because they were classed as "displaced" (persons driven from their homes by prevailing conditions) rather than as "refugees" (persons who would be individually persecuted should they return home). See David A. Albin and Marlowe Hood, eds., *The Cambodian Agony* (Armonk, New York: M.E. Sharpe, Inc., 1987); Elizabeth Becker, *When the War Was Over: the voices of Cambodia's revolution and its people* (New York: Simon and Schuster, 1986); and William Shawcross, *Quality of Mercy: Cambodia, Holocaust, and Modern Conscience* (New York: Simon and Schuster, 1984). On refugee issues, see United States General Accounting Office, *Multilateral Relief Efforts in Border Camps*, Report NSIAD-91-99FS (Washington, D.C.: GAO, January 1991), 1-4.

9. Facilitating a settlement, Vietnam announced the withdrawal of its armed forces from Cambodia in September 1989. (*Los Angeles Times*, February 10, 1989, 15. *New York Times*, June 18, 1989, 1. United Nations, *UN Chronicle* [New York: UN Department of Public Information, December 1989], 21. *New York Times*, January 16, 1990, 1; June 5, 1990, A10, July 19, 1990, A1; August 29, 1990, A1; and September 10, 1990, A1.) For the text of the Perm Five peace plan, see United Nations Document A/45/472, August 31, 1990. The UN Security Council endorsed the plan in Resolution 668 of September 20, 1990.

10. *Financial Times*, October 21, 1991, 17; United Nations Document A/46/608, October 30, 1991.

11. United Nations Document S/23097, September 30, 1991; *World Refugee Survey, 1992* (Washington, D.C.: US Committee for Refugees, 1992), 20; United Nations Documents S/23331, December 30, 1991, 3, and S/23331/Add.1, January 6, 1992.

12. United Nations Documents S/23458, January 24, 1992, 2; S/23613, February 19, 1992; and S/23613/Add.1, February 26, 1992. The proposed budget did not include funds for rebuilding Cambodia's ruined infrastructure.

13. *Washington Post*, April 22, 1992, A24 and June 14, 1992, A30. *New York Times*, April 12, 1992, 22.

14. *New York Times*, June 1, 1993, A9; June 4, 1993, A1; June 15, 1993, A3; August 3, 1993, A5; and August 4, 1993, A5. *Far Eastern Economic Review*, June 10, 1993, 18–23.

15. L. S. Stavrianos, *The Balkans since 1453* (New York: Holt, Rinehart, Winston, 1958), 771-784.

16. *New York Times*, September 2, 1991, 3.

17. *New York Times*, July 4, 1991, A1. The UN sooned embargoed arms to all six Yugoslav republics, but the resolution lacked enforcement provisions (*New York Times*, September 26, 1991, A6). Relentless and indiscriminate shelling during the 86-day siege of Vukovar in northern

Croatia presaged similar treatment for many other cities and towns in both Croatia and Bosnia (*New York Times*, November 18, 1991, A3).
18. Vance's persistent efforts supplemented those of the European Community. The EC sent unarmed civilian observers into Serbia in July 1991, and into Croatia two months later, without appreciable effect. In January 1992, five peace observers died when their helicopter was shot down over northern Croatia by a Yugoslav Air Force fighter. (*New York Times*, July 29, 1991, A3; December 3, 1991, A8; and January 8, 1992, A1. *Washington Post*, September 1, 1991, A24.)

For the initial mandate and authorization of UNPROFOR, see United Nations Documents S/23280, December 11, 1991; S/23592, February 15, 1992; and S/RES/743, February 21, 1992. UNPROFOR deployed along the cease-fire lines inside Croatia, leading critics to charge that the UN was helping Serbia consolidate its military gains and free military resources for other conquests.

19. United Nations Document S/23777, April 2, 1992, 1.

20. *Washington Post*, January 15, 1992, A17.

21. *New York Times*, December 13, 1991, A6; December 23, 1991, A1; January 2, 1992, A3; March 3, 1992, A9; May 6, 1992, A10. *Washington Post*, May 17, 1992, A26.

22. *New York Times*, April 5, 1992, 3; April 7, 1992, A3; July 24, 1992, A1; June 5, 1993, A1.

23. Serbian militias routinely and systematically raped and impregnated Bosnian Muslim women in an apparent policy of slow-motion genocide intended to make their victims socially and psychologically incapable of bearing the next generation of Muslim young. (Grace Halsell, "Women's Bodies a Battlefield in War for 'Greater Serbia'," *The Washington Report on Middle East Affairs*, April/May 1993, 8–9. Anna Quindlen, "Gynocide," *New York Times*, March 10, 1993, A19. Elaine Sciolino, "Abuses by Serbs the Worst Since Nazi Era," *New York Times*, January 20, 1993, A8, citing the Bush Administration's final human rights report.)

24. The Council authorized member states to take "all measures necessary to facilitate" the delivery of assistance (*New York Times*, May 16, 1992, 3; August 11, 1992, A6; and August 12, 1992, A8).

25. For details of the Vance-Owen plan, see United Nations, Security Council, *Report of the Secretary General on the Activities of the International Conference on the Former Yugoslavia*, United Nations Document S/25050, January 6, 1993, annex V.

26. Serb forces drove villagers who survived initial assaults into regional centers and then besieged the centers. UN forces played a constant and wearying game of access with Serbian and, later, Croat militias in an effort to bring food and medicines into these areas. (See, for example, *New York Times*, November 20, 1992, A1; February 19, 1993, A3; March 4, 1993, A8; March 12, 1993, A8; May 10, 1993, A8; July 1, 1993, A3; and August 25, 1993, A6.)

27. In May 1988, organized resistance in the northern city of Hargeisa, led by members of the Isaak clan, led to the slaughter of up to 5,000

mostly civilian Isaaks by the Somali Army; 300,000 others fled into Ethiopia. The United States cut off military aid. (*New York Times*, September 8, 1989, 1, and *Washington Post*, February 18, 1990, A23.)

28. Helicopters carrying US Marines trained in special operations lifted off the amphibious assault ships *USS Guam* and *USS Trenton*, sooner than planned, as the embassy came under rocket attack. They were refueled twice in mid-air by tanker aircraft flown down from Bahrain, more than 2,000 kilometers to the north. The tightly choreographed mission was completed without loss of life (*New York Times*, January 6, 1991, A3, and *Washington Post*, January 9, 1991, 8).

29. *New York Times*, January 30, 1991, A2; The *Economist*, November 16, 1991, 56; *New York Times*, December 8, 1991, A1; and United Nations Document S/23696, March 11, 1992, 4, 11. Perhaps 20,000 Somalis died in the fighting to oust Siad Barre. The renewed fighting killed another 30,000 people and drove at least 100,000 more into exile, this time to northern Kenya, itself seared by the drought then afflicting all of East Africa (*Washington Post*, November 22, 1991, 36, and February 7, 1992, A22).

30. For texts of the cease-fire notes, see United Nations Document S/23696, Annexes I and III, 19-20, 24-25.

31. *New York Times*, April 26, 1992, 15, and July 20, 1992, A3.

32. United Nations, Security Council Resolution 775, August 28, 1993. *New York Times*, November 2, 1992, A1.

33. Lt. Col. T. A. Richards, USMC, "Marines in Somalia," *US Naval Institute Proceedings*, May 1993, 133–136.

34. *New York Times*, January 7, 1993, A9; January 8, 1993, A1; January 16, 1993, 2; February 25–26, 1993, A1. Somali factions signed a formal peace accord in late March that provided for a transitional national government, disarmament of all factions by the end of June, and sanctions against violators (*Washington Post*, March 28, 1993, A22).

35. *Washington Post*, June 6, 1993, A29, and June 12, 1993, A1. *New York Times*, June 7, 1993, A3; June 14, 1993, A6; and June 18, 1993, A1. UNOSOM II was led by an American, its force commander was from Turkey, a member of NATO, and his deputy was America. This arrangement eased US concerns about leaving 4,000 US logistics troops in Somalia under UN command. (A separate, 1,300-member rapid reaction force also remained, but under US command.) Disagreement over the operation's use of force led the commander of the Italian contingent to take independent initiatives that prompted the UN to seek his recall, which the Italian government refused (New York Times, July 12, 1993, A8; July 14, 1993, A6; and July 17, 1993, 3). Although critical of Italian actions, in its own emerging policies the United States reserved the right to second-guess orders given US forces that might be placed under UN command in the future (New York Times, August 18, 1993, A1).

Bibliography

Books, Reports, Articles

AAI Corporation. *"Pioneer* RPV." Company factsheet. Hunt Valley, MD: AAI Corp., 1987.

Abi-Saab, Georges. *The United Nations Operation in the Congo 1960–1964.* Oxford: Oxford University Press, 1978.

Africa Research Bulletin (1985–1990).

Africa South of the Sahara 1991. 20th Edition. London: Europa Publications Ltd., 1990.

Africa South of the Sahara 1992. 21st Edition. London: Europa Publications Ltd., 1991.

Ajami, Fouad. "The End of Arab Nationalism." *The New Republic,* August 12, 1991, 23-27.

_____. *The Arab Predicament.* Cambridge: Cambridge University Press, 1985.

Albin, David A. and Hood, Marlowe, eds. *The Cambodian Agony.* Armonk, New York: M.E. Sharpe, Inc., 1987.

Amin, Sayed Hassan. "The Iran-Iraq War: Legal Implications." *Marine Policy* 6 (July 1982): 193-218.

Aspin, Hon. Les. "Winning the War and Losing the Peace in Saddam Hussein's Iraq." Mimeograph copy of a speech given in New York, December 12, 1991.

Badeeb, Saeed M. *The Saudi-Egyptian Conflict over North Yemen, 1962–1970.* Boulder, Colorado: Westview Press and the Arab-American Affairs Council, 1986.

Bailey, Sydney D. *Four Arab-Israeli Wars and the Peace Process.* New York: St. Martin's Press, 1990.

_____. *How Wars End: The United Nations and the Termination of Armed Conflict 1946–1964, Vol. II.* Oxford: Clarendon Press, 1982.

Barroso, José Manuel Durão. "The Peace Process in Angola: Evolution and Prospects." Text of a speech delivered to the CSIS Study Group on Angola. Washington, D.C.: Center for Strategic and International Studies, February 20, 1991.

Becker, Elizabeth. *When the War Was Over: the voices of Cambodia's revolution and its people.* New York: Simon and Schuster, 1986.

Benvenisti, Meron. *Conflicts and Contradictions.* New York: Villard Books, 1986.

Best, Edward. *US Policy and Regional Security in Central America.* London: Gower and the International Institute for Strategic Studies, 1987.

Blechman, Barry M. and Hart, Douglas. "The Political Utility of Nuclear Weapons." *International Security* 7 (Summer 1982): 132-156.

Bocharov, Gennady. *Russian Roulette: Afghanistan Through Russian Eyes.* New York: Harper Collins Publishers, 1990.

Brookner, Eli. "Radar Imaging for Arms Control." In Kosta Tsipis, David Hafemeister, and Penny Janeway, eds. *Arms Control Verification.* Washington, D.C.: Pergamon-Brassey's, 1986.

Bull, Odd. *War and Peace in the Middle East.* London: Leo Cooper, 1976.

Burns, E.L.M. *Between Arab and Israeli.* London: George G. Harrap, 1962.

Campbell, Kurt and MacFarlane, Neil, eds. *Gorbachev's Third World Dilemmas.* New York: Routledge, 1989.

Child, Jack. *The Central American Peace Process, 1983–1991.* Boulder, Colorado: Lynne Reinner Publishers, 1992.

"Chronology." *Middle East Journal* 43 (Winter 1989).

"Chronology." *Middle East Journal* 44 (Autumn 1990).

"Chronology." *Middle East Journal* 45 (Spring–Fall 1991).

Chubin, Shahram and Tripp, Charles. *Iran and Iraq at War.* London: I.B. Tauris and Co., Ltd., 1988.

Cobban, Helena. *The Making of Modern Lebanon.* Boulder, Colorado: Westview Press, 1985.

Cohen, Raymond. *Negotiating Across Cultures: Common Obstacles in International Diplomacy.* Washington, D.C.: US Institute of Peace, 1991.

Cordesman, Anthony H. and Wagner, Abraham R. *The Lessons of Modern War, Volume I: The Arab-Israeli Conflicts, 1973–1989.* Boulder, Colorado: Westview Press, 1990.

Crocker, Chester. "Peacemaking in Southern Africa: The Namibia-Angola Settlement of 1988." In David D. Newsom, ed. *The Diplomatic Record 1989–1990.* Boulder, Colorado: Westview Press, 1991.

_____. "Southern African Peace Making" *Survival* (May-June 1990): 221-232.

Damrosch, Lori Fisler and Scheffer, David J., eds. *Law and Force in the New International Order.* Boulder, Colorado: Westview Press, 1991.

Dayal, Rajeshwar. *Mission for Hammarskjöld.* Princeton, NJ: Princeton University Press, 1976.

Dayan, Moshe. *Moshe Dayan: Story of My Life.* New York: William Morrow and Co., 1976.

Deng, Francis M. and Zartman, I. William, eds. *Conflict Resolution in Africa.* Washington, D.C.: The Brookings Institution, 1991.

Diehl, Paul F. "Peacekeeping Operations and the Quest for Peace." *Political Science Quarterly* 103, no. 3 (1988): 485-507.

Downs, Anthony. *Inside Bureaucracy.* Boston: Little, Brown, and Company, 1967.

Durch, William J. "The Cuban Military in Africa and the Middle East." *Studies in Comparative Communism 11*, nos. 1 & 2 (Spring-Summer 1978): 34-74.

_____ and Blechman, Barry M. *Keeping the Peace: The United Nations in the Emerging World Order.* Washington, D.C.: The Henry L. Stimson Center, March 1992.

Eban, Abba. *Abba Eban: An Autobiography.* New York: Random House, 1977.

Eisenhower, Dwight D. *White House Years: Waging Peace.* Garden City, New York: Doubleday & Co., 1965.

El-Ayouty, Yassin and Zartman, I. William, eds. *The OAU after Twenty Years.* New York: Praeger Publishers, 1984.

Erskine, Emmanuel. *Mission with UNIFIL.* New York: St. Martin's Press, 1989.

Facts on File. Annual. New York: Facts On File, Inc.

Falk, Richard A. "The Afghanistan 'Settlement' and the Future of World Politics." In Amin Saikal and William Maley, eds. *The Soviet Withdrawal from Afghanistan.* Cambridge: Cambridge University Press, 1989.

Firebrace, James. "The Sahrawi Refugees: Lessons and Prospects." In Richard Lawless and Laila Monahan, eds. *War and Refugees, The Western Sahara Conflict.* London and New York: Printer Publishers, 1987.

Fisher, Roger and Ury, William. *Getting to Yes: Negotiating Agreement Without Giving In.* Boston: Houghton Mifflin Co., 1981.

Fisk, Robert. *Pity the Nation.* New York: Atheneum, 1990.

Forsythe, David P. *The Internationalization of Human Rights.* Lexington, Massachusetts: Lexington Books, 1991.

Fortna, Virginia Page. *Regional Organizations and Peacekeeping.* Occasional Paper No. 11. Washington, D.C.: The Henry L. Stimson Center, October 1992.

Fox, John. "United States Delegation Performance Report on UN-TAG." Text of a speech delivered April 29, 1991. Washington, D.C.: US Department of State, Bureau of International Organization Affairs, mimeograph.

Franck, Thomas. "Theory and Practice of Decolonization: the Western Sahara Case." In Richard Lawless and Laila Monahan, eds. *War and Refugees, The Western Sahara Conflict.* London and New York: Printer Publishers, 1987.

Friedman, Thomas L. *From Beirut to Jerusalem.* New York: Farrar Straus Giroux, 1989.

Fromuth, Peter, ed. *A Successor Vision: The United Nations of Tomorrow.* New York: United Nations Association of the United States, 1988.

Gaffen, Fred. *In the Eye of the Storm, A History of Canadian Peacekeeping.* Toronto: Deneau and Wayne, 1987.

Garthoff, Raymond. *Detente and Confrontation.* Washington, D.C.: The Brookings Institution, 1985.

Geertz, Clifford. *The Interpretation of Cultures.* New York: Basic Books, 1973.

George, Alexander L. "Case Studies and Theory Development: The Method of Structured, Focused Comparison." In Paul Gordon Lauren, ed. *Diplomacy: New Approaches in History, Theory, and Policy.* New York: The Free Press, 1979.

Ghali, Mona. *The Multinational Forces: Non-UN peacekeeping in the Middle East*. Occasional Paper No. 12. Washington, D.C.: The Henry L. Stimson Center, October 1992.

Gilmour, David. *A Fractured Country*. New York: St. Martin's Press, 1983.

Gonzalez, Edward. *Cuba Under Castro: The Limits of Charisma*. Boston: Houghton Mifflin, 1974.

Goulding, Marrack. "The Evolving Role of United Nations Peacekeeping Operations." In *The Singapore Symposium, The Changing Role of the United Nations in Conflict Resolution and Peacekeeping* (DPI/1141). New York: United Nations Department of Public Information, September 1991.

Hägglund, Lt. Gen. Gustav. "Peacekeeping in a Modern War Zone." *Survival* (May–June 1990): 233-240.

Heiberg, Marianne. "Observations on UN Peace Keeping in Lebanon." NUPI Note 305. Oslo, Norway: Norwegian Institute of International Affairs, September 1984.

Heikal, Mohammad H. *Cutting the Lion's Tail: Suez Through Egyptian Eyes*. London: Andre Deutsch, 1986.

Higgins, Rosalyn. *United Nations Peacekeeping, 1946–1967, Documents and Commentary, Vol. I: The Middle East*. London: Oxford University Press, 1969.

––––––––––. *United Nations Peacekeeping, 1946–1967, Documents and Commentary, Vol. II: Asia*. London: Oxford University Press, 1970.

––––––––––. *United Nations Peacekeeping, 1946–1967, Documents and Commentary, Vol. III: Africa*. Oxford: Oxford University Press, 1980.

––––––––––. *United Nations Peacekeeping, 1946–1967, Documents and Commentary, Vol. IV: Europe. New York: Oxford University Press, 1981*.

Hilsman, Roger. *To Move a Nation*. Garden City, New York: Doubleday & Co., 1967.

Hiro, Dilip. *The Longest War: The Iran-Iraq Military Conflict*. London: Grafton Books, 1989.

Holst, Johan Jørgen. "Enhancing Peacekeeping Operations," *Survival* (May–June 1990): 264-275.

Hoskyns, Catherine. *The Congo Since Independence, January 1960–December 1961*. New York: Oxford University Press, 1965.

Hourani, Albert. "Ideologies of the Mountain and the City." In Roger Owen, ed. *Essays on the Crisis in Lebanon*. London: Ithaca Press, 1976.

Hourani, Albert. *Syria and Lebanon*. London: Oxford University Press, 1946.

Hourani, Albert. *The Emergence of the Modern Middle East*. Los Angeles: University of California Press, 1981.

International Defense Review (3/1992): 218.

International Institute for Strategic Studies. *Strategic Survey*. London: IISS, 1985, 1988, 1989, 1991.

James, Alan. *Peacekeeping in International Politics*. New York: St. Martin's Press, 1990.

_____. "The UN Force in Cyprus." *International Affairs* 65 (Summer 1989): 481-500.

_____. "Painful peacekeeping: The United Nations in Lebanon, 1978-82." *International Journal* (October 1983): 613-634.

_____. *The Politics of Peace-keeping*. New York: Frederick A. Praeger, 1969.

Jaster, Robert. *The 1988 Peace Accords and the Future of South-Western Africa*. Adelphi Paper 253. London: International Institute for Strategic Studies, Autumn 1990.

Keesing's Record of World Events. London: Longman, 1989, 1991.

Khalidi, Walid. *Conflict and Violence in Lebanon: Confrontation in the Middle East*. Cambridge, Massachuestts: Center for International Affairs, Harvard University, 1979.

Khouri, Fouad. *The Arab-Israeli Dilemma*. New York: Syracuse University Press, 1985.

Krepon, Michael and Smithson, Amy, eds. *Open Skies, Arms Control, and Cooperative Security*. New York: St. Martin's Press, 1992.

Langston, Bud and Bringle, Don. "The Air View: Operation Praying Mantis." *US Naval Institute Proceedings* (May 1989): 54-65.

Lawless, Richard and Monahan, Laila. *War and Refugees, The Western Sahara Conflict*. London and New York: Printer Publishers, 1987.

Lee, John M.; von Pagenhardt, Robert; and Stanley, Timothy W. *Strengthening United Nations Peacekeeping and Peacemaking: A Summary*. Washington, D.C.: International Economic Studies Institute, April 1992.

Lefever, Ernst W. *Crisis in the Congo, A UN Force in Action*. Washington, D.C.: The Brookings Institution, 1965.

_____ and Joshua, Wynfred. *United Nations Peacekeeping in the Congo: 1960–1964, An Analysis of Political, Executive, and Military Control*. Report prepared for the US Arms Control and Disarmament Agency. Washington, D.C.: The Brookings Institution, 1964.

Legum, Colin, ed. *African Contemporary Record 1986–1987*. New York: Africana Publishing Co., 1988.

_____, ed. *The Battlefronts of Southern Africa*. New York: Africana Publishing Co., 1988.

Leogrande, William M. "From Reagan to Bush: The Transition in US Policy Towards Central America." *Journal of Latin American Studies* 22, no. 3 (October 1990): 595-621.

Lijphart, Arend. *The Trauma of Decolonization: The Dutch and West New Guinea*. New Haven: Yale University Press, 1966.

Lincoff, D. D., ed. *Annual Review of United Nations Affairs*. Dobbs Ferry, New York: Oceana Publications, Inc., 1983, 1985.

Louis, William Roger and Owen, Roger. *Suez 1956: The Crisis and its Consequences*. Oxford: Clarendon Press, 1989.

Lynch, Allen. "Gorbachev's International Outlook." Occasional Paper Series, No. 9. Boulder, Colorado: Westview Press for the Institute for East-West Security Studies, 1989.

Mackinlay, John. "Powerful Peacekeepers." *Survival* (May–June 1990): 241-250.

―――――――. *The Peacekeepers: An Assessment of Peacekeeping Operations at the Arab-Israel Interface*. London: Unwin Hyman, 1989.

Macridis, Roy C. *Contemporary Political Ideologies: Movements and Regimes*, 4th ed. Glenview, Illinois: Scott, Foresman & Co., 1989.

Maddy-Weitzman, Bruce. "Conflict and Conflict Management in Western Sahara: Is the Endgame Near?" *Middle East Journal* 45 (Autumn 1991): 594-607.

Maley, William. "The Geneva Accords of April 1988." In Amin Saikal and William Maley, eds. *The Soviet Withdrawal from Afghanistan*. Cambridge: Cambridge University Press, 1989.

Mandell, Brian S. *The Sinai Experience: Lessons in Multinational Arms Control Verification and Risk Management*. Arms Control Verification Studies No. 3, prepared for the Arms Control and Disarmament Division, Department of External Affairs, Ottawa, Canada, September 1987.

Marchetti, Victor and Marks, John D. *The CIA and the Cult of Intelligence*. New York: Dell Publishing Co., 1974.

Marcum, John. "Africa: A Continent Adrift." *Foreign Affairs* 68, no. 1 (America and the World, 1988–89): 159-179.

Martin, David C. and Walcott, John. *Best Laid Plans*. New York: Simon & Schuster, 1988.

May, Brian. *The Indonesian Tragedy*. London, Boston: Routledge & Kegan Paul, 1978.

McCormick, Shawn. "Angola: The Road to Peace." *CSIS Africa Notes*, No. 125 (June 1991).

McMullen, Christopher J. *Mediation of the West New Guinea Dispute, 1962, A Case Study*. Washington, DC: Institute for the Study of Diplomacy, Georgetown University, 1981.

Miller, Judith and Mylroie, Laurie. *Saddam Hussein and the Crisis in the Gulf*. New York: Random House and Times Books, 1990.

Millman, Joel. "A Force Unto Itself: El Salvador's Army." *New York Times Magazine* (December 10, 1989): 47, 95.

Mills, Susan R. *The Financing of United Nations Peacekeeping Operations*. Occasional Paper No. 3. New York: International Peace Academy, 1989.

Mitchell, Robert. "Peacekeeping and Peacemaking in Cyprus." Background Paper 23. Ottawa: Canadian Institute for International Peace and Security, October 1988.

Molander, Johan. "The Lessons of Iraq: Unconventional Weapons, Inspection and Verification, and the United Nations and Disarmament." Transcript of a briefing given November 13, 1991. Washington, D.C.: The Committee on National Security, 1992.

Neff, Donald. *Warriors at Suez.* New York: Linden Press/Simon & Schuster, 1981.

Nelson, Richard W. "Multinational Peacekeeping in the Middle East and the United Nations Model." *International Affairs* 61 (Winter 1984–85): 67-89.

North, Lisa. *Between War and Peace in Central America: Choices for Canada.* Toronto: CAPA, 1990.

Norton, Augustus R. "Lebanon After Ta'if: Is the Civil War Over?" *The Middle East Journal* 45 (Summer 1991): 457-473.

_____. "The roots of the conflict in Cyprus." In Kjell Skjelsbaek, ed. *The Cyprus Conflict and the Role of the United Nations.* NUPI Report 122. Oslo, Norway: Norwegian Institute of International Affairs, November 1988.

Nutting, Anthony. *No End of a Lesson: The Story of Suez.* London: Constable, 1967.

O'Ballance, Edgar. *The War in the Yemen.* Hamden, Connecticut: Archon Books, 1971.

O'Brien, Conor Cruise. *To Katanga and Back.* New York: Grosset and Dunlap, 1966.

Omar, Rakiya and de Waal, Alex. "Who Prolongs Somalia's Agony?" *New York Times,* February 26, 1992, A21.

Owen, Roger. *Essays on the Crisis in Lebanon.* London: Ithaca Press, 1976.

Parkinson, F. *Latin America, the Cold War, and the World Powers, 1945–1973.* Beverly Hills: Sage Publications, 1974.

Perkins, J. B. "The Surface View: Operation Praying Mantis." *US Naval Institute Proceedings* (May 1989): 66-70.

Quandt, William B. *Decade of Decisions: American Policy Toward the Arab-Israeli Conflict, 1967–1976.* Berkeley and Los Angeles: University of California Press, 1977.

Rabinovitch, Itmar. *The War for Lebanon: 1970–1985.* Ithaca, New York: Cornell University Press, 1985.

Rahmy, Ali Abdel Rahman. *The Egyptian Policy in the Arab World: Intervention in Yemen 1962-67.* Washington, D.C.: University Press of America, 1983.

Rikhye, Indar Jit. *The Sinai Blunder.* London: Frank Cass, 1980.

_____; Egge, Bjørn; and Harbottle, Michael. *The Thin Blue Line: International Peacekeeping and Its Future.* New Haven: Yale University Press, 1977.

Roberts, J. M. *The Pelican History of the World.* Harmondsworth, Middlesex: Penguin Books, Ltd., 1986.

Rothchild, Donald and Hartzell, Caroline. "Great- and Medium-Power Mediations: Angola." *Annals of the American Academy of Political and Social Science 518* (November 1991): 39-57.

Roy, Olivier. *The Lessons of the Soviet/Afghan War*. Adelphi Paper 259. London: International Institute for International Studies, Summer 1991.

Sagan, Scott D. "Nuclear Alerts and Crisis Management." *International Security* 9 (Spring 1985): 99-139.

Salem, Elie A. Speech before the Conference on Lebanon. Washington D.C.: American Task Force on Lebanon, June 27-30, 1991.

Salibi, Kamal. *House of Many Mansions*. Berkeley and Los Angeles: University of California Press, 1988.

Schiff, Ze'ev and Ya'ari, Ehud. *Israel's Lebanon War*. New York: Simon & Shuster, 1984.

Schmidt, Dana Adams. *Yemen, the Unknown War*. New York: Holt, Rinehart and Winston, 1968.

Seale, Patrick. *Asad of Syria: The Struggle for the Middle East*. London: I.B. Tauris, 1988.

Seddon, David. "Morocco at War." In Richard Lawless and Laila Monahan, eds. *War and Refugees, The Western Sahara Conflict*. London and New York: Printer Publishers, 1987.

Segal, David. "The Iran-Iraq War: A Military Analysis." *Foreign Affairs* 66, no. 5 (Summer 1988): 946-963.

Shawcross, William. *Quality of Mercy: Cambodia, Holocaust, and Modern Conscience*. New York: Simon and Schuster, 1984.

Sick, Gary. "Trial by Error: Reflections on the Iran-Iraq War." *Middle East Journal* 43 (Spring 1989): 230-244.

Sifry, Micah and Cerf, Christopher, eds. *The Gulf War Reader*. New York: Random House and Times Books, 1991.

Simon, Herbert A. *Administrative Behavior*, 3rd ed. New York: The Free Press, 1976.

Sivard, Ruth Leger. *World Military & Social Expenditures*, 14th ed. Washington, D.C.: World Priorities, 1991.

Skjelsbaek, Kjell, ed. *The Cyprus Conflict and the Role of the United Nations*. NUPI Report 122. Oslo, Norway: Norwegian Institute of International Affairs, November 1988.

_____ and McDermott, Anthony, eds. *A Thankless Task: The Role of UNIFIL in Southern Lebanon*. NUPI Report 123. Oslo, Norway: Norwegian Institute of International Affairs, December 1988.

Smith, Wayne S. "Lies About Nicaragua." Foreign Policy 67 (Summer 1987): 87-103.

Smithson, Amy. "Multilateral Aerial Inspections." In Michael Krepon and Amy Smithson, eds. *Open Skies, Arms Control, and Cooperative Security*. New York: St. Martin's Press, 1992.

_____. "Open Skies Ready for Takeoff." *Bulletin of the Atomic Scientists* (January-February 1992).

Souresrafil, Behrouz. *The Iran-Iraq War*. Plainview, New York: Guinan Lithographic Co., 1989.

Stavrianos, L. S. *The Balkans since 1453*. New York: Holt, Rinehart, Winston, 1958.

Stevens, Mary Ann, ed. *Annual Review of United Nations Affairs.* Dobbs Ferry, New York: Oceana Publications, Inc., 1973.

Stockwell, John. *In Search of Enemies, A CIA Story.* New York: W.W. Norton & Co., 1978.

Stoessinger, John G. *Financing the United Nations System.* Washington, D.C.: The Brookings Institution, 1964.

The Tower Commission Report. New York: Times Books, 1987.

United Nations Association–National Capital Area. *The Common Defense: Peace and Security in a Changing World.* Washington, D.C.: UNA-USA, June 1992.

Urquhart, Brian. *A Life in Peace and War.* New York: Harper & Row, 1987.

_____. "International Peace and Security: Thoughts on the Twentienth Anniversary of Dag Hammarskjöld's Death." *Foreign Affairs* 60, no. 1 (Fall 1981): 1-16.

_____. *Hammarskjöld.* New York: Alfred A. Knopf, 1972.

_____ and Sick, Gary, eds. *The United Nations and the Iran-Iraq War.* New York: The Ford Foundation, 1987.

von Horn, Carl. *Soldiering for Peace.* New York: David McKay Company, Inc., 1967.

Wagoner, Fred E. *Dragon Rouge: The Rescue of Hostages in the Congo.* Washington, D.C.: National Defense University, 1980.

Wainhouse, David W. *International Peacekeeping at the Crossroads.* Baltimore: The Johns Hopkins University Press, 1973.

_____. *International Peace Observation: A History and Forecast.* Baltimore: The Johns Hopkins University Press, 1966.

West Papua: The Obliteration of a People. London: TAPOL, 1983.

Wiseman, Henry. "The OAU: Peacekeeping and Conflict Resolution." In Yassin El-Ayouty and I. William Zartman, eds. *The OAU After Twenty Years.* New York: Praeger Publishers, 1984.

Wolfe, James H. "United States policy and the Cyprus conflict." In Kjell Skjelsbaek, ed. *The Cyprus Conflict and the Role of the United Nations.* NUPI Report 122. Oslo, Norway: Norwegian Institute of International Affairs, November 1988.

World Refugee Survey, 1992. Washington, D.C.: US Committee for Refugees, 1992.

Yuill, W. A. Douglas. "UNDOF: A Success Story." *Peacekeeping and International Relations* (May–June 1991).

Zartman, I. William. *Ripe For Resolution: Conflict and Intervention in Africa.* New York: Oxford University Press, 1989.

_____ and Berman, Maureen R. *The Practical Negotiator.* New Haven and London: Yale University Press, 1982.

Newspapers and Newsmagazines

Aerospace Daily
Aviation Week and Space Technology
Economist
European Stars and Stripes
Far Eastern Economic Review
Financial Times
Jane's Defence Weekly
Los Angeles Times
New York Times
Washington Post
Washington Times

US Government Documents

US Air Force. Military Airlift Command. Office of the Historian. "MATS Participation in United Nations Peace-Keeping Missions." *MATS/MAC Chronologies*. Scott Air Force Base, Missouri, 1960, 1989.

US Department of State. *The Budget in Brief, Fiscal Year 1993*. February 1992.

——————————. *Bulletin* (1980, 1987, 1988).

US Foreign Broadcast Information Service. *Sub-Saharan Africa*.

US General Accounting Office. *Multilateral Relief Efforts in Border Camps*. Report NSIAD-91-99FS. Washington, D.C.: GAO, January 1991.

US House of Representatives. Committee on Foreign Affairs. *United Nations Peacekeeping in the Middle East, Hearings*. 93rd Cong., 1st sess., December 1973.

——————————. *The US Role in the United Nations, Hearings before the Subcommittee on Human Rights and International Organizations*. 98th Cong., 1st sess, October 1983.

US Senate. Committee on Foreign Relations. *The Western Sahara: The Referendum Process is in Danger*. S. Prt. 102-75, 102d Cong., 2d sess., 1992.

——————————. *Executive Sessions of the Senate Foreign Relations Committee*. 87th Cong., 1st Sess. February 6, 1961. *History Series, Vol. 13, Part 1*.

——————————. *Executive Sessions of the Senate Foreign Relations Committee*. 87th Cong., 2nd Sess. January 18, 1962. *History Series, Vol. 14*, April 1986.

United Nations Documents

General

United Nations. General Assembly. *Unforeseen and Extraordinary Expenses for the Biennium 1990–1991* (A/Res/44/203), December 21, 1989.

_____. *Administrative and Budgetary Aspects of Financing of the United Nations Peace-Keeping Operations:*
    Review of the rates of reimbursement to the governments of troop contributing states (A/45/582), October 10, 1990.
    Review of the background and development of reimbursement to member states contributing troops to peacekeeping operations. Report of the Secretary General, addendum (A/44/605/Add.1), October 12, 1989.
    Report of the Secretary General (A/C.5/44/45), December 5, 1989.
    The feasibility and cost-effectiveness of a reserve stock of equipment...Report of the Secretary General (A/45/493/Add.1), October 30, 1990.

_____. *Comprehensive Review of the Whole Question of Peackeeping Operations in All Their Aspects:*
    Requirements for United Nations Peacekeeping (A/45/217), May 8, 1990.
    Model Agreement Between the United Nations and Member States Contributing Personnel and Equipment to UN Peacekeeping Operations (A/46/185), May 23, 1991.

_____. *Proposed Programme Budget for the Biennium 1992-93, Vol I, part II* (A/46/6/Rev.1), May 24, 1991.

_____. *Report of the Secretary General on the Work of the Organization*
    (A/43/1), September 1988.
    (A/44/1), September 1989.
    (A/45/1), September 1990.
    (A/46/1), September 1991.

_____. *Uniting for Peace* (A/1775), November 3, 1950.

_____. Fifth Committee. *Financial Emergency of the United Nations:*
    Report of the Secretary General (A/C.5/40/16), October 3, 1985.
    Report of the Secretary General (A/C.5/42/31), November 5, 1987.

_____. Fifth Committee. *Scale of Assessments for the Apportionment of the Expenses of the United Nations* (A/C.5/46/L.20), December 19, 1991.

_____. Secretariat. *Financial Regulations and Rules of the United Nations (Series 100)* (ST/SGB/Financial Rules/Rev.3), 1985.

_____. *Status of Contributions as at* 31 December 1991 (ST/ADM/SER.B/364), January 8, 1992. *31 May 1992* (ST/ADM/SER.B/380), June 4, 1992.

_____. Secretary General. "Secretary General announces changes in the Secretariat." Press release (SG/A/479), February 7, 1992.

_____. Secretary General. *An Agenda for Peace: Preventive Diplomacy, Peacemaking, and Peacekeeping* (A/47/277), June 17, 1992.

_____. *The Blue Helmets: A Review of United Nations Peacekeeping*, 2nd ed. New York: UN Department of Public Information, 1990.

_____. *UN Monthly Chronicle* (1980, 1989).

By Peacekeeping Mission (in chapter order)

UNSCOB

United Nations. General Assembly. *[Enabling Resolution]* (A/Res/109), October 21, 1947.

_____. *1st Interim report of the United Nations Special Committee on the Balkans* (A/521), January 9, 1948.

_____. *1st report of the United Nations Special Committee on the Balkans* (A/574), June 30, 1948.

_____. Security Council. *[Report concerning Greek frontier incidents]* (S/360/Rev.1), July 28, 1950.

UNTSO

United Nations. General Assembly. *[Report to the General Assembly from the Palestine Commission]* (A/532), April 10, 1948.

_____. Security Council. *The situation in the Middle East: Report of the Secretary General* (S/21947), November 26, 1990.

UNEF II

United Nations. Security Council. *Report of the Secretary General on the implementation of Security Council resolution 340 (1973)* (S/11052/Rev.1), October 27, 1973, 91.

_____. *Progress report of the Secretary General on the United Nations Emergency Force*
(S/11056/Add. 1), October 30, 1973.
(S/11056/Add.3), November 11, 1973.
(S/11056/Add.6), November 24, 1973.

_____. *Report of the Secretary General on the United Nations Emergency Force,*

    for the period 13 April to 15 July 1975 (S/11758), July 16, 1975.

    for the period 19 October 1976 to 17 October 1977 (S/12416), October 17, 1977.

    for the period 25 October 1977 to 17 October 1978 (S/12897), October 17, 1978.

UNDOF

United Nations. Security Council. [*Report of the Secretary General*] (S/21950), November 19, 1990.

UNOGIL

United Nations. Security Council. *Letter dated 22 May 1958 from the Representative of Lebanon addressed to the President of the Security Council* (S/4007), May 23, 1958.

_____. *Resolution adopted by the Security Council at its 825th meeting on 11 Jun 1958* (S/4023), June 11, 1958.

_____. *Report by the Secretary General on the implementation to date of the resolution of the Security Council of 11 June 1958, on the complaint of Lebanon* (S/4029), June 16, 1958.

_____. *Further report by the Security Council on the implementation of the resolution of the Security Council of 11 June 1958 on the complaint of Lebanon (S/4038), June 28, 1958.*

_____. *1st report of the UN Observation Group in Lebanon* (S/4040), July 3, 1958.

_____. *Interim report of the UN Observation Group in Lebanon submitted through the Secretary General in pursuance of the resolution of the Security Council of 11 June 1958 (S/4023)* (S/4051), July 16, 1958.

_____. *Second interim report of the UN Observation Group in Lebanon submitted through the Secretary General in pursuance of the resolution of the Security Council of 11 June 1958 (S/4023)* (S/4052), July 17, 1958.

_____. *2nd report of the UN Observation Group in Lebanon* (S/4069), July 30, 1958.

_____. *3rd report of the UN Observation Group in Lebanon* (S/4085), August 14, 1958.

UNIFIL

United Nations. Security Council. *Report of the Secretary General on the Interim Force in Lebanon for the period 25 July 1990–22 January 1991* (S/22129), January 23, 1991, and *Addendum* (S/22129/Add. 1), January 28, 1991.

UNYOM

United Nations. Security Council. *Report of the Secretary General on the terms of the disengagement in Yemen* (S/5298), April 29, 1963.

_____. *Report of the Secretary General on Maj. Gen. Carl Von Horn's report on exploratory talks concerning UN observers for Yemen* (S/5321), May 27, 1963.

_____. *Report of the Secretary General on the organization of an observer mission for Yemen* (S/5325), June 7, 1963.

_____. *Letter to the Secretary General from the government of the Yemen Arab Republic* (S/5333), June 17, 1963.

_____. *Letter to the Secretary General from the government of the United Kingdom* (S/5336), June 21, 1963.

_____. *Report of the Secretary General on the functioning to date of the Yemen Observation Mission...* (S/5412), September 4, 1963.

_____. *Report of the Secretary General on the functioning to date of the Yemen Observation Mission...* (S/5447), October 28, 1963.

UNFICYP

United Nations. Security Council. *Resolution adopted by the Security Council at its 1102nd meeting on 4 March 1964* (S/5575), March 4, 1964.

_____. *Letter dated 13 October 1986 from the Secretary-General... containing a further appeal for voluntary contributions for the financing of the UN peacekeeping force in Cyprus* (S/18431, Annex), October 29, 1986.

_____. *Report of the Secretary-General on the United Nations Operation in Cyprus* (S/18491), December 2, 1986.

_____. *Report of the Secretary-General on the UN Operation in Cyprus for the period 1 December 1990–31 May 1991* (S/22665), May 31, 1991.

UNIIMOG

United Nations. General Assembly. *Financing of the United Nations Iran-Iraq Military Observer Group, Report of the Advisory Committee on Administrative and Budgetary Questions* (A/44/874), December 14, 1989.

_____. Security Council. *Resolution adopted by the Security Council at its 2493rd meeting on 31 October 1983* (S/Res/540), October 31, 1983.

_____. *Resolution adopted by the Security Council at its 2750th meeting on 20 July 1987* (S/Res/598), July 20, 1987.

_____. *Report of the Secretary General on the United Nations Iran-Iraq Military Observer Group*
    (S/20862), September 22, 1989.
    (S/21960), November 23, 1990.
    (S/22148), January 29, 1991.

UNIKOM
United Nations. General Assembly. *Financing of the Activities Arising from Security Council Resolution 687 (1991)* (A/45/240/Add.1), April 22, 1991.
_____. *Financing of the Activities Arising from Security Council Resolution 687 (1991): United Nations Iraq-Kuwait Observation Mission* (A/45/1005), April 29, 1991.
_____. Security Council. *Resolution 678 (1991)* (S/Res/678), November 29, 1990.
_____. *Resolution 687 (1991)* (S/Res/687), April 3, 1991.
_____. *Report of the Secretary-General on the Implementation of Paragraph 5 of Security Council Resolution 687 (1991)* (S/22452), April 5, 1991.
_____. *Report of the Secretary-General on the United Nations Iraq-Kuwait Observation Mission*
    (S/22580), May 9, 1991.
    (S/23106), October 2, 1991.
_____. *Note by the President of the Security Council* (S/23699), March 11, 1992.

UNGOMAP
United Nations. General Assembly. *Resolution adopted by the General Assembly: The situation in Afghanistan and its implications for international peace and security* (A/Res/ES-6/2), January 15, 1980.
_____. Security Council. *Letter dated 14 April 1988 from the Secretary General addressed to the President of the Security Council* (S/19834), April 26, 1988.
_____. *Letter dated 22 April 1988 from the Secretary General addressed to the President of the Security Council* (S/19835), April 26, 1988.
_____. *Letter dated 25 April 1988 from the President of the Security Council addressed to the Secretary General* (S/19836), April 26, 1988.
_____. *Implementation of the accords on the settlement of the situation relating to Afghanistan: Report of the United Nations Good Offices Mission in Afghanistan and Pakistan* (S/20465), February 15, 1989.
_____. *The situation in Afghanistan and its implications for international peace and security: Report of the Secretary General* (S/21879), October 17, 1990.

ONUC

United Nations. Security Council. *Resolution adopted by the Security Council at its 873rd meeting on 13 Jul 1960* (S/4387), July 14, 1960.

UNTAG

United Nations. Department of Public Information. *UNTAG in Namibia: A New Nation is Born.* UN Sales No. E.90.I.10. Windhoek and New York: UN, 1990.

_____. Department of Public Information. *Namibia: Chronology 1: Informal Chronology of Contacts of the Secretary-General and his Special Representative for Namibia with Southern African Leaders following the Adoption of Resolution 431 in 1978.* New York: UN, 1988.

_____. Department of Public Information. *Namibia: Chronology 2: Informal Chronology of Security Council Decisions, Secretary General's Reports to the Council and Other Communications.* New York: UN, 1988.

_____. General Assembly. *Financing of the United Nations Transition Assistance Group: Report of the Secretary General* (A/44/856), December 11, 1989.

_____. *Financing of the United Nations Transition Assistance Group: Report of the Secretary General* (A/45/997), April 16, 1991.

_____. *Financing of the United Nations Transition Assistance Group: Report of the Advisory Committee on Administrative and Budgetary Questions* (A/45/1003), April 26, 1991.

_____. Security Council. *Letter dated 10 April 1978 from the Representatives of Canada, France, the Federal Republic of Germany, the United Kingdom of Great Britian and Northern Ireland and the United States of America to the President of the Security Council* (S/12636), April 10, 1978.

_____. *Letter from the Permanent Representative of Cuba to the United Nations to the President of the Security Council* (S/20345), December 22, 1988.

_____. *Report of the Secretary General concerning the implementation of Security Council Resolutions 435 (1978) and 439 (1978) concerning the question of Namibia* (S/20412), January 23, 1989.

_____. *Explanatory statement by the Secretary General concerning his further report (S/20412) concerning the implementation of Security Council Resolutions 435 (1978) and 439 (1978) concerning the question of Namibia* (S/20457), February 9, 1989.

_____. *Report of the Secretary General on the implementation of Security Council Resolution 640 (1989) concerning the question of Namibia* (S/20883), October 6, 1989.

_____. *Report of the Secretary General on the implementation of Security Council Resolution 643 (1989) concerning the question of Namibia* (S/20943), November 3, 1989.

_____. *Further Report of the Secretary General concerning the implementation of Security Council Resolution 435 (1978) concerning the question of Namibia* (S/20967), November 14, 1989.

UNAVEM I

United Nations. General Assembly. *Request for the Inclusion of an additional item in the agenda of the Forty-Third Session, Financing of the United Nations Angola Verification Mission, Addendum, Report of the Secretary General* (A/43/249/Add.1), January 31, 1989.
_____. *Financing of the United Nations Angola Verification Mission, Report of the Secretary General* (A/45/718), November 16, 1990.
_____. *Financing of the United Nations Angola Verification Mission, Report of the Fifth Committee* (A/45/882), December 19, 1990.
_____. Security Council. *Resolution 602 (1987)* (S/Res/602), November 25, 1987.
_____. *Report of the Secretary General in pursuance of Security Council Resolution 602 (1987)* (S/19359), December 18, 1987
_____. *Letter dated 17 December 1988 from the Permanent Representative of Angola to the United Nations addressed to the Secretary General* (S/20336), December 17, 1988.
_____. *Letter dated 17 December 1988 from the Permanent Representative of Cuba to the United Nations addressed to the Secretary General* (S/20337), December 17, 1988.
_____. *Report of the Secretary General* (S/20338), December 17, 1988.
_____. *Letter dated 22 December 1988 from the Permanent Representative of Cuba to the United Nations addressed to the President of the Security Council* (S/20345), December 22, 1988.
_____. *Note verbale dated 22 December 1988 from the Permanent Representative of the United States of America to the United Nations addressed to the Secretary General* (S/20346), December 22, 1988.
_____. *Letter dated 22 December 1988 from the Secretary General addressed to the President of the Security Council* (S/20351), December 23, 1988.
_____. *Interim Report of the Secretary General on the United Nations Angola Verification Mission* (S/20625), May 10, 1989.
_____. *Report of the Secretary General on the United Nations Angola Verification Mission*
    (S/20783), August 11, 1989.
    (S/20955), November 9, 1989.
    (S/21246), April 12, 1990.
    (S/21860), October 10, 1990.

Bibliography 495

_____. *Letter dated 28 May 1991 from Cuba to the United Nations addressed to Secretary General* (S/22644), May 28, 1991.

UNAVEM II

United Nations. *Emergency Aid Contributions Received for Demobilizing Troops in Angola* (IHA/421), October 14, 1991.

_____. General Assembly. *Financing of the United Nations Angola Verification Mission, Report of the Secretary General* (A/45/1028), July 1, 1991.

_____. *Financing of the United Nations Angola Mission, Report of the Advisory Committee on Administrative and Budgetary Question* (A/45/1043), July 31, 1991.

_____. Security Council. *Letter dated 17 May 1991 from the Chargé d'Affaires a.i. of the Permanent Mission of Angola to the United Nations addressed to the Secretary General* (S/22609), May 17, 1991.

_____. *Resolution 696 (1991)* (S/Res/696), May 30, 1991.

_____. *Report of the Secretary General on th United Nations Angola Verification Mission* (S/22627), May 20, 1991.

_____. *Report of the Secretary General in pursuance of Security Council Resolution 696 (1991)* (S/22672), June 4, 1991.

_____. *Report of the Secretary General on the United Nations Angola Verification Mission II (UNAVEM II) for the period 31 May 1991–25 October 1991* (S/23191), October 31, 1991.

_____. *Further report of the Secretary General on the United Nations Angola Verification Mission (UNAVEM II)* (S/23671), March 3, 1992.
Addendum (S/23671/Add.1), March 20, 1992.
(S/24145), June 24, 1992.

MINURSO

United Nations. General Assembly. *Financing of the United Nations Mission for the referendum in Western Sahara:*
Report of the Secretary General (A/45/241/Add.1), May 8, 1991.
Report of the Advisory Committee on Administrative and Budgetary Questions (A/45/1011), May 13, 1991.
Report of the Fifth Committee (A/45/1013), May 16, 1991.

_____. Security Council. *The Situation Concerning Western Sahara: Report of the Secretary General*
(S/21360), June 18, 1990.
(S/22464), April 19, 1991.
(S/22464/Corr. 1), April 22, 1991.
(S/23299), December 19, 1991.
(S/24040), May 29, 1992.

_____. *Report of the Secretary General on the United Nations Mission for the referendum in Western Sahara* (S/23662), February 28, 1992.

ONUCA
United Nations. Department of Public Information. *The United Nations Role in the Central American Peace Process.* New York: UN, May 1990.

_____. *The Peace Process in El Salvador and the United Nations, ONUSAL Fact Sheet No. 1* (July 1991).

_____. General Assembly. *Resolution adopted by the General Assembly, The situation in Central America: Threats to international peace and security and peace initiatives* (A/Res/43/24), January 12, 1989.

_____. *Letter dated 5 April 1989 from the Secretary General addressed to the President of the General Assembly* (A/44/210), April 5 1989.

_____. *Letter dated 6 June 1989 from the Secretary General addressed to the President of the General Assembly* A/44/304, June 6, 1989.

_____. *Letter dated 6 July 1989 from the Secretary General addressed to the President of the General Assembly* (A/44/375), July 7, 1989.

_____. *Letter dated 9 August 1989 from the Permanent Representatives of Costa Rica, El Salvador, Guatemala, Honduras and Nicaragua to the United Nations addressed to the Secretary General* (A/44/451), August 9, 1989.

_____. *Report of the Secretary General on the Situation in Central America, Addendum* (A/44/344/Add. 1), October 9, 1989.

_____. *Financing of the United Nations Observer Group in Central America, Report of the Secretary General* (A/45/833), December 10, 1990.

_____. Security Council. *Letter dated 27 August 1987 from the Permanent Representatives of Costa Rica, El Salvador, Guatemala and Nicaragua to the United Nations addressed to the Secretary General* (S/19085), August 31, 1987.

_____. *Letter dated 24 February 1989 from the representatives of Costa Rica, EL Salvador, Guatemala, Honduras and Nicaragua to the United Nations addressed to the Secretary General* (S/20491), February 27, 1989.

_____. *Letter dated 31 March 1989 from the representatives of Costa Rica, EL Salvador, Guatemala, Honduras and Nicaragua to the United Nations addressed to the Secretary General* (S/20642), May 18, 1989.

_____. *Letter dated 14 April 1989 from the Secretary General addressed to the Ministers of Foreign Affairs of Costa*

Rica, El Salvador, Guatemala, Honduras and Nicaragua (S/20643), May 18, 1989.

_____. *Letter dated 8 May 1989 from the Permanent Representative of Honduras to the United Nations addressed to the Secretary General* (S/20644), May 18, 1989.

_____. *Letter dated 16 May 1989 from the Chargé d'Affaires a.i. of the Permanent Mission of Nicaragua to the United Nations addressed to the Secretary General* (S/20645), May 18, 1989.

_____. *Request for the Inclusion of an Additional Item in the Agenda of the Forty-Fourth Session, Financing of the United Nations Observer Group in Central America, Report of the Secretary General* (A/44/246/Add.1), November 13, 1989.

_____. *Letter dated 12 December 1989 from the Permanent Representative of El Salvador to the United Nations addressed to the Secretary General* (A/44/872), December 12, 1989.

_____. *Letter dated 20 April 1990 from the Secretary General addressed to the President of the Security Council* (S/21259), April 20, 1990.

_____. *Resolution 637 (1989)* (S/Res/637), July 27, 1989.

_____. *Resolution 644 (1989)* (S/Res/644), November 7, 1989.

_____. *Resolution 650 (1990)* (S/Res/650), March 27, 1990.

_____. *Resolution 653 (1990)* (S/Res/653), April 20, 1990.

_____. *United Nations Observer Group in Central America: Report of the Secretary General*
(S/20895), October 11, 1989.
(S/21194), March 15, 1990.
(S/21274), April 27, 1990.
(S/21274/Add.1), May 2, 1990.
(S/21341), June 4, 1990.
(S/21379), June 29, 1990.
(S/21909), October 26, 1990.
(S/22543), April 29, 1991.
(S/23171), October 28, 1991.
(S/23421), January 14, 1992.

ONUSAL

United Nations. Department of Public Information. *ONUSAL: The Peace Process in El Salvador and the United Nations* (DPI/1149A), July 1991.

_____. General Assembly. *Note verbale dated 14 August 1990 from the Chargé d'affaires a.i. of the Permanent Mission of El Salvador to the United Nations addressed to the Secretary General* (A/44/971), August 16, 1990.

_____. *Letter dated 27 January 1992 from the Permanent Representative of El Salvador to the United Nations addressed to the Secretary General* (A/46/864), January 30, 1992.

_____. Security Council. *Resolution 693 (1991)* (S/RES/693), May 20, 1991.

_____. *Security Council Decides to Enlarge Mandate of UN Observer Mission in El Salvador, to Verify and Monitor Peace Agreements.* Press release (SC/5345), January 14, 1992.

_____. *United Nations Observer Mission in El Salvador: Report of the Secretary General* (S/23642), February 25, 1992.

UNTAC
United Nations. General Assembly. *Letter dated 30 October 1991 from the Permanent Representatives of France and Indonesia to the United Nations addressed to the Secretary General* (A/46/608), October 30, 1991.

_____. *Letter dated 18 January 1992 from the Secretary General addressed to the President of th Security Council* (S/23458), January 24, 1992.

_____. *Report of the Secretary General on Cambodia*
(S/23097), September 30, 1991.
(S/23331), December 30, 1991.
(S/23331/Add.1), January 6, 1992.
(S/23613), February 19, 1992. *[Plan for UNTAC]*
(S/23613/Add.1), February 26, 1992.

_____. Security Council. *Resolution 668 (1990)* (S/Res/668), September 20, 1990.

_____. *Resolution 745 (1992) [Establishing UNTAC]* (S/Res/745), February 28, 1992.

UNPROFOR
United Nations. Security Council. *Report of the Secretary General pursuant to Security Council Resolution 721 (1991)* (S/23280), December 11, 1991.

_____. *Further Report of the Secretary General Pursuant to Security Council Resolution 721 (1991)* (S/23592), February 15, 1992.

_____. *Resolution 743 (1992)* (S/RES/743), February 21, 1992.

_____. *Report of the Secretary General Pursuant to Security Council Resolution 743 (1992)* (S/23777), April 2, 1992.

UNOSOM
United Nations. Security Council. *The Situation in Somalia, Report of the Secretary General* (S/23693), March 11, 1992.

Background Interviews

Under-Secretary General Martti Ahtisaari, UN Secretariat
Col. Nils Alstermark, Swedish Mission to the UN
Col. Robert Anderson, US Mission to the UN
Mr. Hedi Annabi, UN Secretariat
Col. Zacharias Backer, Oslo, Norway
Mr. Howard Bamsey, Australian Mission to the UN
Maj. Joseph C. Bebel, US Air Force
Mr. Denis Beissel, UN Secretariat
Mr. Philippe Boullé, Office of the UN Disaster Relief Coordinator
Ms. Marjorie Ann Browne, US Congressional Research Service
Ms. Margaret Carey, UN Development Program
Mr. Christian Castro, US Mission to the UN
Ms. Lois A. Cecsarini, US Department of State
Prof. Chester Crocker, Georgetown University
Mr. Dawit Gebre-Egziabher, Organization of African Unity
Maj. Gen. Göran de Geer, Swedish Ministry of Defense
Mr. Juergen Dedring, UN Secretariat
Deputy Secretary General Hugo de Zela, Organization of American States
Mr. Timour Dmitrichev, UN Secretariat
Mr. John Donovan, US Department of State
Brig. Gen. Ian C. Douglas, Canadian Dept. of National Defence
Ms. Susan Driano, US Department of State
Lt. Col. Dermot Earley, UN Secretariat
Ambassador Jan Eliasson, Swedish Mission to the UN
Ambassador Lars-Göran Engfeldt, Swedish Mission to the UN
Mr. Gerhard Erasmus, Windhoek, Namibia
Mr. John Fox, US Department of State
Col. Douglas Fraser, Canadian Mission to the UN
Col. Sigurd Friis, Norwegian Mission to the UN
Mr. Peter Fromuth, US Mission to the UN
Under-Secretary General Marrack Goulding, UN Secretariat
Mr. Lawrence Grossman, US Mission to the UN
Hon. John H. M. Hagard, Swedish Ministry for Foreign Affairs
Gen. Gustav Hägglund, Finnish Ministry of Defense
Rep. Lee H. Hamilton, US House of Representatives
Lt. Col. Christian Hårleman, International Peace Academy
Dr. Marianne Heiberg, Norwegian Inst. for International Affairs
Maj. Mikael Heinrichs, Finnish Ministry of Defense
Lt. Col. Bo Henricson, Swedish Ministry of Defense
Mr. Leon Hosang, UN Secretariat
Mr. Robert Hughes, US Department of State
Dr. Charles J. Jefferson, US Department of State
Col. Bertil Johansson, Swedish Ministry for Foreign Affairs
Under-Secretary General James Jonah, UN Secretariat
Col. William Jordan, US Department of Defense

Ambassador Philippe Kirsch, Canadian Mission to the UN
Ms. Angela U. Knippenberg, UN Secretariat
Ms. Sheila Kolodny, UN Secretariat
Mr. David Leis, US Department of State
Dr. Ingrid Lehmann, UN Secretariat
Dr. John W. Leland, US Military Airlift Command
Mr. F. T. Liu, International Peace Academy
Mr. Edward C. Luck, UN Association of the USA
Mr. Joseph Manso, US Mission to the UN
Mr. Shawn McCormick, Center for Strategic and Intl. Studies
Mr. Colin McGregor, UN Secretariat
Mr. Craig McKee, US Department of State
Lt. Col. Gerry McMahon, UN Secretariat
Mr. Michael Michalski, US Mission to the UN
Cdr. Markku Moisala, Finnish Mission to the UN
Ms. Donna Nelson, Evergreen Aviation
Lt. Col. Martin H. Ness, Norwegian Department of Defense
Mr. Johan Nordenfelt, UN Secretariat
Dr. Jennifer Noyon, US Department of State
Ambassador Olara A. Otunnu, International Peace Academy
Ms. Lisette Lindahl Owens, Swedish Ministry for Foreign Affairs
Dr. Marc S. Palevitz, US Department of Defense
Mr. William Petersen, US General Accounting Office
Asst Sec'y General Giandomenico Picco, UN Secretariat
Ambassador Thomas R. Pickering, US Mission to the UN
Mr. Frank Record, House Foreign Affairs Committee Staff
Maj. Gen. Indar Jit Rikhye (Ret'd.), US Institute of Peace
Mr. German Santiago Romero-Perez, UNHCR
Mr. Robert Rosenstock, US Mission to the UN
Mr. Peter Rousseau, Office of the Admin. Gen., Windhoek, Namibia
Mr. Behrooz Sadry, UN Secretariat
Ms. Kathryn G. Sessions, UN Association of the USA
Ms. Laurie Lerner Shestak, US Mission to the UN
Lt. Col. Charles R. Snyder, US Department of State
Under-Secretary General Ronald Spiers, UN Secretariat
Lt. Col. David Tanks, US Army (Ret'd.)
Mr. Shashi Tharoor, UN Secretariat
Mr. Franklin N. Thevanaz, UN Secretariat
Mr. Cedric Thornberry, UN Secretariat
Ambassador Klaus Törnudd, Finnish Mission to the UN
Lt. Col. David Underwood, US Department of Defense
Mr. Frank Urbancic, US Mission to the UN
Sir Brian Urquhart, The Ford Foundation
Hon. Cyrus Vance, Simpson, Thacher, & Bartlett
Col. Ahti Vartiainen, Finnish Ministry of Defense
Col. Finn-Goran Wennström, Finnish Ministry of Defense
Mr. Martin Wilkens, Swedish Ministry for Foreign Affairs
Ms. Molly Williamson, US Department of State

Index

About the Authors

William J. Durch is a senior associate at the Henry L. Stimson Center in Washington, D.C. He has taught at Georgetown University, served as assistant director of the Defense and Arms Control Studies Program at the Massachusetts Institute of Technology, and held a research appointment at the Center for Science and International Affairs, Harvard University. He was a foreign affairs officer in the US Arms Control and Disarmament Agency in the Carter administration, joining the government from the staff of the Center for Naval Analyses, Alexandria, Virginia. He holds a BSFS from the Georgetown University School of Foreign Service (1972) and a doctorate in political science from MIT (1988).

Karl Th. Birgisson is an investigative journalist based in Iceland. He holds an AB in philosophy and political science from DePauw University (1986) and has studied international relations at the Paul H. Nitze School of Advanced International Studies, Johns Hopkins University.

Virginia Page Fortna is pursuing a doctorate in government at Harvard University. A former research assistant and program coordinator at the Stimson Center, 1990-92, she holds an AB (international relations) from Wesleyan University (1990).

Mona Ghali works for a human rights monitoring organization based in Jerusalem. She has worked previously as a political risk analyst, focusing on the Middle East. She holds an MA in Middle East studies from the Nitze School of Advanced International Studies (1988), and an SB from the University of Western Ontario (1985).

Brian D. Smith is an independent consultant. He holds a master's degree in government (international relations and national security) from Georgetown University (1991), and an AB in political science from the University of California at Berkeley (1989).